THE
STALINIST
LEGACY

THE
STALINIST
LEGACY

ITS IMPACT ON TWENTIETH-CENTURY WORLD POLITICS

edited by
TARIQ ALI

Haymarket Books
Chicago, IL

First published in 1985 by Lynne Rienner Publishers, Inc.
This edition published in 2013 by Haymarket Books.

Published by:
Haymarket Books
P.O. Box 180165
Chicago, IL 60618
773-583-7884
info@haymarketbooks.org
www.haymarketbooks.org

ISBN: 978-1-60846-219-3

Trade distribution:
In the U.S. through Consortium Book Sales and Distribution, www.cbsd.com
In the UK, Turnaround Publisher Services, www.turnaround-uk.com
In Canada, Publishers Group Canada, www.pgcbooks.ca
In Australia, Palgrave Macmillan, www.palgravemacmillan.com.au
All other countries, Publishers Group Worldwide, www.pgw.com

Special discounts are available for bulk purchases by organizations
and institutions. Please contact Haymarket Books for more information
at 773-583-7884 or info@haymarketbooks.org.

This book was published with the generous support of
the Wallace Global Fund and Lannan Foundation.

Printed in Canada by union labor on recycled paper containing 100 percent
postconsumer waste in accordance with the Green Press Initiative,
www.greenpressinitiative.org.

Library of Congress CIP Data is available.

1 3 5 7 9 10 8 6 4 2

For Peter Uhl and Anna Sabatova, members of Charter 77 in Czechoslovakia, and also for Edmund Baluka, currently in a Polish prison. They have demonstrated that it is possible to fight Stalinism in the name of both socialism and democracy.

Tariq Ali, 1984

Contents

Foreword to the Second Edition

Would the world have been a better place had the Russian Revolution not taken place? I don't think so. Every revolution, successful or unsuccessful, takes us forward, albeit at a snail's pace. To write off these experiences as meaningless (or, as is the fashion today, as crimes) is ahistorical: the result of intoxication with capitalist triumphalism after the fall of 1991. How pathetic all this seems today. Capitalism in yet another crisis and a stagnant US economy overdetermined by Wall Street, where speculative finance and crime regularly shake hands. Socialism was given but a single chance. It failed. Capitalism has failed on several occasions. Logic dictates that socialism will rise again in different shapes and forms in the decades that lie ahead.

History rolls along at its own unpredictable pace: an acceleration forward followed by a long stop and then a reverse movement followed by another long stop. And then forward again. In 49 BCE, as the Roman civil war reached a decisive stage, Julius Caesar understood the historical imperative that in order to defeat Pompey, his last serious rival in the struggle for power, he would have to cross the Rubicon. Once he did, a turning back was impossible. Glorious triumph or an ignominious death awaited him. So it was for the seventeenth-century English revolutionaries who decided after a lengthy debate to execute their king and proclaim a commonwealth. The Jacobins crossed the Rubicon when they sent Louis XVI and Marie Antoinette to the guillotine.

In 1917, the Russian revolutionary leader V. I. Lenin was faced with a similar choice. Despite the advice of his closest collaborators in the leadership of the clandestine Bolshevik Party, and to the horror of other revolutionary and reformist groups on the Russian Left, Lenin decided that the entire pyramid of power had to be toppled. Choices of this sort confront leaders only when they are immersed in a revolutionary wave and surfing on it, they rise to their feet and see the century that lies ahead if they win. As Tsarist Russia degenerated into chaos and the Provisional Government of February was a gripped by a self-induced paralysis, Lenin rose to his feet in the Petrograd Soviet and, in response to a sarcastic question, responded that the Bolsheviks were prepared to take power. They did. A new harbor light appeared on the scene, visible to the entire globe.

Today, a few decades after the collapse of the state brought into being by the October revolution, the common sense of the age (or, to put it in an old-fashioned way, the dominant bourgeois ideology) is that it would have been far better had the Revolution never happened. What is cited is the experience of Stalinism: the random cruelty, the secret police, the gulags, the murder of the old Bolsheviks, the wiping out of all political alternatives, etc. What is interesting is that this was not the view of the *bien pensant* at the time these events were taking place. European bourgeois politicians were, in the main, delighted that, under Stalin, the revolution was settling down. Many left intellectuals and progressives refused to believe the reports coming out of the Soviet Union at the time. How could it be the case? They resisted the betrayal of their illusions.

But the revolutionaries of 1917 had imagined a different world. They knew Russia was backward. They believed that if the revolution did not spread to Germany and France, at the very least, they would be isolated, with unforeseen consequences. They said so endlessly in public, putting enormous pressure on the fledgling communist parties in Europe. The German communists, feeling the weight of this pressure, organized a premature insurrection in 1919. Even though she had been opposed to the adventure, Rosa Luxemburg, one of the finest minds in the continent, participated in it as a revolutionary and was captured, bayoneted to death, and thrown in the river. The isolation of revolutionary Russia was now complete. Hard reality placed limits on its ambitions.

What if the Bolsheviks had not seized power? The more foolish liberal and conservative historians imagine that the alternative to Lenin and Trotsky was a nice, bourgeois-democratic republic that would form part of the chain referred to as universal democracy, despite the fact that women were barred from voting and property franchises limited male suffrage as well. Not even a truncated democracy was on the agenda. In fact, most of the 'universal democracies' sent troops to try and crush the Revolution. The social forces inside the country that unleashed a civil war were the shattered remnants of Tsarism: the Black Hundreds with their experience of organizing pogroms were at the heart of the White counterrevolution. Their motto was simpleminded, but not ineffective, pandering to centuries of anti-Semitism: the Jews have taken over our country. We have to win it back. Had they done so, a fascist-style military junta would have ruled Russia and pre-empted the Judeocide of the Third Reich by launching a Slav version of the same. This was the alternative that Russia faced at the time, and how deep it went is evident from the following incident.

During the Gorbachev period in the late eighties, Fredric Jameson and I were invited to a film festival in Moscow. Watching a documentary on the Afgantsy (Russian soldiers who had served in Afghanistan), we were both struck by the constant presence in the film of baptisms and funerals conducted by the bearded worthies of the Russian Orthodox Church. Soon afterwards we were hailed by a postgraduate student, a great fan of Jameson's oeuvre and a reader of the *New Left Review*. When he asked what we had thought of the film, I mentioned the obtrusive and disquieting presence of the Church. He was taken aback. 'You must understand that religion goes very deep in our culture. Every Russian is at heart Orthodox.' And the Revolution, I inquired gently? 'Oh, that was organized and carried out by Jews. All the opposition was religious.' Fred and I were aghast. I continued: 'All the opposition? The Mensheviks?' He was patient with us. 'No, of course not. They were Jews too.' We walked away.

The internal defeat of most of the decent impulses of the Revolution had taken place by the late thirties. And yet, contrary to the latest batch of Second World War movies, that conflict was essentially won by a combination of Soviet sacrifices and the US arms industry. The battles of Kursk and Stalingrad were the decisive events on the ground. Had Hitler won, the shape of the world might have been very different today.

To understand what happened to the Soviet Union under Stalin is still relevant today, for the socialism that will arise must never repeat the mistakes of the twentieth century.

Tariq Ali
July 2011

Preface

The legacy of Stalinism is most visible today in the political systems that have been established in the USSR and Eastern Europe, China and Indo-China and in the internal mode of functioning of many Communist Parties as well as various political sects of the far Left. The primary concern of this collection of essays and interviews is to explain the origins of the phenomenon now universally known as Stalinism and to chart its development on a global scale. In an essay in this volume, the late Isaac Deutscher describes Stalinism in a vivid metaphor as the 'mongrel offspring of Marxism and primitive magic'. This may or may not be the case, but the reader is offered a wide choice of texts from which to make up his or her mind.

Part One deals with the roots of the problem: Rakovsky, Trotsky, Mandel and Deutscher provide, in my view, the most convincing explanation, which in terms of quality and sophistication is light years ahead of the numerous expositions of the 'totalitarian theories' so popular among academic Kremlinologists in the West. Michael Löwy devotes an essay to the impact of Stalinism on science and literature, as does Daniel Singer in Part Two, in the form of a lively polemic against the cult figure of Solzhenitsyn.

Part Two explains how the very expansion of the post-capitalist system, via conquest (Eastern Europe) and socialist revolution (Yugoslavia, China, Indo-China) created a convulsive crisis for Stalinism from which it has not yet recovered. This last point is demonstrated with a rare skill and precision by Oliver MacDonald in his essay on the events in Poland. Khrushchev's speech which startled the world communist movement and led to a grave haemorrhaging of Moscow's hegemony is made available in its entirety to a readership which may only have heard of it or, at best, read a few extracts. The Hungarian and Czech revolts against Moscow's tutelage are documented by interviews with two leading participants in the revolt. The inherent conservatism which is embodied in Stalinist theory is well demonstrated by an extract from Fernando Claudin's epic study of the communist movement.

For any editor of a collection of this nature, constraints of space pose serious problems in terms of excluding texts. Since my major objective was to concentrate on the politics of Stalinism, I had to sacrifice material on Stalinist economics and philosophy. The latter discipline is, in any case, virtually defunct, and a bibliography lists the best recent study of economics in the Stalin epoch.

That my choice is not totally arbitrary is demonstrated by an interesting new development, so far unacknowledged in the West. The post-Maoist leadership in China has also felt the need to fill the ideological vacuum that arose out of its break with Moscow and the demythologization of Maoism. The Chinese Institute of Marxism–Leninism has recently (under the able Directorship of Su Shaozhi) started publishing a number of important books by Trotsky, Deutscher, Mandel, Anderson, and so on, in order, presumably, to begin a process of Marxist education inside the Chinese Communist Party. It is too early to predict the results of this innovation, but the impact could well become visible in the following decades. In that sense one can only hope that this modest reader, too, will find an audience not just among students in the West, but also in the East, where much of the material contained in it has been regarded as contraband.

*

Ernest Mandel's essay 'What is the Bureaucracy?' is reprinted here with his kind permission. Deutscher's 'Marxism and Primitive Magic' was published in *Marxism in Our Time* and 'Socialism in One Country' is from his classic biography, *Stalin*. Both are reprinted here with the kind permission of Tamara Deutscher. Rakovsky's letter, 'The "Professional Dangers" of Power', was first published in the *Bulletin of the Opposition* in Soviet Russia in the twenties. A collection of his writings exists in English (*Christian Rakovsky: Selected Writings*, ed. Gus Fagin, London, 1980). Liebman's 'Was Lenin a Stalinist?' is from his *Leninism Under Lenin*, with kind permission from Jonathan Cape. Claudin's reflections on Stalin and the Second World War are from *The Communist Movement* (Penguin Books, 1975). I would also like to thank *New Left Review* for permission to reprint 'The Tragedy of Indian Communism' by K. Damodaran and 'Trotsky's Interpretation of Stalinism' by Perry Anderson. The latter was written specially for this anthology. Thanks are due also to *Socialist Register*, where Roland Lew's article was first published in 1975. Daniel Singer's essay on Solzhenitsyn was published in *The Road to Gdansk* and we are grateful to the author and *Monthly Review Press* for permission to reprint.

Tariq Ali
*London, February
1984*

Introduction

Tariq Ali

In his last published interview, the late E. H. Carr – the doyen of non-Marxist historians of the Russian Revolution – expressed his fear that the re-emergence of Cold War ideology and politics would freeze all attempts to appraise the Revolution objectively:

> One need hardly dwell today on the negative consequences of the Revolution. For several years, and especially in the last few months, they have been an obsessive topic in published books, newspapers, radio and television. The danger is not that we shall draw a veil over the enormous blots on the record of the Revolution, over its cost in human suffering, over the crimes committed in its name. The danger is that we shall be tempted to forget it altogether, and to pass over in silence, its immense achievements . . . Of course, I know that anyone who speaks of the achievements of the Revolution will at once be branded a Stalinist. But I am not prepared to submit to this kind of moral blackmail.[1]

Any attempt to explain or analyse Stalinism must perforce begin by outlining the aims of the Revolution from whose bowels it sprang. The hopes aroused by the victory of the Russian Revolution in 1917 defy quantification. They crossed national frontiers with ease and aroused the working class throughout Europe. In Asia the Russian events provided a tremendous fillip for the burgeoning national movements against colonialism. Overnight the success of the Revolution transformed the size of the audience for socialist ideas. These had until then largely been the preserve, with a few exceptions, of a minuscule stratum of intellectuals and workers. After 1917 they appeared as a practical possibility to millions of people across the globe. Empires felt threatened. Capital trembled. Social democracy split into pro- and anti-revolutionary factions. The fall of Petrograd was, in other words, a universal event. It suddenly brought to life the spectre of which Marx and Engels had written in the *Communist Manifesto*. The rulers of Europe (and large parts of three other continents) buried their complacency as their subjects became increasingly restive.

Crowned heads had, of course, been topped before, but those responsible for these acts had been the unwitting agents of a historical progression. Cromwell believed that he was guided by Providence. Robespierre claimed to be acting in the name of abstract principle. Lenin was not

merely the beneficiary of a different historical time, he was the major
leader of a political party that based itself on a special understanding of
existing social forces. It was their materialist view of history that distinguished the Bolsheviks from all previous revolutionary organizations.
They acted as the conscious agents of a rising social class and were
determined (after considerable theoretical and political turmoil in the
upper reaches of the party) to transform the entire social basis of the state.

When a short, bald man stood up in the Petrograd soviet after the
February Revolution and, in reply to what was intended as a rhetorical
question, stated quietly, without a trace of demagogy, that his party was
prepared to exercise power, he was greeted by cries of disbelief and hoots
of derisory laughter. When, a few months later, the Bolsheviks had won a
majority in the key soviets of Petrograd and Moscow and launched a
successful insurrection, his political rivals were incredulous. There was
good reason for their amazement. Tsarist Russia had been culturally and
economically underdeveloped. The multi-millioned peasantry dwarfed
the tiny working class. Russia had 'fallen' because it had been the
'weakest link' in the chain of European imperialisms. The First World
War had laid bare this vulnerability. The Bolsheviks had pressed home
the advantage: Land, Bread and Peace were the three concrete aims of the
Bolshevik Party that had united a uniformed peasantry, reeling from
defeats on the Eastern Front, with the urban proletariat.

Marx had insisted that a socialist society could only be based on an
industrialized society which possessed the potential of being rapidly
transformed into an economy of abundance. Tsarist Russia was almost
the polar opposite of such an economy. For this reason not a single leader
of a party that based itself on the teachings of Marx believed that it would
be possible to construct 'socialism in one country'. Lenin was to stress
this fact repeatedly after the triumph of the October Revolution:

Both prior to October and during the Revolution, we always said that we regard
ourselves and can only regard ourselves as one of the contingents of the international proletarian army, a contingent which came to the fore, not because of its
level of development and preparedness, but because of Russia's exceptional
conditions; we always said that the victory of the socialist revolution, therefore,
can only be regarded as final when it becomes the victory of the proletariat in at
least several advanced countries. It was in this respect that we experienced the
greatest difficulties. Our banking on the world revolution, if you can call it that,
has on the whole been fully justified. But from the point of the speed of its
development we have endured an exceptionally difficult period; we have seen for
ourselves that the revolution's development in more advanced countries has
proved to be considerably slower, considerably more difficult, considerably more
complicated . . . But . . . this slower . . . development of the socialist revolution in
Western Europe has burdened us with incredible difficulties.[2]

The Civil War in Russia was won by the Bolsheviks, but at tremendous cost. The intervention of the Entente powers proved to be a failure, though it successfully bled the Revolution. Capital lost the Soviet Union, but it was able to limit the revolutionary wave. Bela Kun's short-lived Soviet Republic in Hungary, even if it had survived, could not have decisively strengthened the socio-economic base of the Soviet state. In the capitalist heartlands of the West, the ruling classes successfully deflected mass upsurges by granting important democratic reforms (universal suffrage) and loosened the straitjacket of factory discipline (an eight-hour working day). Where this was not sufficient, capital exacted a heavy revenge for Lenin's success in Petrograd. In Italy, three years after Lenin's remarks quoted above, the blackshirted brigades of Benito Mussolini set fire to working-class clubs and rapidly extinguished all civil liberties. Beneath the admiring gaze of Western politicians, Mussolini established a ruthless capitalist dictatorship, providing Europe with its first experience of fascism.[3] Portugal, Germany and Spain were to follow suit and in that order. Fascism was the punishment which capital inflicted on the working class for toying with the idea of revolution. The net result of all these developments was the total isolation of revolutionary Russia.

Direct military intervention had failed to defeat the Red Army, but the Revolution itself was scarred by the experience: a debilitated economy, a war-weary population, the loss of a whole layer of the most politically conscious workers and mass famines were the inevitable outcome. The economic blockade imposed by capital succeeded in quarantining the Revolution. Stalinism was the outcome of these multi-faceted processes. The preponderance of the peasantry, the weakness of the working class, the total lack of democratic traditions, the failure of the Revolution to spread to even one advanced country in the West, the deaths of Lenin and Sverdlov: all these factors became inextricably linked to each other. The result was a growing passivity and demoralization in the towns. Many workers were absorbed by the growing apparatuses of the party and state. In the conditions that existed at the time this was an event of decisive importance: it led to a qualitative increase in the political and social weight of functionaries. The rapid growth of material privileges that this layer enjoyed relative to the average working-class family was bound to have an effect inside the party and state.

Lenin's last struggle, waged from his sick-bed where he lay paralysed and isolated, was against this growing bureaucratization. He perceived this as a potential cancer which could prove to be extremely dangerous for a young, but already deformed, workers' state.[4] His death in 1924 led to an open factional struggle within the party, the only remaining organism in the country where political issues could still be debated. Stalin had understood even during Lenin's lifetime that Trotsky would pose a threat to bureaucratic hegemony. His entire strategy from 1923 to 1930 was built around developing alliances which could isolate Trotsky and his supporters inside the party, army and youth organizations. The Left Opposition waged a heroic struggle. Its defeat was a result of an objective fact: the Russian working class was exhausted and fresh replacements from the countryside had diluted the *élan* and conscious-ness of the proletariat. The party and state bureaucracy found in Stalin and his faction the ideal ally. A growing merger of party and state apparatuses would soon lead to the extermination of the oppositionists. This coalescing of party and state bureaucracies was demonstrated at one of the last debates which Trotsky attended on the Central Committee of the CPSU:

Molotov: And the party, what do you make of the party?
Trotsky: The party, you have strangled it.
Stalin: These cadres can only be removed through a civil war.[5]

The Civil War was soon launched in earnest. It is often forgotten in the West that the first victims of Stalinism were communist revolutionaries who protested against bureaucratic travesties of the revolutionary pro-cess. In order to stabilize his regime Stalin was to kill more communists and socialists than his absolutist predecessor, the Tsar. The question 'what is Stalinism?' was first asked in whispers by imprisoned veterans of the Revolution. The first political strike against Stalinism was undertaken by old Bolshevik prisoners in the Vorkuta prison camp, where the speech of Socrate Guevorkian exhibited an amazing combination of theoretical clarity and physical courage, two attributes which do not always go together.[6]

Stalinism consolidated its power during the late twenties, thirties and forties, but in changed social conditions. Politically, virtually every non-Stalinist alternative had been physically eliminated and the party itself had become an instrument of the bureaucracy. This had been made possible by flooding the party with raw recruits fresh from the country. There were 430,000 party members in 1920, but only 135,000 of these veterans in 1927 and even fewer ten years later. Like their old Bolshevik leaders they had been consumed by the purges. Hélène Carrère D'Encausse has pointed out that:

There were practically no Old Bolsheviks in 1929 and barely 130,000 members who had experienced in the Party the epic of the Civil War. All the others had joined when debate in the Party had already been contained, when the spirit of discipline had already taken the place of the revolutionary initiative of the heroic years and of the criticism of the first years of the Leninist USSR. This, then, was a new Party, whose heroes, ideals and moral rules were no longer those of the Leninist Party.

At the cultural level also, the transformation of the Party was very important; the newcomers were of a very low intellectual calibre and were completely lacking in political experience. The main criterion on which they had been recruited by the secretaries was that of their blind obedience to the Party's authority, which became the new conception of the *spirit of the Party (Partiinost)*.[7]

On the eve of the Second World War, the majority of Lenin's Central Committee as well as the distinguished military leaders of the Red Army had been executed. Trotsky's life was terminated in his Mexican exile in 1940 by a hired Stalinist assassin. The war years were to provide a critical test for the USSR as well as the bureaucracy. The industrialization of the thirties had been a costly affair, but it had strengthened the economic base of the country. It had also resulted in an amazing degree of upward mobility for numerous workers and peasants. Many workers were absorbed into the state apparatus; many peasants obtained jobs in the towns. The mass purges had, not surprisingly, left behind a mass of vacancies. The bureaucracy thus imposed its will only partially through coercion. The secret police was a crucial pillar of bureaucratic rule. Its position of authority in the Gulag gave its bosses a new importance as well as a certain autonomy. Despite all this the regime rested on a social base. The new Soviet working class undoubtedly felt that it had a stake in the preservation of this regime. The urban workers had by now become the dominant social stratum in Soviet society. Without their active support the Soviet Union could not have survived the Second World War. The crude Slavic nationalism which Stalin deployed as the *leitmotif* to 'unite the nation' indicated the degeneration of the bureaucracy. It was not, however, an explanation for the incredible resistance of the Soviet population. The Nazi occupiers did win some support in certain areas of the USSR, but they could neither generalize nor build upon this support. Nor was the regime overthrown by social strata favouring a restoration of capitalism internally, while continuing to fight the Nazi armies. All the evidence suggests that the war was the single most decisive test for the regime. It survived. The victory of the Red Army at Stalingrad was probably the most decisive triumph in modern history. 'The hopes of civilization rest on the banners of the Red Army,' proclaimed the American General Douglas MacArthur. There can be little doubt that it was the Soviet resistance that prevented the whole of Europe from collapsing before Nazism.

The negative features of the victory were initially felt inside the USSR. It provided Stalinism with a legitimacy it had hitherto established over the corpses of old Bolsheviks. In the post-war years the Stalinist seal was observed on every level: state, economy, culture, army and church. Unable because of its peculiar position to develop its own ideology, Stalinism transformed Marxist theory into a set of pragmatic rules.

History was systematically falsified and rewritten. Natural sciences were obstructed and research suppressed. Women's rights were severely curtailed: divorce legislation was designed to encourage 'family life', the right to abortion was halted; homosexuality was regarded as a perversion, although it was not made illegal. A thinly disguised moral code, reminiscent of Victorian England, was instigated at every level of culture and education, finding its most notorious reflection in Makarenko's socialist realist trilogy *The Road to Life*. With a few changes these books could well serve as the Bible of the Boy Scouts and Girl Guides in contemporary Britain. Stalinism became a synonym for a bureaucratic dictatorship. Its deadening impact gradually resulted in the establishment of an iron monopoly of information, politics, culture, theory, ideology, economics and science.

The Revolution had liberated virtually every oppressed and submerged layer within the old society. In the realms of art and architecture, drama and literature, agitprop and cinema, sex and morals, exciting and innovative impulses were experienced that had no equal before or since. Mayakovsky and Meyerhold, Eisenstein and Tatlin, Kollontai and Lunacharsky, all combined to impel the Revolution to reflect and articulate the enthusiasm of a liberated intelligentsia. One commentator, not known for his sympathy to the Revolution, has recently written: 'With the tolerant and sophisticated Anatole Lunacharsky in charge of cultural affairs and with a high proportion of Bolshevik leaders (Lenin, Trotsky and Bukharin) being intellectuals . . . it was taken for granted that the creative process was not amenable to crude administrative control.'[8] With the advent of Stalinism everything changed. At the 1st Congress of Soviet Writers, Karl Radek, a former Oppositionist who had made his peace (so he thought) with the bureaucracy, proclaimed that: 'Joyce stands on the other side of the barricades . . . Our road lies not through Joyce, but along the highway of socialist realism.'[9] Alas, Radek's own highway was to terminate in a prison camp, where he died a miserable and unrecorded death.

What was true in the realm of culture was multiplied a hundred times over in the political domain. The victory of Stalinism marked a qualitative break in the continuity of the revolutionary process. There was, however, to be no regression to the free market. The breach was carried out essentially on the level of the political superstructures of the state. The economic and social conquests of the Revolution were not simply preserved, they were in reality strengthened. Thus Stalinism could not and did not develop an ideology specific to itself. It paid lip-service to the writings of Marx, Engels and Lenin while simultaneously ensuring their mummification. Stalin's own writings were exclusively derivative in character. A study of his texts in isolation from the epidemic of terror that he unleashed is, accordingly, a pointless exercise. A decisive hallmark of the Stalinist tradition has been that it is based on a lie. Thus a study of the Soviet Constitution of 1936 (the so-called Stalin Constitution) reveals a document which, on paper, is ultra-democratic, but is never applied in practice. The same can be said of the character of many 'theoretical' texts that were produced during the Stalin epoch. The most bizarre demonstration of this can be observed in the names which some of the bureaucratic states adopted: the *Democratic* People's Republic of Korea and *Democratic* Kampuchea are the two most glaring anomalies!

It is now fashionable among historians hostile to all social revolutions (past, present and future) to deny that Stalinism represented anything more than the inevitable outcome of a socialist upheaval. It is almost as fashionable as it was in the thirties for liberals and social democrats to avert their eyes from Stalin's crimes and denounce his opponents. Despite all this it is necessary to emphasize that Stalinism was not preordained, but the outcome of specific international and domestic conditions. This book is an attempt to explain how this came about. It provides a Marxist critique of Stalinism extending from the twenties to the present day. The choice of articles does not indicate any theoretical absolutism on our part. Stalinism is still a live issue and the debate on its origin and nature will ultimately only be resolved by the historical process.

Ever since the Russian Revolution there has been a vigorous debate on its outcome. After 1917 basically three theories developed which attempted to come to grips with the new problems that had been raised on a theoretical and strategic level. In fact on no other question has theory and political strategy been so closely related as in analyses of the nature of the USSR. The oldest theory was proposed by the defeated Mensheviks, who regarded the seizure of power by Lenin and the Bolsheviks as an adventure. Russia was not sufficiently advanced to make a socialist revolution. The Mensheviks believed that only a bourgeois state was possible, given the low level of the productive forces, and only the Mensheviks could ensure that it would be a democratic bourgeois state. The Menshevik argument was developed in a more sophisticated style by the Austrian socialist Otto Bauer, who was in no doubt that the Bolsheviks were laying the basis for a state that would ultimately evolve towards a form of capitalist democracy. In a pamphlet entitled *Bolshevism or Social Democracy* (1920) Bauer characterizes Russia as a state evolving via an agrarian revolution to a bourgeois democracy. His advice to the Bolsheviks was to suppress the contradiction between the economic base (which he saw as capitalist) and the state structure and inaugurate a peaceful transition to a bourgeois republic. This view was based on an economic fatalism that gravely underestimated the autonomy of politics.

Amadeo Bordiga, the father of Italian communism, developed a similar theory after his breach with Moscow in 1922 and advanced the view that the new state was an organ of emerging capitalism. Bordiga advanced some extremely valuable projections of what a socialist society and communism should be, but since the USSR was clearly not that, it therefore followed that it was not socialist. What Bordiga's syllogism obscured was the possibility that there could be a long period of transition from capitalism to socialism in those countries where the economic base was underdeveloped. Both Bordiga and Bauer did not attempt to classify the Soviet Union by inventing a new category. They merely tried to prove that it was a state on the road to capitalism. History has proved somewhat unkind to their theses.

Since the Second World War new attempts at classification have been made. Of these attempts the most enduring has been the project of Tony Cliff and his followers, based essentially in Britain.[10] Cliff developed the view that the Soviet Union was a 'state-capitalist' society and represented the emergence of a new ruling class, which was qualitatively no different from the capitalist classes in the West. Cliff's arguments made it clear that the economic functioning of 'state-capitalism' was not exactly the same as capitalism. His position is therefore, in some respects, much closer to the theorists of a new mode of production than the Leninist definition of state-capitalism.[11] It is not possible in the course of this introduction to do justice either to the views of Cliff and his adherents or to the numerous polemical attacks on them. For the benefit of *aficionados* a select bibliography is provided.

The second group of theorists stated that Stalinist Russia represented a new form of oligarchy which was more regressive than capitalism. The best-known exponents of these views were James Burnham and Max Shachtman, one-time Trotskyist intellectuals in the United States of America. Burnham's *Managerial Society* became a cult volume during the first Cold War (1948–68). The author himself was to end his days as a supporter of the extreme right-wing John Birch Society. Shachtman continued to argue that the USSR represented a totalitarian 'bureaucratic collectivism', but unlike his former collaborator he did not move as far to the right. He defended Kennedy's ill-fated invasion of Cuba and was an early supporter of US intervention in Vietnam. Nor were these views inconsistent with his theoretical beliefs. If American democracy represented the most advanced political form on this planet, then there was nothing wrong or immoral in supporting its attempts to export this 'way of life'. Milovan Djilas was the third important theorist of this tradition. Djilas had been a member of the Central Committee of the Yugoslav Communist Party and a partisan leader in the anti-fascist resistance. He developed his analysis of the USSR after the Tito–Stalin split and later expounded his views in *The New Class*, which became another cold war bestseller. Djilas, however, refused to leave Yugoslavia despite spells in prison. Nor did he recant his beliefs. He is today a partisan – albeit a critical one – of Western capitalism. Thus with exceptions every theorist who sought to invent new modes of production and new laws of development to explain the complexities of Soviet society ultimately ended up as an apologist for capitalism. Many disciples of these theoreticians, we should stress, ultimately refused to follow their leaders. They remained anti-capitalist socialists, but the inconsistencies of their theoretical assumptions became apparent whenever they were confronted with a serious challenge in appraising world politics.

In striking contrast were the views advanced by the third and dominant theoretical school. Trotsky's study of the Soviet Union was started in his Turkish exile as he attempted to utilize the geographical and historical distance between him and the apparatus in Moscow in order to produce an explanation which remains peerless to this very day. Trotsky's theses are now dated in some respects, but his general approach represented a phenomenal advance for classical Marxism. It is not surprising that of all Trotsky's writings it was *The Revolution Betrayed* that was to be challenged from all sides, but despite this it became a reference point for all those who engaged in a serious study of post-revolutionary Russia. Trotsky defined Stalinist Russia as a society in transition with specific relations of production characterized by the permanent contradiction between the collective ownership of the means of production and bourgeois norms of distribution. This view was further developed by Ernest Mandel in a number of essays, polemical exchanges and books. A useful and educative account of Trotsky's analysis of Stalinism is contained in this book.[12] Trotsky's views were formed in the light of a sober reappraisal of the Soviet Union. There is not a trace of wildness or exaggeration in them: no Stalinist crime (not even the murder of his own sons) led him towards emotional fanaticism. On a fundamental level Trotsky's theses have stood the test of time. Once regarded as contraband within the orthodox Communist Parties, they have, since the advent of Eurocommunism, found a growing echo and now almost constitute the 'common sense' of a large section of the Marxist and socialist Left on a global scale.[13]

The three features of Stalinism proper had grown out of the specific conditions that prevailed in the Soviet Union and Europe during the twenties and thirties. Stalinism was a product of the defeat and isolation of the world revolution, a development that it had partially aided by its ineptitude and narrow-mindedness. Accordingly it came to be characterized by: (a) an iron monolithism on every level of the party, the state and the international communist movement; (b) 'socialism in one country' – a theoretical justification of autarchy which turned the writings of Marx and Lenin on their head with catastrophic consequences: (c) the abandonment of internationalism and the global utilization of Communist Parties as the frontier guards of the 'socialist homeland' (the Soviet Union) rather than as the vanguards of their own respective revolutions. This was formalized by the dissolution of the Communist International in 1943. A challenge on any of these three levels would weaken the foundations of classical Stalinism. This process had begun even during the dictator's lifetime. It had been a direct consequence of the choices opened up after the Second World War.

The triumphant march of the Red Army to Berlin was reminiscent of Napoleon's sweep across Europe. Whereas Bonaparte had authorized certain transformations, essentially on the level of the political and legal superstructures, he had not permanently altered the social and economic landscape of the conquered territories. What would Stalin do? The accords reached between the Soviet bureaucracy and the capitalist democracies at Teheran, Yalta and Potsdam are currently being re-analysed by Western ideologues as instances of craven capitulation on the part of the West. Such an approach is typically ahistorical, serving the needs of the new Cold War, and it can be dismissed without too much difficulty.

The United States emerged as the strongest capitalist state as the war drew to a close. It demonstrated its new power by firing a nuclear shot across Stalin's bows: the victims of this cynical display of *realpolitik* were the people who died or suffered at Hiroshima and Nagasaki. The atomic explosions established the new status of the United States, but they could not, on their own, solve the problems that confronted capitalism in Europe. It was not simply that the possessing classes had been (with the exception of Britain) gravely enfeebled. The fact was that in a number of Nazi-occupied countries important sections of these classes had willingly collaborated with their German counterparts. Vichy France was the most notorious of this class-before-nation solidarity, but by no means the only one of its kind. In a number of Eastern European countries the old ruling classes had either been weakened and damaged beyond repair (Hungary, Rumania, Bulgaria) or had virtually disappeared (Yugoslavia, Poland, Czechoslovakia) as a result of the collapse of their state apparatuses during the military defeats they had suffered as a result of Nazi occupation and liberation struggles. In Greece and Italy the Resistance had been dominated by the Communist Parties and insurrectional upheavals were clearly on the agenda. The Western leaders were only too aware of these realities. Yalta and Potsdam was the price they were prepared to pay for retaining capitalism in Italy, Greece and even France (where the situation was more complicated). Eastern Europe was accepted as the Russian 'sphere of influence' – a vague phrase which meant that Stalin would be within his rights to prevent the establishment of regimes that threatened the security of the Soviet Union. In this fashion the West abandoned the old rulers in Eastern Europe to the military superiority of the Red Army. The one country where 'influence' was intended to be shared on a 'fifty-fifty' basis between the USSR and the West was Yugoslavia. Tito, however, had other ideas and his partisans were not prepared to make concessions to those who had been obstructing the anti-Nazi resistance. Stalin's attempts to persuade Tito to accept the restoration of a nominal monarchy ended in failure. Yugoslavia's revolution was indigenous, a fact of decisive importance in understanding the subsequent evolution of Yugoslav–Soviet relations.

The important question remained: how would the Soviet bureaucracy change the social and political structures of Eastern Europe? The indecision in Moscow can be seen if we divide Soviet policy towards Eastern Europe into two distinct stages. The first was a period of empirical solutions. The main accent of this phase, which lasted from 1945 to 1947, was on reparations and a pillaging of the economies of the Eastern European countries, while their respective bourgeoisies still held effective economic power. Capitalist production relations were utilized to rebuild the shattered Soviet economy. The second stage was a response to a US initiative. When the Americans hurled the Marshall Plan at a weakened and shattered Europe, the Soviet Union was faced with an unavoidable choice. The aim of the Marshall Plan was no less than the restoration, revival and reconstruction of a severely weakened capitalist economy. The Stalinist rejection of the Plan marked the second phase of Soviet Eastern European policy. In order to push the Americans back into their own orbit the USSR had to consolidate its long-term position in Eastern Europe. This could only be done by a decisive leap which qualitatively transformed the social and economic structure of the so-called 'buffer states' and ended the process of milking their economies. The Marshall Plan revived capitalism in Western Europe despite Washington's awareness of the potential dangers in this process. Rebuilding German capitalism meant reviving the old pre-war rivals of American capital. It was the existence of the USSR that propelled capital to act against its own competitive instincts. On the other side, too, the Stalinist bureaucracy was fully aware of what a transformed Eastern Europe could signify. For that reason the social transformation of Eastern Europe (with the exception of Yugoslavia and Albania) was achieved at the expense of not just the old bourgeoisies, which was inevitable, but also by curtailing, limiting and even preventing any mass initiatives from below. Capitalism was destroyed overnight, but so was any hope of socialist democracy. The

Stalinist model was imposed wholesale on Eastern Europe. While most of the countries in question were largely rural in character, one had a more developed economy than the USSR itself. This was Czechoslovakia. The imposition of primitive Stalinism upon an advanced working class led to disastrous consequences, highlighting the deep crisis in which Stalinism was soon to find itself. The Czech resistance had been widespread and popular; the Czech communists were largely based on the strong traditions of the working class; the Czech people had welcomed the Red Army as liberators. They were not to escape the horse-medicine of the Soviet bureaucracy. The process was movingly described many years later by the French philosopher, Jean-Paul Sartre:

> Czechoslovakia could have been the first power to accomplish a successful transition from an advanced capitalist economy to a socialist economy, offering the proletariat of the West, if not a model, at least an embodiment of its own revolutionary future. It lacked nothing, neither the means nor the men; if genuine workers' control was possible anywhere, it was in Prague and Bratislava.
>
> To its misfortune, the manipulators in Moscow, manipulated by their own manipulations, could not even understand the idea of such a socialism. They imposed their *system* instead. This imported, disadapted model, with no real foundations in the country, was sustained from the outside by the solicitude of the 'elder brother'. It was installed as an idol − that is to say, a fixed sort of unconditional demands, indisputable, undisputed, inexplicable, unexplained . . .
>
> Let there be no misunderstanding: the men of 1945 were convinced revolutionaries and most of them remained so, but the system forbade them the experience of building socialism themselves. In order to change them, the experience would have had to take them as they were; the system took them as they were not. Instead of presenting itself as an open set of problems calling for both a rational transformation of structures and a constant modification of ideas (in other words a reciprocal and dialectical interaction of practice and theory), it posed with incredible complacency as a gracious gift of providence, a socialism without tears − in other words, without revolution or any contestation whatever. The tasks were already defined; it only remained to execute them. All knowledge was already complete: it only remained to memorize it.[14]

The decision to transform the social order was a bureaucratic *fiat*, imposed from above. It did, however, provoke a certain degree of enthusiasm from below, especially in the towns. Important layers of the working class were prepared to give the new regimes a breathing space in return for the important social rights that they were being given. Andrej Wajda's sensitive and intelligent film *Man of Marble* is an accurate portrayal of the contradictory tensions that existed within the working class during the late forties and fifties. The extension of post-capitalist states broke the post-1917 embargo on the Soviet Union. Simultaneously and contrary to appearances at the time, it also *weakened* the hegemony of Stalinism. 'Socialism in one country' – how was this possible any longer? Stalin perceived at an early stage that the success of the revolution in Yugoslavia and the assimilation process of Eastern Europe meant that there were new autonomous and semi-autonomous centres of power. The monopoly of the Soviet bureaucracy as the only basis of authority for the world communist movement had been objectively broken. Tito's truculence and the final split between him and Stalin led to fears that Eastern Europe might follow suit. The purges and show trials of the thirties were now repeated throughout Eastern Europe. The anti-God then had been Trotsky. It was now Tito, who was described as a 'Trotskyite counter-revolutionary', 'agent of imperialism', and so on. The aim of the new purges was to remove every potential alternative to classical Stalinism inside the Communist Parties. The death of Stalin in 1953 halted the process, but confirmed the dead autocrat's fears.

The first outbreak of working-class opposition to bureaucratic rule erupted in East Berlin, where striking workers demanded basic democratic rights: freedom of speech, press and organization. The revolt was crushed by Soviet tanks. Meanwhile, inside the Soviet Union, Stalin's successors were seeking to humanize the system. Khrushchev's speech at the 20th Party Congress (see p. 221) was, despite its obvious flaws, a devastating blow for Stalinism on a global scale. Within Eastern Europe there ensued an uprising in Hungary (again crushed by Russian tanks) and an upsurge in Poland in 1956. The latter led to the first major victory for a current that became known as 'reform communism' and brought Gomulka to power. It was the triple failure of Polish 'reform communism' to deliver the political goods (1956, 1970, 1976) that led to the emergence of Solidarity in 1980 and 1981, symbolizing the distance that the workers had travelled since 1953.

The crisis of Stalinism was to receive a new and decisive blow in the Far East. The victory of the Chinese Communist Party in 1949 was the result of a protracted struggle against indigenous reaction and Japanese occupation, which had started in the twenties. It could hardly be argued that Mao Zedong's partisans lacked mass support. In its own way the Chinese Revolution was in social terms an almost direct reversal of the 1917 model. Mao's forces had mobilized the peasantry and had come to power in 1949 on the basis of a gigantic peasants' upsurge. They had then liberated the cities, many of which had remained under Japanese or Kuomintang occupation for decades. While the peasants were fully mobilized, the urban proletariat was almost demobilized as a class until after the revolution, which lent the Chinese revolutionary process certain specific features. What concerns us here, however, is the undeniable fact that Mao's forces made their own revolution in the face of Stalin's open scepticism and minuscule material aid from Moscow. It was only following the success of the Chinese Communist Party in 1949 that Soviet economic aid was forthcoming after several weeks of hard negotiations between Mao and Stalin in Moscow. This was to be a crucial determinant in aiding the development of Chinese industry. When the Sino-Soviet ideological dispute erupted a decade and a half later, all Soviet aid and economic advisers were withdrawn at a stroke. The Chinese Revolution transformed the relationship of forces both on a world scale and within the non-capitalist bloc. China, the world's largest state, could not be treated as a Yugoslavia of the East. The phenomenal advances of the Eighth Route Army had, in practice, buried 'socialism in one country'. Moscow's hegemony remained unchallenged for many years, but subterranean tensions indicated that the multiplication of authoritative centres of power posed real problems for the heirs of Stalin from the very beginning.

The one organizational framework through which all ideological disputes could be peacefully settled no longer existed. The Comintern had been dissolved in 1943, prior to the success of the Yugoslav, Vietnamese and Chinese revolutions. The international communist movement had no centralized press in which all contentious issues could be debated. This, too, was one of the legacies of Stalinism. Tito and Mao had broken in practice with many aspects of classical Stalinism, but their ideological formation had been as members of the Stalinist family. They could never break totally with their past. This meant that there was never any real search for an alternative which might have provided a totally different set of criteria for running the state. Ironically enough a Communist International was needed far more at this stage of the world revolution than it had been in the twenties, when not a single Communist Party was in a real position to challenge Moscow's hegemony, with the result that the Stalinization of the USSR was replicated with ease inside the International and its constituent organizations. This dependence was symbolized in 1943 in the decision to disband, which was taken in Moscow without even the gesture of convening a World Congress, Such an action would have been impossible if there had been even one other centre of power. It would not have been possible for Tito and Mao to have been cast out of a Comintern without serious repercussions inside the movement as a whole. The fact that Mao never attempted to organize a new International revealed the extent of his dependence on a number of crucial ideological formulae of Stalinism. Both the Yugoslav and Chinese communists had made their revolutions by breaking *in practice* with Moscow. The failure to break with Stalinism *in theory* was to create a tragic disjuncture in the revolution at the very moment of its success. The mode of organization, best expressed in the complete equation between the party and state, the monopoly of politics and information, that characterized Chinese society, was not dissimilar to the USSR in the late twenties and early thirties.

This raises a gamut of questions which have yet to be satisfactorily resolved. Is it the case that economic backwardness necessitates a Stalinist-type political structure? Is not a one-party state the inevitable outcome of a revolution in an underdeveloped country? Is it a pure accident that every single revolution has resulted in a monolithic state, with the very partial exception of Castro's Cuba? If we were to look solely at what exists today, then we would have no choice but to agree, however reluctantly, that the answer to all these questions must be a sad 'yes'. To do so, however, would be to accept an ultra-objectivist, one-sided view of historical development. This leads to a blind worshipping of accomplished facts and can be utilized to justify every disaster: Stalin, the purges, the so-called 'Great Proletarian Cultural Revolution', the horrors of Pol Pot, the self-parodying Stalinism of Kim-il-Sung, the débâcle in Afghanistan and the saloon-bar quality of the shoot-outs in Tirana. To suggest that all these events were inevitable is to fall prey to a political myopia of the worst sort. In our opinion all these horrendous occurrences could have been avoided. They were not essential to either making or preserving the gains of all these revolutions.

It has been argued that these processes were necessary in order to establish regimes that were intrinsically unpopular and could only survive by creating a dictatorship over the proletariat and poor peasants. This certainly applies to Stalin, who came to power on the basis of liquidating large number of cadres and members of the party that had made the revolution. The cases of Ho Chi Minh, Mao Tse-tung, Josip Broz Tito and Fidel Castro are somewhat different. Could the Chinese revolution have succeeded if the Chinese Communist Party had not commanded mass support? Why was it that the United States explicitly sabotaged elections in Vietnam in 1956 as agreed to by the Geneva Accords of 1954? Eisenhower gave an honest answer to this when he told a questioner that if there were elections, 'Ho Chi Minh would win 80 per cent of the vote'. If Tito had organized a poll in Yugoslavia in 1948, who would the people have voted for? The answer to this can be elicited from the fact that Tito armed his entire population in readiness for any attack from Stalin. Which US-sponsored dictator in the 'third world' has ever done that? Why was Fidel Castro able to stay in power despite continuing attempts to overthrow him by the United States – economic blockades, military invasion, CIA attempts at his assassination and so on? The Chinese, Yugoslavian and Cuban regimes have survived over the years because of indigenous popular support, and not through the presence of a foreign army.

The weakness of post-revolutionary governments has lain in their complete failure to institutionalize mass participation and control in the political and economic life of the country. It is here that the distinctive ideological thrust of Stalinism has come into full play. Both Tito and Mao broke with the Soviet Union, but neither was capable of a real break on the question of implementing some form of socialist democracy. 'Self-management' in the Yugoslav economy was not a fake, but could only have real meaning if there were self-management within the political sphere. Mao's demagogic appeals to the 'spirit of the Paris Commune' during the 'Cultural Revolution' did unleash mass mobilizations, but for the explicit purpose of resolving a factional struggle inside the Chinese Communist Party.[15] In neither case were the people given any real say in the reorganization of society. The 'model' used in virtually every case was based on a variant of Stalinist Russia. If that model had been a different one there is very little doubt that the third world revolutions would have benefited greatly.

We can now return to the real object of our study: the Soviet Union. Even if we accept all the objectivist arguments for the unavoidable growth of bureaucratic power in that country, it is undeniable that the conditions which facilitated the rise of Stalinism have now disappeared. The USSR is neither isolated nor a backward social formation. The level of culture and the standard of living is higher than ever before. Every worker is guaranteed the right to work and mass unemployment of the Western variety simply does not exist. The *gulag* is a powerful but distant memory for the bulk of the population. Khrushchev and Brezhnev moved the USSR into a post-Stalin era since the death of the dictator thirty years ago. Despite the very real changes, however, Soviet society remains undemocratic and continues to be ruled by a bureaucratic elite which jealously safeguards its power and privileges. The USSR has not even returned to the stage which existed during Lenin's lifetime, especially in relation to intellectual and cultural freedoms.[16]

Post-Stalinist interregnum in the USSR

The death of Stalin posed a fundamental problem for his successors. How should they rule this vast country and maintain discipline in Eastern Europe? In the eleventh century, the monk Nestor had bemoaned in the Russian primary chronicle: 'The land is large and rich, but there is no order.' Stalin's heirs set their minds towards establishing an order that would simultaneously dispense with primitive Stalinism, attempt to integrate all the crucial layers of Soviet society and preserve the monopoly of power which the bureaucracy enjoyed. It is in this context that Khrushchev's speech to the 20th Party Congress should be seen. It was undoubtedly an audacious move, and scared the party hierarchy, which feared that it might lead to massive disturbances. Khrushchev went ahead despite the opposition of a majority of the Central Committee. The consequent breach inside Eastern Europe and the world communist movement marked the beginning of a profound crisis in Stalinism. Khrushchev had insisted that the speech was vital to prevent an explosion from below and offer some hope to the victims of Stalin. His primary concern was the Soviet Union. The 'thaw' was accompanied by a determined attempt to weaken social tensions by reducing differentials and improving the living standards of the majority of the population – a policy picturesquely described by the old *muzhik* as 'goulash communism'. This went hand-in-glove with a systematic termination of the reign of terror that had characterized classical Stalinism. Political prisoners were released in droves and the camps were disbanded. The arbitrariness which had been a hallmark of the old system was replaced by restoring the confidence of the demoralized and atomized cadres of the CPSU. Instead of a terroristic monolithism, with every move dependent on the whims of Stalin, a slow move towards *bureaucratic* pluralism was undertaken. Within the party hierarchies on both state and provincial levels, discussion was encouraged once again. Ideological absolutism was discouraged and the slogan of the Hungarian leader, Janos Kadar, 'Those who are not against us are with us', summed up this new approach. The security services were slimmed down and deprived of the virtual autonomy they had enjoyed under Stalin.

The bedrock of the post-Stalinist era was in the sphere of domestic policies. The political stability that has characterized the USSR since 1956 (compared to Eastern Europe and China) can only be understood by studying the steady rise in living standards. This point was made very firmly by the well-known Soviet dissident, Zhores Medvedev, who lives in London:

> The economic situation in the country remains below expectations, but is improving slowly all the time. There is no unemployment, but on the contrary a shortage of labour – which creates greater variety of job-choice for workers. The average working family can easily satisfy its immediate material needs: apartment, stable employment, education for children, health care and so on. The prices of essential goods – bread, milk, meat, fish, rent – have not changed since 1964. The cost of television or radio sets and other durable items has actually been reduced (from unduly high previous levels). In fact, there is now an excess of cash in people's hands, and consumer demand for items which a few years ago were not deemed vital remains unsatisfied. So inflation does exist, but for inessentials. The result is that there are few real signs of *economic* discontent in the working class . . .[17]

This improvement in living conditions has not been confined to the dominant Russian nationality, but has extended to the population as a whole. The Brezhnev leadership was only too aware of the national dimension within the Soviet system. It is the Baltic Republics that have the highest living standards today, a Central Asian peasant is better off than a Russian collective farmer and there is no qualitative difference between a provincial town in the Ukraine or in Russia.

However, only a crass economism could compel one to view the situation complacently. It is the existence of a bureaucracy and the *nomenklatura* structure of privileges that acts as a massive road-block on the path of any meaningful democratization. National tensions in the Caucasian Republics have not been lessened by the economic advantages they have enjoyed. In October 1980 there were massive demonstrations in Estonia. This coincided with a letter sent to Brezhnev by 365 Georgian intellectuals, including members of the Academy of Sciences, protesting against the 'russification drives' which 'lead to a gradual loss of the national rights of the Georgian people that were won in the struggle against Tsarism, contradict Leninist nationalities policy and constitute a violation of the constitutional status of the Georgian people'. These contradictions extend into the CPSU itself, where they fester, creating the basis for future explosion. How could it be otherwise when the Communist Party was written into the 1977 Brezhnev Constitution as 'the leading and directing force of Soviet society, the nucleus of its political system' (Chapter 1, Article 6). Thus no serious discussion took place about reviving the long-extinct power of soviets, since that would have meant a formal structure of representation and periodic elections. This would have threatened the power of the bureaucracy by signalling the end of its political monopoly. Here the old Stalinist methods were humanized, but not altered in any fundamental way.[18] By the time Brezhnev died, the post-Stalinist phase over which he had so diligently presided also came to an end. There were a number of major scandals involving corruption at a high level, and the low-productivity levels in the factories were beginning to produce new strains. Bureaucratic pluralism had given party bureaucrats a security that they had not enjoyed under Stalin, but it had increased the gulf between the *nomenklatura* and the needs of ordinary citizens as well as enabling local chiefs to organize their own networks based on patronage.

More fundamentally we can say that the Brezhnev era with its relaxations on the cultural level and the considerable improvement in the conditions of life has had an enormous effect on the post-war generations. Those born after 1950 have not experienced the traumas and fears of the Stalin period. The younger generation enjoys a self-confidence which is more reminiscent of their grandparents than of their parents. They are bound to exert a new pressure (and on every level) for democratic freedoms and a loosening of the ideological monopoly of the bureaucracy as well as its capacity for social control. The very successes of Brezhnev have created the conditions for a new period of turbulence. The fact that the USSR is an advanced industrial society places its economic base in a situation of confrontation with an outmoded and primitive political structure. Even on the question of improving productivity in the factories, a number of liberal journals within the Soviet Union have hinted that some degree of workers' control will be necessary in place of the present system of 'one-man management'. An unusual poll of 900 factory workers throughout the USSR was carried out by the Komsomol in 1977. It discovered that 'only isolated individuals opposed the idea of electing the factory executive' and 'some 76 per cent of those who favoured elections maintained that under such a system production would become more efficient, management would improve and become more responsible for their jobs.'[19]

Yuri Andropov was elected General Secretary of the CPSU at a time when the worsening international situation coincided with the need for an audacious new offensive on the domestic front. His death at the beginning of 1984 delayed reforms as the gerontocracy re-established its grip. Upon the policies that are devised by the post-Chernenko-leadership will depend the future of the bureaucratic system. All final judgements will, therefore, have to wait as history is still in the process of being made. Yet upon its resolution could depend the very future of socialism and the continued existence of the human race.

Stalinism was presented by its apologists as 'socialism', the first stage on the long road to communism. This theme was eagerly seized upon by the ruling classes in the West which sought to equate the socialist project with the crimes of Stalinism. This remains a central myth of capitalist ideologists to this very day. To state this fact is not to imply that it can be easily conjured away. The crimes have been too great, the confusion engendered has gone too deep, the resultant cynicism become too widespread in the European working class, to disappear at a stroke. No book, anthology, article or poem, speech or TV play can effectively challenge this equation of Stalinism (or its modified and muted successors) and socialism. Relief will only come with direct experience and knowledge that proves the opposite. The populations of both East and West will have to see with their own eyes a system that preaches and practises both socialism and democracy (political pluralism, freedom of speech, access to media, right to form a trade union, cultural liberty) before a massive shift in consciousness can take place. Such a society, which could be glimpsed in Dubcek's Czechoslovakia, would not simply bury Stalinism and exorcize its ghosts. It would also offer the most profound and meaningful challenge to the priorities of the capitalist order in the West, which survives largely because of the continuous besmirching of socialism in the East. The price paid for these survivals has not been a small

one: two World Wars, genocide against colonial peoples, institutionalized misery in the 'third world' and the threat of a nuclear conflagration
that could obliterate all life on this planet.

The aim of this anthology is to stimulate discussion rather than
foreclose debate but, above all, to challenge the simplistic cold war or-
thodoxies currently prevalent at the Sorbonne, Cambridge and Harvard.

NOTES TO INTRODUCTION

1. E. H. Carr, 'The USSR and the West', *New Left Review*, 111, September
   1978.
2. V. I. Lenin, 'Report to the 7th All-Russia Congress of Soviets', December
   1919, Moscow, *Collected Works*, vol. 30, p. 207.
3. Winston Churchill told Italian journalists in Rome in 1927 that, 'if I had been
   an Italian, I am sure I would have been wholeheartedly with you from start to
   finish in your triumphant struggle against the bestial appetites and passions of
   Leninism.' Quoted in Ralph Miliband, *Capitalist Democracy in Britain*,
   London, 1983, p. 47. Lord Reith, the hallowed father-figure of the BBC, was
   another admirer of Mussolini and Hitler!
4. The most precise account of this last critical phase of Lenin's life is contained in
   Moshe Lewin, *Lenin's Last Struggle*, London, 1968.
5. This exchange took place on 1 August 1927 and is quoted in Ernest Mandel,
   Trotsky: A Study in the Dynamic of His Thought, London, 1979.
6. See 'M.B.', 'Trotskyists at Vorkuta', p. 187.
7. Hélène Carrère D'Encausse, *Stalin: Order Through Terror*, London, 1981.
8. Max Hayward, 'Literature in the Soviet Period' in Auty and Obolensky (eds),
   An Introduction to Russian Language and Literature, Cambridge, 1979.
9. Radek's servility may well have been tongue-in-cheek, though the cultured old
   Bolshevik had become a time-server. The most notorious thought-policeman
   was Zhdanov, who was to describe his literary theories thus: 'Comrade Stalin
   described our writers as "engineers of human minds". What does it mean?
   What duties does this title impose on you? It means that truthfulness and
   historical concreteness of artistic depiction must be combined with the task of
   ideological remoulding and re-education of the toiling people in the spirit of
   socialism. This method in fiction and in literary criticism is what we call
   Socialist Realism.'
10. Tony Cliff is the pen name of Ygael Gluckstein, a Palestinian Marxist, who
    settled in Britain after the Second World War. Cliff was to break with
    Trotskyist orthodoxy in the early fifties and found the International Socialists,
    the forerunners of the British Socialist Workers' Party. Cliff's best-known
    work, *Russia: A Marxist Analysis*, has gone through several editions. In sharp
    contrast to Burnham, Shachtman and Djilas, Cliff remains an intransigent
    revolutionary committed to the victory of socialism.
11. For Lenin state-capitalism did not refer to a new socio-economic formation,
    but to a mode of functioning of capitalism under the control of a workers'
    state.

12. Perry Anderson, 'Trotsky's Interpretation of Stalinism', p. 118.

13. This can be attested by the fact that a number of Trotsky's writings, as well as critical works by Ernest Mandel, Perry Anderson, Pierre Frank and Wang Fan-Hsi, have been officially published in Peking.

14. Jean-Paul Sartre, 'Czechoslovakia: The Socialism That Came In from the Cold' in *Between Existentialism and Marxism*, London, 1974.

15. See Livio Maitan, *Party, Army and Masses in China*, London, 1970. An additional point, however, needs to be made. However limited the aim and scope of these mobilizations they undoubtedly aided in politicizing the masses to a certain extent. The fact that the Chinese dissidents are, in their majority, Marxists can be traced to this turbulent period in Chinese politics. The cultural atrocities and loss of life during the 'cultural revolution' should not lead us to unduly facile analogies with the Stalinist purges of the Thirties.

16. For an example of these see Victor Serge, *Year One of the Russian Revolution*, London, 1972.

17. Zhores Medvedev, 'Russia Under Brezhnev', *New Left Review*, 117, September 1979.

18. The 1977 Constitution abandoned all talk of soviets, even on paper. The party was recognized as the only political organism of the state. Its membership had been just under 7 million in 1952 at the 19th Congress. At the 26th Congress in 1981 it stood at almost 18 million! The expansion was most noticeable in the collective farm sector and among industrial workers of the big towns. Thus any rise in social tensions or an outbreak of radical political demands would find an immediate reflection inside the CPSU itself.

19. Cited by the distinguished Sovietologist, Dr Bohdan Krawchenko of the University of Alberta, in a paper delivered to the Marx Centenary Conference in Winnipeg, Canada, in March 1983.

Part 1

The Roots of the Problem

1. Social Relations in the Soviet Union

Leon Trotsky

In the industries state ownership of the means of production prevails almost universally. In agriculture it prevails absolutely only in the Soviet farms, which comprise no more than 10 per cent of the tilled land. In the collective farms cooperative or group ownership is combined in various proportions with state and private ownership. The land, although legally belonging to the state, has been transferred to the collectives for 'perpetual' use, which differs little from group ownership. The tractors and elaborate machinery belong to the state; the smaller equipment belongs to the collectives. Each collective farmer moreover carries on individual agriculture. Finally, more than 10 per cent of the peasants remain individual farmers.

According to the census of 1934, 28.1 per cent of the population were workers and employees of state enterprises and institutions. Industrial and building-trade workers, not including their families, amounted in 1935 to 7.5 million. The collective farms and cooperative crafts comprised, at the time of the census, 45.9 per cent of the population. Students, soldiers of the Red Army, pensioners and other elements directly dependent upon the state, made up 3.4 per cent. Altogether, 74 per cent of the population belonged to the 'socialist sector', and 95.8 per cent of the basic capital of the country fell to the share of this 74 per cent. Individual peasants and craftsmen still comprised, in 1934, 22.5 per cent, but they had possession of only a little more than 4 per cent of the national capital!

Since 1934 there has been no census; the next one will be in 1937. Undoubtedly, however, during the last two years the private enterprise sector has shrunk still more in favour of the 'socialist'. Individual peasants and craftsmen, according to the calculations of official economists, now constitute about 10 per cent of the population – that is, about 17 million people. Their economic importance has fallen very much lower than their numbers. The Secretary of the Central Committee, Andreyev, announced in April 1936: 'The relative weight of socialist production in our country in 1936 ought to reach 98.5 per cent. That is to say, something like an insignificant 1.5 per cent still belongs to the nonsocialist sector.' These optimistic figures seem at first glance an unanswerable proof of the 'final and irrevocable' victory of socialism. But woe to him who cannot see social reality behind arithmetic!

The figures themselves are arrived at with some stretching: it is sufficient to point out that the private allotments alongside the collective farms are entered under the 'socialist' sector. However, that is not the crux of the question. The enormous and wholly indubitable statistical superiority of the state and collective forms of economy, important though it is for the future, does not remove another and no less important question: that of the strength of bourgeois tendencies within the 'socialist' sector itself, and this not only in agriculture but in industry. The material level already attained is high enough to awaken increased demands in all, but wholly insufficient to satisfy them. Therefore, the very dynamic of economic progress involves an awakening of petty bourgeois appetites, not only among the peasants and representatives of 'intellectual' labour, but also among the upper circles of the proletariat. A bare antithesis between individual proprietors and collective farmers, between private craftsmen and state industries, does not give the slightest idea of the explosive power of these appetites, which imbue the whole economy of the country, and express themselves, generally speaking, in the desire of each and every one to give as little as possible to society and receive as much as possible from it.

No less energy and ingenuity is being spent in solving money-grubbers' and consumers' problems than upon socialist construction in the proper sense of the word. Hence derives, in part, the extremely low productivity of social labour. While the state finds itself in continual struggle with the molecular action of these centrifugal forces, the ruling group itself forms the chief reservoir of legal and illegal personal accumulations. Masked as they are with new juridical norms, the petty bourgeois tendencies cannot, of course, be easily determined statistically. But their actual predominance in economic life is proven primarily by the 'socialist' bureaucracy itself, that flagrant *contradictio in adjecto*, that monstrous and continually growing social distortion, which in turn becomes the source of malignant growths in society.

The new constitution – wholly founded, as we shall see, upon an identification of the bureaucracy with the state, and the state with the people – says: '. . . the state property – that is, the possessions of the whole people'. This identification is the fundamental sophism of the official doctrine. It is perfectly true that Marxists, beginning with Marx himself, have employed in relation to the workers' state the terms *state*, *national* and *socialist* property as simple synonyms. On a large historic scale, such a mode of speech involves no special inconveniences. But it becomes the source of crude mistakes, and of downright deceit, when applied to the first and still unassured stages of the development of a new society, and one moreover isolated and economically lagging behind the capitalist countries.

In order to become social, private property must as inevitably pass through the state stage as the caterpillar in order to become a butterfly must pass through the pupal stage. But the pupa is not a butterfly. Myriads of pupae perish without ever becoming butterflies. State property becomes the property of 'the whole people' only to the degree that social privilege and differentiation disappear, and therewith the necessity of the state. In other words: state property is converted into socialist property in proportion as it ceases to be state property. And the contrary is true: the higher the Soviet state rises above the people, and the more fiercely it opposes itself as the guardian of property to the people as its squanderer, the more obviously does it testify against the socialist character of this state property.

'We are still far from the *complete* abolition of classes,' confesses the official press, referring to the still existing differentiation of city and country, intellectual and physical labour. This purely academic acknowledgement has the advantage that it permits a concealment of the income of the bureaucracy under the honourable title of 'intellectual' labour. The 'friends' – to whom Plato is much dearer than the truth – also confine themselves to an academic admission of survivals of the old inequality. In reality, these much put-upon 'survivals' are completely inadequate to explain the Soviet reality. If the differences between city and country have been mitigated in certain respects, in others they have been considerably deepened, thanks to the extraordinarily swift growth of cities and city culture – that is, of comforts for an urban minority. The social distance between physical and intellectual labour, notwithstanding the filling out of the scientific cadres by newcomers from below, has increased, not decreased, during recent years. The thousand-year-old caste barriers defining the life of every man on all sides – the polished urbanite and the uncouth *muzhik*, the wizard of science and the day labourer – have not just been preserved from the past in a more or less softened form, but have to a considerable degree been born anew, and are assuming a more and more defiant character.

The notorious slogan: 'The cadres decide everything', characterizes the nature of Soviet society far more frankly than Stalin himself would wish. The cadres are in their very essence the organs of domination and command. A cult of 'cadres' means above all a cult of bureaucracy, of officialdom, and aristocracy of technique. In the matter of playing up and developing cadres, as in other matters, the soviet regime still finds itself compelled to solve problems which the advanced bourgeoisie solved long ago in its own countries. But since the Soviet cadres come forward under a socialist banner, they demand an almost divine veneration and a continually rising salary. The development of 'socialist' cadres is thus accompanied by a rebirth of bourgeois inequality.

From the point of view of property in the means of production, the differences between a marshal and a servant girl, the head of a trust and a day labourer, the son of a people's commissar and a homeless child, seem not to exist at all. Nevertheless, the former occupy lordly apartments, enjoy several summer homes in various parts of the country, have the best automobiles at their disposal, and have long ago forgotten how to shine their own shoes. The latter live in wooden barracks often without partitions, lead a half-hungry existence, and do not shine their own shoes only because they go barefoot. To the bureaucrat this difference does not seem worthy of attention. To the day labourer, however, it seems, not without reason, very essential.

Superficial 'theoreticians' can comfort themselves, of course, that the distribution of wealth is a factor secondary to its production. The dialectic of interaction, however, retains here all its force. The destiny of the state-appropriated means of production will be decided in the long run according as these differences in personal existence evolve in one direction or the other. If a ship is declared collective property, but the passengers continue to be divided into first, second and third class, it is clear that, for the third-class passengers, differences in the conditions of life will have infinitely more importance than that juridical change in proprietorship. The first-class passengers, on the other hand, will propound, together with their coffee and cigars, the thought that collective ownership is everything and a comfortable cabin nothing at all. Antagonisms growing out of this may well explode the unstable collective.

The Soviet press relates with satisfaction how a little boy in the Moscow zoo, receiving to his question, 'Whose is that elephant?' the answer: 'The state's', made the immediate inference: 'That means it's a little bit mine too.' However, if the elephant were actually divided, the precious tusks would fall to the chosen, a few would regale themselves with elephantine hams, and the majority would get along with hooves and guts. The boys who are done out of their share hardly identify the state property with their own. The homeless consider 'theirs' only that which they steal from the state. The little 'socialist' in the zoological garden was probably the son of some eminent official accustomed to draw inferences from the formula: *'L'état – c'est moi.'*

If we translate socialist relations, for illustration, into the language of the market, we may represent the citizen as a stockholder in a company which owns the wealth of the country. If the property belonged to all the people, that would presume an equal distribution of 'shares', and consequently a right to the same dividend for all 'shareholders'. The citizens participate in the national enterprise, however, not only as 'shareholders', but also as producers. On the lower stage of communism, which we have agreed to call socialism, payments for labour are still made according to bourgeois norms – that is, in dependence upon skill, intensity, and so on. The theoretical income of each citizen is thus composed of two parts, a + b – that is, dividend + wages. The higher the technique and the more complete the organization of industry, the greater is the place occupied by a as against b, and the less is the influence of individual differences of labour upon standard of living. From the fact that wage differences in the Soviet Union are not less, but greater than in capitalist countries, it must be inferred that the shares of the Soviet citizen are not equally distributed, and that in his income the dividend as well as the wage payment is unequal. Whereas the unskilled labourer receives only b, the minimum payment which under similar conditions he would receive in a capitalist enterprise, the Stakhanovist or bureaucrat receives 2a + b, or 3a + b, etc., while b also in its turn may become 2b, 3b, etc. The differences in income are determined, in other words, not only by differences of individual productiveness, but also by a masked appropriation of the products of the labour of others. The privileged minority of shareholders is living at the expense of the deprived majority.

If you assume that the Soviet unskilled worker receives more than he would under a similar level of technique and culture in a capitalist enterprise – that is to say, that he is still a small shareholder – it is necessary to consider his wages as equal to a + b. The wages of the higher categories would be expressed with the formula: 3a + 2b, 10a + 15b, etc. This means that the unskilled worker has one share, the Stakhanovist three, the specialist ten. Moreover, their wages in the proper sense are related as 1 : 2 : 15. Hymns to the sacred socialist property sound under these conditions a good deal more convincing to the manager or the Stakhanovist, than to the rank-and-file worker or collective peasant. The rank-and-file workers, however, are the overwhelming majority of society. It was they, and not the new aristocracy, that socialism had in mind.

'The worker in our country is not a wage slave and is not the seller of a commodity called labour power. He is a free workman' (*Pravda*). For the present period this unctuous formula is unpermissible bragging. The transfer of the factories to the state changed the situation of the worker only juridically. In reality, he is compelled to live in want and to work a definite number of hours for a definite wage. Those hopes which the worker formerly had placed in the party and the trade unions, he transferred after the Revolution to the state created by him. But the useful functioning of this implement turned out to be limited by the level of technique and culture. In order to raise this level, the new state resorted to the old methods of pressure upon the muscles and nerves of the worker.

There grew up a corps of slave drivers. The management of industry became superbureaucratic. The workers lost all influence whatever upon the management of the factory. With piecework payment, hard conditions of material existence, lack of free movement, with terrible police repression penetrating the life of every factory, it is hard indeed for the worker to feel himself a 'free workman'. In the bureaucracy he sees the manager, in the state, the employer. Free labour is incompatible with the existence of a bureaucratic state.

With the necessary changes, what has been said above relates also to the country. According to the official theory, collective farm property is a special form of socialist property. *Pravda* writes that the collective farms 'are in essence already of the same type as the state enterprises and are consequently socialistic', but immediately adds that the guarantee of the socialist development of agriculture lies in the circumstance that 'the Bolshevik Party administers the collective farms'. *Pravda* refers us, that is, from economics to politics. This means in essence that socialist relations are not as yet embodied in the real relations among men, but dwell in the benevolent heart of the authorities. The workers will do very well if they keep a watchful eye on that heart. In reality the collective farms stand halfway between individual and state economy, and the petty bourgeois tendencies within them are admirably helped along by the swiftly growing private allotments or personal economies conducted by their members.

Notwithstanding the fact that individual-tilled land amounts to only 4 million hectares, as against 108 million collective hectares – that is, less than 4 per cent – thanks to the intensive and especially the truck-garden cultivation of this land, it furnishes the peasant family with the most important objects of consumption. The main body of horned cattle, sheep and pigs is the property of the collective farmers, and not of the collectives. The peasants often convert their subsidiary farms into the essential ones, letting the unprofitable collectives take second place. On the other hand, those collectives which pay highly for the working day are rising to a higher social level and creating a category of well-to-do farmers. The centrifugal tendencies are not yet dying, but on the contrary are growing stronger. In any case, the collectives have succeeded so far in transforming only the juridical forms of economic relations in the country – in particular the methods of distributing income – but they have left almost without change the old hut and vegetable garden, the barnyard chores, the whole rhythm of heavy *muzhik* labour. To a considerable degree they have left also the old attitude to the state. The state no longer, to be sure, serves the landlords or the bourgeoisie, but it takes away too much from the villages for the benefit of the cities, and it retains too many greedy bureaucrats.

For the census to be taken on 6 January 1937, the following list of social categories has been drawn up: worker; clerical worker; collective farmer; individual farmer; individual craftsman; member of the liberal professions; minister of religion; other nonlabouring elements. According to the official commentary, this census list fails to include any other social characteristics only because there are no classes in the Soviet Union. In reality the list is constructed with the direct intention of concealing the privileged upper strata, and the more deprived lower depths. The real divisions of Soviet society, which should and might easily be revealed with the help of an honest census, are as follows: heads of the bureaucracy, specialists, etc., living in bourgeois conditions; medium and lower strata, on the level of the petty bourgeoisie; worker and collective farm aristocracy – approximately on the same level; medium working mass; medium stratum of collective farmers; individual peasants and craftsmen; lower worker and peasant strata passing over into the *lumpenproletariat*; homeless children, prostitutes, etc.

When the new constitution announces that in the Soviet Union 'abolition of the exploitation of man by man' has been attained, it is not telling the truth. The new social differentiation has created conditions for the revival of the exploitation of man in its most barbarous form – that of buying him into slavery for personal service. In the lists for the new census personal servants are not mentioned at all. They are, evidently, to be dissolved in the general group of 'workers'. There are, however, plenty of questions about this: Does the socialist citizen have servants, and just how many (maid, cook, nurse, governess, chauffeur)? Does he have an automobile at his personal disposal? How many rooms does he occupy? etc. Not a word in these lists about the scale of earnings! If the rule were revived that exploitation of the labour of others deprives one of political rights, it would turn out, somewhat unexpectedly, that the cream of the ruling group are outside the bounds of the Soviet constitution. Fortunately, they have established a complete equality of rights . . . for servant and master! Two opposite tendencies are growing up out of the depth of the Soviet regime. To the extent that, in contrast to a decaying capitalism, it develops the productive forces, it is preparing the economic basis of socialism. To the extent that, for the benefit of an upper stratum, it carries to more and more extreme expression bourgeois norms of distribution, it is preparing a capitalist restoration. This contrast between forms of property and norms of distribution cannot grow indefinitely. Either the bourgeois norm must in one form or another spread to the means of production, or the norms of distribution must be brought into correspondence with the socialist property system.

The bureaucracy dreads the exposure of this alternative. Everywhere and all the time – in the press, in speeches, in statistics, in the novels of its *littérateurs*, in the verses of its poets, and, finally, in the text of the new constitution – it painstakingly conceals the real relations both in town and country with abstractions from the socialist dictionary. That is why the official ideology is all so lifeless, talentless and false.

State capitalism?

We often seek salvation from unfamiliar phenomena in familiar terms. An attempt has been made to conceal the enigma of the Soviet regime by calling it 'state capitalism'. This term has the advantage that nobody knows exactly what it means. The term 'state capitalism' originally arose to designate all the phenomena which arise when a bourgeois state takes direct charge of the means of transport or of industrial enterprises. The very necessity of such measures is one of the signs that the productive forces have outgrown capitalism and are bringing it to a partial self-negation in practice. But the outworn system, along with its elements of self-negation, continues to exist as a capitalist system.

Theoretically, to be sure, it is possible to conceive a situation in which the bourgeoisie as a whole constitutes itself a stock company which, by means of its state, administers the whole national economy. The economic laws of such a regime would present no mysteries. A single capitalist, as is well known, receives in the form of profit, not that part of the surplus value which is directly created by the workers of his own enterprise, but a share of the combined surplus value created throughout the country proportionate to the amount of his own capital. Under an integral 'state capitalism', this law of the equal rate of profit would be realized, not by devious routes – that is, competition among different capitals – but immediately and directly through state bookkeeping. Such a regime never existed, however, and, because of profound contradictions among the proprietors themselves, never will exist – the more so since, in its quality of universal repository of capitalist property, the state would be too tempting an object for social revolution.

During the war, and especially during the experiments in fascist economy, the term 'state capitalism' has most often been understood to mean a system of state interference and regulation. The French employ a much more suitable term for this – *étatisme*. There are undoubtedly points of contact between state capitalism and 'state-ism', but taken as systems they are opposite rather than identical. State capitalism means the substitution of state property for private property, and for that very reason remains partial in character. State-ism, no matter where – in Italy, Mussolini, in Germany, Hitler, in America, Roosevelt, or in France, Léon Blum – means state intervention on the basis of private property, and with the goal of preserving it. Whatever be the programmes of the government, state-ism inevitably leads to a transfer of the damages of the decaying system from strong shoulders to weak. It 'rescues' the small proprietor from complete ruin only to the extent that his existence is necessary for the preservation of big property. The planned measures of state-ism are dictated not by the demands of a development of the productive forces, but by a concern for the preservation of private property at the expense of the productive forces, which are in revolt against it. State-ism means applying brakes to the development of technique, supporting unviable enterprises, perpetuating parasitic social strata. In a word, state-ism is completely reactionary in character.

The words of Mussolini: 'Three-fourths of Italian economy, industrial and agricultural, is in the hands of the state' (26 May 1934), are not to be taken literally. The fascist state is not an owner of enterprises, but only an intermediary between their owners. These two things are not identical. *Popolo d'Italia* says on this subject: 'The corporative state directs and integrates the economy, but does not run it (*dirige e porta alla unità l'economia, ma non fa l'economia, non gestisce*), which, with a monopoly of production, would be nothing but collectivism' (11 June 1936). Towards the peasants and small proprietors in general, the fascist bureaucracy takes the attitude of a threatening lord and master. Towards the capitalist magnates, that of a first plenipotentiary. 'The corporative state,' correctly writes the Italian Marxist, Feroci, 'is nothing but the sales clerk of monopoly capital . . . Mussolini takes upon the state the whole risk of the enterprises, leaving to the industrialists the profits of exploitation.' And Hitler in this respect follows in the steps of Mussolini. The limits of the planning principle, as well as its real content, are determined by the class dependence of the fascist state. It is not a question of increasing the power of man over nature in the interests of society, but of exploiting society in the interests of the few. 'If I desired,' boasts Mussolini, 'to establish in Italy – which really has not happened – state capitalism or state socialism, I should possess today all the necessary and adequate objective conditions.' All except one: *the expropriation of the class of capitalists.* In order to realize this condition, fascism would have to go over to the other side of the barricades – 'which really has not happened' to quote the hasty assurance of Mussolini, and, of course, will not happen. To expropriate the capitalists would require other forces, other cadres and other leaders.

The first concentration of the means of production in the hands of the state to occur in history was achieved by the proletariat with the method of social revolution, and not by capitalists with the method of state trustification. Our brief analysis is sufficient to show how absurd are the attempts to identify capitalist state-ism with the Soviet system. The former is reactionary, the latter progressive.

Is the bureaucracy a ruling class?

Classes are characterized by their position in the social system of economy, and primarily by their relation to the means of production. In civilized societies, property relations are validated by laws. The nationalization of the land, the means of industrial production, transport and exchange, together with the monopoly of foreign trade, constitute the basis of the Soviet social structure. Through these relations, established by the proletarian revolution, the nature of the Soviet Union as a proletarian state is for us basically defined.

In its intermediary and regulating function, its concern to maintain social ranks, and its exploitation of the state apparatus for personal goals, the Soviet bureaucracy is similar to every other bureaucracy, especially the fascist. But it is also in a vast way different. In no other regime has a bureaucracy ever achieved such a degree of independence from the dominating class. In bourgeois society, the bureaucracy represents the interests of a possessing and educated class, which has at its disposal innumerable means of everyday control over its administration of affairs. The Soviet bureaucracy has risen above a class which is hardly emerging from destitution and darkness, and has no tradition of dominion or command. Whereas the fascists, when they find themselves in power, are united with the big bourgeoisie by bonds of common interest, friendship, marriage, etc., the Soviet bureaucracy takes on bourgeois customs without having beside it a national bourgeoisie. In this sense we cannot deny that it is something more than a bureaucracy. It is in the full sense of the word the sole privileged and commanding stratum in the Soviet society.

Another difference is no less important. The Soviet bureaucracy has expropriated the proletariat politically in order by methods of *its own* to defend the social conquests. But the very fact of its appropriation of political power in a country where the principal means of production are in the hands of the state, creates a new and hitherto unknown relation between the bureaucracy and the riches of the nation. The means of production belong to the state. But the state, so to speak, 'belongs' to the bureaucracy. If these as yet wholly new relations should solidify, become the norm and be legalized, whether with or without resistance from the workers, they would, in the long run, lead to a complete liquidation of the social conquests of the proletarian revolution. But to speak of that now is at least premature. The proletariat has not yet said its last word. The bureaucracy has not yet created social supports for its dominion in the form of special types of property. It is compelled to defend state property as the source of its power and its income. In this aspect of its activity it still remains a weapon of proletarian dictatorship.

The attempt to represent the Soviet bureaucracy as a class of 'state capitalists' will obviously not withstand criticism. The bureaucracy has neither stocks nor bonds. It is recruited, supplemented and renewed in the manner of an administrative hierarchy, independently of any special property relations of its own. The individual bureaucrat cannot transmit to his heirs his rights in the exploitation of the state apparatus. The bureaucracy enjoys its privileges under the form of an abuse of power. It conceals its income; it pretends that as a special social group it does not even exist. Its appropriation of a vast share of the national income has the character of social parasitism. All this makes the position of the commanding Soviet stratum in the highest degree contradictory, equivocal and undignified, notwithstanding the completeness of its power and the smoke screen of flattery that conceals it.

Bourgeois society has in the course of its history displaced many political regimes and bureaucratic castes, without changing its social foundations. It has preserved itself against the restoration of feudal and guild relations by the superiority of its productive methods. The state power has been able either to cooperate with capitalist development, or put brakes on it. But in general the productive forces, upon a basis of private property and competition, have been working out their own destiny. In contrast to this, the property relations which issued from the socialist revolution are indivisibly bound up with the new state as their repository. The predominance of socialist over petty bourgeois tendencies is guaranteed, not by the automatism of the economy – we are still far from that – but by political measures taken by the dictatorship. The character of the economy as a whole thus depends upon the character of the state power.

A collapse of the Soviet regime would lead inevitably to the collapse of the planned economy, and thus to the abolition of state property. The bond of compulsion between the trusts and the factories within them would fall away. The more successful enterprises would succeed in coming out on the road of independence. They might convert themselves into stock companies, or they might find some other transitional form of property – one, for example, in which the workers should participate in the profits. The collective farms would disintegrate at the same time, and far more easily. The fall of the present bureaucratic dictatorship, if it were not replaced by a new socialist power, would thus mean a return to capitalist relations with a catastrophic decline of industry and culture.

But if a socialist government is still absolutely necessary for the preservation and development of the planned economy, the question is all the more important, upon whom the present Soviet government relies, and in what measure the socialist character of its policy is guaranteed. At the 11th Party Congress in March 1922, Lenin, in practically bidding farewell to the party, addressed these words to the commanding group: 'History knows transformations of all sorts. To rely upon conviction, devotion and other excellent spiritual qualities – that is not to be taken seriously in politics.' Being determines consciousness. During the last fifteen years, the government has changed its social composition even more deeply than its ideas. Since of all the strata of Soviet society the bureaucracy has best solved its own social problem, and is fully content with the existing situation, it has ceased to offer any subjective guarantee whatever of the socialist direction of its policy. It continues to preserve state property only to the extent that it fears the proletariat. This saving fear is nourished and supported by the illegal party of Bolshevik-Leninists, which is the most conscious expression of the socialist tendencies opposing that bourgeois reaction with which the Thermidorian bureaucracy is completely saturated. As a conscious political force the bureaucracy has betrayed the revolution. But a victorious revolution is fortunately not only a programme and a banner, not only political institutions, but also a system of social relations. To betray it is not enough. You have to overthrow it. The October Revolution has been betrayed by the ruling stratum, but not yet been overthrown. It has a great power of resistance, coinciding with the established property relations, with the living force of the proletariat, the consciousness of its best elements, the impasse of world capitalism, and the inevitability of world revolution.

The question of the character of the Soviet Union not yet decided by history

In order better to understand the character of the present Soviet Union, let us make two different hypotheses about its future. Let us assume first that the Soviet bureaucracy is overthrown by a revolutionary party having all the attributes of the old Bolshevism, enriched moreover by the world experience of the recent period. Such a party would begin with the restoration of democracy in the trade unions and the soviets. It would be able to, and would have to, restore freedom of Soviet parties. Together with the masses, and at their head, it would carry out a ruthless purgation of the state apparatus. It would abolish ranks and decorations, all kinds of privileges, and would limit inequality in the payment of labour to the life necessities of the economy and the state apparatus. It would give the youth free opportunity to think independently, learn, criticize and grow. It would introduce profound changes in the distribution of the national income in correspondence with the interests and will of the worker and peasant masses. But so far as concerns property relations, the new power would not have to resort to revolutionary measures. It would retain and further develop the experiment of planned economy. After the political revolution – that is, the deposing of the bureaucracy – the proletariat would have to introduce in the economy a series of very important reforms, but not another social revolution.

If – to adopt a second hypothesis – a bourgeois party were to overthrow the ruling Soviet caste, it would find no small number of ready servants among the present bureaucrats, administrators, technicians, directors, party secretaries and privileged upper circles in general. A purgation of the state apparatus would, of course, be necessary in this case too. But a bourgeois restoration would probably have to clean out fewer people than a revolutionary party. The chief task of the new power would be to restore private property in the means of production. First of all, it would be necessary to create conditions for the development of strong farmers from the weak collective farms, and for converting the strong collectives into producers' cooperatives of the bourgeois type – into agricultural stock companies. In the sphere of industry, denationalization would begin with the light industries and those producing food. The planning principle would be converted for the transitional period into a series of compromises between state power and individual 'corporations' – potential proprietors, that is, among the Soviet captains of industry, the émigré former proprietors and foreign capitalists. Notwithstanding that the Soviet bureaucracy has gone far towards preparing a bourgeois restoration, the new regime would have to introduce in the matter of forms of property and methods of industry not a reform, but a social revolution.

Let us assume – to take a third variant – that neither a revolutionary nor a counter-revolutionary party seizes power. The bureaucracy continues at the head of the state. Even under these conditions social relations will not jell. We cannot count upon the bureaucracy's peacefully and voluntarily renouncing itself on behalf of socialist equality. If at the present time, notwithstanding the too obvious inconveniences of such an operation, it has considered it possible to introduce ranks and decorations, it must inevitably in future stages seek support for itself in property relations. One may argue that the big bureaucrat cares little what are the prevailing forms of property, provided only they guarantee him the necessary income. This argument ignores not only the instability of the bureaucrat's own rights, but also the question of his descendants. The new cult of the family has not fallen out of the clouds. Privileges have only half their worth, if they cannot be transmitted to one's children. But the right of testament is inseparable from the right of property. It is not enough to be the director of a trust; it is necessary to be a stockholder. The victory of the bureaucracy in this decisive sphere would mean its conversion into a new possessing class. On the other hand, the victory of the proletariat over the bureaucracy would insure a revival of the socialist revolution. The third variant consequently brings us back to the two first, with which, in the interests of clarity and simplicity, we set out.

To define the Soviet regime as transitional, or intermediate, means to abandon such finished social categories as *capitalism* (and therewith 'state capitalism') and also *socialism*. But besides being completely inadequate in itself, such a definition is capable of producing the mistaken idea that from the present Soviet regime *only* a transition to socialism is possible. In reality a backslide to capitalism is wholly possible. A more complete definition will of necessity be complicated and ponderous.

The Soviet Union is a contradictory society halfway between capitalism and socialism, in which: (a) the productive forces are still far from adequate to give the state property a socialist character: (b) the tendency toward primitive accumulation created by want breaks out through innumerable pores of the planned economy; (c) norms of distribution preserving a bourgeois character lie at the basis of a new differentiation of society; (d) the economic growth, while slowly bettering the situation of the toilers, promotes a swift formation of privileged strata; (e) exploiting the social antagonisms, a bureaucracy has converted itself into an uncontrolled caste alien to socialism; (f) the social revolution, betrayed by the ruling party, still exists in property relations and in the consciousness of the toiling masses; (g) a further development of the accumulating contradictions can as well lead to socialism as back to capitalism; (h) on the road to capitalism the counter-revolution would have to break the resistance of the workers; (i) on the road to socialism the workers would have to overthrow the bureaucracy. In the last analysis, the question will be decided by a struggle of living social forces, both on the national and the world arena.

Doctrinaires will doubtless not be satisfied with this hypothetical definition. They would like categorical formulae: yes – yes, and no – no. Sociological problems would certainly be simpler, if social phenomena always had a finished character. There is nothing more dangerous, however, than to throw out of reality, for the sake of logical completeness, elements which today violate your scheme and tomorrow may wholly overturn it. In our analysis, we have above all avoided doing violence to dynamic social formations which have had no precedent and have no analogies. The scientific task, as well as the political, is not to give a finished definition to an unfinished process, but to follow all its stages, separate its progressive from its reactionary tendencies, expose their mutual relations, foresee possible variants of development, and find in this foresight a basis for action.

2. The 'Professional Dangers' of Power

Christian Rakovsky

Dear Comrade Valentinov,

In your 'Meditations on the Masses' of 8 July, in examining the problems of the 'activity' of the working class, you speak of a fundamental question, that of the conservation, by the proletariat, of its directing role in our state. Although all the political claims of the opposition aim to this end, I agree with you that all has not been said on this question. Up to the present, we have always examined it coupled with the whole problem of the taking and conserving of political power; to make it clearer, it should have been taken separately, as a question which has its own value and importance. The reality of events has brought it to the fore.

The opposition as against the party will always retain as one of its merits – a merit which nothing can remove – the fact that it has, in good time, sounded the alarm on the terrible decline of the spirit of activity of the working classes, and on their increasing indifference towards the destiny of the dictatorship of the proletariat and of the Soviet state.

That which characterizes the flood of scandal which has become public, that which constitutes its greatest danger, is precisely this passivity of the masses (a passivity greater even among the communist masses than among the non-party masses) towards the unprecedented manifestations of despotism which have emerged. Workers witnessed these, but let them pass without protest, or contented themselves with a few remarks, through fear of those who are in power or because of political indifference. From the scandal of Chubarovsk (to go back no further) to the abuses of Smolensk, of Artiemovsk, etc. . . . . the same refrain is always heard: *'We have known for some time'* . . . Thefts, prevarications, violence, orgies, incredible abuse of power, unlimited despotism, drunkenness, debauchery: all these are spoken of as known facts, not for a month, but for years, and also as things that everyone tolerates without knowing why.

I do not need to explain that when the world bourgeoisie vociferates on the vices of the Soviet Union, we can ignore it with a quiet disdain. We know too well the moral purity of governments and parliaments in the whole bourgeois world. But they are not the ones on whom we are to model ourselves. With us, it is a *workers'* state. No one today can ignore the terrible consequences of the political indifference of the working class. Moreover, the question of the causes of this indifference and that of the means to eliminate it is considered to be a fundamental one. However, this obliges us to consider it in a fundamental way, scientifically, by submitting it to a profound analysis. Such a phenomenon merits our full attention.

The explanations which you give of this are doubtless correct: each of us has already laid them bare during our talks: they already form part of our platform (that is, the platform of the Left opposition of 1927). Nonetheless the interpretations and the remedies proposed to emerge from this painful situation have had and still have an empirical character; they refer to each particular case and do not get to the basis of the question.

To my mind this has come about because the question itself is a new one. Up to the present we have witnessed a great number of cases where the spirit of initiative of the working class has become weakened and declined almost to the level of political reaction. But these examples became apparent to us, as much here as abroad, during a period when the proletariat was battling still for the conquest of political power.

We could not have a previous example of a decline of proletarian ardour in a period when it already had power for the simple reason that in history our case is the first where the working class has retained power for such a time. Up until now, we have known what could happen to the proletariat, that is, the vacillations of spirit which occur when it is an oppressed and exploited class; but it is only now that we can evaluate on the basis of fact, the changes of its mental state when it takes over *the control*.

This political position (of directing class) is not without its dangers: rather, the dangers are very great. I do not refer here to the objective difficulties due to the whole complex of historical conditions, to the capitalist encirclement on the outside, and the pressure of the petty bourgeois inside the country. No, I refer to the inherent difficulties of any new directing class, consequent on the taking and on the exercise of power itself, on the ability or inability to make use of it.

You will understand that these difficulties would continue to exist up to a certain point, even if we allowed, for a moment, that the country was inhabited only by proletarian masses and the exterior was made up solely of proletarian states. These difficulties might be called the 'professional dangers' of power. In fact, the situation of a class which is fighting to wrest control and that of a class holding control in its hands is different. I repeat that when I spoke of dangers, I did not think of the relationships to other classes, but more of those which are created within the ranks of the victorious class itself.

What does a class on the offensive represent? The maximum of unity and cohesion. All spirit of trade or clique, let alone personal interests, becomes secondary. All initiative is in the hands of the militant mass itself and of its revolutionary vanguard, which is bound to the mass in a very close, organic relationship.

When a class takes power, one of its parts becomes the agent of that power. Thus arises bureaucracy. In a socialist state, when capitalist accumulation is forbidden by members of the directing party, this differentiation begins as a functional one; it later becomes a social one. I am thinking here of the social position of a communist who has at his disposal a car, a nice apartment, regular holidays, and is receiving the maximum salary authorized by the party; a position which differs from that of the communist working in the coal mines and receiving a salary of fifty to sixty roubles per month. As regards workers and employees, you know that they are divided into eighteen different categories . . .

Another consequence is that certain functions formerly satisfied by the party as a whole, by the whole class, are now become the attributes of power, that is, only of a certain number of persons in the party and in this class. The unity and cohesion which formerly were the natural consequences of the struggle of the revolutionary class cannot now be maintained except by the application of the whole system of measures which have for their aim the preservation of the equilibrium between the different groups of this class and of this party, and to subordinate these groups to the fundamental goal.

But this constitutes a long and delicate process. It consists in educating politically the dominant class in such a way as to make it capable of holding the state apparatus, the party and the syndicates, of controlling and of directing these organisms. I repeat this: it is a question of education. No class has been born in possession of the art of government. This art can only be acquired by experience, thanks to the errors committed, that is, by each learning from his errors. No Soviet constitution, be it ideal, can insure to the working class an exercise without obstacle of its dictatorship and of its control over the government if the proletariat does not know how to utilize its rights under the constitution. The lack of harmony between the political capacities of any given class, its administrative ability and its judicial constitutional form that it establishes for its own use after the taking of power, is an historical fact. It can be observed in the evolution of all classes, in part also in the history of the bourgeoisie. The English bourgeoisie, for example, fought many battles, not only to remake the constitution according to its own interests, but also to be able to profit from its rights and in particular, fully and without hindrance of its right to vote. One of Charles Dickens' books, *Pickwick Papers*, contains many incidents of this period of English constitutionalism during which the directing group, assisted by its own administrative apparatus, overturns into the ditch coaches bringing to the ballot boxes the opposition's supporters, to prevent them from arriving in time to vote.

This process of differentiation is perfectly natural for the triumphant, or almost triumphant, bourgeoisie. In effect, in the wider sense of the term, the bourgeoisie is made up of a series of groups and even economic classes. We recognize the existence of the upper middle and lower (petty) bourgeoisie: we know that there exists a financial bourgeoisie, a commercial bourgeoisie, an industrial bourgeoisie and an agricultural bourgeoisie. After events such as wars and revolutions, regroupings take place within the ranks of the bourgeoisie itself; new strata appear, begin to play the role which is properly theirs, as for example the proprietors, the acquisitors of national goods, the *nouveaux riches*, as they are called, who appear after every war of a certain length. During the French Revolution, during the period of the Directory, these *nouveaux riches* became one of the factors of the reaction.

Generally speaking, the history of the victory of the third estate in France in 1789 is extremely instructive. Firstly, this third estate was itself made up of extremely disparate elements. It included all who did not belong to the nobility or the clergy; thus it included not only all the various branches of the bourgeoisie, but equally the workers and the poor peasants. It was but gradually, after a long struggle, after armed intervention repeated many times over, that the whole third estate acquired in 1792 the legal possibility of participating in the administration of the country. The political reaction which began even before Thermidor consisted in this, *that the power began to pass both formally and effectively into the hands of an increasingly restricted number of citizens.* Little by little, first by the force of circumstances and then legally, the popular masses were eliminated from the government of the country.

It is true that the pressure of reaction made itself felt initially along the seams joining together sections of classes which constituted the third estate. It is equally true that if we examine a particular group of the bourgeoisie, it does not show class cleavages as clear as those which, for example, are seen separating the bourgeoisie and the proletariat, that is, two classes playing a role entirely different in production. Moreover, in the course of the French Revolution, during its period of decline, power intervened not only to eliminate, following the lines of differentiation, social groups which but yesterday marched together and were united by the same revolutionary aim, but it disintegrated equally more or less homogeneous masses. By functional specialization the given class gave birth, out of its ranks, to circles of high functionaries; such is the result of fissures which were converted, thanks to the pressure of the counter-revolution, into yawning gulfs. Following on this the dominant class itself produced contradictions in the course of the conflict.

The contemporaries of the French Revolution, those who participated and even more the historians of the following period, were preoccupied by the question of the causes of the degeneration of the Jacobin party.

More than once Robespierre warned his partners against the consequences which the *intoxication of power* could bring. He warned them that, holding power, they should not become *too presumptuous*, 'bigheaded', as he said, or as we would say now infected with 'Jacobin vanity'. However, as we shall see later, Robespierre himself contributed largely to the loss of power from the hands of the petty bourgeoisie which leaned on the Parisian workers.

We will not mention here all the facts given by contemporaries concerning the diverse causes of the decomposition of the Jacobin party, such as, for instance, their tendency to enrich themselves, their participation in contracts, in supplies, etc. Let us rather mention a strange and well-known fact: the opinion of Babeuf according to which the fall of the Jacobins was much facilitated by the noble ladies with whom they had entangled themselves. He addressed the Jacobins as follows: 'What are you doing, pusillanimous plebeians? Today they hug you in their arms, tomorrow they will strangle you.' (If the motorcar had existed at the time of the French Revolution, we would also have had the factor of the 'motor-harem', indicated by Comrade Sosnovsky as having played a very important role in the formation of the ideology of our bureaucracy of soviets and the party.)

But what played the most important role in the isolation of Robespierre and the Jacobin Club, that which cut them off completely from the working and petty bourgeois masses, was, in addition to the liquidation of all the elements of the left, beginning with the enraged, the Herbertists and the Chaumettists (of all the Commune of Paris in general), the gradual elimination of the elective principle and its replacement by the principle of *nominations*.

The sending of commissioners to the armies or to the cities where the counter-revolution was once more gaining ground was not only legitimate but defensible. But when, little by little, Robespierre began to replace the judges and the commissioners of the different sections of Paris which, up until then, had been elected in the same way as the judges; when he began to name the presidents of the revolutionary committees and even began to substitute by functionaries all the leadership of the communes, he could not but reinforce the bureaucracy and kill popular initiative by all these measures. Thus the Robespierre regime, instead of developing the revolutionary activities of the masses, already oppressed by the economic crisis and, even more, by the shortage of food, aggravated the situation and facilitated the work of the anti-democratic forces.

Dumas, the president of the revolutionary tribunal, complained to Robespierre that he could not find people to serve as jurors for the tribunal, as no one wished to carry out this function. Robespierre himself experienced this indifference of the Parisian masses when, on the 10th Thermidor, he was led wounded and bleeding through the streets of Paris without any fear that the popular masses would intervene in favour of yesterday's dictator.

From the evidence given, it would seem ridiculous to attribute Robespierre's fall and the defeat of the revolutionary democracy to the *principle of nominations*. However, this did without any doubt accelerate the action of the other factors. Among these a decisive role was played by the difficulties of supplying food and munitions, due largely to the two years of bad crops (as also to the consecutive perturbations at the transformation of the large rural properties of the nobility into small peasant culture), to the constant rise of the price of bread and meat, to the fact that the Jacobins did not at first wish to have recourse to administrative measures to repress the avidity of speculators and rich peasants. And when they finally decided, under the pressure of the masses, to vote the law of the maximum, this law, operating in the conditions of the free market and of capitalist production, inevitably acted as a palliative.

Let us now move on to the reality in which we live.

I believe that it is first necessary to indicate that when we use expressions such as 'the party' and 'the masses' we must not lose sight of the significance which these terms have acquired in the last ten years. The working class and the party – not now *physically* but *morally* – are no longer what they were ten years ago. I do not exaggerate when I say that the militant of 1917 would have difficulty in recognizing himself in the militant of 1928. A profound change has taken place in the anatomy and the physiology of the working class. In my opinion it is necessary to concentrate our attention on the study of the modifications in the tissues and in their functions. Analysis of the changes which have occurred will have to show us the way out of the situation which has been created. I do not present this analysis here; I will limit myself to a few remarks.

In speaking of the working class it is necessary to find an answer to a whole series of questions, for example: What is the proportion of workers actually employed in our industry who have entered it after the Revolution, and what is the proportion of those who worked in it previously? What is the proportion of those who previously participated in the revolutionary movement, have taken part in strikes, have been deported, imprisoned, or have taken part in the war or served in the Red Army? What is the proportion of workers employed in industry who work regularly? How many work only on occasion? What is the proportion in industry of semi-proletarian elements, semi-peasants, etc. . . .

If we penetrate into the depths of the proletariat, of the semi-proletariat and of the working masses in general we will find there whole strata of the population who can hardly be said to be with us. I do not refer only to the workless, who constitute an ever-increasing danger which, in any case, has been clearly signalled by the opposition. I am thinking of the masses reduced to penury, or the semi-pauperized who, thanks to the derisory subsidies allocated by the state, are on the borders of pauperism, theft and prostitution.

We cannot imagine how people but a few steps from us live at times. Sometimes we encounter phenomena whose existence would not have been suspected in a Soviet state, and we get the impression of having suddenly discovered an abyss. It is not a question of pleading the case of Soviet power, by invoking the fact that it has not succeeded in getting rid of the doubtful heritage passed on by the Tsarist and capitalist regime. No: it is simply that in our own time, under the present regime, we discover the existence, within the body of the working class, of crevices into which the bourgeoisie would be able to push this end of the wedge.

During a certain period under the bourgeois regime, the thinking part of the working class carried with it this numerous mass, including the semi-vagabonds. The fall of the capitalist regime was to have brought about the liberation of the *whole proletariat*. The semi-vagabond elements made the bourgeoisie and the capitalist state responsible for their situation; they considered that the revolution should bring a change in their condition. But these people are now far from satisfied; their situation has been improved little if at all. They are beginning to regard Soviet power and that part of the working class in industry, with hostility. They are especially becoming the enemies of the functionaries of the soviets, of the party and of the syndicates. They can sometimes be heard referring to the summits of the working class as the 'new nobility'.

I will not stop to consider here the differentiation which power has introduced into the bosom of the proletariat, and which I qualified above as 'functional'. The function has modified the organism itself; that is to say, that the psychology of those who are charged with the diverse tasks of direction in the administration and the economy of the state, has changed to such a point that not only objectively, but subjectively, not only materially, but morally, they have ceased to be a part of this very same working class. Thus, for example, a factory director playing the 'satrap' despite the fact that he is a communist, despite his proletariat origin, despite the fact that he was a factory worker a few years ago, will not epitomize the best qualities of the proletariat in the eyes of the workers. Molotov may, to his heart's delight, put a sign of equality between the dictatorship of the proletariat and. our state with its bureaucratic degenerations, and what is more with the brutes of Smolensk, the swindlers of Tashkent and the adventurers of Artiomovsk. By doing this he only succeeds in discrediting without satisfying the legitimate discontent of the workers.

If we move on to the party itself, in addition to all the overtones which can be found in the working class, it is necessary to add those from other classes. The social structure of the party is far more heterogeneous than that of the proletariat. It has always been so – with the difference, of course, that when the party had an intense ideological life, it fused this social amalgamation into a single alloy, thanks to the struggle of a revolutionary class in action. But power is a cause, in the party as much as in the working class, of the same differentiation revealing the seams existing between the different social strata.

The bureaucracy of the soviets and of the party constitutes a new order. We are not concerned with isolated cases, of failings in the conduct of a comrade, but rather of a new social category, to whom a whole treatise should be given.

On the project of the programme of the Communist International, I wrote to Leon Davidovitch (Trotsky) among other things:

As regards Chapter 4 (The Transitory Period). The way in which the role of the Communist Parties is formulated in the period of the dictatorship of the proletariat is somewhat weak. Without doubt this vague manner of speaking of the role of the party towards the working class and the state is not the result of hazard. The antithesis existing between the bourgeois democracy is clearly indicated; but not a word is said to explain what the party must do to bring about, concretely, this proletarian democracy. 'Attract the masses and get them to participate in construction', 're-educate its proper nature' (Bukharin makes a point of developing this last idea, among others, more especially in connection with the cultural revolution): these are true statements from a historical point of view, and have been known for a long time; but they are reduced to platitudes if they are not combined with the accumulated experience of ten years of proletarian dictatorship. 'It is here that the question arises of methods of leadership, methods which play such an important role.'

But our leaders do not like to speak of these, being afraid that it might become evident that they themselves have still a long way to go before they 're-educate their proper nature'. If I were charged with the writing of a project of a programme for the Communist International, I would have given much space, in this chapter (The Transitory Period), to the theory of Lenin on the state during the dictatorship of the proletariat and of the role of the party in the creation of a proletariat and of the role of the party in the creation of a proletarian democracy, such as it should have been and not one where there exists a bureaucracy of the soviets and of the party as at present.

Comrade Preobrazhensky has promised to consecrate a special chapter in his book *The Conquests of the Dictatorship of the Proletariat in the Year XI of the Revolution* to the Soviet bureaucracy. I hope that he will not forget the role of the bureaucracy of the party, which plays a much greater role in the Soviet state than that of its sisters, the soviets themselves. I have expressed the hope to him that he will study this specific sociological phenomenon under all its aspects. There is no communist pamphlet which, in relating the treason of social democracy in Germany on 4 August 1914, does not at the same time stress the fatal role which the top bureaucracy of the party and of the syndicates played in the history of the fall of that party. On the other hand, little has been said, and that in very general terms only, on the role played by our party and the Soviet state. It is a sociological phenomenon of the first order, which cannot however be understood and appreciated in its entirety, if its consequences in changing the ideology of the party and of the working class are not examined.

You ask what has happened to the spirit of revolutionary activity of the party and of our proletariat? Where has their revolutionary initiative gone? Where have their ideological interests, their revolutionary values, their proletarian pride gone? You are surprised that there is so much apathy, weakness, pusillanimity, opportunism and so many other things that I could add myself? How is it that those who have a worthy revolutionary past, whose personal honesty cannot be held in doubt, who have given proof of their attachment to the Revolution on more than one occasion, can have been transformed into pitiable bureaucrats? Whence comes this terrible 'Smerdiakovschina' (*The Karamazov Brothers*) of whom Trotsky speaks in his letter on the declarations of Krestinsky and of Antonov-Ovseenko?

But if it can be expected that those who have transferred from the bourgeoisie, the intellectuals, the 'individuals' in general, retrogress in terms of ideas and morality, how can we explain a similar phenomenon in respect of the working class? Many comrades have noted the fact of its passivity and cannot hide their feeling of deception.

It is true that other comrades, during a certain wheat-harvesting campaign, have seen evidence of the robust revolutionary attitude, proving that class reflexes still exist in the party. Recently comrade Ischenko has written to me (or more exactly has written in theses which he has equally sent to other comrades) that the wheat-harvesting and the self-criticism are due to the resistance of the proletarian section of the party. Unfortunately it has to be said that this is not correct. These two facts result from a combination arranged in high places and are not due to the pressure of workers' criticism; it is for political reasons and sometimes for group, or I should say faction reasons, that some of the top men

in the party pursue this line. It is possible to speak of only one form of
proletarian pressure – that guided by the opposition. But it has to be
clearly said, this pressure has not been sufficient to maintain the opposition inside the party; further, it has not succeeded in changing its
political line. I agree with Leon Davidovitch who has shown, in a series of
irrefutable examples, the true and positive revolutionary role which
certain revolutionary movements have played by their defeat: the Commune in Paris, the insurrection of December 1905 in Moscow. The first
ensured the maintenance of the republican form of government in
France; the second opened the road to constitutional reform in Russia.
However, the effects of such conquering defeats are of short duration if
they are not reinforced by a new revolutionary upsurge.

The most unhappy fact is that no reflex action occurs either from
within the party or the masses today. For two years there was an
exceptionally bitter struggle between the opposition and the high circles
of the party; over the last two months events have occurred which should
have opened the eyes of the most blind. However, up till now no one has
the impression that the masses of the party have intervened.

Just as comprehensible is the pessimism of certain comrades, which I
can sense throughout your questions.

Babeuf, after he was released from the prison at Abbaye, looked about
him and began to ask himself what had happened to the people of Paris,
the workers of the faubourgs St-Antoine and St-Marcea, those who on
14 July 1789 had taken the Bastille, on 10 August 1792 the Tuileries,
who had laid siege to the Convention on 30 May 1793, not to speak of
numerous other armed interventions. In one single phrase, in which can
be sensed the bitterness of the revolutionary, he summed up what he felt:
'It is more difficult to re-educate the people in the love of Liberty than to
conquer it.'

We have seen why the people of Paris forgot the attraction of Liberty.
Famine, unemployment, the liquidation of the revolutionary cadres
(numbers of whom had been guillotined), the elimination of the masses
from the direction of the country, all this brought about such an
overwhelming moral and physical inertia in the masses that it was
thirty-seven years before the people of Paris and the rest of France started
a new revolution. Babeuf formulated his programme in two words (I refer
here to his programme of 1794): 'Liberty and an elected Commune'.

I must now make a confession: I have never let myself be taken in by the
illusion that it would be sufficient for the leaders of the opposition to
present themselves in party meetings and in workers' reunions, to win the
masses over to the opposition. I have always considered such hopes,
coming especially from the leaders of Leningrad (this applies particularly
to Zinoviev and Kamenev) as a sort of survival from the period when they

mistook ovations and official approbation for the expression of the true sentiment of the masses and attributed them to their imagined popularity.

I will go further: this explains to me the quick about-turn which occurred in their conduct. They went over to the opposition, hoping to take power quickly. It was with this aim that they rejoined the opposition of 1923 (the first opposition being that of Trotsky in Moscow). When one of the 'group without leaders' reproached Zinoviev and Kamenev of having let fall their ally Trotsky, Kamenev answered: 'We needed Trotsky to govern; to enter into the party he is a dead weight.' However, the premise should have been that the work of educating the party and the working class was a long and difficult task, and that it was that much more so because men's minds have first of all to be cleansed of all the impurities introduced into them by the practices of the soviets and of the party and by the bureaucratization of these institutions.

We must not lose sight of the fact that the majority of the members of the party (not to speak of the young communists) have a most erroneous conception of the tasks, functions and structure of the party, to wit the conception taught them by the bureaucracy in its example, its practical conduct and its stereotyped formulae. All the workers who rejoined the party after the Civil War, entered it for the most part after 1923 (the Lenin Levy); they had no idea what the party regime was like previously. The majority of them lack the revolutionary class education acquired in the real-life struggle for the construction of socialism. But as our bureaucracy has reduced this effort to an empty phrase, the workers are unable to acquire any part of this education. I naturally exclude, as an abnormal method of class education, the fact that our bureaucracy, by lowering real wages, by worsening conditions of work, by favouring the development of unemployment, forces the workers to struggle and awakens their class consciousness; but then this is hostile to the socialist state.

According to the concept of Lenin and of us all, the task of the party leaders consists precisely in keeping the party and the working class from the corrupting influence of privileges, of favours, of special rights inherent in power through its contact with remnants of the ancient nobility and of the petty bourgeoisie; we should have been prepared against the nefarious influence of the NEP, against the temptation of the ideology and morality of the bourgeoisie.

At the same time we had the hope that the party leadership would have created a new, truly worker-and-peasant apparatus, new, truly proletarian syndicates, a new morality of daily life. We have to recognize it frankly, clearly and with a high and intelligible voice: the apparatus of the party has not accomplished this task. It has shown in this double task of preservation and education the most complete incompetence; it has become bankrupt; it is insolvent. We have been convinced for a long time, and the last eight months in particular should have proved to all, that the leadership of the party is advancing on a most perilous road. And it continues to follow this road.

The reproaches which we are addressing to it do not concern so much the quantitative as the qualitative side of work. This has to be emphasized, otherwise we will once more be submerged by a flood of statistics on the innumerable and total successes achieved by the apparatus of the party and of the soviets. It is high time to put an end to this statistical charlatanism. Study the reports of the 15th Party Congress. Read that of Kossior on organizational activity. What do you find? I quote literally: 'The prodigious development of democracy in the party . . . The organizational activity of the party has widened considerably.' And then, to back all this up: statistics, more statistics and again more statistics. And this was being said at the time when there were in the files of the Central Committee documents proving the terrible disintegration of the apparatus of the party and of the soviets, of persecutions, of a reign of terror imposed upon the lives of militants and workers.

. This is how *Pravda* of 11 April characterizes the power of the bureaucracy: 'Opportunist elements, idle, hostile and incompetent, spend their time in chasing the last Soviet inventors beyond the frontiers of the USSR, in case a great blow may be struck against such elements, with all our strength, with all our determination, with all our courage . . .' Nonetheless, knowing our bureaucracy, I would not be surprised to hear again someone speaking of the 'enormous and prodigious' development of the activity of the masses and of the party, of the organizational work of the Central Committee implanting democracy . . . I am convinced that the bureaucracy of the party and of the soviets actually existing will continue with the same success to cultivate around itself such suppurating abcesses, in spite of the noisy trials which took place last month. This bureaucracy will not change merely through being submitted to a cleansing. Naturally I do not deny the relative utility and the absolute necessity of such a cleansing. I merely wish to underline that it is not only a question of a change of personnel but primarily of a change in methods.

In my opinion, the first condition necessary to make the leadership of our party capable of exercising an educative role is to reduce the size and functions of this leadership. Three-quarters of the apparatus should be done away with. The tasks of the remaining quarter should have strictly determined limits. This should apply equally to the tasks, the functions and the rights of the central organisms. The members of the party must recover their rights which have been trampled on and be given worthwhile guarantees against the despotism to which the directing circles have accustomed us.

It is difficult to conceive what is happening in the lower ranks of the party. It is especially in the struggle against the opposition that the ideological mediocrity of these cadres has manifested itself, as has the corrupting influence which they exercise on the proletarian masses of the party. If, at the top, there existed a certain ideological line, a specious and erroneous line mixed, it is true, with a strong dose of bad faith, in the lower ranks on the other hand demagogy of the worst order has been employed against the opposition. The agents of the party have not hesitated to utilize anti-semitism, xenophobia, hate of intellectuals, etc. I am convinced that all party reform which is based on the bureaucracy is Utopian.

To summarize: while noting, like you, the lack of spirit of revolutionary activity among the masses in the party, I see nothing surprising in this phenomenon. It is the result of all the changes which have taken place in the party and in the proletariat itself. It is necessary to re-educate the working masses and the party masses within the framework of the party and of the syndicates. This process will be long and difficult, but inevitable. It has already started. The struggle of the opposition, the expulsion of hundreds and hundreds of comrades, the imprisonments and deportations, while having done little as yet for the communist education of our party, have in any case had more effect than the whole apparatus taken together. In reality the two factors cannot even be compared: the apparatus has wasted the party capital handed down by Lenin, not only in a useless way but in one which has caused difficulty. It has demolished while the opposition was building.

Up until now, I have reasoned abstractly from the facts of our economic and political life which have been analysed in the platform of the opposition. I have deliberately done so, since my task was to underline the changes which have occurred in the composition and psychology of the party and of the proletariat in relation to the taking of power itself. These facts have perhaps given a unilateral character to my exposition. But without proceeding to give a preliminary analysis, it would be difficult to understand the origin of the economic and political errors committed by our leadership in that which concerns the peasants and the problems of industrialization, the inner regime of the party, and finally, of the administration of the state.

Astrakhan, 6 August 1928

3. What is the Bureaucracy?

Ernest Mandel

The genesis of the bureaucratic phenomenon

The problem of bureaucracy within the working-class movement poses itself in its most immediate form as the problem of the *apparatus* of working-class organizations: the problem of full-timers and petty-bourgeois intellectuals who come to occupy the middle or top functions within the working-class organizations.

As long as these organizations are limited to tiny groups, to political sects or self-defence groups of limited numerical strength, there is no apparatus, there are no full-timers and the problem does not arise. At the very most, there is the problem of the relationship with petty-bourgeois intellectuals who come to aid in the formation of this as yet embryonic working-class movement.

However, the very growth of the movement, the appearance of mass political or trade-union organizations, is inconceivable without the creation of an apparatus of full-timers and functionaries; and the very existence of an apparatus carries within itself a potential danger of bureaucratization. From the very beginning there comes into play one of the fundamental roots of the bureaucratic phenomenon – the division of labour within capitalist society.

The division of labour within capitalist society reserves the manual work involved in day-to-day production for the proletariat, and the production and assimilation of culture for other social classes. It's tiring work, exhausting both physically and intellectually, does not allow the proletariat in its entirety to acquire and assimilate the objective sciences in their most advanced form or to maintain a continuous political and social activity: the status of the proletariat under the rule of capital is one of scientific and cultural underdevelopment.

The development of the working-class movement brings about the creation of an apparatus and functionaries, whose specialized knowledge is necessary to fill the gaps caused by this status of the working class and is an absolutely indispensable condition for further continuation of the class struggle.[1]

To put it very crudely, it is this specialization that gives rise to the phenomenon of bureaucracy: as soon as a number of individuals are involved in political or trade-union activity as professionals, on a full-time basis, there exists the latent possibility of bureaucratization.

This specialization, in a commodity-producing society, also gives birth, at a deeper level, to the phenomena of fetishism and reification. In a society based on an extreme division of labour and of generalized commodity production, the fact that people are imprisoned in a tiny sector of global social activity tends to find its ideological expression in their attitudes: they come to consider their activities as ends in themselves and become more and more unable to understand society as a whole. Organizational structures, originally conceived as means for attaining certain social goals, come to be regarded as aims in themselves – particularly by those who are identified with them most obviously and directly, who live permanently within them and draw their livelihood from them, those who make up the apparatus: the full-timers, the potential bureaucrats.

We will now proceed to examine the psychological and ideological basis for the creation of working-class bureaucracy: the dialectic of partial conquests.

The dialectic of partial conquests

This dialectic manifests itself in the attitudes and activity of those who subordinate the pursuit of the struggle of the working class for the conquest of power and the radical transformation of society – building a socialist world – to the defence of such working-class conquests as have already been achieved. At the international level, they see the defence of the Soviet Union, China and/or other workers' states as of greater importance than the extension of the international revolution. For such people, the existence of workers' states in a world dominated by imperialism is an aim in itself. What has been achieved there for them constitutes socialism, and they therefore believe it imperative to subordinate all new struggles to its defence. This constitutes a fundamentally conservative world outlook.

The famous sentence in the *Communist Manifesto* which says that the proletariat has nothing to lose but its chains puts forward a very profound thesis, which should be taken as one of the fundamentals of Marxism: the proletariat is given the historic task of transforming the capitalist society into a communist one precisely because it possesses nothing to defend.

But at the moment this is not absolutely the case, that is to say, as soon as a part of the proletariat (the working-class bureaucracy, the labour aristocracy which forms within the proletariat in the imperialist countries) acquires an organization or a superior standard of living in place of its original state of total deprivation, there emerges the danger of a new frame of mind. The pros and cons of every new action now come to be weighed and balanced: might not the projected move forward, instead of achieving something new, result in the loss of what has already been gained?

This is a fundamental root of bureaucratic conservatism, found already in the social democratic movement before the First World War and in the bureaucracy of the Soviet Union even prior to the extreme peak of the Stalinist era.

The dialectic of partial conquests is a dialectic reflecting real problems and not a false contradiction that can be resolved by a formula.

While bureaucratic conservatism clearly harms the interests of the proletariat and therefore socialism, because it refuses to wage and support revolutionary struggle in the capitalist countries and the world as a whole, the initial cause of this attitude (the need to defend working-class achievements) reflects a real dilemma. The reason why we call this attitude conservative is because it assumes *a priori* that any revolutionary leap forward, whether on a national or an international level, threatens the gains of the working class. It is this assumption which underlines the deep and permanent conservatism of both the reformist and Stalinist bureaucracies.

The dialectic of partial conquests, linked to the phenomenon of fetishization characteristic for a society of generalized commodity production organized around an extreme division of labour, expresses an important aspect of the process of bureaucratization. As such it is inherent in the development of the working-class movement in the historical stage of the decay of capitalism and transition towards a socialist society.

The real solution to the problem of bureaucracy lies not in trying to abolish it through decrees or magical formulae, but in creating the best subjective and objective conditions for it to wither away.

Bureaucratic privileges

As materialists we cannot, of course, separate the problem of the bureaucracy from that of its material interests: this bureaucracy enjoys material privileges and is determined to defend them. However, to reduce the problem of bureaucracy solely to this particular aspect would not help us to understand its origin and subsequent development. For example, the degree of bureaucratization of the Communist Parties that are not in power (for example PCF, PCI) or of the Communist Parties in semi-colonial countries (such as Brazil) could not be explained with this simple model. On the other hand, we see in these cases the ideology of partial conquests clearly at work: identification of the aims with the means, of the bureaucrat with the organization. This identification, as we have said, gives rise to deep conservatism and this conservatism often comes into violent opposition with the interests of the working-class movement.

Just as we should avoid a vulgar materialist explanation, we should equally avoid the opposite, psychologistic error. The psychological tendency to conservatism on the part of leaders and other functionaries is clearly related to both the material advantages and privileges and the power and authority which their status bestows upon them. When we look at the nature of bureaucratic privileges as manifested in the first organizations of the working class, the trade unions and social democratic parties, we can note two different aspects:

1. Leaving the place of production, especially in the conditions prevailing at that time (twelve-hour working day, total absence of social security, etc.), in order to become a full-timer represented for a worker an unquestionable social promotion, a certain degree of individual self-emancipation. It would be wrong to equate this with 'bourgeoisification' or the creation of a privileged social layer. The early secretaries of working-class organizations spent a considerable part of their lives in prison and lived in more than modest material circumstances. All the same, from an economic and social point of view, they lived better than the rest of the workers at the time.

2. At the psychological level, it is obviously infinitely more satisfying for a socialist or communist militant to spend all his time fighting for his ideas than to spend his days performing mechanical work in some factory, knowing that the result of his labour will only serve to enrich the class enemy.

The phenomenon of social and personal promotion unquestionably contains the potential seeds of bureaucratization. Those who occupy such positions quite simply want to carry on occupying them; they will defend their status against anybody who wants to establish instead a rota system, whereby each member of the organization would at some time fill these posts.

While social privileges are not very tangible at the beginning, they become considerable once the mass organizations gain a position of strength within capitalist society. There is then the question of electing advisers, MPs and trade-union secretaries who are capable of negotiating directly with the bosses – and thus, to some extent, of coexisting with them. Similar considerations apply when appointing newspaper editors or representatives to take part in the additional activities through which the organization intervenes at all social levels.

This produces a genuine dialectic which cannot be reduced to a trivial contradiction. For example, when the movement starts producing a paper and therefore needs an editor, it faces a real dilemma. If it applies the rule designed by Marx to prevent the formation of a bureaucracy – that the salary of a full-timer should be equal to that of a skilled worker – it risks a process of professional selection in reverse. The most politically conscious militants will accept the logic of this rule, but many talented journalists who are in a position to earn a lot more elsewhere will be continuously tempted to take up the more lucrative option. So long as they are not sufficiently committed they will be in danger of getting re-absorbed into the bourgeois milieu and thus being lost to the workers' movement.

This holds true for other professions as well. For example, in towns administered by the labour movement the same problem holds in relation to architects, engineers or doctors. A strict application of Marx's rule would in most cases lead to the elimination of all those whose political consciousness is insufficiently developed, but who might be professionally better skilled.

It is impossible inside a capitalist society, with its prevalent norms and values, to build a perfect communist system of human relations even within the workers' movement. This may just be possible for a nucleus of highly conscious revolutionaries, but a large workers' movement is much more firmly integrated into capitalist society and communist principles are thus much more difficult to put into practice within it. Consequently there is a tendency for the obstacles specifically erected against the danger of bureaucratization to be gradually abandoned.

In this historic phase of capitalist decay, the dialectic of partial conquests assumes its fully developed form of conscious integration into bourgeois society together with the politics and logic of class collaboration. All obstacles to bureaucratization disappear, privileges multiply, the social democratic leaders no longer give a part of their parliamentary salary to the organization – indeed, these functionaries come to represent a client layer inside the working class. From this point on, bureaucratic deformation can only leap forward towards bureaucratic degeneration.

The bureaucratization of the workers' states

A similar three-phase process can be found at work in the bureaucratization of the workers' states during the period of transition from capitalism to socialism. At first there are only the privileges of authority and the political advantages stemming from the monopoly of power over the state apparatus. Then follow the bureaucratic privileges of a material and cultural nature. Finally, complete degeneration takes place: the political leadership no longer attempts to check the growth of bureaucracy, consciously integrates itself into it and becomes its motor, striving for further increase of privileges. This process leads to the monstrous excesses of the Stalinist era.

Here are some examples to illustrate the scope of these privileges. At the peak of the Stalinist era, a system of 'fixed bank accounts' was instituted whereby a certain number of top bureaucrats could claim unlimited credit while their bank balances remained always the same. The only limit to spending was the relative lack of goods. For these people, communism really existed in the midst of a still poor society. Post-Stalin literature is full of concrete examples of top artists and party leaders who owned such accounts. Then there is the case of 'special shops' which sold goods generally unavailable to the 'normal' consumer. These shops appeared in Stalin's time and continued to exist in most workers' states up to 1956–7. Patronized by party and state officials, their existence was kept carefully hidden from the rest of the population – their fronts were disguised to look like ordinary houses. There existed a real hierarchy among these functionaries: the lowest on the bureaucratic ladder had to pay the full price of goods, those higher up only half the price while the top bureaucrats – those with 'fixed bank accounts' – could take anything they fancied without having to pay at all.

During 1947–8, which was a time of want and misery in the workers' states, CP bureaucrats in countries like Germany used to receive parcels from the Soviet Union containing silk or wool stockings, butter, sugar, etc. The care with which the hierarchy was respected is quite amusing: the size and content of the parcels strictly reflected the rank of the receiver. It would be comic, were it not really tragic, to find in a situation of generalized famine such a rigid application of the bureaucratic mind, which elevates the hierarchy into a sacred principle. However, it is only logical to find even in such petty instances all the paraphernalia of bureaucratic degeneration.

Some wrong solutions

The most important lesson that should be drawn from this brief study of the problem of the origin of bureaucracy in the working-class movement is that one must carefully distinguish between the following:

1. the germs of bureaucratization which are inherent in the development of the working-class mass organizations;

2. full and complete bureaucratization, as found in the various reformist and Stalinist parties and in the Soviet state.

If one does not make a distinction between the two and consequently rejects any form of mass organization for the workers' movement, on the assumption that it will inevitably degenerate, then one is forced to conclude that the self-emancipation of the proletariat is impossible. By refusing to recognize the dialectic between spontaneity and organization, such a procedure is defeatist from the outset.

This confusion of the two poles of the bureaucratic phenomenon characterizes various 'ultra-Left' groups. Some of them argue that, because of the danger inherent in the very presence of an apparatus and full-timers, one should therefore rule out any role for 'professional revolutionaries'. Their thesis could be summarized by the phrase: the first professional revolutionary who appeared within the working-class movement prefigured the future Stalin. The real question, however, is whether a workers' emancipation movement is possible *at all* without some permanent organizational structures – not in some imagined ideal situation but in capitalist society such as it is.

A movement which did not seek to create professional revolutionaries – from, and linked to, the working class – would be incapable of moving beyond the most primitive workers' defence groups. Such a movement would be incapable of carrying the class struggle beyond the most spontaneous and immediate demands. It would certainly not be able to overthrow capitalism and liberate the proletariat, thus opening the way for socialism. History shows that this option is never taken and that there is not a single country where the working class, out of fear of bureaucrat-ization, continues to cling to organizational primitivism after some experience of the class struggle. On the contrary, historical practice shows that a workers' movement which refuses to organize and does not select and systematically educate its cadres, only falls under the ideologi-cal and organizational domination of bourgeois and petty-bourgeois intellectuals, who reproduce within the movement the pattern of cultural monopoly which they already exercise in capitalist society at large. So there is really no choice at all: wanting to avoid the pitfalls of 'incipient' bureaucratization, one falls into even worse pitfalls.

These 'ultra-Left' groups do not understand that the choice is not between an organizational form which is totally free from the bureau-cratic danger and one that contains it in embryo. The only real choice is between developing real organized working-class autonomy (involving the potential danger of bureaucracy) and leaving the workers' organiz-ations under the ideological sway of the bourgeoisie. A working-class organization whose members are only manual workers engaged full-time in the productive process is far more easily conquered by bourgeois politics and ideology than an organization which makes a conscious effort to educate and select the most conscious workers and form them into professional revolutionists.

Another false solution, which stems again from not seeing the problem as a dialectical one, was produced by the 'Socialisme ou Barbarie' group.[2] They argued that the way to prevent bureaucratization in the workers' states was to abolish all wage differentials. But what would be the objective result of this measure? Eliminating overnight all differences in wages in a society dominated by material scarcity would mean eliminating those incentives that make people want to learn new skills. Once the possession of a professional skill no longer guarantees even a modestly improved standard of living, then only the most politically conscious elements, who understand the objective social necessity of raising professional skills, would make the effort to acquire them. Consequently the development of the productive forces would be slower and the state of scarcity would last longer. The objective causes for the growth of bureaucracy (low development of productive forces, cultural underdevelopment of the proletariat) would last longer and the result would be exactly the opposite of that hoped for. By maintaining some modest difference in wages, skills increase and so does the material basis favourable to the withering away of bureaucratization and privileges. Once again one is faced with a dialectical process requiring a dialectical solution.

The revolutionary Marxist solution

Marx did not see clearly all the aspects of the bureaucratic problem, because there had not been sufficient historical precedents. Nevertheless, armed solely with the experience of the Paris Commune, he drew up two very simple but fundamental rules which contain nearly all the safeguards against bureaucratization developed to this day by the workers' movement:

1. *The political functionaries of a workers' state must have wages on a par with those of skilled workers.* For Marx the aim of this rule was to prevent careerism, that is, seeking public office for the sake of personal advancement.

2. *All officials should be elected and subject to the right of recall at any time by those who elected them.* This principle (supplemented by Lenin's rota system rule) will further the withering away of the state, as classes disappear and each citizen gains concrete experience in carrying out administrative functions.

The revolutionary Marxist solution to the problem of bureaucracy is to be found in Lenin's theory of the revolutionary party, and in Trotsky's theory of the workers' state and the vanguard's role in the struggle against its bureaucratization. This solution is based on a clear understanding of the objective nature of the tendency in the working-class movement towards bureaucratization and provides the movement with effective means to combat this tendency.

Lenin's theory of the party was first developed in *What is to be Done?*. But after the Russian working class underwent its first revolutionary experience of large-scale mass action – in 1905 – Lenin himself found it necessary to deepen his analysis. The true Leninist theory of the party thus includes two elements. In the first place, what he wrote at the beginning of the century, in *What is to be Done?*, about the creation of the nucleus of the revolutionary party in conditions of clandestinity. Secondly, what he wrote after the Russian proletariat's first mass revolutionary experience – the experience of mass parties, trade unions and soviets. To understand Lenin's theory of the party is to understand both the need for vanguard detachments and parties, which can only organize a small minority of the working class, and at the same time the need for the vanguard party to be integrated into the masses and not substitute itself for them nor take upon itself tasks which can only be executed by the masses themselves. The thesis that the emancipation of the proletariat can only be accomplished *by the proletariat itself* must not be modified, either in theory or in practice, to mean that it is the revolutionary party's task to emancipate the proletariat and to establish the workers' state on behalf of the proletariat – first in the latter's name and then, in certain historical situations, against it.

In this dialectic between the vanguard and the masses, it is necessary to insist on the fact that the party can accomplish its historical tasks *only if it is actively supported by the majority of the proletariat*. But this active support of the masses for a revolutionary party can only occur at *exceptional* though *historically determined* moments, which means that the party must remain a minority party as long as there is not a revolutionary situation.[3]

The true Leninist theory of the party lies in its global understanding of the dialectical relationship between the party and the masses. This dialectic implies a definite type of organization and a definite conception of the professional revolutionary. The latter must never be separated permanently from the masses; he must always be ready to return to the factory floor and cede his place to another comrade, in order that he too can acquire the necessary experience. This is the theory of the rota system, which establishes a real 'circulation of life-blood' between the proletariat and its vanguard.

The same fundamental principles apply for the workers' states in transition from capitalism to socialism. Here, although Lenin initially developed a number of important observations and theses on the problem of bureaucratization of workers' states (indeed, in 1921–2 he was much more aware of the danger than Trotsky), it has mainly been

Trotsky and the Trotskyist movement who have provided the revolutionary Marxist solution to the problem.

While a tendency to bureaucratic deformation is inevitable in a backward and isolated society, it is not inevitable that this tendency should lead to the monstrous degeneration of the Stalinist era. In these conditions, the role of the subjective factor is once again decisive. The revolutionary vanguard must fight against the danger of bureaucratization at all levels:

– *at the level of the political organization of the state*, it must foster workers' democracy and encourage direct intervention of the masses in the running of the state;

– *at the international level*, it must support the development of the world revolution which, by breaking the isolation of the workers' states, will be the most effective antidote to bureaucratization. If a proletarian vanguard free from moral and physical exhaustion succeeded in taking power, it would be able to take over the leading role in the spread of the world revolution: this is what Trotsky called the third aspect of the theory of Permanent Revolution.

– *at the economic level*: any radical separation of the function of accumulation from the function of production, any radical separation of the real, living working class from control over the social surplus product – whether through an ultra-centralized state bureaucracy or whether through free functioning of 'market laws' – must be avoided at all costs. Democratically centralized, planned workers' management of the economy is the historical answer to this problem.

Marx's analysis of the experience of the Paris Commune

Perhaps the best way to introduce this topic is to consider the lessons drawn by Marx from his study of the Paris Commune. The most striking feature of this first attempt at building a workers' state was the effort made (more instinctively than consciously) by the Commune leaders to *destroy* the permanent state apparatus bequeathed by the previous ruling classes (the absolute monarchy and the successive bourgeois regimes). In his analysis Marx isolated three main preconditions for the success of this project (two of which have already been mentioned):

1. The salaries of the Commune functionaries were not higher than those of skilled workers;

2. these functionaries were elected and could be recalled at any time by those who elected them;

3. the third requirement was alluded to by Marx and subsequently made explicit by Lenin: *an end to the separation of the legislative and*

executive functions. This separation, which is the fundamental characteristic of the bourgeois state, was suppressed in this new state which was already not quite a state – that is, the creation of the workers' state marked the beginning of the withering away of the state. Right from the beginning, workers were involved not only in the legislative functions of the state but also in the execution of laws – right from the beginning the proletariat was involved in the exercise of power.

This first experiment in the creation of a workers' state also produced the first effective measures against bureaucratization: the withering away of the state must coincide with the withering away of the state apparatus. The three rules drawn up by Marx should be seen as the basic safeguard against the bureaucratization of any democratic structure – whether of state, trade union or party. While Marx did not live to see the bureaucratic deformation of mass working-class parties and of workers' states and thus could not provide a full analysis of the problem, the passage he wrote nevertheless constituted for long the key weapons for the struggle against bureaucracy.

Kautsky's Parallel

The next major contribution to the analysis of the bureaucratic phenomenon we owe to Kautsky. At the end of the last century Kautsky wrote a book called *The Origins of Christianity*, in which he raised the following question: after the working-class seizure of power, is there not a danger that this power may be surrendered into the hands of a bureaucracy? This was the first time that the problem was posed so clearly (though it is true that anarchists had previously alluded to it). Kautsky asked: is there not a possibility that the working-class movement could undergo a process of bureaucratization similar to that which the Catholic Church underwent after its consolidation as a dominant force in society? Kautsky went on to compare what had happened to the Catholic Church after it became a state church (in the fourth century AD, under Constantine the Great) with what could happen to the workers' party and state after the victory of the working-class movement.

This comparison was not the fruit of Kautsky's theoretical labour alone. He drew inspiration from two sources. Engels, in his introduction to *The Class Struggles in France*, had already compared the persecution suffered by the working-class movement to that of another movement sixteen hundred years earlier. In spite of harsh repression, Christianity had gone from strength to strength until this movement of the oppressed, bitterly fought by the ruling classes, progressively reached all social classes and ended victorious.

Another possible source of inspiration was the anarcho-syndicalist movement represented by Most.[4] Starting from Engels' remarks, Most concluded that workers' organizations become bureaucratized as they develop in the same way that the Church had done in the course of its historical development.

Faced with the parallel, Kautsky grasped and posed the problem correctly. Of course, he knew that a complete parallel between the workers' movement and the Catholic Church was not possible, nevertheless he saw that the conquest of power would confront the working-class movement with a problem of bureaucracy analogous to that undergone by the Catholic Church after its arrival in power. Kautsky's answers are interesting, since they differ considerably from the ones given by Marx and remind us of those later produced by Trotsky.

Kautsky argued that the parallel would be perfectly tenable if the historical conditions under which the working class came to power resembled those under which the Church had triumphed. The Catholic Church had risen to power at a time when the forces of production were on the decline. Under similar conditions the workers' movement could not avoid bureaucratization either. But, in reality, the conditions would in its case be the exact opposite. For socialism means a tremendous development of productive forces which lays the foundation for the withering away of the division of labour and a revolution in the cultural level of the masses. Given these conditions, the victory of the bureaucracy is historically inconceivable.

Kautsky's answer is thus on the whole correct. But he overlooked the possibility, a possibility nobody considered at the time, that the working class might take power not in an advanced capitalist country but in a country that had only begun in the last few decades to shake off the fetters of a semi-feudal social order. In this case the absence of the factors mentioned by Kautsky – material plenty, cultural revolution – that would act as a brake on the development of bureaucracy, coupled to the low cultural level of the masses and a numerically weak working-class, might allow a temporary victory of the bureaucracy.

Trotsky's polemic against Lenin's conception of the party

The third phase in the development of the analysis of the bureaucratic problem is rather 'delicate' for those communists who are both Leninists and Trotskyists, since it is marked by Trotsky's polemic against Lenin's theory of the revolutionary party. In this debate Trotsky was undoubtedly wrong, as he himself later acknowledged. However, while the internal logic of Trotsky's argument is far from perfect, his conclusions nevertheless appear as an acute premonition of subsequent events. In 1903 Trotsky wrote that a theory in which the party substitutes for the proletariat in carrying out the fundamental tasks risks thereafter substi-

tuting the Central Committee for the party, the Secretariat for the Central
Committee, and, finally, the General Secretary for the Secretariat, so that
in the end one man alone is given the mission of realizing the great tasks of
the Revolution.

This argument represents a perfectly correct condemnation of all
substitutionist theories – but has, of course, little to do with Lenin's real
theory of the party.[5]

In Stalin's time, however, this substitutionist theory effectively became
the official theory of the Russian Communist Party. Bureaucrats in the
workers' states are always surprised when, if challenged, they cannot find
a single line in Lenin's writings which says that the dictatorship of the
proletariat is to be exercised by the party, that the party should nationalize the means of production, that the party should govern the workers'
state, etc., etc. This is because they have been brought up in a political
spirit which transfers to the party the tasks of the proletariat. Lenin, on
the contrary, always envisaged these tasks as being accomplished *by the
proletariat under the leadership of the party* – which is a very different
matter.

The theory which allows the party to usurp the place of the proletariat
leads in a natural way to situations in which the party comes to execute
these tasks against the will of the great majority of the proletariat. For
example, this theory justifies the Soviet intervention in Hungary in 1956
and the violent suppression of the general strike in which 95 per cent of
the Hungarian workers took part. In other words, 'dictatorship of the
proletariat' was exercised against 95 per cent of the proletariat!

In 1903 Trotsky's critique of the substitutionist theory, while absolutely correct, appeared an abstract exercise in polemic, because no one in
particular – certainly not Lenin – held such substitutionist positions.
Thirty years later, however, the substitutionist theory became the semi-
official doctrine of the Soviet bureaucracy (semi-official only because the
Stalinist bureaucracy never quite dared to reject openly and completely
Lenin's theoretical heritage).

Rosa Luxemburg's struggle against the German
trade-union bureaucracy

The fourth phase in the analysis of the bureaucratic phenomenon is very
important, because for the first time it was applied to an already formed
bureaucracy: that of the German trade unions. We owe this development
to Rosa Luxemburg who, between 1907 and 1914, waged an open
struggle against the German trade-union bureaucracy and the growing
general bureaucratization of the German social democratic mass movement.

Rosa Luxemburg drew on the experience of the revolution of 1905, particularly as it affected the most industrialized parts of Tsarist Russia: the industrial sectors of Poland, Lettonia, the Ukraine and Petrograd. She found in all these cases that the working class enters a political or trade-union movement *en masse* only at times of revolutionary upheaval. Consequently, this indicates the need for a political strategy towards millions of workers who have never had the formative experience of belonging to an established working-class organization. Given that the activity of these workers cannot be channelled via the usual organizational forms, news ones are required: forms of organization which would have greater flexibility than a trade union or a party and which would unite in action a much larger mass of the proletariat.

History has supported Luxemburg's theory by showing in practice the usefulness of the soviet organizational form in times of revolutionary upheaval. Soviets constitute an extremely flexible form, since each soviet is related to the specific local situation. It is sufficient to look at the first soviets in the 1905 Russian revolution, the workers' and soldiers' councils in the German revolution of 1918, or the committees formed during the Spanish revolution in order to realize their rich potential. Specific to a given situation, they were always formed in order to solve a practical task posed by the revolution at a given historical moment. Soviets are the only organizational form capable of uniting *all* workers, whether previously organized or unorganized, in action for a specific revolutionary task.

Consequently, they should not be seen as permanent institutional structures applicable to all historical situations. Similarly, if one has understood their real nature, then one can see how dogmatic it is to give them the same label in all countries and in all situations. One can then see the absurdity of Maoist groups which, repeating the Stalinist 'third-period' tactics, want immediately to set up soviets in countries like Belgium or the United States. Mesmerized by labels, they are blind to the real problem: what organizational form is best adapted to the aspirations of a given working class, in a given country, at a given time; to the possibilities of a decisive development of working-class consciousness.

Rosa Luxemburg called attention to another aspect of the problem of bureaucracy. The trade-union bureaucracy, once its period of formation has been completed, tends to become an extremely conservative force which constitutes a growing obstacle to the development of the class struggle. Her personal experience of the German trade-union movement enabled her to see this process more clearly and long before either Lenin or Trotsky; she was therefore able to predict the counter-revolutionary role this bureaucracy was to play a few years later. While other working-class militants stressed at the time only the most immediately visible aspect of this problem – the opportunistic nature of this bureaucracy –

Luxemburg documented its process of integration into the bourgeois state, its identification with certain 'bourgeois-democratic' institutions and its concern with its own privileges, especially those of a material nature.

In 1914 Lenin used Luxemburg's theory of bureaucratic degeneration in order to explain the general state of degeneration of European social-democracy and the reasons for the treachery of the Second International in face of the imperialist war.

However, in her concern with the need to wage the anti-bureaucratic struggle, Luxemburg went too far in underestimating the objective importance of these organizations for maintaining a minimal level of class consciousness in the 'normal' periods of capitalism. Even in the most advanced capitalist countries, the alternatives are not a revolutionary working class on the one hand and a working class regimented by bureaucratic trade unions on the other. There is also the very real possibility of an atomized working class without any organization or any class consciousness. When criticizing the counter-revolutionary and bureaucratic aspects of trade unions, one must also bear in mind that they represent at the same time the guarantee of a minimal class combativity for the broad masses within capitalist society.

It is necessary to emphasize this point, because on the periphery of the Trotskyist movement there is an ultra-Left current which does not distinguish between the two polar aspects of the problem and consequently draws the following equation:

mass trade union movement = reactionary bureaucracy = betrayal

forgetting that the mass trade-union movement is the objective expression of the collective force of the class during the period of social calm. When such people say that in the advanced capitalist countries trade unions have become institutions of 'social welfare', dealing mainly with pensions and family allowances, they are to a certain extent correct. But one must not forget that if the trade unions did not exist, workers would have to solve all these 'welfare' problems on an individual basis. The relationship of forces would then be much more unfavourable to them and they would not have any chance of winning against the employees. The function of trade unions is, in the last analysis, to bring the *collective* force of the working class to bear in this day-to-day dialogue with the bosses. Furthermore, when the class struggle accelerates its pace, trade unions can become formidable class weapons.

It is necessary to start from this dual nature of the trade-union bureaucracy in order to understand why, after fifty years of repeated betrayals by the bureaucracy, the workers remain strongly attached to these organizations. The workers know very well that trade unions are crucial to their day-to-day struggle against the capitalist bosses and that therefore it is not in their interest to abandon them.

Lenin's theses on the degeneration of social democracy

The fifth phase in the analysis of the bureaucratic phenomenon is constituted by Lenin's theses on the degeneration of the Second International and the betrayal of social democracy at the outbreak of the First World War. Lenin explained this by two factors:

1. The appearance of a bureaucracy inside the trade unions and social democratic parties, which controls these organizations and is committed to the privileges it has acquired both within them and outside (MPs, mayors, journalists, etc.).

2. The sociological roots of this bureaucratic layer are to be found in the 'labour aristocracy', that is, in that part of the working class inside the imperialist countries that has been won over to the bourgeoisie by means of colonial 'super-profits'.

Lenin's theory has been a 'dogma' for revolutionary Marxists for nearly half a century. We must now re-examine it critically, for at least two reasons:

1. There are things that are difficult to explain by this theory. For example, it is difficult to explain the nature of the trade-union bureaucracy in the United States solely by the existence of a 'labour aristocracy' corrupted by colonial super-profits. True, American capital invested abroad brings home profits but these constitute a negligible sum compared to the total wage bill of the American working class, and certainly not a sufficiently large fraction to account for the existence of a trade-union bureaucracy that rules over more than 17 million wage-earners. Present-day France has practically no colonies left and draws a very limited profit from its former colonial territories, and yet the bureaucratization of the French working-class movement has not correspondingly diminished.

2. The second reason is even more important. When we examine the economic conditions of existence of the working class throughout the world, we see that the real 'labour aristocracy' is no longer constituted inside the proletariat of an imperialist country but rather by the proletariat of the imperialist countries as a whole in relation to that of the colonial and semi-colonial countries. For example, the wage of an English worker is ten times larger than the wage of a black South African worker, while the wage differential of two English workers is 1:2 at most. Imperialist exploitation has produced a tremendous wage

differential between the workers of imperialist and underdeveloped countries and this factor plays a significant role in the political corruption of certain layers of the proletariat inside the advanced capitalist countries.

There are other reasons why we should use the concept of 'labour aristocracy' with great discretion. For example, in the history of the European working-class movement it is often the so-called 'labour aristocracy', that is, the best-paid layers of the proletariat, that has acted as the spearhead of the communist movement. The German Communist Party became a mass party in the early twenties by winning over the metal-workers, who were the best-paid section of the German working class at the time. The same is true in the case of France: the growth of the PCF after 1934 was based on its growth among workers of large enterprises, where wages were among the highest in the country. Thus it was the Renault workers rather than the textile workers of the North of France who joined the Communist Party in large numbers; the latter have remained faithful to social democracy.

Rather than mechanically applying Lenin's concept of 'labour aristocracy', we should emphasize his global analysis of the increasing symbiosis of the trade-union bureaucracy and the bourgeois state.

Trotsky's theory of the degeneration of the Soviet workers' state

Trotsky's theory of the degeneration of the Soviet workers' state, a society in transition from capitalism to socialism, constitutes the sixth phase in the development of an understanding of the bureaucratic phenomenon. Trotsky's main contribution was to transform the theories of bureaucratization of workers' organizations into a coherent theory of the bureaucracy in a workers' state. Though recognizing the importance of objective factors in this bureaucratization process, Trotsky also recognized that degeneration was by no means inevitable.[6] It should have and could have been combated, through a conscious effort by the Bolshevik Party. The great tragedy of the development of the Soviet Union was the total lack of understanding of the bureaucratic phenomenon by the majority of the Bolshevik Party at the decisive moments in its history. If a concrete understanding of the problem had been reached by 1922–3, when preventive measures were still possible, the history of the Soviet Union could have followed quite another course. Industrialization could have started earlier, the proletariat could have become more numerous, the alliance between the proletariat and the poor peasants could have been based upon producers' cooperatives founded upon superior technology, and therefore higher productivity and income than those of the private peasants; proletarian democracy could have been extended; the international revolution could have been successful in a number of countries. If one disregards the subjective factors and considers the whole process to have been inevitable, then one certainly cannot understand what the Left opposition's struggle against the rise of Stalinism was all about.[7]

Other important aspects of Trotsky's theory of the bureaucratization of the Soviet state are his positions on industrialization, planning and workers' self-management.

In the early twenties, a confrontation developed between the leadership of the Bolshevik Party, led at the time by Lenin and Trotsky, and a tendency inside the party – the so-called workers' opposition led by Shlyapnikov and Kollontai. The present-day supporters of this wing of the party maintain that if this tendency had won no bureaucratization would have taken place.[8]

But this conclusion is totally wrong and what Trotsky said at the time remains quite correct. One only needs to recall the state of Soviet factories in 1921. Three-quarters empty and manned by only a few of the 1917 veterans, they were producing practically nothing. This disastrous economic situation did not allow the Soviet worker much scope for combating the re-emergence of petty-commodity production, on the basis of barter between an extremely weak industrial sector and an increasingly discontented peasantry. To believe that in such conditions the answer to the problem of bureaucracy lay in giving power to the small groups of workers still working in the factories is to endow self-management with magic powers. Such a belief ignores fundamental realities: if the working class is to manage factories, then these must be functioning; if the working class is to direct the state and society, then it must exist in some strength and be employed; if this class is to show a minimum of political initiative, it must have a full stomach and some leisure time. Only on the basis of a minimal development of the productive forces and a functioning degree of workers' democracy can a struggle against bureaucracy be a real possibility.[9]

Though Trotsky underrated the institutional aspect of the problem with which he hardly dealt, he saw quite clearly that the first imperative was to increase production, to set production back into motion with the maximum possible speed, in order to strengthen the proletariat numerically, to combat the tendency towards private accumulation, to provide the masses with basic food and shelter, and to create the minimum material basis for enough workers' democracy for the proletariat to begin to play a growing direct role in the direction of the economy and the state.

The invocation of a self-management and workers' control which were impossible in the social and economic reality of 1921 is simply so much rhetoric.

The bureaucracy in the worker's states

Marxists studying Eastern Europe encounter difficulties which indicate a basic problem: the theoretical framework required to analyse societies moving from capitalism to socialism does not yet fully exist.

We know Marx's ideas on socialism and, while it is difficult to define closely what socialism is, we know quite well what it is not. Any serious Marxist can see that socialism has not yet been achieved either in the Soviet Union or in any other of the workers' states. But this statement does not solve the problem, because between capitalism and socialism there is inevitably, as Marxists from Marx himself to Lenin and Trotsky have recognized, a period of transition. And given that we have only elements of a theory of transitional societies, it is extremely difficult to decide which developments are due to bureaucratic degeneration and which are historically inevitable.

Numerous bourgeois, social-democratic and 'ultra-Left' ideologues argue that the survival of market categories (money, commodities, trade, etc.) in the Soviet Union automatically classifies the Soviet Union as a capitalist country, because a market economy implies a capitalist system of production. This is a serious mistake. While Marxists would agree that a fully developed socialist mode of production is one in which commodity production is no longer present, they also realize that the overthrow of capitalism does not result in its immediate abolition. The existence of commodity production in the Soviet Union does not mean that the Soviet Union is a capitalist country but rather a country in which socialism has not yet been fully realized. One of the characteristics of all societies in transition from capitalism to socialism, however advanced they may be, will probably be the survival to a greater or lesser degree, of market categories. Capitalism is characterized not by *elements* of commodity production, but by *universal* commodity production which does not exist in the Soviet Union.

Anarchists argue, in similar vein, that the continued existence of the state (an instrument of class struggle) in the Soviet Union points to the continued existence of exploitation and therefore capitalism. Lenin has already dealt with these arguments in his *State and Revolution*. The fact that the existence of the state indicates the existence of classes and class conflict in these countries does not prove that they are capitalist. On the contrary, in the transitional period from capitalism to socialism the state, in so far as it represents the dictatorship of the proletariat, is absolutely necessary to the building of socialism.

These arguments show that it is necessary to abstract from the historical specificities of the individual workers' states and to investigate at a more general level the problematic of transitional societies.

The general problematic of transitional societies

From an economic point of view, a society in transition from capitalism to socialism is principally defined by the suppression of private ownership of the means of production (industry, land, transport, banks, etc.), the monopoly of external trade and the introduction of planning into the economy. Thereby, production is no longer fundamentally governed by the law of value. It is no longer market forces or competition between different capitals which basically distribute economic resources between various sectors of output. Consequently, there arises a fundamental contradiction between the mode of production, which is clearly no longer capitalist, and the mode of distribution, which basically remains a bourgeois one. In his *Critique of the Gotha Programme*, Marx analysed at great length the continuing survival of social inequalities in the transitional period and even into the first stage of socialism. These inequalities he attributed to the survival of bourgeois norms of distribution (material incentives, the struggle to maximize wages, inequality in consumption, etc.).[10]

This crucial contradiction of the transitional period derives from the fact that the socialist mode of production presupposes a much higher stage of development of the productive forces than exists today on a world scale – a stage of material plenty that would render unnecessary the bourgeois aspect of the norms of distribution. This means that the historical task of the transitional society is twofold: it has to destroy the ideological residues of the old society based on class division, money economy and the trend to individual enrichment and, *at the same time*, it has to bring about an important new growth of the productive forces, to a level which will make possible a full development of plenty for all mankind.

It is the imperative necessity to realize these two tasks simultaneously which is the source of all the main contradictions of the transitional period, resulting in: (1) the partial survival of commodity production at the same time as it progressively withers away; (2) the survival of class divisions (peasantry, working class, urban petty bourgeoisie) at the same time as they too begin to wither away; (3) the survival of a state under the dictatorship of the proletariat, which at the same time starts to wither away – a state whose main function is to prevent a return of the old ruling class and to regulate the day-to-day economic activity which will ensure the socialist accumulation vital to the building of the new society. Clearly, the rapidity with which commodity production, social classes and the state wither away does not depend only on the domestic class struggle, but also on the international balance of forces, or the international class struggle.

The withering away of the state coexists, therefore, with the need for coercive direction of the economic process. Hence – a point most difficult to accept – certain bureaucratic deformations are inevitable.

These bureaucratic deformations would not be inevitable were the proletariat as a whole in a position, as soon as it takes power, to direct collectively, as a class, all spheres of social life. Unfortunately this is not the case. Those who refuse to acknowledge this fact only give undue historical credit to capitalism. For capitalism (which precedes the transitional period) alienates workers in all domains and, by subjecting them to an eight-, nine- or ten-hour working day (including time lost in going to and from the work place) denies them the systematic cultural development that would enable them to take on immediately the running of society as a whole. As long as the working day is not drastically reduced, the most elementary material conditions for workers' management of society do not exist, so that a certain delegation of power is inevitable – which in turn leads to partial bureaucratic deformations. What a transitional society needs is to find an ideal rhythm for the growth of its productive potential – one that will reduce the amount of social tension and at the same time will allow the progressive withering away of all the negative features inherited from the old society.

The problem of analysing the bureaucratically degenerated workers' state can now be posed in the following way. Fifty years after the creation of the Soviet Union, there are no signs whatsoever of the withering away of the features of class society. On the contrary, they are being progressively reinforced. The state dominates all spheres of social life. Partial commodity production and growing social inequality have been consolidated. Bureaucratic deformations, culminating in the total political expropriation of the working class, have become institutionalized.

If the problem is posed in this light, then one can proceed to a structural analysis of the historical origins, the inner logic and the unfolding of bureaucratic degeneration in the Soviet Union.

The origin of bureaucratic degeneration in the workers' states

As indicated above, the inevitability of bureaucratic deformation in the transitional societies is linked, in the last analysis, to two fundamental factors: insufficient development of productive forces, and the survival of capitalist features in the post-revolutionary society. To these two we should now add two more factors that lie at the roots of Stalinist degeneration. In the countries in which capitalism has been smashed, we find not only that the level of economic development was too low to ensure a rapid achievement of the state of abundance required for socialism, but also that this level was much lower than that of the industrialized capitalist countries. Hence the transitional societies were forced to accomplish the tasks of socialist accumulation *at the same time* as those of 'primitive accumulation' – notably industrialization. (This is what Preobrazhensky called 'primitive socialist accumulation'.) It was foreseen neither by Marx nor by other Marxists that the revolution would triumph first in a backward country, while the advanced countries would remain capitalist for a whole historical epoch. The fact that this is what in reality occurred has had a whole series of disastrous results in the last fifty years.

The Revolution, it was believed prior to 1917, would either take place simultaneously throughout an important part of the world or, failing that, it would at least capture the most advanced capitalist countries first. In the latter case, the non-socialist sector of the world would not significantly influence the development of the new social order, whether through military pressure, through ideological pull, or through a higher standard of living.

But the isolated victory of the Revolution in a backward country meant that this country had to defend itself against the military aggression or threat of aggression of all the advanced capitalist countries and to spend an important part of its national social surplus product for this purpose. At the same time, the higher standard of living in industrialized capitalist countries exerted a strong ideological attraction upon significant sections of the population. These two 'unforeseen factors', supplementing those which had already been foreseen by Marxists as 'normal' for a transitional society, lie at the roots of the bureaucratic degeneration. This is the fundamental historical explanation for developments in the Soviet Union after October. No Bolshevik leader in the period from 1917 to 1923 foresaw this evolution. And yet Lenin and Trotsky, and other leaders at various periods in their lives, understood well how the isolation of the Revolution in a backward country could provoke dangers unpredicted by Marxist theory.

The historical genesis of the Soviet bureaucracy therefore cannot be viewed either as a wicked plot or as the inevitable outcome of the specific socio-economic formation.[11] These two poles are mediated by an increasing political passivity of the Soviet proletariat during the 1920s. It is this decisive *mediation* that explains how the intense political and economic activity of the Soviet proletariat in 1917 to 1919 became gradually transformed into its total political expropriation ten or fifteen years later. The increasing political passivity of the Soviet proletariat was determined by a whole series of historical factors: the physical elimination of a great part of the workers' vanguard during the civil war; disappointment following the failure of the world revolution; generalized hunger and

misery; weakening of the institutions of workers' power, etc. Lenin saw
the danger during the last years of his life and started to fight them. From
1923 on, Trotsky and the Left opposition argued for an economic policy
at home and an internationalist strategy abroad that would objectively
help the Soviet proletariat to resume its political activity. These proposals, which contained no illusions about some miraculous quick solution,
were designed to create a situation where a faster development of
productive forces would go hand in hand with the revival of the political
climate of the first post-revolutionary years, in which soviets were
actually functioning and the proletariat had a direct role in the management of enterprises.

The strategy of the Left opposition, squarely based on a Marxist
analysis of the epoch, took into account (as Lenin had done from 1920
on) the growing danger of a dictatorship of the bureaucracy. It was a
tragedy that the majority of the Bolshevik cadres, despite all their
experience, failed to understand the correctness of the opposition's
proposals. Such a catastrophic ideological breakdown is unfortunately
not infrequent in the history of the working-class movement.[12] True,
between 1923 and 1936 most of the old Bolshevik leaders came to realize
the monstrous nature of bureaucratic power; but this realization came
too late. Their failure to perceive the real danger in time, coupled with
their inability to see the historical significance of the factional struggles in
which they took part, meant that the process of bureaucratic degeneration proceeded uninterrupted.

However, to rest content with this explanation only would mean
falling into subjectivism: it is necessary first to find the historical causes of
this tragic failure. The Bolshevik Party apparatus became the uncon-
scious instrument of a bureaucratic social stratum; this was made
possible only because the party itself had become bureaucratized.
The party apparatus, which was heavily integrated into the state
apparatus, had already gone through the first phase of bureaucratic
degeneration. It was thus against both its ideological and its material
interests to combat a process in which it was to a considerable degree
itself implicated.

One can go on at great length – as many analysts, from Souvarine to
Deutscher, have done – about how Stalin's victory was historically
inevitable or about the tactical errors committed by Trotsky.[13] But it is
much more important to recognize how a whole series of *political and
institutional errors* committed by the Bolshevik Party aided the process of
integration of party and state apparatuses and their simultaneous
bureaucratization, so that the party became sociologically incapable of
acting as a brake on this process.

1. *The ban on factions inside the party.* The prohibition of factions inside the party meant the beginning of the end of internal party democracy. Freedom of expression inevitably implies the right to the formation of tendencies: these equally inevitably can turn into factions, particularly when bureaucratization is under way, since this results in a systematic generalization of political differences.

2. *The introduction of the single-party practice.* Contrary to a widespread belief, nothing in Lenin's writings suggests that the period of the dictatorship of the proletariat allows for only one party. Nor is such a principle to be found in the Soviet constitution. Up to 1921 a number of parties (Left-Menshevik, Social-Revolutionaries, Anarchists) enjoyed legal existence, so long as they did not align themselves openly with military counter-revolution. A number of soviets were led by these parties (for example the rubber factory in Moscow was under Menshevik leadership) and elections were carried out on the basis of different slates representing different parties. However, from 1920 onwards, although no law was passed to that effect, the single-party principle became a practice. The banning of factions within the Bolshevik Party logically led to the suppression of other tendencies in the working-class movement. The fact that the single-party principle is entirely absent from Lenin's writings has been completely obliterated by the ideology of Stalinism. What Lenin did say was that the dictatorship of the proletariat was impossible without a Bolshevik Party, but that is something quite different.

The Bolshevik Party made the mistake of believing that, although the civil war was over and social tensions were beginning to diminish, the introduction of NEP with its attendant dangers required an accentuation of political repression and more centralization. The ban on other parties was based on the fear that they might be used by the bourgeoisie and the peasantry to overthrow the new social order. However, history shows that the best way to combat the danger of capitalist restoration is the continuous political activity of the proletariat. Therefore it was absolutely vital to create conditions favourable to the political reactivation of the proletariat – whereas the suppression of proletarian democracy encouraged the bureaucratization that Lenin wanted above all to avoid.

3. The third, and perhaps the most serious, institutional error was *the failure to understand the organic links between Soviet power, collective ownership and the need for 'primitive socialist accumulation'* (that is, for competition with the private sector of the economy).[14] The party believed that this competition would be won by the state enterprises through their higher economic productivity. Consequently, great emphasis was placed on individual productivity, which demanded a high degree of centraliz-

ation at the level of the enterprise, leading to the principle of one-man management. Aware of the possibilities for bureaucratic misuse inherent in this principle, the Bolsheviks provided a number of safeguards: (a) a high degree of trade-union autonomy; (b) the 'troika' system within the factory, whereby the powers of the factory manager were strictly controlled by the party and the trade unions (this in practice often turned into control by the party secretary and the trade-union secretary); (c) a very advanced social legislation designed to prevent abuses by the managers. In this last domain, the Soviet Union in the twenties was a model; workers could not be sacked by the managers, overtime could not be imposed, etc.

What Lenin and the other party leaders did not realize was that all these safeguards depended, in the last instance, on the health of the political power. As the party and the state came ever more under the control of the bureaucracy, the struggle of the workers – already extremely passive – to maintain these safeguards against the increasingly exorbitant power of the bureaucracy became more and more difficult. In the period after 1927, Stalin in fact removed all the various safeguards without meeting any significant resistance from the Soviet working class. First he got rid of the 'troika' system and instituted absolute powers for the manager. Then he suppressed all trade-union autonomy. Lastly he even abolished much of the progressive social legislation, introducing piece-work, overtime, Stakhanovism, and all the other aspects of abusive practices against the labour force.

If the Bolshevik Party had understood the problem in time, at the start of the twenties – if it had allowed the existence of factions within the party and other Soviet parties and at the same time had encouraged in a systematic fashion the growth of workers' self-management – then the resistance to bureaucratization would have been immeasurably greater. There can be no doubt that these historical factors played a far more important role than the tactical errors made by Trotsky and the Left opposition. But even if both these factors – Soviet democracy and workers' self-management – had been present, this in itself would not in the long run have prevented the victory of the bureaucracy, if working-class passivity had continued as a result of failure to achieve a correct orientation of economic and international policies. Only the conjunction of these institutional reforms with a more rapid industrialization, a step-by-step collectivization of agriculture, and a conduct of the international revolution which permitted victory in countries like Germany and China would have effectively and lastingly prevented the triumph of the bureaucracy. Then the historical evolution would have been different: internal democracy within the party would have survived, multi-party political life would have been maintained, workers' management of the economy would have been institutionalized and strengthened. A

Congress of Workers' Councils and not a handful of bureaucrats would have taken all the great decisions determining the basic orientation of the planned economy.

The conclusions of this brief historical study can be summarized as follows: In order to prevent the unavoidable tendency to bureaucratization in a workers' state (especially a backward one) from being transformed into institutional bureaucratic degeneration, a combination of three fundamental factors is necessary: (1) state institutions of soviet power, that is, genuine workers' democracy; (2) economic and social policies designed with a view to increasing the socio-economic weight, the 'self-activity' and the consciousness of the proletariat at all levels, that is, with a view to improving the balance of forces between the proletariat and the other social classes (this includes a development of the productive forces and of the standard of living of the proletariat); (3) an international extension of the socialist revolution.

The nature of the bureaucracy in the workers' states

Under certain historical conditions, when the balance of forces is very unfavourable to the proletariat, the bureaucracy may acquire a considerable autonomy – at first sight a quasi-total one. *But this autonomy can never be complete.* The bureaucracy can never separate itself completely from the mode of production which gives it birth and create a qualitatively new mode of production. The autonomy of the bureaucracy is limited by the mode of production into which it is inserted and it is this mode of production rather than its own sectoral interests that dictates its priorities.[15] One should distinguish very carefully between the demands of the historically objective socio-economic system within which this bureaucracy functions and its interests as a socially privileged layer.[16]

For a long period, Trotsky characterized the overall policy of the bureaucracy by the notion of *bureaucratic centrism*: the social nature of the bureaucracy leads it to move from one extreme to another, so that the internal logic of this centrism can only be grasped by an overall analysis of the conjunctural oscillations.[17]

Bureaucratic rule in general, even after the degeneration has gone to the point where a hardened bureaucratic social layer has appeared, is characterized by *the dual nature of the bureaucracy.*

The first aspect reflects its relation to a society and mode of production that is no longer capitalist, that is indeed radically opposed to capitalism. This aspect explains the forced collectivization of the Soviet peasantry, the heroic resistance against Nazism and the destruction of capitalism in the countries occupied by the Red Army on a permanent basis.[18]

This first aspect of the dual nature of the bureaucracy is related to the fact that this social stratum has acquired its privileges on the basis of the previous destruction of the old ruling class. These privileges can develop only within the framework of a non-capitalist mode of production. They are incompatible with the victory of private property over the means of production. The restoration of capitalism in the Soviet Union (which, for those who do not believe in 'peaceful roads' in reverse, cannot happen unless a violent class war is unleashed and won by counter-revolution) could allow some bureaucrats to own factories. But this act would also signify an end to their existence as bureaucrats and their transformation into capitalists with quite different social attitudes. The economic attitude of the bureaucracy as a social layer is not dictated by the laws of competition, of profit maximization and of accumulation of capital, but by quite different motivations related to their role in the transitional period.[19]

The second aspect of the dual nature of the bureaucracy is its fundamentally conservative social outlook: its desire to maintain the status quo in the international arena and hold back the advance of the world revolution. Indeed, the advance of the world revolution spells the end of the historic usurpation by the bureaucracy of the economic and political power of the proletariat. The reactivation of the international proletariat poses a threat to the bureaucratic hegemony.

The dual nature of the bureaucracy represents a permanent combination of these two contradictory aspects characteristic of the bureaucracy in power in the workers' states; it defends the non-capitalist nature of the workers' states and at the same time it fears and fights world revolution and thereby undermines the socio-economic basis of the workers' state.

Its fundamental conservatism should not be interpreted narrowly: when necessary this bureaucracy does not hesitate to cross national boundaries and extend its power over other countries – provided this can be accomplished without the proletariat becoming re-politicized on a dangerous scale in the process.[20]

The need for a political revolution in the workers' states
What revolutionary strategy follows from the contradictory nature of the bureaucracy in power in the workers' states?

This social layer, conscious of its interests and privileges, will not simply abandon them under the pressure of an objective evolution – the development of productive forces and the growth of the numerical and cultural strength of the world proletariat – that continuously modifies the balance of forces at its expense and makes its hegemony increasingly difficult to maintain. Only a political revolution will smash the power of the bureaucracy and institute the power of the proletariat. This does not mean that such a revolution will necessarily have to be long and violent. The historical examples available (Berlin 1953, Budapest 1956, Czechoslovakia 1968) show that when a process of political revolution is initiated, and a growing mobilization of the working class takes place, with factory occupations, the election of workers' councils, etc., then the local bureaucracy virtually melts away. Only military intervention from outside is capable of halting such a political revolution. And in the case of the USSR itself, of course, there could be no such outside intervention. One may thus be rather optimistic about the way in which the political revolution will be achieved. After all, what social base could the bureaucracy call on to defend it? Who would be prepared in the long run to fight at its side against the proletariat?

This vulnerability of the bureaucracy is an indication of what is meant by a *political* revolution in contradistinction to a *social* one. In a social revolution, the mode of production is changed and power passes from one class to another. A political revolution, on the other hand, leaves the mode of production fundamentally unchanged and power passes from one layer of a class to another layer of the same class.[21]

The effect of a political revolution in the workers' states would be to give the existing mode of production a new content: bureaucratized management of production is incompatible with the exercise of proletarian democracy. But the main framework of the economy – collective property, planning, the survival of some market mechanisms, etc. – would not be transformed. They would acquire a new meaning, but would not be destroyed and replaced by others. Consequently the form of the state would undergo a transformation but its social nature would remain the same.[22]

The bureaucracy: a social layer or a class?

The conclusion that the power of the bureaucracy will be smashed through a political rather than a social revolution stems from the fact that it is not a class rooted in the production process but a social layer growing out of the proletariat. This definition is not a question of a play on words: it is of crucial importance in formulating the correct strategy for the international working-class movement.

The widespread confusion regarding the nature of this social layer is caused by its social mode of existence, which resembles in certain outward characteristics that of a class: the monopoly of power, material privileges, collective identity, etc.[23] To call this bureaucracy a class does not allow a correct understanding of the reality of the world revolution and leads to insoluble contradictions on the theoretical and methodological plane. If the bureaucracy is a class, then either this class constituted itself as a class and took power only after the revolution, or it existed as a class before the revolution and the revolution was in fact its seizure of power.

The implications of these alternatives are quite different and have to be carefully distinguished. Take the argument that the bureaucracy exists as a class before it takes power and that in the capitalist countries it consists of the leadership of the Communist Parties. To Marxists this proposition is a theoretical monstrosity: what is the relationship of the communist leadership in capitalist countries to the process of production? But this simple 'mistake' can have extremely damaging political consequences. For example, according to this theory, a strike led by the PCI or PCF would no longer be an instance of the class struggle between the proletariat and the bourgeoisie but between the bureaucracy and the bourgeoisie – in this case the proletariat would have to adopt a 'class alliance', or even worse. Similarly, any national liberation struggle – the struggle in Vietnam, for example – would no longer be seen as a struggle between imperialism and the masses but between the bureaucracy and the imperialist bourgeoisie. This theoretical position, we see, totally distorts actual reality. For Marxists, a strike led by the Italian or French Communist Party is an instance of the class struggle between the proletariat and the bourgeoisie. True, the CP bureaucracy attempts to bend the strike to its own aims, but thereby the struggle does not become a three-cornered struggle between three classes; it is still a struggle between the proletariat and the bourgeoisie.

The logic of this position (the position that the leaderships of the Western Communist Parties form classes in embryo) is, in the last instance, the logic of abstention from the class struggle; in essence it is a counter-revolutionary position. There are groups who argue that the war in Vietnam is a war between two imperialist camps (likewise the Korean war in the early fifties); that the Cuban revolution is of no interest to revolutionaries because it is led by a new exploiting class, so that the conflict between Cuba and USA imperialism is one between two exploiting classes, in which the proletariat should take no sides; and so on. Now, whether we like it or not, anti-imperialist and class struggles in many countries are led by Communist Parties and it is our duty to support those struggles (which does not mean that we abstain from pointing out that as long as these struggles are led exclusively by Stalinists they have a slim chance of success; that we do not have to fight against Stalinism, etc.).

Then there are those who see in the bureaucracy of the workers' states a new social class historically progressive in relation to the bourgeoisie. This position would lead the proletariat to support another class, the bureaucracy, in its struggle against the bourgeoisie and imperialism, that is, it denies the proletariat the leading role in the world revolution. [24] Consequently the political groups which start off with this premise entertain serious illusions about the revolutionary potential of the bureaucracy. But who can really believe that the present policy of, for example, the French Communist Party, is directed towards the conquest of power?

Let us now turn to the position which claims that the bureaucracy constituted itself as a class after the revolution and let us examine what kind of politics flows from this. When one looks at the theoreticians of the 'new exploiting class' (people like Djilas, Burnham, etc.) one finds that in most cases their revolt against Stalin and the post-Stalin Stalinists has resulted in scepticism towards the working class, adulation of bourgeois democracy, denial of Marxism. Their denunciation of the Kremlin has only turned them towards Washington.[25] These people have in effect crossed the class lines and joined the bourgeoisie. Nothing more needs to be said about this thesis.

There are others – most notably the Polish comrades Kuron and Modzelewski – who also characterize the bureaucracy as a social class but do so within the framework of a Marxist analysis denouncing capitalism and bourgeois democracy and expressing a firm belief in the historical role of the proletariat. In the case of these comrades the problem is more one of terminology than of politics.

In 1939 Trotsky wrote on this problem:

Let us begin by posing the question of the nature of the Soviet state not on the abstract-sociological plane but on the plane of concrete-political tasks. Let us concede for the moment that the bureaucracy is a new 'class' and that the present regime in the USSR is a special system of class exploitation. What new political conclusions follow for us from these definitions? The Fourth International long ago recognized the necessity of overthrowing the bureaucracy by means of a revolutionary uprising of the toilers. Nothing else is proposed or can be proposed by those who proclaim the bureaucracy to be an exploiting 'class'. The goal to be attained by the overthrow of the bureaucracy is the re-establishment of the rule of the soviets, expelling from them the present bureaucracy. Nothing different can be proposed or is proposed by the leftist critics. It is the task of the regenerated soviets to collaborate with the world revolution and the building of a socialist society. The overthrow of the bureaucracy presupposes the preservation of state property and planned economy. Herein is the nub of the whole problem.

Needless to say, the distribution of productive forces among the various branches of the economy and generally the entire content of the plan will be drastically changed when this plan is determined by the interests not of the bureaucracy but of the producers themselves. But inasmuch as the question of overthrowing the parasitic oligarchy still remains linked with that of preserving the nationalized (state) property, we call the future revolution *political*. Certain of our critics (Ciliga, Bruno and others) want, come what may, to call the future revolution *social*. Let us grant this definition. What does it alter in essence? To those tasks of the revolution which we have enumerated it adds nothing whatsoever.

Our critics as a rule take the facts as we long ago established them. They add absolutely nothing essential to the appraisal either of the position of the bureaucracy and the toilers, or of the role of the Kremlin on the international arena. In all these spheres, not only do they fail to challenge our analysis, but on the contrary they base themselves completely upon it and even restrict themselves entirely to it. The sole accusation they bring against us is that we do not draw the necessary 'conclusions'. Upon analysis it turns out, however, that these conclusions are of a purely terminological character. Our critics refuse to call the degenerated workers' state – a workers' state. They demand that the totalitarian bureaucracy be called a ruling class. The revolution against this bureaucracy they propose to consider not political but social. Were we to make them these terminological concessions, we would place our critics in a very difficult position, inasmuch as they themselves would not know what to do with their purely verbal victory. It would therefore be a piece of monstrous nonsense to split with comrades who on the question of the sociological nature of the USSR have an opinion different from ours, insofar as they solidarize with us in regard to the political tasks.[26]

The difference is, however, not purely terminological, because Kuron and Modzelewski are led by their analysis to a number of incorrect conclusions:

1. They are forced to introduce a qualitative difference between the central political bureaucracy and the so-called technocracy; these two become for them distinct classes.

2. They are led to attribute to the bureaucracy a class aim (production for production's sake) which has in fact already been partially abandoned (see note 10 below).

3. They are led to adopt a 'national' analysis of the bureaucratic phenomenon and fail to understand the international role of the Russian bureaucracy.

These three factors put together lead them to underestimate the capacity of the bureaucracy for further adaptation and repression.

Conclusion

In conclusion, let us stress that the one basic truth that must never be lost sight of is that the fundamental struggle in the world today is the struggle between the bourgeoisie and the proletariat. The bureaucracy intervenes in this struggle only to distort it. The only way to eliminate both the bureaucracy and the bourgeoisie is to lead to its logical conclusion both the working-class and the anti-imperialist revolutionary struggle. Only the widest possible spread of the world revolution can ultimately guarantee the destruction of the bureaucracy's power.

The problem of bureaucracy has already been partially answered by history. All the victorious revolutions since 1945 have posed more or less directly the problem of bureaucracy: the Yugoslav Revolution by its attempt at self-management; the Chinese Revolution in the distorted form of the 'Cultural Revolution'; the Cuban Revolution most explicitly and deliberately in its attacks against bureaucracy. As Marx said: history poses only those problems it can solve. Today both the objective and subjective conditions seem to be ripe for solving the problem of bureaucracy. On the one hand, we are witnessing a widespread expansion of the world revolution and a tremendous development of the world productive forces. On the other hand, revolutionary militants in both capitalist and workers' states have become aware of the fundamental importance of this problem for the socialist revolution. There is thus no doubt that any new proletarian revolution will have consciously to confront the problem of bureaucracy and to solve it in the most effective way.

NOTES TO CHAPTER 3

1. The absence of organizational structures would condemn the working-class movement to a level of mediocrity that would make its victory appear as a historical regression from the advances made by the capitalist system of production. Indeed, if in the aftermath of a successful revolution the new society were to do away with all specialists and technicians not directly involved in the material sphere of production, it would regress to a level of primitive communism which would in turn quickly disintegrate through a new process of social differentiation. Instead of eliminating the danger of bureaucratization, this procedure would revive it – only under more insidious conditions.

   The creation of an apparatus is indispensable even for reasons of simple efficiency; it is impossible to organize, say, 50,000 people without a minimal infrastructure.

2. This group broke from the French section of the Fourth International in 1949, and published the review *Socialisme ou Barbarie* until the mid-sixties. They were the ideological mentors of the Solidarity group in Britain.

3. The numerical size of social democratic parties, far from being an obstacle to their bureaucratization, is in fact a major cause of it. It is far easier to prevent the bureaucratization of an organization which only recruits members who already have a basic minimum of political consciousness, experience and activity since this makes it impossible for the phenomenon of 'clientalism' to appear on any large scale.

4. Around 1891–2 a number of ultra-Left groups of more or less anarchist orientation developed inside the German social democratic movement. This 'Berlin Left' is little known in the working-class movement. No black-and-white judgement on it is possible: Lenin himself was forced after 1914 to change his previously uncomplimentary assessment and came to view in these oppositional groupings a first semi-conscious reaction against the growing reformism and corruption of the social democratic movement.

5. In the preface to the second edition of *What is to be Done?*, Lenin specifically emphasizes this point: the moment the vanguard detaches itself from the proletariat it falls into complete adventurism and arbitrariness. A small group of bureaucrats sits around a table and decides how, at a given historical moment, the proletariat ought to act. Such procedure banishes the basic objective criterion of revolutionary socialist practice: the class-consciousness of the proletariat and what it is in fact prepared to do.

6. These objective factors could be summarized as: insufficient level of development of the productive forces; cultural and numerical underdevelopment of the proletariat; isolation of the victorious revolution with the retreat of the world revolution; the general state of scarcity prevailing in the country, etc.

7. Deutscher never quite grasped this point: for him the men who made up the Left opposition were heroes condemned to lose and whose destiny was to prepare a very distant future.

8. Recent attempts to rehabilitate this tendency have come from various quarters: (1) 'ultra-Left groups (e.g. *Socialisme ou Barbarie*), who cherish a 'Prophetic' text published by Kollontai in 1921; (2) Yugoslav ideologues, who defend its struggle against Lenin's democratic centralism – a somewhat surprising position given the hyper-centralization of the political power structure in that country; (3) some members of the 'Pabloite' tendency, which is not surprising given their belief in self-management as a universal panacea for all problems in the society of transition from capitalism to socialism, especially bureaucracy.

9. The example of Yugoslavia shows that a purely formal system of self-management limited to the factory level, is insufficient for fighting bureaucracy.

10. In pre-capitalist societies, these norms of distribution either do not apply or are present only in an embryonic form. In feudal society, for example, the quantity of goods at the disposal of an individual is not so much a function of his income as of his social status.

11. From a subjective point of view the actors in this drama were to a great extent unaware of what was at stake. Trotsky once suggested that if someone in 1920 had been able to show Stalin that he was going to suppress all forms of workers' power, and to destroy the Bolshevik Party and the Communist International, it is quite possible that Stalin would have committed suicide. The same is true of the other party leaders who rejected the Left opposition platform and allied themselves with Stalin.

12. Every time the working class is confronted with a new and unforeseen major problem, a considerable section of its best cadres fail to respond to it correctly. One example was the failure, after 1909–10, to understand the nature of the coming imperialist war and period of revolution and the underlying causes of the imminent social democratic betrayal. This inability to come to grips with the new situation lasted for a number of years even among those who later came to constitute the new Communist Parties.

13. Those who go in for analyses of this type generally try to prove two mutually exclusive theses: 1. that Trotsky's mistakes allowed Stalin's victory; 2. that Stalin's victory was inevitable due to objective conditions in the Soviet Union

at the time. This was particularly clear in the case of Isaac Deutscher, in whose works we find the two theses systematically interlinked.

14. This failure derives from the opposition between the need to accumulate and the need to defend the producers as 'consumers' characteristic of the transitional period. Within the framework of 'market socialism', the immediate economic interests of the producers may come into conflict with the fundamental principles of a socialist economy, even in democratically managed enterprises. Examples of this can be found in Yugoslavia, where a democratically elected workers' council can vote to lay off 25 per cent of the labour force in order to improve the wages of the rest of the workers. This shows that the coincidence of interests between individual groups of workers and the proletariat as a whole is not automatic.

15. One cannot attribute all the monstrous errors committed by the bureaucracy to its desire to defend its privileges. Thus it was clearly not in the interest of Stalin and the Soviet bureaucracy to decrease agricultural production for twenty-five years. In other countries, for example Yugoslavia, the bureaucracy has shown itself perfectly capable of maintaining relatively friendly relations with the peasantry.

16. The Polish activists Kuron and Modzelewski make a theoretical mistake by arguing that giving priority to heavy industry is a fundamental feature of the bureaucracy. It in fact merely represents one particular phase of bureaucratic rule – a phase which has already been left behind in some countries, for example the Soviet Union. This mistake is dangerous, because it can lead to the belief that the bureaucracy will have no material basis once heavy industry loses its preferential position in the national economy.

17. Many people in the twenties attempted to characterize the bureaucracy on the basis of its right-wing policy of concessions to the peasantry and were consequently quite unable to explain the turn of 1928 and the brutal elimination of the *kulaks*. Similarly, those who identified the bureaucracy with violent police dictatorship and large-scale concentration camps could hardly explain Yugoslavia in the sixties.

18. The theory according to which the Soviet Union is a workers' state while the 'people's democracies' are capitalist gives a completely incomprehensible view of reality: how can one reasonably maintain that the Czechoslovak economic system is qualitatively different from the one in the Soviet Union but identical to that of the capitalist countries? That the East German economy is qualitatively different from that of the USSR but of the same social nature as that of West Germany?

19. For Marx the notion of 'state capitalism', that is, the complete suppression of intra-capitalist competition, was inconceivable: capitalism cannot exist except as *different* capitals. The total suppression of competition would put an end to the accumulation of capital and economic growth under capitalism, as its motor would have disappeared.

20. Stalinists justify the USSR's refusal to extend the revolution into countries like France, Italy, Greece or Yugoslavia by reference to the Yalta agreement, which the USSR allegedly had to respect under the American threat of unleashing another World War. This justification 'forgets' that the revolution did not

respect the division of the world into power-blocs and was successful in Yugoslavia, China and Cuba. Each success of the revolution provoked an international tension but in the end imperialism had to accept the *fait accompli.*

21. To Marx, the years of 1830 and 1848 in France were examples of political revolutions: state power changed hands between various layers of the same class (financial bourgeoisie, industrial bourgeoisie). The industrial bourgeoisie had to fight arms in hand to wrench political power from the financial bourgeoisie – hence the revolution of February 1848. But the 1848 revolution was fundamentally different from that which brought the Paris Commune into existence: in the latter case, state power passed temporarily out of the hands of the bourgeoisie and into the hands of the proletariat.

22. The definition of the nature of the state rests, in the last analysis, exclusively on its relationship to a given mode of production. The change from fascism to bourgeois democracy in Germany in 1945 involved a considerable change in the form of the state without any change in the mode of production. So did the change between the Second Empire and the Third Republic in France. The fact that many forms of state power are possible *within* a given economic formation does not mean that the change from one to another can necessarily be made in a reformist or gradual fashion.

23. The tendency among certain Marxists in Eastern Europe to characterize the bureaucracy as a class springs from the desire to draw a line of demarcation between themselves and the reformist currents which believe in the strategy of alliance with one wing of the bureaucracy against another.

24. This theory is based on the refusal to recognize what Lukacs called the fundamental idea of Leninism: the actuality of the revolution. In the last century, the proletariat could play a secondary role, supporting the progressive classes against the reactionary ones. But what is on the agenda today is a *proletarian revolution,* carried out by the working class itself.

25. See Pierre Frank's introduction to 'An Open Letter to Communist Party Members' by Kuron and Modzelewski in *Revolutionary Marxist Students in Poland Speak Out,* Merit, 1968.

26. Leon Trotsky, *In Defense of Marxism,* Merit, 1965, p. 4.

4. 'Socialism in One Country'

Isaac Deutscher

Stalin first formulated his ideas on socialism in one country in the autumn of 1924. Belief in socialism in one country was soon to become the supreme test of loyalty to party and state. In the next ten or fifteen years nobody who failed that test was to escape condemnation and punishment. Yet, if one studies the 'prolegomena' to this article of Stalinist faith, one is struck by the fact that it was first put forward by Stalin almost casually, like a mere debating point, in the 'literary discussion'. For many months, until the summer of the next year, none of Stalin's rivals, neither the other triumvirs nor Trotsky, thought the point worth arguing. Nor was Stalin's own mind fixed. In his pamphlet *The Foundations of Leninism*, published early in 1924, he stated with great emphasis that, though the proletariat of one country could seize power, it could not establish a socialist enconomy in one country.

But the overthrow [these are Stalin's words] of the power of the *bourgeoisie* and establishment of the power of the proletariat in one country does not yet mean that the complete victory of socialism has been ensured. The principal task of socialism – the organization of socialist production – has still to be fulfilled. Can this task be fulfilled, can the final victory of socialism be achieved in one country, without the joint efforts of the proletarians in several advanced countries? No, it cannot. To overthrow the *bourgeoisie* the efforts of one country are sufficient; this is proved by the history of our revolution. For the final victory of socialism, for the organization of socialist production, the efforts of one country, particularly of a peasant country like Russia, are insufficient; for that, the efforts of the proletarians of several advanced countries are required.[1]

In his *Problems of Leninism*, however, which he wrote later in the same year, Stalin corrected himself and asserted the opposite. He withdrew the first edition of his *Foundations of Leninism* from circulation and re-nounced it as apocryphal. He was at first hardly aware of the weight that circumstances were soon to give to his 'socialism in one country'. He reached his formula gropingly, discovering, as it were, a new continent, while he believed himself to be sailing for quite a different place.

His immediate purpose was to discredit Trotsky and to prove for the *n*th time that Trotsky was no Leninist. Searching in Trotsky's past, the triumvirs came across the theory of 'permanent revolution', which he had formulated in 1905. They started a polemic against it; and it was in the course of that polemic that Stalin arrived at his formula. Since his 'socialism in one country' thus originated as a counter to Trotsky's 'permanent revolution', it is proper to sum up and analyse the two formulas in their bearing upon each other.

Trotsky had borrowed his theory from Marx and applied it to the Russian Revolution.[2] He spoke of the 'permanency' of the revolution in a double sense: the revolution, he foresaw, would be driven by circumstances to pass from its anti-feudal (bourgeois) to its anti-capitalist (socialist) phase. Contrary to the then accepted Marxist view, not the advanced Western European countries but backward Russia would be the first to set out along the road to socialism. But Russia alone would not be able to advance far upon that road. The revolution could not stop at her national frontiers. It would have to pass from its national to its international phase – this was to be the second aspect of its 'permanency'. Under the impact of Russia Western Europe, too, would become revolutionized. Only then could socialism be established on a broad international basis. The progress of mankind, so Trotsky argued, was now hampered not only by the capitalist mode of production but also by the existence of nation-states. The final outcome of the revolutionary transformation could only be One World, one socialist world. There was, however, a disquieting question mark in this prognostication. What will happen – Trotsky asked in 1906 – if the revolution fails to spread from Russia to Western Europe? His grim answer was that it would then either succumb to a conservative Europe or become corroded in its economically and culturally primitive Russian environment.

Until 1917, it will be remembered, this theory was Trotsky's personal contribution to Marxist thought, rejected by Bolsheviks as well as by Mensheviks. On one or two occasions Lenin vaguely sketched a not dissimilar view of the future; but, on the whole, his policy was firmly based on the premise that the Russian Revolution would confine itself to its anti-feudal objectives. It was on this point that he denied its 'permanency'. Nevertheless he, too, did believe that the bourgeois revolution in Russia would stimulate a socialist revolution in Western Europe; and that then, but only then, might Russia also, with the help of the 'advanced countries', move forward towards socialism. What Lenin denied was not the international character of the revolution but Russia's intrinsic capacity to embark upon socialism before Western Europe. He reproached Trotsky with 'overlooking' the peasantry, because only if one ignored the peasantry's attachment to individual property could one assume that a peasant country like Russia would by itself pass from the bourgeois to the socialist revolution.

In 1917, it will be remembered, Lenin changed his mind. In all essentials the thesis of the permanent revolution (though not, of course, its somewhat bookish nomenclature) was adopted by his party. The revolution did in fact pass from the anti-feudal to the anti-capitalist phase. To the very last Lenin and his followers expected it also to spread beyond Russia. Meanwhile they looked upon their own country as upon a besieged fortress, spacious and powerful enough to hold out. They believed that an important advance could be made in organizing the internal life of that fortress on socialist lines. Spurring on his followers to the job, Lenin (and Trotsky) emphatically pointed to the possibilities of socialist experiment opening before them. But essentially Lenin thought of socialist society in international terms. We have seen that early in 1924 Stalin, too, was still arguing that 'for the final victory of socialism, for the organization of socialist production, the efforts of one country, particularly of a peasant country like Russia, are insufficient'. He now stated that the efforts of Russia alone would suffice for the *complete* organization of a socialist economy. A socialist economy – this had so far been taken for granted – was conceivable only as an economy of plenty. This presupposed a highly developed industry capable of ensuring a high standard of living for the whole people. How then, the question arose, could a country like Russia, whose meagre industry had been reduced to wrack and ruin, achieve socialism? Stalin pointed to Russia's great assets: her vast spaces and enormous riches in raw materials. A proletarian government could, in his view, through its control of industry and credit, develop those resources and carry the building of socialism to a successful conclusion, because in this endeavour it would be supported by a vast majority of the people, including the peasants.

This, the most essential, part of Stalin's formula was very simple. It proclaimed in terms clear to everybody the self-sufficiency of the Russian Revolution. It was true that Stalin begged many a question. He did not even try to meet the objections to his thesis that were raised later by his critics. One objection that most peasants, attached as they were to private property, were certain to put up the strongest resistance to collectivism, he simply dismissed as a heretical slander on the peasantry. Nor did he seriously consider the other argument that socialism was possible only on the basis of the intensive industrialization already achieved by the most advanced Western countries; and that Russia by herself would not be able to catch up with those countries. According to his critics, socialism could beat capitalism only if it represented a higher productivity of labour and higher standards of living than had been attained under capitalism. The critics deduced that if productivity of labour and standards of living were to remain lower in Russia than in the capitalist countries then socialism would, in the long run, fail even in Russia. Nor did Stalin ever try to refute their forecast that in an economy of scarcity, such as an isolated Russian economy would be, a new and glaring material inequality between various social groups was certain to arise.

But, whatever the flaws in Stalin's reasoning, flaws that were obvious only to the most educated men in the party, his formula was politically very effective. It contained, at any rate, one clear and positive proposition: we are able to stand on our own feet, to build and to complete the building of socialism. This was what made the formula useful for polemical and practical purposes. It offered a plain alternative to Trotsky's conception. For a variety of reasons, however, Stalin did not present his thesis in that plain and clear-cut form. He hedged it round with all sorts of reservations and qualifications. One reservation was that the victory of socialism in Russia could not be considered secure so long as her capitalist environment threatened Russia with armed intervention. Socialism in a single state could not be beaten by the 'cheap goods' produced in capitalist countries of which his critics spoke; but it might be defeated by force of arms. In the next few years Stalin himself constantly held that danger before Russia's eyes and thereby seemed to weaken his own case. Moreover, he went on to express, though with ever decreasing confidence, a belief in the proximity of international revolution. He proclaimed the absolute self-sufficiency of Russian socialism in one half of his thesis and disclaimed it in the other.

The strangeness of that passionate ideological dispute does not end here. As the controversy developed, Stalin ascribed to his critics the view that it was not possible to build socialism in Russia. He then presented the issue as one between those who believed in the 'creative force' of the revolution and the 'panic mongers' and 'pessimists'. Now the issue was not as simple as that. His critics were beyond question not guilty of the things imputed to them. They, too, asserted that it was possible and necessary to organize the country's economy on socialist lines. Trotsky in particular had, since the end of the civil war, urged the Politburo to begin gearing up the administration for planned economy; and in those early days he first sketched most of the ideas that were later to be embodied in the five-year plans.[3]

The student of the controversy may thus often have the uncanny feeling that its very object is indefinable; that, having aroused unbounded passion and bitterness, it simply vanishes into thin air. Stripped of polemical distortions and insinuations, the debate seems in the end, to the student's astonishment, to centre on a bizarre irrelevancy. The point was not whether socialism could or should be built but whether the building could be *completed* in a single isolated state. Metaphorically speaking, the antagonists did not argue whether it was possible or desirable to erect the edifice they wanted; nor did they disagree about the materials of which it was to be built or even about its shape. Ostensibly, the only point at issue was whether it would be possible to cover the edifice with a roof. Stalin's yes was as emphatic as his opponents' no.[4] Both sides still agreed that the 'roof' was not to be laid for a very, very long time yet, that classless socialism would not be achieved within the lifetime of one or even two generations. Both sides also agreed that hostile forces might wreck the building at any stage of their work on it – they constantly saw the shadow of war falling across Russia. Finally, Stalin, like his critics, professed to believe that long before the time came to put on the roof, the problem he had posed would cease to exist, because revolution in the West would free socialist Russia from isolation.

It might seem then that it was preposterous for the disputants, who were men of action, to pose the problem as they had posed it; and that, on their own showing, they could have travelled a very, very long way together, leaving their differences to professional scholastics to thrash out. Was the whole dispute, then, a mere smoke-screen for a clash of personal ambitions? No doubt the personal rivalries were a strong element in it. But the historian who reduced the whole matter to that would commit a blatant mistake. He would still have to explain why 'socialism in one country' split the ranks of Bolshevism from top to bottom, why it became an issue of such deadly earnest for a whole Russian generation, why it determined the outlook of a great nation for a quarter of a century. The other suggestion which is often made, that socialism in one country was invented to allay the suspicions of foreign governments, alarmed by 'subversive' activities directed from Moscow, is even more pointless. When Stalin formulated his thesis, his name was still almost unknown abroad; and, even later on, the desire to allay foreign suspicions did not prevent him from making statements on communism in Europe that made the flesh of many a Conservative abroad creep.

As sometimes happens in important disputes, where both sides are strongly committed to certain common principles, so in this controversy, too, its explanation cannot be found in the literal meaning of the disputants' words, certainly not in their zealous reiteration of 'common' principles, but must rather be sought in the subtle, often imperceptible, shifts in the emphasis of their arguments. The explanation is further to be found in the state of mind and the moods of the milieu in which the disputants act and which they address. In the last resort, the doctrinal controversy grows out of those moods; and they – the moods – form the sounding-board that imparts a significant ring to the seemingly indistinguishable formulas that are bandied about. The audience that listens to the disputants is left unmoved by their professions of common principle; it treats these as part of a customary ritual. But it pricks up its ears at the different hints and allusions thrown out by either side; and it avidly absorbs all their undertones and unspoken conclusions. It quickly learns to tell the operative part of any formula from the reservations and escape clauses that seem to contradict it.

Now the operative part of Stalin's thesis, the thing that was really new and striking in it, was the assertion of the self-sufficiency of the Russian Revolution. All the rest was a repetition of traditional Bolshevik truisms, some of which had become meaningless and others embarrassing, but all of which had to be repeated, because they had the flavour of doctrinal respectability. The thing that was new in Stalin's argument represented a radical revision of the party's attitude. But the revision was undertaken in a manner that seemed to deny the very fact of revision and to represent it as a straight continuation of an orthodox line of thought, a method familiar from the history of many a doctrine. We shall not lead the reader further into the thick of this dogmatic battle. Suffice it to say that Stalin did his best to graft his formula on to the body of doctrine he had inherited from Lenin.

More important than the dogmatic intricacies is the fact that now, in the seventh and eighth years of the revolution, a very large section of the party, probably its majority, vaguely and yet very definitely felt the need for ideological stocktaking and revision. The need was emotional rather than intellectual; and those who felt it were by no means desirous of any open break with Bolshevik orthodoxy. No revolutionary party can remain in power seven years without profound changes in its outlook. The Bolsheviks had by now grown accustomed to running an enormous state, 'one-sixth of the world'. They gradually acquired the self-confidence and the sense of self-importance that come from the privileges and responsibilities of power. The doctrines and notions that had been peculiarly theirs when they themselves had been the party of the under-dog did not suit their present outlook well. They needed an idea or a slogan that would fully express their newly won self-confidence. 'Socialism in one country' did it. It relieved them, to a decisive extent, of a sense of their dependence on happenings in the five-sixths of the world that were beyond their control.

It gave them the soothing theoretical conviction that, barring war, nothing could shake their mastery over Russia: the property-loving peasantry, the industrial weakness of the nation, its low productivity and even lower standard of living, all these implied no threat of a restoration of the *ancien régime*.

Whoever, like Trotsky, and later on Zinoviev and Kamenev, dwelt on the dangers to the revolution inherent in all those circumstances, offended the complacency of the party.

Below this psychological attitude, which was confined to the rulers, there was a much broader undercurrent: the party and the working classes had grown weary of the expectation of international revolution which had been the daily bread of Bolshevism. That expectation was dashed in 1917, 1918, and 1920. It rose again in 1923, during the turmoil in Germany. This time the deferment of hope made the heart of the party sick. 'The European working classes are letting us down; they listen to their social democratic leaders and tremble over the fleshpots of capitalism' – such was, roughly, the comment of many a politically minded worker on the daily news from the West. It was a galling thought, one which was inseparable from Trotsky's 'permanent revolution', that in spite of all this the fortunes of Russian communism should still be regarded as ultimately dependent on the victory or defeat of communism abroad. There was something that hurt the national *amour propre* in the usual talk about 'backward' Russia and 'advanced' Europe, even though party speakers illustrated such talk with weighty comparative statistics on Russian poverty and Western wealth. The average Bolshevik wished for nothing more than to push such thoughts from his mind; and Stalin, as it were, did that for him.

What Stalin told the party was, roughly, this: Of course we are looking forward to international revolution. Of course we have been brought up in the school of Marxism; and we know that contemporary social and political struggles are, by their very nature, international. Of course we still believe the victory of the proletariat in the West to be near; and we are bound in honour to do what we can to speed it up. But – and this was a very big, a highly suggestive 'but' – do not worry so much about all that international revolution. Even if it were to be delayed indefinitely, even if it were never to occur, we in this country are capable of developing into a fully fledged, classless society. Let us then concentrate on our great constructive task. Those who tell you that this is utopia, that I am preaching national narrow-mindedness, are themselves either adventurers or pusillanimous social democrats. We, with our much despised *muzhiks*, have already done more for socialism than the proletariat of all other countries taken together; and, left alone with our *muzhiks*, we shall do the rest of the job.

Stripped of its terminological pretensions and pseudo-dialectical profundity, Stalin's theory reduces itself to this plain and 'sound' colloquialism. But it was as its author that Stalin now established himself as an ideologue in his own right. He was no longer just the General Secretary, the administrative magician of the party: he was the author of a new dogma as well. To old, educated Bolsheviks this was the surprise of their life. When, at one of the party meetings of those days, Stalin involved himself in a theoretical argument, he was interrupted by a half-amused and half-indignant remark from the old Marxist scholar Ryazanov: 'Stop it, Koba, don't make a fool of yourself. Everybody knows that theory is not exactly your field.' The condescending irony of the educated Marxists did not, however, prevent 'socialism in one country' from becoming the national creed. For all its triteness, Stalin's innovation had its weight and its *raison d'être*. Doctrines may, broadly speaking, be classed into two categories: those that, starting from a long train of intellectual ideas, strike out boldly into a remote uncharted future; and those that, though they are neither deeply rooted in ideas nor original in their anticipations, sum up a powerful and hitherto inarticulate trend of opinion or emotion. Stalin's theory obviously belonged to that second category.

The truly tragic feature of Russian society in the twenties was its longing for stability, a longing which was only natural after its recent experiences. The future had little stability in store for any country, but least of all for Russia. Yet the desire at least for a long, very long, respite from risky endeavours came to be the dominant motive of Russian politics. Socialism in one country, as it was practically interpreted until the late twenties, held out the promise of stability. On the other hand, the very name of Trotsky's theory, 'permanent revolution', sounded like an ominous warning to a tired generation that it should expect no Peace and Quiet in its lifetime. The warning was to come true, though not in the way its author expected; but it could hardly have been heeded.

In his argument against Trotsky, Stalin appealed directly to the horror of risk and uncertainty that had taken possession of many Bolsheviks. He depicted Trotsky as an adventurer, habitually playing at revolution. The charge, it need hardly be said, was baseless. At all crucial moments – in 1905, 1917, and 1920 – Trotsky had proved himself the most serious strategist of the revolution, showing no proneness to light-minded adventure. Nor did he ever urge his party to stage any *coup* in any foreign country, which cannot be said of Stalin. Trotsky firmly believed that Western European communism would win by its own intrinsic momentum, in the ordinary course of the class struggle, in which outside initiative or assistance, though important at times, could play only a subordinate role. In weighing the chances of communism in the West, Stalin was more sceptical; and his scepticism was to grow as the years passed by. Be that as it may, the epithet 'adventurer' stuck to the ideologue of the 'permanent revolution'. Stalin went further and charged Trotsky with a fondness for terror which had allegedly horrified Lenin. This charge, too, was unfair, especially in Stalin's mouth. Trotsky had not shrunk from using terror in the civil war; but he can be said to have been as little fond of it as a surgeon is fond of bloodshed. Yet in the circumstances just described the charge had a vague and yet distinct eloquence. People afraid of the continuation of the terror were led to believe that the man who had laid the charge against Trotsky was himself at least liberal minded.

The remarkable trait in Stalin was his unique sensibility to all those psychological undercurrents in and around the party, the untalked of hopes and tacit desires, of which he set himself up as a mouthpiece. In this he was very different from the other triumvirs. At the beginning of the controversy over 'permanent revolution' they acted in unison; towards its end they were already poles apart. As Zinoviev and Kamenev admitted later, they started the campaign in order to discredit Trotsky with outdated quotations from Lenin against the 'permanent revolution'; at heart they had no quarrel with its basic tenets, which had become the household ideas of the party. Their attacks upon Trotsky's theory were therefore strangely unreal; they were confined to pointless quibbling over long-forgotten episodes of the days of pre-revolutionary exile. They did not even dream of opposing Trotsky with a positive doctrine of their own. It was otherwise with Stalin. What for him, too, had begun as ideological shadow-boxing developed into a real ideological struggle. The debating-point became the issue. He came to feel a real hatred for his opponent's views; and because of this he had to counter with something positive. He sensed which of his arguments evoked the strongest response from the mass of party officials and workers, that vast human sounding-board which was his *vox dei*. The sounding-board proved unexpectedly responsive to 'socialism in one country'. As happens with revelationists, a figment of his mind, the vision of socialism in one country, took possession of him; but it did so because it corresponded to the things that were latent in so many other minds.

For a long time Zinoviev and Kamenev were unaware of the change that had occurred in their partner. They shrugged their shoulders over his quaint insistence on the possibility of fully fledged socialism in a single country; but they treated the whole thing as a mere stick with which their intellectually inferior partner chose to beat Trotsky; and they did not bother to have a close look at it. They did not object even when, in March and April of 1925, Stalin asked the 14th Party Congress to give formal sanction to this thesis and obtained it. It was only next autumn, nearly a year after he had put forward his view, that they awakened to its significance and criticized it as the abandonment of traditional Bolshevism in favour of national communism. Trotsky did not challenge the dogma until 1926, when it had already gained wide acceptance.

The practical implications of Stalin's doctrine were not yet clear. Bolshevism had now reached a most important landmark of its post-revolutionary history; but so far the change affected its attitude of mind rather than its attitude in action. The broad lines of the change can be summed up as follows: hitherto Bolshevism looked upon Russia as upon a periphery of modern civilization. On that periphery the revolution started; there socialism had found its practical pioneers. From there came the impulses for revolutionary change in West and East. Russia's role in the world-wide transformation of society was seen as that of the powerful initiator of the whole movement. But Western Europe still remained the real centre of modern civilization; and, in the old Bolshevik view, it was there in the centre and not on the periphery that the forms of a new social life were eventually to be forged. The whole process was seen in terms of a double impact: first of Russia upon the West and then of the socialist West upon Russia.

In Stalin's doctrine Russia no longer figures as a mere periphery of the civilized world. It is within her own boundaries that the forms of a new society are to be found and worked out. It is her destiny to become the centre of a new civilization, in all respects superior to that capitalist civilization that is defending itself, with so much power of resistance, in Western Europe. This new view of the future undoubtedly reflected the exasperation of Russian communism at its own isolation; but it gilded that isolation with dazzling prospects. Exhausted and disillusioned, Bolshevik Russia was withdrawing into her national shell, feasting her sore eyes on the vistas of socialism in one country.

NOTES TO CHAPTER 4

1. This quotation is taken from the English edition of J. Stalin, *Problems of Leninism* (p. 157), published in Moscow in 1945.

2. Trotsky first developed this theory in his famous pamphlet, *Itogi i Perspektivy Ruskoi Revolutsii*, published in 1906. He gave the most complete exposition of his theory in *Permanentnaya Revolutsya*, written in 1928, after his deportation to Alma Ata, and published abroad in 1930.

3. N. Bukharin in his *Kritika Ekonomicheskoi Platformy Oppositsii*, entirely devoted to a criticism of Trotsky's, Piatakov's and Preobrazhensky's economic ideas, quotes Trotsky's letter to the Central Committee (8 October 1923), in which Trotsky summed up his policy as follows: 'Planned economy; severe concentration of industry; severe reduction of costs' (p. 54). In his *Novyi Kurs*, published later in the year, Trotsky urged the subordination of financial and monetary policy to the needs of industrialization (ibid., pp. 71–2). This brought upon him the charge that he advocated the 'dictatorship of industry' and 'super-industrialization'. See N. Bukharin, op. cit., pp. 3, 53–4.

4. At a later stage of the debate, in January 1926, Stalin thus formulated his view: 'We mean the possibility of solving the contradictions between the proletariat and the peasantry with the aid of the internal forces of our country, the possibility of the proletariat assuming power and using that power to build a complete socialist society in our country, with the sympathy and the support of the proletariat of other countries, but without the preliminary victory of the proletarian revolution in other countries.

'Without such a possibility, the building of socialism is building without prospects, building without being sure that socialism will be built. It is no use building socialism without being sure that we can build it, without being sure that the technical backwardness of our country is not an *insuperable* obstacle to the building of a complete Socialist society. To deny such a possibility is to display lack of faith in the cause of building socialism, to abandon Leninism.' See J. Stalin, *Problems of Leninism* (English edition), p. 160.

5. Marxism and Primitive Magic

Isaac Deutscher

Plekhanov once wrote that if historical circumstances create the need for a certain political function to be performed they also supply the 'organ' capable of performing it. If the need for the 'function' is deeply rooted in the conditions of an epoch, the epoch is sure to bring forth not just óne but at least several individuals with the minds, the characters and the wills needed to perform the function. As a rule, circumstances allow only one or, at the most, a few of a whole group of potential leaders to move to the front of the stage; and so the historical record contains the evidence only of their capabilities and deeds. The fact that one individual has already filled the place of the actual leader debars other potential leaders from revealing themselves – they are condemned to remain in obscurity.

Plekhanov applied this theory not only to politics. He argued, for instance, that if Leonardo da Vinci had not lived to produce his master-pieces, this would not have altered the broad trend of the artistic ideas of the Renaissance, because this trend had sprung from the social conditions and from the intellectual and moral climate of the age. Only the 'individual features' of the trend would have been different. The same is true of the great scientific discoveries which bear the name of a single man. Such discoveries are the outcome of the stage of development which a certain branch of science has reached at a particular time, and it is more or less a matter of chance which individual actually makes them. Indeed, it often happens that several leading scientists make a discovery almost simultaneously and independently of one another.

To return to political history: if, for instance, a certain General Bonaparte had been killed in a battle before he had time to become First Consul and Emperor of revolutionary France, another general would have filled his place with essentially the same effect. There were in France at that time several military leaders capable of this. Bonaparte's rise prevented those potential Napoleons from becoming actual ones. The 'organ' capable of performing the historical 'function' had been supplied; and there was no room for duplication. That 'function' consisted in giving an authoritarian and yet revolutionary government – the rule of a 'good sword' – to a nation which had tried out and abandoned the republican-plebeian democracy of the Jacobins but still refused to countenance the restoration of the pre-revolutionary order.

Plekhanov's argument has given rise to considerable controversy, into which it is not proposed to enter here. Suffice it to say that even among Marxists, who broadly accepted Plekhanov's view, there have been many 'deviations' from it.

Trotsky, for instance, in his *History of the Russian Revolution*, attempted to strike a balance between the general Marxist philosophy of history – which sees the collective forces of social classes and groups as the decisive agents in any historical process – and his own view that Lenin's individual role in the Russian revolution was unique, that is to say that no other Bolshevik leader would have been qualified to perform it. However, Trotsky 'deviated' even further from the classical Plekhanovist view. In a private letter to an old Bolshevik friend which he wrote from his exile in Alma Ata, he stated bluntly and without inhibition: 'You know that without Lenin the October Revolution would not have won.'[1] Thus, while in his published writings he tried to adjust his own view of Lenin's role with Plekhanov's theory, privately he appears to have taken an attitude diametrically opposed to it.

The story of Stalin's career seems calculated to resolve the controversy in favour of Plekhanov.

Hardly any of Stalin's contemporaries, comrades and rivals alike, regarded him at first as in any way suited to the role he was to play. He appeared to them to have none of the gifts which make a great leader, Bolshevik or otherwise. His ascendancy came as a complete surprise. Trotsky wrote of Stalin that he detached himself like a shadow from a Kremlin wall to succeed Lenin. This impression was shared by Zinoviev, Kamenev, Rykov, Tomsky, Bukharin, and also by nearly all the leaders of the non-Russian Communist Parties.[2] Lenin alone was more discerning in his appraisal of the man, for although eventually he advised his followers to depose Stalin from the post of the party's General Secretary, he nevertheless described both Stalin and Trotsky as the 'two ablest men' in the Central Committee.

Why was it that nearly everyone who had known Stalin before and during his rise was so utterly wrong about his chances?

The typical Bolshevik leader of the Leninist era was, as a rule, a Marxist theorist, a political strategist, a fluent writer, and an effective orator, in addition to being some sort of organizer. Stalin did not count at all as a theorist.[3] He was to the end a political tactician rather than a strategist: he showed his mastery in short-term manoeuvre rather than in long-term conception, although his genius for tactics did more than compensate his weakness as a strategist. He was cumbersome and ineffective as a writer and speaker. Only as an exceptionally gifted organizer had he made his mark in Lenin's lifetime. His contemporaries and rivals had reason therefore to think that he was unfit to be Lenin's successor.

Their mistake lay in the assumption that Bolshevik Russia after Lenin needed the type of leadership which Lenin had provided and which Lenin's closest associates might have provided collectively or individually. They misjudged the changing circumstances and the new need of the time; and so they failed to see that the man who might not have been qualified to act as the leader in one phase of the revolution might be eminently suited for that role in the subsequent phase.

We know that among those changing circumstances Bolshevik Russia's political isolation in the world and mental self-isolation from it were the most important. The isolation was not of Stalin's making – it was a consequence of events preceding his ascendancy. He merely took the situation as it was. He was reconciled to it and inwardly free to act within its framework; and therefore he thrived on it. Most of his rivals were unreconciled to Russia's isolation, incapable of overcoming their internationalist habits of thought, and not disposed to frame policies consistently within the context of isolation. They were at odds with the root fact of the new time; and they were undone by it.

The same is true of Stalin's as against his rivals' attitude in the dilemma of proletarian democracy *versus* autocracy, the other crucial issue in the transition from Leninism to Stalinism. It was not Stalin who had destroyed the proletarian democracy of the early phase of the revolution. It had withered even before 1923–4; at most, Stalin delivered the *coup de grâce*.

His rivals, however, could not shed their democratic habits. They were not inwardly reconciled to the fact that, struggling for the preservation of its revolution, Bolshevism had deprived the working classes of freedom of political expression. They were entangled in their own regrets, scruples, and second thoughts. They looked back longingly to the democratic origins of the revolution. Stalin did nothing of the sort. They were therefore not fitted to act effectively within the new, undemocratic framework of the Bolshevik state. He was. They were crushed by that framework, while he proceeded to build around it his autocratic system of government.[4]

The trend of the time found in Stalin its 'organ'. If it hadn't been Stalin it would have been another.

A similar view when expressed about other historical figures may seem implausible; but it is exceptionally convincing in the case of Stalin.

When it is said that the general trend of the Renaissance would not have been different without Leonardo da Vinci and that at the most some of its 'individual features' would have been different, one immediately thinks of the 'Last Supper' and 'Mona Lisa', and one wonders: Would the trend really not have been different? Was the contribution of Leonardo (or of Michelangelo) merely one of its 'individual features'?

When one is told that another French general of the period of the Directory could have filled the place of Napoleon, one cannot help thinking about Napoleon's *élan*, intellectual brilliance, and romantic appeal; and one wonders just how much Napoleon's individual characteristics counted in the general course of events.

But when one contemplates Stalin, that grey, inconspicuous, almost faceless character, one is more than inclined to see in him but the vehicle of anonymous forces at work in the background. He appears as the embodiment of Anonymity itself, Anonymity which rose to the pinnacle of power and fame and even there remained true to itself – utterly impersonal and therefore utterly elusive.

When the struggle between Stalin and Trotsky is viewed only in terms of individual gifts and talents, Stalin's victory over his rival remains inexplicable. Stalin had not a single gift that Trotsky did not possess in the same or in a much higher degree; in addition Trotsky had conspicuous talents which Stalin altogether lacked. It was no exaggeration when Lenin, a great judge of men, described Trotsky as 'the ablest' of all the Bolshevik leaders.

It is often said that Trotsky did not have Stalin's flair for organization. Nobody who has studied the history of the Red Army can seriously entertain that view. In so far as any single individual may be credited with this achievement, Trotsky was the true organizer of the army. He created it 'from nothing' after the old army had collapsed, dissolved, and left a military vacuum. To fill the vacuum with a new army demanded a genius for organization and administration superior to that required for making even the most effective use of an already existing and well-established army. After the Red Army had come into being there was hardly a military authority, Russian or non-Russian, Bolshevik or anti-Bolshevik, who did not describe Trotsky's feat as 'truly Napoleonic'.[5]

It is also said that Stalin was superior to Trotsky as a political tactician. Again, it is enough to study from original sources the tactical manoeuvres which Trotsky carried out on the eve of the October Revolution, and during the revolution itself, to realize that this too is incorrect. As the operational leader of the Bolshevik insurrection, Trotsky almost alone – Lenin was then in hiding – lulled and hypnotized all the enemies of the Bolshevik Party into a state of utter inactivity, and even into complicity with the Bolsheviks. He won the insurrection almost without firing a shot: its most hostile eye-witnesses did not put the number of casualties on both sides at more than ten.

Stalin, on the other hand, made no mark as a tactician in 1917; and, as the records of the Bolshevik Central Committee show, he did not put forward a single tactical idea throughout that year.

Yet it is true that, in his struggle against Stalin, Trotsky was always tactically inferior.

The question must therefore be asked: What made Trotsky, the genius in tactics of 1917, into the inferior tactician of 1924–7? And what made Stalin, the indifferent tactician of 1917, into the master of the later years?

The answer may be found in the different general conditions of the two periods, in consequence of which Trotsky, not Stalin, was in his element in 1917, while Stalin, not Trotsky, was in his some years later.

Stalin was fitted for his role not merely and not even primarily by his great talents for organization and tactics. His background, his experience and his cast of mind had prepared him to lead Bolshevism in the break with its democratic origins and through the decades of its isolation and self-isolation. For the 'function' of such a leadership he was the most perfect 'organ'.

He had spent all his years inside Russia, mostly in his native Caucasus on the borders of Europe and Asia, where he had been insulated from the direct influences of Western European Marxism. This was his weakness during the Leninist period, when Bolshevism was staking its future on revolution in the West. But this was also the source of his extraordinary strength when the revolution was withdrawing into its national shell. He, who had hardly ever looked beyond that shell, found little or no difficulty in divorcing Bolshevism from the Western Marxist outlook.

His rivals had, like Lenin, lived as émigrés in Germany, France, and other European countries. There, for many years, they listened with enthusiasm to the great speeches of Jaurès and Bebel, the pioneers and prophets of French and German socialism. They absorbed the teachings of Kautsky and Guesde, the leading expounders of Marxism. They viewed with admiration and envy the scores of great socialist newspapers and journals, which were openly published and read by the million, while the Russian revolutionaries could bring out only a few small clandestine sheets, which they smuggled into Russia with much difficulty and great danger to themselves. They watched with rapture the parliamentary strength, and the political and educational institutions, of Western Marxism, the massive trade unions, the 'powerful' and openly conducted strikes, the May Day demonstrations, etc., etc. They were held spellbound by the 'might' of European Marxism.

Then came the great collapse of 1914, when, despite all the previous professions of anti-militarism and internationalism, the power of the Western parties was harnessed to the war machines of the belligerent governments. But the Russian émigrés still believed that the inherent 'class consciousness' and power of the Western proletariat would overcome this 'betrayal' and its consequences. They found it hard to shed this belief even some years after they had themselves become Russia's rulers.

Stalin had known none of their enthusiasms and none of their illusions. He had never sat at the feet of Jaurès, Bebel, Kautsky, and Guesde. He had never had any first-hand impression of the apparent might of the Marxist movement in the West. Even during the Leninist era when he too expressed hope for the spread of the revolution, he was merely adopting what was then the conventional Bolshevik idiom. When that hope was shattered, his inward balance was not upset. Unlike many old Bolsheviks, he did not feel that the Russian revolution and its makers were now suspended over an abyss. Even as early as the beginning of 1918 he had expressed icy scepticism about the revolutionary movements of the West, and brought upon his head a rebuke from Lenin. Paradoxically, Stalin's ignorance of the West led him to a more realistic appreciation of its revolutionary potentialities than that which other Bolshevik leaders, including Lenin, had reached after many years of first-hand observation and study.

The democratic orientation of the early Bolshevik leaders was also up to a point bound up with the Western Marxist tradition. Under the Tsar Bolshevism could exist and work only underground. Any underground movement, if it is to be effective, must be led in a more or less authoritarian manner. It must be strictly disciplined, hierarchically organized, and centrally controlled. Nearly all Russian revolutionary movements (and all the Resistance movements in Nazi-occupied Europe of 1940–45 as well) were characterized by such features. The chiefs of any clandestine party must exalt the idea of strict discipline and strong leadership on which survival of such a party largely depends. In his time Lenin exalted the principle of strong leadership with all the emphasis and over-emphasis peculiar to him.

Yet even the underground Bolshevik organization of Tsarist days was by no means the monolithic body the Stalinist legend depicted.

The Bolshevik émigrés had before their eyes the example of the Western labour organizations, in which free debate flourished and democratic procedures were strictly observed, even if in fact most of those organizations too were effectively controlled by centralized and self-willed caucuses. The Bolshevik emissary who, on a false passport, travelled between Western Europe and Russia, was often torn between the democratic outlook of the Western parties and the clandestine authoritarianism of his own movement. He dreamed of the day when his party too would emerge into the open, freely debate its affairs, adopt democratic procedures, and freely elect its leaders. Whenever the Bolshevik Party did emerge into the open, if only for a short spell as in 1905,

Lenin did indeed infuse democracy into it. And from 1917 to 1920 inner-party democracy flourished in Bolshevik ranks.

Stalin's political outlook had been formed exclusively by clandestine Bolshevism. He had been one of those disciplinarian committee-men who had jealously guarded the Bolshevik organization from infiltration by alien elements and *agents provocateurs*. In a clandestine organization the rank and file could not freely elect their leaders – often they could not even be allowed to know who the leaders were. The committee-man not unnaturally sensed in any attempt at democratization the threat of disruption and the danger of exposure to the political police.

This outlook of the old underground leader remained with Stalin throughout his lifetime. He regarded, as he himself said later, the turbulent, open debates in which the party indulged between 1917 and 1920 as a waste of time and a drain on the party's efficiency and striking power. Of course, he too had to speak occasionally, in deference to precept, about the need for inner-party democracy. But he never even began to realize that genuine freedom of criticism and the open clash of opinion might be a creative ferment keeping a party mentally alive and vigorous.

Having risen to power, he carried the habits of clandestine Bolshevism to a grotesque extreme, and transplanted them into the Soviet state and into the life of a whole nation, in which, anyhow, all democratic impulses had become atrophied.

Finally, Stalin was as if predestined to become the chief mouthpiece of Bolshevism when it was absorbing the Russian 'way of life' and the sombre heritage of the Tsarist past. In that heritage the Greek Orthodoxy was a dominant element. Stalin had imbibed it in his youth. True, many a Russian revolutionary received his education in an Orthodox Seminary, especially in the Caucasus. Nor need a revolutionary trained in his youth to be a priest preserve the theological cast of mind for the rest of his life. But Stalin did preserve it in an extraordinary degree.

Before he imposed the Greek Orthodox style and manner upon the Bolshevik Party, that style and manner had in his own mind imposed themselves upon his Marxism and atheism. He presented the Marxist and Leninist formulae in the accent, the intonation, and sometimes even the idiom of Greek Orthodoxy, which made those formulae sound less alien to the 'backward' Russian masses. Indeed, he made Bolshevism appear as something like a new emanation of the old and indefinable spirit of the Church, long before he rehabilitated the Church itself for reasons of expediency.

It is enough, for instance, to read Stalin's famous oath of fealty to Lenin, that strange litany which he intoned after Lenin's death and in which he began every invocation with the refrain 'We swear to Thee,

Comrade Lenin', to feel with almost physical immediacy the ex-pupil of the monks, trained in the delivery of sermons and funeral orations, emerging in the disciple of Lenin and overtopping the Marxist.

This is only the most striking instance of that amalgamation of Marxism and Greek Orthodoxy which was characteristic of Stalin and Stalinism. Even in his most sophisticated writings, up to his last essay on the 'Economic Problems of Socialism in the USSR', he gave his arguments an inimitable scholastic twist, as if he were dealing not with the realities of political power and social life but with the theological interpretation of dogma.

If the trend of the Russian revolution was towards national self-centredness, autocracy, and quasi-ecclesiastical orthodoxy, then Stalin was its ideal agent. But these political formulae, correct in themselves, have not yet touched the innermost psychological springs of Stalinism, which may have to be sought far below political consciousness, in the imagination and the instincts of a primitive people.

The Russia of the early and middle 1920s was at an extremely low level of civilization. Barefoot and illiterate *muzhiks*, most of whom tilled their tiny plots of land with wooden ploughs, still formed the overwhelming majority of the nation. There were also the tribes of mountaineers in the Caucasus, and the nomad-shepherds and semi-nomads of the Asiatic provinces – all submerged in an even more ancient way of life.

The sheer weight of these elements was great. True enough, in the events of 1917 the industrial workers of Petrograd (Leningrad) and Moscow were the decisive actors. But their political ascendancy came to an end with the ebbing of the revolution and with the physical dispersal of the metropolitan working class during the civil wars. In the years of Stalin's rise the upsurge of rural Russia and of her Asiatic and semi-Asiatic fringes was one of the most striking features of Russian life.

Much of the thinking and imagination of rural Russia was still below the level even of Greek Orthodoxy or of any organized religious thought. It was immersed in the primitive magic of rudimentary society. We know from the investigators of the earliest phases of civilization and from the Freudists how many remnants of primitive magic may be traced in the imagination and behaviour even of modern and relatively educated nations. But we also know that primitive magic expressed man's helplessness amid the forces of nature which he had not yet learned to control; and that, on the whole, modern technology and organization are its deadliest enemies. On the technological level of the wooden plough primitive magic flourishes.

Under Lenin Bolshevism had been accustomed to appeal to the reason, the self-interest, and the enlightened idealism of 'class-conscious' industrial workers. It spoke the language of reason even when it appealed to the *muzhiks*. But once Bolshevism had ceased to rely on revolution in the West, once it had lost the sense of its own elevation above its native environment, once it had become aware that it could only fall back on that environment and dig itself in, it began to descend to the level of primitive magic, and to appeal to the people in the language of that magic.

In Stalin the world of primitive magic was perhaps even more strongly alive than the tradition of Greek Orthodoxy. In his native Georgia the tribal way of life, with its totems and taboos, had survived into his own day. The Caucasus had been the meeting ground of Oriental and Greek mythologies, which had permeated native poetry and folklore. We know even from official Soviet biographies how strongly these worked upon the mind of the young Stalin; and, according to all the evidence, his deeply emotional, unsophisticated sensitivity to folk legend remained with him to the last. Quite recently, Mr Budu Svanidze, Stalin's nephew, has told us what a strong hold some of the tribal Georgian taboos had on Stalin in his mature years. Incidentally, Mr Svanidze, who was once his uncle's courtier and is still his admirer, relates this with the tribesman's pride rather than with any intention to detract from Stalin's greatness.

He dwells in particular on the fact that Stalin was powerfully swayed by the Georgian traditions of blood feud. He describes, for instance, a pre-revolutionary incident when Stalin refused to sing a certain song in the presence of two Georgian party members, because the song was about a blood feud in which the ancestors of his two comrades had been involved as enemies. When someone remarked that his scruples were ridiculous and that the two Georgians 'were no longer savage moun-taineers or feudal princes' but members of the same revolutionary party, 'Stalin replied: "It makes no difference. We Georgians have our own code of a tooth for a tooth, an eye for an eye, a life for a life – the law of the Khevsures, which obliges us to take vengeance. Revolutionaries or not, comrades or not, the law still binds us. No Georgian ever forgives an offence or an insult to himself, to his family, or to his forebears. Never!"'

Mr Svanidze goes on to say that in the great purges of 1936–8 Stalin was influenced once again by the traditions of 'the tribe of the Khevsures, who gave to Georgia its basic customs, above all the law of vengeance and vendetta'. While Stalin was brooding over the decision to start the purges, he went to the Crimea, retired into solitude, but took with him his nephew in order to have by his side, again in accordance with the primordial Georgian custom, a man of his tribe before embarking upon the blood feud.

It is difficult to dismiss all this as petty gossip, as one might otherwise be inclined to do, when one considers how much of the spirit of primitive magic Stalin brought with him into Bolshevism.

The most characteristic landmark of Stalinist Moscow, indeed of Stalinist Russia, was the Lenin Mausoleum in the Red Square, to which long queues of Russian peasants and visitors from the most remote Asiatic corners of the USSR made their pilgrimage to see the mummy of the founder of Bolshevism. The Mausoleum had been set up despite the protests of Krupskaya, Lenin's widow, and of other members of the Central Committee. To old Bolsheviks its mere sight was an offence to their dignity, and — so they thought — an insult to the maturity of the Soviet people. The Mausoleum was the monument which primitive magic erected to itself in the very heart of the Russian Revolution, the totem pole and the shrine of Stalinism. It had its fascination for the Soviet people; it was for them a place of pilgrimage during nearly thirty years. (And Stalin's oath of fealty to the dead Lenin had all the undertones of a funeral homage to a deceased tribal chief.)

Under Stalin the story of Bolshevism came to be rewritten in terms of sorcery and magic, with Lenin and then Stalin as the chief totems.

In the tribal cults there can be no graver sin than to offend the totem; and so in the Stalin cult whoever had at any time disagreed or quarrelled with Lenin was guilty of sacrilege. (Stalin himself, of course, was quite cynical about this. He knew the real history of all the inner party controversies; and he himself had had his disagreements with Lenin. But this was the manner in which the story of the party had to be presented in order to help to secure his own immunity from criticism and attack.)

Stalin's opponents, Bukharin and others, had to be charged with the attempt to murder the ancestral totem — the cardinal sin in primitive magic. They were indeed accused of having attempted to assassinate not only Stalin but Lenin also; and the charge was brought against them twenty years after the alleged attempt. The whole atmosphere of the purge trials, with their countless accusations, their incredible confessions, and all the violent curses thrown at the defendants by prosecutors, judges, and witnesses, can never be fully explained, whatever the plausible political explanations, in terms other than those of primitive magic.

And what was Stalin himself, the remote, inaccessible ruler, the Life-giving Sun, the Father of all the two hundred millions of Soviet citizens, if not the totem whom the tribe considers as its forebear and with whom all the members of the tribe must feel themselves in a close personal relationship?

Something like a belief in the transmigration of the political souls of great leaders was essential to the Stalin cult: Lenin was the 'Marx of his time'; Stalin was the 'Lenin of his time'. This motif too sprang from the inner recesses of the primitive imagination.

In recent years the world was taken aback by the irrational campaign designed to convince the Soviet people that the Russians, and the

Russians alone, had been the initiators of all the epoch-making ideas and of all the modern technical discoveries. The campaign may have been dictated by cold political calculation, by the desire to enhance Russia's self-confidence in the conflict with the West. In respect of its claims, the campaign has by no means been unique. Almost every Western nation has at one time or another boosted itself by means of chauvinistic self-adulation. But the grotesque form which the self-adulation has assumed in Russia transcends the experience of any modern chauvinism. It goes back to that remote epoch when the tribe cultivated a belief in its own mysterious powers which set it apart from and above all other tribes.

Similarly, the fear instilled in Soviet citizens of contamination by contact with the West has been in its violence and irrationality reminiscent of the taboo – it suggests the savage's dread of incest.

Stalinism is a complex phenomenon, which needs to be viewed from many angles. But when it is seen from the angle from which we are now viewing it, it appears as the mongrel offspring of Marxism and primitive magic.

Marxism has its inner logic and consistency: and its logic is modern through and through. Primitive magic has its own integrity and its peculiar poetic beauty. But the combination of Marxism and primitive magic was bound to be as incoherent and incongruous as is Stalinism itself. Stalin was exceptionally well equipped to embody that combination and to reconcile in some degree the irreconcilables. But he did not himself create the combination. It was produced by the impact of a Marxist revolution upon a semi-Asiatic society and by the impact of that society upon the Marxist revolution.

NOTES TO CHAPTER 5

1. The writer found this letter in the Trotsky Archives at Harvard.
2. This was, of course, even more true of the anti-communists. Thus the Menshevik *Sotsialisticheskii Vestnik* wrote after Stalin's death: 'We, who have known personally and often quite closely the leaders of the Bolshevik Party since 1903, and who have met also Stalin as early as 1906 and later have wondered more than once how it happened that all of us . . . could so underrate him. Nobody thought of him as an eminent political worker . . .' (*Sotsialisticheskii Vestnik*, February–March 1953.)
3. It is possible to prove from the internal evidence of Stalin's writings that he became acquainted with Marx's *Das Kapital* only towards the end of his life.
4. It is interesting to note here the view of Mr R. Abramovich, the Menshevik veteran who could well celebrate now the fifty years' jubilee of his uninterrupted and increasingly vehement struggle against Bolshevism. In the article from the *Sotsialisticheskii Vestnik*, quoted above, Mr Abramovich (we assume he is its author) writes: 'Thinking about the past it seems to us that the basic reason of

our common, evidently incorrect appraisal of Stalin's personality was that we thought in terms of a democratic system, and strangely enough not only we, the Mensheviks, the opponents of the dictatorship, but also its adherents did so.'

5. This is, for instance, how General Ludendorff and General Hoffmann, the outstanding commanders of the German Army in the First World War and Trotsky's enemies during the Brest-Litovsk period, described his military achievement.

6. Trotsky's Interpretation of Stalinism

Perry Anderson

Trotsky's interpretation of the historical meaning of Stalinism, to this day the most coherent and developed theorization of the phenomenon within the Marxist tradition, was constructed in the course of twenty years of practical political struggle against it. His thought thus evolved in tension with the major conflicts and events of these years, and can be conveniently periodized into three essential phases.

1. Trotsky's early writings on the subject date from the inner-party struggle that broke out in the CPSU after the Civil War. They do not name Stalinism as such. Their focus is what party tradition called 'bureaucratism'. *The New Course* (1923) is the key text of this period. In it, Trotsky took over the two major terms of what had been Lenin's explanations of this before his death. Bureaucratism, Lenin had argued, was rooted in the *lack of culture* of the Russian masses, rural or urban, that deprived them of the necessary aptitudes for competent post-war administration, and in the petty-commodity and subsistence character of the *agrarian economy*, whose immense dispersal of the primary producers rendered inevitable an over-centralization of the state apparatus in Russia. Trotsky subjoined a third cause – the inevitable contradiction between the immediate and long-term interests of the working class, amid the great shortages and dire exigencies of post-war construction. More significantly, however, he insisted that bureaucra*tism* was not 'only the aggregate of the bad habits of office-holders', but represented 'a social phenomenon – a definite system of administration of men and things'.[1] The main locus of this phenomenon was the state apparatus, but the latter – by absorbing 'an enormous quantity of the most active party elements'[2] – was infecting the Bolshevik Party itself. The expression of this contamination was the increasing dominance of the central apparatus within the party, operating through an appointments system, repressing democratic debate, and dividing the old guard from the rank-and-file and younger generation. This development posed the danger of a 'bureaucratic degeneration'[3] of the old guard itself. Bureaucratism was thus – here Trotsky broke clearly beyond Lenin's analysis – 'not a survival of some preceding regime, a survival in the process of disappearing; on the contrary, it is an essentially new phenomenon, flowing from

the new tasks, the new functions, the new difficulties and the new mistakes of the party'.[4]

2. *The New Course* warned of the dangers of bureaucratism prior to the victory of Stalin's grouping within the CPSU. After the consummation of that victory, Trotsky's oppositional writings in the later twenties attempt to provide a more comprehensive explanation of the phenomenon. *The Third International after Lenin* (1928) is probably the most important text for his views in this intermediary phase of his thought. There, he attributes the defeat of the Left opposition within Russia, which sealed the triumph of a bureaucratic internal regime, to *the downswing of the international class struggle* – above all, the disasters that had overtaken the German Revolution in 1923 and the Chinese Revolution in 1927, respectively on the West and East flanks of the USSR. The shift in the world balance of class forces to the advantage of capital was inevitably translated into an increase in alien social pressures on the Bolshevik Party itself, within Russia. These were in turn compounded by the failure of Stalin's faction to pursue rapid industrialization in the USSR to date, which would have strengthened the countervailing weight of the Soviet proletariat. After the effects of the First Five-Year Plan became visible, Trotsky modified this claim to argue that the new 'labour aristocracy' created by Stakhanovism, above the mass of the working class, objectively functioned as a support of the bureaucratic regime within the party. Stalin's own faction, which had won its victory on the social-patriotic slogan of 'socialism in one country', Trotsky still characterized as a Centre, poised between the party Right (Bukharin –Rykov–Tomsky) and the Left, the creature of the permanent apparatus of the CPSU. In his autobiography *My Life* (1929), he sketched what he saw as the social-psychological mechanisms that had converted so many revolutionaries of 1917 into functionaries of this regime – 'the liberation of the philistine in the Bolshevik' – as the *élan* of the insurgent masses declined in the aftermath of the Civil War, and fatigue and apathy set in, creating a period of generalized 'social reaction' in the USSR. In subsequent essays on Stalin's industrialization drive, Trotsky extended the notion of a factional 'Centre' into the more far-ranging category of Stalinist *centrism* – arguing that while centrism was an inherently unstable phenomenon in capitalist countries, a posture midway between reform and revolution in the labour movement, reflecting shifts from Left to Right or vice-versa in mass pressures, in the USSR it could acquire a durable material basis in the bureaucracy of the new workers' state. The abrupt zig-zags of Stalin's policies at home and abroad, from appeasement to all-out war on the *kulaks*, from class conciliationism to ultra-Leftism in the Third International, were the logical expression of this centrist character of his regime, subject to complex and contradictory

class pressures on it. The decisive court of these pressures, however, was international, not national.

3. Trotsky's interpretation of Stalinism, hitherto still fragmentary and tentative in many respects, became systematic and conclusive from 1933 onwards. The reason, of course, was the triumph of Nazism in Germany, which convinced Trotsky that the Comintern – for whose rectification of line he had fought down to the last moment – was now irrecuperable, and with it the Stalinized CPSU itself. The decision to found a new International was thus the immediate impulse for his frontal engagement with the problem of the nature of Stalinism, which for the first time now became the direct object of extended theoretical interpretation in itself, rather than an issue treated in the course of texts discussing many other questions, as previously. The crucial essay that provides nearly all the main themes of Trotsky's mature thought on Stalinism was written within a few months of Hitler's seizure of power: *The Class Nature of the Soviet State* (1933). In it, he set out the four fundamental theses that were to be the basis of his position down to his death.

Firstly, the role of Stalinism at home and abroad had to be distinguished. *Within* the USSR, the Stalinist bureaucracy played a contradictory role – defending itself *simultaneously* against the Soviet working class, from which it had usurped power, and against the world bourgeoisie, which sought to wipe out all the gains of the October Revolution and restore capitalism in Russia. In this sense, it continued to act as a 'centrist' force. *Outside* the USSR, by contrast, the Stalinized Comintern had ceased to play any anti-capitalist role, as its débâcle in Germany had now irrevocably proved. Hence 'the Stalinist apparatus could completely squander its meaning as an international revolutionary force, and yet preserve part of its progressive meaning as the gate-keeper of the social conquests of the proletarian revolution.'[5] Soon afterwards, Trotsky would argue that the Comintern performed an actively *counter-revolutionary* role in world politics, colluding with capital and shackling labour in the interests of protecting the Stalinist monopoly of power in Russia itself, which would be threatened by the example of any victory of a socialist revolution, creating a proletarian democracy, elsewhere.

Secondly, within the USSR Stalinism represented the rule of a bureaucratic *stratum*, emergent from and parasitic upon the working class, not a new *class*. This stratum occupied no independent structural role in the process of production proper, but derived its economic privileges from its confiscation of political power from the direct producers, within the framework of nationalized property relations.

Thirdly, the administration over which it presided remained typologically a *workers' state*, precisely because these property relations – embodying the expropriation of the expropriators achieved in 1917 – persisted. The identity and legitimacy of the bureaucracy as a political 'caste' depended on its defence of them. Therewith, Trotsky dismissed the two alternative accounts of Stalinism most widespread in the labour movement in the 1930s (which had emerged within the Second International during the Civil War itself) – that it represented a form of 'state capitalism' or of 'bureaucratic collectivism'. The iron dictatorship exercised by the Stalinist police and administrative apparatus over the Soviet proletariat was not incompatible with the preservation of the proletarian nature of the state itself – any more than the Absolutist dictatorships over the nobility had been incompatible with the preservation of the nature of the feudal state, or the fascist dictatorships exercised over the bourgeois class were with the preservation of the nature of the capitalist state. The USSR was indeed a *degenerated* workers' state, but a 'pure' dictatorship of the proletariat – conformable to an ideal definition of it – had never existed in the Soviet Union in the first instance.

Fourthly and finally, Marxists should adopt a two-fold stance towards the Soviet state. On the one hand, there was now no chance of the Stalinist regime either reforming itself or being reformed peacefully, within the USSR. Its rule could only be ended by a revolutionary overthrow from below, destroying its whole machinery of privilege and repression, while leaving intact the social property relations over which it presided – if now within the context of a proletarian democracy. On the other hand, the Soviet state had to be defended *externally* against the constant menace of aggression or attack by the world bourgeoisie. Against this enemy, the USSR – incarnating as it did the anti-capitalist gains of October – needed the resolute and unconditional solidarity of revolutionary socialists everywhere. 'Every political tendency that waves its hand hopelessly at the Soviet Union, under the pretext of its "non-proletarian" character, runs the risk of becoming the passive instrument of imperialism'.[6]

These four corner-stones of Trotsky's account of Stalinism remained stable down to his assassination. It was on them that he erected the major edifice of his study of Soviet society under Stalin – the book entitled *Where is Russia Going?* (1936: misleadingly translated as *The Revolution Betrayed*). In this work, Trotsky presented a panoramic survey of the economic, political, social and cultural structures of the USSR in the mid-thirties, combining a wide range of empirical materials with a deeper theoretical foundation for his analysis of Stalinism. The whole phenomenon of a repressive workers' bureaucracy he now anchored in the category of scarcity (*nuzhda*), basic to historical materialism since Marx's formulation of it in *The German Ideology*.

The basis of bureaucratic rule is the poverty of society in objects of consumption, with the resulting struggle of each against all. When there are enough goods in a store, the purchasers can come whenever they want to. When there are few goods, the purchasers are compelled to stand in line. When the lines are very long, it is necessary to appoint a policeman to keep order. Such is the starting point of the power of the Soviet bureaucracy. It 'knows' who is to get something and who has to wait.[7]

So long as scarcity prevailed, a contradiction was inevitable between socialized relations of production and bourgeois norms of distribution: it was this contradiction that fatally produced and reproduced the constraining power of the Stalinist bureaucracy.

Trotsky then went on to explore each side of the contradiction, assessing and emphasizing the grandeur of Soviet industrial development, however barbaric the methods the bureaucracy employed to drive it forward, while at the same time meticulously exposing the vast gamut of economic, cultural and social inequalities generated by Stalinism, and providing statistical estimates of the size and distribution of the bureaucratic stratum in the USSR itself (some 12–15 per cent of the population). This bureaucracy had betrayed world revolution, even if it still felt subjectively loyal to it; yet it remained an irreconcilable enemy in the eyes of the world bourgeoisie, so long as capitalism was not restored in Russia. The *dynamic* of its regime was equally contradictory: on the one hand, the very development it had promoted at break-neck pace within the USSR was rapidly increasing the economic and cultural potential of the Soviet working class, its capacity to rise up against it, while on the other hand its own parasitism was increasingly an impediment to further industrial progress. However spectacular the accomplishments of the Five-Year Plans, Trotsky warned, they still left *social productivity of labour* far behind that of Western capitalism, in a gap that would never be caught up until a shift to *qualitative* growth was achieved, which bureaucratic misrule precisely blocked.

The progressive role of the Soviet bureaucracy coincides with the period devoted to introducing into the Soviet Union the most important elements of capitalist technique. The rough work of borrowing, imitating, transplanting and grafting, was accomplished on bases laid down by the revolution. There was, thus far, no question of any new word in the sphere of technique, science or art. It is possible to build gigantic factories according to a ready-made pattern by bureaucratic command – although, to be sure, at triple the normal cost. But the farther you go, the more the economy runs into problems of quality, which slips out of the hands of a bureaucracy like a shadow. The Soviet products are as though branded with the grey label of indifference. Under a nationalized economy, *quality* demands a democracy of producers and consumers, freedom of criticism and initiative.[8]

Technological superiority would rest with imperialism so long as Stalinism persisted, and assure it victory in any war with the USSR – unless a revolution in the West broke out. The task of Soviet socialists was to accomplish a *political* revolution against the entrenched bureaucracy beforehand, whose relation to the socio-economic revolution of 1917 would be as the change of power in 1830 or 1848 was to the upheaval of 1789 in France, in the cycle of bourgeois revolutions.

In the final two years of his life, as the Second World War started, Trotsky reiterated his basic perspectives in a series of concluding polemics with Rizzi, Burnham, Schachtman and other proponents of the notion of 'bureaucratic collectivism'. The working class was in no way congenitally incapable of establishing its own sovereign rule over society. The USSR – 'the most transitional country in a transitional epoch' – lay between capitalism and socialism, gripped by a ferocious police regime that yet still defended in its own fashion the dictatorship of the proletariat. But Soviet experience was an 'exceptional refraction' of the general laws of transition from capitalism to socialism, in a backward country surrounded by imperialism – not a modal type. The contradictory role of Stalinism at home and abroad had been confirmed by the most recent episodes of international politics: its counter-revolutionary sabotage of the Spanish Revolution (beyond its control), contrasted with its revolutionary abolition of private property in the border regions of Poland and Finland incorporated by it into the USSR. The duty of Marxists to defend the Soviet Union against capitalist attack remained undiminished. Disillusionment and fatigue were no excuses for renouncing the classical perspectives of historical materialism.

Twenty-five years in the scales of history, when it is a question of profoundest changes in economic and cultural systems, weigh less than an hour in the life of man. What good is the individual who, because of empirical failures in the course of an hour or a day, renounces a goal that he set for himself on the basis of the experience and analysis of his entire previous lifetime?[9]

Another forty years on, we are still only a few hours into that lifetime. Do these hours – which subjectively seem so long – give us reasons to question Trotsky's basic judgements? How should we assess the legacy of his overall perspective on Stalinism?

The merits of Trotsky's interpretation, it might be said, are three-fold. Firstly, it provides a theory of the phenomenon of Stalinism in a long *historical* temporality, congruent with the fundamental categories of classical Marxism. At every point in his account of the nature of the Soviet bureaucracy, Trotsky sought to situate it in the logic of successive modes of production and transitions between them, with corresponding class powers and political regimes, that he inherited from Marx, Engels or Lenin. Hence his insistence that the proper optic for defining the relation of the bureaucracy to the working class was the antecedent and analogous relationships between absolutism and aristocracy, fascism and bourgeoisie; just as the relevant precedents for its future overthrow would be political risings such as those of 1830 or 1848 rather than a new 1789. Because he could think of the emergence and consolidation of Stalin in a historical time-span of this epochal character, he avoided the explanations of hasty journalism and improvised confections of new classes or modes of production, unanchored in historical materialism, which marked the reaction of many of his contemporaries.

Secondly, the *sociological* richness and penetration of his survey of the USSR under Stalin had no equal in the literature of the Left on the subject. *Where is Russia Going?* remains a topical masterpiece to this day, by the side of which the collected articles of Schachtman or Kautsky, the books by Burnham or Rizzi or Cliff, appear strikingly thin and dated. The major advances in detailed empirical analysis of the USSR since Trotsky's time have largely come from professional scholars working in Sovietological institutions after the Second World War: Nove, Rigby, Carr, Davies, Hough, Lane and others. Their findings have essentially developed rather than contradicted Trotsky's account, providing us with far greater knowledge of the inner structures of the Soviet economy and the Soviet bureaucracy, but without an integrated theory of it such as that bequeathed by Trotsky.

Thirdly, Trotsky's interpretation of Stalinism was remarkable for its *political* balance – its refusal of either adulation or commination, for a sober estimate of the contradictory nature and dynamic of the bureaucratic regime in the USSR. In Trotsky's lifetime, it was the former attitude that was unusual on the Left, amidst the intoxicated enthusiasm not only of Communist Parties but of so many other observers of the Stalinist order in Russia. Today, it is the latter attitude that is the more unusual, amid the apoplectic denunciation not only by so many observers on the Left but even within certain Communist Parties of the Soviet experience as such. There is little doubt that it was Trotsky's firm insistence – so unfashionable in later years, even among many of his own followers – that the USSR was in the final resort a workers' state that was the key to this equilibrium. Those who rejected this classification for the notions of 'state capitalism' or 'bureaucratic collectivism' were invariably left with the difficulty of defining a political attitude towards the entity they had so categorized. For if one thing was evident about 'state capitalism' or 'bureaucratic collectivism' in Russia, it was that it lacked any vestige of the democratic liberties to be found in 'private capitalism' in the West. Should not, therefore, socialists support the latter in a conflict between the two, as far the lesser – because 'non-totalitarian' – evil? The logic of these interpretations, in other words, always ultimately tended (though with individual, less consistent exceptions) to shift their adherents to the Right. Kautsky, father of 'state capitalism' and 'bureaucratic collectivism' alike in the early 1920s, is emblematic of this trajectory; Schachtman ended his career applauding the US war in Vietnam in the 1960s. The contrasting solidity and discipline of Trotsky's interpretation of Stalinism has only acquired retrospective relief from the attempts to rethink Stalinism that followed it.

At the same time, like all historical judgements, Trotsky's theorization of Stalinism was to reveal certain limits after his death. What were these? Paradoxically, they concern less the 'internal' balance-sheet of Stalinism, than its 'external' record. Domestically, Trotsky's diagnosis of the motor and the brake on Russian economic development, so long as bureaucratic rule persisted, proved extraordinarily accurate. Enormous material progress was to be registered in the Soviet Union in the four decades after he died; but labour productivity has revealed itself more and more as the Achilles heel of the economy, as he predicted. As the epoch of extensive growth has come to an end, over-centralized authoritarian planning has proved increasingly unable to effect a transition to qualitative, intensive growth: a slow-down threatening an entropic crisis for the regime, if unresolved. The durability of the Soviet bureaucracy itself, surviving well past Stalin, has been greater, of course, than Trotsky imagined in some of his conjunctural writings; although not a real 'longevity' in terms of the historical time of which he spoke at the end of his life. Part of the reason for this persistence has probably been the very social promotion of sectors of the Soviet working class through the channels of the bureaucratic regime itself, the proletarian recruitment of so many of whose cadres has often been emphasized by subsequent scholars (Nove, Rigby). Another part, of course, has lain in the political atomization and cultural stunning of the greatly enlarged working class that emerged during the thirties – its lack of any pre-Stalinist memory, which Trotsky underestimated. But by and large, the portrait of Russian society he drew nearly half a century ago remains arrestingly accurate and contemporary in its vision today.

Abroad, however, Trotsky's diagnosis of Stalinism proved more fallible. There were two reasons for this discrepancy in his prognostications. Firstly, he erred in qualifying the external role of the Soviet bureaucracy as simply and unilaterally 'counter-revolutionary', whereas in fact it was to prove profoundly *contradictory* in its actions and effects abroad, just as much as it was at home. Secondly, he was mistaken in thinking that Stalinism represented merely an 'exceptional' or 'aberrant' refraction of the general laws of transition from capitalism to socialism, that would be confined to Russia itself. The structures of bureaucratic power and mobilization pioneered under Stalin proved to be both more *dynamic* and more *general* a phenomenon on the international plane than Trotsky ever imagined. He ended his life predicting that the USSR would be defeated in a war with imperialism, unless revolution broke out in the West. In fact, for all Stalin's own criminal blunders, the Red Army threw back the Wehrmacht and marched victoriously to Berlin, with no aid from a Western revolution. European fascism was essentially destroyed by the Soviet Union (242 German divisions deployed on the Eastern Front to no more than 22 on the first Western front in Italy). Capitalism was abolished over one half of the Continent, by bureaucratic fiat from above – the Polish and Finnish operations extended to the Elbe. Thereafter, the permanent threat of the 'socialist camp' acted as the decisive accelerator of bourgeois decolonization in Africa and Asia in the post-war epoch. Without the Second World of the 1940s and 1950s, there would have been no Third World in the 1960s. The two major forms of historical progress registered within world *capitalism* in the past fifty years – the defeat of fascism, the end of colonialism – have thus been directly dependent on the presence and performance of the USSR in international politics. In this sense, it could be argued that, paradoxically, the exploited classes *outside* the Soviet Union may have benefited more directly from its existence than the working class inside the Soviet Union – that on a world-historical scale the decisive costs of Stalinism have been internal, the gains external. Even the new consumer prosperity of the Western working classes, the other major advance of post-war capitalism, has owed much (not all) to the Keynesian arms economies created to meet the Soviet challenge in the Cold War. Yet these effects have, of course, been largely objective and involuntary processes, rather than the products of conscious intentions of the Soviet bureaucracy (even the destruction of fascism, which certainly formed no part of Stalin's plans in 1940). They testify, none the less, to the contradictory logic of a 'degenerated workers' state', colossally distorted, yet still persistently anti-capitalist, which Trotsky wrongly suspended at the Soviet frontier-posts. By the late 1960s, the USSR had even achieved something like that strategic parity with imperialism which he had thought impossible under bureaucratic rule, and therewith proved capable of extending vital economic and military aid to socialist revolutions and national liberation movements abroad – assuring the survival of the Cuban Revolution, permitting the victory of the Vietnamese Revolution, securing the existence of the Angolan Revolution. Such entirely conscious and deliberate actions, in diametric contrast to Stalin's options in Spain, Yugoslavia or Greece, were precisely those Trotsky had ruled out for the Soviet Union, when he pronounced it an unequivocally and ubiquitously counter-revolutionary force beyond its own borders.

The second disconfirmation of Trotsky's interpretation was more radical. For him, Stalinism was essentially a bureaucratic *apparatus*, erected above a broken working class, in the name of the 'national-reformist' myth of 'socialism in one country'. The foreign parties of the Comintern, after 1933, he judged to be simply subordinate instruments of the CPSU, incapable of making a socialist revolution in their own countries because to do so would be to act against Stalin's directives. The most he would concede was that – in absolutely exceptional cases – insurgent masses might *compel* such parties to take power, against their own will. At the same time, he looked forward above all to the industrialized West as the theatre of successful socialist advance, inspired by anti-Stalinist parties, in the wake of the Second World War. In fact, as we know, history took another turn. Revolution did spread, but to the backward regions of Asia and the Balkans. Moreover, these revolutions were uniformly organized and led by local Communist Parties professing loyalty to Stalin – Chinese, Vietnamese, Yugoslav, Albanian – and modelled in their internal structures on the CPSU. Far from being passively propelled by the masses in their countries, these parties actively mobilized and vertically commanded the masses in their assault on power. The states they created were to be manifestly cognate (not identical: affinal) with the USSR, in their basic political system. Stalinism, in other words, proved to be not just an apparatus, but a *movement* – one capable not only of keeping power in a backward environment dominated by scarcity (USSR), but of actually winning power in environments that were yet more backward and destitute (China, Vietnam) – of expropriating the bourgeoisie and starting the slow work of socialist construction, even against the will of Stalin himself. Therewith, one of the equations in Trotsky's interpretation undoubtedly fell. Stalinism as a broad phenomenon, that is, a workers' state ruled by an authoritarian bureaucratic stratum, did not merely represent a *degeneration* from a prior state of (relative) class grace: it could also be a spontaneous *generation* produced by revolutionary class forces in very backward societies, without any tradition of either bourgeois or proletarian democracy. This possibility, whose realization was to transform the map of the world after 1945, was never envisaged by Trotsky.

In these two critical respects, then, Trotsky's interpretation of Stalinism encountered its limits. But they remain consonant with his central thematic emphasis – the contradictory nature of Stalinism, hostile at once to capitalist property and to proletarian liberty. His error was, ironically, only to have thought that this contradiction could be confined to the USSR itself: whereas 'Stalinism in one country' was to prove a contradiction in terms. In pointing out the ways in which Stalinism continued to act as an 'international revolutionary factor' here, it should not be necessary to recall at the same time the ways in which it also continued to act as an international *reactionary* factor. Every unpredictable gain had an incalculable price. The multiplication of bureaucratized workers' states, each with its own sacred national egoism, has inexorably led to economic, political and now even armed conflicts between them. The military shield the USSR can extend to socialist revolutions or national liberation forces in the Third World also objectively increases the dangers of global nuclear war. The abolition of capitalism in Eastern Europe has unleashed the furies of nationalism against Russia, which has in turn responded to popular aspirations in the region with the most purely reactionary series of external interventions, repressive and regressive, of the Soviet bureaucracy anywhere in the world. Above all, however, while the basic Stalinist model of a transition beyond capitalism may have propagated itself successfully across the backward zones of Eurasia, its very geographical extension and temporal prolongation – complete with the repetition of dementia like the Yezhovschina in the 'Cultural Revolution' and 'Democratic Kampuchea' – have deeply tarnished the very idea of socialism in the advanced West, its absolute negation of proletarian democracy inhibiting the working class from an assault on capitalism within the structures of bourgeois democracy, and thereby decisively *strengthening* the bastions of imperialism in the late twentieth century. *Rien ne se perd*, alas. We have still to settle accounts with the immense skein of international consequences and connections, progressive and regressive, revolutionary and counter-revolutionary, that followed from the fate that befell the October Revolution, that give rise to the phenomenon we still call Stalinism today.

NOTES TO CHAPTER 6

1. *The New Course*, Ann Arbor, 1965, p. 45.
2. ibid.
3. ibid., p. 22.
4. ibid., p. 24.
5. *The Class Nature of the Soviet State*, London, 1968, p. 4.
6. ibid., p. 32.
7. *The Revolution Betrayed*, New York, 1945, p. 112.
8. ibid., p. 276.
9. *In Defense of Marxism*, New York, 1965, p. 15.

7. Was Lenin a Stalinist?

Marcel Liebman

The interpretation offered by most historians of Russian communism possesses the merit, if not of truthfulness, at least of clarity. Convinced of the basic Machiavellianism of the founder of Russian communism, and of the servile submission of his supporters, they see in the beginnings of the Soviet regime the apparent justification of a familiar and banal thesis: Lenin, the man of organization and of the party, had in view only the triumph of his faction. Identifying socialism with the rule of the vanguard, Lenin – clever, crafty and free from all scruples – spoke in a democratic way when that was needed, relied, when this seemed useful, upon the spontaneous action of the masses, pretended to be converted to the libertarian philosophy of the soviets, and even allowed himself to borrow some slogans from the anarchists. When, however, by means of tactical subtleties and tricks against which the pathetic naïvety of his opponents proved helpless, Lenin had gained power, he hastened to throw off the disguise that he had assumed. After reproaching the Provisional Government for failing to convene the Constituent Assembly, and then, having allowed it to meet, observed with chagrin that the results of the election constituted a repudiation of Bolshevism, Lenin dispersed the Assembly. After proclaiming his devotion to democratic freedoms, he lost no time in stifling them, and after announcing his intention of establishing a Soviet and socialist regime, he made haste, not content with installing his own party alone in power, to prohibit and persecute the other socialist parties. So rapid, almost immediate, a disavowal of the Bolshevik programme by the Bolsheviks themselves, and by Lenin of his own ideas, must surely prove, by the irrefutable testimony of facts, that the Leninist doctrine, a totalitarian plan, *necessarily* had to give rise, once victorious, to a totalitarian state – and Leninism and Stalinism were really one and the same.

To quote Leonard Schapiro, a well-known supporter of this view: 'The malignant figure of the General Secretary, Stalin, has become only too familiar in its portrayal by disappointed oppositionists, defeated by the apparatus which he controlled. But it was Lenin, with their support, who equipped him with the weapons, and started him upon his path.' Raymond Aron says the same thing: 'In the case of the Soviet regime, the monopoly of the party and of ideology [in other words, totalitarianism, M.L.] is the essence itself of Bolshevism . . .'

Facts are of decisive importance in judging the nature of Leninism – so decisive that it is indispensable to examine them with very close attention and, refusing to be satisfied with half-truths, to study the actual circumstances that presided over the degeneration of the Soviet regime and the coming of the Bolshevik monolith and Soviet totalitarianism. Was Leninism responsible for this process, or was Leninism itself among its victims? This is, in a sense, what all the argument is about.

The Constituent Assembly and its dissolution

The convening of a Constituent Assembly figured in the programme of all the Left parties in Russia, and especially in that of the Social Democrats, Bolsheviks included. While they did not make it the axis of their propaganda, since they mobilized themselves and the masses in the name of Soviet power ('All Power to the Soviets!') Lenin's supporters and Lenin himself had, between February and October 1917, presented the convening of a Constituent Assembly as one of the aims of their activity. On 25 October, at the moment of the seizure of power, Lenin told the delegates to the Second All-Russia Congress of Soviets that 'the Soviet government . . . will ensure the convocation of the Constituent Assembly at the time appointed.' The Council of People's Commissars itself acknowledged, through Lenin, its provisional character, 'until the Constituent Assembly is convened'.

During the first weeks following the insurrection Lenin had occasion to confirm these assurances.[1] The elections did indeed take place: they were held on and after 12 November 1917, in an atmosphere of great freedom. The first results that came in confirmed the verdict of elections held previous to the October rising, and favoured the Bolsheviks; but when the results arrived from the provinces they did not support the optimistic impression thus given. As they came to hand they revealed more and more clearly the great success won by the Socialist Revolutionaries, and especially by their Right wing. In the end, the Assembly was made up as follows: SRs, 299 seats; Ukrainian SRs, eighty-one; Left SRs, thirty-nine; Bolsheviks, 168; Mensheviks, eighteen; Constitutional Democrats, fifteen; the remaining eighty-three seats being divided among small parties, mostly non-Russian nationalists.

The opponents of the Soviet regime thus enjoyed a comfortable majority in the Assembly, and the Bolshevik government found itself confronted with a dilemma which the party's Central Committee was obliged to discuss at its meeting on 29 November. To judge by the minutes, the discussion was very confused. Though Lenin was present, he took no part in this discussion, which came to no decision, so great was

the uncertainty and irresolution among the Bolsheviks. Their disappointment was all the greater because they had entered with zeal, and
sometimes with real enthusiasm, into the election campaign, in which the
party militants had shown tremendous activity.

The moderate socialist parties – the SRs and Mensheviks – called for
the Assembly to be convened at once; they saw it, and not the soviets, as
the sole legitimate depository of sovereignty. The bourgeois politicians
carried on agitation, former ministers in the Provisional Government
striving vainly to bring about on their own a meeting of members of the
Assembly. Finally, the first counter-revolutionary forces, which were
starting to gather in the south of Russia – especially the 'Volunteer
Army', concentrated in the Don region – included only a single point
in their meagre political programme: all power to the Constituent
Assembly.

The Bolsheviks were still divided. They had already formed their
elected deputies to the Assembly into a parliamentary group, and this
group had chosen a bureau, consisting of Kamenev, Rykov, Ryazanov,
Larin, Milyutin and Nogin – all of them important figures known for
their 'moderate' outlook. They were, as a whole, in favour of allowing the
Assembly to meet, and, doubtless, of respecting its rights. On 11 December the Central Committee discussed the question afresh, and Lenin
proposed that the bureau of the Bolshevik group in the Assembly –
described as 'the Right-wing tendency' – be dissolved. He was unsuccessful, the Central Committee preferring not to vote on his resolution. The
Central Executive Committee of the All-Russia Congress of Soviets
decided soon afterwards that the Constituent Assembly should meet on 5
January 1918, but Lenin almost at once revealed the reasons behind his
attitude of distrust towards the Assembly: his 'Theses on the Constituent
Assembly', written on 12 December, were published in *Pravda* of 26
December. For the first time, explicitly at any rate, he stated that the
imminent confrontation of the two bodies, the Constituent Assembly and
the Congress of Soviets, and the possible clash between them, was
nothing less than a confrontation and clash between classes, with the
proletarian institution facing the bourgeois one. To this fundamental
conception he added arguments relating more closely to the circumstances in which the Constituent Assembly had been elected. It could not
reflect in its composition, he claimed, the split that had taken place
between the Right SRs, hostile to the Soviet government, and the Left
SRs, who had decided to support the new regime. The election had taken
place, too, before the people, especially those in the rural areas, had really
become aware of the October Revolution, or at least of what it implied.
Finally, the beginning of counter-revolutionary action, and so of civil
war, had made it impossible to observe normal electoral procedures.

Lenin declared that the slogan 'All power to the Constituent Assembly!' had become '*in fact* the slogan of the Cadets and the Kaledinites [the followers of the "White" General Kaledin, M.L.] and of their helpers'. He concluded that 'the Constituent Assembly . . . must inevitably clash with the will and interests of the working and exploited classes which on 25 October began the socialist revolution against the bourgeoisie. Naturally, the interests of this revolution stand higher than the formal rights of the Constituent Assembly . . .'

When the Constituent Assembly met, on 5 January 1918, with the Right S R Chernov in the chair, it was invited by the Bolshevik group of deputies to ratify the principal measures taken by the Soviet government, which amounted to acknowledging its legitimacy. The motion put down to this effect was rejected by 237 votes to 138. The Bolshevik and Left S R deputies then walked out of the Assembly, never to return. The debates went on all through the night of 5–6 January. Soon after five in the morning, the commander of an armed detachment, the anarchist Zheleznyakov, carrying out the government's instructions, ordered the Assembly to stop working – 'because the guard is tired', he explained. Without attempting to resist, the members of the Assembly dispersed. They were never to reassemble, a decree of the Soviet government having dissolved the Constituent Assembly. The reaction of public opinion, especially of its most active element, showed great indifference to what had occurred, though on 5 January the Bolsheviks had briskly dispersed a large demonstration in support of the Assembly. It was to be the last of its kind.

The question of the fate meted out by the Soviet government to the Constituent Assembly, the only assembly freely elected by universal suffrage that Russia ever knew, can be considered in a number of ways. The first of these is to state, absolutely, that there is no democracy without consultation of the citizens as a whole and respect for the will of the majority that emerges from this. If this point of view is accepted, it means *ipso facto* condemning the attitude of the Russian communists, and of Lenin in particular. If, however, one chooses a different approach, refusing to adopt an absolute, and therefore *abstract*, judgement, certain observations have to be made regarding the political and social forces that clashed with each other on the occasion of and in connection with the meeting of the Constituent Assembly. From this standpoint, no doubt is possible: the industrial proletariat and the masses it led were *against* the Constituent Assembly and for the soviets; the bourgeoisie and the conservative or reactionary elements were, on the contrary, against the soviets and *for* the Constituent Assembly. On the former of these propositions the testimony of Oskar Anweiler, the chief Western historian of the soviets as an institution, is all the more convincing because his attitude is not one of indulgence towards the Bolsheviks. He is quite categorical: 'The soviets were seen by the masses as "their" organ, and it would have been impossible to mobilize them against the soviets in the name of the Constituent Assembly.'

Socially, supporters and opponents of the Constituent Assembly also present another kind of differentiation. At the elections to the Assembly the Bolsheviks received massive votes not only in the industrial towns but also in those country districts and sectors of the front that were near urban centres. It was also observed that, in the countryside, the Bolsheviks obtained their best results in the villages and localities situated along the railway lines – wherever, in fact, the communications network made it possible to spread, through the agency of workers and soldiers, the message of the revolution, and, consequently, to stir up the peasants politically.

The Assembly, when it met, was dominated by the huge contingent of SRs – who, as we shall see, were neither socialist nor revolutionary. This party, having lost its Left wing, represented, on the contrary, an increasingly conservative force. It had just chosen a new president, belonging to the Left Centre tendency, in the person of its most esteemed leader, Chernov, who had been Minister of Agriculture in the Provisional Government. But the SR group in the Assembly was much further to the Right than the leadership of the party. The principal historian of the SR Party considers that the members of the SR group's steering committee in the Assembly could be 'regarded, and not without reason, as the worst enemies of the revolution'. The same writer describes thus the predominant social composition of the Assembly: 'Men of prestige and experience . . . experts in agronomy or administration, peasants who were looked up to by their communities.' To translate and sum up, this was an 'assembly of notables' which, by its origins and aspirations, justified the hope and trust placed in it by the conservative camp. Thus, while the confrontation between the soviets and the Constituent Assembly corresponded, on the plane of principle, to the distinction between revolutionary democracy and parliamentary democracy, it signified in social and political reality the opposition between two hostile worlds: that of the bourgeoisie and its allies, and that of the proletariat and its supporters.

Finally, the question 'Soviets or Constituent Assembly?' transcends the historical and geographical limitations in which we have hitherto considered it, for it is not confined either to the year 1917 or to Russia. When we think of the great social clashes of modern times, we observe, in France and Germany as in Russia, that the revolutionary dynamic has always been blocked by the paralysing or braking force of the election mechanism, even in its democratic form of universal suffrage. This happened in 1848 in Paris, when the proletariat attacked in the streets and the bourgeoisie answered with rifle-fire – and with votes. This happened in 1871, too, when the National Assembly was able, in face of the Commune, to boast of a democratic legitimacy that the workers of Paris did not have: *they* were not representatives of the nation's sovereign will. Every time, universal suffrage crushes beneath numbers, and by virtue of that force of inertia which the revolution is in revolt against, the revolution's own *élan*.[2] The revolutionary is a bad voter, and the voter a poor revolutionary. This is confirmed by an event geographically and historically nearer than those mentioned to the Bolshevik Revolution: the German Revolution of 1918. The political and social struggle that developed amid the ruins of the Hohenzollern empire assumed the same outlines and gave rise to the same divisions as in Russia. In Berlin, conservatives who had, the day before, been staunch supporters of a semi-autocratic monarchy and a semi-feudal order, proclaimed themselves overnight republicans and democrats, supporters of 'popular sovereignty'; in other words, quite concretely, of a national Constituent Assembly. The 'Freikorps' themselves, forerunners of the Nazis, made their members swear an oath of allegiance to this democratic institution. And it was the Spartacists who opposed the convening of such an Assembly and countered the very principle of it with their demand for a 'democracy of councils'. In their paper, the *Rote Fahne*, they presented the Constituent Assembly as 'the bourgeois solution', whereas Workers' and Soldiers' Councils were 'the socialist one'.

In Russia, moreover, though the dissolution of the Constituent Assembly was actually effected by the Bolsheviks, who were in power, this deed was approved by the Left SRs and by the anarchists, both of which groups were alien to Leninist doctrine, but who were also in favour of very thorough-going democracy.

In the last analysis, what causes surprise is not that Lenin assumed the responsibility of dissolving the Constituent Assembly, but that he took so long in deciding to do this, and had such difficulty in identifying the terms in which the dilemma – for there was a dilemma – presented itself, namely: Constituent Assembly *or* soviets. It is simplistic to attribute Lenin's conduct in this matter to that Machiavellianism which some writers see as his second nature, if not his first. In reality, in this field as in many others, he was not guided by any previously determined strategy. In one of his last writings, reviewing the events of 1917, he acknowledged that he had been inspired by a dictum of Napoleon's: 'Napoleon, I think, wrote: *"On s'engage et puis ... on voit."* Rendered freely this means: "First engage in a serious battle and then see what happens." Well, we did ...' In January 1918 he told the congress of Russia's railwaymen: 'We had not acted according to plan.' In 1917 Lenin had, indeed, committed himself to the soviets, to restarting the revolutionary offensive, to launching a fresh assault by the proletariat upon the positions of the bourgeoisie – in fact, he had opted, as we have seen, for 'permanent revolution'. But when he did this he did not cease to be, in many respects, a man of Russian and international Social Democracy for whom the conquests of the Revolution formed part of the classic programme of demands of the labour movement – which included the securing of a *constitutional* regime in autocratic or semi-autocratic states, and of universal suffrage where the electoral law still included property qualifications.

Had Lenin, wholly absorbed in day-to-day revolutionary activity, not noticed what, today, with the hindsight of history, seems so obvious – that the very notion of entrusting power, *all* power, to the soviets, popular institutions which did not provide for the representing of all classes, ruled out any notion of making a Constituent Assembly elected by the population as a whole the sovereign organ of state power in Russia? What seems now so plain evidently seemed much less so to Lenin. He did not immediately grasp the constitutional implications of the revolutionary dynamic which, making the conquests of February look trivial, and in any case anachronistic, hurling the soviets into attack on the newly established order and the masses into attack on the soviets, the peasants into attack on the land and the workers on the factories, caused the idea of permanent revolution, conceived by Marx and Trotsky, to become the ruling principle of the Russia of 1917. It is not accidental that we find Lenin so hesitant in characterizing the events of this period. Today it appears to us that with each leap forward made by the revolution – the struggle for Soviet power against the Provisional Government, the liquidation of the latter, the breaking of the alliance with the Western bourgeois democracies, support for workers' control and dissolution of the Constituent Assembly – the revolution, transcending its bourgeois limits, intensified its character as a *socialist* revolution. Lenin, however, hesitated on this point, groping his way, and sometimes contradicting himself.

He was later to refer to 'setting up the Soviet state system' and 'getting out of the imperialist war' as the essential preliminary 'tasks of our revolution in the sphere of socialist construction'. In the period when the Constituent Assembly was dissolved, speaking in January 1918 to the Third All-Russia Congress of Soviets, he declared: 'Today, when the Soviets are in power ... there can be no question of a bourgeois-democratic revolution.' Yet the question of the bourgeois revolution was so much in Lenin's mind that he often identified the transition from the bourgeois to the socialist revolution with the setting-up in June 1918 of the 'Committees of Poor Peasants', which, breaking the unity of the peasant camp, introduced the class struggle into the countryside. In *The*

Proletarian Revolution and the Renegade Kautsky he asserted unequivocally that 'our revolution is a bourgeois revolution *as long* as we march with the peasants *as a whole*'. And to the 8th Party Congress, in March 1919, he said that it was 'from the moment the Poor Peasants' Committees began to be organized' that 'our revolution became a *proletarian* revolution'.

These approximations and varying definitions will surprise only those who wish to see in Lenin an infallible master and omniscient planner – whether providential or diabolical – of revolutionary strategy. This he was not. He was not even the real theoretician of the revolution, but 'merely' the maker of it. And it was his absorption in practical activity that, doubtless, prevented him in 1917 from deducing theoretical conclusions from the lessons of events. Hence the *theoretical* hesitancy of his approach to the problem of the Constituent Assembly – which he made up for, and very greatly, by his boldness in practice.

The Bolshevik Party and the socialist parties

Linear *schemata* are the most alluring. Here is one example. In their thirst for power, the Bolsheviks, almost as soon as they had become masters of the situation, proceeded to eliminate their political opponents. Dealing first of all with the Constitutional Democrats,[3] they then turned to suppress the socialist parties. Totalitarian Leninism: that is the thesis which Leonard Schapiro sums up perfectly in his classic history of the Communist Party of the Soviet Union: 'The refusal to come to terms with the socialists and the dispersal of the Constituent Assembly led to the logical result that revolutionary terror would now be directed not only against traditional enemies, such as the bourgeoisie and right-wing opponents, but against anyone, be he socialist, worker or peasant, who opposed Bolshevik rule.'

'The refusal to come to terms with the socialists.' This is how the writer summarizes an important episode of the Russian Revolution – the attempt, on the morrow of the October insurrection and the establishment of Soviet power, to form a broad coalition socialist government, which would have prevented communist monolithism from appearing and developing. The question is too heavy with implications not to be looked at carefully.

One observation must be made at the outset. The history of relations between the Bolsheviks and the moderate socialist parties does not begin in October 1917. Even without going back to the pre-revolutionary period, it must be kept in mind that divergence between the Leninists, on the one hand, and the SRs and Mensheviks, on the other, marked the entire evolution of events in Russia between February and October 1917: it was a complete divergence, bringing the two camps into conflict on *all* the problems of the revolution, and, in the last analysis, on the fundamental question: was it or was it not necessary to trust the bourgeoisie, allowing that class to establish its authority and, indeed, encouraging it to do so? It was because the Bolsheviks and the moderate socialist parties disagreed on this vital point that the October rising took place *against* those parties, and because of this that they did not content themselves with holding aloof from it, but denounced it, and would have crushed it if their weakness had not been as great as their disapproval and anger. Hardly had the sovereignty of the soviets, as the source of state power, been proclaimed, during the night of 25–26 October 1917, than the Mensheviks and SRs refused to recognize it, and walked out of the All-Russia Congress of Soviets – most of them never to return.

It might be concluded that this refusal and this walk-out, confirming a disagreement that related to the very nature of the new regime, must make impossible any collaboration between parties that were thenceforth each other's adversaries, despite the similarity of their titles.

Was all possibility of a compromise between Bolsheviks and moderate socialists – moderate in their socialism but not at all, as we shall see, in their hatred of Bolshevism – finally ruled out from that moment, and with it the possibility of a coalition government? An initiative taken by the railwaymen's trade union brought the question up. On 29 October, this union issued an ultimatum which was mainly aimed at Lenin's government. The railwaymen called for the formation of a coalition including all the parties represented in the soviets: if this did not take place, they would call a general railway strike throughout the country. That same day, the Bolshevik Central Committee (with Lenin absent) met to examine the railwaymen's 'proposal'. They decided to take part in the conference that was to be held to discuss the question of a coalition, and were all the better disposed to do this because, in the words of the resolution unanimously voted by those present, they considered it 'necessary to enlarge the basis of the government'. A delegation was nominated to carry on the negotiations: significantly, it consisted of three Right-wing Bolsheviks: Ryazanov, Sokolnikov and Kamenev. The two last-named spoke at the Central Committee meeting in favour of including *all* socialist groups in the future government, even those of the extreme Right tendency. Furthermore, the Bolshevik leaders decided to enlarge the Central Executive Committee of the Soviets by adding to it delegates from 'the parties which left the Congress', this to be done on a basis of proportional representation.

On 1 November the negotiators reported to their colleagues on the Central Committee on how the 'coalition conference' was going. Kamenev, Sokolnikov and Ryazanov mentioned the demand made by the moderate socialists to have the Central Executive Committee of the soviets enlarged by adding a strong contingent of *bourgeois* representatives, members of the Municipal Councils of Petrograd and Moscow, a demand which called in question the *Soviet* character of the new regime. This move by the moderate socialists caused Lenin to take a hostile line towards the conference – and all the more so because the Bolshevik delegates reported another condition laid down by the SRs and Mensheviks: that on no account must Lenin or Trotsky be a member of the coalition. He formally proposed that the negotiations be 'suspended'. This proposal, however, was rejected by ten votes to four, and the Bolshevik delegates accordingly continued their efforts to form a coalition government.

At the next day's meeting of the Central Committee Lenin won some ground. His motion challenging 'the opposition within the Central Committee' was passed by ten votes to five. This 'opposition', whose central figure was Kamenev, had shown its hand in the Central Executive Committee of the Congress of Soviets. Kamenev was chairman of this important body. Anticipating the course of the negotiations, he had proposed that the Council of People's Commissars resign and be replaced by a coalition government. He was supported by a strong contingent of leading Bolsheviks, including Nogin, a member of the party's Central Committee and People's Commissar for Industry and Commerce, Rykov, also a member of the Central Committee, Milyutin, People's Commissar for Agriculture, and Teodorovich, People's Commissar for Food – not to mention Zinoviev, once more allying himself with Kamenev. The 'moderate' tendency was thus still strong among the party's leaders. When Lenin put down a motion declaring that 'to yield to the ultimatums and threats of the minority in the soviets means finally rejecting not only Soviet power but democracy itself, for such concessions signify fear by the majority to make use of its majority', the discussion led to an indecisive battle. The first vote showed six for Lenin's motion and six against; second vote showed seven for and seven against; a third vote had to be taken, from which Lenin emerged as the victor by one vote – eight for, seven against.

Defeated, the minority decided to leave the Central Committee, raising the slogan: 'Long live the Government of the Soviet parties!' This minority included one-third of the leadership: Kamenev, Zinoviev, Rykov, Nogin and Milyutin. Several People's Commissars also resigned from their posts, so great was their desire to find a basis of agreement with the moderate socialists. Although this hope of theirs was nothing extraordinary – for, as the American historian R. Daniels points out, at the time of the October insurrection the Bolsheviks as a whole had no notion of ruling the country alone, and the Left communists themselves, despite their habitual radicalism, were in favour of a coalition, provided that the

Bolsheviks held a majority in it – the stubbornness of their attitude was more so. The agreement they wanted would have been possible only if the mood of the Mensheviks and SRs had been similar to that of most of the Bolsheviks. The marriage of convenience that they wanted proved to be out of the question, however, because the Bolshevik suitors found themselves faced only with hostility, contempt and refusal to compromise.

Speaking in the name of his party, a Socialist Revolutionary declared: 'For us a government with Bolsheviks participating is unthinkable.' And he went on to proclaim that 'the country will not forgive them the blood that has been shed.' The Mensheviks endorsed this view. On the morning of 30 October, when the discussion was resumed, the representatives of the two moderate socialist parties put forward demands that might have been more appropriate coming from victors than from vanquished. The Bolsheviks must undertake to disarm the Red Guards and to allow Kerensky's troops to enter the capital without resistance! When, however, news was received of the defeat of the anti-Bolshevik rising of the officer-cadets in Petrograd, a section of the SRs – but not all of them – showed greater modesty. They said they were ready to contemplate the possibility of allowing a few Bolsheviks to participate in the government, as individuals – this tolerant attitude not extending, however, to either Trotsky or Lenin.[4]

Negotiations were resumed, on this basis, on 1 November, with Bolshevik delegates present who were still ready, as we have seen, to offer the most far-reaching concessions to their interlocutors. The SRs admitted that it was only their military setbacks that led them to take part in the work of the conference. Next day, however, the SRs and Mensheviks jointly announced their decision not merely to 'suspend' the talks but to put an end to them altogether. The American historian Radkey concludes in this connection: 'The Socialist Revolutionary Party at the outset had taken an intransigent stand, departing from it only under the spur of disaster and even then demanding that their adversaries come round by the back way to share in power the plenitude of which they already possessed.' It is hard to conceive a greater lack of realism or more complete absurdity of conduct. In fact, however, the policy followed by the SRs and the Mensheviks during the coalition talks was laughable only in appearance. It corresponded to a logic that the same writer has summed up very well: 'In the last analysis it was the Bolshevik commitment to the Soviet form of government which wrecked the negotiations.'

That was the root of the problem. Only a minority (even though a substantial one) of the Bolshevik leadership were ready to sacrifice *the Soviet regime* to the anti-Soviet attitude of the moderate socialists. The rest were unwilling to accept such a surrender, even though they were no less desirous of widening the composition of the government. As for Lenin, he was neither more nor less uncompromising than most of his colleagues – merely more clear-sighted. That he was not intransigent or intent on monopolizing power for his own party is shown by his efforts to bring the Left SRs into the government. It is elsewhere than in the abortive attempt to form a coalition between the Bolsheviks and their socialist opponents that we must seek for the origins of communist monolithism.

Socialist Revolutionaries, Mensheviks and anarchists

And so, apart from the brief period of collaboration between the Bolsheviks and the Left SRs, the Leninists, often against their will, concentrated the whole of state power in their own hands, with no share held by other socialist parties. Furthermore, the new regime moved towards prohibition and suppression of these parties. This attitude on the part of the Bolsheviks towards their socialist opponents, as also towards the anarchists who in some circumstances acted as their allies, seems, indeed, to show a culpable desire for power, a fatal tendency towards monolithism.

The case of the Socialist Revolutionaries is at first sight the most disturbing, since Lenin had expressed concern to base himself on the majority of the population and needed, therefore, to obtain the support of the peasantry, whose political spokesman was, traditionally, the SR Party. In January 1918, addressing the 3rd All-Russia Congress of Soviets, Lenin said: 'In Russia only that power could last for any length of time that would be able to unite the working class and the majority of the peasants, all the working and exploited classes, in a single inseparably interconnected force fighting against the landowners and the bourgeoisie.'

Compared with this consideration, others, based upon the revolutionary past of the SR Party, might appear trivial, especially as this past, made up of struggles that were often ineffectual, though always heroic, was remote from and unrelated to the social character and political orientation of the SRs as they actually were when the Bolsheviks took power. We have seen how they turned their backs on the Congress of Soviets. This decision was not due merely to the fact that, in October, they had lost their majority to the Bolsheviks. It was not just the majority in the soviets that they rejected, but *the Soviet regime itself*. In September 1917 the newspaper *Izvestiya*, which they controlled, had written that 'the useful life of the soviets is coming to an end', and, a month later: 'When the autocracy and the bureaucratic regime collapsed, we created the soviets as a sort of shelter in which democracy could seek temporary refuge. Now we are about to build a more suitable edifice to replace this shelter, and it is natural that the people should move to a more comfortable home.'

It was not surprising that the SRs should have preferred, in the autumn of 1917, to the poverty of the Soviet 'temporary shelter', the comfort of new premises – those, no doubt, which they visualized the Constituent Assembly as occupying. Everything impelled them towards such a preference, starting with their social basis, which their principal and most scrupulous historian describes like this: 'The core of the Socialist Revolutionary Party was the rural intelligentsia: the village scribes, the children of the priests, the employees of the *zemstvos* and cooperatives, and, above all, the village schoolteachers.' These typically petty-bourgeois elements soon came, as the year 1917 wore on, to line up with the Constitutional Democrats, who themselves had become converted to a conservative and even reactionary outlook. This was the reason why the SRs refused, between February and October, to support the demands that had figured in their own programme since the party's foundation, and why they opposed, sometimes violently, the attempts made by the peasantry to divide up the large estates.

The fact is that a large segment of the Populist [i.e., SR] intelligentsia had become Kadets [Constitutional Democrats] without admitting it. They clung to the old SR label even though the old faith was gone . . . The last thing wanted by these people who continued to call themselves Socialist Revolutionaries was a social revolution, for it would halt the war, jeopardize their status in life, and enrage the Kadets, to whom they looked up in a worshipful admiration.

In the Constituent Assembly their group was to represent 'one of the most conservative elements in Russian society'. The SRs continued to be a peasants' party certainly, but, as E. H. Carr says, one that was concerned more specifically with the interests of the *well-to-do* peasants which they protected to the best of their ability during the distribution of land that followed the Bolsheviks' accession to power.

This, then, was the Socialist Revolutionary Party. Revolutionary before 1917, conservative between February and October, it showed itself to be counter-revolutionary from the very first days, even the first hours, of the Soviet regime. It was on 26 October 1917 that the majority of the Central Committee of the SR Party resolved to undertake, forthwith, *armed* action against the Bolsheviks. This decision, kept secret at the moment when it was taken, was made public at the 4th Congress of the SR Party, held openly in Petrograd in December 1917. The carrying out of the plan was entrusted to the party's most influential figure, Abraham Gotz, who had received more votes than anyone else in the election to the party's central committee. It turned out very soon, however, that Gotz could not count on the SR activists in order to put his counter-revolutionary plan into effect. He therefore turned, first, to the Cossacks stationed in the capital, and then, when they refused to commit themselves, to the training schools of the 'junkers', the officer-cadets, who were well-known for their conservative loyalties. The cadets accepted the assurances of the monarchist Purishkevich, with whom Gotz had made a pact that was doubtless decisive in rendering armed action possible. This was the background of the rising of the officer-cadets which disturbed the calm of Petrograd on 29 October, and which the Red Guards put down without much difficulty. Faced with this defeat, several of the SR leaders made their way to the front, to join forces with elements of the Army which they expected to launch an offensive against the Bolsheviks in the immediate future. The former Minister for Agriculture, Chernov, who was regarded as more to the Left than to the Right among the SRs, was there already, working hard to promote a speedy reconquest of the capital.

I shall not trace in detail the counter-revolutionary activities of the SRs before and after the dissolution of the Constituent Assembly; but it is certain that the SRs were pioneers on the counter-revolutionary side in the launching of the Civil War. In November 1917 their military commission planned to kidnap Lenin and Trotsky, entrusting this scheme to a group of officers. And if the demonstration in support of the Constituent Assembly which they organized in January 1918 in the streets of Petrograd was peaceful, this was not because the SRs had wanted it to be an unarmed one, but merely because they had not been able to obtain arms. The plan originally conceived by the party's leaders envisaged, on the contrary, a violent attempt to bring down the Soviet government: 'For weeks all preparations had been made with this end in view. But by the new year it was evident that a strictly military coup could not succeed.'

After the dissolution of the Constituent Assembly, the SRs decided to supplement their methods of action with a weapon taken from their party's old traditions: that of individual terrorism. In the spring they hatched a plot to assassinate Lenin. In June 1918 one of their men killed the Bolshevik leader Volodarsky, and, a month later, another killed Uritsky, also an important figure in the government camp. Altogether, in the Civil War that ravaged the country from July onwards, the SRs played a very prominent role. Already in May, at their 8th Conference, they had resolved 'to overthrow the Bolshevik dictatorship and to establish a government based on universal suffrage and willing to accept Allied assistance in the war against Germany'. The SRs took part on a large scale in all the anti-Bolshevik governments that were set up in Russia, often predominating in them. They took part in such governments even when these proclaimed and carried out a clearly reactionary programme. This was the case, for example, with the 'Provisional

All-Russia Government' formed in the autumn of 1918, whose pro-gramme was 'to develop the productive forces of the country with the help of private Russian and foreign capital, and to stimulate private initiative and enterprise'.

What was left of the socialist and revolutionary past of this organiz-ation, in which its old leader Chernov, despite his hatred of the Bolshe-viks, 'was horrified by the progress made by the monarchists and by the weakness of the moderate ones among us in consenting to a coalition with the antidemocratic forces'? This conversion of numerous SRs to monarchism was nothing new in the autumn of 1918. Jacques Sadoul, in a letter sent from Moscow in April of that year, summed up in these words what had emerged from his talks with SR leaders: 'Without so far admitting it publicly, many of them affirm, in private conversation, the need for a restoration of the monarchy.'

It is true that a change took place in February 1919, after months of civil war, in the attitude of certain SRs in Moscow and in Samara, where they had participated in an anti-communist government. They decided to seek a *rapprochement* with the Soviet regime: but their party's 9th Conference, held secretly in the capital, replied by denouncing these 'conciliators', who thereupon left the SR Party. Meanwhile, the Bolshe-viks had responded to this turn on the part of a minority of the SRs by relegalizing their party, which they had banned in June 1918. This gesture of toleration was to remain without a future, however, for the waverings and hesitations of a few individual SRs, amid the tumult of Civil War, did nothing to alter the basic fact that, in the conflict between classes that preceded and followed the October Revolution, the SR Party chose the banner of counter-revolution, and fought for it with all the violence that was typical of the period. The 'intolerance' the Bolsheviks showed in relation to the SRs was a reply to this decisive choice made by the latter. The case of the Mensheviks differs considerably from that of their SR allies. They were no less anti-Bolshevik than the SRs but their opposition had necessarily to take other forms, owing to their weakness and also to the very nature of their party.

At the moment when Soviet power was established, the Mensheviks looked quite discredited. A party of the towns, the election results showed that they had lost all their popularity there. A working-class party, they had lost the support among the proletariat that they had enjoyed in the first months following the February Revolution. In October 1917 the Mensheviks seemed to be a political formation without any social basis. A grouping that included some eloquent politicians and brilliant intellectuals, they seemed, in their almost pathetic weakness, like ghosts from a world that had passed away. Besides this weakness, which contrasted with the still firm roots possessed by the SRs in the country-

side, another point of difference between the SRs and the Mensheviks
was the political character of the latter. In many ways their party was a
grouping of genuine *moderates*. Their long dispute with the Bolsheviks,
since the foundation of Russian Social Democracy, testified to their
caution and concern for legality. After having shown, before the
February Revolution, that they were very timid revolutionaries, they had
proved between February and October that they were mediocre politicians. Their defeat was so absolute that they seemed to have no future at
all before them. However, they were to discover and display in adversity
that energy in which they had been so sadly lacking during their brief
period in power.

During the negotiations organized by the railwaymen's union with a
view to the forming of a coalition government, the Menshevik representative began by declaring that the only language appropriate for
talking to the Bolsheviks was that of guns. Since, however, the art of war
had never been the Mensheviks' strong point, they agreed to sit down at
the conference table. When the SRs decided to terminate the negotiations
most of the Mensheviks concurred. Martov, who since his return to
Russia in May 1917 had led the Left wing of the party, and disagreed
profoundly with its Right-wing leadership, condemned this attitude.

In December 1917, at an extraordinary congress of the Menshevik
Party which was publicly convened in Petrograd, Martov and his group
strengthened their position at the expense of the Right tendency led by
Lieber. Whereas the latter called on his comrades to join in a 'fighting
alliance of all anti-Bolshevik forces', Martov, after demonstrating that
this extreme view was held by a minority only, secured approval for his
own viewpoint, one which was so hedged about with qualifications as to
amount almost to a mere muddle: approval, subject to reservations, of
participation in the soviets was accompanied by a statement of loyalty to
the Constituent Assembly. Martov explained that it was impossible to
join the anti-communist camp, since that would mean a complete break
with the working class, 'now under the sway of utopias and illusions',
that is, of Bolshevism. His comrade Dan acknowledged, more prosaic-
ally, that since the attempt to overthrow the Bolsheviks 'by force of arms'
had 'failed', it was now necessary to take up 'the position of conciliation'.

During the winter of 1917–18 and the spring of 1918 the Mensheviks
reappeared in the Central Executive Committee of the Soviets, where
they formed a very small group – half a dozen out of nearly 350 delegates.
Their speakers also took part in the discussions at the All-Russia Congresses of Soviets, and on all such occasions Martov denounced with
remarkable vigour the policy being followed by the Bolshevik government. The Menshevik opposition was far from being a tame and respect-
ful one.

The Menshevik newspapers, which continued to be published openly, even though under difficult conditions,[5] also attacked various aspects of communist policy. They reproved the Soviet government for employing officers of the Tsarist Army in the Red Army, and also the first attempts made to subject the working class to labour discipline. In the spring of 1918 this Menshevik press was quite important, including daily papers as well as periodicals. It gave support to the party's candidates when they put themselves forward for election to the soviets – and they succeeded in getting substantial votes as the country's economic difficulties intensified. In Tambov, for instance, the Mensheviks even managed to win the majority in the town soviet. In other cases they declined to take part in elections, or were prevented from doing so by the Bolsheviks.

In May 1918 the Menshevik Party held a new conference – officially and openly – at which they condemned the Allied intervention in Russia (a step to the Left) but also confirmed their devotion to the Constituent Assembly (a step to the Right). The majority of the party, except for a conservative wing which supported the counter-revolution, increasingly gave the impression of trying, in the Civil War that was beginning, to remain above the battle and retain a certain neutrality. Thus, when, at the end of May, the Czechoslovak Legion in Russia, which was being transferred to the Western Front in order to continue fighting Germany, became involved in an armed clash with the Bolsheviks, the Mensheviks, on being asked by trade unionists among the railwaymen what attitude they should take up, advised them to stay neutral. When this advice was felt to be too vague, the Menshevik Central Committee explained that the neutral attitude to be maintained should be 'friendly to the Czechs and hostile to the Bolsheviks'.

Whatever the difficulties experienced by Martov and his friends in deciding on a coherent policy that could rally the support of all the different tendencies among the Mensheviks, the Soviet government took a decision of major importance in relation to them and to the SRs. On 14 June 1918, a decree was issued expelling the representatives of these two parties from the All-Russia Congress of Soviets and from its Central Executive Committee, and calling on all local and regional soviets to follow this example. Communist monolithism, favoured by the 'waiting' policy of the Mensheviks and provoked by the frankly counter-revolutionary conduct of the SRs, had taken a decisive step forward.

After the summer of 1918, with the rapid development of the Civil War, the Mensheviks found it very hard to form themselves into a comparatively homogeneous group. A series of divergences appeared among them which it was not easy to reconcile, and which their traditional lack of organization and discipline prevented them from overcoming. There were the minorities at the two extremes. One of these, led by

Lieber, stood for armed struggle against the Bolsheviks, and in some cases actually participated in this struggle. The party's Central Committee expelled those members who took an active part in the counter-revolution, but this decision seems neither to have been applied to all the Mensheviks concerned nor to have been made effective, since the counter-revolutionary Mensheviks in outlying parts of the country continued to regard themselves as members and representatives of the party. On the extreme Left was another minority, which advocated and practised *rapprochement* with the Soviet government and even with the Communist Party. In the centre, the majority of the Central Committee gathered around Martov, who recovered, after 1917, the stature as a leader that he had lost in the pre-October period.

Martov's attitude towards the Soviet government, and by implication that of the majority of the Mensheviks, has been described by a perceptive and well-disposed biographer as 'semi-loyal'. Paradoxically, it was after the party had been banned that their leader drew closer to the communist regime. His attitude, and that of his party, during the Civil War period, were defined at a conference held by the Menshevik Central Committee in Moscow during five days in October 1918. By the final resolution the Menshevik leaders undertook to support Lenin's government in so far as it was defending the gains of the revolution, but to oppose its policy of immediate socialization, the dictatorship of the Bolshevik Party and the exercise of terror. This conversion was subject, however, to reservations so subtle that it is uncertain whether everyone concerned was capable of grasping what they implied. Thus, the conference stated that the party was 'obliged to take the Soviet regime as point of departure in its struggle, accepting it as reality and not as a principle', while at the same time remaining faithful to 'the idea of popular sovereignty, universal suffrage and the Constituent Assembly'. The resolution expressed the hope that the situation would evolve in such a way as to make possible in the near future resumption of the struggle for the Constituent Assembly.

Despite its subtlety and contradictoriness, this document, when made public, produced a good impression on the Bolshevik leaders, and they were not long in responding to it. On 30 November a decree of the CEC of the soviets – actually, of the government – announced the 'relegalization' of the Menshevik Party. It was at this period – *but only at this period* – that the Menshevik Central Committee 'definitively' separated itself from the party's extreme Right element, who were still actively participating in the counter-revolution.

In 1919, especially in the second half of that year, the Mensheviks were thus able to make their appearance once more in the soviets, even though in small numbers only, and to defend their ideas, even though with very limited resources. As a constitutional opposition, they developed their policy in three directions: defence of 'Soviet legality' and struggle against the Red Terror; demands for measures of economic liberalization; and support for the restoration of independent trade unions and the rights of the working class. On economic matters the Mensheviks called in July 1919 for a relaxation of 'War Communism'. In a pamphlet which was circulated openly, which they had been encouraged to produce by an important Bolshevik, the economist Larin, and which they had the happy idea of entitling *What Is To Be Done?* the Mensheviks argued for a series of measures of liberalization that constituted an anticipation of the New Economic Policy.

The Mensheviks chiefly made their mark, however, during 1919 and 1920, by their defence of the rights of labour and the independence of the trade unions. The comparatively strong position they held before 1918 in certain trade-union organizations and their concern to maintain this position in face of pressure and coercion which, in many instances, emanated from the new rulers, account for their policy of defence of the trade unions, which was accompanied by a striving to safeguard the working class from a worsening of its standard of living – both being concerns that accorded with the traditional Menshevik line. Undoubtedly, as a result of the government's increasing unpopularity, and the loosening of revolutionary tension as the Civil War drew towards its close, the Mensheviks recovered a certain basis among the workers. This was reflected in the gains they made in some elections to the soviets. In 1920, for example, they won forty-six seats in the Moscow soviet, 205 in that of Kharkov, 120 in Yekaterinoslav, and fifty in Tula. They had an official headquarters in Moscow and published several papers legally, and at public meetings Menshevik speakers sometimes took the floor to oppose the representatives of the Bolshevik Party.

At the same time, the spirit of toleration shown by the communists must not be exaggerated. Even during the time when the Mensheviks were legal their freedom was highly precarious and subject to vexations, discriminations and methods of intimidation, in the form of arrests for brief periods. Nevertheless, in the words of Martov's biographer, 'outright repressions, arrests and expulsions from Soviets were the exception rather than the rule.' This toleration, with occasional lapses, was subjected to a severe test in May 1920, when Menshevik trade unionists organized a meeting in honour of a delegation from the British trade unions which was visiting Moscow. The speeches made at this meeting were critical, of course, of the government's policy. That was in order; but what was perhaps not, and certainly looked like an act of provocation, was that the organizers of the meeting allowed their platform to be used by the SR leader Chernov, that veteran leader of the counterrevolution, who was wanted by the police. The authorities took a month

residue of anarchists remained. According to Victor Serge, they constituted an appreciable force there in the autumn of 1918, and were planning to start an armed rising against the Soviet power. While there were many pro-Soviet anarchists who cooperated with the Bolsheviks, others engaged in acts of revolt of various kinds. Some anarchists took part in the rising in Moscow in July 1918 led by the Left SRs, and in September 1919, helped by SRs, they blew up the headquarters of the Moscow Communist Party while an important meeting was in progress, causing the death of twelve members of the local Bolshevik Committee. Over fifty people were wounded, including Bukharin. On the other hand, when Yudenich's counter-revolutionary forces approached Petrograd, one month after the explosion in Moscow, some anarchists, who must have belonged to a different tendency, enlisted in the workers' forces that undertook the defence of the city.

It was in the Ukraine, however, that the most important conflict took place between communists and anarchists. Relations between the two groups included phases of precarious collaboration, based on their common hatred of the 'White' forces, which were especially strong in the Ukraine; and also phases of violent antagonism, caused by the desire for independence on the part of Nestor Makhno's forces and the determination of the Red Army command to impose upon these anarchists its own authority, which tended, in the Ukraine as everywhere else, towards centralism. The to-ings and fro-ings of the bloody struggle cannot be described here, any more than we can here examine the claim that the 'Makhnovists' revealed at certain moments in the Ukraine a 'capacity for organization' that Victor Serge confirms. Their antipathy to all political parties and the fact that they banned these wherever they established their power − a ban which applied indiscriminately to both Bolshevik and non-Bolshevik organizations − did not facilitate their dealings with the communist government. The latter was, in any case, not at all disposed to tolerate the existence of a 'counter-authority' in the Ukraine. In November 1920 the Red Army brutally smashed what remained of Makhno's forces, putting a bloodstained close to an episode of the Russian revolution that still awaits its real historian.

That cannot be said of the drama of Kronstadt, which the American historian of Russian anarchism, Paul Avrich, has analysed in a book in which sympathy for the cause of the rebel sailors does not interfere with either the rigour of the account given or the lucidity of the analysis made. The merits of this work are not slight, since the field is one in which, to an unusual degree, passionate feelings have distorted the argument. Even today, more than fifty years after the event, communists of various allegiances, Trotskyites of different schools, and anarchists of all colours and shades clash over Kronstadt, in controversies that are rarely conducted with honesty, are often rowdy and are always absolutely useless, as the Leninists (of both the 'communist' and the 'Trotskyist' kind) endeavour to dodge the real problems, while the 'anarchists' fail to present them in other than emotional terms. All that can be done here is to offer a very brief and summary account, relying mainly on Avrich's book.

The attitude taken up by the communist government towards the Kronstadt rising cannot be understood unless the event is placed in its context. At the moment of the rising the government's situation was really disastrous. Addressing the 10th Congress of the Communist Party while the rising was in progress, Lenin described thus the condition of the essential, if not the only, social basis of the Soviet regime: 'our proletariat has been largely declassed' owing to the 'terrible crises' and 'extreme want and hardship'. In the same period he described the working class as 'uncommonly weary, exhausted and strained', adding that 'never has its suffering been so great and acute'. The state of the countryside caused Lenin even more anxiety. 'The crisis in peasant farming,' he warned, 'is coming to a head.'

There were, indeed, 50,000 peasants in open revolt in Tambov province alone, and in the Ukraine nearly thirty partisan detachments, some of them over a thousand strong, were operating against the Soviet power. The big strikes that had broken out in Petrograd at the end of February (and, shortly before that, in Moscow itself) showed that the industrial workers were not immune to the current unrest. Finally, on the international plane the situation was far from reassuring: peace had not yet been signed with Poland, and the forces of the 'White' General Wrangel, amounting to some tens of thousands, though defeated and obliged to leave Russian soil, were still not far away, standing ready to resume the Civil War should opportunity arise.

Does this mean that no other means but force was open to the Moscow government in order to deal with the rising? This cannot be said. The communist representatives sent to Kronstadt to restore order behaved with clumsiness and arrogance, inflaming angry feelings rather than calming them down. Was this because they felt themselves to be in a hostile and alien setting? The bulk of the Kronstadt sailors were certainly not what they had been at the time when they formed the spearhead of the revolution. Their social composition was markedly more 'peasant' than in 1917. This was, indeed, why the sailors at the naval base were particularly concerned about the misery in the rural areas. As for their state of mind, this was more than ever marked by anarchistic inclinations – reluctance to submit to any authority, desire for freedom and independence, what the Bolshevik Dybenko, who knew the sailors well, having long been one himself, called their 'eternally rebellious spirit'.

The uneasiness felt by the communists is thus easily explained. Nevertheless, the charges they levelled against the rebels, whom they presented as counter-revolutionaries linked with, or manipulated by, the Mensheviks, the SRs and the émigré 'Whites', had little connection with reality. The Mensheviks, constituting an opposition that was still legal, or semi-legal, refused to endorse the revolt. The SRs, in the person of Chernov, offered the rebels their services, but these were declined for the time being at any rate. As for the counter-revolutionary émigré circles, they did, it is true, prepare to launch an operation directed at the Kronstadt naval base, control of which they saw as invaluable, even indispensable, if they were to be in a position to rekindle the Civil War: but there is nothing to show that the Kronstadt sailors took any part in these preparations, or that they even knew about them. After the suppression of the revolt, however, the 'Provisional Revolutionary Committee' of Kronstadt, or what was left of it, did make an agreement with the Paris 'Whites', and its principal figure, the sailor Petrichenko, worked actively for their 'Russian National Centre' in the spring of 1921, carrying on counter-revolutionary activities on their behalf in Petrograd.

What is essential is the programme of the rebellion and its ideology. The Kronstadt programme consisted of a set of political demands supplemented by some economic ones. The rebels wanted, above all, restoration of liberties, an end to the monopoly of power held by the communists, restoration of all rights to the anarchists, the 'Left Socialist Parties' and the trade unions, and fresh elections, by secret ballot. Freedom of enterprise should, they declared, be given back to the peasants and craftsmen.

We shall not describe the course of the battle between the communist troops and the rebel sailors, a plebeian force in which officers played no part but which had been joined by quite a few Bolsheviks. It was a hard fight with heavy losses on both sides. The subsequent repression was severe.[6] In the last analysis we must ask ourselves, like Paul Avrich: 'What government would long tolerate a mutinous navy at its most strategic base, a base which its enemies coveted as a stepping-stone for a new invasion?'

The dramatic quality of 'Kronstadt' does not lie in the repression that followed it so much as in its political significance. The Soviet government had found itself compelled to act against men who were only asking for application of the principles on which that government had based its authority, and this was happening after the close of a civil war that the Soviet government had won. It amounted to 'defeat in victory'. Discouragement and bitterness were sown among those anarchists in Russia who, in spite of everything, had still clung to the hope of possible collaboration with the communists.[7]

The Left Socialist Revolutionaries offer the interesting peculiarity that they were the only party to have collaborated in government with the Bolshevik Party. The revolutionary wing within the SR Party did not actually secede from it until after the October Revolution. After the seizure of power the Bolsheviks invited them to enter the Council of People's Commissars. Lenin showed 'surprising patience' with them, offering three portfolios, including the vital one of agriculture, but was rebuffed. When the Bolshevik People's Commissar of Agriculture, Milyutin, resigned as a result of his dispute with the Central Committee on the question of coalition, Lenin approached the Left SRs again, but without any better success. Eventually, however, on 12 December 1917, agreement was reached, the Left SRs receiving seven People's Commissariats as against the eleven held by the Bolsheviks, and a Left SR being appointed deputy-head of the Cheka.

During the three months that they remained in the government, the Left SRs, whose social basis was mainly the middle peasantry, and whose political tendencies were somewhat akin to syndicalism, especially as regards their hostility to centralism, strove mainly to exert a moderating influence on their Bolshevik partners. They were reluctant to use violent methods to combat counter-revolution. The immediate cause of their departure from the government was the signing of the peace treaty of Brest-Litovsk, to which they were, as a whole, strongly opposed. Efforts were made to overcome this divergence, which was not entirely a question of a split between Bolsheviks and Left SRs, since the Bolsheviks themselves were divided on the issue. On 23 February 1918, at the crucial moment in the discussion on whether or not to sign the treaty, the Bolshevik and Left SR groups in the Central Executive Committee of the Soviets held a joint meeting to seek a compromise. It is interesting to note that the anarchist members of the CEC were also invited to this meeting.

After their 'ministers' had resigned, the Left SRs continued for some time to maintain relatively friendly relations, or at any rate to continue certain forms of cooperation, with the Bolsheviks. Their representatives still sat as members of the commissions of the CEC engaged in drawing up a draft of a new constitution, to supervise the 'land committees' in a number of provinces, and to occupy important posts in the Cheka. Alongside these overt forms of cooperation were others, more discreet, such as the organization of struggle against the German occupying forces in the Ukraine. What destroyed all possibilities of agreement or compromise between the two parties was the government's agrarian policy, especially the setting-up of the 'Committees of Poor Peasants' and the dispatch of workers' detachments into the countryside for the purpose of requisitioning foodstuffs. These measures aroused opposition not only among the *kulaks* but also among the middle peasants, who were the chief clientele of the Left SRs. The latter protested vigorously against these measures, but got no satisfaction, and this caused the final and complete break with the Bolsheviks.

As true revolutionaries, the heirs and successors of the terrorist tradition of the Narodnaya Volya, the Left SRs expressed their opposition with the utmost violence. In July 1918 they assassinated Count Mirbach, the German Ambassador, in the hope of restarting the war between Russia and Germany, and at the same time launched in the streets of the capital a revolt against their erstwhile allies. They too had gone over to the camp of counter-revolution, and, in this direction as in so many others, all chance of cooperation between Bolsheviks and non-Bolsheviks was finally ended.[8]

Leninism and the opposition

If we consider what is understood today by the 'Soviet model', at least in the field of political institutions, we observe that it signifies, very largely, the one-party system. The most innovatory, or most revisionist, wing of the communist world (the confusion of these terms having became practically inextricable in the Stalinist and post-Stalinist imbroglio) may contemplate, in its bolder moods, a revision of the concept of the single party, redefining its role and functions in society. Never, though, does it question, in the countries where the communists are in power, the idea, which has indeed become sacrosanct, that state power must be identified with, or at least based upon, a political organization that knows no rival. This concept of the single party occupies such a place in the 'Soviet model', and the latter has been so easily identified with the political and institutional realization of Leninism, that it is essential to analyse with some care the historical factors that governed the emergence and consolidation, in the Soviet Russia of Lenin's time, of the single party, the sole wielder of political power.

Faced with the situation created by the Civil War directed against the bourgeoisie, which had been ousted not only from power but also, to a large extent, from political life itself as a result of the dictatorship of the proletariat, and faced with the counter-revolutionary attitude adopted by some of the socialist parties and the refusal, at first practically unanimous, of these parties to accept the legitimacy of the Soviet regime, what solution did Lenin advocate? Did he, under the pressure of events, work out a theory of political power which affirmed the need for a single proletarian party? Certainly not – if only for the simple reason that, after taking power, Lenin proved incapable, in an almost physical, material sense, of conceiving any theoretical system at all. In default of any Leninist doctrine inspired by the lonely exercise of power, we can only note that, in his writings and speeches before the Revolution, Lenin had never suggested anything remotely resembling a single-party system – and then proceed to study what he said, wrote and did in the period subsequent to October 1917. Let us recall, in this connection, that we have seen that he opposed the entry of the Mensheviks and Right S Rs into the Soviet government *after* they had – not content with displaying all through 1917 their pusillanimity and inclination to side with the bourgeoisie – refused to recognize the sovereignty of the soviets, and that, in contrast to this, he showed himself anxious to add to the Bolshevik team of People's Commissars representatives of the Left S Rs who, despite reservations, *had* accepted the new state.

It is true that monolithism does not consist only, or mainly, in keeping one's political opponents in opposition, but also, and above all, in depriving them, first, of any right to express themselves, and eventually of all possibility of existence. Now, freedom of expression was allowed to the Right S R and Menshevik parties by the Soviet government for several months. It vanished when these parties were banned, in June 1918, in circumstances that have already been explained. Until then the press of the socialist (or ex-socialist) opposition had been, at best tolerated, at worst (and most often) harassed, but certainly not muzzled or suppressed. Here are some relevant facts.

The Moscow anarchist paper *Burevestnik* wrote in April 1918: 'We have come to the limit! Bolsheviks having lost their senses have betrayed the proletariat and have attacked the anarchists. They have joined the Black Hundred generals, the counter-revolutionary bourgeoisie . . . Our November is still ahead.' The Left Menshevik paper *Novaya Zhizn*, edited by Maxim Gorky, published between October 1917 and its suppression in July 1918 a series of highly inflammatory articles which nevertheless did not bring down upon it the thunderbolts of the state. It denounced the 'vanity of Lenin's promises . . . the extent of his madness', and described the Council of People's Commissars as an 'autocracy of savages'. Furthermore, it said: 'Lenin and his acolytes think they have licence to commit every crime,' and, regarding Lenin himself: 'He is an incurable madman, signing decrees as head of the Russian government instead of undergoing hydrotherapeutic treatment under the care of an experienced alienist.' And *to the Right* of papers like this were the organs of the Right S Rs and the 'orthodox' Mensheviks.

All the same, we do not find in Lenin any categorical statement (let alone any theoretical reflection) about 'freedom of the press', any more than about the question of the rights of parties, and certainly nothing about either the right of an opposition press to exist, or the negation of this right. Apart from incidental remarks, thrown off in the heat of debate and of a more or less polemical nature, we chiefly have from his pen on this subject a 'draft resolution on freedom of the press' written barely a week after the taking of power and not published until long after Lenin's death. According to this document, 'For the workers' and peasants' government, freedom of the press means liberation of the press from capitalist oppression, and public ownership of paper mills and printing presses; equal right for public groups of a certain size (say, numbering 10,000) to a fair share of newsprint stocks and a corresponding quantity of printers' labour.' For the present, Lenin demanded restrictions on the freedom of the bourgeois press, declaring before the CEC: 'We cannot provide the bourgeoisie with an opportunity for slandering us.' This attitude met with vigorous opposition among the Bolsheviks themselves, and when a prominent party member, Larin, put down a motion criticizing the restrictions imposed by the government on press freedom, the CEC, although dominated by Bolsheviks, rejected it by a majority of only two.

Generally speaking, Lenin linked the problem of press freedom with that of political freedom in general, relating these freedoms to the situation in the Civil War,[9] and adopting a class viewpoint on the whole question. '"Liberties" and democracy not for all, but for the working and exploited masses, to emancipate them from exploitation.' There was nothing in all this that implied systematic and final banning of the opposition socialist press. Although the measures taken by the Bolshevik rulers during the Civil War were certainly dangerous in their severity and their pragmatic character, they cannot seriously be judged in isolation from their context and without extending our field of observation to include cases other than that of the communist government. If we look, for example, at German Social Democracy, which was born and developed in a climate of great freedom of expression, and which had allowed the most diverse tendencies within it to exist and even to flourish, we are surprised to see that its leaders, when they found themselves in especially serious circumstances of political crisis, paid hardly more heed to 'freedom of the press' than did the Russian communists. During the First World War, even before they came to power, Ebert and his colleagues of the German party leadership deprived the Left tendency, by a veritable act of violence, of the papers that it had long been in control of. Once installed in state power in November 1918, these same Social Democratic leaders did their best, during the development of the revolutionary crisis, to prevent the Spartacist and Independent Left Socialist papers from being published.

The case of the German revolution of November 1918 deserves attention from the angle of this problem of freedom of the press and its use in a revolutionary period. It illustrates, indeed, the disastrous consequences for the socialist cause that can result from the existence of the big de facto press monopoly enjoyed by the bourgeoisie and made use of by it in crisis situations, not to mention more normal ones. As Pierre Broué observes, in his book on the German revolution:

After November [1918], thanks to the watchword of 'freedom of the press' put about by the Social Democrats and the forces behind them, the supplying of information remained in the hands of the enemies of the working class. While the *Vossische Zeitung, Berliner Tageblatt, Kreuzzeitung* and the rest [the very papers that were to applaud the murder of Karl Liebknecht and Rosa Luxemburg, depicting this as the providential elimination of 'criminals pure and simple', M.L.] continued to appear, backed by substantial funds, the revolutionary workers' organisations, which could count on nothing but the workers' contributions, were obliged to remain silent, or to express themselves only with very inadequate means, in face of the coalition that was crushing them . . . It is easily appreciated that, under these conditions, almost the entire press . . . joined in orchestrating a systematic campaign to discredit the Workers' and Soldiers' Councils.

The measures of prohibition and intimidation adopted by the Bolsheviks, and recommended by Lenin, certainly do not provide a *solution* to the very real problem posed by freedom of the press in a revolutionary period. To represent them, however, as proof of a deliberate striving for totalitarianism is to close one's eyes to the reality of a revolution. This amounts to advising revolutionaries to answer the massive pressure exerted by the bourgeoisie (not to mention its violence) with the Franciscan virtues of renunciation, resignation and humility.

The press is only a vehicle of opinions and interests, the means of expression of organizations, notably of political bodies, and it is Lenin's attitude to the latter that is of fundamental interest in our present context. In this connection Lenin's attitude to the anarchists constitutes a special case. E. H. Carr considers that 'from the time of *State and Revolution* onwards Lenin always showed a certain tenderness for anarchists'.

Though Professor Carr's formulation is questionable, his opinion is basically quite justified. To be sure, reiterating his previously expressed views, Lenin declared in the spring of 1918, in *The Immediate Tasks of the Soviet Government*, that 'anarchism and anarcho-syndicalism are *bourgeois* trends . . . irreconcilably opposed . . . to socialism, proletarian dictatorship and communism,' but this statement surprises us if we compare it with numerous indulgent, complaisant or even favourable references that he made to anarchists, if not to anarchism. In January 1918 he had already spoken of 'the new, fresh trend in anarchism [which] was definitely on the side of the Soviets'. It was above all in August 1919, however, in a letter to Sylvia Pankhurst, that Lenin revealed his sympathy for a certain form of anarchism: 'Very many anarchist workers,' he wrote, 'are now becoming sincere supporters of Soviet power, and that being so, it proves them to be our best comrades and friends, the best of revolutionaries, who have been enemies of Marxism only through misunderstanding, or, more correctly, not through misunderstanding but because the official socialism prevailing in the epoch of the Second International (1889–1914) betrayed Marxism . . .' In *'Left-Wing' Communism,' An Infantile Disorder,* Lenin, again referring to the attitude of the anarchists towards socialism before 1914 admitted that 'the anarchists rightly pointed to the opportunist views on the state prevalent among most of the socialist parties'.[10] Acknowledging that 'the old division' between socialists and anarchists had 'proved to be outdated', since 'the working-class movement in all countries followed a new line, not the line of [either] the anarchists and [that is, or] the socialists, but one that could lead to the dictatorship of the proletariat', Lenin quite logically called upon the anarchist workers to join the ranks of the Third International, even considering that 'the measure in which genuinely Communist Parties succeed in winning mass proletarian elements, rather than intellectual and petty-bourgeois elements, away from anarchism is a criterion of the success of those parties.'

This unconcealed sympathy towards anarchism, shown in a period when clashes with other Marxist socialist trends were, on the contrary, becoming sharper, did not, however, suffice to ensure relatively harmonious cooperation between the Bolsheviks and the various libertarian tendencies. This failure resulted from the variety of such tendencies and the very pronounced contradictions that led some anarchists to take up a certain position *within* the Soviet order while others, as we have seen, opposed it violently. Faced with these divergences, Lenin could only make a distinction between the 'ideological' anarchists and the rest. Lasting cooperation between communists and anarchists was also hindered by the contrast between the strength of the former and the comparative weakness of the latter. As has been said, the Kronstadt revolt and its suppression was to draw a line of blood between them. It is to be observed, however, that, even in Kronstadt, the rebels showed a certain sympathy with Lenin, whereas they felt violent hatred for Trotsky. After the revolt had been crushed, when the communists recovered possession of the base, they discovered, for instance, that in the offices the rebels had occupied, though portraits of Trotsky had been torn down, those of Lenin had been allowed to remain. Lenin took the trouble, in September 1921, to arrange for all the better-known anarchists who had not committed acts of violence against the state to be released from prison, on condition that they left the country at once. Moreover, Lenin met Nestor Makhno, during the summer of 1918, and showed himself conciliatory and even friendly towards him, saying that 'if only one-third of the Anarchist-Communists were like you, we communists would be ready, under certain well-known conditions, to join with them in working towards a free organization of producers.'

No less significant is the fact that Lenin kept in touch with Kropotkin, although the latter had taken up a patriotic attitude during the war and supported Russia's participation in that conflict alongside the Entente countries. The two men met from time to time, and corresponded. Lenin showed 'considerable respect' for the great anarchist leader. The latter said that 'our aims seem to be the same' but that their methods differed greatly, and proposed that he supply Lenin with reports on the injustices committed by the Soviet authorities. Lenin agreed to this, and Kropotkin sent him such reports until his death in February 1921.[11]

Let mention finally be made of a number of attempts that were pursued during the Civil War to bring communists and anarchists together, with a view to complete legalization of the libertarian movement. Kamenev and Alfred Rosmer took part in these moves. The anarchists were called upon to check their ranks and carry out a purge of the unbalanced and uncontrollable elements that were so numerous among them, along with some actual counter-revolutionaries. As Victor Serge records, however, 'the majority of the anarchists gave a horrified refusal to this suggestion of organization and enrolment ... Rather than that, they would disappear, and have their press and premises taken off them.'

Thus, whereas Lenin's attitude towards the anarchists, immediately after the October Revolution and in the first years of the Soviet regime, showed more goodwill than sectarianism, his policy in relation to the moderate socialists was one of great sternness. Here we touch upon a question of major importance – whether it was possible for the communists to coexist with a socialist opposition that accepted the essential foundations of the Soviet regime, as did the Mensheviks, in contrast to the SRs. That such coexistence would inevitably have been very difficult is obvious. The Civil War and the exacerbation of relations between classes and parties was bound to cause a strengthening of the extremes and threaten to ruin any tendency favouring conciliation. This was what happened with the Mensheviks. That their heterogeneity, with the presence inside the complex Menshevik 'family' of trends that were Rightist and sometimes counter-revolutionary, made worse by a long tradition of toleration and indiscipline, must have intensified these difficulties is not to be denied. Lenin was not altogether wrong when he declared that 'there is *no* definite line of demarcation' between Rights and Lefts among the Mensheviks, and that, 'although they verbally "condemn" their "Rights", even the best of the Mensheviks and SRs, in spite of all they say, are actually *powerless* compared with them'. It remains true, however, that he did nothing – quite the contrary – to overcome these difficulties, and appears to have resigned himself to them rather easily, thus obliging the Mensheviks to play the role of a less and less tolerated opposition, and progressively eliminating them from all sectors of public life.

The 5th All-Russia Congress of Soviets, in July 1918, was the last at which the opposition was present in strength. At the next Congress, held four months later, there were 933 communist delegates out of the total of 950. Although the Mensheviks had played no part in the rising of the Left SRs, they suffered for it as well – and along with them, Soviet democracy. The policy thereafter followed by Leninism in power towards the Mensheviks can be summed up as follows: total subordination to the requirements of the Civil War; conviction that, in such a period, neutrality is out of the question; and treatment of Mensheviks and Right SRs as though they were the same. The first point corresponds to an unchallengeable logic which was affirmed by Lenin on numerous occasions. In face of the exigencies of the struggle against the 'Whites', he said, the distinction between Left Mensheviks and Right Mensheviks inevitably became unimportant. 'Even supposing,' he said to the Central Trade-Union Council in April 1919, 'the Menshevik Central Committee is better than the Mensheviks in Tula who have been definitely exposed as fomentors of strikes – in fact I have no doubt some of the regular members of the Mensheviks Committee are better – in a political struggle, when the White guards are trying to get us by the throat, is it possible to draw distinctions? ... In two years' time, perhaps, after we have beaten Kolchak, we shall examine this matter, but not now.'

Moreover, in view of the gravity of the situation in which the communist rulers found themselves, with the ephemeral but sometimes spectacular and apparently decisive advances made by the counter-revolutionary forces, Lenin refused to allow that there could be any neutrality in the conflict. 'He who is not for us is against us.'

That, in these circumstances, the Bolshevik rulers should not have been greatly disposed to welcome the subtleties of the resolutions passed by the Mensheviks, and Martov's 'semi-loyalism', goes without saying. But this did not prevent them from taking note of the turn made by the Mensheviks in October 1918, and hailing it as a positive act, since they agreed to 'regularize' the party's position. Lenin considered that they should 'take into account and make use of the turn'. He stressed that 'many of the slogans of this struggle [against the SRs and Mensheviks, M.L.] have now become frozen and petrified and prevent us from properly assessing and taking effective advantage of the new period, in which a change of front has begun among these democrats, a change in our direction'. And he concluded that 'it would be ... foolish ... to insist only on tactics of suppression and terror in relation to the petty-bourgeois democrats ...'

In December 1918 he reaffirmed: 'We must not now turn them [the

Mensheviks] away, on the contrary, we must meet them halfway and give them a chance to work with us.' This joint work had definite limits, however: Lenin was agreeable, at this moment, to maintaining 'good neighbourly relations' with Mensheviks, but he added immediately: 'We are quite willing to legalize you, Menshevik gentlemen,' though 'we reserve state power for ourselves, *and for ourselves alone.*' There would be, so to speak, a division of labour between Mensheviks and communists: the latter would hold power, while the former, assuming they collaborated loyally, would be assigned *practical* tasks.[12]

Lenin never went any further than this towards conciliation with the Mensheviks, and soon resumed an extremely severe attitude towards their party as a whole. His severity increased as the ending of the Civil War revealed the ruined state of the country and the stark isolation of the Communist Party. In March 1919 he told the 8th Party Congress that 'the Mensheviks are the worst enemies of socialism'. In December of the same year, addressing the Congress of Soviets, he accused the Mensheviks of wanting to see a return to bourgeois democracy, and exclaimed: 'when we hear people who profess sympathy with us making such declarations we say to ourselves, "Yes, the terror and the Cheka are absolutely indispensable."' This meant suggesting, at least, that the terror and the Cheka might be used against the Menshevik party. Above all, with the introduction of the New Economic Policy and the all-round political crisis nothing mattered any more but coercion, unity and discipline. Unity and discipline, as we shall see, for the communists themselves, and coercion for the Mensheviks. In and after 1922 Lenin frequently instructed his colleagues, especially in the People's Commissariat for Justice, to intensify repression against the Mensheviks, calling on the Political Bureau to wage a 'relentless struggle against' what he called 'the most dangerous *de facto* accomplices of the White Guards', and recommending that 'the application of the death sentence should be extended (commutable to deportation) . . . to all forms of activity by the Mensheviks, SRs and so on.'

What accounts for the almost entirely negative, and occasionally terroristic, attitude taken up by Lenin towards the Mensheviks is the hostility, almost repulsion, that their principal activities inspired in him. He blamed them especially for their legalism and their condemnation of the use of terror when only ruthless struggle against reaction could save the regime, and, more generally, their continual uncertainty – 'the spineless vacillation bringing them to serve Kolchak' – the zigzags of an unstable and wavering policy which Lenin attributed to the fundamentally petty-bourgeois character of the Mensheviks' social basis. More concretely, the Mensheviks exasperated Lenin by their social agitation and their readiness to encourage the workers to go on strike to protect their immediate interests. The successes they achieved in this field testified to a recovered popularity that made them more dangerous than they had ever been since October 1917. Their activity, carried on during a phase of retreat and setbacks, threatened to intensify the crisis of the regime. The weakness of the Communist Party itself, a prey to its own divisions, tipped the scale in favour of a policy of force; and what was left of the Menshevik Party was finally liquidated.

What is most striking, however, in Lenin's attitude, and calls for most severe criticism, is the 'amalgam' that he kept making between the Mensheviks and the Right SRs. Enough has been said on the differences between these two parties for it to be unnecessary to prove how deeply mistaken it was to treat them as being essentially the same. It was understandable that he should say, in November 1920, that 'the Soviet regime would *most certainly* have been overthrown if Mensheviks, reformists, petty-bourgeois democrats had remained in our party, or even if they had remained in any considerable numbers in the central Soviet bodies'. But to eliminate them completely from the public life of Soviet Russia and destroy them as a party was fatal to Soviet democracy. This destruction of the Menshevik Party was indeed one of the worst symptoms of the malady from which this democracy was suffering. It was doubly wrong and doubly unjust to identify the Mensheviks with the SRs, who had degenerated politically into enemies of the revolution. The two parties had certainly been closely associated in 1917. On the morrow of the October Revolution, however, the SRs markedly intensified their conservative tendencies, and got rid of their Left wing, so that they fell into the arms of the counter-revolution. The Mensheviks, on the contrary, made a turn to the Left shortly after the establishment of the Soviet regime, reducing their former Right-wing leadership to minority status and transforming the fiercely anti-Bolshevik element into a marginal tendency in the party. This development brought the Mensheviks closer to their Marxist origins and caused them gradually to resume contact with the working class.

This *rapprochement* between Menshevism and the working class took place during a period of ebb-tide in the revolution. Being in many ways the opposite of Bolshevism, it was not possible for Menshevism to find a social basis and a certain degree of strength except in a period of retreat and defeat, just as Bolshevism could advance only in a period of workers' victories and revolutionary advance. The corollary applies, also, that Menshevism found an echo, from 1920 onwards, only in a working class that had been largely de-classed and was in any case weakened and demoralized. These circumstances nevertheless do not alter the fact that the Menshevik movement, in so far as its existence was tolerated, became once more the political voice of a *working-class* reality. Yet Lenin, in an arbitrary way, described Menshevism as something petty-bourgeois pure and simply. In fact, with the limited means at their disposal, and despite the precarious conditions in which they had to act, the Mensheviks strove to undertake active defence of the workers' material conditions. They were behind a number of strikes that occurred, including the very big one in Petrograd shortly before the Kronstadt rising. Lenin considered that these strikes were against the interests of the proletarian state. Even so, during the great debate about the trade unions that was held in the Communist Party he admitted that the degree of bureaucracy that prevailed in the regime justified a policy of pressure by the workers' own organizations. The Mensheviks, while endeavouring to defend the poor remnants of trade-union independence that still remained, came forward to take the place of the trade unions, now enfeebled and much bureaucratized. Their old familiarity with trade-union activity helped them to play this role. Lenin sometimes denounced the demands raised by the Russian workers as evidence of an egoistic attitude at a time when the Soviet power (or what was left of it) could be saved only by sacrifice. Faced with the rising wave of discontent, the reaction of the communist leaders, headed by Lenin, was often to denounce the petty-bourgeois mentality which had evidently not disappeared, and was still doing harm. However, this argument was facile and dangerous. The Leninist rulers, backs to the wall, never made a serious attempt to introduce any mechanism of 'social defence' apart from the institutions of repression that operated during the Civil War. They did not really permit the working class to develop any autonomous activity in pursuit of its own demands. In this sphere, Lenin opted for an authoritative and even authoritarian line.

There is, however, one reservation to be made, and it is a serious one. Lenin never depicted what he considered to be a necessity as being either a virtue or as a really lasting system. On the contrary, some remarks of his – incidental, certainly – allow us to assume that the existence of a plurality of parties accorded better with his political plans. In March 1919, addressing the Party Congress, he said that 'for a long time these [petty-bourgeois, M.L.] parties are bound to take one step forward and two steps back', and appeared to be resigned to this. Even more clearly, he acknowledged during the discussions at the 10th Congress of the Communist Party, in 1921, the congress that placed restrictions on freedom within the Bolshevik organization, that 'the choice before us is not whether or not to allow these parties to grow – they are inevitably engendered by petty-bourgeois economic relations. The only choice before us, and a limited one at that, is between the forms of concentration and coordination of these parties' activities.' The formulation is vague and far from satisfactory, but it certainly does not suggest a desire to eliminate the opposition parties once for all. One cannot discern any totalitarian or monolithic scheme here; nevertheless, what Leninism actually *did* contributed to bring such a development about. It banned the legal opposition constituted by the Menshevik Party – an irreparable mistake which the tragic circumstances of the Civil War explain, but which the very principle of proletarian democracy puts beyond justification.

According to Pierre Broué, Lenin was thinking, during the final weeks of his active life, of legalizing the Menshevik Party. Unfortunately, however, he gives no source for this important claim. Victor Serge alleges categorically that 'in May 1922 Lenin and Kamenev were considering the revival of some degree of press freedom', but also gives no authority for the statement. It would seem, on the contrary, that Lenin was in favour of strengthening repression of the Menshevik Party. Did he perhaps – as a result of the illness that kept him away from the exercise of state power, and gave him the opportunity to discover the latter's grave imperfections – become aware, belatedly but clearly, of the defects of increasing monolithicity? Nothing in Lenin's last writings gives grounds for claiming this – at least so far as what has been published is concerned – despite the considerable interest and almost prophetic quality of some of these writings. At most one may observe that in an instruction addressed to his secretaries in February 1923 Lenin asked for information on 'the present situation (the election campaign, the Mensheviks, suppression, national discord)'. There is not enough here for the slightest conclusion to be drawn, and any assumption based upon it, in the present state of our knowledge, is entirely conjectural and unwarranted. It will be observed, nevertheless, that this note was written in the very last weeks of Lenin's active life, when he was attempting a final assault on some especially pernicious forms of political arbitrariness. To this must be added certain facts regarding the relations between Martov and Lenin and how these developed during Lenin's illness.

The relations between Lenin and Martov constitute a subject that the historian and sociologist can study only with the help of the psychologist. We know for certain that the Bolshevik leader felt for his Menshevik rival a degree of admiration and of friendship that was unusual for him. As the struggle between factions and parties developed, however, Lenin had come to employ unrestrained verbal violence against Martov. Even the internationalist attitude taken up by the latter during the war – 'centrist' in character, to be sure – did not suffice to shelter him from attack after attack, and neither did his opposition to the conservative policy followed by the Menshevik leadership during 1917. When virulently attacked by Martov, Lenin replied with the crudest invective, calling his opponents a 'lackey of the bourgeoisie' and 'a rogue', accusing him of 'refined corruption', 'hypocrisy' and 'treachery' because he had said that the Civil War was dividing the working class itself.

And yet Lenin's incredibly hard attitude was compatible with some ambiguous feelings. Lunacharsky, writing in 1923 at a time when the expression of any sort of sympathy with Martov was not calculated to bring approval in Soviet Russia, said that in the spring of 1917 Lenin 'dreamed of an alliance with Martov'. What is certain is that Lenin showed in his last years definite solicitude for his old opponent. In October 1921 Martov, suffering from the tuberculosis that was to kill him two years later, asked permission to leave Russia in order to attend the congress that the Independent Socialist Party of Germany was to hold at Halle, to decide whether or not to join the Third International. Although Martov intended to speak, in the name of the Mensheviks, against joining the Comintern, he was given his passport. The Communist Party's Political Bureau had favoured refusal, but Lenin's personal intervention had reversed their decision. Martov never returned to Russia, but settled in Berlin, laid low by his illness. (In the winter of 1919–20 Lenin had sent him the best doctor obtainable in Moscow.) Martov's biographer relates, on the authority of the memoirs of Svidersky, a former People's Commissar for Agriculture, that during Lenin's last illness he showed an 'obsession to get together with Martov: paralysed and having lost his speech, Lenin would point at Martov's books on his shelves and demand that a driver take him to Martov.' The testimony of Krupskaya is doubtless more reliable, though the freedom of expression she enjoyed after her husband's death was also more limited. She records that 'Vladimir Ilyich was already seriously ill when he said to me once sadly: "They say Martov is dying too",' and takes the opportunity to mention Lenin's warm attitude towards his old associate.

This incursion into the history of personal relations is bound up with one of the most serious historical problems that Leninism presents, namely, Lenin's inability to allow the existence, alongside of his own party, of an opposition group that might have checked or prevented the growth of monolithism. Professor Carr has depicted this growth as something that was practically inevitable, but such a view reflects, perhaps, a determinism that is excessively rigid. It is true that the possibility of coexistence between a revolutionary ruling power and a diversified and flexible structure that would enable a legal opposition to the Communist Party to express itself must be subject to very grave difficulties that an historian may confuse with irresistible fatality. But Lenin had shown on a number of occasions that he did not resign himself to any fatalities. If he had realized, between 1918 and 1922, the need for a proletarian democracy to preserve, as an essential constituent, the right of opposition, would he not have striven to overcome even those obstacles that were apparently most refractory? In the last analysis Victor Serge is right when he says that 'if the revolution is to be well served . . . it must be constantly on guard against its own abuses, excesses, crimes and reactionary elements. It therefore has a vital need for criticism, opposition and civic courage on the part of those who carry it out.' Actually, the complete suppression of Menshevism by the Leninist ruling power had *two* victims – Russian social democracy, with its ambivalent nature (bourgeois-democratic in ideology, proletarian in its basis) and also Bolshevism itself, the vitality of which proved unable to resist the ravages of orthodoxy and monolithism.

NOTES TO CHAPTER 7

1. For example, on 8 November 1917, in connection with the powers to be given to the local soviets.
2. A similar development was seen in France in 1968.
3. The Constitutional-Democratic Party was banned on 1 December 1917. Its papers continued to appear, though not without difficulty, until the summer of 1918.
4. At a colloquim held at Cambridge, Mass., on the fiftieth anniversary of the Russian Revolution, two historians, Messrs Fainsod and Geyer, neither of whom has ever shown any tenderness towards the communists, agreed in saying that the Bolsheviks 'ostensibly favoured a coalition of socialist parties and were forced to govern alone only because the other parties refused to cooperate'.
5. As had happened with the Bolshevik press after the 'July days' of 1917, the Menshevik papers were often obliged, in order to continue to appear despite measures banning or suspending them, to change their titles.
6. The communists shot some of their prisoners, even several months after the end of the revolt, and many of the Kronstadt men were sent to detention camps, where they encountered relatives of theirs who had been arrested as hostages.
7. When he heard the sound of the cannonade that heralded the Bolshevik onslaught against Kronstadt, the American anarchist Alexander Berkman, an active supporter of the line of collaboration with the communists, murmured: 'Something has died within me.' That was true not only of him.
8. It should here be noted that, unlike what had happened in June 1918 with the Mensheviks and Right SRs, the Left SRs were not excluded as a party from the soviets in July. Even at that stage a relatively substantial section of them declared for continued cooperation with the Bolsheviks. The Left SRs were also spared by the wave of Red Terror that swept over Moscow in September. However, their political role became quite insignificant.
9. 'At moments when the country is in danger, when Kolchak has reached the Volga and Denikin Orel, there can be no freedoms,' said Lenin in September 1920.

10. In his 'Theses on the Tasks of the Second Congress of the Communist International' Lenin was to mention again the 'perfectly legitimate hatred of the opportunism and reformism of the parties of the Second International' that was found among the anarchists before the First World War.

11. Kropotkin's funeral was the occasion of a great demonstration organized by Moscow's anarchists, some of whom were released from prison for twenty hours so as to be able to attend. Lenin himself is said to have proposed to Kropotkin's family that he be given a national funeral, but they declined. At the funeral Alfred Rosmer delivered a speech, in the name of the Executive Committee of the Third International, in which he avoided all polemical allusions – whereas the anarchist speakers did not miss the opportunity to attack the government. Their addresses were printed and circulated legally, in 40,000 copies. The authorities transformed Kropotkin's house into a museum devoted to his memory.

12. In March 1920 Lenin advised Kamenev how to deal with Martov and Dan, who had been elected to the Moscow Soviet: 'I think you should "wear them out" with *practical* assignments: Dan – *sanitary inspection*, Martov – control over *dining rooms.*'

8. Stalinist Ideology and Science

Michael Löwy

It is impossible to study the relationship between ideology and science in Marxism without referring to the 'Stalinist phenomenon' and, more specifically, to its manifestations in the period between 1948 and 1953. Stalinism is a social and political fact which goes far beyond Josef Vissarionovich Stalin and the 'personality cult': it refers to the formation of a bureaucratic social stratum which originated within the proletariat and/or the Russian labour movement and which congealed into a separate category with its own distinct interests and social practices. In my opinion, this stratum is not so much a class in the Marxist sense of the term (as defined by its position in the process of production) as a social order (*Stand*) or 'estate' (in the sense of the three 'estates' of pre-revolutionary France) defined in terms of politico-ideological criteria. In that sense it is analogous to the order of the clergy in pre-capitalist societies. In both cases – the bureaucratic social order in post-capitalist societies and the clerical order in pre-capitalist societies – membership of a politico-ideological institution (party or church) confers power and privileges: hence the crucial importance of ideological monolithism, hunting out heresies, excommunications and scholastic dogmatism. Stalinist doctrine is the expression of this social stratum's standpoint. As it is not a social class, it is incapable of creating a new social world vision: it simply distorts and misrepresents Marxism, transforming it into an ideology designed to perpetuate the power of an established political and social system and the domination of a privileged social *Stand*. The bureaucracy thus produces a 'vulgar Marxism' analogous to the 'vulgar political economy' of bourgeois thought. In other words it produces a Marxism that is directly subordinated to its own political and social interests. In order to exercise its hegemony the bureaucracy must necessarily present its own standpoint as that of the proletariat itself. This disparity or distortion creates the need for ideological occultation: the bureaucracy must at all costs conceal the discrepancy between its own perspective and that of the proletariat from the proletariat (and sometimes from itself via a process of self-mystification). Although it was born in the USSR, Stalinism also manifests itself as an ideological reflection in the organized communist movement outside the USSR and thus takes on the proportions of a world-wide phenomenon.

Because of its basic characteristics, Stalinism relates to knowledge in a very instrumental way: it tends to turn it into ideology and to abolish its relative autonomy. In the field of social and historical science we need only mention the caricatural example of the *History of the CPSU (B). Short Course* which was constantly rewritten in the light of changes in the party line and the disappearance or retrospective 're-evaluation' of disgraced Bolshevik leaders, etc.

With Stalinism, a new and unprecedented phenomenon appears in Marxism: an attempt to 'ideologize' the natural sciences themselves. It is true that Engels and Lenin ventured into the field of the natural sciences, but (rightly or wrongly, it is irrelevant here) they did so in order to develop philosophical considerations relating to natural facts (their dialectical or materialist character) and not in order to impose ideological norms on research in the natural sciences as such. The idea that the existing natural sciences are 'bourgeois' is quite alien to classic Marxist thought: it is a Stalinist theoretical innovation that might be described as an inverted positivism. Whereas positivism wanted to 'naturalize' the political and social sciences, Stalinism attempts to 'politicize' the natural sciences. Both fail to recognize the specificity of the human sciences and the methodological differences between them and the natural sciences.

The most perfect expression of this Stalinist notion is of course the Lysenko Affair. The facts are well known and we need only refer the reader to the vast literature devoted to the subject from Julian Huxley's early work to more recent studies by the Soviet biologist Zhores Medvedev and the French communist philosopher Dominique Lecourt.[1] We will restrict ourselves to an examination of its 'methodological' aspects, taking the Lysenkoist doctrine of the relationship between science and ideology as an extreme example of a reductionist approach that purports to be based upon Marxism.

The first significant episode in the 'Lysenko Affair' took place in December 1936 when Lysenko's supporters clashed with the majority of the geneticists who worked with Vavilov (the founder of the Lenin Academy of Agricultural Sciences). In this confrontation Lysenko's 'philosophical' *éminence grise* Prezent distinguished himself by accusing the Soviet geneticists of being 'Trotskyist saboteurs fawning on the latest reactionary proposals of foreign scientists'. This denunciation (which is worthy of a *sycophant* in Marx's sense of the term) did not fall upon deaf ears in the period of the great purges: several of the geneticists (Meister, Levit, Gorbanov and Muralov) were arrested in 1938 and Vavilov himself was deported in 1940.[2] This was not, however, a definitive victory for Lysenko and in any case the affair was restricted to the USSR:

it did not take on the proportions of an overall theorization of the sciences and their social status.

Lysenkoism did not become a major issue until 1948 when the Cold War conjuncture of confrontation between the two blocs led to clampdowns and ideological monolithism on both sides: witchhunts in the West and Zhdanovism in the East. By generalizing the ideological confrontation to all spheres of intellectual life – philosophy, literature, art, music, the social and natural sciences – Zhdanov reduced culture to a narrow political battle, dividing everything along 'class' lines: proletarian music and bourgeois music, proletarian biology and so on *ad nauseam*. As early as 1947, Zhdanov bourgeois biology and was denouncing 'Mendelo-Morganism' (that is, modern genetics) as a striking example of how bourgeois science provides fideism and clericalism with new arguments that have to be mercilessly exposed in his famous pamphlet *On Literature, Music and Philosophy*.[3]

Such was the context for the famous session of the USSR Academy of Agricultural Science in July–August 1948, for the complete triumph of Lysenko and his supporters and for the eclipse of Soviet genetics for a long time to come. The decision to impose Lysenkoism as an official 'scientific doctrine' was taken at the highest level of the CPSU: by Stalin himself. If we are to believe Lysenko, Stalin not only inspired 'all branches of the science of society and nature' and 'showed us how to develop the Michurian materialist theory of biology' but also discovered 'several of the most important laws of biology'.[4]

It was, then, in 1948 that Lysenko formulated his doctrine of the two sciences in biology. The simplicity and coherence of his argument are perfect: 'In the present epoch of struggle between two worlds the two opposing and antagonistic trends, penetrating nearly all branches of biology, are particularly sharply defined.' An explicit connection is made between the Cold War (the struggle between two worlds) and its scientific corollary. According to Lysenko, the conflict is between socialist biological science, 'a Soviet biological science founded by Michurin, a science new in principle', and 'the representatives of reactionary biological science – Neo-Darwinians, Weissmanists, or, which is the same, Mendelist-Morganists' who 'uphold the so-called chromosome theory of heredity'.[5]

In his excellent study of Lysenkoism, Dominique Lecourt defines it as the ideology of a stratum of cadres in agricultural production.[6] As a description of the origins of the phenomenon that is probably accurate enough but it is only when it is adopted by the Stalinist state bureaucracy that Lysenkoism takes on its true proportions. As Lysenko never tires of saying, until 1948 his followers 'were in a minority in the Lenin Academy of Agricultural Sciences. But the situation in the Academy has now changed sharply thanks to the interest taken in it by the party, the government and Comrade *Stalin* personally.'[7] In reality (and as Lecourt himself accepts) Lysenkoism becomes a state ideological system from 1948 onwards.[8]

Its relationship with the 'class enemy' (that is, 'bourgeois' genetics and its supporters in the USSR) is not one of scientific debate but one of ideological denunciation. The sycophantic Prezent says so quite explicitly in his memorable intervention during the pseudo-debate at the Academy of Agricultural Sciences in 1948: 'They [the Morganists] want a discussion. But we shall not discuss with the Morganists (*applause*): we shall continue to expose them as adherents of an essentially false scientific trend, a pernicious and ideologically alien trend, brought to our country from foreign shores.'[9] As for the unfortunate geneticists, they had to make a 'Galilean' self-criticism at the end of the debate and abjure their 'pernicious foreign ideology'. They did so by evoking strictly political reasons which had nothing to do with the scientific problems in question. Academician Zhukovsky: 'The speech I made the day before yesterday, at a time when the Central Committee had drawn a dividing line between the two trends in biological science, was unworthy of a member of the Communist Party and of a Soviet scientist.' The geneticist Alikhanian: 'It is important to realize that we must be on this side of the scientific barricades, with our party and with our Soviet science ... When I leave this session the first thing I must do is to review not only my attitude towards the new, Michurian science, but my entire earlier activity.'[10] Biological science has to submit not only to a philosophical doctrine (*diamat*, as formulated by Stalin in the *Short Course*), but also to a political ideology (the Cold War ideology of the two worlds) and even to the conjunctural 'line' established by the Central Committee of the party. The pseudo-Marxist façade of crude sociological reductionism (the class character of trends in biology) masks the way in which science is being completely instrumentalized by a totalitarian bureaucratic apparatus.

It should not be forgotten that the two-sciences 'theory' was extended to other natural sciences. In physics, for example, quantum mechanics is criticized as being 'bourgeois' and even in 1953 N. A. Maximov can write that 'the theory of relativity is manifestly anti-scientific'.[11] Linus Pauling's work on the chemical bond and molecular structure is rejected in favour of the 'dialectical materialist' chemistry of Chelintsev, the would-be Lysenko of chemistry. But it is no accident that this project should 'privilege' biology: of all the natural sciences it is probably the most 'vulnerable' to ideologies in that it is so close to the 'hot' frontier with the human sciences. We need only recall how Darwin's theories continued to provoke ideological polemics (religious, social and political) until the beginning of the twentieth century whereas physics and chemistry were able to develop in a much more 'neutral' and asceptic universe.

In studying the Lysenko Affair it is difficult to avoid comparing the accusations made against the Soviet geneticists with Galileo's fate at the hands of the Inquisition (and several authors, including Medvedev, have made the comparison). In both cases, a dominant social order (*Stand*) integrates a doctrinal interpretation of natural phenomena into its system of ideological hegemony and uses its 'secular arm' to crush any scientific attempt to question that interpretation. The ideologization of the natural sciences is not, however, an absolute necessity for the post-capitalist bureaucratic *Stand*, as it was for the pre-capitalist clerical estate: after 1964 Mendelian genetics was 'rehabilitated' in the USSR and Lysenko was removed from his post as Director of the Institute of Genetics.

The phenomenon of Lysenkoism was not restricted to the USSR: thanks to the communist movement, it spread throughout the world. Of the European countries, France and England were the most deeply involved in the polemic.[12]

In England, at least one communist scientist – J. B. S. Haldane, the celebrated biologist and geneticist – dared to reject the party's new biological doctrine and to proclaim his support for Mendelian genetics. Haldane's attitude was, however, very defensive, as can be seen from the title of his article in The Modern Quarterly, the communist intellectuals' theoretical review: 'In Defence of Genetics'. Haldane does not attack Lysenko's theses directly and goes so far as to concede that 'We have a lot to learn from Soviet geneticists. We must realize that there is a lot of quite unjustifiable idealism and mechanicism in our basic concepts . . . Until I read Lysenko's speeches, I had not recognized the idealistic character of Mendel's formulation of his results.'[13] The important point, however, is that he is not prepared to accept the rejection of the advances of Mendelian genetics in the name of ideological or 'philosophical' arguments. He describes himself as a Darwinian, despite Darwin's social ideas, and adds that 'similarly, I am a Mendelist-Morganist, although Mendel used an idealistic terminology and Morgan wrote of the mechanisms of heredity.'[14]

Unfortunately, this reasoned, independent position is an exception. The most notorious case is that of J. D. Bernal, the eminent scientist and historian of science. In a very important book on the social function of science published in 1939, Bernal soberly recognizes the limitations of Soviet science and notes the absence of any critical attitude in research:

A critical attitude is the fruit of long experience and well-established schools, its absence one of the faults of youthful enthusiasm which only time and experience can correct. A certain part is played here by the long period in which Soviet science was cut off from the rest of the world . . . It is only by the comparison of the work of a very large number of scientists that a fully critical attitude can be developed.[15]

He also stresses that 'It need hardly be said that dialectical materialism is in no sense a substitute for science; it is no royal road to science. Induction and proof remain as they were.'[16] In a footnote he refers to the 1936–8 controversy between Lysenko and the Soviet geneticists (Vavilov), commenting that 'This controversy has been magnified out of all proportion . . . the geneticists were . . . criticized for . . . neglecting cytoplastic and environmental factors, whose importance was probably exaggerated by their critics.'[17]

Astonishingly enough, in 1949 Bernal joins in the Lysenkoist chorus in totally uncritical fashion, using arguments that are diametrically opposed to those put forward in his major work of the thirties:

1. Far from criticizing the break between Soviet science and that of the rest of the world, Bernal now praises the Lysenkoists as 'scientists of the new socialist world' who refuse to assimilate the 'bourgeois science of the capitalist world'.[18]

2. Turning to the 'scientific' role of dialectical materialism, Bernal now explains the controversy between the geneticists and the Lysenkoists in the Academy of Science in terms of a conflict between 'the narrow science of academic specialists and the comprehensive science of dialectical materialism'.[19]

3. Finally, he accuses the genetics he defended against the 'exaggerated criticisms' of the Lysenkoists in 1939 of leading to racism: 'The connection of orthodox genetics with eugenics, with Malthusianism, and with theories of race superiority and ultimately with Nazism are not accidental.'[20] J. D. Bernal concludes his article by asking the Soviet geneticists to square the circle: 'It should be the task of Marxist geneticists to reformulate in those terms the body of experimental facts hitherto associated with orthodox genetics'.[21]

From 1949 onwards a number of communist scientists and intellectuals are mobilized to provide philosophical, political, ideological and empirical justifications for Lysenkoism.[22] In June 1949 a Conference of Marxist Scientists meets in London. In his conference report on 'Dialectical Materialism and Science', the philosopher and epistemologist Maurice Cornforth refers to 'a conflict of two trends of science – the science of the capitalist world and the science of the socialist world'. In a polemical reference which is probably directed against Haldane he attacks the 'revisionist way [which is] uncritically to accept the particular formulations being made by bourgeois scientists and to try to dress them up in a dialectical terminology' and stresses that 'the task of leadership, in the sphere of the sciences, too, devolves upon this [Communist] Party'.[23]

The year 1949 also sees the publication of an important scientific (and political) attack on Lysenkoism in Julian Huxley's *Soviet Genetics and World Science*. D. M. Ross, professor of zoology at University College London and a member of the CPGB, replies with a critical review in *The Modern Quarterly*. According to Ross, Huxley's ideas are, of course, 'typical of the ideological confusion of the bourgeois scientists of our time'. But the most interesting feature of his article is the argument he puts forward for those communist scientists who dare to doubt the validity of Lysenko's 'socialist science' (the target is again Haldane, the black sheep of the family, but presumably the argument also applies to all those who reacted in similar fashion):

> This book ... deserves particularly close study by all those who remain loyal to socialist principles and believe that these principles are being applied in the Soviet Union, and who yet retain reservations about Lysenko's biology. Huxley's book will show such readers that if one rejects Michurian biology because all the facts support Mendelism, one must in consequence believe that the leadership of Soviet Society is entrusted to a group of incompetent, perverted, ignorant, unscrupulous and ambitious men ... It is good that serious socialists should be presented in this way with the implications of accepting any of the usual arguments against Lysenko.[24]

Translated into the language of the sixteenth century, the argument would be roughly as follows: if you believe that the earth revolves around the sun simply because all the facts support that view, you must in consequence believe that the Pope, his Cardinals and the Inquisition are a group of incompetent, ignorant and unscrupulous men. Will the heretic repent when he sees the terrible consequences of his impiety? (Irony apart, there is a very real basis to this analogy: the similarities between the clerical estate and the bureaucratic estate.)

The Modern Quarterly's eminent English zoologist does not seem to realize that his argument is double-edged and might backfire on him: given that the facts show that Lysenko is wrong and that the geneticists are right, it would indeed seem that the leadership of Soviet society is entrusted to a group of men with all the unsavoury characteristics he enumerates. In any case, it would be difficult to find a better illustration of the fact that Lysenkoism is a legitimate child of Stalinism and Zhdanovism, a political and ideological phenomenon that has very little to do with biological science.

But it was in France that Lysenkoism had its greatest influence on communist intellectuals. There were a few exceptions, notably the biologist Marcel Prenant, who went no further than trying to 'reconcile'

Lysenko and genetics, but it was in France that the two-sciences doctrine found its most systematic formulations. The starting point was the publication of a dossier on the famous July–August session of the Academy of Agricultural Sciences in the cultural journal *Europe*. Paradoxically, Aragon's preface to the dossier was entitled 'De la libre discussion des idées' ('On the Free Discussion of Ideas'). While he admits that he is neither a scientist nor a biologist, Aragon has no hesitations about venturing on to the slippery ground of the sociology of the natural sciences:

It is the bourgeois (sociological) nature of science that prevents the creation of a purely scientific biology, that prevents the scientists of the bourgeoisie from making certain discoveries. *For sociological reasons they cannot accept the principles behind those discoveries*. In the USSR, the Michurians and Lysenko cannot regard the bitter struggle being waged against them by the 'national' Mendelists as a *biological*, scientific struggle that concerns biologists alone. They naturally regard it as a sociological (*sic*) struggle waged by scientists who are under the sociological (*sic*) influence of the bourgeoisie . . . as an effect of bourgeois survivals in the USSR.[25]

These themes are developed by various authors in a number of increasingly vehement articles published in the PCF's review *La Nouvelle Critique* between 1948 and 1953. The tone becomes especially vehement in 1949, when the review organized a conference on 'Bourgeois science and proletarian science' and published the proceedings in pamphlet form.

Let us look briefly at the characteristics of the 'two-sciences' doctrine. It represents a reductionist attempt to identify the natural sciences with ideology, an attempt to ideologize scientific discourse. An editorial entitled 'Science, a Historically Relative Ideology' in *La Nouvelle Critique* states explicitly that

Science is a social product . . . Science is therefore a historically relative ideology. There is at the moment a conflict between two practices: bourgeois practice . . . and proletarian (socialist) practice. These two practices define two fundamentally contradictory sciences: bourgeois science and proletarian science. Michurin's discoveries and Lysenko's work are products of proletarian science. Taking a proletarian stance in science and adopting the criteria of proletarian science are preconditions for objectivity in scientific debate.[26]

In this context scientific activity obviously loses all its autonomy and is immediately reduced to its supposed 'class' basis. Some of *La Nouvelle Critique*'s polemicists, such as Gérard Vassails, do seem to accept that there is a certain continuity between bourgeois and Soviet science at the level of the mathematical and physical sciences in so far as 'facts, laws and tested mathematical theories can move intact from one to the other'. But this aspect is immediately dismissed as secondary: the main point is not

the continuity but the radical novelty of the proletarian natural sciences
and their infinite superiority. And in order to avoid any possible confusion between Soviet physics and capitalist physics, which can look
deceptively similar, Vassails adds this stirring metaphor:

The vast superiority of proletarian science is not apparent to those who
concentrate on the part rather than the whole, on the current state of things and
not their movement. Such people ignore the warnings given them by Michurian
biology and conclude that there is no basic difference between the physical and
mathematical sciences in the USSR and in the capitalist countries. They make the
same mistake as those who identify sunrise with sunset: the light may well be
equally strong, but sunset brings darkness and sunrise brings daylight.[27]

For similar reasons, the distinction between the natural sciences and
the social sciences disappears: they are all ideologized under the aegis
of the same tutelary institution, namely the Soviet state and party.
Thus, according to the party's representative at La Nouvelle Critique's
conference,

In a country where man has at last become master of his own destiny . . . the
bourgeois distinction between natural and human sciences is meaningless. In the
Soviet Union, all the sciences are coordinated and harmonized by the unity of the
political principle which is guiding the Soviet Union in its march towards
communism. The intervention of the Bolshevik Party into any science is the
unmistakable sign of the unity of human knowledge.[28]

Auguste Comte's dream of a unified science which abolishes all
differences between nature and society is coming true, albeit in what
might be termed an inverted fashion (because it is subject to ideological
imperatives).

The doctrine of the two sciences is further characterized by its use of an
appeal to authority to close the debate: Roma locuta, causa finita. The
ultimate authority is of course Stalin himself. Lysenko never tires of
stressing his theoretical and scientific debt to the Secretary General. On
15 December 1949 he writes in Izvestia that the discoveries made by
Soviet biologists would have been impossible without 'Stalin's teaching
about gradual, concealed, unnoticeable qualitative changes leading to a
rapid radical change'. Francis Cohen cites this passage from Lysenko in
an article in La Nouvelle Critique in 1950 and analyses it from the
standpoint of the two-sciences doctrine: 'This quotation calls for a few
comments . . . firstly, it shows us the process whereby proletarian science
is elaborated . . . it is based upon experimentation and then interpretation in the light of Marxist-Leninist theory and specifically Chapter IV
of the History of the CPSU (B).'[29] The Short Course – and especially
Chapter 4 on diamat, which was written by Stalin himself – is absolutely
central to the Soviet epistemology of science. It is a sort of summa

theologica which not only inspires the historical and social sciences but also becomes a source of discoveries in the natural sciences. Francis Cohen's answer to those who, like Marcel Prenant, dare to question the pertinence of Stalin's writings for biological science and reject the appeal to authority, is 'For a communist, and for the reasons that Desanti has expounded, *Stalin is the highest scientific authority in the world.*' Which sheds an interesting light on the appeal to authority!

Doubting a statement made in such circumstances means doubting the obvious efficacy, correctness and unity of Stalinism. It means assimilating a proletarian scientist who is committed to the building of communism to an irresponsible bourgeois scientist who is working in isolation without any theory to guide him.

This remarkable and paradigmatic article ends with the following statement, which provides a wonderful illustration of how Stalinism conflates ideological struggle and scientific debate in the natural sciences:

There can no more be compromises in scientific matters than there can be compromises in the trade union struggle or in the struggle for peace. The struggle of the working class goes on in laboratories too. In every domain, the road to victory has been shown by the one country where the working class is in power, by its Bolshevik Party and by Josef Stalin, the workers' guide and *the greatest scientist of our time.*[30]

The final corollary of this conception of the natural sciences is the impossibility of dialogue: there is no point in entering into a scientific debate with the representatives of bourgeois science. In 1953 Francis Cohen attacks those who insist on the need for open debate:

It might be objected that there can be no truly open debate if the Morganists cannot defend their point of view . . . But if we allow them to go on developing their reactionary scientific theories indefinitely aren't we simply putting a brake on the development of science? After twenty years of discussion, the reactionary and non-scientific character of the Mendelo-Morganist *theories* has been demonstrated both theoretically and experimentally. It has also been demonstrated that any scientist worthy of the name who really wants progress to be made in science must adopt the ideological standpoint of Marxism-Leninism, 'the science of the laws of the development of nature and society' (Stalin). Soviet scientists cannot tolerate the intervention of conceptions which contradict the dialectical reality of nature. One such conception is that of the non-influence of environment on heredity, an absurdity which is also the basis for formal genetics. It would be an abuse of the word freedom to allow such restrictive dogmas into the debate.[31]

In some articles the attack on bourgeois science is extended to all its traditional methods, including the experimental method itself. Thus, according to Francis Cohen, 'Bourgeois science has become an obstacle to progress. Its methods have become ossified and sclerotic. They were once progressive, but they are now obsolete and reactionary. We are forced to conclude that the classical experimental method is unable to solve the new problems facing science.'[32] This is, however, an extreme position, and one which is not necessarily shared by all supporters of the two-sciences doctrine.

The pseudo-sociologism of the formula of 'class' science ('bourgeois' and 'proletarian' science) in fact masks something else: it is not so much a question of finding a significant link between social classes and scientific production as of linking science with a *state* or *bloc of states*: the USA and Western Europe versus the USSR. It is not so much a matter of 'class' science as of *state* science: the sociological reductionism is merely a cover for an overtly politic-ideological operation which is connected with the inter-state confrontations of the Cold War.

But why should this doctrine have been so successful in France? Why should France have provided its most systematic theoretical developments? Quite apart from the privileged links between French communism and the USSR and the party's considerable intellectual influence, one further factor deserves mention: the weight of the positivist tradition in French academic circles (this also applies to England). Not even communist intellectuals escape that tradition completely. Take the example of a party publication on Marx and Comte (1937). The main criticism addressed to Comte by the author (Lucy Prenant) is that his positivism is inconsistent: 'To a certain extent, Comte betrayed all that was best in his doctrine and other positivists have been more consistent.'[33] According to Lucy Prenant, Marx and Comte are in agreement as to one important point: 'For both Marx and Comte, the sciences can only be synthesized by an explanation of history, and that explanation must in its turn lead to political action: applied history.' She also thinks that in some senses Comte comes 'very close to the concept of dialectics'. For example, 'he constantly tries to combine dynamics and statics. The very slogan of positivism – "Order and Progress" – represents a synthesis which transcends the antagonism between obsolete and progressive.'[34] Paradoxically, it is this positivist side to the ideology of the French labour movement that makes it so 'vulnerable' to the *inverted positivism* of Lysenkoism: both ideologies are on common ground in that they postulate that there are no fundamental methodological frontiers between the social and historical sciences on the one hand and the social sciences on the other. This also explains why the reaction against Lysenkoism and the two-sciences doctrine is itself coloured by positivism. This is especially true of Althusser's line of argument.

The fact remains that, despite the ideological delirium that surrounded the two-sciences doctrine in France and England, a real problem was being raised by communist scientists and intellectuals: the problem of the social and political conditions which determine the orientation of scientific research and the application of its results. They were quite right not to concentrate on scientific research in the abstract and to denounce its subordination to the profit motive in capitalist countries and its use for warlike ends. Their mistake – which was taken to absurd lengths and which became an extreme form of ideological obscurantism – was to extend such considerations to the *content* of the natural sciences, as though the discoveries of atomic physics were somehow invalidated by the murderous use made of them at Hiroshima or by the FBI's control over American laboratories. By applying the same ritual and incantatory condemnation to two radically distinct spheres, they turned the doctrine of the two natural sciences into a grotesque caricature of Marxist sociology of knowledge which could serve the interests of the Stalinist bureaucracy alone.

It is in reaction against the ideological delirium of the fifties that Louis Aragon elaborated his conception of science and of Marxism as science in the sixties – once he had got over what he calls the 'shock' of the 20th Congress. His 'self-criticism', made somewhat late in the day in the preface to *For Marx* (1965), is not directed against Lysenkoism alone (and as an intellectual militant of the PCF he considers himself partly responsible for Lysenkoism): it questions the very possibility of establishing a link between science and the class struggle:

In our philosophical memory [this time] remains the period of intellectuals in arms . . . slicing up the world, arts, literatures, philosophies, sciences with the pitiless demarcation of class – the period summed up in caricature by a single phrase, a banner flapping in the void: 'bourgeois science, proletarian science'. To defend Marxism, imperilled as it was by Lysenko's 'biology', from the fury of bourgeois spite, some leaders had relaunched this old 'Left-wing' formula, once the slogan of Bogdanov and the Proletkult. Once proclaimed, it dominated everything . . . we had been made to treat science, a status claimed by every page of Marx, as merely the first-comer among ideologies.[35]

But does this critique imply a break with Stalinism? Paradoxically, the starting point for Althusser's argument is in fact Stalin, who, despite 'his implacable system of government', did have the merit of 'reducing the madness to a little more reason'; thanks to 'the few simple pages in which he reproached the zeal of those who were making strenuous efforts to prove language a superstructure, we could see that there were limits to the use of the class criterion'.[36] Stalin can thus to some extent be absolved of having fathered the two-sciences doctrine, which is generously ascribed to the theoretical leftists of the 'historicist-humanist interpretation of Marxism' who

proclaimed a radical return to Marx (the young Lukács and Korsch) and worked out a theory which put Marx's doctrine into a directly expressive relationship with the working class. From this period, too, dates the famous opposition between 'bourgeois science' and 'proletarian science', in which triumphed an idealist and voluntarist interpretation of Marxism as the exclusive product and expression of proletarian practice.[37]

Althusser's 1965 position is in fact a symmetrical inversion of the PCF's line in 1948–53. They share the same basic error: a failure to recognize the relative but essential difference between history and nature, between social and natural science, a difference which explains why there can be neither a 'proletarian' genetics nor a 'purely scientific' history of the 1917 Revolution (in other words a history with no partisan presuppositions). We have defined Lysenkoism as an 'inverted positivism': when it is mechanically inverted it logically enough produces the neo-positivism of Althusser. Althusser makes no secret of his admiration of Auguste Comte, 'the only mind worthy of interest'[38] produced by French philosophy in 'the 130 years following the revolution of 1789', and for Durkheim who, along with Comte, is 'one of the few great minds' that French philosophy can 'salvage from its own history'.[39]

The positivist dimension of Althusserian Marxism can be seen quite clearly in the concept of the 'epistemological break' (which is borrowed from Gaston Bachelard's work on the constitution of the natural sciences). According to Althusser, Marx inaugurated a new science, the science of history, by making an epistemological break with ideology, as represented by bourgeois political economy (as we have seen, this does not correspond with Marx's own conception of his relationship with his predecessors). Given that he denies the existence of any epistemological link between Marxist science and the proletariat, Althusser has to present the split between Marx and his predecessors as a purely intellectual phenomenon to be ascribed to Marx's genius alone.[40]

Because he ignores the socially conditioned character of the social sciences Althusser makes no methodological distinction between natural and historical science. He can therefore constantly compare Marx with Lavoisier by stressing the similarity – or better still, the *epistemological identity* – between their discoveries: 'In order to understand Marx *we must treat him as one scientist among others* and apply to his scientific work *the same epistemological and historical concepts* we would apply to others: in this case to Lavoisier. Marx thus appears as the founder of a science, comparable with Galileo or Lavoisier.'[41] But how can the author of the Eleventh Thesis on Feuerbach ('The philosophers have only *interpreted* the world in various ways; the point, however, is to *change* it') be treated as one scientist among others?

Althusser does sometimes seem to realize that there is a problem here: '"economic science" is especially exposed to the pressures of ideology: the sciences of society do not have the serenity of the mathematical sciences. As Hobbes put it, geometry unites men, social science divides them. "Economic science" is the arena and the prize of history's great political battles'.[42] A closer reading of the text suggests, however, that for Althusser the 'pressures of ideology' only affect bourgeois economists: Marx represents a science which is free from pressure and which is serene (like geometry perhaps?) and simply restates 'in a new domain [history] the requirements which have long been imposed on the practices of those sciences which have achieved autonomy', namely the natural sciences. Which brings us back to neo-positivism.

Althusser is obviously right to stress the specificity of scientific practice (in the knowledge of history) and its autonomy from the social structure and historical conditions. But he makes the mistake of making its autonomy absolute by transforming it into independence, separation . . . Such is the implication of his criticisms of Gramsci and his Italian disciples who 'define as historical the conditions for all knowledge concerning a historical object'.[43] For Althusser, a science (be it natural or social) has its own history and is totally independent of social and political history: it is not affected by the class struggle and it is not part of 'the historical bloc'.[44] The history of economic science is, in his eyes, analogous with that of the science of chemistry: its status as a scientific discipline results from a brilliant discovery which establishes an epistemological break between science and ideology and which has nothing to do with any given social class and its world vision. Althusser does not seem to suspect that the link between Marxism and the revolutionary proletariat might not be quite the same as that between Lavoisier and the revolutionary bourgeoisie of 1789. The point is not that the bourgeoisie guillotined the famous scientist but that there was no epistemological link between the discovery of oxygen and the struggles and aspirations of the Third Estate. Althusser's work, like that of the positivist-Marxists of the Second International, is a classic example of faulty reasoning.

To sum up: Althusser recognizes only two possibilities:

1. Social science as a practice independent of social struggle and free of any class connection (a thesis he defends).

2. Social science as the immediate, exclusive expression of a social class: in the case of Marxism, the proletariat (a thesis which he wrongly attributes to the theoretical leftists).

He seems unaware of the fact that there is a third variant, which in my view is the only way to account for the reality of the process of socio-scientific knowledge: the science of history (or society) is necessarily located within a class standpoint, but in its own sphere of activity it is relatively autonomous (I will return to this point in the conclusion).

Althusser's 1965 position is still Stalinist in that he identifies the standpoint of the proletariat with that of the party apparatus. His legitimate desire to preserve the independence and dignity of science from the changing political imperatives of that apparatus takes the form of a refusal to admit that there is any link between Marxist science and a class standpoint. The acceptance of the Stalinist 'party spirit' in 1949–53 and the refusal to relate Marxist theory to the proletariat in 1965 derive from the same error: the proletarian standpoint is confused with a bureaucratic caricature of that standpoint.

In so far as that identification has been shaken – probably by the events of May 1968 – Althusser has to some extent been able to go beyond the quasi-positivist (or neo-Stalinist) conceptions of 1965. In a text on the Young Marx, for instance (written in 1970 and subsequently published in *Essays in Self-Criticism*), he accepts that 'it is therefore necessary to abandon the theoretical position of the ruling class, and take up a position from within which these mechanisms [of exploitation and domination] become visible: the proletarian standpoint.'[45] It is only in 1976 that he begins to make a serious attack on Stalinism in his introduction to Dominique Lecourt's *Proletarian Science?* and it is only in 1978 that he begins to question the bureaucratic workings of the party in *What must change in the Party*.[46]

NOTES TO CHAPTER 8

1. Julian Huxley, *Soviet Genetics and World Science: Lysenko and the Meaning of Heredity*, London, 1949; Zhores Medvedev, *The Rise and Fall of T. D. Lysenko*, New York, 1969; Dominique Lecourt, *Lysenko, Histoire réelle d'une science prolétarienne*, Paris, 1976; tr. *Proletarian Science? The Case of Lysenko*, London, 1977.
2. Lecourt, op. cit., p. 63; tr. p. 49.
3. London, 1950.
4. Article in *Pravda*, 8 March 1953.
5. *The Situation in Biological Science: Proceedings of the Lenin Academy of Agricultural Sciences of the USSR Session: 31 July–7 August 1948*, Verbatim Report, Moscow, 1949, pp. 18–19.
6. Lecourt, op. cit., p. 99; tr. p. 76.
7. *The Situation*, op. cit., p. 30.
8. Lecourt, op. cit., p. 160; tr. p. 122.
9. *The Situation*, op. cit., pp. 602–3.
10. *The Situation*, op. cit., pp. 618, 620, 621.
11. *Voprossy Filosofi*, no. 3, 1948.
12. Lecourt, op. cit., pp. 151–2; tr. p. 115.
13. J. B. S. Haldane, 'In Defence of Genetics', *The Modern Quarterly*, vol. IV, no. 3, Summer 1949, pp. 201, 195.

14. ibid., p. 198.
15. J. D. Bernal, *The Social Function of Science*, London, 1944, p. 230 (first edition, London, 1939).
16. ibid., p. 231.
17. ibid., p. 237.
18. J. D. Bernal, *The Modern Quarterly*, vol. IV, no. 3, Summer 1949, pp. 211–13.
19. ibid., p. 209.
20. ibid., p. 217.
21. ibid., p. 217.
22. Cf. the articles by J. L. Fyfe, P. W. Brian, J. Kennedy and C. McLeod in *The Modern Quarterly*, and the joint statement made by I. Campbell, A. McPherson, A. Suddaby and P. Trent on 'The Value of Marxism to the Modern Natural Scientist'.
23. Maurice Cornforth, *Dialectical Materialism and Science*, London, 1949, pp. 19, 22.
24. *The Modern Quarterly*, vol. V, no. 4, Autumn 1950, p. 376.
25. Louis Aragon, 'De la libre discussion des idées', *Europe*, October 1948, no. 33–4, p. 26.
26. *La Nouvelle Critique*, no. 15, April 1950, p. 48.
27. Gérard Vassails, 'Atome et politique' in *Science bourgeoise et science prolétarienne*, Paris, 1950, pp. 30, 33.
28. Raymond Guyot, 'Conclusions', *Science bourgeoise et science prolétarienne*, p. 46.
29. Francis Cohen, 'Mendel, Lyssenko et le rôle de la science', *La Nouvelle Critique*, no. 13, February 1950, p. 61.
30. ibid., pp. 62, 70. The article on 'Staline, savant d'un type nouveau' by J. T. Desanti was published in *La Nouvelle Critique*, no. 11, December 1949. It includes the following subheadings: 'La science stalinienne, science universelle', 'La science stalinienne, science rigoureuse'. Desanti was a member of the PCF at this time and made a further contribution to the argument by authority in another essay entitled 'La science, idéologie historiquement relative': 'Proletarian statesmen and the leaders of Communist Parties can and must intervene in science. Because of their function and their historical role they are in possession of a science without which they would not be statesmen. It is in the name of that science that they make their interventions . . . The boost given to Michurian science is an excellent example' (*Science bourgeoise et science prolétarienne*, p. 9). J. T. Desanti has commented on his past in an afterword to Dominique Desanti's *Les Staliniens*, Paris, 1975
31. Francis Cohen, 'La Biologie soviétique et nos tâches scientifiques', *La Nouvelle Critique*, no. 44, March 1953, p. 119.
32. Francis Cohen, 'Génétique classique et science mitchourinienne', *Science bourgeoise et science prolétarienne*, pp. 38, 39.
33. Lucy Prenant, agrégée de l'université, 'Karl Marx et Auguste Comte', *À la lumière du marxisme*, vol. 2, *Karl Marx et la pensée moderne*, Paris, 1937, Part 1, p. 37.
34. Prenant, op. cit., pp. 65, 66.

35. Louis Althusser, *Pour Marx*, Paris, 1965, p. 12; tr. *For Marx*, London, 1969, p. 22.
36. Althusser, op. cit., p. 12; tr. p. 22.
37. Louis Althusser, *Lire le Capital*, Paris, 1965, vol. 1, p. 104; tr. *Reading Capital*, London, 1970, p. 140.
38. Althusser, *Pour Marx*, p. 16; tr. p. 25.
39. Louis Althusser, *Lénine et la philosophie*, Paris, 1970, p. 13; tr. 'Lenin and Philosophy', *Lenin and Philosophy and Other Essays*, London, 1971, p. 33. As we saw in Chapter 5, Lukács never claimed that Marxism was the 'direct expression' or 'exclusive product' of proletarian practice. On the contrary, he claimed it was a standpoint which corresponded rationally to the historical interests of the proletariat.
40. Cf. Norman Geras, 'Althusserian Marxism: An Exposition and Assessment', *New Left Review*, 71, February–March 1972.
41. Althusser, *Lire le Capital*, vol. 2, p. 119; tr., p. 153.
42. Althusser, *Lire le Capital*, vol. 2, tr., p. 185.
43. Althusser, *Lire le Capital* vol. 2, p. 77; tr., p. 122.
44. Althusser, *Lire le Capital* vol. 2, p. 93; tr., p. 133.
45. Louis Althusser, *Éléments d'autocritique*, Paris, 1976; tr. *Essays in Self-Criticism*, London, 1976, p. 161.
46. *New Left Review*, 109, May–June 1978.

Part 2

Stalinism in Crisis

9. The Trotskyists in Vorkuta Prison Camp[1]

'M.B.'

During the middle and at the end of the 1930s, the Trotskyists formed a quite disparate group at Vorkuta; one part of them kept its old name of 'Bolshevik-Leninists'. There were almost 500 at the mine, close to 1,000 at the camp of Oukhto-Petchora, and certainly several thousand altogether around the Petchora district.

The orthodox Trotskyists were determined to remain faithful to the end to their platform and their leaders. In 1927, following the resolutions of the 15th Congress of the party, they were excluded from the Communist Party and, at the same time, arrested. From then on, even though they were in prison, they continued to consider themselves communists; as for Stalin and his supporters, 'the apparatus men', they were characterized as renegades from communism.

Among these 'Trotskyists' were also found people who had never formally belonged to the CP and did not join the Left Opposition, but who tied their own fate with it to the very end – even when the struggle of the Opposition was most acute.

In addition to these genuine Trotskyists, there were in the camps of Vorkuta and elsewhere more than 100,000 prisoners who, members of the party and the youth, had adhered to the Trotskyist Opposition and then at different times and for diverse reasons (of which the principal were, evidently, the repressions, unemployment, persecutions, exclusion from schools and university faculties, etc.) were forced to 'recant their errors' and withdraw from the Opposition.

The orthodox Trotskyists arrived at the mine during the summer of 1936 and lived in a compact mass in two large barracks. They categorically refused to work in the pits; they worked only on the surface, and for only eight hours, not the ten or twelve required by the regulations as the other prisoners were forced to do. They did so on their own authority, in an organized manner, openly flouting the camp regulations. In the main they had already served nearly ten years in deportation.

In the beginning, they were sent into political isolators and then afterwards exiled to Solovka; finally, they arrived at Vorkuta. The Trotskyists formed the only group of political prisoners who openly criticized the Stalinist 'general line' and offered organized resistance to the jailers.

The different groups
Nevertheless, there were significant divergences within this group. Some considered themselves disciples of Timothy Sapronov (ex-secretary of the Supreme Soviet) and insisted on being called 'Sapronovists' or 'democratic-centralists'. They claimed to be more to the left than the Trotskyists and thought that the Stalinist dictatorship had already reached the stage of bourgeois degeneration by the end of the 1920s, and that the *rapprochement* of Hitler and Stalin was very probable. Nevertheless, in the event of war, the 'Sapronovists' declared themselves for the defence of the USSR.

Among the 'Trotskyists' were also found partisans of the 'Right Wing', that is to say of Rykov and of Bukharin, as well as followers of Shliapnikov and of his 'Workers' Opposition' platform.

But the great majority of the group was made up of authentic Trotskyists, supporters of L. D. Trotsky. They openly defended the so-called Clemenceau thesis: 'the enemy is in our country. It is first necessary to get rid of the reactionary government of Stalin and only after that to organize the defence of the country against the external enemies.'[2]

In spite of their differences, all of these groups at the mine lived in a friendly enough fashion under one common denominator, 'the Trotskyists'. Their leaders were Socrate Guevorkian, Vladimir Ivanov, Melnais, V. V. Kossior and Trotsky's ex-secretary, Posnansky.

Portraits of leaders
Guevorkian was a calm man, very balanced, reasonable, full of good sense. He spoke without hurry, weighing his words, without any affectation or theatrical gestures. Up to the time of his arrest, he had worked as an expert for the Russian Association of the Centres of Scientific Research of the Institute of Human Sciences. He was an Armenian, and, at this time, was at least forty. His younger brother was imprisoned with him.

Melnais, a Lett, was a little younger than Guevorkian. After having been a member of the Central Committee of the Young Communists, he studied at the Faculty of Physics and Mathematics of the University of Moscow, where, in 1925–7, he headed a very important group (several hundred people) of Opposition students. At University meetings, when Melnais intervened, the Stalinists stirred up a storm of hues and cries, preventing him from speaking. But obstinately, doggedly, Melnais waited; when the howlers were out of breath, exhausted and silent, the chairman of the meeting rang the bell and told him, 'Your time is up!'

Melnais replied, 'Excuse me, that was your time. You have conducted yourselves like devils and you have screamed; I have been silent. Now, it is my turn to speak.' He then spoke to the audience.

At the end of 1927, Melnais was one of the first members of the Opposition at the University to be arrested. His arrest provoked an explosion of indignation among the students. The revolting details of the arrest were repeated in the corridors and classrooms of the University. Melnais was married and lived in a private apartment. His wife, also a student, was pregnant. During the night, her labour pains started. Having phoned for an ambulance, Melnais nervously paced to and fro in the apartment, waiting for the doctor. Hearing the doorbell ring, he eagerly opened the door and let in three people dressed in civilian clothes. 'This way please, my wife is really in pain,' he said, showing the way.

'Just one minute!' one of the men stopped him. 'For a moment we are not interested in your wife, but in you,' and he showed him a warrant for his arrest. The doctor and ambulance men arrived very soon; Melnais' wife was taken to the hospital . . . and he to the Lubianka prison.

Melnais had been imprisoned ever since. In political isolators and in exile, he spent a lot of time working on economic problems and soon turned out to be an eminent and talented economist.

Vladimir Ivanov was a hearty man, with the round and full face of a successful merchant, with a big black moustache and intelligent grey eyes. In spite of his fifty years, one sensed in him a strong will and the strength of a bear. An old Bolshevik and member of the Central Committee, Ivanov, until his arrest, directed the Eastern Chinese railroad. He, as well as his wife, had belonged to the 'Democratic Centralist' group and were among the supporters of Sopranov. When the 15th Congress decided that belonging to the Opposition and to the party was incompatible, Ivanov quit the ranks of the Opposition, but this did not save him; he was arrested after the assassination of Kirov.

Camp 'trial'

At the camp, he was in charge of the narrow railroad that linked the mine of Vorkuta to the Oussa River. In 1936, following directives from headquarters, the NKVD of the camp concocted a charge accusing Ivanov of sabotage of this laughing-stock of a railroad, sixty kilometres long. A special jury of the high tribunal of the Autonomous Soviet Republic of Komis came to the camp. In secret session, after having read the indictment, they said to Ivanov: 'What can you say to justify yourself?'

'You have your orders,' he replied. 'You are assigned to carry out all the necessary formalities and to cowardly enforce them with the death penalty. You are forced to do this. You know as well as I that these accusations are manufactured from whole cloth, and have been prepared by compliant Stalinist police functionaries. So, don't complicate your job; do your business. As for me, I refuse to participate in your juridical comedy.' Then he said, pointing a finger at three false witnesses taken from among the common criminals: 'Why don't you ask them? In return for a package of *makhorka* they will not only tell you that I am a saboteur, but also a parent of the Mikado.'

The tribunal could get no more out of him; they could only interrogate the hand-picked 'witnesses'. The examination at the hearing was cut short. On the other hand, the deliberation of the jury lasted a very long time. First a telephone call, then a long wait for the answer, and finally, the sentence was pronounced: 'Deserves the highest penalty; but taking into account this ... and that ... sentence is commuted to ten years' imprisonment at hard labour.' And with shifting eyes, not daring to look at Ivanov, the members of the jury quickly collected their papers and departed trembling. The false witnesses approached Ivanov, seeking to justify themselves. 'Get out of my way, you dirty swine!' he roared, and returned to his barracks.

Kossior was a middle-aged man, very short (almost a dwarf), with a large head. Before his arrest, he occupied a leading post in the management of the Petroleum industry. His brother, Stanislas Kossior, then sat on the Politburo, and, at the same time, was secretary of the Central Committee of the Ukrainian Communist Party. (He was later liquidated by Stalin. His case was mentioned by Khrushchev in his report to the 20th Congress.) In the camp, V. V. Kossior worked in the boiler room, carrying coal in a wheelbarrow to keep the boiler going. Also at the camp were both his wives, the first, a Ukrainian from whom he was divorced, and the second, a Russian whom he had married in exile.

Posnansky, a handsome, well-built man about thirty-five to thirty-eight years old, was deeply interested in music and chess. Trotsky's second secretary, Grigoriev, was also at Petchora.

Trotskyists confer
In the autumn of 1936, soon after the frame-up trials against the leaders of the Opposition, Zinoviev, Kamenev and the others, the entire group of 'orthodox' Trotskyists at the mine got together to confer with one another.

Opening the meeting, Guevorkian addressed those present: 'Comrades! Before beginning our meeting, I ask you to honour the memory of our comrades, guides and leaders who have died as martyrs at the hands of the Stalinist traitors of the revolution.'

The entire assembly stood up. Then, in a brief and very trenchant speech, Guevorkian explained that it was necessary to examine and resolve the key problem: what should be done and how should they conduct themselves from now on?

It is now evident that the group of Stalinist adventurers have completed their counter-revolutionary *coup d'état* in our country. All the progressive conquests of our revolution are in mortal danger. Not twilight shadows, but those of deep black night envelop our country. No Cavaignac spilled as much working class blood as has Stalin. Physically annihilating all the opposition groups within the party, he aims at total personal dictatorship. The party and the whole people are subjected to surveillance and to summary justice by the police apparatus. The predictions and the direst fears of our opposition are fully confirmed. The nation slides irresistibly into the thermidorian swamp. This is the triumph of the centrist petty-bourgeois forces, of which Stalin is the interpreter, the spokesman, and the apostle. No compromise is possible with the Stalinist traitors and hangmen of the revolution. Remaining proletarian revolutionaries to the very end, we should not entertain any illusion about the fate awaiting us. But before destroying us, Stalin will try to humiliate us as much as he can. By throwing political prisoners in with common criminals, he strives to scatter us among the criminals and to incite them against us. We are left with only one means of struggle in this unequal battle: the hunger strike. With a group of comrades, we have already drawn up a list of our demands of which many of you are already informed. Therefore, I now propose to you that we discuss them together and make a decision.

The demands

The meeting lasted only a short time; the question of the hunger strike and of concrete demands had already been debated for some months by the Trotskyists. Some Trotskyist groups in other camps (Oussa station, Tchibiou, Kotchmess, etc.) had also been discussing the matter and had sent their agreement to support the demands and to participate in the hunger strike. These demands were ratified unanimously by those present. They stipulated:

1. Abrogation of the illegal decision of the NKVD, concerning the transfer of all Trotskyists from administrative camps to concentration camps. Affairs relating to political opposition to the regime must not be judged by special NKVD tribunals, but in public juridical assemblies.

2. The work day in the camp must not exceed eight hours.

3. The food quota of the prisoners should not depend on their norm of output. A cash bonus, not the food ration, should be used as a production incentive.

4. Separation, at work as well as in the barracks, of political prisoners and common criminals.

5. The old, the ill and women political prisoners should be moved from

the polar camps to camps where the climatic conditions were more favourable.

It was recommended, at the time of the meeting, that the sick, the invalids, the old should not participate in the hunger strike; however, all those in question energetically rejected this proposal.

The meeting did not decide the day on which the hunger strike should begin; a five member directorate, headed by Guevorkian, was delegated to inform the other Trotskyist groups spread over the immense territory containing the camps of Oukhto-Petchora.

Three weeks later, 27 October 1936, the massive hunger strike of the political prisoners began, a strike without precedent and a model under Soviet camp conditions. In the morning, at reveille, in almost every barrack, prisoners announced themselves on strike. The barracks occupied by the Trotskyists participated 100 per cent in the movement. Even the orderlies struck. Close to 1,000 prisoners, of whom half worked in the mine, participated in this tragedy, which lasted more than four months.

The first two days, the strikers stayed in their usual places. Then the camp administration busied itself in isolating them from the rest of the prisoners, concerned lest the latter followed their example. In the tundra, forty kilometres from the mine, on the banks of the Syr-Iaga River, there were primitive half-demolished barracks, which previously had been used during the preliminary boring of the mines. In great haste, these barracks were put into makeshift condition; a call was sent out to the inhabitants of the region, who, with their teams of reindeer, transported the hunger strikers there, where they soon numbered about 600. The others were brought together not far from Tchibiou.

After having isolated the strikers, the GPU took measures to prevent the movement from spreading in the country and from becoming known outside the frontiers. The prisoners were deprived of the right of corresponding with their families; the salaried employees of the camp lost their holidays and their right to leave. Attempts were made to incite the other prisoners against the strikers. At the mine there were food reserves beyond what was required to sustain those who worked in the pits; the camp administration contended that it had to use up its large reserves of fat and sugar, intended for the underground workers, for artificial feeding of the Trotskyists.

At the end of the first month of the strike, one of the participants died of exhaustion; two others died during the third month. The same month, two strikers, non-orthodox Trotskyists, voluntarily gave up striking. Finally, just a few days before the end of the strike, still another striker died.

The strike is won

Having begun at the end of October 1936, the hunger strike lasted 132 days, ending in March 1937. It culminated with the complete victory of the strikers who received a radiogram from the headquarters of the NKVD, drawn up in these words: 'Inform the hunger strikers held in the Vorkuta mines that all their demands will be satisfied.'

The Trotskyists were then taken back to the mine, received food reserved for the sick and, after a period of time, they went back to work, but only above ground; certain of them worked in the office of the director of the mine, in the capacity of paid workers, book-keepers, economists, etc. Their work day did not exceed eight hours; their food ration was not based on their production norm.

New arrivals

But little by little the other prisoners' interest in the strikers began to diminish. Everyone's interest was now focused on the new trial at Moscow, which was being broadcast by radio; besides, new prisoners began arriving at the end of June. Their stories described mass arrests, outrages, executions without trial behind the walls of the NKVD, and this all over the country. At the beginning, no one wanted to believe this, particularly since the new arrivals spoke unwillingly and rather enigmatically. But little by little, the bonds between them became tighter and the conversations franker. Without letup, new prisoners arrived from Russia; old friends and acquaintances discovered each other: it no longer was possible not to believe the stories.

In spite of these obvious facts, a certain number of prisoners waited with impatience for the autumn of 1937 and the twentieth anniversary of the October Revolution; they hoped, on this occasion as in 1927, that the government would declare a large-scale amnesty, particularly since a little while earlier the very promising 'Stalinist Constitution' had been adopted. But the autumn brought bitter disillusions.

Brutal repressions

The harsh regime of the camps grew abruptly worse. The sergeants and their assistants in maintaining order – common criminals – having received new orders from the camp director, armed themselves with clubs and pitilessly beat the prisoners. The guards, the watchmen close to the barracks, tormented the prisoners. To amuse themselves during the night they fired on those who went to the toilets. Or else, giving the order, 'On your bellies', they forced the prisoners to stretch out, naked, for hours on the snow. Soon there were massive arrests. Almost every night, GPU agents appeared in the barracks, called out certain names and led away those called.

Certain Trotskyists, including Vladimir Ivanov, Kossior and Trotsky's son, Serge Sedov, a modest and likeable youth, who had imprudently refused to follow his parents into exile in 1928, were taken in a special convoy to Moscow. We can only believe that Stalin was not satisfied simply to hurl them into the tundra; his sadistic nature thirsted not only for blood; he wished first to immeasurably humiliate them and torture them, coercing them into false self-accusations. Ivanov and Kossior disappeared without trace behind the walls of the Lubianka prison. As for Serge Sedov, after a 'treatment' at the Lubianka, he was 'tried' at Sverdlovsk, where he had worked as an engineer at the electric station; according to the newspaper stories, 'he recalled having devoted himself to acts of sabotage' and other 'crimes', for which he was condemned to be shot.[3]

Towards the end of the autumn, about 1,200 prisoners found themselves in the old brickfield; at least half of these were Trotskyists. They were all lodged in four large barracks; their food ration was 400 grams of bread a day although they did not receive this every day. The barracks were surrounded by a barbed wire fence. Nearly a hundred freshly recruited guards, supplied with automatic arms, watched the prisoners day and night.

The prisoners arrested at the mine, at Oussa and in other nearby camps were taken to an old brickyard. Those arrested in more distant camps – at Petchora, Ijme, Kojve, Tchibiou, etc. – were kept near Tchibiou.

The whole winter of 1937–8 some prisoners, encamped in barracks at the brickyard, starved and waited for a decision regarding their fate. Finally, in March, three NKVD officers, with Kachketine at their head, arrived by plane at Vorkuta, coming from Moscow. They came to the brickyard to interrogate the prisoners. Thirty to forty were called each day, superficially questioned five to ten minutes each, rudely insulted, forced to listen to vile name-calling and obscenities. Some were greeted with punches in the face; Lieutenant Kachketine himself several times beat up one of them, the old Bolshevik, Virab Virabov, a former member of the Central Committee of Armenia.

The 'convoys'

At the end of March, a list of twenty-five was announced, among them Guevorkian, Virabov, Slavine, etc. . . . To each was delivered a kilo of bread and orders to prepare himself for a new convoy. After fond farewells to their friends, they left the barracks, and the convoy departed. Fifteen or twenty minutes later, not far away, about half a kilometre, on the steep bank of the little river Verkhniaia Vorkuta (Upper Vorkuta), an abrupt volley resounded, followed by isolated and disorderly shots; then all grew quiet again. Soon, the convoy's escort passed back near the barracks. And it was clear to all on what sort of convoy the prisoners had been sent.

Two days later, there was a new call, this time of forty names. Once more there was a ration of bread. Some, out of exhaustion, could no longer move; they were promised a ride in a cart. Holding their breath, the prisoners remaining in the barracks heard the grating of the snow under the feet of the departing convoy. For a long time there was no sound; but all, on the watch, still listened. Nearly an hour passed in this way. Then, again, shots resounded in the tundra; this time, they came from much further away, in the direction of the narrow railway which passed three kilometres from the brickyard. The second 'convoy' definitely convinced those remaining behind that they had been irremediably condemned.

The executions in the tundra lasted the whole month of April and part of May. Usually one day out of two, or one day out of three, thirty to forty prisoners were called. It is characteristic to note that each time, some common criminals, repeaters, were included. In order to terrorize the prisoners, the GPU, from time to time, made publicly known by means of the local radio, the list of those shot. Usually these broadcasts began as follows: 'For counter-revolutionary agitation, sabotage, brigandage in the camps, refusal to work, attempts to escape, the following have been shot . . .' followed by a list of names of some political prisoners mixed with a group of common criminals.

One time, a group of nearly a hundred, composed mainly of Trotskyists, was led away to be shot. As they marched away, the condemned sang the Internationale, joined by the voices of hundreds of prisoners remaining in camp.

Women not spared

At the beginning of May, a group of women were shot. Among them were the Ukrainian communist, Choumskaia, the wife of I. N. Smirnov, a Bolshevik since 1898 and ex-People's Commissar (Olga, the daughter of Smirnov, a young girl, apolitical, passionately fond of music, had been shot a year before in Moscow); the wives of Kossior, of Melnais, etc. . . . one of these women had to walk on crutches. At the time of execution of a male prisoner his imprisoned wife was automatically liable to capital punishment; and when it was a question of well-known members of the Opposition, this applied equally to any of his children over the age of twelve.

In May, when hardly a hundred prisoners remained, the executions were interrupted. Two weeks passed quietly; then all the prisoners were led in a convoy to the mine. There it was learned that Yezhov had been dismissed, and that his place had been taken by Beria . . .

Among the survivors of the old brickyard, several orthodox Trotskyists found that they had escaped execution. One of these, the engineer R., was very close to Guevorkian and was one of the five leaders who had organized the great hunger strike. At the mine, it was said that R. had saved his life at the cost of treason to his comrades; these suspicions were probably well founded since after the executions, R. enjoyed the confidence of the camp administration and rose to the rank of a director.

NOTES TO CHAPTER 9

1. The fate of the Left Opposition and its followers in Stalin's camps has never been fully recorded since there were few survivors. Yet these veteran Bolsheviks were the first dissidents from within the social system established in October 1917. This account is by a Menshevik prisoner, who did not agree with the Oppositionists, but could not fail to be moved by their courage. The article appeared under the initials 'M.B.' in the October–November issue of the Russian Mensheviks' paper in exile *The Socialist Messenger*. It was reprinted in the December 1962 issue of the French-language journal *Quatrième Internationale*.

2. The author of the article distorts Trotskyist thought on this question. The 'Clemenceau thesis' enunciated in 1926–7, when the opposition was still in the Bolshevik Party, meant that they did not renounce the struggle to change the line of the Party and of the State in time of war. In an article dated 25 September 1939, anticipating the war between the USSR against Nazism, Trotsky wrote: 'While arms in hand they deal blows to Hitler, the Bolshevik-Leninists will at the same time conduct revolutionary propaganda against Stalin preparing his overthrow at the next and perhaps very near stage.'

3. The author is in error. Sedov was never tried in public nor did he confess. Roman Rosdolsky met him in Lubianka prison in February 1937. Sedov told Rosdolsky that they had tried to force him to testify against his father. His refusal led to liquidation.

10. Stalin and the Second World War

Fernando Claudin[1]

The judgements of certain Western historians and politicians who are champions of the 'free world' and enjoy pointing out the 'tricks' by means of which Stalin obtained his satellites and the other aims of his world strategy, while idealizing the policy of Roosevelt, show not only a lack of objectivity but also ingratitude. If the 'free world' did not lose some of its finest flowers in the crisis, there can be no doubt that it owes this to Stalin. It is true that no hypothesis on the course that history might have taken, rather than the one it did take, can be proved. It would be idle to argue that if the Soviet leader – who was also the supreme commander of the world communist army – had placed the European revolution among the priorities of his strategy, then that revolution would inevitably have triumphed. On the other hand, it can certainly be argued that Stalin, with the help of Western communist leaders who faithfully applied his policies, made an invaluable contribution to solving the difficult problem which faced the leaders of Anglo-American capitalism from 1939 onwards – how to defeat their dangerous German rivals while still avoiding the danger of revolution in the vital centres of European capitalism.

Trotsky undoubtedly took an excessively optimistic view of the revolutionary situation which would be created in Europe as the result of a Second World War. This optimism derived from his view of the state of capitalism, the exhaustion of its historic capacity to develop the forces of production, etc. However, his prophecy that the Second World War could result in revolution on a European scale was not an extremist fantasy. It expressed a real possibility, and one which the bourgeoisie realized from the first day of the war. This possibility arose not out of the fact that the capitalist system had reached the limiting stage postulated by Trotsky – who was here repeating the mistake of Lenin's analysis during the First World War – but out of the method it was forced to adopt in order to carry out a 'readjustment' of its structures and pass on to a new stage of development.

The Second World War was the most serious crisis which the capitalist and imperialist system had experienced in its whole history. Yet, at the same time, it revealed spectacularly, even while the war was on, but even more afterwards, the vitality which the system considered as a whole still possessed, the enormous potential of its industrial, technical and scientific structures, its ability to manipulate the masses and keep them in subjection to the values, ideologies and political attitudes necessary for the survival of the system. It demonstrated the political intelligence of the old ruling classes, and their skill in manoeuvre, the fruit of centuries of experience. Like the war of 1914–18 and the economic crisis of 1929, the Second World War showed – on a much larger scale – that the 'death-throes' of dying capitalism would last a good while longer. (The prolongation of the agony gave official Marxism the time and opportunity to fit it into a learned scheme of periodization. It was first claimed that the 'general crisis' of capitalism had begun with the 1914–18 war and the Russian Revolution. After the Second World War, since the patient was still alive, it was decided that the inter-war period was only the 'first stage' of the 'general crisis'. This first stage was followed by a second, which began with the war of 1939–45. In 1960 it was ruled that the second stage was over and the 'third' beginning. How many more 'stages' will we see?)

The global vitality of capitalism, however, included ossified structures which came into sharp conflict with the movement of the system, which was based on three power-centres, Germany, Japan and, above all, the United States. The control exercised by old Anglo-French capitalism over vast colonial territories and over the backward areas of southern and eastern Europe was a serious obstacle to the expansive potential of these centres. Anglo-French capitalism, threatened in its most precious interests, was not prepared to yield without a struggle. For American capitalism, which had a large field of expansion at hand in Latin America and could more easily advance into the Anglo-French colonial territories, the problem did not present itself as one involving war. For German and Japanese capitalism, however, the only way open was the traditional one of war.

From the point of view of the five main capitalist powers, the Second World War, like the first, was a war for markets, colonies and raw materials, and at the same time it meant the transition of the system as a whole to a new phase, that of state monopoly capitalism. The three powers which were in the lead in this new phase had designs not only on Anglo-French territory (in addition to the colonial territories of Holland and Belgium), but also on Soviet territory. The fact that the United States tried to achieve this objective by alliance with its future victims, while its dangerous rivals tried to do it by military conquest, gave great political and military advantages to the former, but made no essential difference to the nature of the aims of one side or the other.

After the experience of the years 1917–20 the bourgeoisie in all countries was fully aware of the dangers involved in the terrible operation which the horrifying logic of the system now again made necessary. The danger appeared all the greater in view of the existence of the Soviet state with its army and the Communist International. It is true that by the outbreak of war the European revolutionary movements had been defeated and forced underground in almost all the countries of the European continent, but how would the masses react to the effects of this new slaughter? Would not the communist cells which still existed be able to take advantage of the situation? After all in 1917 the Bolsheviks had only been a handful of revolutionaries.

Each bourgeoisie looked at these unknown factors differently, in the light of the internal situation of its own country. German capitalism was sure of itself, once the labour movement and the Communist Party had been crushed in its country. It thought that military victory would allow it to destroy by similar means any seeds of revolution in the rest of Europe. Japanese capitalism took a very similar view, since it too had reduced its labour movement to impotence. On a quite different basis – a reformist integration of the proletariat unequalled in the capitalist world – the United States was in a more favourable position than any other power to face the test of war. The British bourgeoisie could not feel the same confidence, as the great strike of 1926 had emphasized, but the Labour Party at least offered a fairly solid guarantee. This situation looked very different in France. It was clear that in the system of industrial capitalism France was the weakest link. Added to the obsolescence of its political and economic structures was the radicalization of the proletariat, shown by the social explosion of 1936, the hegemonic position acquired by the Communist Party within the labour movement and the spread of communist influence among large groups of intellectuals and other social sectors. The French Communist Party's exemplary moderation during the period of the Popular Front was not enough to dispel the fears of the bourgeoisie: was it a temporary tactic or a basic change in the party? Italy, which had undergone considerable capitalist development under fascism, was an unknown from the point of view of the solidity of the bourgeoisie. It seemed clear that its situation could not offer the security of Germany, but, equally visibly, it did not contain any element as disturbing as French communism.

Outside the industrial capitalist zone, situations capable of turning into revolutionary crises under the impact of the world war were numerous: the Asian colonies, the republics of Latin America, the backward states of eastern and southern Europe. The most serious and most obvious threat from the point of view of world capitalism, however, apart from the entry of the USSR into the war, lay in the possible coincidence of fascist defeat (and Soviet victory) and a proletarian revolution in France, which would mark the beginning of a process which could end in revolution over the whole continent of Europe. The British and American bourgeoisie were fully aware of this danger, and their whole policy, all their strategic plans and military operations throughout the war, were profoundly influenced by it, particularly in the last stages of the conflict, when the presence of the Soviet Union, now the first military power in Europe, poised for victory, made itself felt everywhere. At this period the French resistance appeared a considerable force, led largely by the communists, the possibility of revolution could be clearly seen in Italy and it became a fact in Yugoslavia and Greece.

The Americans and the British were in agreement on two fundamental aims, the need to defeat their rivals and save capitalist and industrialist Europe from proletarian revolution. They were also naturally in agreement about the need to forestall or crush, as the case might be, any threat of revolution in other parts of the world, and especially in China. They might differ over the means to achieve these ends, but on the ends themselves their views were identical. Contradictory interests came into play above all in connection with the colonial problem, but that was a question for the future rather than an immediate problem. The community of interests in the most important aims, together with the crumbling British empire's heavy dependence on the United States, was a solid bond for the Anglo-American alliance. The difficult problem lay in the contradiction between their two principal aims, since the defeat of Nazi Germany was a necessary condition for a·revolution in Europe and the internal logic of the anti-fascist war pointed the peoples of the European continent in the direction of revolution. A similar problem faced the Anglo-American alliance in the Pacific war, especially in connection with China. In the minds of the leaders in Washington and London, however, the Far Eastern problem was less dramatic than the problem in Europe. At that time they underestimated the chances of the Chinese Communists and the other revolutionary movements in Asia.

The necessity to forestall revolution in Europe logically forced the governments of Great Britain and the United States to seek a compromise with Germany, and, as is well known, they devoted all their efforts to this right up to the outbreak of war. But the logic of German imperialism was quite different: for it, military victory on the European continent and in the British Isles would enable it to achieve simultaneously two aims: to remove for an indefinite period any threat of revolution in Europe and also to secure an economic and political basis for future expansion. This programme of German imperialism represented for the British and Americans no less a threat, and above all a much more immediate and precise one, than the possibility of revolution in Europe. Faced with the unavoidable necessity of defeating Germany in order to protect its vital interests, the Anglo-American alliance was obliged to explore another course which might combine the defeat of Germany with the preservation of capitalism in France: a wide-ranging agreement with the Soviet state and the communist movement. This possibility showed itself first at the time of the Popular Front, but its first important demonstration, which showed how far the Soviets could go in this direction, was the German–Soviet pact, in support of which the Kremlin did not hesitate to force the Communist Parties to abandon their anti-fascist strategy. Nevertheless, this action was not entirely conclusive, because the Soviet Union had signed the pact with Germany in a position of weakness, and it was not therefore a sufficient basis to predict Soviet behaviour in a position of strength, such as they would enjoy if the Nazis were defeated. But the British and Americans had no alternative to this course, though they combined it with the elementary precaution of acting in such a way that the USSR would be weakened to the maximum in its duel with Germany.

Experience was to show, as we have seen, that the compromise desired by Washington and London was perfectly possible. It enabled them to overcome the underlying contradiction between their main European aims, the defeat of Germany and the prevention of continental revolution. They were less successful in Asia, but the responsibility for that was not Stalin's.

From 1943 onwards, the possibility of a revolutionary outcome to the anti-fascist war in Europe was clearly visible in four countries, France, Italy, Yugoslavia and Greece. The defeat of Germany came into sight at the same time, together with the important part to be played in that defeat by the Soviet armies, whose general offensive developed rapidly on all fronts during the summer of that year. It was the year when most of the British and American press shouted its warnings, and when the leaders of the Anglo-American coalition demanded the dissolution of the Comintern and the clear acceptance by the Communist Parties of a political line excluding any prospect of revolution. It was the year in which Stalin willingly accepted these demands, since they did not affect his strategic and political aims, and indeed could be useful to him as bargaining counters in the great negotiation with the Allies. The Yugoslav communists resisted Moscow's instructions; the Greek communists hesitated, and during 1944 made concessions to Moscow which were to prove fatal to them. Thorez and Togliatti accepted Stalin's line unconditionally, since anyway it coincided with the neo-reformist turn in these leaders' political views which had begun at the time of the Popular Front. The leading groups in these two parties, which had been formed in these views, offered no resistance. From this point the possibility of revolutionary development in France and Italy was seriously threatened; the position was as it would have been in Russia in the course of 1917, if

Lenin's 'April Theses' had been rejected by the Bolshevik Party. The bourgeois revolution would have consolidated itself, one way or another, but the proletarian revolution would not have taken place, and historians and revolutionaries would still be arguing whether the possibility had really existed and whether or not Lenin was a Leftist adventurer, as they are twenty-five years later about France and Italy.

The simple fact that the argument continues without any sign of being settled is sufficient proof that historical scholarship has found the famous possibility solid enough. It was not fantasies which aroused the fear of the French and Italian bourgeoisie and their American protectors in those years. The bourgeois Italy which had emerged from the Risorgimento had known no more serious national crisis than the one which began in 1943, and the same can be said of France since the Paris Commune. The national disaster of 1940 had spotlighted the weakness of French capitalism. The state collapsed and was replaced by a caricature state in the service of the occupier; the calamities of war were increased by the humiliation of a shameful defeat and the German occupation.

The causes of all this were clear: out-of-date social and economic structures, rotten and impotent parliamentarism, colonial parasitism and technical backwardness. The ruling classes and their political groupings were discredited. It was they who bore the full responsibility for the disaster. But the most serious aspect of the situation from the point of view of the French bourgeoisie was the clear shift to the Left which took place in the proletariat and other sectors of society, reflecting a realization of the causes of the crisis and the location of responsibility. The reason why the masses quickly turned to the Communist Party, in spite of its absurd policies during the period 1939–41, and why the party acquired leading positions in the resistance, was that the most active and advanced sectors, expressing the still confused movement among the masses, were looking for a radical solution to the crisis of the bourgeois system.

The same phenomenon unfolded in Italy. The responsibility of the fascist regime for the national crisis was inextricably bound up with that of the big industrialists and landowners, who had shown themselves incapable, in fifteen years of dictatorship, of overcoming the chief weakness of Italian capitalism, the underdevelopment of the south, and had led the country into colonial adventures and imperialist wars. The fascist dictatorship itself, however, was also the result and the proof of the impotence of the Italian bourgeois democracy which emerged from the Risorgimento. The ruling classes of the peninsula had failed with both these forms of government, and the formidable mass movement which followed the fall of Mussolini, with its clear inclination to the Left, and the striking advance of the Communist Party, were a reflection, even sharper than in France, of the tendency towards a revolutionary solution of the national crisis.

Never before in the history of either of these countries had the real movement so strongly or so objectively challenged the bourgeois order. Never before had the mass of the workers, the intellectuals, the whole society, lived through such an exemplary demonstration of the need for a new economy, a new state, for the rule of a new social class. Could the Communist Party fail to consider the socialist alternative without losing its *raison d'être*? Could it let such an opportunity as this go by without carrying the critique written into events by the real movement over on to the level of political theory and action?

Two aspects of the problem must be distinguished here. One is the exploration to the full of the objective situation, of common experience to raise the political consciousness of the masses and create an informed desire for revolutionary change, the working-out of tactics and a strategy which could organize and prepare the forces capable of imposing such a change, with the principal aim of a seizure of power, *not by the Communist Party, but by a combination of all the social and political forces willing to support a socialist alternative.* This was the inescapable duty of any Marxist revolutionary party in a situation of radical national crisis, such as existed in France and Italy in 1940–45.

This was independent of the other aspect of the problem, the question whether such a course would result in victory for the revolution. This question could not be answered except in the course of the action itself; only the action, in combination with other factors, could create the favourable situation, the relation of forces which would make possible the decisive step, the seizure of power. (In April 1917 no one could guarantee, nor did Lenin ever claim, that conditions favourable to a seizure of power by the Bolsheviks would inevitably come into being. The April policy was not the only factor which determined the emergence of these conditions in October, but without that policy those conditions would not have existed.) The leaders of the Communist Parties of France and Italy, who controlled the general line of their parties during the Second World War from Moscow, under Stalin's direct control, 'solved' the problem on the very first day, immediately, that is, the United States and Great Britain became the allies of the USSR. In France and Italy there could be no socialist outcome; the aim was to be the restoration of bourgeois democracy.

Such an abdication, such a denial in practice of what communists thought they were and continued to proclaim that they were, required theoretical and practical justifications of comparable weight. As long as the war lasted, the principal justification, which absorbed all the others put forward from time to time, could be reduced to the following schema:

(a) The victory of Hitler's Germany would mean the destruction of the Soviet Union and the crushing for an indefinite period of the working-class movement in Europe; (b) therefore, the principal aim must be victory over Germany; (c) to ensure the defeat of Germany, the essential condition was to ensure the solidarity of the anti-Hitler coalition; (d) raising the problem of a socialist perspective, making the aim the seizure of power by the proletariat, would inevitably lead to a confrontation with the Western Allies which would threaten the chances of victory; (e) therefore, it was impossible, at the present stage, to consider the socialist alternative.

This reasoning presented itself as indisputable, the product of simple common sense. Only hardened Leftists, Trotskyites and other irresponsible elements – 'Hitlero-Trotskyites' in Thorez's language – could question such basic truths. The motives which led the majority of active communists, notably those of France and Italy, to accept this common-sense logic have already been mentioned. The initial propositions (a) and (b) were, of course, indisputable. On the other hand, proposition (c), from which (d) and (e) derived, contained a thesis which was much less indisputable. This maintained that the cohesion of the anti-Hitler coalition – understood as the alliance of the United States and Great Britain with the Soviet Union and the alliance of Germany's European bourgeois rivals with the working-class and anti-fascist movement – was an indispensable condition of victory. This view excluded the possibility that there could develop in the course of the war a new relation of forces based on an alliance of the Soviet Union with the liberation movements of the European peoples which would be capable of ensuring the defeat of Germany and upsetting the plans of the Anglo-American imperialists. The exclusion of this possibility *a priori* was reflected in the refusal to adopt a policy which could help to create it. As the official Soviet history recognizes, this possibility took tangible form towards the end of 1943 and the beginning of 1944, when the Allied landing on the continent was no longer necessary to ensure the defeat of Germany. Its essential aim was to save Western Europe from revolution. Would this aim have been achieved if the policies of the French and Italian Communist Parties had been different, if they had been like that of the Yugoslav communists?

The possibility of carrying on the struggle on two fronts was given a practical demonstration in Yugoslavia from 1941 onwards. The main enemy was the fascist occupier and his quislings, and the secondary target was the Allied enemy, which was trying, while the war was still being fought, to establish the foundations for a restoration of the regime of the bourgeoisie and large landowners and of the country's dependence on Anglo-American imperialism. This strategy also proved itself just as effective in the war against Hitler as the strategy which attempts had been made to justify in the name of simple common sense: the scale of operations carried out by the Yugoslav liberation army against the occupier far surpassed that of the operations of the French and Italian resistance. Paradoxically, the strategy inspired by simple common sense recoiled against its main apparent justification, to obtain the greatest efficiency in the fight against the occupier. The practical effect of the refusal of the French and Italian Communist Parties to give a revolutionary content to the war of national liberation in order to avoid a conflict with the policy of the Western Allies and the national bourgeoisie was not only to make it easier for the Allies and the bourgeoisie to restore the bourgeois order, but also to lead to a failure to mobilize against the invader energies and forces among the people which could only have been brought into action by revolutionary fervour, an awareness of struggling for social emancipation, for the power of the workers. We have seen in detail in the previous pages how common-sense logic led the Communist Parties of France and Italy to subordinate themselves, the proletariat and all the forces of the Left to the leadership of the Western Allies and the bourgeois wing of the resistance, whose policy was to reduce to the minimum the participation of the working-class and popular forces. The 'national unity', urged as more powerful because it was broader, proved in practice both narrower and weaker than the revolutionary national unity created in the struggle in Yugoslavia.

It is hardly necessary to explain that the type of confrontation, and the way it was linked to common action, would vary with the development of the war in Europe and other sectors, and in each country. The first necessity was for the struggle to be political, avoiding armed conflict as much as possible, especially in conditions unfavourable for the revolutionary forces. The Yugoslavs provided a model of political intelligence in the way in which they understood the dialectic of confrontation and common action, combining the open political struggle with united actions when possible, armed confrontations with the Chetniks and negotiations with the royal government and the Allies. At the same time as they were creating their own power and building a revolutionary army, they allowed the old English fox to think that he could obtain by negotiation what he could not take by force. They even managed to get weapons delivered to them by the Western Allies before receiving Soviet supplies.

The problem for the Italian and French communists – assuming that they were interested in a revolutionary policy – was not, of course, to imitate the Yugoslav strategy, but to work out their own strategy of confrontation and common action. Nevertheless the Yugoslav example indicated some of the essential conditions for tactics of this sort. The first of these was the formation of the working-class and Left-wing anti-fascist forces into an independent movement, with its own programme and its own completely autonomous armed forces; the second, the creation of a new popular power in the course of the war against Hitler by encouraging, as far as circumstances allowed, the direct participation of the masses in the new power. Other equally important aspects could be mentioned, but this has already been done in the section on the struggle in Yugoslavia. Was it really true that the situation in France and Italy made a similar course impossible?

It is significant that in the face of the Yugoslav criticisms at the founding meeting of the Cominform the French and Italian communist leaders did not even try to assert the impossibility of this. They evaded the core of the problem by claiming that if they had tried to take power the British and American armies would have intervened to prevent them. This was evading the core of the problem, because they were being criticized, not for not trying to take power, but for following, from as early as 1941, a policy which implied the abandonment in advance of any such aim, a policy, indeed, which adopted the opposite aim, the restoration of bourgeois democracy, a policy of subordination to the bourgeois Allies. The danger of intervention by the British and American armies did not arise in France until the summer of 1944. What stopped the French Communist Party from having a policy in the previous three years designed to prepare the working class, ideologically, politically and organizationally, for a struggle to give a socialist ending to the unprecedented crisis of bourgeois France? Why, instead of helping to tie the resistance to Gaullist leadership and the old system of the bourgeois parties, did it not support and lead the opposing tendencies present in the resistance? Why, when faced with the restoration of the old power which Gaullism represented, did it not fight, right from the start, for the creation of a new power arising out of the resistance and based ultimately on the mass of the workers? Many signs showed the depth of the revolutionary current (at a time when the masses believed that the Communist Party was the party of revolution). In spite of the ultra-opportunist policy of the PCF during those three years, the liberation meant that, in many areas, as non-communist historians admit, the working-class and popular forces had power within their reach; the masses flocked to the Communist Party and supported the Left-wing movements in the Socialist Party, the unions and other organizations. These signs also made it starkly clear, in retrospect, that if a different policy had been followed in the previous period the level of consciousness of the movement, its fighting spirit and its desire to enforce a radical change would have been much stronger. But, even starting from the level reached by the movement in the months after the liberation, was there not a possibility of directing it towards revolutionary goals? This is a question which the leaders of the PCF have always avoided. To Left-wing criticisms they have always replied, and continue to reply, that the combination of conditions favourable to a takeover of power did not exist. That, however, was not the question. The question lies in the fact that the party followed a policy designed to eliminate any possibility of the emergence of conditions favourable to a takeover of power, not only by the party, but also by the whole of the revolutionary wing of the resistance. Their policy was that of a fire brigade at the outbreak of a fire. In the period between the liberation of Paris and the capitulation of Germany (almost a year), no one except the Communist Party and the unions it controlled could have prevented the gathering development of the mass movement. In reply to the Gaullist policy of abolishing the committees of liberation and the patriotic militias, the embryo of the dual power created by the resistance, the PCF could have organized strikes, factory occupations, mass demonstrations and other forms of action. It could have encouraged the transformation of the liberation committees into direct organs of the masses, supported by the organs of workers' power in industry. The party had the power to promote movements of this type and to encourage the unity of the Left around a programme of socialist democracy. The problem of power could be considered realistically only in the context of a policy intended to strengthen the mass movement, dissipate illusions about Gaullism and the Allies (illusions created by the party itself during the preceding period), etc.

But, as we have seen, the policy of the PCF was quite different. It cooperated with de Gaulle in the elimination of the resistance, it told the working class that it would have to tighten its belt in order to restore the capitalist economy; it held back – which was perhaps worse – the liberation movement in the French colonies; it disseminated illusions about the peaceful, parliamentary road; it continued to idealize the Allies. This was a new version of the traditional reformist, nationalist policy of the Right wing of French social democracy.

In Italy the possibility of carrying out a policy which dialectically combined the war against Hitler with the struggle for a socialist outcome became actual with the fall of Mussolini, when, in Togliatti's words, the old foundations of the bourgeois state collapsed, including its military organization, and there began the largest popular insurrection in the whole history of Italy, which was led principally by communists, socialists and progressive intellectuals. When Togliatti landed at Naples in 1944, the need to choose between two policies, confusedly reflected in the conflict between anti-fascism and the King, Badoglio and the Allies, began to appear. One policy attempted to associate the working-class parties and the petty-bourgeois Left against the monarchy, the traditional

Right and the Allies; the other tried instead to weaken the contradictions, to form a closer association of Left and Right, working class and bourgeoisie, under the sole command of the Allied military authorities and behind the slogan 'First win the war'. The first political line might have led to the formation of the new 'historical bloc' discussed by Gramsci. The second, the policy of 'national unity', in the event eased the task of the old ruling classes and led finally to the restoration and modernization of Italian capitalism.

It was not 'national unity', but 'national differentiation', which could have upset the game of the old ruling classes, which had been plain since the fall of Mussolini. It could have revealed to the masses the forces which were genuinely struggling for the social and political renewal of Italy, its national independence, and those which were working for the return of the big industrialists and the landowners, with the aim of placing Italy in subjection to a new imperialism. 'National unity' did not, in spite of Togliatti's claims, give the working class the leading role; it merely gave it the illusion of that role. Real control was in other hands. In order to make themselves a real hegemonic class, the working class would have had to combine *in action* the problem of national liberation with that of agrarian revolution in the south and the islands, with the struggle for *socialist* democracy. Togliatti's strategy – a reproduction of that adopted by the Comintern in the Spanish revolutionary war – dissociated these aims at the very time that the real movement, the serious crisis of social and political structures, the awakening of the masses, was tending to join them in a single revolutionary process. During the two years between the Allied landings and the rising in the north the PCI did nothing to organize the struggle of the peasant masses for the land, and opposed the tendencies in favour of fighting for a socialist solution which began to emerge within the great proletarian movement in the north. The policy of 'national unity' consisted in practice of holding back the mass movement in order to avoid the break-up of the coalition government and any confrontation with the Anglo-American military authorities.

The movement of the masses, asserting itself at every level as an autonomous power, with its own programme, was the only force ultimately capable of preventing the restoration of traditional power which gradually took place. The military presence of the Allies would have required, of course, different methods from those used by the Yugoslavs, an essentially political type of confrontation. But the presence and attitude of the Anglo-American military authorities was, on the other hand, a living lesson which the working-class and anti-fascist Left could have used to increase the national consciousness awakened by the war of liberation, by demanding full and unrestricted recognition of Italian sovereignty, the right of the people to free choice of their organs of government and a promise by the Anglo-American military authorities not to interfere in Italian internal affairs.

The essential obstacle to the development of a strategy to push ahead with the fight for the land and for other revolutionary changes did not lie in the Italian situation. It lay in the PCI leadership's submission to the line laid down by Moscow. Such a strategy could have extended the foundations of dual power and increased the political isolation of the Allies and the Right. It could have created a powerful independent movement of the working-class parties and the Left-wing anti-fascist forces, and made it possible to connect the great proletarian rising in the north with the revolutionary movement in the south. If the Yugoslav communists had followed Stalin's instructions as contained in Dimitrov's message of March 1942, similar 'obstacles' would have arisen in Yugoslavia.

Togliatti and Thorez more than once referred to the example of Greece to justify their policies. The catastrophe of the Greek resistance could, however, have been avoided, in spite of Stalin's unbelievable treachery, if the Greek communist leaders had resisted Soviet pressure and not capitulated at a moment when they were in control of almost the whole country and were backed by a seasoned popular army. Eighteen months later, in much less favourable conditions, they took up the struggle again and were able to hold out for three years, with foreign aid which bore no relation to the size of the American intervention and effectively ended in 1948. If the Greek communist leaders had not given way to Stalin in December 1944 and January 1945, the British expeditionary force would have found itself in an unenviable situation.

In the early months of 1945 Germany was nearly defeated. The Soviet armies, with the addition of sizeable detachments from Bulgaria, Romania and Poland – and of course the Yugoslav liberation army – possessed a decisive military superiority over the forces of the Western Allies in Europe. The United States was tied up, for how long it was impossible to say, in the war in the Pacific. It was the moment when the democratic and reforming ideals of the resistance enjoyed the maximum of popular enthusiasm. What would have happened if in this situation the working-class movements of France and Italy had gone over to the offensive in support of the power of the workers and the whole Left, with a programme of democratic and socialist changes (not 'communist' power or a 'Soviet' programme)? Would the West have intervened? Could Roosevelt or Truman have faced the political consequences of taking over Hitler's role as chief enemy of the European Left? From a military point of view, could they even have made the attempt? (The danger could not be ignored, just as in 1917 it was impossible to ignore the danger of an intervention by the German armies, which did take place and almost crushed the Russian Revolution. It is hard to think of any revolution secure against all danger. There was, however, one notable difference in the situation of 1944–5, which was that the real danger came not so much from a possible intervention by the capitalist armies as from the very likely failure to intervene of the armies which were regarded as the standard-bearers of the October Revolution. This is what happened in Greece. On the other hand, it should be admitted that the case of Greece itself shows how difficult such operations were in the situation of that time.)

But conjectures and questions about what might or might not have happened in the past must stop. History was decided at Yalta, when the 'areas of influence' were shared out. Stalin laid down the law to the Communist Parties without meeting any resistance, except from some future heretics in the underdeveloped countries. In the centres of capitalism communist neo-reformism fell in step with the 'grand alliance'.

When we began our analysis of Stalin's strategy during the Second World War, we referred to one of the factors which affected it the most, to which we must now briefly return. The foreign policy of the Soviet bureaucracy could not do other than reflect, in some form, its domestic policy. After wiping out the best representatives of the October Revolution, after destroying proletarian democracy and depriving the people for many years of all political life, after discrediting the socialist ideal in the eyes of the Soviet workers by proclaiming that this regime of poverty and police dictatorship was finished, socialism, in short, after polluting the sources which could have kept alive the revolutionary spirit and formed an internationalist class-consciousness, the Soviet leaders were incapable of giving the war against Hitler's Germany a revolutionary or socialist character. This fact was independent of all the other reasons we have analysed (strategic considerations, interest in maintaining the 'grand alliance', etc.), which were anyway strongly conditioned by the internal situation. Continuing therefore in the same direction, and starting from the type of social consciousness which their ideological mystifications and political opportunism had formed, the Stalinist leaders gave the war the only character they could give it, that of a patriotic war. Hitlerism was first and foremost the new face of the traditional enemy, the 'Teuton', who dared to attack *Belikaia Rossiia* – as the new national anthem called it – and not the grave-digger of the German working-class movement and the Spanish revolution. 'They are not fighting for us,' said Stalin in a moment of sincerity during an interview with Ambassador Harriman, 'they are fighting for Mother Rus.'

In the minds of millions of *muzhiks* and worker-*muzhiks* the Stalin myth was closely mingled with that of the great Tsars, combined with traditional patriotism, the glories of the past, a revived religion. Stalin and the party skilfully used every means to build these springs of patriotism into the new state, and Lenin was ritually invoked on every occasion to increase the prestige of the new Lenin. From the point of view of the international aims of the war, the Soviet leaders did not add a comma to the aims proclaimed by the Allied capitalist powers, national liberation for the peoples of Europe and democracy.

More accurately, they added one element, which was not exactly revolutionary or even progressive – pan-Slavism, the call for the unity of the Slav peoples. The transparent intention of this call, apart from its immediate effect as a rallying-cry against the traditional enemy of pan-Germanism, was to prepare ideologically for the future construction of the protective barrier. Europe was going through its second disastrous war twenty years after the end of the first. It was clear proof that national frontiers had become an anachronism hindering the development of the productive forces, making a lasting peace impossible and constituting a permanent source of rivalries and conflict. Had not the moment come to call on the European proletariat to fight for the socialist United States of Europe, the idea of which had been launched by the Bolshevik Party at the beginning of the 1914–18 war and taken up by the Comintern in 1923? But the Slav idea replaced the European socialist idea. The Slavs must unite; the other peoples of Europe could stay in their national shells.

We shall not dwell on these aspects of Stalin's policy, which other authors – in particular Isaac Deutscher – have examined in detail. Deutscher has raised another problem of considerable interest. The victory of a socialist revolution throughout Europe would have meant the end of the isolation of the Russian Revolution, but Stalin feared the effects of the interpenetration of the Soviet system and socialism in the areas of industrial capitalism. He thought, not without justification, that this would endanger the political and ideological basis of the bureaucratic and totalitarian system built on the basis of isolation. From being an objective influence on the system, isolation had become a necessary condition for its survival and for the privileges of its ruling class. Subsequent developments have confirmed Deutscher's view. Stalin and his successors have made every effort to maintain the isolation of Soviet society, not only from the West, but also from the other countries of the 'socialist camp'. Genuine contact between Russia and the 'people's democracies' – free travel and free exchange of ideas – could easily have become another source of ferment inside Russia. Stalin had therefore to keep in being two 'iron curtains', one separating Russia from her own zone of influence, the other separating that zone from the West.

As we have seen, the ill-starred European proletarian revolution had to overcome many obstacles to make its way through the great crisis of the 1940s. Victory at the end of the second decade of the century was denied it by the absence of a socialist party independent of the bourgeoisie. Victory at the beginning of the fifth decade would have required a party independent both of the bourgeoisie and of the 'fatherland of socialism'.

The main justification for the policy of 'national unity' disappeared with the capitulation of Germany in the spring of 1945, but the collaboration of the Communist Parties in the bourgeois governments of France and Italy (and of a number of other European capitalist states) continued and, as we have shown, contributed to the restoration of the capitalist economy and its political superstructures. A new justification now became necessary, and this time it could not be merely, or essentially, tactical.

To fill this need use was made of the doctrine of 'new democracy' or 'people's democracy', created to meet another urgent necessity, that of defining the regimes which began to establish themselves in the countries liberated by the Soviet armies. The paradox was that while revolution had been avoided with skill and delicacy in France and Italy – where 'the working class and its allies were better organized than the forces of reaction and had a clear superiority over the ruling groups of monopoly capitalism and its political agents' (the quotation is from Soviet historians) – in the Eastern European countries it had been encouraged by the same *raison d'état* which had blocked it in the West. It was obvious that the defensive barrier could not be built on capitalist structures.

The historic defeat of fascism, the Yugoslav revolution, the revolutionary process begun in other East European countries as a result of their liberation by the Soviet army and the formation of the satellite system, the emergence of the USSR as a world power, the increased strength of the Western Communist Parties: all this hid from communists – who at that period lived in the euphoric dream described at the beginning of this essay – and not only from them, the serious implications for the further struggle for socialism of the frustration of the revolution in Europe. Shortly afterwards, the Chinese Revolution and, later, the collapse of the old colonial system had a similar effect. But if we see events in a historical perspective, it can be seen very clearly that this victory of the international bourgeoisie, this abdication of European communism at the moment of its greatest influence – at the most favourable conjuncture in the half-century since the October Revolution – has had an unhappy influence on the subsequent course of world events. It was the last, and most serious, effect of the ideological decay of the Communist International, and is one of the main objective causes of the present crisis of the communist movement.

1. Fernando Claudin was a leading member of the Spanish Communist Party from the late thirties until his expulsion in 1965. He was a member of the Politburo from 1947 to 1965. This extract is taken from his classic work, *The Communist Movement: From Comintern to Cominform*, published in English by Penguin Books in 1975. The book is an extremely informative account of Stalinist foreign policy.

11. The First Breach:
The Excommunication of Yugoslavia

Josip Broz Tito et al.

1. Tito places the Soviet–Yugoslav dispute in a global ideological context, 20 January 1951

The path which we followed was at first that of complete reliance on the Soviet Union, and the clash between us and the Soviet leaders stemmed from the real relationship existing between the Soviet Union and other socialist states – in this particular case, Yugoslavia. The method of relationship between socialist states as practised by the Soviet Union was unacceptable to us not simply because it involved ourselves – Yugoslavia, a geographically small socialist state – but on general grounds, since we saw from the very outset that this was something very deep-rooted, involving the whole future development of socialism throughout the world, which was not in keeping with the teaching of Marx, Engels, and Lenin. We could not naturally know at first where all this would lead to, but we saw that it was wrong, and we thought that, by resisting such a standpoint in the specific case of Yugoslavia, we might promote a discussion on a basis of equality, that is, that the leaders of the Soviet Union would see that it was the wrong path. We thought that their mistakes regarding Yugoslavia stemmed from a lack of knowledge about conditions in our country which was the product of wrong or misleading information about Yugoslavia, and so on. But no; it later became clear over a period of three years – for the clash did not start with the revolution but long before, we might even say, from the war years – that things went much deeper than that, and that the leaders of the Soviet Union were applying in their international policy methods which are quite wrong and anti-socialist, in other words, that they had strayed from the path of socialism in the form conceived in broad outline by our great teachers Marx, Engels, and Lenin.

Our party has helped all progressive people in the world – not only socialists and communists but others – to look at the matter differently today. In many countries of Western Europe there are more and more people who breathe more freely today and see that it is possible to achieve socialism not in the way wanted by the rulers of the Soviet Union, but in the way which working folk in every country want it. I think this is a great service rendered by our party which, through the example it has set, has given the impulse to make others think and feel that there are revolutionary forces latent in their countries able to build socialism without some armed power bringing it to them at bayonet point. For never in history has real freedom been brought at bayonet point, and still less can socialism be built in this way.

2. Kardelj in Skupština accuses the USSR of continuing its aggressive policy towards Yugoslavia, 27 February 1951

There exist in the world today a number of danger-spots making for war. I want to refer particularly to the one which most directly concerns us and which threatens the independence, peace, and socialist construction of Yugoslavia, namely the USSR's hegemonistic policy towards Yugoslavia, and also the hostile policy pursued against Yugoslavia by some neighbouring governments in the service of Soviet foreign policy . . .

The whole responsibility for this state of affairs rests with the USSR and the governments under its influence. The Yugoslav government has done everything in its power to normalize relations between our country and the countries of the Soviet bloc. I should like to remind you that Comrade Tito and other official representatives of the Yugoslav government have taken every opportunity from 1948 down to the present to stress Yugoslavia's readiness for a normalization of relations and Yugoslavia's peaceful cooperation with the countries of the Soviet bloc, on one condition – that such cooperation should be based on respect for the independence of the peoples of Yugoslavia and non-intervention in our internal affairs . . .

We do not ask of the Soviet government that it should have a liking for the way we are building socialism. We have no liking for their unsocialistic methods which, furthermore, compromise the idea of socialism. We do not reproach them for failing to criticize that system. But what we demand from the Soviet government is this; that they should behave with due respect for the independence of the peoples of Yugoslavia and their desire to work in peace, and without threatening anyone, for the great task of building socialism and increasing the prosperity of our working people.

3. Molotov at Polish CP rally predicts 'the liquidation of the Tito–Fascist clique', 21 July 1951: excerpt

Obvious to all is the fate of Yugoslavia, which fell by means of deceit into the hands of spies and provocateurs who betrayed their people and sold them out to the Anglo–American imperialists. Now all see that the Tito, Kardelj and Ranković gang have already re-established the capitalist system in Yugoslavia, deprived the people of its revolutionary victory, and transformed the nation into a weapon of the aggressive imperialist powers.

Realizing that the Yugoslav people hate this hired gang of criminals who stole its way to power, it holds itself in power by bloody terror and fascist methods of ruling. This cannot continue long. The people of Yugoslavia will find a way to freedom and liquidation of the Titoist–fascist regime.

4. Tito replies to Molotov's charges by accusing the Soviet leaders of genocide, 27 July 1951: excerpt

A few days ago the well-known Soviet leader Molotov found it necessary to go to Poland and there deliver a slanderous, warmongering speech aimed primarily against our country and its leaders. I shall tell you the reason why he attacked us, but first I should like to explain why it was Poland he went to. He went to Poland, Comrades, because it is not exactly all a bed of roses for them there, because he wanted to threaten them and tell the Poles what they could expect if they dared to follow Yugoslavia's example. The threats he uttered there against us are really aimed primarily against the Poles, as I believe that he should know very well by now that we are not afraid of his threats. He knows that, Comrades.

In this speech of his he, of course, hurled all sorts of threats and violent insults against the leaders of our country. He dubbed us, in customary style, spies and criminals who were murdering their people. But in this charge of theirs that we are criminals I see nothing else than their wish to cover up their own crimes. They have been murdering in Albania, Bulgaria, Hungary, Romania, Poland, and Czechoslovakia – not to mention Russia itself. And since this is the case, then they need to accuse *us* of murdering, so as to cover up their own deeds in this way. But which Cominformists have we killed up to now, which of those handful of wretches whom we could have ground into dust have we destroyed? Not one! Why should we kill anyone? Let them do what they want, let them then build socialism and think about themselves. What moral right has Molotov to throw in our face that we are criminals, that we are murdering the people and extirpating it? What right has he to speak – he who is one of the chief leaders of a country where an unheard-of crime of genocide has been committed, where whole nations have been annihilated in the face of the whole world? Where is the German Republic of the Volga, where one of the most gifted of peoples used to live? It is in the forests of Siberia! Where is the Tartar Crimean Republic? It does not exist any more; it is in Siberia, vanished amidst the forests and swamps! Where are the Chechens of the Caucasus? They no longer exist – they have been driven out of the hills where, as a free people, they had been fighting for centuries for their liberty; they have disappeared into Siberia, swallowed up in the gigantic forests where they must slowly die, for they cannot support the climate. Where are the thousands and tens of thousands of Estonian, Latvian and Lithuanian citizens? They do not exist any more; every day they are being sent to Siberia, to labour there in the hardest conditions and to perish from the face of the earth. This fate awaits every country and people which lets itself fall into their clutches. Who, then, is the criminal, who commits genocide, and who destroys peoples and carries out mass murders? Yes, Comrades – the answer is not difficult. So they have no moral right to throw such an insult in our face . . .

Molotov has threatened that we shall disappear, that all the leaders of our country whom he has dubbed criminals will be swept away, and that the people will see to that. He said that because he knows that our people do not like to keep quiet. But I should like to see him here, I should like him to come here among us and say what he wants to you, while I shall say what I want, and then we shall see whom you believe. He has uttered this threat against us not only indeed to frighten the peoples of this country, but also if need be to frighten those amongst us who are not properly informed. But our people, Comrades, do not let themselves be frightened by any threats.

5. Yugoslavia complains to the UN of hostile activities by the USSR, 9 November 1951

1. The government of the Union of Soviet Socialist Republics has been instigating, organizing and exercising for more than three years – both directly and through the governments of Hungary, Bulgaria, Romania and Albania, as well as the governments of Czechoslovakia and Poland – all-round aggressive pressure against Yugoslavia for the purpose of encroaching upon her sovereignty and threatening her territorial integrity and national independence. These hostile actions have manifested themselves in all spheres of international relations. They have also broken up the basic conventional links between states, so that the existing diplomatic relations are merely nominal. It is clear that such actions are creating a situation endangering the maintenance of international peace.

2. The government of the FPRY has done everything in its power to avoid the worsening of relations and to avoid being provoked. In spite of very grave offences, the government of the FPRY has limited itself to customary and direct, but unfortunately unsuccessful, diplomatic steps. Only when it had become crystal clear that these hostile actions actually amounted to a system of aggressive pressure, which was being intensified according to plan, the government of the FPRY began to draw attention to this situation in the course of the debates of the General Assembly of

the United Nations on problems regarding the maintenance of peace. When all this failed to produce the desired effect, the government of the FPRY published its 'White Book'. None of the accused governments has even attempted to deny or contradict the facts brought out in the 'White Book', but, on the contrary, all of them have continued to increase the aggressive pressure in all spheres.

3. Consequently, the government of the FPRY deems it necessary to draw the attention of the General Assembly formally to the existing situation, fraught with danger for peace, which has been brought about, and which is being deliberately aggravated, by the government of the USSR, and under its instigation, by the governments of Bulgaria, Hungary, Romania, and Albania, and also those of Czechoslovakia and Poland.

4. The facts are:

5. That the government of the USSR has organized and thoroughly carried out, together with the six aforementioned governments, an economic blockade against the FPRY. Some of the above-mentioned states have already severed even all postal and railway connections with Yugoslavia, thus violating not only their treaties with Yugoslavia, but also international conventions;

6. That the government of the USSR has been pursuing for more than three years, together with the six aforementioned governments, a crude campaign of incitement against the FPRY, which, as regards its scope and forms, has no parallel in international relations. The direct purpose of this propaganda is the creation of a war psychosis. The aim of this propaganda is to incite the hatred of the peoples of the aforementioned countries against Yugoslavia, and to stir up, among the Yugoslavs, agitation, excitement, and insecurity. In order to augment the effect of this propaganda which is being waged on the radio and in the press, the highest representatives of the government and of the army of the USSR, and of the other six states, are, in their public and official addresses, not only insulting the state and government of the FPRY, but are also launching direct exhortations to the Yugoslavs to revolt and overthrow their legal government;

7. That, with the same aim in view, they are organizing spying, subversive and terroristic activities against Yugoslavia. Special centres for the training of terroristic groups have been set up. Such groups are being sent into Yugoslavia from Bulgaria, Hungary, and Albania, with the direct assistance of state organs, for the purpose of committing acts of diversion and sabotage, in order to weaken the defensive power of Yugoslavia;

8. That, with the same aim in view, members of the Yugoslav minorities are being removed on a large scale from areas where they have been living for centuries. This is not only an inhuman act, but is also a violation of the truce agreements and peace treaties, under which the governments of the respective countries have pledged themselves to respect human rights and to refrain from discrimination;

9. That the governments of Bulgaria and Hungary are, in contradiction with the provisions of the peace treaties, imposing their citizenship upon Yugoslav citizens born in those parts of Yugoslavia that Bulgaria and Hungary, as allies of Hitler, occupied during the war;

10. That, by withdrawing ambassadors and ministers from Belgrade and indulging in discriminatory practices and acts contrary to the law of nations and established international practice against Yugoslav diplomats – groundless rejections of diplomatic notes and failure to answer them; misuse of diplomatic correspondence for slanderous and abusive attacks on the FPRY – the aforementioned governments are not only rendering it impossible to solve even the most insignificant disputes through diplomatic channels, but are also jeopardizing the nominal maintenance of diplomatic relations;

11. That the governments of the USSR and of the other six States have unilaterally abrogated forty-six political, economic, cultural, and other agreements and conventions concluded with Yugoslavia;

12. That the governments of Bulgaria, Hungary, and Romania, supported by the government of the USSR, have arbitrarily violated the military clauses of the peace treaties, by increasing the numerical strength of their armies and strengthening the quantity and quality of their armaments. Demonstrative troop movements and manoeuvres have been taking place in the frontier areas bordering on the FPRY. The number and location of the troops of the USSR in Hungary and Romania are lending a much more dangerous character to these ostentatious provocations and are obviously encouraging them, because the provocations are increasing in number and intensity, so that many Yugoslav frontier guards and citizens have been killed and wounded in the course of incidents which have taken place along all the borders of the aforementioned states. Not only the number of incidents, but also the manner in which these incidents are being carried out, are proof of the intention to intensify the prevailing tension.

13. All these and similar actions of the governments of the USSR, Hungary, Romania, Bulgaria, and Albania, as well as the governments of Czechoslovakia and Poland, violate the generally accepted principles

regarding relations among nations, as set forth in the United Nations Charter.

14. All the attempts that the government of the FPRY has made so far in order to settle peacefully the questions under dispute, as well as the proposal of the government of the FPRY to conclude agreements for a lasting peace and non-aggression with each of the neighbouring states, submitted by Mr Edvard Kardelj, Minister for Foreign Affairs, at the meeting of the General Assembly of the United Nations on 25 September 1950, have remained unsuccessful. On the contrary, the governments of the states responsible for this state of affairs are constantly aggravating these relations, so that in October 1951, on the eve of the session of the General Assembly of the United Nations, they have been refusing even to accept notes regarding grave incidents, in which Yugoslav citizens were murdered on Yugoslav territory by agents of the said states.

15. The government of the FPRY, having exhausted all normal diplomatic means for the elimination of a situation fraught with danger for international peace, and, bearing in mind that this situation is worsening, has the honour to request the General Assembly of the United Nations, in accordance with Article 10 of the United Nations Charter, that the following item: 'Hostile activities of the government of the USSR and the governments of Bulgaria, Hungary, Romania, and Albania, as well as the governments of Czechoslovakia and Poland, against Yugoslavia', should be placed on the agenda of the General Assembly, so that the Assembly may discuss it and make recommendations which it may find appropriate.

12. Secret Report to the 20th Party Congress of the CPSU[1]

Nikita S. Khrushchev

Special Report by Nikita S. Khrushchev, First Secretary of the
Communist Party of the Soviet Union. Delivered at the Closed
Session of the 20th Congress of the Communist Party of the Soviet
Union. (24–25 February 1956)

Comrades! In the report of the Central Committee of the party at the 20th
Congress, in a number of speeches by delegates to the Congress, as also
formerly during the plenary CC/CPSU sessions, quite a lot has been said
about the cult of the individual and about its harmful consequences.

After Stalin's death the Central Committee of the party began to
implement a policy of explaining concisely and consistently that it is
impermissible and foreign to the spirit of Marxism-Leninism to elevate
one person, to transform him into a superman possessing supernatural
characteristics, akin to those of a god. Such a man supposedly knows
everything, sees everything, thinks for everyone, can do anything, is
infallible in his behaviour.

Such a belief about a man, and specifically about Stalin, was cultivated
among us for many years.

The objective of the present report is not a thorough evaluation of
Stalin's life and activity. Concerning Stalin's merits, an entirely sufficient
number of books, pamphlets and studies had already been written in his
lifetime. The role of Stalin in the preparation and execution of the
socialist revolution, in the Civil War, and in the fight for the construction
of socialism in our country, is universally known. Everyone knows this
well.

At present, we are concerned with a question which has immense
importance for the party now and for the future – with how the cult of the
person of Stalin has been gradually growing, the cult which became at a
certain specific stage the source of a whole series of exceedingly serious
and grave perversions of party principles, of party democracy, of revolutionary legality.

Because of the fact that not all as yet realize fully the practical
consequences resulting from the cult of the individual, the great harm
caused by the violation of the principle of collective direction of the party

and because of the accumulation of immense and limitless power in the hands of one person, the Central Committee of the party considers it absolutely necessary to make the material pertaining to this matter available to the 20th Congress of the Communist Party of the Soviet Union.

Allow me first of all to remind you how severely the classics of Marxism-Leninism denounced every manifestation of the cult of the individual. In a letter to the German political worker, Wilhelm Bloss, Marx stated:

From my antipathy to any cult of the individual, I never made public during the existence of the International the numerous addresses from various countries which recognized my merits and which annoyed me. I did not even reply to them, except sometimes to rebuke their authors. Engels and I first joined the secret society of communists on the condition that everything making for superstitious worship of authority would be deleted from its statute. Lassalle subsequently did quite the opposite.

Sometime later Engels wrote: 'Both Marx and I have always been against any public manifestation with regard to individuals, with the exception of cases when it had an important purpose; and we most strongly opposed such manifestations which during our lifetime concerned us personally.'

The great modesty of the genius of the Revolution, Vladimir Ilyich Lenin, is known. Lenin had always stressed the role of the people as the creator of history, the directing and organizational role of the party as a living and creative organism, and also the role of the Central Committee.

Marxism does not negate the role of the leaders of the working class in directing the revolutionary liberation movement.

While ascribing great importance to the role of the leaders and organizers of the masses, Lenin at the same time mercilessly stigmatized every manifestation of the cult of the individual, inexorably combated the foreign-to-Marxism views about a 'hero' and a 'crowd', and countered all efforts to oppose a 'hero' to the masses and to the people.

Lenin taught that the party's strength depends on its indissoluble unity with the masses, on the fact that behind the party follows the people – workers, peasants and intelligentsia. 'Only he will win and retain power,' said Lenin, 'who believes in the people, who submerges himself in the fountain of the living creativeness of the people.'

Lenin spoke with pride about the Bolshevik Communist Party as the leader and teacher of the people; he called for the presentation of all the most important questions before the opinion of knowledgeable workers, before the opinion of their party; he said: 'We believe in it, we see in it the wisdom, the honour, and the conscience of our epoch.'

Lenin resolutely stood against every attempt aimed at belittling or weakening the directing role of the party in the structure of the Soviet state. He worked out Bolshevik principles of party direction and norms of party life, stressing that the guiding principle of party leadership is its collegiality. Already during the pre-revolutionary years, Lenin called the Central Committee of the party a collective of leaders and the guardian and interpreter of party principles. 'During the period between congresses,' pointed out Lenin, 'the Central Committee guards and interprets the principles of the party.'

Underlying the role of the Central Committee of the party and its authority, Vladimir Ilyich pointed out: 'Our Central Committee constituted itself as a closely centralized and highly authoritative group.'

During Lenin's life the Central Committee of the party was a real expression of collective leadership of the party and of the nation. Being a militant Marxist-revolutionist, always unyielding in matters of principle, Lenin never imposed by force his views upon his co-workers. He tried to convince; he patiently explained his opinions to others. Lenin always diligently observed that the norms of party life were realized, that the party statute was enforced, that the party congresses and the plenary sessions of the Central Committee took place at the proper intervals.

In addition to the great accomplishments of V. I. Lenin for the victory of the working class and of the working peasants, for the victory of our party and for the application of the ideas of scientific communism to life, his acute mind expressed itself also in this – that he detected in Stalin in time those negative characteristics which resulted later in grave consequences. Fearing the future fate of the party and of the Soviet nation, V. I. Lenin made a completely correct characterization of Stalin, pointing out that it was necessary to consider the question of transferring Stalin from the position of the Secretary General because of the fact that Stalin is excessively rude, that he does not have a proper attitude towards his comrades, that he is capricious and abuses his power.

In December 1922, in a letter to the Party Congress, Vladimir Ilyich wrote: 'After taking over the position of Secretary General, Comrade Stalin accumulated in his hands immeasurable power and I am not certain whether he will be always able to use this power with the required care.'

This letter – a political document of tremendous importance, known in the party history as Lenin's 'testament' – was distributed among the delegates to the 20th Party Congress. You have read it and will undoubtedly read it again more than once. You might reflect on Lenin's plain words, in which expression is given to Vladimir Ilyich's anxiety concerning the party, the people, the state, and the future direction of party policy.

Vladimir Ilyich said:

> Stalin is excessively rude, and this defect, which can be freely tolerated in our midst and in contacts among us communists, becomes a defect which cannot be tolerated in one holding the position of the Secretary General. Because of this, I propose that the comrades consider the method by which Stalin would be removed from this position and by which another man would be selected for it, a man who, above all, would differ from Stalin in only one quality, namely, greater tolerance, greater loyalty, greater kindness and more considerate attitude toward the comrades, a less capricious temper, etc.

This document of Lenin's was made known to the delegates at the 13th Party Congress, who discussed the question of transferring Stalin from the position of Secretary General. The delegates declared themselves in favour of retaining Stalin in this post, hoping that he would heed the critical remarks of Vladimir Ilyich and would be able to overcome the defects which caused Lenin serious anxiety.

Comrades! The Party Congress should become acquainted with two new documents, which confirm Stalin's character as already outlined by Vladimir Ilyich Lenin in his 'testament'. These documents are a letter from Nadezhda Konstantinovna Krupskaya to Kamenev, who was at that time head of the Political Bureau, and a personal letter from Vladimir Ilyich Lenin to Stalin.

I will now read these documents:

> Lev Borisovich!
> Because of a short letter which I had written in words dictated to me by Vladimir Ilyich by permission of the doctors, Stalin allowed himself yesterday an unusually rude outburst directed at me. This is not my first day in the party. During all these thirty years I have never heard from any comrade one word of rudeness. The business of the party and of Ilyich are not less dear to me than to Stalin. I need at present the maximum of self-control. What one can and what one cannot discuss with Ilyich I know better than any doctor, because I know what makes him nervous and what does not, in any case I know better than Stalin. I am turning to you and to Grigory as much closer comrades of V.I. and I beg you to protect me from rude interference with my private life and from vile invectives and threats. I have no doubt as to what will be the unanimous decision of the Control Commission, with which Stalin sees fit to threaten me; however, I have neither the strength nor the time to waste on this foolish quarrel. And I am a living person and my nerves are strained to the utmost.
>
> N. KRUPSKAYA

Nadezhda Konstantinovna wrote this letter on 23 December 1922. After two and a half months, in March 1923, Vladimir Ilyich Lenin sent Stalin the following letter:

To Comrade Stalin: 5 March 1923
Copies for: Kamenev and Zinoviev.

Dear Comrade Stalin!

You permitted yourself a rude summons of my wife to the telephone and a rude reprimand of her. Despite the fact that she told you that she agreed to forget what was said, nevertheless Zinoviev and Kamenev heard about it from her. I have no intention to forget so easily that which is being done against me, and I need not stress here that I consider as directed against me that which is being done against my wife. I ask you, therefore, that you weigh carefully whether you are agreeable to retracting your words and apologizing or whether you prefer the severance of relations between us.

Sincerely: LENIN

(*Commotion in the hall.*)

Comrades! I will not comment on these documents. They speak eloquently for themselves. Since Stalin could behave in this manner during Lenin's life, could thus behave towards Nadezhda Konstantinovna Krupskaya – whom the party knows well and values highly as a loyal friend of Lenin and as an active fighter for the cause of the party since its creation – we can easily imagine how Stalin treated other people. These negative characteristics of his developed steadily and during the last years acquired an absolutely insufferable character.

As later events have proven, Lenin's anxiety was justified: in the first period after Lenin's death, Stalin still paid attention to his advice, but later he began to disregard the serious admonitions of Vladimir Ilyich.

When we analyse the practice of Stalin in regard to the direction of the party and of the country, when we pause to consider everything which Stalin perpetrated, we must be convinced that Lenin's fears were justified. The negative characteristics of Stalin, which, in Lenin's time, were only incipient, transformed themselves during the last years into a grave abuse of power by Stalin, which caused untold harm to our party.

We have to consider seriously and analyse correctly this matter in order that we may preclude any possibility of a repetition in any form whatever of what took place during the life of Stalin, who absolutely did not tolerate collegiality in leadership and in work, and who practised brutal violence, not only towards everything which opposed him, but also towards that which seemed, to his capricious and despotic character, contrary to his concepts.

Stalin acted not through persuasion, explanation and patient cooperation with people, but by imposing his concepts and demanding absolute submission to his opinion. Whoever opposed this concept or tried to prove his viewpoint and the correctness of his position was doomed to removal from the leading collective and to subsequent moral and physical annihilation. This was especially true during the period following the 17th Party Congress, when many prominent party leaders and rank-and-file party workers, honest and dedicated to the cause of communism, fell victim to Stalin's despotism.

We must affirm that the party had fought a serious fight against the Trotskyites, rightists and bourgeois nationalists, and that it disarmed ideologically all the enemies of Leninism. This ideological fight was carried on successfully, as a result of which the party became strengthened and tempered. Here Stalin played a positive role.

The party led a great political-ideological struggle against those in its own ranks who proposed anti-Leninist theses, who represented a political line hostile to the party and to the cause of socialism. This was a stubborn and a difficult fight but a necessary one, because the political line of both the Trotskyite-Zinovievite bloc and of the Bukharinites led actually towards the restoration of capitalism and capitulation to the world bourgeoisie. Let us consider for a moment what would have happened if in 1928–9 the political line of Right deviation had prevailed among us, or orientation towards 'cotton-dress industrialization', or towards the *kulak*, etc. We would not now have a powerful heavy industry, we would not have the *kolkhozes*, we would find ourselves disarmed and weak in a capitalist encirclement.

It was for this reason that the party led an inexorable ideological fight and explained to all party members and to the non-party masses the harm and the danger of the anti-Leninist proposals of the Trotskyite opposition and the rightist opportunists. And this great work of explaining the party line bore fruit; both the Trotskyites and the rightist opportunists were politically isolated; the overwhelming party majority supported the Leninist line and the party was able to awaken and organize the working masses to apply the Leninist party line and to build socialism.

Worth noting is the fact that, even during the progress of the furious ideological fight against the Trotskyites, the Zinovievites, the Bukharinites and others, extreme repressive measures were not used against them. The fight was on ideological grounds. But some years later, when socialism in our country was fundamentally constructed, when the exploiting classes were generally liquidated, when the Soviet social structure had radically changed, when the social basis for political movements and groups hostile to the party had violently contracted, when the ideological opponents of the party were long since defeated politically – then the repression directed against them began.

It was precisely during this period (1935–7–8) that the practice of mass repression through the government apparatus was born, first against the enemies of Leninism – Trotskyites, Zinovievites, Bukharinites, long since politically defeated by the party – and subsequently also against many honest communists, against those party cadres who had borne the heavy load of the Civil War and the first and most difficult years of industrialization and collectivization, who actively fought against the Trotskyites and the rightists for the Leninist party line.

Stalin originated the concept 'enemy of the people'. This term automatically rendered it unnecessary that the ideological errors of a man or men engaged in a controversy be proven; this term made possible the usage of the most cruel repression, violating all norms of revolutionary legality, against anyone who in any way disagreed with Stalin, against those who were only suspected of hostile intent, against those who had bad reputations. This concept 'enemy of the people' actually eliminated the possibility of any kind of ideological fight or the making of one's views known on this or that issue, even those of a practical character. In the main, and in actuality, the only proof of guilt used, against all norms of current legal science, was the 'confession' of the accused himself; and, as subsequent probing proved, 'confessions' were acquired through physical pressures against the accused. This led to glaring violations of revolutionary legality and to the fact that many entirely innocent persons, who in the past had defended the party line, became victims.

We must assert that, in regard to those persons who in their time had opposed the party line, there were often no sufficiently serious reasons for their physical annihilation. The formula 'enemy of the people' was specifically introduced for the purpose of physically annihilating such individuals.

It is a fact that many persons who were later annihilated as enemies of the party and people had worked with Lenin during his life. Some of these persons had made errors during Lenin's life, but, despite this, Lenin benefited by their work; he corrected them and he did everything possible to retain them in the ranks of the party; he induced them to follow him.

In this connection the delegates to the Party Congress should familiarize themselves with an unpublished note by V. I. Lenin directed to the Central Committee's Political Bureau in October 1920. Outlining the duties of the Control Commission, Lenin wrote that the commission should be transformed into a real 'organ of party and proletarian conscience'.

As a special duty of the Control Commission there is recommended a deep, individualized relationship with, and sometimes even a type of therapy for, the representatives of the so-called opposition – those who have experienced a psychological crisis because of failure in their Soviet or party career. An effort should be made to quiet them, to explain the matter to them in a way used among comrades, to find for them (avoiding the method of issuing orders) a task for which they are psychologically fitted. Advice and rules relating to this matter are to be formulated by the Central Committee's Organizational Bureau, etc.

Everyone knows how irreconcilable Lenin was with the ideological enemies of Marxism, with those who deviated from the correct party line. At the same time, however, Lenin, as is evident from the given document, in his practice of directing the party demanded the most intimate party contact with people who had shown indecision or temporary non-conformity with the party line, but whom it was possible to return to the party path. Lenin advised that such people should be patiently educated without the application of extreme methods.

Lenin's wisdom in dealing with people was evident in his work with cadres.

An entirely different relationship with people characterized Stalin. Lenin's traits – patient work with people, stubborn and painstaking education of them, the ability to induce people to follow him without using compulsion, but rather through the ideological influence on them of the whole collective – were entirely foreign to Stalin. He discarded the Leninist method of convincing and educating, he abandoned the method of ideological struggle for that of administrative violence, mass repressions and terror. He acted on an increasingly larger scale and more stubbornly through punitive organs, at the same time often violating all existing norms of morality and of Soviet laws.

Arbitrary behaviour by one person encouraged and permitted arbitrariness in others. Mass arrests and deportations of many thousands of people, execution without trial and without normal investigation created conditions of insecurity, fear and even desperation.

This, of course, did not contribute towards unity of the party ranks and of all strata of working people, but, on the contrary, brought about annihilation and the expulsion from the party of workers who were loyal but inconvenient to Stalin.

Our party fought for the implementation of Lenin's plans for the construction of socialism. This was an ideological fight. Had Leninist principles been observed during the course of this fight, had the party's devotion to principles been skilfully combined with a keen and solicitous concern for people, had they not been repelled and wasted but rather drawn to our side, we certainly would not have had such a brutal violation of revolutionary legality and many thousands of people would not have fallen victim to the method of terror. Extraordinary methods would then have been resorted to only against those people who had in fact committed criminal acts against the Soviet system.

Let us recall some historical facts.

In the days before the October Revolution, two members of the Central Committee of the Bolshevik Party – Kamenev and Zinoviev – declared themselves against Lenin's plan for an armed uprising. In addition, on 18 October they published in the Menshevik newspaper, *Novaya Zhizn*, a statement declaring that the Bolsheviks were making preparations for an uprising and that they considered it adventuristic. Kamenev and Zinoviev thus disclosed to the enemy the decision of the Central Committee to stage the uprising, and that the uprising had been organized to take place within the very near future.

This was treason against the party and against the Revolution. In this connection, V. I. Lenin wrote: 'Kamenev and Zinoviev revealed the decision of the Central Committee of their party on the armed uprising to Rodzyanko and Kerensky . . .' He put before the Central Committee the question of Zinoviev's and Kamenev's expulsion from the party.

However, after the Great Socialist October Revolution, as is known, Zinoviev and Kamenev were given leading positions. Lenin put them in positions in which they carried out most responsible party tasks and participated actively in the work of the leading party and Soviet organs. It is known that Zinoviev and Kamenev committed a number of other serious errors during Lenin's life. In his 'testament' Lenin warned that 'Zinoviev's and Kamenev's October episode was of course not an accident.' But Lenin did not pose the question of their arrest and certainly not their shooting.

Or, let us take the example of the Trotskyites. At present, after a sufficiently long historical period, we can speak about the fight with the Trotskyites with complete calm and can analyse this matter with sufficient objectivity. After all, around Trotsky were people whose origin cannot by any means be traced to bourgeois society. Part of them belonged to the party intelligentsia and a certain part were recruited from among the workers. We can name many individuals who, in their time, joined the Trotskyites; however, these same individuals took an active part in the workers' movement before the Revolution, during the Socialist October Revolution itself, and also in the consolidation of the victory of this greatest of revolutions. Many of them broke with Trotskyism and returned to Leninist positions. Was it necessary to annihilate such people? We are deeply convinced that, had Lenin lived, such an extreme method would not have been used against any of them.

Such are only a few historical facts. But can it be said that Lenin did not decide to use even the most severe means against enemies of the Revolution when this was actually necessary? No; no one can say this. Vladimir Ilyich demanded uncompromising dealings with the enemies of the Revolution and of the working class and when necessary resorted ruthlessly to such methods. You will recall only V. I. Lenin's fight with the Socialist Revolutionary organizers of the anti-Soviet uprising, with the counter-revolutionary *kulaks* in 1918 and with others, when Lenin without hesitation used the most extreme methods against the enemies. Lenin used such methods, however, only against actual class enemies and not against those who err, and whom it was possible to lead through ideological influence and even retain in the leadership. Lenin used severe methods only in the most necessary cases, when the exploiting classes were still in existence and were vigorously opposing the Revolution, when the struggle for survival was decidedly assuming the sharpest forms, even including a Civil War.

Stalin, on the other hand, used extreme methods and mass repressions at a time when the Revolution was already victorious, when the Soviet state was strengthened, when the exploiting classes were already liquidated and socialist relations were rooted solidly in all phases of national economy, when our party was politically consolidated and had strengthened itself both numerically and ideologically.

It is clear that here Stalin showed in a whole series of cases his intolerance, his brutality and his abuse of power. Instead of proving his political correctness and mobilizing the masses, he often chose the path of repression and physical annihilation, not only against actual enemies, but also against individuals who had not committed any crimes against the party and the Soviet government. Here we see no wisdom but only a demonstration of the brutal force which had once so alarmed V. I. Lenin.

Lately, especially after the unmasking of the Beria gang, the Central Committee looked into a series of matters fabricated by this gang. This revealed a very ugly picture of brutal wilfulness connected with the incorrect behaviour of Stalin. As facts prove, Stalin, using his unlimited power, allowed himself many abuses, acting in the name of the Central Committee, not asking for the opinion of the Committee members nor even of the members of the Central Committee's Political Bureau; often he did not inform them about his personal decisions concerning very important party and governmental matters.

Considering the question of the cult of the individual, we must first of all show everyone what harm this caused to the interests of our party.

Vladimir Ilyich Lenin had always stressed the party's role and significance in the direction of the socialist government of workers and peasants; he saw in this the chief precondition for a successful building of socialism in our country. Pointing to the great responsibility of the Bolshevik Party, as ruling party of the Soviet state, Lenin called for the most meticulous observance of all norms of party life; he called for the realization of the principles of collegiality in the direction of the party and the state.

Collegiality of leadership flows from the very nature of our party, a party built on the principles of democratic centralism. 'This means,' said Lenin, 'that all party matters are accomplished by all party members – directly or through representatives – who, without any exceptions, are subject to the same rules; in addition, all administrative members, all directing collegia, all holders of party positions are elective, they must account for their activities and are recallable.'

It is known that Lenin himself offered an example of the most careful observance of these principles. There was no matter so important that Lenin himself decided it without asking for the advice and approval of the majority of the Central Committee members or of the members of the Central Committee's Political Bureau. In the most difficult period for our party and our country, Lenin considered it necessary regularly to convoke congresses, party conferences and plenary sessions of the Central Committee at which all the most important questions were discussed and where resolutions, carefully worked out by the collective of leaders, were approved.

We can recall, for an example, the year 1918 when the country was threatened by the attack of the imperialistic interventionists. In this situation the 7th Party Congress was convened in order to discuss a vitally important matter which could not be postponed – the matter of peace. In 1919, while the Civil War was raging, the 8th Party Congress convened which adopted a new party programme, decided such important matters as the relationship with the peasant masses, the organization of the Red Army, the leading role of the party in the work of the soviets, the correction of the social composition of the party, and other matters. In 1920 the 9th Party Congress was convened which laid down guiding principles pertaining to the party's work in the sphere of economic construction. In 1921 the 10th Party Congress accepted Lenin's New Economic Policy and the historical resolution called *About Party Unity*.

During Lenin's life, party congresses were convened regularly; always when a radical turn in the development of the party and the country took place, Lenin considered it absolutely necessary that the party discuss at length all the basic matters pertaining to internal and foreign policy and to questions bearing on the development of party and government.

It is very characteristic that Lenin addressed to the Party Congress as the highest party organ his last articles, letters and remarks. During the period between congresses, the Central Committee of the party, acting as the most authoritative leading collective, meticulously observed the principles of the party and carried out its policy.

So it was during Lenin's life. Were our party's holy Leninist principles observed after the death of Vladimir Ilyich?

Whereas, during the first few years after Lenin's death, Party Congresses and Central Committee plenums took place more or less regularly, later, when Stalin began increasingly to abuse his power, these principles were brutally violated. This was especially evident during the last fifteen years of his life. Was it a normal situation when over thirteen years elapsed between the 18th and 19th Party Congresses, years during which our party and our country had experienced so many important events? These events demanded categorically that the party should have passed resolutions pertaining to the country's defence during the Patriotic War and to peacetime construction after the war. Even after the end of the war a Congress was not convened for over seven years. Central Committee plenums were hardly ever called. It should be sufficient to mention that during all the years of the Patriotic War not a single Central Committee plenum took place. It is true that there was an attempt to call a Central Committee plenum in October 1941, when Central Committee members from the whole country were called to Moscow. They waited two days for the opening of the plenum, but in vain. Stalin did not even want to meet and talk to the Central Committee members. This fact shows how demoralized Stalin was in the first months of the war and how haughtily and disdainfully he treated the Central Committee members.

In practice, Stalin ignored the norms of party life and trampled on the Leninist principle of collective party leadership.

Stalin's wilfulness *vis-à-vis* the party and its Central Committee became fully evident after the 17th Party Congress which took place in 1934.

Having at its disposal numerous data showing brutal wilfulness towards party cadres, the Central Committee has created a party commission under the control of the Central Committee Presidium; it was charged with investigating what made possible mass repressions against the majority of the Central Committee members and candidates elected at the 17th Congress of the All-Union Communist Party (Bolsheviks).

The commission has become acquainted with a large quantity of materials in the NKVD archives and with other documents and has established many facts pertaining to the fabrication of cases against communists, to false accusations, to glaring abuses of socialist legality, which resulted in the death of innocent people. It became apparent that many party, Soviet and economic activists, who were branded in 1937-8 as 'enemies', were actually never enemies, spies, wreckers, etc., but were always honest communists; they were only so stigmatized and, often, no longer able to bear barbaric tortures, they charged themselves (at the order of the investigative judges – falsifiers) with all kinds of grave and unlikely crimes.

The commission has presented to the Central Committee Presidium lengthy and documented materials pertaining to mass repressions against the delegates to the 17th Party Congress and against members of the Central Committee elected at that Congress. These materials have been studied by the Presidium of the Central Committee.

It was determined that of the 139 members and candidates of the party's Central Committee who were elected at the 17th Congress, ninety-eight persons, that is, 70 per cent, were arrested and shot (mostly in 1937–8). (*Indignation in the hall.*) What was the composition of the delegates to the 17th Congress? It is known that 80 per cent of the voting participants of the 17th Congress joined the party during the years of conspiracy before the Revolution and during the Civil War; this means before 1921. By social origin the basic mass of the delegates to the Congress were workers (60 per cent of the voting members).

For this reason, it was inconceivable that a congress so composed would have elected a Central Committee a majority of whom would prove to be enemies of the party. The only reason why 70 per cent of the Central Committee members and candidates elected at the 17th Congress were branded as enemies of the party and of the people was because honest communists were slandered, accusations against them were fabricated, and revolutionary legality was gravely undermined.

The same fate met not only the Central Committee members but also the majority of the delegates to the 17th Party Congress. Of 1,966 delegates with either voting or advisory rights, 1,108 persons were arrested on charges of anti-revolutionary crimes, in other words, decidedly more than a majority. This very fact shows how absurd, wild and contrary to common sense were the charges of counter-revolutionary crimes made out, as we now see, against a majority of participants at the 17th Party Congress. (*Indignation in the hall.*)

We should recall that the 17th Party Congress is historically known as the Congress of Victors. Delegates to the Congress were active participants in the building of our socialist state; many of them suffered and fought for party interests during the pre-Revolutionary years in the conspiracy and at the civil-war fronts; they fought their enemies valiantly and often nervelessly looked into the face of death.

How, then, can we believe that such people could prove to be 'two-faced' and had joined the camps of the enemies of socialism during the era after the political liquidation of Zinovievites, Trotskyites and rightists and after the great accomplishments of socialist construction? This was the result of the abuse of power by Stalin, who began to use mass terror against the party cadres.

What is the reason that mass repressions against activists increased more and more after the 17th Party Congress? It was because at that time Stalin had so elevated himself above the party and above the nation that he ceased to consider either the Central Committee or the party.

While he still reckoned with the opinion of the collective before the 17th Congress, after the complete liquidation of the Trotskyites, Zinovievites and Bukharinites, when as a result of that fight and socialist victories the party achieved unity, Stalin ceased to an ever greater degree to consider the members of the party's Central Committee and even the members of the Political Bureau. Stalin thought that now he could decide all things alone and all he needed were statisticians; he treated all others in such a way that they could only listen to and praise him.

After the criminal murder of Sergei M. Kirov, mass repressions and brutal acts of violation of socialist legality began. On the evening of 1 December 1934, on Stalin's initiative (without the approval of the Political Bureau – which was passed two days later, casually), the Secretary of the Presidium of the Central Executive Committee, Yenukidze, signed the following directive:

1. Investigative agencies are directed to speed up the cases of those accused of the preparation or execution of acts of terror.

2. Judicial organs are directed not to hold up the execution of death sentences pertaining to crimes of this category in order to consider the possibility of pardon, because the Presidium of the Central Executive Committee of the USSR does not consider as possible the receiving of petitions of this sort.

3. The organs of the Commissariat of Internal Affairs are directed to execute the death sentences against criminals of the above-mentioned category immediately after the passage of sentences.

This directive became the basis for mass acts of abuse against socialist legality. During many of the fabricated court cases, the accused were charged with 'the preparation' of terroristic acts; this deprived them of any possibility that their cases might be re-examined, even when they stated before the court that their 'confessions' were secured by force, and when, in a convincing manner, they disproved the accusations against them.

It must be asserted that to this day the circumstances surrounding Kirov's murder hide many things which are inexplicable and mysterious and demand a most careful examination. There are reasons for the suspicion that the killer of Kirov, Nikolayev, was assisted by someone from among the people whose duty it was to protect the person of Kirov.

A month and a half before the killing, Nikolayev was arrested on the grounds of suspicious behaviour but he was released and not even searched. It is an unusually suspicious circumstance that when the Chekist assigned to protect Kirov was being brought for an interrogation, on 2 December 1934, he was killed in a car 'accident' in which no other occupants of the car were harmed. After the murder of Kirov, top functionaries of the Leningrad NKVD were given very light sentences, but in 1937 they were shot. We can assume that they were shot in order to cover the traces of the organizers of Kirov's killing. (*Movement in the hall.*)

Mass repressions grew tremendously from the end of 1936 after a telegram from Stalin and Zhdanov, dated from Sochi on 25 September

1936, was addressed to Kaganovitch, Molotov and other members of the Political Bureau. The content of the telegram was as follows:

> We deem it absolutely necessary and urgent that Comrade Yezhov be nominated to the post of People's Commissar for Internal Affairs. Yagoda has definitely proved himself to be incapable of unmasking the Trotskyite–Zinovievite bloc. The OGPU is four years behind in this matter. This is noted by all party workers and by the majority of the representatives of the NKVD.

Strictly speaking, we should stress that Stalin did not meet with and, therefore, could not know the opinion of party workers.

This Stalinist formulation that the 'NKVD is four years behind' in applying mass repression and that there is a necessity for 'catching up' with the neglected work directly pushed the NKVD workers on the path of mass arrests and executions.

We should state that this formulation was also forced on the February–March plenary session of the Central Committee of the All-Union Communist Party (Bolsheviks) in 1937. The plenary resolution approved it on the basis of Yezhov's report, *Lessons Flowing from the Harmful Activity, Diversion and Espionage of the Japanese-German-Trotskyite Agents*, stating:

> The plenum of the Central Committee of the All-Union Communist Party (Bolsheviks) considers that all facts revealed during the investigation into the matter of an anti-Soviet Trotskyite centre and of its followers in the provinces show that the People's Commissariat of Internal Affairs has fallen behind at least four years in the attempt to unmask these most inexorable enemies of the people.

The mass repressions at this time were made under the slogan of a fight against the Trotskyites. Did the Trotskyites at this time actually constitute such a danger to our party and to the Soviet state? We should recall that in 1927, on the eve of the 15th Party Congress, only some 4,000 votes were cast for the Trotskyite–Zinovievite opposition while there were 724,000 for the party line. During the ten years which passed between the 15th Party Congress and the February–March Central Committee plenum, Trotskyism was completely disarmed; many former Trotskyites had changed their former views and worked in the various sectors building socialism. It is clear that in the situation of socialist victory there was no basis for mass terror in the country.

Stalin's report at the February–March Central Committee plenum in 1937, *Deficiencies of Party Work and Methods for the Liquidation of the Trotskyites and of Other Two-Facers*, contained an attempt at theoretical justification of the mass terror policy under the pretext that as we march forward towards socialism class war must allegedly sharpen. Stalin asserted that both history and Lenin taught him this.

Actually Lenin taught that the application of revolutionary violence is necessitated by the resistance of the exploiting classes, and this referred to the era when the exploiting classes existed and were powerful. As soon as the nation's political situation had improved, when in January 1920 the Red Army took Rostov and thus won a most important victory over Denikin, Lenin instructed Dzerzhinsky to stop mass terror and to abolish the death penalty. Lenin justified this important political move of the Soviet state in the following manner in his report at the session of the All-Union Central Executive Committee on 2 February 1920:

We were forced to use terror because of the terror practised by the Entente, when strong world powers threw their hordes against us, not avoiding any type of conduct. We would not have lasted two days had we not answered these attempts of officers and White Guardists in a merciless fashion; this meant the use of terror, but this was forced upon us by the terrorist methods of the Entente.

But as soon as we attained a decisive victory, even before the end of the war, immediately after taking Rostov, we gave up the use of the death penalty and thus proved that we intend to execute our own programme in the manner that we promised. We say that the application of violence flows out of the decision to smother the exploiters, the big landowners and the capitalists; as soon as this was accomplished we gave up the use of all extraordinary methods. We have proved this in practice.

Stalin deviated from these clear and plain precepts of Lenin. Stalin put the party and the NKVD up to the use of mass terror when the exploiting classes had been liquidated in our country and when there were no serious reasons for the use of extraordinary mass terror.

This terror was actually directed not at the remnants of the defeated exploiting classes but against the honest workers of the party and of the Soviet state; against them were made lying, slanderous and absurd accusations concerning 'two-facedness', 'espionage', 'sabotage', preparation of fictitious 'plots', etc.

At the February–March Central Committee plenum in 1937 many members actually questioned the rightness of the established course regarding mass repressions under the pretext of combating 'two-facedness'.

Comrade Postyshev most ably expressed these doubts. He said:

I have philosophized that the severe years of fighting have passed. Party members who have lost their backbones have broken down or have joined the camp of the enemy; healthy elements have fought for the party. These were the years of industrialization and collectivization. I never thought it possible that after this severe era had passed Karpov and people like him would find themselves in the camp of the enemy. (Karpov was a worker in the Ukrainian Central Committee whom Postyshev knew well.) And now, according to the testimony, it appears that Karpov was recruited in 1934 by the Trotskyites. I personally do not believe that in 1934 an honest party member who had trod the long road of unrelenting fight against enemies for the party and for socialism would now be in the camp of the enemies. I do not believe it . . . I cannot imagine how it would be possible to travel with the party during the difficult years and then, in 1934, join the Trotskyites. It is an odd thing . . .

(*Movement in the hall.*)

Using Stalin's formulation, namely, that the closer we are to socialism the more enemies we will have, and using the resolution of the February–March Central Committee plenum passed on the basis of Yezhov's report, the *provocateurs* who had infiltrated the state-security organs together with conscienceless careerists began to protect with the party name the mass terror against party cadres, cadres of the Soviet state and the ordinary Soviet citizens. It should suffice to say that the number of arrests based on charges of counter-revolutionary crimes had grown ten times between 1936 and 1937.

It is known that brutal wilfulness was practised against leading party workers. The party statute, approved at the 17th Party Congress, was based on Leninist principles expressed at the 10th Party Congress. It stated that, in order to apply an extreme method such as exclusion from the party against a Central Committee member, against a Central Committee candidate and against a member of the Party Control Commission, 'it is necessary to call a Central Committee plenum and to invite to the plenum all Central Committee candidate members and all members of the Party Control Commission'; only if two-thirds of the members of such a general assembly of responsible party leaders find it necessary, only then can a Central Committee member or candidate be expelled.

The majority of the Central Committee members and candidates elected at the 17th Congress and arrested in 1937–8 were expelled from the party illegally through the brutal abuse of the party statute, because the question of their expulsion was never studied at the Central Committee plenum.

Now, when the cases of some of these so-called 'spies' and 'saboteurs' were examined, it was found that all their cases were fabricated. Confessions of guilt of many arrested and charged with enemy activity were gained with the help of cruel and inhuman tortures.

At the same time, Stalin, as we have been informed by members of the Political Bureau of that time, did not show them the statements of many accused political activists when they retracted their confessions before the military tribunal and asked for an objective examination of their cases. There were many such declarations, and Stalin doubtless knew of them.

The Central Committee considers it absolutely necessary to inform the

Congress of many such fabricated 'cases' against the members of the party's Central Committee elected at the 17th Party Congress.

An example of the vile provocation, of odious falsification and of criminal violation of revolutionary legality is the case of the former candidate for the Central Committee Political Bureau, one of the most eminent workers of the party and of the Soviet Government, Comrade Eikhe, who was a party member since 1905. (*Commotion in the hall.*)

Comrade Eikhe was arrested on 29 April 1938, on the basis of slanderous materials, without the sanction of the Prosecutor of the USSR, which was finally received fifteen months after the arrest.

Investigation of Eikhe's case was made in a manner which most brutally violated Soviet legality and was accompanied by wilfulness and falsification.

Eikhe was forced under torture to sign ahead of time a protocol of his confession prepared by the investigative judges, in which he and several other eminent party workers were accused of anti-Soviet activity.

On 1 October 1939, Eikhe sent his declaration to Stalin in which he categorically denied his guilt and asked for an examination of his case. In the declaration he wrote: 'There is no more bitter misery than to sit in the jail of a government for which I have always fought.'

A second declaration of Eikhe has been preserved which he sent to Stalin on 27 October 1939; in it he cited facts very convincingly and countered the slanderous accusations made against him, arguing that this provocatory accusation was on the one hand the work of real Trotskyites whose arrests he had sanctioned as First Secretary of the West Siberian Krai Party Committee and who conspired in order to take revenge on him, and, on the other hand, the result of the base falsification of materials by the investigative judges.

Eikhe wrote in his declaration:

On October 25 of this year I was informed that the investigation in my case had been concluded and I was given access to the materials of this investigation. Had I been guilty of only one hundredth of the crimes with which I am charged, I would not have dared to send you this pre-execution declaration; however, I have not been guilty of even one of the things with which I am charged and my heart is clean of even the shadow of baseness. I have never in my life told you a word of falsehood, and now, finding my two feet in the grave, I am also not lying. My whole case is a typical example of provocation, slander and violation of the elementary basis of revolutionary legality . . .

. . . The confessions which were made part of my file are not only absurd but contain some slander towards the Central Committee of the All-Union Communist Party (Bolsheviks) and towards the Council of People's Commissars, because correct resolutions of the Central Committee of the All-Union Communist Party (Bolsheviks) and of the Council of People's Commissars which were not made on my initiative and without my participation are presented as hostile acts of counter-revolutionary organizations made at my suggestion . . .

I am now alluding to the most disgraceful part of my life and to my really grave guilt against the party and against you. This is my confession of counter-revolutionary activity . . . The case is as follows: Not being able to suffer the tortures to which I was submitted by Ushakov and Nikolayev – and especially by the first one – who utilized the knowledge that my broken ribs have not properly mended and have caused me great pain, I have been forced to accuse myself and others.

The majority of my confession has been suggested or dictated by Ushakov, and the remainder is my reconstruction of NKVD materials from Western Siberia for which I assumed all responsibility. If some part of the story which Ushakov fabricated and which I signed did not properly hang together, I was forced to sign another variation. The same thing was done to Rukhimovich, who was at first designated as a member of the reserve net and whose name later was removed without telling me anything about it; the same was also done with the leader of the reserve net, supposedly created by Bukharin in 1935. At first I wrote my name in, and then I was instructed to insert Mezhlauk. There were other similar incidents.

. . . I am asking and begging you that you again examine my case, and this is not for the purpose of sparing me but in order to unmask the vile provocation which, like a snake, wound itself around many persons in a great degree due to my meanness and criminal slander. I have never betrayed you or the party. I know that I perish because of vile and mean work of the enemies of the party and of the people, who fabricated the provocation against me.

It would appear that such an important declaration was worth an examination by the Central Committee. This, however, was not done, and the declaration was transmitted to Beria while the terrible maltreatment of the Political Bureau candidate, Comrade Eikhe, continued.

On 2 February 1940, Eikhe was brought before the court. Here he did not confess any guilt and said as follows:

In all the so-called confessions of mine there is not one letter written by me with the exception of my signatures under the protocols, which were forced from me. I have made my confession under pressure from the investigative judge, who from the time of my arrest tormented me. After that I began to write all this nonsense . . . The most important thing for me is to tell the court, the party and Stalin that I am not guilty. I have never been guilty of any conspiracy. I will die believing in the truth of party policy as I have believed in it during my whole life.

On 4 February Eikhe was shot. *(Indignation in the hall.)*

It has been definitely established now that Eikhe's case was fabricated; he has been posthumously rehabilitated.

Comrade Rudzutak, candidate-member of the Political Bureau, member of the party since 1905, who spent ten years in a Tsarist hard-labour camp, completely retracted in court the confession which was forced from him. The protocol of the session of the Collegium of the Supreme Military Court contains the following statement by Rudzutak:

... The only plea which he places before the Court is that the Central Committee of the All-Union Communist Party (Bolsheviks) be informed that there is in the NKVD an as yet not liquidated centre which is craftily manufacturing cases, which forces innocent persons to confess; there is no opportunity to prove one's non-participation in crimes to which the confessions of various persons testify. The investigative methods are such that they force people to lie and to slander entirely innocent persons in addition to those who already stand accused. He asks the Court that he be allowed to inform the Central Committee of the All-Union Communist Party (Bolsheviks) about all this in writing. He assures the Court that he personally had never any evil designs in regard to the policy of our party because he had always agreed with the party policy pertaining to all spheres of economic and cultural activity.

This declaration of Rudzutak was ignored, despite the fact that Rudzutak was in his time the chief of the Central Control Commission, which was called into being in accordance with Lenin's concept for the purpose of fighting for party unity. In this manner fell the chief of this highly authoritative party organ, a victim of brutal wilfulness; he was not even called before the Central Committee's Political Bureau because Stalin did not want to talk to him. Sentence was pronounced on him in twenty minutes and he was shot. *(Indignation in the hall.)*

After careful examination of the case in 1955, it was established that the accusation against Rudzutak was false and that it was based on slanderous materials. Rudzutak has been rehabilitated posthumously.

The way in which the former NKVD workers manufactured various fictitious 'anti-Soviet centres' and 'blocs' with the help of provocatory methods is seen from the confession of Comrade Rozenblum, party member since 1906, who was arrested in 1937 by the Leningrad NKVD.

During the examination in 1955 of the Komarov case Rozenblum revealed the following fact: When Rozenblum was arrested in 1937, he was subjected to terrible torture during which he was ordered to confess false information concerning himself and other persons. He was then brought to the office of Zakovsky, who offered him freedom on condition that he make before the court a false confession fabricated in 1937 by the NKVD concerning 'sabotage, espionage and diversion in a terroristic centre in Leningrad'. *(Movement in the hall.)* With unbelievable cynicism, Zakovsky told about the vile 'mechanism' for the crafty creation of fabricated 'anti-Soviet plots'.

Rozenblum stated:

In order to illustrate it to me, Zakovsky gave me several possible variants of the organization of this centre and of its branches. After he detailed the organization to me, Zakovsky told me that the NKVD would prepare the case of this centre, remarking that the trial would be public. Before the Court were to be brought four or five members of this centre: Chudov, Ugarov, Smorodin, Pozern, Shaposhnikova (Chudov's wife) and others together with two or three members from the branches of this centre . . .

. . . The case of the Leningrad centre has to be built solidly, and for　; reason witnesses are needed. Social origin (of course, in the past) and the party standing of the witness will play more than a small role.

'You, yourself,' said Zakovsky, 'will not need to invent anything. The NKVD will prepare for you a ready outline for every branch of the centre; you will have to study it carefully and to remember well all questions and answers which the Court might ask. This case will be ready in four–five months, or perhaps a half year. During all this time you will be preparing yourself so that you will not compromise the investigation and yourself. Your future will depend on how the trial goes and on its results. If you begin to lie and to testify falsely, blame yourself. If you manage to endure it, you will save your head and we will feed and clothe you at the government's cost until your death.'

This is the kind of vile things which were then practised. *(Movement in the hall.)*

Even more widely was the falsification of cases practised in the provinces. The NKVD headquarters of the Sverdlov Oblast 'discovered' the so-called 'Ural uprising staff' – an organ of the bloc of rightists, Trotskyites, Social Revolutionaries, church leaders – whose chief supposedly was the Secretary of the Sverdlov Oblast Party Committee and member of the Central Committee, All-Union Communist Party (Bolsheviks), Kabakov, who had been a party member since 1914. The investigative materials of that time show that in almost all krais, oblasts and republics there supposedly existed 'Rightist Trotskyite, espionage-terror and diversionary-sabotage organizations and centres' and that the heads of such organizations as a rule – for no known reason – were first secretaries of oblast or republic Communist Party committees or central committees.

Many thousands of honest and innocent communists have died as a result of this monstrous falsification of such 'cases', as a result of the fact that all kinds of slanderous 'confessions' were accepted, and as a result of the practice of forcing accusations against oneself and others. In the same manner were fabricated the 'cases' against eminent party and state workers – Kossior, Chubar, Postyshev, Kosarev and others.

In those years repressions on a mass scale were applied which were based on nothing tangible and which resulted in heavy cadre losses to the party.

The vicious practice was condoned of having the NKVD prepare lists of persons whose cases were under the jurisdiction of the Military Collegium and whose sentences were prepared in advance. Yezhov would send these lists to Stalin personally for his approval of the proposed punishment. In 1937–8, 383 such lists containing the names of many thousands of party, Soviet, Komsomol, Army and economic workers were sent to Stalin. He approved these lists.

A large part of these cases are being reviewed now and a great part of them are being voided because they were baseless and falsified. Suffice it to say that from 1954 to the present time the Military Collegium of the Supreme Court has rehabilitated 7,679 persons, many of whom were rehabilitated posthumously.

Mass arrests of party, Soviet, economic and military workers caused tremendous harm to our country and to the cause of socialist advancement.

Mass repressions had a negative influence on the moral-political condition of the party, created a situation of uncertainty, contributed to the spreading of unhealthy suspicion, and sowed distrust among communists. All sorts of slanderers and careerists were active.

Resolutions of the January plenum of the Central Committee, All-Union Communist Party (Bolsheviks), in 1938 had brought some measure of improvement to the party organizations. However, widespread repression also existed in 1938.

Only because our party has at its disposal such great moral-political strength was it possible for it to survive the difficult events in 1937–8 and to educate new cadres. There is, however, no doubt that our march forward toward socialism and toward the preparation of the country's defence would have been much more successful were it not for the tremendous loss in the cadres suffered as a result of the baseless and false mass repressions in 1937–8.

We are justly accusing Yezhov for the degenerate practices of 1937. But we have to answer these questions:

Could Yezhov have arrested Kossior, for instance, without the knowledge of Stalin? Was there an exchange of opinions or a Political Bureau decision concerning this?

No, there was not, as there was none regarding other cases of this type.

Could Yezhov have decided such important matters as the fate of such eminent party figures?

No, it would be a display of naivety to consider this the work of Yezhov alone. It is clear that these matters were decided by Stalin, and that without his orders and his sanction Yezhov could not have done this.

We have examined the cases and have rehabilitated Kossior, Rudzutak, Postyshev, Kosarev and others. For what causes were they arrested and sentenced? The review of evidence shows that there was no reason for this. They, like many others, were arrested without the prosecutor's knowledge.

In such a situation, there is no need for any sanction, for what sort of a sanction could there be when Stalin decided everything? He was the chief prosecutor in these cases. Stalin not only agreed to, but on his own initiative issued, arrest orders. We must say this so that the delegates to the Congress can clearly undertake and themselves assess this and draw the proper conclusions.

Facts prove that many abuses were made on Stalin's orders without reckoning with any norms of party and Soviet legality. Stalin was a very distrustful man, sickly suspicious; we know this from our work with him. He could look at a man and say: 'Why are your eyes so shifty today?' or 'Why are you turning away so much today and avoiding looking at me directly in the eyes?' The sickly suspicion created in him a general distrust even toward eminent party workers whom he had known for years. Everywhere and in everything he saw 'enemies', 'two-facers' and 'spies'. Possessing unlimited power, he indulged in great wilfulness and choked a person morally and physically. A situation was created where one could not express one's own will.

When Stalin said that one or another should be arrested, it was necessary to accept on faith that he was an 'enemy of the people'. Meanwhile, Beria's gang, which ran the organs of state security, outdid itself in proving the guilt of the arrested and the truth of materials which it falsified. And what proofs were offered? The confessions of the arrested, and the investigative judges accepted these 'confessions'. And how is it possible that a person confesses to crimes which he has not committed? Only in one way — because of application of physical methods of pressuring him, tortures, bringing him to a state of unconsciousness, deprivation of his judgement, taking away of his human dignity. In this manner were 'confessions' acquired.

When the wave of mass arrests began to recede in 1939, and the leaders of territorial party organizations began to accuse the NKVD workers of using methods of physical pressure on the arrested, Stalin dispatched a coded telegram on 20 January 1939, to the committee secretaries of oblasts and krais, to the central committees of republic Communist Parties, to the People's Commissars of Internal Affairs and to the heads of NKVD organizations. This telegram stated:

The Central Committee of the All-Union Communist Party (Bolsheviks) explains that the application of methods of physical pressure in NKVD practice is permissible from 1937 on in accordance with permission of the Central Committee of the All-Union Communist Party (Bolsheviks) . . . It is known that all bourgeois intelligence services use methods of physical influence against the representatives of the socialist proletariat and that they use them in their most scandalous forms.

The question arises as to why the socialist intelligence service should be more humanitarian against the mad agents of the bourgeoisie, against the deadly

enemies of the working class and of the *kolkhoz* workers. The Central Committee
of the All-Union Communist Party (Bolsheviks) considers that physical pressure
should still be used obligatorily, as an exception applicable to known and
obstinate enemies of the people, as a method both justifiable and appropriate.

Thus, Stalin had sanctioned in the name of the Central Committee of
the All-Union Communist Party (Bolsheviks) the most brutal violation of
socialist legality, torture and oppression, which led as we have seen to the
slandering and self-accusation of innocent people.

Not long ago – only several days before the present Congress – we
called to the Central Committee Presidium session and interrogated the
investigative judge Rodos, who in his time investigated and interrogated
Kossior, Chubar and Kosarev. He is a vile person, with the brain of a bird,
and morally completely degenerate. And it was this man who was
deciding the fate of prominent party workers; he was making judgements
also concerning the politics in these matters, because, having established
their 'crime', he provided therewith materials from which important
political implications could be drawn.

The question arises whether a man with such an intellect could alone
make the investigation in a manner to prove the guilt of people such as
Kossior and others. No, he could not have done it without proper
directives. At the Central Committee Presidium session he told us: 'I was
told that Kossior and Chubar were people's enemies and for this reason I,
as an investigative judge, had to make them confess that they are
enemies.' *(Indignation in the hall.)*

He would do this only through long tortures, which he did, receiving
detailed instructions from Beria. We must say that at the Central Committee Presidium session he cynically declared: 'I thought that I was
executing the orders of the party.' In this manner, Stalin's orders concerning the use of methods of physical pressure against the arrested were in
practice executed.

These and many other facts show that all norms of correct party
solution of problems were invalidated and everything was dependent
upon the wilfulness of one man.

The power accumulated in the hands of one person, Stalin, led to
serious consequences during the Great Patriotic War.

When we look at many of our novels, films and historical 'scientific
studies', the role of Stalin in the Patriotic War appears to be entirely
improbable. Stalin had foreseen everything. The Soviet Army, on the
basis of a strategic plan prepared by Stalin long before, used the tactics of
so-called 'active defence', in other words tactics which, as we know,
allowed the Germans to come up to Moscow and Stalingrad. Using such
tactics, the Soviet Army, supposedly thanks to Stalin's genius, turned to
the offensive and subdued the enemy. The epic victory gained through the

armed might of the land of the Soviets, through our heroic people, is ascribed in this type of novel, film and 'scientific study' as being completely due to the strategic genius of Stalin.

We have to analyse this matter carefully because it has a tremendous significance not only from the historical, but especially from the political, educational and practical point of view. What are the facts of this matter?

Before the war, our press and all our political-educational work was characterized by its bragging tone: When an enemy violates the holy Soviet soil, then for every blow of the enemy we will answer with three blows, and we will battle the enemy on his soil and we will win without much harm to ourselves. But these positive statements were not based in all areas on concrete facts, which would actually guarantee the immunity of our borders.

During the war and after the war, Stalin put forward the thesis that the tragedy which our nation experienced in the first part of the war was the result of the 'unexpected' attack of the Germans against the Soviet Union. But, comrades, this is completely untrue. As soon as Hitler came to power in Germany he assigned to himself the task of liquidating communism. The fascists were saying this openly: they did not hide their plans.

In order to attain this aggressive end, all sorts of pacts and blocs created, such as the famous Berlin–Rome–Tokyo Axis. Many facts from the pre-war period clearly showed that Hitler was going all out to begin a war against the Soviet state, and that he had concentrated large armed units, together with armoured units, near the Soviet borders.

Documents which have now been published show that by 3 April 1941, Churchill, through his Ambassador to the USSR, Cripps, personally warned Stalin that the Germans had begun regrouping their armed units with the intent of attacking the Soviet Union.

It is self-evident that Churchill did not do this at all because of his friendly feeling towards the Soviet nation. He had in this his own imperialistic goals – to bring Germany and the USSR into a bloody war and thereby to strengthen the position of the British Empire.

Just the same, Churchill affirmed in his writings that he sought to 'warn Stalin and call his attention to the danger which threatened him'. Churchill stressed this repeatedly in his dispatches of 18 April and on the following days. However, Stalin took no heed of these warnings. What is more, Stalin ordered that no credence be given to information of this sort, in order not to provoke the initiation of military operations.

We must assert that information of this sort concerning the threat of German armed invasion of Soviet territory was coming in also from our own military and diplomatic sources; however, because the leadership was conditioned against such information, such data was dispatched with fear and assessed with reservation.

Thus, for instance, information sent from Berlin on 6 May 1941, by the Soviet military attaché, Captain Vorontsov, stated: 'Soviet citizen Bozer ... communicated to the deputy naval attaché that, according to a statement of a certain German officer from Hitler's headquarters, Germany is preparing to invade the USSR on 14 May through Finland, the Baltic countries and Latvia. At the same time Moscow and Leningrad will be heavily raided and paratroopers landed in border cities . . .'

In his report of 22 May 1941, the deputy military attaché in Berlin. Khlopov, communicated that: '. . . the attack of the German Army is reportedly scheduled for 15 June, but it is possible that it may begin in the first days of June . . .'

A cable from our London Embassy dated 18 June 1941 stated: 'As of now Cripps is deeply convinced of the inevitability of armed conflict between Germany and the USSR, which will begin not later than the middle of June. According to Cripps, the Germans have presently concentrated 147 divisions (including air force and service units) along the Soviet borders . . .'

Despite these particularly grave warnings, the necessary steps were not taken to prepare the country properly for defence and to prevent it from being caught unawares.

Did we have time and the capabilities for such preparations? Yes, we had the time and capabilities. Our industry was already so developed that it was capable of supplying fully the Soviet Army with everything that it needed. This is proven by the fact that, although during the war we lost almost half of our industry and important industrial and food-production areas as the result of enemy occupation of the Ukraine, Northern Caucasus and other western parts of the country, the Soviet nation was still able to organize the production of military equipment in the eastern parts of the country, install there equipment taken from the western industrial areas, and to supply our armed forces with everything which was necessary to destroy the enemy.

Had our industry been mobilized properly and in time to supply the Army with the necessary material, our wartime losses would have been decidedly smaller. Such mobilization had not been, however, started in time. And already in the first days of the war it became evident that our Army was badly armed, that we did not have enough artillery, tanks and planes to throw the enemy back.

Soviet science and technology produced excellent models of tanks and artillery pieces before the war. But mass production of all this was not organized, and, as a matter of fact, we started to modernize our military equipment only on the eve of the war. As a result, at the time of the enemy's invasion of the Soviet land we did not have sufficient quantities either of old machinery which was no longer used for armament production or of new machinery which we had planned to introduce into armament production.

The situation with anti-aircraft artillery was especially bad; we did not organize the production of anti-tank ammunition. Many fortified regions had proven to be indefensible as soon as they were attacked, because the old arms had been withdrawn and new ones were not yet available there.

This pertained, alas, not only to tanks, artillery and planes. At the outbreak of the war we did not have sufficient numbers of rifles to arm the mobilized manpower. I recall that in those days I telephoned to Comrade Malenkov from Kiev and told him, 'People have volunteered for the new Army and demand arms. You must send us arms.' Malenkov answered me, 'We cannot send you arms. We are sending all our rifles to Leningrad and you have to arm yourselves.' (*Movement in the hall.*)

Such was the armament situation.

In this connection we cannot forget, for instance, the following fact. Shortly before the invasion of the Soviet Union by the Hitlerite army, Kirponos, who was chief of the Kiev Special Military District (he was later killed at the front), wrote to Stalin that the German armies were at the Bug River, were preparing for an attack and in the very near future would probably start their offensive. In this connection, Kirponos proposed that a strong defence be organized, that 300,000 people be evacuated from the border areas and that several strong points be organized there: anti-tank ditches, trenches for the soldiers, etc.

Moscow answered this proposition with the assertion that this would be a provocation, that no preparatory defensive work should be undertaken at the borders, that the Germans were not to be given any pretext for the initiation of military action against us. Thus, our borders were insufficiently prepared to repel the enemy.

When the fascist armies had actually invaded Soviet territory and military operations began, Moscow issued the order that the German fire was not to be returned. Why? It was because Stalin, despite evident facts, thought that the war had not yet started, that this was only a provocative action on the part of several undisciplined sections of the German Army, and that reaction might serve as a reason for the Germans to begin the war.

The following fact is also known. On the eve of the invasion of the territory of the Soviet Union by the Hitlerite army, a certain German citizen crossed our border and stated that the German armies had received orders to start the offensive against the Soviet Union on the night of 22 June at three o'clock. Stalin was informed about this immediately, but even this warning was ignored.

As you see, everything was ignored: warnings of certain Army commanders, declarations of deserters from the enemy army, and even the open hostility of the enemy. Is this an example of the alertness of the chief of the party and of the state at this particularly significant historical moment?

And what were the results of this carefree attitude, this disregard of clear facts? The result was that already in the first hours and days the enemy had destroyed in our border regions a large part of our Air Force, artillery and other military equipment; he annihilated large numbers of our military cadres and disorganized our military leadership; consequently we could not prevent the enemy from marching deep into the country.

Very grievous consequences, especially in reference to the beginning of the war, followed Stalin's annihilation of many military commanders and political workers during 1937–41 because of his suspiciousness and through slanderous accusations. During these years repressions were instituted against certain parts of military cadres beginning literally at the company and battalion commander level and extending to the higher military centres; during this time the cadre of leaders who had gained military experience in Spain and in the Far East was almost completely liquidated.

The policy of large-scale repression against the military cadres led also to undermined military discipline, because for several years officers of all ranks and even soldiers in the party and Komsomol cells were taught to 'unmask' their superiors as hidden enemies. (*Movement in the hall.*) It is natural that this caused a negative influence on the state of military discipline in the first war period.

And, as you know, we had before the war excellent military cadres which were unquestionably loyal to the party and to the Fatherland. Suffice it to say that those of them who managed to survive, despite severe tortures to which they were subjected in the prisons, have from the first war days shown themselves real patriots and heroically fought for the glory of the Fatherland; I have here in mind such comrades as Rokossovsky (who, as you know, had been jailed), Gorbatov, Maretskov (who is a delegate at the present Congress), Podlas (he was an excellent commander who perished at the front), and many, many others. However, many such commanders perished in camps and jails and the Army saw them no more.

All this brought about the situation which existed at the beginning of the war and which was the great threat to our Fatherland.

It would be incorrect to forget that, after the first severe disaster and defeat at the front, Stalin thought that this was the end. In one of his speeches in those days he said: 'All that which Lenin created we have lost forever.'

After this Stalin for a long time actually did not direct the military operations and ceased to do anything whatever. He returned to active leadership only when some members of the Political Bureau visited him and told him that it was necessary to take certain steps immediately in order to improve the situation at the front.

Therefore, the threatening danger which hung over our Fatherland in the first period of the war was largely due to the faulty methods of directing the nation and the party by Stalin himself.

However, we speak not only about the moment when the war began, which led to serious disorganization of our Army and brought us severe losses. Even after the war began, the nervousness and hysteria which Stalin demonstrated, interfering with actual military operations, caused our Army serious damage.

Stalin was very far from an understanding of the real situation which was developing at the front. This was natural because, during the whole Patriotic War, he never visited any section of the front or any liberated city except for one short ride on the Mozhaisk highway during a stabilized situation at the front. To this incident were dedicated many literary works full of fantasies of all sorts and so many paintings. Simultaneously, Stalin was interfering with operations and issuing orders which did not take into consideration the real situation at a given section of the front and which could not help but result in huge personnel losses.

I will allow myself in this connection to bring out one characteristic fact which illustrates how Stalin directed operations at the fronts. There is present at this Congress Marshal Bagramian, who was once the chief of operations in the headquarters of the south-western front and who can corroborate what I will tell you.

When there developed an exceptionally serious situation for our Army in 1942 in the Kharkov region, we had correctly decided to drop an operation whose objective was to encircle Kharkov, because the real situation at that time would have threatened our Army with fatal consequences if this operation was continued.

We communicated this to Stalin, stating that the situation demanded changes in operational plans so that the enemy would be prevented from liquidating a sizable concentration of our Army.

Contrary to common sense, Stalin rejected our suggestion and issued the order to continue the operation aimed at the encirclement of Kharkov, despite the fact that at this time many Army concentrations were themselves actually threatened with encirclement and liquidation.

I telephoned to Vasilevsy and begged him: 'Alexander Mikhailovich, take a map' – Vasilevsky is present here – 'and show Comrade Stalin the situation which has developed.' We should note that Stalin planned operations on a globe. (*Animation in the hall.*) Yes, comrades, he used to take the globe and trace the front line on it. I said to Comrade Vasilevsky:

'Show him the situation on a map; in the present situation we cannot continue the operation which was planned. The old decision must be changed for the good of the cause.'

Vasilevsky replied, saying that Stalin had already studied this problem and that he, Vasilevsky, would not see Stalin further concerning this matter, because the latter didn't want to hear any arguments on the subject of this operation.

After my talk with Vasilevsky, I telephoned to Stalin in his villa. But Stalin did not answer the telephone and Malenkov was at the receiver. I told Comrade Malenkov that I was calling from the front and that I wanted to speak personally to Stalin. Stalin informed me through Malenkov that I should speak with Malenkov. I stated for the second time that I wished to inform Stalin personally about the grave situation which had arisen for us at the front. But Stalin did not consider it convenient to raise the phone and again stated that I should speak to him through Malenkov, although he was only a few steps from the telephone.

After 'listening' in this manner to our plea, Stalin said: 'Let everything remain as it is!'

And what was the result of this? The worst that we had expected. The Germans surrounded our Army concentrations and consequently we lost hundreds of thousands of our soldiers. This is Stalin's military 'genius'; this is what it cost us. (*Movement in the hall.*)

On one occasion after the war, during a meeting of Stalin with members of the Political Bureau, Anastas Ivanovich Mikoyan mentioned that Khrushchev must have been right when he telephoned concerning the Kharkov operation and that it was unfortunate that his suggestion had not been accepted.

You should have seen Stalin's fury! How could it be admitted that he, Stalin, had not been right! He is after all a 'genius', and a genius cannot help but be right! Everyone can err, but Stalin considered that he never erred, that he was always right. He never acknowledged to anyone that he made any mistake, large or small, despite the fact that he made not a few mistakes in the matter of theory and in his practical activity. After the Party Congress we shall probably have to re-evaluate many wartime military operations and to present them in their true light.

The tactics on which Stalin insisted without knowing the essence of the conduct of battle operations cost us much blood until we succeeded in stopping the opponent and going over to the offensive.

The military know that already by the end of 1941, instead of great operational manoeuvres flanking the opponent and penetrating behind his back, Stalin demanded incessant frontal attacks and the capture of one village after another.

Because of this, we paid with great losses – until our generals, on whose shoulders rested the whole weight of conducting the war, succeeded in changing the situation and shifting to flexible-manoeuvre operations, which immediately brought serious changes at the front favourable to us.

All the more shameful was the fact that, after our great victory over the enemy which cost us so much, Stalin began to downgrade many of the commanders who contributed so much to the victory over the enemy, because Stalin excluded every possibility that services rendered at the front should be credited to anyone but himself.

Stalin was very much interested in the assessment of Comrade Zhukov as a military leader. He asked me often for my opinion of Zhukov. I told him then, 'I have known Zhukov for a long time; he is a good general and a good military leader.'

After the war Stalin began to tell all kinds of nonsense about Zhukov, among others the following, 'You praised Zhukov, but he does not deserve it. It is said that before each operation at the front Zhukov used to behave as follows: he used to take a handful of earth, smell it and say, "We can begin the attack," or the opposite, "The planned operation cannot be carried out."' I stated at that time, 'Comrade Stalin, I do not know who invented this, but it is not true.'

It is possible that Stalin himself invented these things for the purpose of minimizing the role and military talents of Marshal Zhukov.

In this connection, Stalin very energetically popularized himself as a great leader; in various ways he tried to inculcate in the people the version that all victories gained by the Soviet nation during the Great Patriotic War were due to the courage, daring and genius of Stalin and of no one else. Exactly like Kuzma Kryuchkov he put one dress on seven people at the same time. (*Animation in the hall.*)

In the same vein, let us take, for instance, our historical and military films and some literary creations; they make us feel sick. Their true objective is the propagation of the theme of praising Stalin as a military genius. Let us recall the film, *The Fall of Berlin*. Here only Stalin acts; he issues orders in the hall in which there are many empty chairs and only one man approaches him and reports something to him – that is Poskrebyshev, his loyal shield-bearer. (*Laughter in the hall.*)

And where is the military command? Where is the Political Bureau? Where is the government? What are they doing and with what are they engaged? There is nothing about them in the film. Stalin acts for everybody; he does not reckon with anyone; he asks no one for advice. Everything is shown to the nation in this false light. Why? In order to surround Stalin with glory, contrary to the facts and contrary to historical truth.

The question arises: And where are the military, on whose shoulders rested the burden of the war? They are not in the film; with Stalin in it, no room was left for them.

Not Stalin, but the party as a whole, the Soviet government, our heroic Army, its talented leaders and brave soldiers, the whole Soviet nation – these are the ones who assured the victory of the Great Patriotic War. (*Tempestuous and prolonged applause.*)

The Central Committee members, ministers, our economic leaders, leaders of Soviet culture, directors of territorial-party and Soviet organizations, engineers, and technicians – every one of them in his own place of work generously gave of his strength and knowledge towards ensuring victory over the enemy.

Exceptional heroism was shown by our hard core – surrounded by glory is our whole working class, our *kolkhoz* peasantry, the Soviet intelligentsia, who under the leadership of party organizations overcame untold hardships and, bearing the hardships of war, devoted all their strength to the cause of the defence of the Fatherland.

Great and brave deeds during the war were accomplished by our Soviet women who bore on their backs the heavy load of production work in the factories, on the *kolkhozes*, and in various economic and cultural sectors; many women participated directly in the Great Patriotic War at the fronts; our brave youth contributed immeasurably at home to the defence of the Soviet Fatherland and to the annihilation of the enemy.

Immortal are the services of the Soviet soldiers, of our commanders and political workers of all ranks; after the loss of a considerable part of the Army in the first war months they did not lose their heads and were able to reorganize during the progress of combat; they created and toughened during the progress of the war a strong and heroic Army and not only withstood the pressures of the strong and cunning enemy but also smashed him.

The magnificent and heroic deeds of hundreds of millions of people of the East and of the West during the fight against the threat of fascist subjugation which loomed before us will live centuries and millennia in the memory of thankful humanity. (*Thunderous applause.*)

The main role and the main credit for the victorious ending of the war belong to our Communist Party, to the armed forces of the Soviet Union, and to the tens of millions of Soviet people raised by the party. (*Thunderous and prolonged applause.*)

Comrades, let us reach for some other facts. The Soviet Union is justly considered as a model of a multi-national state because we have in practice assured the equality and friendship of all nations which live in our great Fatherland.

All the more monstrous are the acts whose initiator was Stalin and

which are rude violations of the basic Leninist principles of the nationality policy of the Soviet state. We refer to the mass deportations from their
native places of whole nations, together with all communists and Komsomols without any exception; this deportation action was not dictated by
any military considerations.

Thus, already at the end of 1943, when there occurred a permanent
break-through at the fronts of the Great Patriotic War benefiting the
Soviet Union, a decision was taken and executed concerning the deportation of all the Karachai from the lands on which they lived.

In the same period, at the end of December 1943, the same lot befell the
whole population of the Autonomous Kalmyk Republic. In March 1944,
all the Chechen and Ingush peoples were deported and the Chechen-
Ingush Autonomous Republic was liquidated. In April 1944, all Balkars
were deported to faraway places from the territory of the Kabardino-
Balkar Autonomous Republic and the Republic itself was renamed the
Autonomous Kabardian Republic.

The Ukrainians avoided meeting this fate only because there were too
many of them and there was no place to which to deport them. Otherwise, he would have deported them also. (*Laughter and animation in the
hall.*)

Not only a Marxist-Leninist but also no man of common sense can
grasp how it is possible to make whole nations responsible for inimical
activity, including women, children, old people, communists and Komsomols, to use mass repression against them, and to expose them to misery
and suffering for the hostile acts of individual persons or groups of
persons.

After the conclusion of the Patriotic War, the Soviet nation stressed
with pride the magnificent victories gained through great sacrifices and
tremendous efforts. The country experienced a period of political enthusiasm. The party came out of the war even more united; in the fire of the
war, party cadres were tempered and hardened. Under such conditions
nobody could have even thought of the possibility of some plot in the
party.

And it was precisely at this time that the so-called 'Leningrad affair'
was born. As we have now proven, this case was fabricated. Those who
innocently lost their lives included Comrades Voznesensky, Kuznetsov,
Rodionov, Popkov, and others.

As is known, Voznesensky and Kuznetsov were talented and eminent
leaders. Once they stood very close to Stalin. It is sufficient to mention
that Stalin made Voznesensky first deputy to the chairman of the Council
of Ministers and Kuznetsov was elected Secretary of the Central Committee. The very fact that Stalin entrusted Kuznetsov with the supervision
of the state-security organs shows the trust which he enjoyed.

How did it happen that these persons were branded as enemies of the people and liquidated?

Facts prove that the 'Leningrad affair' is also the result of wilfulness which Stalin exercised against party cadres. Had a normal situation existed in the party's Central Committee and in the Central Committee Political Bureau, affairs of this nature would have been examined there in accordance with party practice, and all pertinent facts assessed; as a result, such an affair as well as others would not have happened.

We must state that, after the war, the situation became even more complicated. Stalin became even more capricious, irritable and brutal; in particular his suspicion grew. His persecution mania reached unbelievable dimensions. Many workers were becoming enemies before his very eyes. After the war, Stalin separated himself from the collective even more. Everything was decided by him alone without any consideration for anyone or anything.

This unbelievable suspicion was cleverly taken advantage of by the abject *provocateur* and vile enemy, Beria, who had murdered thousands of communists and loyal Soviet people. The elevation of Voznesensky and Kuznetsov alarmed Beria. As we have now proven, it had been precisely Beria who had 'suggested' to Stalin the fabrication by him and by his confidants of materials in the form of declarations and anonymous letters, and in the form of various rumours and talks.

The party's Central Committee has examined this so-called 'Leningrad affair'; persons who innocently suffered are now rehabilitated and honour has been restored to the glorious Leningrad party organization. Abakumov and others who had fabricated this affair were brought before a court; their trial took place in Leningrad and they received what they deserved.

The question arises: Why is it that we see the truth of this affair only now, and why did we not do something earlier, during Stalin's life, in order to prevent the loss of innocent lives? It was because Stalin personally supervised the 'Leningrad affair', and the majority of the Political Bureau members did not, at that time, know all of the circumstances in these matters and could not therefore intervene.

When Stalin received certain material from Beria and Abakumov without examining these slanderous materials he ordered an investigation of the 'affair' of Voznesensky and Kuznetsov. With this, their fate was sealed.

Instructive in the same way is the case of the Mingrelian nationalist organization which supposedly existed in Georgia. As is known, resolutions by the Central Committee, Communist Party of the Soviet Union, were made concerning this case in November 1951 and in March 1952. These resolutions were made without prior discussion with the Political

Bureau. Stalin had personally dictated them. They made serious accusations against many loyal communists. On the basis of falsified documents, it was proven that there existed in Georgia a supposedly nationalistic organization whose objective was the liquidation of the Soviet power in that republic with the help of imperialist powers.

In this connection, a number of responsible party and Soviet workers were arrested in Georgia. As was later proven, this was a slander directed against the Georgian party organization.

We know that there have been at times manifestations of local bourgeois nationalism in Georgia as in several other republics. The question arises: Could it be possible that, in the period during which the resolutions referred to above were made, nationalist tendencies grew so much that there was a danger of Georgia's leaving the Soviet Union and joining Turkey? (*Animation in the hall, laughter.*)

This is, of course, nonsense. It is impossible to imagine how such assumptions could enter anyone's mind. Everyone knows how Georgia has developed economically and culturally under Soviet rule.

Industrial production of the Georgian Republic is twenty-seven times greater than it was before the Revolution. Many new industries have arisen in Georgia which did not exist there before the Revolution: iron smelting, an oil industry, a machine-construction industry, etc. Illiteracy has long since been liquidated, which, in pre-Revolution Georgia, included 78 per cent of the population.

Could the Georgians, comparing the situation in their republic with the hard situation of the working masses in Turkey, be aspiring to join Turkey? In 1955, Georgia produced eighteen times as much steel per person as Turkey. Georgia produces nine times as much electrical energy per person as Turkey. According to the available 1950 census, 65 per cent of Turkey's total population are illiterate, and, of the women, 80 per cent are illiterate. Georgia has nineteen institutions of higher learning which have about 39,000 students; this is eight times more than in Turkey (for each 1,000 inhabitants). The prosperity of the working people has grown tremendously in Georgia under Soviet rule.

It is clear that, as the economy and culture develop, and as the socialist consciousness of the working masses in Georgia grows, the source from which bourgeois nationalism draws its strength evaporates.

As it developed, there was no nationalistic organization in Georgia. Thousands of innocent people fell victim to wilfulness and lawlessness. All of this happened under the 'genial' leadership of Stalin, 'the great son of the Georgian nation', as Georgians like to refer to Stalin. (*Animation in the hall.*)

The wilfulness of Stalin showed itself not only in decisions concerning the internal life of the country but also in the international relations of the Soviet Union.

The July plenum of the Central Committee studied in detail the reasons for the development of conflict with Yugoslavia. It was a shameful role which Stalin played here. The 'Yugoslav affair' contained no problems which could not have been solved through party discussions among comrades. There was no significant basis for the development of this 'affair'; it was completely possible to have prevented the rupture of relations with that country. This does not mean, however, that the Yugoslav leaders did not make mistakes or did not have shortcomings. But these mistakes and shortcomings were magnified in a monstrous manner by Stalin, which resulted in a break of relations with a friendly country.

I recall the first days when the conflict between the Soviet Union and Yugoslavia began artificially to be blown up. Once, when I came from Kiev to Moscow, I was invited to visit Stalin, who, pointing to the copy of a letter lately sent to Tito, asked me, 'Have you read this?'

Not waiting for my reply, he answered, 'I will shake my little finger – and there will be no more Tito. He will fall.'

We have dearly paid for this 'shaking of the little finger'. This statement reflected Stalin's mania for greatness, but he acted just that way: 'I will shake my little finger – and there will be no Kossior'; 'I will shake my little finger once more and Postyshev and Chubar will be no more'; 'I will shake my little finger again – and Voznesensky, Kuznetsov and many others will disappear.'

But this did not happen to Tito. No matter how much or how little Stalin shook, not only his little finger but everything else that he could shake, Tito did not fall. Why? The reason was that, in this case of disagreement with the Yugoslav comrades, Tito had behind him a state and a people who had gone through a severe school of fighting for liberty and independence, a people which gave support to its leaders.

You see to what Stalin's mania for greatness led. He had completely lost consciousness of reality; he demonstrated his suspicion and haughtiness not only in relation to individuals in the USSR, but in relation to whole parties and nations.

We have carefully examined the case of Yugoslavia and have found a proper solution which is approved by the peoples of the Soviet Union and of Yugoslavia as well as by the working masses of all the people's democracies and by all progressive humanity. The liquidation of the abnormal relationship with Yugoslavia was done in the interest of the whole camp of socialism, in the interest of strengthening peace in the whole world.

Let us also recall the 'affair of the doctor-plotters'. (*Animation in the hall.*) Actually there was no 'affair' outside of the declaration of the woman doctor Timashuk, who was probably influenced or ordered by someone (after all, she was an unofficial collaborator of the organs of state security) to write Stalin a letter in which she declared that doctors were applying supposedly improper methods of medical treatment.

Such a letter was sufficient for Stalin to reach an immediate conclusion that there are doctor-plotters in the Soviet Union. He issued orders to arrest a group of eminent Soviet medical specialists. He personally issued advice on the conduct of the investigation and the method of interrogation of the arrested persons. He said that the academician Vinogradov should be put in chains, another one should be beaten. Present at this Congress as a delegate is the former Minister of State Security, Comrade Ignatiev. Stalin told him curtly, 'If you do not obtain confessions from the doctors we will shorten you by a head.' (*Tumult in the hall.*)

Stalin personally called the investigative judge, gave him instructions, advised him on which investigative methods should be used; these methods were simple – beat, beat and, once again, beat.

Shortly after the doctors were arrested, we members of the Political Bureau received protocols with the doctors' confessions of guilt. After distributing these protocols, Stalin told us, 'You are blind like young kittens; what will happen without me? The country will perish because you do not know how to recognize enemies.'

The case was so presented that no one could verify the facts on which the investigation was based. There was no possibility of trying to verify facts by contacting those who had made the confessions of guilt.

We felt, however, that the case of the arrested doctors was questionable. We knew some of these people personally because they had once treated us. When we examined this 'case' after Stalin's death, we found it to be fabricated from beginning to end.

This ignominious 'case' was set up by Stalin; he did not, however, have the time in which to bring it to an end (as he conceived that end), and for this reason the doctors are still alive. Now all have been rehabilitated; they are working in the same places they were working before; they treat top individuals, not excluding members of the government; they have our full confidence; and they execute their duties honestly, as they did before.

In organizing the various dirty and shameful cases, a very base role was played by the rabid enemy of our party, an agent of a foreign intelligence service – Beria, who had stolen into Stalin's confidence. In what way could this *provocateur* gain such a position in the party and in the state, so as to become the First Deputy Chairman of the Council of Ministers of the Soviet Union and a member of the Central Committee of the Political Bureau? It has now been established that this villain had climbed up the government ladder over an untold number of corpses.

Were there any signs that Beria was an enemy of the party? Yes, there were. Already in 1937, at a Central Committee plenum, former People's Commissar of Health Kaminsky said that Beria worked for the Mussavat intelligence service. But the Central Committee plenum had barely concluded when Kaminsky was arrested and then shot. Had Stalin examined Kaminsky's statement? No, because Stalin believed in Beria, and that was enough for him. And when Stalin believed in anyone or anything, then no one could say anything which was contrary to his opinion; anyone who would dare to express opposition would have met the same fate as Kaminsky.

There were other signs, also. The declaration which Comrade Snegov made to the party's Central Committee is interesting. (Parenthetically speaking, he was also rehabilitated not long ago, after seventeen years in prison camps.) In this declaration, Snegov writes: 'In connection with the proposed rehabilitation of the former Central Committee member, Kartvelishvili-Lavrentiev, I have entrusted to the hands of the representative of the Committee of State Security a detailed deposition concerning Beria's role in the disposition of the Kartvelishvili case and concerning the criminal motives by which Beria was guided.'

In my opinion, it is indispensable to recall an important fact pertaining to this case and to communicate it to the Central Committee because I did not consider it as proper to include in the investigation documents.

On 30 October 1931, at the session of the Organizational Bureau of the Central Committee, All-Union Communist Party (Bolsheviks), Kartvelishvili, secretary of the Transcaucasian Krai Committee, made a report. All members of the executive of the Krai Committee were present; of them I alone am alive.

During this session, J. V. Stalin proposed a motion at the end of his speech recommending that the organization of the secretariat of the Transcaucasian Krai Committee should be: first secretary, Kartvelishvili; second secretary, Beria (it was then, for the first time in the party's history, that Beria's name was mentioned as a candidate for a party position). Kartvelishvili answered that he knew Beria well and for that reason refused categorically to work together with him. Stalin proposed then that this matter be left open and that it be solved in the process of the work itself. Two days later a decision was arrived at that Beria would receive the party post and that Kartvelishvili would be deported from the Transcaucasus.

This fact can be confirmed by Comrades Mikoyan and Kaganovich, who were present at that session.

The long, unfriendly relations between Kartvelishvili and Beria were widely known; they date back to the time when Comrade Sergo was active in the Transcaucasus; Kartvelishvili was the closest assistant of

Sergo. The unfriendly relationship impelled Beria to fabricate a 'case' against Kartvelishvili. It was characteristic of such cases that Kartvelishvili should be charged with a terroristic act against Beria.

The indictment in the Beria case contains a discussion of his crimes. Some things should, however, be recalled, especially since it is possible that not all delegates to the Congress have read this document. I wish to recall Beria's bestial disposal of the cases of Kedrov, Golubev, and Golubev's adopted mother, Baturina – persons who wished to inform the Central Committee concerning Beria's treacherous activity. They were shot without any trial and the sentence was passed *ex post facto*, after the execution.

Here is what the old communist, Comrade Kedrov, wrote to the Central Committee through Comrade Andreyev (Comrade Andreyev was then a Central Committee secretary):

I am calling to you for help from a gloomy cell of the Lefortovsky prison. Let my cry of horror reach your ears; do not remain deaf; take me under your protection; please, help remove the nightmare of interrogations and show that this is all a mistake.

I suffer innocently. Please believe me. Time will testify to the truth. I am not an *agent provocateur* of the Tsarist Okhrana; I am not a spy; I am not a member of an anti-Soviet organization of which I am being accused on the basis of denunciations. I am also not guilty of any other crimes against the party and the government. I am an old Bolshevik, free of any stain; I have honestly fought for almost forty years in the ranks of the party for the good and prosperity of the nation . . .

. . . Today I, a 62-year-old man, am being threatened by the investigative judges with more severe, cruel and degrading methods of physical pressure. They (the judges) are no longer capable of becoming aware of their error and of recognizing that their handling of my case is illegal and impermissible. They try to justify their actions by picturing me as a hardened and raving enemy and are demanding increased repressions. But let the party know that I am innocent and that there is nothing which can turn a loyal son of the party into an enemy, even right up to his last dying breath.

But I have no way out. I cannot divert from myself the hastily approaching new and powerful blows.

Everything, however, has its limits. My torture has reached the extreme. My health is broken, my strength and my energy are waning, the end is drawing near. To die in a Soviet prison, branded as a vile traitor to the Fatherland – what can be more monstrous for an honest man? And how monstrous all this is! Unsurpassed bitterness and pain grips my heart. No! No! This will not happen; this cannot be, I cry. Neither the party, nor the Soviet government, nor the People's Commissar, L. P. Beria, will permit this cruel, irreparable injustice. I am convinced that, given a quiet, objective examination, without any foul rantings, without any anger and without the fearful tortures, it would be easy to prove the baselessness of the charges. I believe deeply that truth and justice will triumph. I believe. I believe.

The old Bolshevik, Comrade Kedrov, was found innocent by the Military Collegium. But, despite this, he was shot at Beria's order. (*Indignation in the hall.*)

Beria also handled cruelly the family of Comrade Ordzhonikidze. Why? Because Ordzhonikidze had tried to prevent Beria from realizing his shameful plans. Beria had cleared from his way all persons who could possibly interfere with him. Ordzhonikidze was always an opponent of Beria, and he told Stalin so. Instead of examining this affair and taking appropriate steps, Stalin allowed the liquidation of Ordzhonikidze's brother and brought Ordzhonikidze himself to such a state that he was forced to shoot himself. (*Indignation in the hall.*)

Beria was unmasked by the party's Central Committee shortly after Stalin's death. As a result of the particularly detailed legal proceedings, it was established that Beria had committed monstrous crimes and he was shot.

The question arises why Beria, who had liquidated tens of thousands of the party and Soviet workers, was not unmasked during Stalin's life. He was not unmasked earlier because he had utilized very skilfully Stalin's weaknesses; feeding him with suspicions, he assisted Stalin in everything and acted with his support.

Comrades: The cult of the individual acquired such monstrous size chiefly because Stalin himself, using all conceivable methods, was intent on the glorification of his own person. This is supported by numerous facts. One of the most characteristic examples of Stalin's self-glorification and of his lack of even elementary modesty is the edition of his *Short Biography*, which was published in 1948.

This book is an expression of the most dissolute flattery, an example of making a man into a godhead, of transforming him into an infallible sage, 'the greatest leader, sublime strategist of all times and nations'. Finally, no other words could be found with which to lift Stalin up to the heavens.

We need not give here examples of the loathsome adulation filling this book. All we need to add is that they all were approved and edited by Stalin personally and some of them were added in his own handwriting to the draft text of the book.

What did Stalin consider essential to write into this book? Did he want to cool the ardour of his flatterers who were composing his *Short Biography*? No! He marked the very places where he thought that the praise of his services was insufficient. Here are some examples characterizing Stalin's activity, added in Stalin's own hand:

In this fight against the sceptics and capitulators, the Trotskyites, Zinovievites, Bukharinites and Kamenevites, there was definitely welded together after Lenin's death, that leading core of the party . . . that upheld the great banner of Lenin, rallied the party behind Lenin's behests, and brought the Soviet people into the broad road of industrializing the country and collectivizing the rural economy. The leader of this core and the guiding force of the party and the state was Comrade Stalin.

Thus writes Stalin himself! Then he adds: 'Although he performed his task as leader of the party and the people with consummate skill and enjoyed the unreserved support of the entire Soviet people, Stalin never allowed his work to be marred by the slightest hint of vanity, conceit or self-adulation.'

Where and when could a leader so praise himself? Is this worthy of a leader of the Marxist-Leninist type? No. Precisely against this did Marx and Engels take such a strong position. This also was always sharply condemned by Vladimir Ilyich Lenin.

In the draft text of his book appeared the following sentence: 'Stalin is the Lenin of today.'

This sentence appeared to Stalin to be too weak, so, in his own handwriting, he changed it to read: 'Stalin is the worthy continuer of Lenin's work, or, as it is said in our party, Stalin is the Lenin of today.'

You see how well it is said, not by the nation but by Stalin himself.

It is possible to give many such self-praising appraisals written into the draft text of that book in Stalin's hand. Especially generously does he endow himself with praises pertaining to his military genius, to his talent for strategy.

I will cite one more insertion made by Stalin concerning the theme of the Stalinist military genius. He writes:

The advanced Soviet science of war received further development at Comrade Stalin's hands. Comrade Stalin elaborated the theory of the permanently operating factors that decide the issue of wars, of active defence and the laws of counter-offensive and offensive, of the cooperation of all services and arms in modern warfare, of the role of big tank masses and air forces in modern war, and of the artillery as the most formidable of the armed services. At the various stages of the war Stalin's genius found the correct solutions that took account of all the circumstances of the situation.

(Movement in the hall.)

And, further, writes Stalin: 'Stalin's military mastery was displayed both in defence and offence. Comrade Stalin's genius enabled him to divine the enemy's plans and defeat them. The battles in which Comrade Stalin directed the Soviet armies are brilliant examples of operational military skill.'

In this manner was Stalin praised as a strategist. Who did this? Stalin himself, not in his role as a strategist but in the role of an author–editor, one of the main creators of his self-adulatory biography. Such, comrades, are the facts. We should rather say shameful facts.

And one additional fact from the same *Short Biography* of Stalin. As is known, *The Short Course of the History of the All-Union Communist Party (Bolsheviks)* was written by a commission of the party Central Committee.

This book, parenthetically, was also permeated with the cult of the individual and was written by a designated group of authors. The fact was reflected in the following formulation on the proof copy of the *Short Biography* of Stalin: 'A commission of the Central Committee, All-Union Communist Party (Bolsheviks), under the direction of Comrade Stalin and with his most active personal participation, has prepared a *Short Course of the History of the All-Union Communist Party (Bolsheviks).*'

But even this phrase did not satisfy Stalin. The following sentence replaced it in the final version of the *Short Biography*: 'In 1938 appeared the book, *History of the All-Union Communist Party (Bolsheviks), Short Course*, written by Comrade Stalin and approved by a commission of the Central Committee, All-Union Communist Party (Bolsheviks).'

Can one add anything more? (*Animation in the hall.*)

As you see, a surprising metamorphosis changed the work created by a group into a book written by Stalin. It is not necessary to state how and why this metamorphosis took place.

A pertinent question comes to our mind: If Stalin is the author of this book, why did he need to praise the person of Stalin so much and to transform the whole post-October historical period of our glorious Communist Party solely into an action of 'the Stalin genius'?

Did this book properly reflect the efforts of the party in the socialist transformation of the country, in the construction of socialist society, in the industrialization and collectivization of the country, and also other steps taken by the party which undeviatingly travelled the path outlined by Lenin? The book speaks principally about Stalin, about his speeches, about his reports. Everything without the smallest exception is tied to his name.

And when Stalin himself asserts that he himself wrote the *Short Course of the History of the All-Union Communist Party (Bolsheviks)*, this calls at least for amazement. Can a Marxist-Leninist thus write about himself, praising his own person to the heavens?

Or let us take the matter of the Stalin Prizes. (*Movement in the hall.*) Not even the Tsars created prizes which they named after themselves.

Stalin considered the best to be a text of the national anthem of the Soviet Union which contains not a word about the Communist Party; it contains, however, the following unprecedented praise of Stalin: 'Stalin brought us up in loyalty to the people. He inspired us to great toil and achievements.'

In these lines of the anthem, the whole educational, directional and inspirational activity of the great Leninist party is ascribed to Stalin. This is, of course, a clear deviation from Marxism-Leninism, a clear debasing and belittling of the role of the party. We should add for your information that the Presidium of the Central Committee has already passed a resolution concerning the composition of a new text of the anthem, which will reflect the role of the people and the role of the party. (*Loud, prolonged applause.*)

And was it without Stalin's knowledge that many of the largest enterprises and towns were named after him? Was it without his knowledge that Stalin monuments were erected in the whole country – these 'memorials to the living'? It is a fact that Stalin himself had signed, on 2 July 1951, a resolution of the USSR Council of Ministers concerning the erection on the Volga-Don Canal of an impressive monument to Stalin; on 4 September of the same year he issued an order making thirty-three tons of copper available for the construction of this impressive monument.

Anyone who has visited the Stalingrad area must have seen the huge statue which is being built there, and that on a site which hardly any people frequent. Huge sums were spent to build it at a time when people of this area had lived since the war in huts. Consider, yourself, was Stalin right when he wrote in his biography that '. . . he did not allow in himself . . . even a shadow of conceit, pride, or self-adoration'?

At the same time Stalin gave proofs of his lack of respect for Lenin's memory. It is not a coincidence that, despite the decision taken over thirty years ago to build a Palace of Soviets as a monument to Vladimir Ilyich, this palace was not built, its construction was always postponed and the project allowed to lapse.

We must not forget to recall the Soviet government resolution of 14 August 1925, concerning 'the founding of Lenin prizes for educational work'. This resolution was published in the press, but to this day there are no Lenin prizes. This, too, should be corrected. (*Tumultuous, prolonged applause.*)

During Stalin's life – thanks to known methods which I have mentioned, and quoting facts, for instance, from the *Short Biography* of Stalin – all events were explained as if Lenin played only a secondary role, even during the October Socialist Revolution. In many films and in many literary works the figure of Lenin was incorrectly presented and inadmissibly depreciated.

Stalin loved to see the film, *The Unforgettable Year of 1919*, in which he was shown on the steps of an armoured train and where he was practically vanquishing the foe with his own sabre. Let Klimenti Yefremovich, our dear friend, find the necessary courage and write the truth about Stalin; after all, he knows how Stalin had fought. It will be difficult for Comrade Voroshilov to undertake this, but it would be good if he did it. Everyone will approve of it, both the people and the party. Even his grandsons will thank him. (*Prolonged applause.*)

In speaking about the events of the October Revolution and about the Civil War, the impression was created that Stalin always played the main role, as if everywhere and always Stalin had suggested to Lenin what to do and how to do it. However, this is slander of Lenin. (*Prolonged applause.*)

I will probably not sin against the truth when I say that 99 per cent of the persons present here heard and knew very little about Stalin before the year 1924, while Lenin was known to all; he was known to the whole party, to the whole nation, from the children up to the greybeards. (*Tumultuous, prolonged applause.*)

All this has to be thoroughly revised so that history, literature and the fine arts properly reflect V. I. Lenin's role and the great deeds of our Communist Party and of the Soviet people – the creative people. (*Applause.*)

Comrades! The cult of the individual has caused the employment of faulty principles in party work and in economic activity; it brought about rude violation of internal party and Soviet democracy, sterile administration, deviations of all sorts, covering up of shortcomings and varnishing of reality. Our nation gave birth to many flatterers and specialists in false optimism and deceit.

We should also not forget that, due to the numerous arrests of party, Soviet and economic leaders, many workers began to work uncertainly, showed over-cautiousness, feared all which was new, feared their own shadows and began to show less initiative in their work.

Take, for instance, party and Soviet resolutions. They were prepared in a routine manner, often without considering the concrete situation. This went so far that party workers, even during the smallest sessions, read their speeches. All this produced the danger of formalizing the party and Soviet work and of bureaucratizing the whole apparatus.

Stalin's reluctance to consider life's realities and the fact that he was not aware of the real state of affairs in the provinces can be illustrated by his direction of agriculture.

All those who interested themselves even a little in the nation's affairs saw the difficult situation in agriculture, but Stalin never even noted it. Did we tell Stalin about this? Yes, we told him, but he did not support us. Why? Because Stalin never travelled anywhere, did not meet city and *kolkhoz* workers; he did not know the actual situation in the provinces.

He knew the country and agriculture only from films. And these films had dressed up and beautified the existing situation in agriculture. Many films so pictured *kolkhoz* life that the tables were bending from the weight of turkeys and geese. Evidently, Stalin thought that it was actually so.

Vladimir Ilyich Lenin looked at life differently; he was always close to the people; he used to receive peasant delegates and often spoke at factory gatherings; he used to visit villages and talk with the peasants.

Stalin separated himself from the people and never went anywhere. This lasted ten years. The last time he visited a village was in January 1928, when he visited Siberia in connection with grain deliveries. How then could he have known the situation in the provinces?

And when he was once told during a discussion that our situation on the land was a difficult one and that the situation in cattle breeding and meat production was especially bad, a commission was formed which was charged with the preparation of a resolution called 'Means Toward Further Development of Animal Breeding in Kolkhozes and Sovkhozes'. We worked out this project.

Of course, our proposals of that time did not contain all possibilities, but we did chart ways in which animal breeding on *kolkhozes* and *sovkhozes* would be raised. We had proposed then to raise the prices of such products in order to create material incentives for the *kolkhoz*, MTS and *sovkhoz* workers in the development of cattle breeding. But our project was not accepted and in February 1953 was laid aside entirely.

What is more, while reviewing this project Stalin proposed that the taxes paid by the *kolkhozes* and by the *kolkhoz* workers should be raised by 40 billion rubles; according to him the peasants are well off and the *kolkhoz* worker would need to sell only one more chicken to pay his tax in full.

Imagine what this meant. Certainly, 40 billion rubles is a sum which the *kolkhoz* workers did not realize for all the products which they sold to the government. In 1952, for instance, the *kolkhozes* and the *kolkhoz* workers received 26,280 million rubles for all their products delivered and sold to the government.

Did Stalin's position, then, rest on data of any sort whatever? Of course not. In such cases facts and figures did not interest him. If Stalin said anything, it meant it was so — after all, he was a 'genius', and a genius does not need to count, he only needs to look and can immediately tell how it should be. When he expresses his opinion, everyone has to repeat it and to admire his wisdom.

But how much wisdom was contained in the proposal to raise the agricultural tax by 40 billion rubles? None, absolutely none, because the proposal was not based on an actual assessment of the situation but on the fantastic ideas of a person divorced from reality.

We are currently beginning slowly to work our way out of a difficult agricultural situation. The speeches of the delegates to the 20th Congress please us all; we are glad that many delegates deliver speeches, that there are conditions for the fulfilment of the sixth Five-Year Plan for animal husbandry, not during the period of five years, but within two to three years. We are certain that the commitments of the new Five-Year Plan will be accomplished successfully. (*Prolonged applause.*)

Comrades! If we sharply criticize today the cult of the individual which was so widespread during Stalin's life and if we speak about the many negative phenomena generated by this cult which is so alien to the spirit of Marxism-Leninism, various persons may ask: How could it be? Stalin headed the party and the country for thirty years and many victories were gained during his lifetime. Can we deny this? In my opinion, the question can be asked in this manner only by those who are blinded and hopelessly hypnotized by the cult of the individual, only by those who do not understand the essence of the revolution and of the Soviet state, only by those who do not understand, in a Leninist manner, the role of the party and of the nation in the development of the Soviet society.

The Socialist Revolution was attained by the working class and by the poor peasantry with the partial support of middle-class peasants. It was attained by the people under the leadership of the Bolshevik Party. Lenin's great service consisted of the fact that he created a militant party of the working class, but he was armed with Marxist understanding of the laws of social development and with the science of proletarian victory in the fight with capitalism, and he steeled this party in the crucible of revolutionary struggle of the masses of the people.

During this fight the party consistently defended the interests of the people, became its experienced leader, and led the working masses to power, to the creation of the first socialist state. You remember well the wise words of Lenin that the Soviet state is strong because of the awareness of the masses that history is created by the millions and tens of millions of people.

Our historical victories were attained thanks to the organizational work of the party, to the many provincial organizations, and to the self-sacrificing work of our great nation. These victories are the result of the great drive and activity of the nation and of the party as a whole; they are not at all the fruit of the leadership of Stalin, as the situation was pictured during the period of the cult of the individual.

If we are to consider this matter as Marxists and as Leninists, then we have to state unequivocally that the leadership practice which came into being during the last years of Stalin's life became a serious obstacle in the path of Soviet social development. Stalin often failed for months to take up some unusually important problems, concerning the life of the party and of the state, whose solution could not be postponed. During Stalin's leadership our peaceful relations with other nations were often threatened, because one-man decisions could cause, and often did cause, great complications.

In the last years, when we managed to free ourselves of the harmful practice of the cult of the individual and took several proper steps in the sphere of internal and external policies, everyone saw how activity grew before their very eyes, how the creative activity of the broad working masses developed, how favourably all this acted upon the development of economy and of culture. (*Applause.*)

Some comrades may ask us: Where were the members of the Political Bureau of the Central Committee? Why did they not assert themselves against the cult of the individual in time? And why is this being done only now?

First of all, we have to consider the fact that the members of the Political Bureau viewed these matters in a different way at different times. Initially, many of them backed Stalin actively because Stalin was one of the strongest Marxists and his logic, his strength and his will greatly influenced the cadres and party work.

It is known that Stalin, after Lenin's death, especially during the first years, actively fought for Leninism against the enemies of Leninist theory and against those who deviated. Beginning with Leninist theory, the party, with its Central Committee at the head, started on a great scale the work of socialist industrialization of the country, agricultural collectivization and the cultural revolution.

At that time Stalin gained great popularity, sympathy and support. The party had to fight those who attempted to lead the country away from the correct Leninist path; it had to fight Trotskyites, Zinovievites and Rightists, and the bourgeois nationalists. This fight was inevitable.

Later, however, Stalin, abusing his power more and more, began to fight eminent party and government leaders and to use terroristic methods against honest Soviet people. As we have already shown, Stalin thus handled such eminent party and government leaders as Kossior, Rudzutak, Eikhe, Postyshev and many others.

Attempts to oppose groundless suspicions and charges resulted in the opponent falling victim of the repression. This characterized the fall of Comrade Postyshev.

In one of his speeches Stalin expressed his dissatisfaction with Postyshev and asked him, 'What are you actually?'

Postyshev answered clearly, 'I am a Bolshevik, Comrade Stalin, a Bolshevik.'

This assertion was at first considered to show a lack of respect for Stalin; later it was considered a harmful act and consequently resulted in

Postyshev's annihilation and branding without any reason as a 'people's enemy'.

In the situation which then prevailed I often talked with Nikolai Alexandrovich Bulganin; once when we two were travelling in a car, he said, 'It has happened sometimes that a man goes to Stalin on his invitation as a friend. And, when he sits with Stalin, he does not know where he will be sent next – home or to jail.'

It is clear that such conditions put every member of the Political Bureau in a very difficult situation. And, when we also consider the fact that in the last years the Central Committee plenary sessions were not convened and that the sessions of the Political Bureau occurred only occasionally, from time to time, then we will understand how difficult it was for any member of the Political Bureau to take a stand against one or another unjust or improper procedure, against serious errors and shortcomings in the practices of leadership.

As we have already shown, many decisions were taken either by one person or in a roundabout way, without collective discussion. The sad fate of Political Bureau member Comrade Voznesensky, who fell victim to Stalin's repressions, is known to all. It is a characteristic thing that the decision to remove him from the Political Bureau was never discussed but was reached in a devious fashion. In the same way came the decision concerning the removal of Kuznetsov and Rodionov from their posts.

The importance of the Central Committee's Political Bureau was reduced and its work was disorganized by the creation within the Political Bureau of various commissions – the so-called 'quintets', 'sextets', 'septets' and 'novenaries'. Here is, for instance, a resolution of the Political Bureau of 3 October 1946:

Stalin's Proposal:
  1. The Political Bureau Commission for Foreign Affairs ('Sextet') is to concern itself in the future, in addition to foreign affairs, also with matters of internal construction and domestic policy.
  2. The Sextet is to add to its roster the Chairman of the State Commission of Economic Planning of the USSR, Comrade Voznesensky, and is to be known as a Septet.
  Signed: Secretary of the Central Committee, J. Stalin.

What a card player's terminology ! (*Laughter in the hall.*) It is clear that the creation within the Political Bureau of this type of commissions – 'quintets', 'sextets', 'septets' and 'novenaries' – was against the principle of collective leadership. The result of this was that some members of the Political Bureau were in this way kept away from participation in the most important state matters.

One of the oldest members of our party, Klimenti Yefremovich

Voroshilov, found himself in an almost impossible situation. For several years he was actually deprived of the right of participation in Political Bureau sessions. Stalin forbade him to attend the Political Bureau sessions and to receive documents. When the Political Bureau was in session and Comrade Voroshilov heard about it, he telephoned each time and asked whether he would be allowed to attend. Sometimes Stalin permitted it, but always showed his dissatisfaction.

Because of his extreme suspicion, Stalin toyed also with the absurd and ridiculous suspicion that Voroshilov was an English agent. (*Laughter in the hall.*) It's true – an English agent. A special tapping device was installed in his home to listen to what was said there. (*Indignation in the hall.*)

By unilateral decision, Stalin had also separated one other man from the work of the Political Bureau – Andrei Andreyevich Andreyev. This· was one of the most unbridled acts of wilfulness.

Let us consider the first Central Committee plenum after the 19th Party Congress when Stalin, in his talk at the plenum, spoke about Vyacheslav Mikhailovich Molotov and Anastas Ivanovich Mikoyan and suggested that these old workers of our party were guilty of some baseless charges. It is not impossible that had Stalin remained at the helm for another several months, Comrades Molotov and Mikoyan would not have delivered any speeches at this Congress.

Stalin evidently had plans to finish off the old members of the Political Bureau. He often stated that Political Bureau members should be replaced by new ones.

His proposal, after the 19th Congress, concerning the election of twenty-five persons to the Central Committee Presidium, was aimed at the removal of the old Political Bureau members and the bringing in of less experienced persons so that these would extol him in all sorts of ways.

We can assume that this was also a design for the future annihilation of the old Political Bureau members and, in this way, a cover for all shameful acts of Stalin, acts which we are now considering.

Comrades! In order not to repeat errors of the past, the Central Committee has declared itself resolutely against the cult of the individual. We consider that Stalin was excessively extolled. However, in the past Stalin doubtless performed great services to the party, to the working class and to the international workers' movement.

This question is complicated by the fact that all this which we have just discussed was done during Stalin's life under his leadership and with his concurrence; here Stalin was convinced that this was necessary for the defence of the interests of the working classes against the plotting of enemies and against the attack of the imperialist class.

He saw this from the position of the interest of the working class, of the interest of the labouring people, of the interest of the victory of socialism and communism. We cannot say that these were the deeds of a giddy despot. He considered that this should be done in the interest of the party, of the working masses, in the name of the defence of the revolution's gains. In this lies the whole tragedy!.

Comrades! Lenin had often stressed that modesty is an absolutely integral part of a real Bolshevik. Lenin himself was the living personification of the greatest modesty. We cannot say that we have been following this Leninist example in all respects.

It is enough to point out that many towns, factories and industrial enterprises, *kolkhozes* and *sovkhozes*, Soviet institutions and cultural institutions have – if I may express it so – been treated like private property and accorded the names of this or that government or party leader who was still active and in good health. Many of us participated in the action of assigning our names to various towns, rayons, enterprises and *kolkhozes*. We must correct this. (*Applause.*)

But this should be done calmly and slowly. The Central Committee will discuss this matter and consider it carefully in order to prevent errors and excesses. I can remember how the Ukraine learned about Kossior's arrest. The Kiev radio used to start its programmes thus: 'This is Radio (in the name of) Kossior.' When one day the programmes began without naming Kossior, everyone was quite certain that something had happened to Kossior, that he probably had been arrested.

Thus, if today we begin to remove the signs everywhere and to change names, people will think that these comrades in whose honour the said enterprises, *kolkhozes* or cities are named also met some bad fate and that they have also been arrested. (*Animation in the hall.*)

How is the authority and the importance of this or that leader judged? On the basis of how many towns, industrial enterprises and factories, *kolkhozes* and *sovkhozes* carry his name. Is it not about time that we eliminate this 'private property' and 'nationalize' the factories, the industrial enterprises, the *kolkhozes* and the *sovkhozes*? (*Laughter, applause, voices: 'That is right.'*) This will benefit our cause. After all, the cult of the individual is manifested also in this way.

We should, in all seriousness, consider the question of the cult of the individual. We cannot let this matter get out of the party, especially not to the press. It is for this reason that we are considering it here at a closed Congress session. We should know the limits; we should not give ammunition to the enemy; we should not wash our dirty linen before their eyes. I think that the delegates to the Congress will understand and assess properly all these proposals. (*Tumultuous applause.*)

Comrades! We must abolish the cult of the individual decisively, once and for all; we must draw the proper conclusions concerning both ideological-theoretical and practical work. It is necessary for this purpose:

First, in a Bolshevik manner to condemn and to eradicate the cult of the individual as alien to Marxism-Leninism and not consonant with the principles of party leadership and the norms of party life, and to fight inexorably all attempts at bringing back this practice in one form or another.

To return to and actually practise in all our ideological work the most important theses of Marxist-Leninist science about the people as the creator of history and as the creator of all material and spiritual good of humanity, about the decisive role of the Marxist party in the revolutionary fight for the transformation of society, about the victory of communism.

In this connection we will be forced to do much work in order to examine critically from the Marxist-Leninist viewpoint and to correct the widely spread erroneous views connected with the cult of the individual in the sphere of history, philosophy, economy and of other sciences, as well as in literature and the fine arts. It is especially necessary that in the immediate future we compile a serious textbook of the history of our party which will be edited in accordance with scientific Marxist objectivism, a textbook of the history of Soviet society, a book pertaining to the events of the Civil War and the Great Patriotic War.

Secondly, to continue systematically and consistently the work done by the party's Central Committee during the last years, a work characterized by minute observation in all party organizations, from the bottom to the top, of the Leninist principles of party leadership, characterized, above all, by the main principle of collective leadership, characterized by the observance of the norms of party life described in the statutes of our party, and, finally, characterized by the wide practice of criticism and self-criticism.

Thirdly, to restore completely the Leninist principles of Soviet socialist democracy, expressed in the Constitution of the Soviet Union, to fight wilfulness of individuals abusing their power. The evil caused by acts violating revolutionary socialist legality which have accumulated during a long time as a result of the negative influence of the cult of the individual has to be completely corrected.

Comrades! The 20th Congress of the Communist Party of the Soviet Union has manifested with a new strength the unshakable unity of our party, its cohesiveness around the Central Committee, its resolute will to accomplish the great task of building communism. (*Tumultuous applause.*)

And the fact that we present in all their ramifications the basic problems of overcoming the cult of the individual which is alien to Marxism-Leninism, as well as the problem of liquidating its burdensome consequences, is evidence of the great moral and political strength of our party. (*Prolonged applause.*)

We are absolutely certain that our party, armed with the historical resolutions of the 20th Congress, will lead the Soviet people along the Leninist path to new successes, to new victories. (*Tumultuous, prolonged applause.*)

Long live the victorious banner of our party – Leninism! (*Tumultuous, prolonged applause ending in ovation. All rise.*)

NOTE TO CHAPTER 12

1. It is easy today to forget or seriously underestimate the impact which Khrushchev's 'secret' speech had on the international communist movement. The sensational suppression of the cult of Stalin shook every single Communist Party in the world, with the possible exception of Albania. Khrushchev's speech was an act of remarkable audacity for a leader trained in Stalinist traditions and imbued with bureaucratic habits. It is now accepted that Khrushchev delivered his speech in the face of opposition from the majority of the Politburo. He appealed over its head directly to the delegates attending the 20th Party Congress of the Communist Party of the Soviet Union. This was to prove successful and ensure Khrushchev's ascendancy within the apparatus. The delegates were hardly a critical mass: they were (in the traditions of Stalinism) selected rather than elected. Despite this they had, in their own way, suffered from the uncertainties (such as life or death) of the Stalin era. Moreover in most one-party states of the Stalinist variety all the social and political contradictions that mark the social formation, tend to be reflected *inside* the party. Since the party monopolizes all politics, then, on occasion, politics from below affect the party. Khrushchev's speech reflected the mood amongst ordinary party members. The process of de-Stalinization was severely limited by the bureaucracy, but its effect on a global scale was dramatic. The Poznan rebellion led to the first of many crises that have afflicted Polish communism. The explosion in Budapest that followed in the same year (1956) was the first decisive indication that the Stalinist system in Eastern Europe was in a state of crisis: it was the de-Stalinizer Khrushchev who sent in the tanks to crush the Hungarian uprising.

Once Khrushchev had denounced Stalin and his 'excesses' he had also unwittingly ended the sacred monolithism that characterized Stalinist parties. If Stalin was guilty, then no one could be regarded as infallible. The Sino-Soviet split and the birth of 'Eurocommunism' in the West were the logical outcome.

13. Maoism, Stalinism and the Chinese Revolution

Roland Lew

Stalinism and the Chinese Communist Party

The socialist movement in China – as a mass movement, at least – was from its very beginning dependent upon the Russian Revolution. It began under the influence of the thunderclap of October 1917, and this starting-point in China which was a culmination in Russia caused the two movements to follow different courses. Chinese communism was Leninist from the outset, but what might have seemed to be a short cut – China's revolutionaries being spared twenty years of struggle to shake off 'reformism' – proved eventually a source of troubles. What gave Leninism its strength and precision was, in fact, its having matured in the course of struggles, both ideological and practical, in which it confronted and even clashed with other socialist trends, and had plenty of time to test out both the absolute adversary (Tsardom) and the bourgeois 'allies', who first vacillated and then defaulted.

From this history, prosaic or glorious, often harsh, but relatively linear (without the party being destroyed at any stage), Leninism emerged stronger, all the more so because it attracted to itself in 1917 a cohort of radicals, many of them talented, who by joining it enriched Leninism still further, and broadened its outlook (Trotsky typified these newcomers). As regards the road to revolution, Leninism had the benefit of thorough experience, and it was on this basis that Lenin was able to get accepted, if not easily then at least quickly, the sharp turn he made in April 1917. On the other hand, Bolshevism lacked previous experience of 'socialist construction', whereas the Chinese communists were to benefit from that which was accumulated by their northern neighbour.

Chinese communism wished to be Leninist, but its Leninism was *vague* and *poorly assimilated*, revolving around these few themes: (1) the decisive role of the working class as the active force in the social revolution; (2) the party as a gathering of the conscious vanguard, and conceived as a carbon-copy of the Russian 'elder-brother' party; and (3) the importance of the USSR, the first workers' state, which became the guide and example to be followed.

The Chinese Communist Party resulted from the conjuncture of radicalized sections of the bourgeois intellectuals – at once radicalized and frustrated by the revolution of 1911 and its failure, and exasperated by the plundering of China and its transformation into a semi-colony – with Leninism, which seemed to them the theory and the credible means for bringing about the real emancipation of their country. Communism meant the way to the liberation and independence of China, to genuine economic development, and at the same time revealed to them the historical 'subject' that was to accomplish these tasks – the proletariat. Between 1921 and 1927, like the Bolshevik Party down to 1917, the Communist Party of China (CPC) developed as essentially, and sometimes even exclusively, a party of the workers, its view being that the latter, by themselves, would be able to overthrow the social order in China. So far as Chen Tu-hsiu, the party leader, was concerned – and the same applied to his comrades, including Mao down to 1925 or 1926 – all attention and concern was focused upon the working class, while the peasantry was neglected and even despised, being assigned, in any case, a very subordinate role. (There were some exceptions: Peng Pai, Mao after 1925–6, and others.)

Apart from these few borrowings from Leninism, the nascent CPC was affected by a number of problematics and influences that reflected the complexity of China itself, the force of traditional forms of social behaviour and thought (Confucianism, etc.) and also by differing attitudes to modernization seen as Westernization or to modernization seen as not implying, or as transcending, Westernization. The unifying axis of the party, that which in those days gave it coherence, was its attitude to the USSR, and, furthermore, its organizational and political assimilation to the 'great brother-party'. Aware of its weaknesses and limitations, the CPC subordinated itself to the CP of the USSR and to the Comintern, which became its mentors. This circumstance was to govern the troubled history of the Chinese communist movement from 1921 to 1935. Looking at things through Soviet spectacles meant bringing into play in China policies that were contradictory or ill-adapted to the tasks of the Chinese Revolution.

Mao, as a 'middle cadre' of the party, was deeply affected by the experiences of his party between 1921 and 1927. Like all the other militants, he followed the directives of the Comintern without understanding what lay behind them and without grasping the reasons for changes in strategy which were comprehensible only on the basis of the situation in Russia. What was going on in that country was the gradual Stalinization of the communist movement, which meant covering up and concealing classical Marxism and its interpretation by Lenin. Stalinism became the Leninism of the CPC, and this 'telescoping' was to prevent the Chinese communist leaders from appreciating the specific nature of Stalinism in the Russian and international settings, and the character and scope of its break with Leninism – above all, with the central category of 'world revolution'.

This telescoping process was all the more effective because the CPC did not become a fully coherent structure until after the defeat of 1927. Before that date, the Chinese communists followed the behests of the Comintern, either hesitantly or with conviction,[1] they exercised no independent judgement of their own, and, besides, the Soviet advisers on the spot (Borodin, etc.)[2] were there to maintain direct and continuous supervision of the Chinese party's policy.

The 1927 defeat destroyed the CPC and threw its leading structures into confusion. After the departure or expulsion of Right and Left Oppositionists (1927–9), only two trends were left in the CPC. First, a Stalinist wing, dominant between 1928 and 1935, selected and imposed by Moscow, which had a view of China and the world that was articulated but false (divorced from reality) and represented close assimilation to Stalinism, or, more precisely, surrender thereto. For this wing it was recognition of the hegemony of the Russian party and of the central role of the USSR, bulwark of socialism, that had to be defended at all costs. This was a 'world-wide' outlook, to be sure, but one which was centred on the defence of a particular state, the USSR, from the standpoint of whose interests the whole world situation was evaluated. Here also, and above all, there was assimilation to that form of 'Soviet' bureaucratism which expressed the basis and essence of Stalinism – a process of perpetuating bureaucratic structures, which was favoured by the formation in Moscow itself of a team devoted to the USSR, resulting from selection through intense factional struggle: the 'Twenty-eight Bolsheviks'.[3]

Secondly, there was the Mao trend, which emerged gradually, slowly and modestly from 1927 onward. Marginal in relation to the first trend, it had only a regional basis, and no influence, at the outset, on the leadership of the party. Less structured politically than the Stalinist group, it was also less well-armed and poorer in political training – but, paradoxically, it was protected by its very ideological poverty. Being more closely associated with social action it was less disposed to employ schemata which were coherent but false, and, above all, it was by virtue of its practical activity more aware of the inadequacy of these schemata.

Thus, the 1927 defeat reduced the CPC to a sect upon which Stalinism, in process of consolidation in the USSR, was to swoop in order to carry out an activity of assimilation that would leave militants with only the choice (if there was any choice at all now!) between leaving the party (or being expelled from it), submitting, or accepting a silent 'marginality', facilitated by geographical remoteness. This last attitude was the one taken up by Mao.

Integration into Stalinism was effected in two senses – positively by internalizing the specifically Russian bureaucratic system, and negatively by hiding Leninism away – but it expressed itself especially in defence of the Soviet 'bastion'. This was the most fundamental and least perverted reason for the hegemony of Stalinism and for the impact of the theory of 'socialism in one country'. Gramsci showed, as early as 1926, the profound meaning for the communists outside Russia of their acceptance of this theory.

In his letter to Togliatti of 26 October 1926 Gramsci criticized him not for supporting the Soviet leadership (Stalin and Bukharin) against the Left Opposition but for the bureaucratic form of his support. He declared: '. . . today, that is, nine years after October 1917, it is no longer the fact that the Bolsheviks *have taken power* that can revolutionize the masses in the West, for this is a situation that has already been accomplished and has produced all its effects; today, what has an ideological and political impact is the conviction (if it exists) that the proletariat, once it has come to power, *can build socialism.*'[4] Undoubtedly it was this motive that explained why Gramsci accepted (with some qualifications) the theory of 'socialism in one country' – and along with him the great majority of communist militants. Stalinism represented the conjuncture between a process of bureaucratization which remained within the setting of a transition to socialism – a process embodied in the narrow but coherent concept of 'socialism in one country' – and the extraordinary appeal which this 'socialist construction' (actually, to a large extent distorted) had for the international proletariat, or at least for its communist wing. From this standpoint Bettelheim is probably right when he points[5] to the unifying and mobilizing value of this slogan for the Russian party: in a period of retreat, it was a credible project (even if in fact an unrealizable one) and the credibility it possessed (even more, the fascination it exerted) affected the world communist movement, probably contributing to Stalin's easy victory over Trotsky. The latter was particularly conscious of the absurdity of a project to build socialism in a single country, and a very backward one at that: he saw this as not only absurd, moreover, but also reactionary, in that it implied renunciation of the world revolution. But Trotsky did not perceive, or did not fully perceive, that this proposition – 'building socialism in one country' – provided a real response, in the short run at least, to the ebbing of the revolutionary tide.

Unquestionably, the USSR became thus established as the 'pole of reference' above all because it was building a socialist society, or what was regarded as such: hence the way the Five-Year Plans were hailed . . . While, as a result, Stalin and the Comintern were able to impose on the world's Communist Parties strategic directives that were dubious or wrong, and were even seen to be so (by Mao among others), the USSR remained nevertheless the obligatory reference-point, the only acceptable and accessible model, and the 'weight' of the USSR and its leader Stalin was for this reason all the more substantial. Hence the hegemony exercised by the USSR and the ease with which leaders and rank-and-file alike in the Communist Parties accepted the most varied and inconsistent instructions. This submissiveness was especially striking in China. Between 1924 and 1927 the CPC followed the Rightist line of subordination to the Kuomintang (which was supposed to represent the progressive national bourgeoisie), leading to the tragic defeat of 1927. Between 1927 and 1934, still under Moscow's orders, three ultra-Left lines were applied, in a situation so absurd that it calls for a brief explanation. The first of the ultra-Left lines, that of Chu Chiu-pai, came immediately after the 1927 defeat. It was a 180-degree turn, the purpose of which was to get Stalin off the hook: the party's meagre surviving forces were hurled into the adventurist revolt in Canton and the no less adventurist 'Autumn Harvest Rising' (imposed upon, and led by, Mao). All this quickly ended in débâcle – in a period, moreover, when the international line was still Rightist.

The years 1928–9 were years of uncertainty in the USSR. The Bukharinist Right was in process of being beaten. Yet in 1928, at the 6th World Congress of the Comintern, practically coinciding with the 6th Congress of the CPC, also held in Moscow, a moderate course was still promulgated (and was favourably received by Mao in the mountains where he had taken refuge). In 1929–30, however, what was actually implemented was a new ultra-Left line, under the leadership of Li Li-san, corresponding to the ultra-Leftism of the Comintern as a whole in the period 1929–34. Once more the CPC was obliged to throw its skeletal forces into attacks on the cities of China, in a conquest-of-power strategy. The result was that it lost its last remaining militants in the cities. Curiously enough, the party of the proletariat was attempting, all alone, to seize power not in order to establish the dictatorship of the proletariat but in the context of a 'bourgeois-democratic' revolution. But what was more important, and worse, was that this attempt was undertaken in the midst of a period of ebb-tide, even regression, of the revolution. Li Li-san spoke of an impetuous upsurge of the masses because in Moscow they 'saw' this proletarian breakthrough going on throughout the world, and in China especially.

The result was another catastrophe, for which Li Li-san was made the scapegoat and dismissed. As, however, the Comintern was still in an ultra-Left phase, the ultra-Leftism of Li Li-san was followed by the ultra-Leftism of Wang Ming, leader of the 'Twenty-eight Bolsheviks' and most Stalinist of China's communists. He in turn applied an offensive policy, and attacked the Mao trend, which was sharply rebuked, isolated and made to submit. At the end of 1934, on the eve of the 'Long March' (which was in fact a long flight) and of Mao's accession to power, the CPC was nothing more than a Stalinist party, doomed to suffer the vicissitudes of the Comintern's directives and thereby cut off from all contact with the working class.

The effect of Stalinism on Chinese communism was not, however, merely negative. Stalinism presented itself as, and shaped the CPC as, a Marxist trend, and so maintained – in a caricatural way, to be sure, but really, nevertheless – *the proletariat* as its reference-point. This was a paradoxical but decisive consequence of Stalinist influence: because its roots were in the *workers'* state, it had to maintain a corresponding outlook – distorted and 'ideological', but with a certain minimum of consistency and conviction. This 'Marxism' was to be the reference-point of generations of communist militants. This system of thought (this superstructure of a power-system) prevented, if necessary by physical 'liquidation', any open and living application of Marxism, while maintaining a proletarian political framework. And it was in this impoverished and restricted ideological setting, and by using what remained in it of Leninism, that Mao's specific line was to emerge, showing peculiar features that were sometimes alien to Marxism, even to Stalinist Marxism (if that makes sense), but nevertheless internalizing in a consistent way an orientation that was proletarian and socialist.

Thus, in China, Stalinism both formed and deformed the local Marxism, and remained as the horizon of Chinese communism, as a conception through which it was necessary to pass even in order to take one's distance from it. Stalin's Russia was the embodiment of hope and of a transferable model of socialist construction – and also, it confidently expected, the 'great rear', the ally, the source of support . . .[6]

Where, then, is Maoism to be placed? In that political space which was both opened and shut by Stalinism. But it was also rooted in the contradictions of Chinese society, even while being profoundly shaped by the Russian Revolution and by Leninism: here too what is involved is a relation of absence-and-presence.

Most important, Maoism did not begin to assume concrete forms until the setting was that of the counter-revolution of 1927 and the problems this presented. In other words, Maoism was at first only a particular, conjunctural response to the way Chinese society had got into a dead end, a situation the effects of which gradually became general, as a result of the 1927 setback.

The effect of Maoism, which will be examined later, also transcends the limits of China, in so far as it is *in fact* a response to the crisis of the 'world revolution'. This is so only objectively, however, but not consciously: Stalinism fills the whole of 'revolutionary' space, distorting this and excluding every alternative, so that the space of the 'revolution' can be occupied only *marginally*, rather than in opposition to Stalinism.

Maoism began like that, as a marginal movement, localized both regionally and politically, remote from the working class, but, what made up for this, rooted in an original way in another Chinese reality: the countryside. And this 'distance' from Stalinism was of far-reaching importance. From his first days as leader of the party, in 1935, Mao's authority was accepted, even tolerated, rather than truly approved by the Comintern. The CPC, having been largely destroyed, no longer interested Stalin. Besides, the CPC on the march (in flight) was far away, difficult of access: what was happening over there signified little. So, let Mao or anybody else lead the CPC . . .

Furthermore, even with Mao, the appearances (and not only the appearances) of total agreement with Moscow were kept up, especially after the CPC proposed, apparently after strong pressure from Moscow, a united anti-Japanese front of the CPC and the Kuomintang. Accepted reluctantly by Mao, the alliance with Chiang Kai-shek, in accordance with the world-wide 'People's Front' line, showed that the Chinese communist leader wished to appear an orthodox Stalinist. The real situation was more complex.

Stalin's underestimation of the CPC, which was obvious already in the 1930s (though in the Comintern press of that period the influence of the Chinese brother-party was exaggerated), and even a certain contempt for it, continued until 1948. And yet as early as 1937–8 the Chinese revolutionaries had become a real force, which was considerable by 1945, and were even on the road to power in 1947–8. Down to that time, however, they continued to be treated by Moscow as a negligible quantity,[7] or, at best, as a *masse de manœuvre* to be employed in a diplomatic game.

In spite of this, Mao, being unable to rise above Stalinism, adopted it to some extent, while also 'getting round' it, so to speak.

1. He accepted Stalinism because he was unable to define and characterize it, and had, besides, no rich Marxist experience of his own, comparable to the history of Bolshevism.

2. He adopted Stalinism, too, because he lacked the conceptual means, the political strength and the ideological prestige, even within his own party, to put forward any alternative. This was why he concealed or played down for so long the distinctiveness of his own ideas.

3. But, above all, and this is the main point, his thinking was bounded by the horizon of Stalinism, as I have already stressed, and for this reason,

though he might produce an original strategic plan for China, he was incapable of expanding it into a new international conception (and, indeed, he showed no inclination to do so).

Thus, Maoism developed somewhere outside Stalinism and Leninism[8] in a space of its own which gave it a specific character as a 'concrete totality' which integrated the constraints, old and new, of Chinese society, and the lessons drawn from China's two abortive revolutions (1911 and 1925–7) – in short, taking up a Chinese problematic while remaining rooted in the proletarian ideology, but without a proletariat. Maoism was, consequently, a bastard solution – but perhaps the only solution – to the twofold· crisis of Chinese society and of the Chinese Communist Party.

The Maoist road to revolution: China and the revolution
In China the revolution was over-determined by an accumulation of tensions resulting from the particular effects of the break-up of a traditional society and from the various aspects, both negative and positive, of imperialist penetration, especially in its latest form, the Japanese invasion, and the accelerated collapse of Chinese society on the morrow of the Second World War. It was these experiences – more destructuring in their effect (rending the social fabric) than restructuring (re-establishing a stable society) – that made of twentieth-century China a powder-barrel. And it was this over-determination – the confluence of all these effects towards a socialist revolution – that explains why a conception so woolly, so lacking in Marxist rigour, as Maoism could come into being.

Maoism, lacking in rigour, was also well weak in its grasp of problems of such importance as the significance of Stalinism and the nature of the world revolution, and was unable to make·a precise analysis of Chinese society and its classes, etc.

What this signified can be made clearer, perhaps, by means of a contemporary analogy. If the strategy of establishing revolutionary *focos* had proved adequate to lead Latin America to socialism in the 1960s, in the wake of the Cuban Revolution, the Marxism that would have resulted would doubtless have presented the same 'practical' and 'summary' aspect as we see in Maoism. But in fact the failure of the *foco* strategy showed that the ground was less favourable. It was indispensable to go over everything again from scratch, subjecting to close analysis local capitalism and its relations with imperialism, the class contradictions, the methods used by the ruling classes, etc. In short, a 'summary' form of Marxism proved quite inadequate to the situation.

From this, however, it must not be concluded that Maoism, carried along by a process of 'permanent revolution', was enabled to carry through an *easy* revolution.

After 1927, of the three main classes of Chinese society, two, the working class and the bourgeoisie, were out of the running as revolutionary 'subjects'. The urban working class had been crushed: a proletariat which had shown no less dynamism and determination than its Russian counterpart, and had formed the basis for the growth of the Communist Party, disappeared as an independent force for more than twenty years.

For its part, the bourgeoisie had failed to constitute itself as a homogeneous and resolute class: this is the clearest lesson to be drawn from the counter-revolution of 1927. The bourgeoisie had gone over to the counter-revolution. Or, more precisely, the Kuomintang, its political representative, had not detached itself (perhaps could not have done) from the other dominant social forces: the landlords, the compradors, the warlords – in short, an amalgam the impurity of which tarnished the brightness of the bourgeois radicalism that Lenin thought he had perceived in Sun-Yat-sen-ism. The hybrid character of the Kuomintang was incarnate in its new leader Chiang Kai-shek, who united in his person the modernistic businessman and the leader of a traditional sect. At village level the unifying axis of this party was maintenance of the social *status quo* and defence of the landlords. In the towns, however, it tended to favour industrial development, in which the state played an important role. It was this activity in the towns that most clearly revealed the bourgeois nature of the Kuomintang and the capitalist (even rising-capitalist) tendency of Chinese society, and also made more apparent the distorted character of the alliance between the bourgeoisie and the most conservative class of all, the landlords.

What remained, then, was the huge peasant mass – more than a class, a many-faceted world, sunk in thousand-year-old networks of social and cultural relations, scattered among hundreds of thousands of villages all over China. It was without any social representation, unlike its Russian counterpart, which had found in Narodism channels for the voicing of its demands, and intellectuals to express them.

The Chinese peasantry was diverse, but was above all deprived of any social leadership, this being the most noteworthy result of the break-up of traditional society and the disappearance of the mandarinate. The landlords (when they were not absentees), together with the rich peasants, dominated the villages, to be sure, but without giving expression to the peasants' demands: they did not so much weld rural society together as live at its expense.

Was the rural world of China in a state of crisis in the twentieth century? Here we must be precise and must distinguish: more than the peasantry, it was agriculture that was in crisis. An increasingly numerous peasantry cultivated an agricultural area that grew only slightly, and the yield from which also increased only slowly. This had been the case for at least two centuries, made worse and worse by the steady increase in population.[9] A deterioration that was slow but steady was going on: and this increasingly difficult situation was made even harder by all the additional factors that were present in greater or less degree: usury, ground-rent, famine, the warlords and bandits, taxation . . .

But while there was great poverty and real crisis, what was typical of the countryside was comparative lethargy, punctuated by savage, sporadic revolts: a certain resistance to oppression, but, in the main, tolerance or resignation in the face of poverty that was experienced as a gradual degradation.[10] Furthermore, the peasants were still extremely atomized, and their horizon rarely extended beyond the walls of their own village: the peasantry was everything but an organized class, conscious of possessing a particular interest of its own. If it constituted a revolutionary force, this was only as a *potential* which required an impulse from without if it was to develop consistent activity. As such it could not, therefore, take the place of the working class of the towns, which had been laid prostrate, for it lacked, in itself, comparable dynamism and coherence. The peasantry was to be for the revolutionaries as much a problem as an asset: a very difficult problem that must be mastered before the peasants' revolutionary potentialities could be deployed.

Accordingly, the relationship between the CPC and the peasantry would never be what it had been with the proletariat in the days down to 1927, when the party had indeed been the party of the working class, inspiring and organizing that class. Moreover, the basic reality of Chinese communism, namely, a workers' party led by intellectuals, was smashed in 1927. What was left was a structured party: one that had lost its basis, but a party all the same. It was confronted by no peasant party: the political space of the peasantry was virgin territory, which Maoism, in search of a new way forward, was consciously to occupy.

The multiplicity of the causes of revolution (over-determination) did not diminish the importance of the revolutionary party and its methods: quite the contrary, despite an allegation which is often met with.[11] While China was undoubtedly pregnant with revolution – like other countries, where, however, no revolution took place – to bring this revolution about required a definite instrument, adapted to special and unforeseen situations (absence of the proletariat, etc.), a party that was ready, also, to react adequately to new events. To put the matter more concretely, the party of the revolution had, after 1927, first and foremost to survive, and that was not easy. It had to survive, but also to strike root in a new social foundation the support of which would enable it to go on existing. If it was to continue as the party of the revolution, however, it must retain its proletarian point of reference, and without a working-class basis that would be hard to achieve. Above all, the party had to maintain its *cohesion*, in fact, to continue to function as a *party* and not as a heterogeneous conglomerate: and this, too, was not a simple matter.

In the 1930s, besides, there were two other problems that needed to be solved successfully: the war against Japan, which necessitated a correct appreciation of the party's anti-imperialist role; and defence of the party's independence against Stalinist pressure for subordinating it to the Kuomintang. This created a delicate situation: without actually breaking with Stalinism, it was necessary to set the party at a certain distance from it.

Here, then, was a complex and difficult task, which called not so much for an acute conception of Marxism as for great political and organizational talent.

Maoism meant insistence on revolution in a counter-revolutionary situation, with all that that implied in terms of voluntarism, but also the power to perceive everything that objectively favoured re-emergence of the revolution. But Maoism also meant a brake on the revolution, or rather a tendency to compel the revolution to follow a determined path, with precisely-defined phases. Maoism meant, as has been said, an impoverished but adequate view of revolution – impoverished indeed, but above all turned inwards upon China, and showing, at this level, a rich understanding of the peculiarities of China, an unusual sense of the impulses at work in the masses, and great skill in military strategy and tactics. And it meant also a revolutionary sense which Stalinism had, if not warped, then at least narrowed.

At the outset, the action undertaken by the Chinese leader was nothing but a gamble: would he be able to hold out under the difficult circumstances of the countryside and in a period of counter-revolution? Or, rather, it was a tireless search to discover the conditions and mediations that would safeguard the space – social, political, and geographical – of the revolution.

It was from this special situation that Maoism as a specific trend emerged: one that was both genuine and yet also a denaturing and twisting of Leninism and to a certain extent even (and fortunately!) of Stalinism.

With Maoism the revolution was the more genuine and creative in proportion as it was Chinese, and the more Chinese it was the farther it departed from Leninism, accepting Stalinism as its only international horizon (or its lack of an international horizon – this was the separation between China and the world, the introversion, that was characteristic of Maoism), while partly rejecting Stalinism in its *local* strategy.

While Mao was wrong to confine his conception to a 'revolution by stages', when in fact, as will be seen, the movement revealed an irresistible dynamic of permanent revolution that justified Trotsky's forecasts, he was nevertheless superior to Trotsky, in relation to China at least, in his outstanding and highly Leninist sense of 'concrete analysis of the concrete situation' and his capacity to bring forth solutions to problems that seemed insoluble (or at least were considered so by Marxists) such as revolutionizing the world of the peasant smallholders, finding forms suitable for relations between the party and the petty-bourgeois masses, etc. Mao's imagination exploited every possible means to cause communism to rise again in the apparently preposterous setting of exclusively peasant Soviets. But he had, above all, an amazing intuition: *properly worked upon*, the world of the peasantry could serve as an excellent terrain for the revolution, not just because it was all that was available, but by virtue of its own value.

For Trotsky, the peasant Soviets were the rearguard of a struggle against a counter-revolution which, starting from the cities, spread gradually over the land of China, and the Russian revolutionary saw this circumstance as offering no great future for these Soviets. He conceived that they might be able to survive, here and there, but for him their isolation from the proletariat doomed them, if they failed to recover contact with the working-class world, to the worst anti-proletarian peasant deviations, petty-bourgeois in social content.[12]

Mao argued differently. For him, the counter-revolution would never succeed in crushing the revolution in the huge expanse of China: this would take too much time, and the time-factor was important, for the class contradictions in China and the greed of the imperialists would not leave Chiang Kai-shek free to destroy the revolution at leisure. Thus, Mao declared in his letter of 5 January 1930 to Lin Piao:

While the imperialist contention over China becomes more intense, both the contradiction between imperialism and the whole Chinese nation and the contradictions among the imperialists themselves develop simultaneously on Chinese soil, thereby creating the tangled warfare which is expanding and intensifying daily and giving rise to the continuous development of the contradictions among the different cliques of China's reactionary rulers . . . In the wake of the contradictions between imperialism and China's national industry comes the failure of the Chinese industrialists to obtain concessions from the imperialists, which sharpens the contradiction between the Chinese bourgeoisie and the Chinese working class, with the Chinese capitalists trying to find a way out by frantically exploiting the workers, and with the workers resisting . . . Once we understand all these contradictions, we shall see in what a desperate situation, in what a chaotic state, China finds herself. We shall also see that the high tide of revolution against the imperialists, the warlords and the landlords is inevitable, and will come very soon. All China is littered with dry faggots, which will soon be aflame. The saying, 'A single spark can start a prairie fire', is an apt description of how the current situation will develop.[13]

Meanwhile one had to hold on, to prepare for this revolutionary future, building bases (the Soviets) as firmly as possible wherever this could be done – in the South, and then, when it was no longer possible to hold out there, in some other part of China: in the North, whether by choice or by force of circumstances[14] mattered little. The most important thing was to hold on.

And events justified Mao. This analysis of his, both implicit and explicit, is the only aspect of Maoist strategy that has world-wide significance. This aspect was, too, the earliest to show itself, in 1928–30, revealing that this poorly educated leader was capable of great intellectual acuteness as well as of undeniable revolutionary faith. Mao's capacity for concrete analysis was his strength, expressed in a definite talent, regardless of theoretical limitations, for finding the practical mediations between the end (to hold on) and the means (the Soviets, leadership and organization of the peasants, the Red Army). Beyond question, Mao showed in this respect, a kinship with, even a resemblance to, Lenin.

Let us bring together in a few strokes the elements that gave coherence to Maoism, a coherence that was only gradually established:

1. Mao started from the conviction that the Kuomintang had failed to accomplish its tasks. Thereby that party had exhausted its role in history; and even when Mao was saying the opposite (in 1938, for instance), the Communist Party's practice was based on this conviction.

2. The urban working class had been finally destroyed as an organized and active force: struck to the ground in the cities, it was no longer the vanguard of the revolution, and other social forces must take over from it.

3. The poor peasantry was, in this situation, the only social force at the disposal of the revolution, while at the same time it was the most fundamental element in Chinese society.

4. The revolution thus became a 'revolutionary peasant war' (1927–37): what was at stake in this conflict, on the economic and social plane, was agrarian reform, but the basic aim was to transform the peasantry into a revolutionized element in society.

5. The task of the revolution in China was to carry through the unfinished work of the bourgeoisie – to rescue China from stagnation, which implied bringing about national unity, industrialization, agrarian reform, and national independence.

6. In realizing these aims, one example alone was credible, that of socialist construction in the USSR. As already mentioned, the USSR, the first workers' state, came to be seen as the model, the guarantor and perhaps the supporter in economic development. This accounts for the impact made by Stalin on Mao, even though the Soviet dictator's directives inspired only reserve and mistrust.

7. Because the future lay with industrialization, and so with the town and the proletariat, the leaders of the CPC adopted, or rather maintained, the proletariat as their pole of reference.

8. The instrument appropriate to this special situation, in which a 'proletarian horizon' dominated although no actual proletariat was present, was the party: more than merely the instrument, indeed, it was the guarantor.

9. The history of Maoism was thus the history of its special methods, and especially of its 'substitutism':[15] one class, the peasantry, took the place of another, the proletariat, which was absent but continued to be the pole of reference, and this reference was maintained by *the Communist Party*, which substituted itself for the missing class and acted in its stead. This substitution was more negative – a matter of avoiding contamination of the party by the peasantry's petty-bourgeois tendencies – than positive, in the sense of effectively taking the place of the working class. Thus, a little nucleus of communist cadres (themselves sons of bourgeois, landlords or rich peasants) took into their hands alone the proletarian task in the name of which they mobilized, inspired and led the peasantry, as a revolutionary force both acting and acted upon.

Along with this strategic conception went the means for realizing it.

1. While the party was the master-planner and the peasantry the social force for carrying out the party's aim, the agent for transforming these peasants into communists was the army, and the general framework for this work was the Soviets (or, after 1937, with a change of name: 'the liberated areas'). This army was adapted to the performance of different roles, both resistance and going over to the offensive, which called for appropriate military strategy and tactics, guerrilla warfare and regular army operations. The internal regulations of the army were designed to alter the ways of thinking of the peasant soldiers (who were sometimes peasants who had become bandits before they joined the Red Army), 'deruralizing' them to some extent. The Soviets ('the Red bases'), structures that embodied the hegemony of the communists, rather as in a state system, also provided the setting for organizing, activizing and rendering conscious the whole peasant community.

2. The party's centralism, and later (in 1942), the 'rectification campaigns', served not only to safeguard the proletarian line and keep the party up to its tasks, but also provided forms for social control and activization of the party members, and methods whereby heterogeneous (and rarely proletarian) social groups were homogenized and shaped in the same mould. In the last analysis, the 'rectification campaigns' (which must not be divorced from the party's centralism) were the 'terrain' on which specific constraints (particularly those which concerned social provenance) were directed towards the constitution of a revolutionary instrument that would be communist and proletarian.

The specific nature of Maoism can be clarified more precisely by considering some 'moments' in which it has revealed itself in typical fashion, namely, its methodology, its conception of the stages of the revolution, and its form of hegemony (its bureaucratism).

Methodology

When we examine *On Practice* and *On Contradictions* we penetrate to the heart of Mao's thinking. These are not perhaps works of lofty philosophical quality, expressing theoretical thought of wide scope and solid foundations, but they do offer certain original features. It seems to me, moreover, that where a number of important points are concerned, Mao returns to the original inspiration of Marx, after decades in which this had been neglected and even falsified. (These writings are dated 1937, at the height of the reign of Stalinist dogmatism.) If we take into account the conditions in which Mao's work was carried out, in isolation from the sources of living Marxism, subject to contamination by Stalinist distortions, and with only a limited body of translations of Marx's works as its basis, it must be seen as a remarkable achievement in the field of theory.

Only a few Marxist theoreticians have followed Marx in applying his essential methodology: one may mention the 'Italian' trend, with Labriola and Gramsci, and the German-speaking thinkers of the 1920s, Korsch and Lukács; but all of these, together with their problematics, were unknown to Mao.[16] On the other hand Mao had retained a certain contact with the work of Lenin as thinker and practitioner of the communist movement, and Lenin, too, had, through his study of Hegel, undertaken a methodological dialogue with Marxism. Lenin's *Philosophical Notebooks* of 1914–15, consisting of notes and comments on Hegel's writings, had been partly translated into Chinese, and they served as the essential link between Marxist dialectics and Mao's working out of his own dialectical conception on the basis of the theoretical materials and experience at his disposal. Let me explain this more fully.

What has been called the 'Marxist dialectical tradition' is the form of theoretical structuring which runs all through the evolution of Marxism, with Marx himself as its chief representative. At the heart and centre of this problematic lies the determining role of the dialectical method. It was on the basis of a relation to Hegelian dialectics – a complex relation which is still subject to lively discussion – that the original form of Marxist dialectics took shape. In the *Theses on Feuerbach* (1845), which Mao knew, and also in Marx's economic writings – *Capital*, the *Grundrisse* (which Mao did not have), etc. – we can see a method being applied. This method is undoubtedly one of the fundamentals of Marxism, and the one on which Mao concentrated: there can be no theory that is not also practice, and vice versa. The basis for Marxist methodology is *praxis*, practical work.

Accordingly, Mao begins his exposition by analysing 'practice' – an approach that expresses a profound understanding of Marxism. Contrary to the claim made by hosts of Marxists, from Kautsky to the Social Democrats of today, and including Bernstein and the Stalinist movement, there is no Marxist metaphysics, that is, Marxism has no ontological basis. Practice and practice alone is there at the outset. To have grasped that was a great achievement on Mao's part. But perhaps it will be said that this achievement was a mere triviality? Certainly not! For Kautsky, for the Austro-Marxists, for the younger Lenin (before the *Philosophical Notebooks*), for the entire Stalinist movement (which was, nevertheless, the reference-point for the Chinese communists), and for many others, though practice is essential it is not the *point of departure*. At the start, as the basis, are various forms of metaphysics – Darwinian (in Kautsky's case), sociological or mechanistic, depending on the particular writer – and through this metaphysics is imposed the imprint of the surrounding type of society, whether bourgeois or (in the USSR) bureaucratic.[17]

For many sinologists of the English-speaking world, Maoism is a 'Chinese' version of Stalinism, and they find it hard, therefore, to perceive what is original in Mao. They concentrate on the simple and, as they see it, 'summary' aspect of Mao's thought. His originality in fact lies elsewhere, in his rejection of metaphysics, on the basis of the primacy of 'practice'. (As we shall see later, a certain 'dose' of metaphysics does reappear, all the same, in the text and the problematic of *On Contradictions*.)

For Mao there is no *a priori* materialism: 'Knowledge begins with experience – this is the materialism of the theory of knowledge.'[18] Here is an extraordinary statement, which comes straight out of the problematic of praxis (Marx's famous *Theses on Feuerbach*, of 1845) and stands in opposition to Stalinist Marxism. The latter is centred, like the Lenin of *Materialism and Empiriocriticism* (1909), on the doctrine of the primacy of matter, in the sense of the existence of matter before mind. For Marx explicitly and for Mao implicitly, this is a metaphysical thesis, a discussion that remains enclosed within bourgeois categories. Practice alone, the work of praxis, provides the key to the questions man asks himself.

Man's knowledge depends mainly on his activity in material production, through which he comes gradually to understand the phenomena, the properties and the laws of nature, and the relations between himself and nature; and through his activity in production he also gradually comes to understand, in varying degrees, certain relations that exist between man and man. *None of this knowledge can be acquired apart from activity in production* (my emphasis, R. L.).[19]

And Mao also says that 'dialectical materialism . . . emphasizes the dependence of theory on practice, emphasizes that theory is based on practice and in turn serves practice.'[20] Further, he brings into the sphere of cognition the 'class standpoint': 'In class society everyone lives as a member of a particular class, and every kind of thinking, without exception, is stamped with the brand of a class.'[21] There is thus an 'absolute' starting point, practice, and a particular standpoint, membership of a certain class, which can be correct when it rises to the level of universality, that is, when it transcends the social limitations of the individuals concerned, to grasp what is required for great transformations of society.

While knowledge begins with experience (practice), 'the second point is that knowledge needs to be deepened, that the perceptual stage of knowledge needs to be developed to the rational stage – this is the dialectics of the theory of knowledge.'[22] Practice is only a starting point. Dialectics is conceptual. 'Concepts are no longer the phenomena, the separate aspects and the external relations of things; they grasp the essence, the totality and the internal relations of things.'[23]

The political function of this passage is clear. For Mao, the CPC possesses a practice, and it is on this that the party's activity must be based, not on stereotyped (Mao's word is 'formalistic') conceptions. But it is necessary to go beyond experience and strive toward theorization, that is, rational knowledge. Confining oneself to practice leads to empiricism, to subordination to whatever is immediately present. Criticism of these two errors recurs in many of the writings of Mao and of other communist leaders.

Now Mao – he, and not the leaders imposed by Moscow – had applied a creative political line, and by showing, in addition, that he was capable of developing theory, he legitimized his position as party leader. Thus, in face of the reproach of empiricism and pragmatism frequently levelled at him, his philosophical writings were not merely useful in relation to a particular situation, they represented a simple but genuine 'reappropriation' of Marxism. This was not altogether the case, however, with the essay in which Mao analysed the process of rational cognition, his study of contradictions.

On Contradictions bears the date August 1937, and so was written a month later than *On Practice*. Like its predecessor this work is said to have been presented in lecture form to the 'Institute for Resistance to Japan' (Kangda). In it Mao sets contradiction at the centre of the theory of cognition. Here, too, despite appearances, there is no mere platitude. It was indeed far from platitudinous, in 1937, to centre the theory of dialectics not on a rigid set of laws, the famous 'laws of dialectics', but on a close analysis of contradictions. And it was equally unusual to refer, in support of this exercise, mainly to the Lenin of the *Philosophical Notebooks* (1914–15) rather than to the still somewhat mechanistic author of *Materialism and Empiriocriticism* (1909).[24]

Further, it seems to me that the reference to Lenin's *Philosophical Notebooks* was the only one that could give a semblance of legitimacy to Mao's views. The essay touches on philosophical discussions in the Soviet Union but does not reproduce the exposition that was orthodox at that time – unlike the essay entitled *Dialectical Materialism*[25] which is attributed to Mao but seems to have been written earlier.

Putting the stress on the analysis of contradictions gave new life to dialectics and made it once again an instrument of analysis that could grasp a complex, living, many-sided reality. Here again, in order to defend the living, multiform, paradoxical practice of the CPC under his leadership, Mao could not rest satisfied with the dried-up thing that was later to be nicknamed 'Diamat'. I have already pointed out that he ascribes an essential role to the analysis of contradictions. 'There is internal contradiction in every single thing, hence its motion and development. Contradictoriness within a thing is the fundamental cause of its development, while its interrelation and interactions with other things are secondary causes.'[26] Thus, there is no question of 'laws of dialectics' that are all of 'equal' significance: one element, the movement of contradictions, is predominant.[27]

Furthermore, Mao defines the different forms of contradiction: 'the universality of contradiction, the particularity of contradiction, the principal contradiction and the principal aspect of a contradiction, the identity and struggle of the aspects of a contradiction, and the place of antagonism in contradiction.'[28] This 'detailed' conception of dialectics is essential to Maoist theory, and is to be found throughout the history of the CPC down to the present time.

Once again it seems to me that, over and above the circumstantial motives that were certainly relevant, we can see here a methodology that is deeply rooted in reality, but also, and much more, a *Weltanschauung*. What is characteristic of this conception is, no less than the (certainly original) analysis of the forms of contradiction, the ontological view of the world that Mao presents. Contradiction becomes the world-principle, the essence of all that exists. 'The universality or absoluteness of contradiction has a twofold meaning. One is that contradiction exists in the process of development of all things, and the other is that in the process of development of each thing a movement of opposites exists from beginning to end.'[29] A view of history from beginning to end, a veritable teleology, one might say![30] Here we see the metaphysical aspect of Mao's thinking which was mentioned above, and which is basically alien to Marx's thought. Marx declined to be a new Hegel, a thinker about the meaning of history and founder of the ontology of what exists and of its 'becoming'. Contradiction is for Marx the movement of concrete history, of the concrete 'becoming' of concrete societies: it is *never* an ontological principle. I shall come back later to this metaphysical aspect of Mao's thought, which differs from his conception in *On Practice*.

Mao also distinguishes, moreover, the specificity of contradictions: 'The particular essence of each form of motion is determined by its own particular contradiction.'[31] And he defines the ways in which specific contradictions are resolved:

The contradiction between the great masses of the people and the feudal system is resolved by the method of democratic revolution; the contradiction between the colonies and imperialism is resolved by the method of national revolutionary war; the contradiction between the working class and the peasant class in socialist society is resolved by the method of collectivization and mechanization in agriculture; contradiction within the Communist Party is resolved by the method of criticism and self-criticism; the contradiction between society and nature is resolved by the method of developing the productive forces.[32]

Furthermore, Mao considers that it is necessary to distinguish among contradictions between that which is the principal contradiction and the ones that are secondary. Thus, in China: 'At such a time, the contradiction between imperialism and the country concerned becomes the principal contradiction, while all the contradictions among the various classes within the country ... are temporarily relegated to a secondary and subordinate position.'[33] Here we find the methodological justification of Maoist strategy. This strategy, and even Maoist tactics as well, would always base itself on this principle – concentrate against the principal enemy of the moment while dealing tactfully with the enemy (persons, things, social tendencies) that is for the time being secondary, and even, if possible, making use of this enemy.

Mao emphasizes, finally, the uneven development of contradictions. He makes more precise his definition of the identity of opposites.

Identity, unity, coincidence, interpenetration, interpermeation, interdependence (or mutual dependence for existence), interconnection or mutual cooperation – all these different terms mean the same thing, and refer to the following two points: first, the existence of each of the two aspects of a contradiction in the process of the development of a thing presupposes the existence of the other aspect, and both aspects coexist in a single entity; second, in given conditions each of the two contradictory aspects transforms itself into its opposite. This is the meaning of identity.[34]

And he adds, regarding antagonism: 'Antagonism is one form, but not the only form, of the struggle of opposites.'[35]

As we see, his is a rich, subtle conception devised as an instrument for strategy, for action – but with an underlying element of metaphysics to which I shall turn.

How are we to evaluate Mao's Marxism on the basis of his two philosophical essays? I have mentioned his references to Lenin and Marx; but what about his relation to Chinese thought, to Chinese culture? This is a difficult question.

Mao has never denied the powerful impression made upon him by Chinese culture and thought. Educated as he was by reading the classical works of Chinese literature,[36] it was not until he was about eighteen that he came under his first Western influences.

Quite recently, in 1971, in the discussion about Lin Piao and in order to refute the theory of the 'Genius', Mao recalled the early influence of Confucius upon him, but as a stage which he passed through and left behind.[37]

Westernizing influence came to Mao through a few direct readings of translations of European works. Thus, Mao's marginal notes on the book by the German neo-Kantian Paulsen on ethics have been preserved. In these notes one may or may not discern elements of dialectical thinking (very embryonic, in any case).[38]

But was this way of approaching the new Western culture, whether precociously dialectical or not, rooted in Chinese civilization? And in what particular source?

Let us try to particularize this question. As has been said, Mao's dialectics is a reappropriation of the Marxist conception of praxis, but includes an ontological view of contradiction which separates Mao from Marx (perhaps less so from Engels). Can China's cultural tradition throw light on this paradox? In general,

in China's past, the dialectical and even materialist elements in Chinese thought formed a soil favourable to the implantation of Marxism . . . In the first place,

Chinese culture, more than any other, retains an essentially practical, quasi-pragmatic aspect, and it is correct to speak, in connection with it, of the 'prestige of the concrete' . . . This often empirical thinking has no taste for abstraction, classification or generalization . . . : things must correspond to the names given them . . .[39]

This is the 'anti-metaphysical side of Chinese thought'.[40]

Moreover, 'the pragmatic element in Chinese thought, which values only effectiveness and utility, prefigures the thesis that Mao was to emphasize so strongly, that a theory is true only if it is verified by practice'.[41] Thus, in continuity with Confucian and also with Taoist culture, but altering radically the sphere of its application, Mao was able to some extent to make the leap to a Marxist conception of praxis for which every question always comes back to practice, to theoretical practice, to human practice — and not to *a priori* metaphysics.

Mao could find embryonic notions for this theory of contradictions in the Chinese conception of Yin and Yang.[42] It is noteworthy that he refers to a (very embryonic) Chinese dialectics: 'The dialectical world outlook emerged in ancient times both in China and in Europe. Ancient dialectics, however, had a somewhat spontaneous and naïve character . . .'[43]

The French sinologist Michelle Loi, who quotes this passage, comments that: 'according . . . to Mao Tse-tung . . . primitive Taoist thought (called the doctrine of the "two elements", of I-ching) was a rudimentary dialectical materialism like that of Heraclitus, which he distinguishes both from "metaphysics" and from idealist dialectics *à la* Hegel.'[44] Still on the subject of Yin and Yang:

> This conception of the world is neither monist nor fixist. Every phenomenon, natural or social, presents two opposed and complementary aspects, the Yin and the Yang (male and female, winter and summer, night and day, moon and sun, prudence and vitality), the alternate and reciprocal play of which gives the world its movement, the Tao (the 'way'). Some have considered that this elementary dialectics of Yin and Yang, this very old-established sense of contradiction, provided for the spread of Marxism a much more favourable soil than the other traditional systems of thought in the East.[45]

In other words, in Chinese culture there were some rudiments of 'dialectical thinking', but, as in Europe, a radical leap had to be made in order to arrive at dialectical materialism, which emerged in a quite specific socio-historical setting,[46] that of capitalism in the West.

To say that Mao was able to draw upon a dialectical tradition, but that he had to make the conceptual leap to Western Marxism, and to acknowledge that he not only largely accomplished this task but contributed to reformulating a more dialectical Marxism — more dialectical, at any rate, than the Stalinist tradition in the USSR, which had been imported into China – is quite simply to admit that this non-philosopher possessed very great intellectual acuteness and undeniable creative capacity.

But how, then, are we to account for the metaphysical elements to be found in Mao, so alien to the Chinese tradition and to the original outlook of Marxism, and even differing from Stalinist metaphysics?

Some hypotheses can be offered, without claiming to exhaust this difficult subject. The metaphysical notion of the timeless universality of contradiction, so remote from the 'utilitarian' and 'without any *a priori*' notion of praxis, is essential if we are to understand all the practical activities of Maoism. It gives a special tone to Mao's undertakings marking them off from those of other Marxists, both Chinese and non-Chinese.[47] Maoist praxis has this 'view of the world' as its underlying preconception. By 'view of the world' I mean, like Lukács and Goldmann,[48] the structured and coherent (or partly coherent) set of ideas by which a social group (a class or part of a class) apprehends the world, situating this group in a given society as regards its own place and its relations with other groups, and giving it its 'possible consciousness', that is, the maximum possible understanding of its situation in the world, allowing for the period of history. This 'view of the world', this possible consciousness, can be embodied in thinkers, writers, etc. What view of the world does Mao hold and on behalf of what social group does he express it? As the son of peasants, formed first by Chinese and then by Westernizing ideas, a Marxist cadre in a proletarian party, dealing exclusively with the peasantry but doing this in the name of the proletariat, Mao bears within him a complex 'view of the world' that must be the resultant of these varied influences. Without trying here to sort out the threads, let us ask whether there is not some connection between peasant millennialist notions and 'Maoist millennialism', in the sense of treating as eternal some problematics which in fact are specific (until practice proves them not to be),[49] or which at least are situated temporally and historically: to postulate the eternal movement of contradictions is to come into conflict with the Marxist and Maoist theory of praxis (Mao's own theory in *On Practice*), which refuses to deal with abstract questions, meaning those which have no basis in concrete history. This does not signify that future societies will not possess contradictions that will move them onward, but that it is nonsensical ('metaphysical'), starting from something we can observe today, to project this feature into the whole history of the universe, human and natural, past, present and future.

This relative correspondence between peasant tradition and Maoist theory is perhaps the price paid for a two-sided phenomenon, namely, remoteness from the proletariat, and submergence in the rural world, the latter being conceived not only as where the peasants are but as a horizon, a system of values, a situation from which certain phenomena are absent (town life, industry, etc.).

This proposition can be explained in another way, by means of a somewhat paradoxical comparison. Let us take two conceptions of Marxism that are very distant from each other: Maoism, with its peasant practice, and Western ultra-Leftism,[50] which is centred on the physical presence of an industrial proletariat. These two trends have developed a rather similar conception of praxis, rejecting metaphysics and ontology – especially in Mao's case – and linking every theory with the 'class standpoint'. But Mao, the proletarian leader in a peasant milieu, invokes a proletariat which is absent and works out a dialectics reflecting not the rise and class struggles of a proletariat actually operating on the historical scene, but in fact based on one abstraction and one reality: the abstract theory of an absent proletariat and the reality of an actually present and acting peasantry.

For the ultra-Left, the reality is the proletariat, the millions of German, Dutch or American proletarians. This trend exalts this proletariat, which is indeed present, as a colossal force in bourgeois society. It is upon the transforming practice of this class, and on nothing else, that the ultra-left bases its Marxist programme. Any other consideration is held to be reactionary, or bourgeois metaphysics. There can be no 'ontology' here, but only the observed practice of the proletariat in a defined historical setting, that of bourgeois society and the socialist society developing from it. Each of the concrete, acting classes – the proletariat and the peasantry – thus structures its own distinct 'world-view', even if the class which is taken as the pole of reference is the same, the proletariat. Maoism is perhaps metaphysical because that social group, the working class, which would have enabled it to transcend ontology has set the mark of its *absence* upon the special course taken by the Chinese Revolution.

It remains to consider what this implies. It seems to me to be something important, even if its consequences appear to have been limited before 1949, and even to have been offset, as I have already pointed out (and I shall come back to the point in my conclusion), by everything that tended objectively, even necessarily, to keep the CPC on a Marxist and proletarian line. On the other hand, this particular aspect of Maoism is vital to our understanding of its practice in the last twenty-five years. Maoist ideas about socialist construction are based on the conviction that disequilibrium, perpetual contradiction, is the general norm, and equilibrium the exception: from the 'Great Leap Forward' to the 'Cultural Revolution', this belief has produced certain consequences. What now has to be considered is whether this conception breaks away from Marxism, or is, on the contrary, a deepening of Marxism. This is an open question!

The nature and stages of the revolution

At a very important plenum of the Central Committee held in 1938 Mao made a long speech, only a small part of which appears in the *Selected Works*. In the original text Mao justified at length the party's alliance with the Kuomintang, attributing to the latter the leadership in the struggle against Japan, in terms so flattering that he was unable, a few years later, to reproduce them.[51]

This speech was addressed to the party, but was also intended for non-party circles, and was made as a justification of the policy then being followed. Nevertheless, it did not reflect Mao's real feelings towards the Kuomintang, which were filled with mistrust. Seeking to muster as much power as possible, and not to give up an inch wherever it had established itself, the CPC was in fact fighting for hegemony over all China, even if its struggle was for some years confined to the north of the country.

Seeking out the principal contradiction, the struggle against Japan, and, especially, so as to appear as a dynamic and unifying element in the fight against the invader, Mao emphasized the party's *formal* subordination to the Kuomintang. The main thing for the communist leader was to be seen by the masses as the most resolute fighter, if not the only one really determined to drive out the enemy.

In this context it became possible to restore substance to the party, mobilizing the masses and revolutionizing them. Formulations of the moment, opportunist in style, mattered little: all that signified was the political function they served, and from this standpoint the CPC had great success, becoming once more, in the course of a year or two (1937–8) a force in which the Chinese nation could believe.

Thus, political effectiveness took precedence over correspondence between programme and actual activity. The alliance with Chiang Kaishek had been imposed by Moscow. So be it, Mao must have thought. What advantages can be got from the alliance, and what must be done to ensure that *this* 'united front' does not turn to the party's disadvantage in the way the first one did?

The advantage of the alliance lay in the way that the nation could be brought to acknowledge the outstanding role played by the CPC, so that the latter might take the forefront of the stage. The safeguard against things going wrong consisted in the independence of the party, of the army and of the communist-ruled territories. And then, 'while one can find statements in Mao's writings both before and after [1939] acknowledging the leading role of the bourgeoisie, after 1939 it is clear that these are mere verbal concessions; in fact he envisages that the reality of power will rapidly fall to the communists'.[52] I am not sure that 'rapidly' is right here, but the rest of this statement is unquestionably sound, as can be seen in a work of Mao's which was both important and paradoxical, namely, *On New Democracy* (January 1940).

This piece of writing, which outlined the future prospect as seen by the CPC, needs to be read at several different levels. First of all, in the setting of the anti-Japanese struggle, it was necessary to smile reassuringly upon the urban petty-bourgeoisie. The CPC wished to gather as many social forces as possible around itself. In addition to its main support, the poor and middle peasantry, it aimed to win as allies or to neutralize the other elements in society – the national bourgeoisie of the towns, the rich peasantry and so on.

Mao's famous essay *On New Democracy* synthesized in 1940 Mao's method and what he had achieved. According to him, China was moving towards 'New Democracy', that is, towards a bourgeois order, which must remain China's regime for a long period, and only after which could a socialist stage be conceived.

It is also possible to read this work in a different way, in which it becomes the expression of an *apparently* flawless Stalinist orthodoxy. Talking of revolution by stages and postponing socialism to a distant future – what could be more in line with the directives of the Stalinized Third International, especially after its Seventh Congress (1935)?[53] Here was a Mao whom the USSR and Stalin would find it hard to excommunicate, for he was following the official line. And yet . . .

Finally, the work can be read at a third level, the most important – 'New Democracy' as an expression of Maoism in its most specific, least orthodox aspect in relation to Stalinism.[54] Mao brought in two scarcely orthodox aspects which modified the structure of his essay and, so to speak, made it 'more Left'. 'New Democracy', he said, was part of the struggle for socialism; and the CPC must lead the revolutionary process.[55]

Let me illustrate this with a few quotations. Writing of China since the Russian Revolution, he said: 'Since these events, the Chinese bourgeois-democratic revolution has changed, it has come within the new category of bourgeois-democratic revolutions and, as far as the alignment of revolutionary forces is concerned, forms part of the proletarian-socialist world revolution. Why? Because the first imperialist world war and the first victorious socialist revolution, the October Revolution, have changed the whole course of world history and ushered in a new era.'[56] 'In this era, any revolution in a colony or semi-colony that is directed against imperialism . . . is no longer part of the old bourgeois, or capitalist, world revolution, but is part of the new world revolution, the proletarian-socialist world revolution. Such revolutionary colonies and semi-colonies . . . have become allies of the revolutionary front of world socialism.'[57] 'No matter what classes, parties or individuals in an oppres-

sed nation join the revolution, and no matter whether they themselves are
conscious of the point, or understand it, so long as they oppose imperialism, their revolution becomes part of the proletarian-socialist world
revolution and they become its allies.'[58]

Thus, in face of (Japanese) 'fascism', the socialist forces, with the USSR
at their head, have become guarantors of the stage of 'New Democracy'.
In China itself, 'history has proved that the Chinese bourgeoisie cannot
fulfil this responsibility, which inevitably falls upon the shoulders of the
proletariat'[59] – and by the proletariat must be understood its representative, the CPC.

Looking back to before the age of Stalinism we see here the same logic
as in the discussions among Russian revolutionaries in 1905 about the
nature of the Russian Revolution, and the conclusion drawn by Mao
cannot but recall 1917: the bourgeoisie is incapable of carrying out the
democratic revolution.[60] Finally, a bourgeois revolution led by the
proletariat (by the CPC) would be followed through into a socialist
revolution, just as Trotsky, with his theory of 'permanent revolution',
had seen would happen, and as the Chinese would acknowledge later on
by talking of 'uninterrupted revolution'.

Did Mao really think, in 1940, that the CPC, after imposing 'New
Democracy', would halt there? It seems doubtful. But perhaps he did
sincerely believe in a long bourgeois period under the hegemony of the
CPC, a stage the chief purpose of which would be to develop the
productive forces in a China that was too backward to enter the socialist
phase. If that was indeed so, then Mao changed his ideas after the course
of history had swept China towards socialism.

By insisting on hegemony for the CPC, Mao showed that, in his view,
China was moving in the direction of socialism, with, at first, a stage that
would be bourgeois in social significance, *but under close communist
control*, and so, naturally, without any break in continuity as it went
forward to socialism. Later, from 1958 onward, the Chinese communists
were to speak of 'uninterrupted revolution' in describing the process of
their revolution, and of what might be called 'revolution within the
revolution'.[61] It had become impossible, after the communists had been
in power for almost a decade, to maintain the outlook of 1940 or 1945 in
accounting for what happened in 1949.

With the theory of 'uninterrupted revolution' the Chinese communists
introduced a view of their revolution that was more dialectical, even if the
concept still showed a certain confusion, since it spoke both of an
uninterrupted revolution and of a revolution by stages. The 'stages'
served to justify the positions of 1940 ('New Democracy') and 1945
('Coalition Government'), while 'uninterrupted revolution' explained
the rapid transition to the building of socialism. In short, this was a kind

of compromise between a past that had been traversed under the sign of Stalinism (the 'stages') and the real history of the revolution: an explanation, too, that reminds us of Lenin's abandonment of a conception of revolution by stages in favour of the theory of the bourgeois revolution 'growing over' into the socialist revolution.

However, as we have seen, Maoism had cherished this compromise in its bosom since 1940, when the CPC undertook to preside over a 'bourgeois stage' in China. Was this due to genuine uncertainty, or was it just the obligatory reference to Stalinist orthodoxy of a leader who did not want to break with the USSR? Probably it was both.

The CPC and bureaucracy

Despite the radical novelty of social life in the 'liberated areas', one ought not to underestimate the presence of a bureaucracy in Yenan. According to Mark Selden, who has specially studied Shen Kan Ning, the 'liberated area' round Yenan:

> From 1937 to 1941 government developed so rapidly that flexibility was at a premium even within the bureaucracy; mobilization continued to play a part in campaigns for production, elections, taxation, and so forth; a shortage of skills, primitive channels of communication, a lack of time-sanctioned procedures, and a dearth of supplies hampered administrative regularization; finally, a tradition of direct action and local autonomy militated against absolute bureaucratic control. Nonetheless, the major development in government from 1937 to 1941 was the growing strength and independence of the bureaucracy and the concentration of administrative functions in its hands.[62]

Selden explains:

> By December 1941 the bureaucracy had attained peak development. Communist-controlled portions of the region then encompassed twenty-nine districts with a population of approximately 1,400,000. At this time there were an estimated 7,900 full-time salaried government officials, of whom 'over' 1,000 served at the regional level, 4,021 served at the sub-regional district and sub-district levels, and the remainder served in township governments.[63]

But he mentions a detail which modifies this picture: 'In 1937 and 1938, in addition to meeting subsistence needs, the government paid a top salary of five dollars per month to heads of regional departments and two-and-one-half dollars to district magistrates.'[64]

These three quotations bring us to the heart of a question of central importance: what connection can be found between Maoism and bureaucracy? Selden provides information which, though meagre, is very valuable, about bureaucracy in Yenan. In order to get to grips with this problem we need to distinguish between the different forms of bureaucracy in the Chinese communist system, beginning with the bureaucratization of the party itself.

The CPC experienced very early on a process of internal bureaucratization, resulting from the young party's rapid subordination to the
Third International, itself a huge body that underwent rapid bureaucratization. This process took root and spread in connection with the
bureaucratic excrescence that developed in the first and only workers'
state, the USSR, and parallel with the ebbing of the revolutionary tide
throughout the world, which transformed the Third International into a
mere appendage, a network of supports and defences for the Soviet state.
From the outset, let us note the existence of two interconnected forms of
bureaucracy. First, the bureaucracy in the USSR, with material privileges
(in salaries, etc.) and power of command (management of factories,
administration of the state), and fulfilling functions (either essential or
parasitic, depending on one's theory) at the level of the relations of
production.

Along with this bureaucracy there was the bureaucracy of the international communist movement, that is, the leaderships of the Communist
Parties, who swore by Stalinism and were often selected, or even imposed, by the USSR. This type of bureaucratism differed from the
first-mentioned: it was a form of bureaucracy by proxy, and by assimilation of the Soviet social system, with its foreign policy and its pattern of
industrialization, in return for which this bureaucracy was given 'credit',
the value ascribed to which depended on recognition of the 'first workers'
state', which was 'building socialism in one country extending over
one-sixth of the world'. *This* bureaucracy was not marked out by its
privileges, which were often limited and sometimes non-existent. It
controlled sections of the working-class movement that were of greater
or less importance, in the hope, which was realized for some of its
members, of one day becoming leaders of states 'like the USSR'.

This was the kind of bureaucracy that the CPC knew, and which led
the party until 1935. Even when Mao took over the party leadership, this
bureaucracy continued to exist, being marked by its unconditional
loyalty to the USSR, its lack of understanding of the peasantry, and its
hatred of everything unorthodox. Mao's ambiguous attitude to Stalinism
favoured the more or less 'underground' survival of this trend. It was to
re-emerge in strength after 1949.

A second form of bureaucracy in the CPC was that described by
Selden. This resulted from the existence of a state authority based on a
separate body of men, the officials. But it is certain that the material
privileges of these officials were rather limited: between two and five
dollars – even in poverty-stricken China that was not Byzantine! Besides,
it is clear that the CPC made considerable efforts to immerse these cadres
in rural life so far as possible,[65] and, with the 'rectification campaigns',
they were subjected to pressure and tension which did not facilitate the

consolidation of an authority independent of and separated from the masses.

Nevertheless, these germs of bureaucracy, restricted within the limits of the rural setting, which was too poor to afford privileges, and with a communist movement that depended on support from the peasant population, prefigured the huge bureaucratic system that developed in the People's Republic of China after 1949, and which was violently denounced in the 'Cultural Revolution'.

We must now consider *Maoist bureaucratism* resulting from what I have called, following Deutscher, the (two-fold) process of substitution.[66] It is indeed essential to appreciate the profoundly bureaucratic aspects of Maoism, no less than its permanent struggle against bureaucratism. This paradox can be understood only if we distinguish between the different forms of bureaucratic relationship.

The ties between Maoism and the masses, as they were formed in the late 1920s, appeared originally and, one might add, almost necessarily, as a relationship of hegemony which was the source of a particular form of bureaucratism, precisely because what was involved was a relationship with the masses *and not with a class*. The CPC, a proletarian party, had been formed and developed on the basis of the activity of the proletariat, and had been shaped, in the Marxist style, in close connection with the industrial towns and their working class. Losing its ties with the latter after the defeat of 1927, but succeeding in maintaining the Marxist coherence of its outlook, the CPC under Mao's leadership could only function as a 'substituting' force.

The masses, that vague term, which meant mainly the small peasantry, and to some small degree the urban petty bourgeoisie, took the place of the missing proletariat, and the party, acting on its own, substituted itself for the proletariat as *leader* and master of the revolutionary process.[67] It alone took charge, in the absence of any correspondence between the revolutionary social forces at work (the peasantry instead of the proletariat, the national struggle instead of working-class struggles) and the overall Marxist, and so proletarian, aim of the revolution.

Under the extraordinarily difficult conditions of party work among the poor peasantry, with the conscious risk of deviations (focusing on exclusively peasant aspirations: ownership of land, etc.), the maintenance of a Marxist cadre for the party could only be ensured by an act of will, a superimposition. 'Historical' conditions transformed the national struggle and the agrarian struggle into a movement that was 'objectively' and in its tendency *socialist*: but at the concrete level of the peasants' aspirations 'objectivity' was confined to desire for land and for the invader to be driven out, and did not include any prospect of socialism . . .

The party thus internalized a socialist aim which did not correspond to its social basis. The 'authoritarian' structure of the party, its rigorous centralization, resulted from this difficulty: the party, which, according to the Leninist tradition, was supposed to combine integration of its members in the class with separation of them from it, became transformed in Maoism into a party that was isolated from its own class (the proletariat), but linked with the masses who took the place of that class, while maintaining its Marxist orientation against the spontaneous, non-socialist tendencies coming from its peasant base.

This special relationship is well typified by what is called the 'mass line': listen to the masses and keep going back to them. Listening to the people means preserving deep-going links with them, and this aim, or rather this necessity, has been at the heart of Maoism for nearly half a century. But 'listening to the masses' is something very different from a living dialectic between party and class, which implies a party conceived as the vanguard of a class which bears within itself the socialist aim, even if only in embryonic or confused form. Listening to the masses means also, for Maoism, a way of activizing, of revolutionizing, the various strata of the population. In order to lead them adequately one needs to know them, to understand their needs, to absorb their 'best' elements into the party, sometimes also to refuse to subordinate the party's line of action to various pressures. In other words, Mao advocates a relationship of effective command that can make it possible to work thoroughly upon the deepest layers of society.

From this standpoint, the party, even when most closely linked with the toiling population, is a body that is bureaucratized in an all-round way, in the sense of being separated and hegemonic, and, above all, of giving orders rather than acting as a representative or spokesman.

This form of bureaucratism, corresponding to an effort to maintain the party's proletarian aim, always tended to become transformed into other forms, by adding material privileges to those conferred by the power of command. The phenomenon grew extensively after 1949. During the Yenan period, when the CPC wielded real state power, a bureaucratic authority had already begun to take shape, and this implied privileges, including material ones.

The two forms of bureaucratism continue to fight each other. 'Substitutionist' bureaucratism forms part of the Maoist 'world-view' and is adorned with all possible virtues (the 'mass line'). Not so in the case of the other form of bureaucracy . . .

Maoism's first achievement: The People's Republic of China
Isaac Deutscher pointed out that the process of 'permanent revolution' took on new life and strength with the entry of the communists into the

cities, from 1948–9 onward. This is true, but needs qualification. When the CPC occupied the cities it fundamentally changed its orientation rather than its practice. Mao explained this in his report to the second plenary session of the Central Committee at the 7th Congress of the CPC (5 March 1949): 'From 1927 to the present the centre of gravity of our work has been in the villages – gathering strength in the villages, using the villages in order to surround the cities and then taking the cities. The period for this method of work has now ended. The period of "from the city to the village" and of the city leading the village has now begun. The centre of gravity of the party's work has shifted from the village to the city.'[68] But even if the city had again become the centre of the party's work the working class was not mobilized, though its vital role was strongly reasserted. The conception of the state in 1949 remained within the category of 'New Democracy'. In comparison with the explanations given in 1940 and 1945, however, the tone had changed: the central axis was no longer the necessary bourgeois stage, but the dominant role of the Communist Party, and behind this hegemony loomed a different social order.

The party's declarations became more radical, even if the old formulations were not given up. Thus, Mao, in his article *On People's Democratic Dictatorship* (30 June 1949) spoke of the possibility that 'China can develop . . . from a new-democratic into a socialist and communist society, can abolish classes and realize the Great Harmony.'[69] More sharply still, he insisted that 'all Chinese without exception must lean either to the side of imperialism or to the side of socialism.'[70] These expressions contrasted with the more reserved formulations, often referring to the desirability of capitalist development, found in his earlier writings.

Mao mentioned the reason underlying this new assurance: 'The people have a powerful state apparatus in their hands – there is no need to fear rebellion by the national bourgeoisie.'[71] That was indeed the essential point: the communist movement held power, and it could tolerate – tolerate, and no longer promote! – the existence of a bourgeoisie, without abandoning its socialist aim.

The communist leader Li Wei-han, in his pamphlet *The Struggle for Proletarian Leadership in the Period of the New-Democratic Revolution in China*,[72] spells this out. After distinguishing between the minimum programme ('New Democracy') and the maximum programme (socialism and communism), he notes that 'the new-democratic programme already includes preparations for the development of the democratic revolution, which mainly consist in establishing and consolidating the proletarian leadership of the revolution, thoroughly mobilizing and arming the mass of workers and peasants, establishing and developing the state-owned economy and the cooperative economy of the working people, a thorough carrying out of the revolution, etc.'[73] And as, later, he criticizes those who 'built a "Great Wall" between the democratic revolution and the socialist revolution',[74] employing a phrase of Lenin's, it can be seen that what he has in mind is precisely the Leninist conception of a rapid 'growing over' into the socialist state. But this, it will be said, is an *a posteriori* view of the matter. This is the opinion of Claude Cadart, in his interesting and well-documented *Note sur la Chine de 1949 à 1964*.[75] He challenges the official periodization of the early years of the People's Republic of China, which sets out the two first stages as: (a) Phase of economic reconstruction and socialist revolution (1949–52), and (b) Phase of the first stage in the building of socialism and the First Five-Year Plan (1953–57).

Cadart counterposes to this his own periodization: (a) Phase of the last 'moment' of the regime of people's democratic dictatorship (1949–54), and (b) Phase of socialist revolution (1954–7).[76]

As this discussion deals with points that are essential to the present work, and moreover makes possible a general appreciation of Maoism as it was in 1949, I shall first summarize it and then answer its argument.

For Cadart the official view is incompatible both with the theories of the CPC and with the facts. In the first place, it conflicts with the party's theories, and especially with the original version and the spirit of *On New Democracy*, which assigned an important role to the bourgeoisie.

Thus, 'from 1949 to 1954, and in particular from 1949 to 1952, official truth in China held that the Chinese state, although "led" by the proletariat and based on the alliance between the proletariat and the peasantry, was still a state of the dictatorship of the four classes making up the "people".'[77] It was only in September 1956, at the 8th Congress of the CPC, that Liu Shao-chi declared that, 'with the establishment of the People's Republic of China, the people's democratic dictatorship became in essence a form of the dictatorship of the proletariat.'[78]

There is incompatibility also with the facts, says Cadart. 'Between 1937 and 1949 the line of the CPC was one of class collaboration, in particular of collaboration between the oppressed classes and the bourgeoisie . . . [a line] which had been prepared, on the world scale, by the turn made in 1935–6 by the Comintern and in the foreign policy of the USSR.'[79] I shall discuss these ideas later, but let me remind the reader straight away that I have already pointed to the difference, nay, the gulf, between the line proclaimed and the reality established, which was one of exclusive hegemony of the CPC, in the areas under its control – extending from 1949–50 onward to the whole of China, except Formosa and Hong Kong.

But Cadart brings forward another interesting argument, which seems to be irrefutable:

It was nevertheless in the towns that this line of class collaboration was most obvious between 1937 and 1949, and not only during the war against Japan but also during the 'Third Revolutionary Civil War' . . . While it had hardly any negative effect on the morale of the peasantry, for whom the main enemy was not the bourgeoisie but the landlord class, it did have such an effect, and to a considerable extent, upon the morale of the proletariat of the towns, for whom the main enemy was the bourgeoisie. The unquestionable 'rightism' of the policy being followed at that time by Mao Tse-tung resulted in preventing the urban revolutionary elements *who had remained in the towns* from playing a decisive part in the struggle against the Kuomintang.[80]

Cadart further notes that between 1949 and 1952 'the so-called national bourgeoisie was the object of most careful attention by the CPC. Its profits did not decline, but increased';[81] and 'the old state apparatus was only half-smashed during the years 1949–51'.[82] And he concludes that, 'eventually, it was a bourgeois revolution that the new regime accomplished, or finished accomplishing, in China between 1949 and 1952, much more than a socialist one. The elements of socialism that could be seen appearing here and there were rather negligible.' More plainly still, he affirms that 'this period (1949–54) was for China a period of hesitation between the socialist and the capitalist road, and in any case it is impossible to date from 1 October 1949, or even from the period 1949–52 . . . the triumph of the socialist revolution.'[83]

These stimulating remarks bring us into the heart of the problematic of Marxism in 1949, and discussing them will enable us to deepen our understanding of Maoism.

With the occupation of the cities, I have said, there came an irresistible dynamic of 'permanent revolution', that is, the building of a workers' state which opened a period of socialist construction. It is this statement that must now be explained and justified.

In principle, to be sure, the first years of the regime were placed under the sign of 'New Democracy'. This was certainly the signboard, but behind it lay the hegemonic authority of the CPC; and this state of undivided rule by the Communists raised, in theory and still more in practice, the problem of *socialism*, as we have already seen in Mao's formulation of 1949, quoted above.

For 'New Democracy' to be anything more than a façade for the absolute and exclusive power of the CPC it would have been necessary for it to correspond to a real social and political content, that is, participation in the government by a bourgeois political force *acting independently*. As has been shown, however, the poor and middle peasantry (the petty bourgeoisie) never possessed any political independence but were always represented by the Communist Party, with all the ambiguities resulting from this 'substitutive' relationship.

As for the urban bourgeoisie, when the CPC occupied the big cities, it began expropriating the property of the 'bureaucratic capitalism' of the Kuomintang, and thereby a large section of the economy was automatically nationalized, providing the new rulers with the foundation for socialist industry. It will be objected that an important capitalist element remained. This was important socially and economically, to be sure, but not politically.

That bourgeoisie was not given any political independence by the communists: indeed, for such independence to exist it would have been necessary not merely to grant it, but literally to invent it. The CPC, sole master of the situation, had no interest in, and no intention of, stimulating any independent political activity by the bourgeoisie. It was content, therefore, to establish a fictitious representation for them, a mere screen for its own hegemony. This was not *just* a charade, though, for it also served to provide a little reward for some sections of the bourgeoisie for having, belatedly, taken the road to revolution, or at least of neutrality, and, especially, a bait for these sections, which included cadres that the new republic could not do without.

Cadart's strongest argument is that the working class was not mobilized in the 'third revolution'. This is certainly true. But what does that mean? Simply that for the CPC the working class was not (was no longer?) needed in order to take power, whereas some sections of the petty bourgeoisie brought it support by their activity, and the communists wanted, above all, to inherit a *functioning* economy. This accounts for the right-wing, pro-capitalist emphasis given to policy in the towns between 1945 and 1949.[84]

The real social agent of the revolution was clearly the poor peasantry, and where they were concerned the policy of the CPC was radical and uncompromising (at least from 1946 onward). This indifference – even perhaps a certain disdain – in relation to the working class was certainly very significant, but it would be a mistake to define the CPC's attitude on this basis. Even if the working class was not needed in order to carry through the third revolution, it was indispensable, in the communists' view, for the building of the future republic. This was why, as soon as they arrived in the cities, the CPC began recruiting large numbers of workers, even though it did not mobilize them until some years later. Actually, the discussion revolved around a confusion between two phenomena which, though connected, are nevertheless different, namely: the nature of the new state (the 'workers' state', in the Marxist sense), and the building of socialism. Because the People's Republic was a workers' state from the start, with a class dictatorship established, it was socialism that was being built. That it was a workers' state followed from the fact that the CPC was in power – or, more precisely, from the fact that the CPC had remained (in a substitutive role) a *proletarian* movement. And in this context, the reality of the People's Republic was the rapid transition to socialist construction, in contrast to the decades of 'New Democracy' that had been forecast. The period 1950–52 in China in some ways resembled 1917–18 in Russia, with the workers' state making itself felt in the various spheres of social and economic life. In the countryside agrarian reform was made general, destroying the landlord class and weakening the rich peasantry. In the towns the need for political control led to consolidation of the nationalized sector. And the indispensable mobilization of the working class in order to strengthen the new state, not to mention the CPC's mistrust of the bourgeoisie, led to more and more systematic encroachments on bourgeois property and, in any case, to close control over this being established by the workers' state. The nationalizations of 1951–2, together with the anti-bourgeois campaigns,[85] swept away the fictions of 'New Democracy', along with the illusions of the bourgeoisie, and adjusted the social system to the regime of class dictatorship represented by the rule of the CPC. Thereafter socialism was being built openly, and this was proclaimed, even if belatedly, from 1956 onward. Bourgeois property was tolerated, but on an even smaller scale,[86] the bourgeoisie being reduced to the level (a still quite agreeable one) of *rentiers*, or of executives in their own former enterprises.

We can now see the difference between Mao's 'New Democracy' and what was supposed to have inspired it – the directive of the Stalinist Comintern, which called, at its Seventh Congress (1935), for a 'democratic dictatorship of the workers and peasants' – in other words, a bourgeois regime headed by a coalition of bourgeois and proletarian parties (the latter being provided by the communists). In China this formula signified a coalition between the CPC and the Kuomintang (the latter being seen as a party of the national bourgeoisie and not as the bastard party it actually was), and that in turn implied subordination to the bourgeoisie, with China under the leadership of Chiang Kai-shek. 'New Democracy' certainly looked like that – but only looked: the reality was the deliberate and openly-proclaimed will to communist hegemony, meaning not a coalition or a situation of dual power (which existed between 1937 and 1949 over a large area of China) but all power to the Communist Party. On this basis, clearly, there could only be a rapid 'growing-over' to the socialist revolution, even if Mao was sincerely contemplating a protracted phase of 'New Democracy', as may have been the case. Did not Mao in 1945 justify this prolonged bourgeois phase by saying that capitalism would mean progress? In these words there was more than just an obvious excuse for the moderate policy of that time: there was the solid conviction that, for backward China, capitalism could only be advantageous. However, in China, as elsewhere, a developed capitalism proved unable to emerge, and the 'third revolution' was the penalty for that failure. This was the real foundation, and justification, of the theory of 'permanent revolution': a capitalism embracing all social and economic spheres, including agriculture, would indeed have been desirable, but under the conditions existing in China – and not only in China – this was unattainable, for many reasons, all relating to the confrontation between Chinese traditional society and the imperialist world. The tasks of the bourgeois revolution had therefore to be carried out, whether well or ill, by the socialist revolution. The revolutionary authenticity of Maoism lay not in the precision of its slogans – which were woolly, illusory and sometimes merely cynical: certainly never free from opportunism, through Mao's concern to appear 'a good Stalinist' – but in the means adopted in order to realize its aims. Maoism thus followed a line of advance comparable to Lenin's between 1905 and 1917: the revolution would be bourgeois, but in day-to-day practice it was necessary to safeguard the independence of action of the proletariat and its party, which meant always keeping in the forefront the ultimate aim of socialism. The year 1949 was Mao's 1917: the moment of truth that placed on the agenda the move towards socialism which followed from the whole course of the revolution.

Thus, despite the ambiguities, nuances and insincerities to be found in its programme, Maoism went through to the culmination of its activity in the dictatorship of the proletariat. This it did in circumstances which both facilitated the task (the over-determination of the revolution) and made it more difficult (the concealment of reality by Stalinist doctrine; the absence of the proletariat). From this standpoint, Mao was undoubtedly a Chinese Lenin – the leader without whom, very probably, the revolution would never have succeeded. Whatever one's final judgement on Maoism – I have already spoken of bureaucratism, and will conclude by showing how this grew under the People's Republic – Mao has an achievement to his credit that he shares with only a handful of revolutionaries: Lenin, Trotsky, Castro, Ho Chi Minh. This marks him off from Stalin; and it was a fact that counted for much in the dispute between the two rulers.

While the socialist orientation of the new regime was established from the start, at least *de facto*, it had two other characteristics – a revolutionary proselytism that was soon dropped, and an internalization of the Soviet model, with emphasis on the tendency to bureaucracy inherent in this.

Under the impact of a victory that came sooner than had been expected,[87] and impelled also by the historic scale of their revolution, which smashed capitalist domination over a quarter of mankind, the Chinese communists were seized by an urge to proselytize which was in contrast to their usual isolation and their tradition of confining themselves to China's own problems. The Chinese revolutionaries kindled the flames of a new October, and by their revolutionary fervour made plain the gulf separating Stalinism from its ancestor, Leninism, which had, though canonized, been in fact buried and forgotten.

For Stalin the revolutionary fire blazing up on his Asian frontier, in the country with the largest population in the world, was something unexpected and disquieting. China had been the subject of a deal at Yalta[88] from which he felt confident he had got the best of bargains, and he neither allowed for nor wished for China's advance from the status of 'friend' to that of 'disciple', and still less to that of a regime socially and politically allied to his own. For this to happen would be more of a nuisance than an advantage to the Soviet dictator; and his mistrustful feeling was all the stronger, because of the recent defection by Tito (1948). The Marshal feared nothing so much as a revolution that was independent, dynamic, uncontrolled and expansionist. The fresh revolutionary breeze brought a risk – for the ponderous Russian bureaucracy – of arousing the Russian people from their lethargy, from that passivity and lack of independent activity by the proletariat which had enabled the bureaucratic virus to flourish.

The American threat, which was a very real one, to the young Republic provided the Soviet leader with an excellent card to play in his dealings with the Chinese communists, and compelled the latter to subordinate themselves to the USSR. Although he had failed to control, or at least to restrict, the Chinese Revolution, Stalin tried with some success to keep it within its national framework, reducing the impact of this revolution outside China and so its possible influence on the USSR or other countries. This pressure obliged the Chinese communists to turn inward again upon their own country – which corresponded to a profound tendency in Maoism itself.

And yet, at first, it was not at all self-evident that this would happen. As the Chinese Revolution advanced in its forced march to victory, in 1948–9, it preached to the world its own pattern of development, so remote from Stalinism. Thus, Liu Shao-chi, the party's Number Two at that time, called for revolution throughout Asia, in his speech to the World Federation of Trade Unions in November 1949, a month after the proclamation of the Chinese People's Republic, and put forward China as the example. He stressed especially the hegemony of the working class and the Communist Party and the need for an army led by the party. While 'a broad front' was essential, it 'must not be led by the wavering and compromising national bourgeoisie or petty bourgeoisie or their parties'. For the Chinese leader, 'this way is the way of Mao Tse-tung.'[89]

In 1950 a pamphlet was published in China[90] which upheld the same positions as Liu Shao-chi in 1949, reasserting the decisive role played by China in the revolution in the East, and, what was even worse from Stalin's standpoint, declaring that the Chinese example was valid universally. 'The people's democratic revolution in China has already obtained a great victory, a victory of world-wide historical significance. In the future, the victory of the Chinese Revolution will influence not only the destiny of all the nationalities making up the Chinese people but also the world as a whole, and more particularly the historical destiny of the people of all the other Eastern nations.'[91] Again, later: 'The great victory of the Chinese Revolution struck new and powerful blows at the whole world-wide system of imperialism . . . The general crisis of capitalism has been further accentuated, and the ineluctable day which will see the end of bourgeois domination . . . has been brought even closer. Thus the final victory of the working people and of communism in the entire world will come more quickly.'[92]

Despite the stress on the necessity for 'New Democracy', the tone of the passage is unquestionably that of an anti-capitalist appeal which is, in tendency at least, socialist. And this was no mere verbal proclamation.[93] A revolutionary wind was blowing in this pressing incitement to follow the Chinese road and destroy imperialist domination as quickly as possible. Such fervour, recalling the early years of the Comintern, sounded harshly in Stalin's ears.

It was urgent, therefore, for the Soviet leader to restrict these revolutionary excesses, and in the first place to bring the Chinese Revolution back into the Stalinist framework. And yet, as in all the periods of the history of Maoism, the statements issued by the Soviet and Chinese leaderships seemed to employ the same arguments. The Zhdanovist radicalism of the time in the USSR seemed to echo the radicalism of the Chinese. The difference went deep, however, and was shown first and foremost in the refusal of the Soviet leaders to endorse the claims of Maoism. On the contrary, they stressed the quite specific character of the Chinese Revolution and its inapplicability to other countries in Asia: 'In particular, it is difficult to imagine that other Eastern countries pursuing the path of people's democracy would necessarily be able to count on acquiring one of the Chinese Revolution's most important advantages – a revolutionary army like the one in China.'[94] Furthermore, 'people's democracy [in the Eastern countries] . . . was not faced with the immediate prospect of constructing socialism and, consequently, did not function as a proletarian dictatorship.'[95] Yet it was indeed *this* dictatorship that had been set up by the Chinese Revolution!

The article by Astafiev, 'staff member of the Academy of Sciences', ascribed the credit for the victory in China to Stalin's directives. It is unlikely that Mao found it easy to digest such a statement, which was a flagrant falsehood. What can he have thought of this phrase? 'Comrade Stalin defined the characteristics of the Chinese Revolution, brilliantly predicted its course and indicated the conditions in which it would succeed . . .'[96] This apologia for Stalin's organization of the defeat in 1927 must have stuck in the throats of the Chinese leaders, fostering a secret resentment that was to find open expression ten years or so later, when they accused Stalin of having made mistakes regarding China in the 1920s, the 1930s, the 1940s – at every stage, in fact.

Writings of the period show that the two sides were acutely aware of what divided them.[97] In the situation that then obtained, however, China's posture was one of weakness and seeking for help. The combined effects of the imperialist threat (and the Korean War intensified China's dependence on the USSR) and of Stalin's pressure forced Maoism back inside the confines of China. Proselytizing came to an end. Thereafter[98] only China's national interests were taken into account. At the outset the change was not very perceptible: it became so, gradually, only after Stalin's death.

More than submission to the USSR, what was going on was a process of assimilation of China to the USSR and internalization of the Soviet system by China. With the Sino-Soviet treaty of 1950 the USSR, as sole protector of the new regime, could easily impose its conditions. But in 1950, just as twenty years earlier, the USSR was in any case the only credible *model* – or at least, was seen as such – of rapid and independent economic development, as well as the only possible source of material aid.

Consequently, the threatening presence of the USA forced China to swear allegiance to the 'Soviet elder brother', but this was indeed a decision *forced* upon her, and when Mao said that China 'leaned towards one side' he was expressing an objective condition rather than a genuine choice. It was this situation that caused the Chinese to turn inward upon themselves, a movement that came all the easier because the national tendencies of Maoism predisposed it that way, and also because China's leader had become aware that the world context was one of fixed bi-polarity between the USA and the USSR.

Close identification with the USSR led to China's internalizing the social and economic structures of that country, copying its forms of organization and social leadership and reproducing its ideological clichés (the notorious 'wooden language'). The CPC's past and traditions favoured this process of incorporation. After all, the cult of Mao's personality, and, to a smaller extent, of Stalin's, was widely present in the

Chinese party, and bureaucratism, even though in a specific form, was what formed the web of relations between the party and the masses. As a whole, the state then being constituted in China was pretty similar to that found in the 'People's Democracies of Europe and Asia'.

By copying so closely the Stalinist model and drawing away from the egalitarianism of the Maoist tradition, the People's Republic of China transformed itself into a 'bureaucratically-distorted workers' state'. It was a matter of distortion and not of degeneration: the distinction is important. The revolution was a recent event, and the CPC, which had been through twenty-two years of civil war, had in that period formed many ties with the peasant masses, and had even become merged with them. Its roots in the world of the poor countryfolk were too deep to wither altogether upon contact with the realities and advantages of power. Besides, the Chinese Revolution was too original, and carried forward by fighters of too nationalist a fibre, to be capable of remaining a mere copy – often a caricature at that – of the USSR. The extremely bureaucratic behaviour of the Russian brother-party resulted from the absence, for decades on end, of ties between this party and the masses, and that was not the case with the CPC, which enjoyed a considerable consensus, active or passive, in China's population. Finally, and this was not the least important factor, Mao was the least Stalinist of the cadres of the Chinese party, or, more precisely, the leader whose veneer of Stalinism was the most superficial: in addition to which, the Chinese President felt a mistrust towards Stalin that had been quickened by distressing experiences.

Gradually, therefore, resistance to the Soviet model began to be expressed: 'qualified' appreciations were voiced, then criticisms that were more and more outspoken came to be formulated – though only inside the party – against strict application of the Soviet model. Above all, this questioning arose from doubt as to the capacity of the Soviet model to answer the complex problems, both old and new, of Chinese society. And Mao, the builder of an original revolution, set himself to seek, gropingly, for a specific road of socialist construction, or at least, one that he conceived to be such.

Opposition to Stalinism has grown out of criticism of everything in the USSR which gives particular expression to the situation in that country, everything that is distinctive of it and results from the conditions of its industrialization (considered from a positive angle) and of the collectivization of its agriculture (considered more negatively). This has meant challenging the universality of 'Stalinist socialist construction' and has compelled, willy-nilly, those revolutionaries who possess a certain independence of the USSR (China, Yugoslavia) to look in other directions for the solution of their problems.

These new 'roads to socialism' have departed, no less than Stalinism, from the Leninist conception of a national revolution forming part of a strategy of world revolution. The Chinese Revolution has attempted to put into effect a national form of socialist construction; and this has been the background to the turbulent history of Maoism in the last twenty years.

NOTES TO CHAPTER 13

1. For example, Chen Tu-hsiu, the party's general secretary from 1921 until 1927, disapproved of the CPC's entry into the Kuomintang.
2. Though the CPC's entry into the Kuomintang, and the relations between the parties, with their consequences, might appear to constitute a single strategical scheme, in fact there were several different political projects. The one proposed by Sneevliet was different from that which was put into effect in 1924, and especially in 1925, at the moment of the revolution.
3. On the origins of the group of 'Twenty-eight Bolsheviks', formed from among the students of the Sun Yat-sen University in Moscow, see Yueh Sheng, *Sun Yat-sen University in Moscow and the Chinese Revolution: A Personal Account*, University of Kansas Center for East Asian Studies, 1971. The autobiography of Yueh Sheng, who was a student at the university, shows the close connection between the formation of the 'Twenty-eight' group and the Stalinization of the CPC. This group emerged during the struggle against Trotskyism in the university in 1927–8; was backed by Pavel Mif, Rector of the university, after Bukharin's departure; and took over the leadership of the CPC when (preceded by their mentor, Mif) they returned to China in 1930. They were thus carefully selected young Stalinist cadres, who had proved themselves not on the battleground of the class struggle but in intense factional conflict. After attacking Li Li-san they turned on the 'right opportunists', that is, on Mao, whom they saw as guilty of a petty-bourgeois peasant deviation. (See Yueh Sheng, op. cit., pp. 205 et seq. and 231 et seq.)
4. The letter is included in the appendices to the French edition of M. A. Macciocchi's *Per Gramsci: Pour Gramsci*, Paris, 1974: see p. 389.
5. C. Bettelheim, *Les Luttes de classes en URSS, 1917–1923*, Paris, 1974, pp. 37–8.
6. Cf. Isaac Deutscher, 'Maoism – its Origins and Outlook', in *Socialist Register 1964*, p. 25; reprinted in his *Ironies of History*, London, 1966, pp. 106–7.
7. Everyone has heard of the epithet 'margarine communists' applied by Stalin to the Chinese communists during a conversation in June 1944 with Averell Harriman, the US Ambassador in Moscow (quoted in C. McLane, *Soviet Policy and the Chinese Communists, 1931–1946*, New York, 1958, p. 1). Remarks of a similar sort were uttered by Molotov in the same year when talking to Patrick Hurley and Donald Nelson (ibid., p. 1). Again, in April 1945, Russian officials confirmed to Hurley that in their view the Chinese communists were 'not real communists in the Soviet sense' (ibid., p. 2). Already in late 1937, at the beginning of the Japanese invasion, in the pages of

Pravda and *Izvestiya* 'the Kuomintang, not the communists, received the lion's share of Moscow's praise of China' (ibid., p. 103).

8. 'Mao's party bore, in ideology and organization, little resemblance either to Lenin's party or to Stalin's. Lenin's party had its roots deep in the working class. Mao's was based almost exclusively on the peasantry. The Bolsheviks had grown up within a multi-party system which had existed, half-submerged, in Tsarist Russia . . . The Maoists, living for over twenty years in complete isolation . . . had become wholly introverted . . . Unconventional and revolutionary though their militarism was, it stood in striking contrast to the predominantly civilian character of the Bolshevik Party' (I. Deutscher, *The Unfinished Revolution*, London, 1967, pp. 85–6).

9. Cf. among others: Ho Ping-ti, *Studies on the Population of China, 1368–1953*, Cambridge (Mass.), 1959.

10. On the Chinese peasantry under the Republic, see the writings of L. Bianco: *The Origins of the Chinese Revolution, 1915–1949*, London, 1971; *Peasants and Revolution: the Case of China*, discussion paper (duplicated), 18 May 1973, for Peasants Seminar, University of London Centre of International and Area Studies; 'Les paysans et la révolution: Chine, 1919–1949', in *Politique étrangère*, Paris, No. 2, 1968, pp. 117–41.

11. For example, Graham Peck, *Two Kinds of Time*, p. 189, quoted in Bianco, *The Origins*, op. cit., p. 199: 'In a society like China's, revolution can be a fundamental and entirely natural fact of life, as hard to slow up as a pregnancy.'

12. 'While the revolution is beaten in the cities and in the most important centres . . . there will always be, especially in a country as vast as China, fresh regions, fresh just because they are backward, containing not yet exhausted revolutionary forces . . . But in the period under consideration it is only one form of the dissolution and the liquidation of the Communist Party of China, for, by losing its proletarian nucleus, it ceases to be in conformity with its historical destiny.' (Trotsky, 'The Chinese Question after the 6th Congress' [October 1928], in *Problems of the Chinese Revolution*, London, 1969, pp. 122–3). See also Trotsky, 'Peasant War in China and the Proletariat' (September 1932), in *Writings of Leon Trotsky, 1932*, New York, 1973, pp. 192 et seq.

13. 'A Single Spark Can Start a Prairie Fire', in Mao Tse-tung, *Selected Works* (English version published in China), vol. 1, Peking, 1969, pp. 120–21.

14. This aspect of what happened cannot be left out of account. The 'Long March' went northward more by necessity than by choice. It ended, in Shensi, in a region which, while isolated and difficult of access, was also remote from the heart of China.

15. See Deutscher, *The Unfinished Revolution*, op. cit., p. 87, and his *Socialist Register 1964* article (see note 6); also R. Lew, 'La genèse du maoisme, 1927–1937', in *Mai*, Brussels, May–June 1973.

16. On Mao's intellectual training, see Stuart R. Schram's introduction to his *The Political Thought of Mao Tse-tung*, 2nd edition, London, 1969, and also the same writer's preface to Mao's earliest known work, *Une Étude sur l'éducation physique (1917)*, Paris, 1962.

17. This thesis deserves to be developed at length. A remarkable proof so far as Kautsky is concerned was provided by Karl Korsch, in his (1929) work *Die*

Materialistische Geschichtsauffassung: eine Auseinandersetzung mit Karl Kautsky (reprinted Frankfurt, 1971).

18. Mao Tse-tung, *On Practice*, in *Selected Works* (Peking English edition, op. cit.), vol. I, p. 303.
19. ibid., p. 295.
20. ibid., p. 297.
21. ibid., p. 296.
22. ibid., p. 303.
23. ibid., p. 298.
24. It is not possible here to go in detail into the evolution of Lenin's philosophical views. For a critical assessment, see A. Pannekoek, *Lenin as Philosopher* (New York, 1948), and for a general analysis, see H. Lefebvre, *La Pensée de Lenine*, Paris, 1957.
25. This was published anonymously in 1940. See Schram, *The Political Thought of Mao Tse-tung*, op. cit., pp. 180–94.
26. Mao Tse-tung, *Selected Works* (Peking English edition, op. cit.), vol. I, p. 313.
27. A comparison with orthodox Marxist works of the same period brings this out clearly: cf. for instance, Georges Politzer's classic work: *Principes Elémentaires de philosophie* (Paris, 1961: based on the author's lectures delivered in 1935–6).
28. Mao Tse-tung, *Selected Works* (Peking English edition, op. cit.), vol. I, p. 311.
29. ibid., p. 316.
30. This truly 'cosmic' view of history was to be strongly reaffirmed during the period of the 'Cultural Revolution'. Cf. an editorial of 2 June 1966: 'There will always be contradictions, in a thousand years, in ten thousand years, even in a hundred million years' time. Even when the Earth is destroyed and the Sun extinguished, there will still be contradictions in the Universe.' (Quoted in J. Guillermaz, *Histoire du Parti Communiste Chinois*, vol. 2, *Le Parti Communiste Chinois au pouvoir*, Paris, 1972.)
31. Mao Tse-tung, *Selected Works* (Peking English edition, op. cit.), vol. I, p. 320.
32. ibid., p. 321.
33. ibid., p. 331.
34. ibid., p. 337.
35. ibid., p.343.
36. See Schram, preface to Mao Tse-tung, *Une Étude sur l'éducation physique*, op. cit., and introduction to *The Political Thought of Mao Tse-tung*, op. cit.
37. In Schram, *Mao Tse-tung Unrehearsed*, London, 1974, p. 293.
38. The extracts given by Schram, in *The Political Thought of Mao Tse-tung*, op. cit., p. 26, refute the apologetical notion of a precociously dialectical Mao. Those given by Jerome Chen, in *Mao et la révolution chinoise*, Paris, 1968, pp. 61–2, provide some slight credibility to this thesis.
39. Joël Bel Lassen, *Philosophie et conservation des tomates*, Paris, 1973, p. 37. The book's title conveys plainly enough what the author sees as the utilitarian function of Maoist philosophy.
40. ibid., p. 38.
41. ibid., p. 38.

42. ibid., pp. 43 and 47.

43. Mao Tse-tung, *Selected Works* (Peking English edition, op. cit.), vol. I, p. 315.

44. Michelle Loi, preface to Mao Tse-tung, *De la Pratique*, Paris, 1973, p. 62.

45. J. Chesneaux and M. Bastid, *Des Guerres de l'Opium à la Guerre Franco-Chinoise, 1840–1885* (Vol. I of *Histoire de la Chine*, ed. J. Chesneaux), Paris, 1969, p. 7.

46. As regards Taoism, regarded as a form of idealism (and by some as a form of mysticism), see the paradoxical and controversial thesis of Joseph Needham on the materialist significance of Taoism, in his book *The Grand Titration: Science and Society in East and West*, London, 1969.

47. Except *perhaps* for tendencies observable in Engels.

48. G. Lukács, *History and Class-consciousness*, London, 1971: L. Goldmann, *The Human Sciences and Philosophy*, London, 1969 (French original published 1952); L. Goldmann, *Marxisme et Sciences Humaines*, Paris, 1970.

49. This would be in accordance with the logic of 'Maoist practice'!

50. In which the most significant names include Korsch, Mattick, Ruhle, and Bordiga (who came from not very proletarian Naples).

51. 'The Kuomintang and the Communist Party are the foundation of the Anti-Japanese United Front, but of these two it is the Kuomintang that occupies first place . . . In the course of its glorious history, the Kuomintang has been responsible for the overthrow of the Ch'ing . . . It enjoys the historic heritage of the Three People's Principles; it has had two great leaders in succession – Mr Sun Yat-sen and Mr Chiang Kai-shek . . .' (Schram, *The Political Thought of Mao Tse-tung*, op. cit., p. 228).

52. ibid., p. 68.

53. This was the congress (the last to be held by the Comintern) when a turn to the Right was made, leading to attempts to form 'People's Fronts' in alliance with the petty bourgeoisie.

54. 'New Democracy' was subjected to practical experiment, like most of Mao's conceptions, from 1937 onward in the frontier region of Shen Kan Ning (around Yenan). Profiting by a certain stability that prevailed between 1937 and 1941, 'New Democracy' was put into practice: all classes took part in elections and in institutions, but under the unchallenged hegemony of the CPC. Private property was preserved and a moderate measure of agrarian reform carried out. This policy, applied with strictness between 1937 and 1941 (the two dates correspond to the two elections), barely concealed its real content, which was one of all power in the hands of the communists. From 1941 onward, however, the CPC turned to more radical practices, and was obliged, in a very difficult period of split with the Kuomintang and blockade by the Japanese, to reconsider the system of 'New Democracy'. The traditional order, still in force in the villages, was attacked, and a more thoroughgoing agrarian reform carried out. This was, in a way, a prefiguring of the socialist transcending of 'New Democracy' that was to take place after 1949. Cf. Mark Selden, *The Yenan Way in Revolutionary China*, Cambridge (Mass.), 1971, pp. 121 et seq.

55. To be more precise, some of Mao's formulations were orthodox enough, being the same ones that Stalin had used in his writings of 1926–7, but for Stalin they

were mere formulations without real significance; and, besides, they were not being used ten years later. For Mao they corresponded to a concrete content.

56. Mao Tse-tung, *Selected Works* (Peking English edition, op. cit.), vol. 2, p. 343.
57. ibid., pp. 343–4.
58. ibid., pp. 346–7.
59. ibid., p. 350.
60. Here we must point out, following Schram: 'To be sure, in the original version of "On New Democracy", written in January 1940, Mao included a sentence (now deleted) stating that, if the Chinese bourgeoisie (that is, the Kuomintang) was capable of assuming the responsibility of driving out Japanese imperialism and introducing democratic government, "no one will be able to refuse his admiration".' But Mao added at once that if the bourgeoisie were to fail in this task, the main responsibility for the nation's future would inevitably fall upon the shoulders of the proletariat (*The Political Thought of Mao Tse-tung*, op. cit., p. 68).
61. See Schram, introduction to *The Political Thought of Mao Tse-tung*, op, cit., pp. 98 et seq., and also his introduction to the collection of Mao's writings *Sur la 'Révolution Permanente' en Chine*, Paris, 1963, p. xv ('It is not accidental that these writings are dated 1958, the year of the "Great Leap Forward" regarded as one aspect of the "uninterrupted revolution" . . .').
62. Selden, op. cit., p. 148.
63. ibid., p. 152.
64. ibid., p. 154.
65. The caesura between the periods 1937–41 and after 1941 in the practice of the CPC in Yenan is to be noted. In 1937–41 there was a stable authority, increasing bureaucratization, a moderate agrarian reform, administrative centralization, the status quo in the villages. After 1941 there was struggle against bureaucratization, with decentralization, dynamization of the masses, a certain radicalizing of agrarian policy, agricultural cooperatives, and a challenging of the status quo in the villages. Cf. Selden, op. cit., pp. 121 et seq. and 177 et seq.
66. Deutscher's article in *Socialist Register 1964*, op. cit., and R. Lew, op. cit.
67. On Mao's conception of the party, see Schram, 'The Party in Chinese Communist Ideology', in *China Quarterly*, April–June 1969, p. 2: 'To a large extent, the "Party" was for Mao merely a name for the leading nucleus in another organization . . .'
68. Mao Tse-tung, *Selected Works* (Peking English edition, op. cit.), vol. 4, p. 363.
69. ibid., p. 418.
70. ibid., p. 415.
71. ibid., p. 419.
72. Peking, Foreign Languages Press, 1962.
73. Li Wei-han, op. cit., p. 90.
74. ibid., p. 98.
75. In Cahier 146 (*Régime Interne et Politique Extérieure dans les Pays d'Asie*), Fondation Nationale des Sciences Politiques, Paris, 1966, pp. 269–88.
76. ibid., p. 269.

77. ibid., pp. 272–3.
78. ibid., p. 273.
79. ibid.
80. ibid., p. 274.
81. ibid.
82. ibid.
83. ibid., pp. 274–5.
84. Cf. K. Lieberthal, 'Mao versus Liu? Policy towards industry and commerce, 1946–1949', in China Quarterly, no. 47, July–September 1971: 'In essence, one basis of the policy [of the CPC when they first began to occupy cities] was to import the notions of class struggle from the rural areas into the cities, and to support every demand of the workers as a means of waging this class struggle' (p. 497). After 1948, however, when the communists really started to take over the big cities, their policy changed: 'The real meaning of the new urban policy was that production must be increased so as to enlarge the volume of supplies, munitions and money available to the CPC to wage the civil war' (p. 505). Further, when Liu Shao-chi was sent in 1949 to Tientsin, an industrial centre recently occupied, 'he affirmed the right of capitalists to dismiss workers if keeping them on the payrolls would be uneconomical. He admitted that a workday of more than eight hours would be permissible and stressed the obligation of the workers to maintain labour discipline' (p. 514). Liu also spoke of the capitalists' right to a reasonable profit. Here was undoubtedly a policy of defending, if not of promoting, capitalism.
85. There were campaigns against opponents on the Left, as well. All active Trotskyists were arrested on 24 December 1952. By these campaigns the proletarian and bureaucratic content of the new regime was manifested at one and the same time.
86. This is shown, at the level of ownership of industrial production, by the official figures reproduced in Cadart, op. cit., p. 276:

	1950	1952	1954	1956
Socialist sector	45.3	56	62.8	67.5
Mixed sector	2.9	5.0	12.3	32.5
Private sector	51.8	39.0	24.9	—
Total	100	100	100	100

87. 'In order to smash Chiang Kai-shek's offensive we must plan on a long-term basis', wrote Mao on 20 July 1946 (Selected Works, Peking English edition, op. cit., vol. 4, p. 90). Already in May 1947, however, he noted that 'The march of events in China is faster than people expected' (ibid., p. 138).
88. Cf. the article by Thai Quang Trung in Le Monde Diplomatique, March 1975: 'L'Asie, les illusions de Roosevelt et la synthèse de Yalta': '. . . Stalin, who distrusted the Chinese communists, behaved towards China as if that country was not for a long time yet to emerge from its divided state and become a viable power. He also intended to advance Soviet power as far as possible in East Asia, considering that China was bound to fall into the American sphere of influence. And, to the Americans' prospect of a united China, playing the

stabilizing role of a structure of equilibrium in East Asia, Stalin preferred the reality of a Soviet-American agreement on a divided China.'

89. Liu's speech is in *Marxism and Asia, 1853–1964*, edited by Stuart R. Schram and H. Carrère d'Encausse, London, 1969, pp. 271–2.

90. An extract is given in ibid., pp. 274 et seq.

91. ibid., p. 276.

92. ibid., p. 277.

93. This was the period of a 'hard' policy in relations with the countries of the Third World. The Chinese communists showed little interest in the 'bourgeois' governments of these countries, even when they were 'neutralist'. Cf. Cadart, op. cit., p. 277.

94. Russian article, dated November 1951, reproduced in Schram and Carrère d'Encausse, op. cit., p. 274.

95. ibid., p. 273.

96. ibid., p. 268.

97. See in this connection the article by P. Bridgham, A. Cohen, L. Joffe, etc., written in September 1953, in their capacity as 'propaganda analysts' for the CIA (which also has its place among the sinologists of the English speaking world), on 'Mao's road and Sino-Soviet relations', which was reprinted in *China Quarterly*, no. 52, October–December 1972. As an appendix to their article, these writers give the Chinese version (dated 15 December 1949) and the Russian version (17 September 1950) of the opening paragraphs of an article by Chen Po-ta (who was at that time very close to Mao), entitled 'Stalin and the Chinese Revolution' (op. cit., pp. 695 et seq.). The differences are significant, and include the following:

CHINESE VERSION		RUSSIAN VERSION
p. 695.	'Comrade Mao Tse-tung is correct.'	Missing.
p. 696.	'Comrade Mao Tse-tung's views on the nature and tactics of the Chinese revolution were *completely identical* with those of Stalin.'	'Comrade Mao Tse-tung, in [matters relating to] problems regarding the nature of the revolution and its strategy [the Chinese version says 'tactics'! – R.L.] *followed* Stalin.'
p. 697.	*'It was a great misfortune for our party that the opportunists, in the interests of disseminating the various erroneous viewpoints and proposals, either intentionally or unintentionally kept back Stalin's works on China. But, despite this situation, Comrade Mao Tse-tung has been able to reach the same conclusions as Stalin on many fundamental problems through his independent thinking based*	Suppressed in the Russian version. How could they have been unaware of Stalin's views?!

> *on the fundamental revolution-*
> *ary science of Marx, Engels,*
> *Lenin and Stalin. Thus, the*
> *correctness of Mao himself and*
> *his comrades-in-arms was main-*
> *tained.'* [A patently ironical
> passage! – R.L.]

98. No precise date can be given, but the new line was clearly apparent at the time
of the Bandoeng conference in 1955.

14. The Peculiarities of Vietnamese Communism

Pierre Rousset

In political and ideological terms, relations between the Vietnamese communist movement and Stalinism are both complex and contradictory. From the outset, the future of Vietnamese communism was determined by its relations with Comintern on the one hand and the nationalist movement on the other hand.

In the 1930s Vietnamese Marxism was represented by several parties. There was, of course, the Communist Party of Indo-China, which subsequently became the Vietnam Workers' Party and then the Communist Party of Vietnam (CPV), which now rules the Socialist Republic.[1] But there were also Left Opposition groups which joined Leon Trotsky's Fourth International and independent groups such as that led by Nguyen An Ninh. In the 1930s these groups were able to play a significant role, but the CPV finally took over the leadership of the national liberation movement and Vietnamese Marxism therefore came to be identified with that party. This essay will therefore deal mainly with the CPV.

The situation prevailing in the 1930s does, however, shed some light on the problems raised by an analysis of the CPV's relationship with Stalinism. The first nucleus of the Communist Party was formed between 1925 and 1930, during, that is, the period of the Stalinization of the Communist International. The Communist Party of Indo-China (CPI) was officially founded in 1930 when three different groups merged, largely at the urgings of Nguyen Ai Quoc – the future Ho Chi Minh – who was then acting as the Comintern's regional envoy. It remained loyal to the Stalinist International throughout the thirties and rejected proposals for the formation of a new International. The debate was all the more clear-cut in that it took place against the background of the Popular Front in France – the ruling colonial power in Vietnam. Moscow and the Parti Communiste Français (PCF) both supported the Popular Front Government. Despite some disagreements the CPV seems to have followed suit. The Trotskyist groups opposed its policies and particularly its line on the colonial question. The debate in Vietnam appears to have reproduced that between the Left Opposition and the PCF, a Stalinist party if ever there was one.

Was, then, the CPV always a Stalinist party or did it become one in the thirties? Despite appearances to the contrary, this is not in fact the case. *The CPV considered itself part of the Stalinist Comintern but never became a Stalinist party as such.* In other words, it was never subordinated to the interests of the Soviet bureaucracy in either political or organizational terms.[2] To that extent, the evolution of the CPV resembles that of the Communist Party of China (CPC).

The best way to understand how the party has been marked both by its own national experience and by its membership of the Moscow-led 'socialist camp' is to analyse its history. That also allows us to grasp how it could promote the interests of the revolutionary struggle in Vietnam itself (and go against the international line of the Soviet bureaucracy if need be) without ever trying to provide an overall alternative to Stalinism.

Deep national roots

A vital characteristic of the CPV is that it has always been deeply rooted in the social and national reality of the country. The emergence of the Vietnamese communist movement was the expression both of international factors (the Russian Revolution, the French labour movement and the Chinese Revolution of 1925–7) and of the development of a strong and long-standing nationalist movement. Its development reflected the formation of new social strata (a rural and urban proletariat and semi-proletariat and a new intelligentsia) and the ripening of an overall social crisis which objectively placed a revolutionary response to colonial domination on the agenda.

It is worth stressing that the situation of the CPV was very different to that of many Third World Communist Parties which developed late and were little more than off-shoots of Comintern. They were all the more dependent upon Moscow in that they were never deeply rooted in the national reality of their own countries. The CPV's situation was therefore very different to that of the Communist Party of Algeria (CPA), most of whose members were of French descent. The CPA was thus organically linked with the PCF, the party in the colonial metropolis. Because of the PCF's position on the colonial question it became divorced from the national movement. In contrast, the CPV was founded by Vietnamese and its members were Vietnamese. Although it enjoyed a certain authority because of its links with the Comintern, the PCF remained an external influence.

Vietnamese communism took shape slowly in the second half of the 1920s, at a time when the nationalist movement was in a state of transition (to that extent, the process of its formation differs from that of its Chinese equivalent). French colonialism met with stubborn and lasting resistance from both popular and traditionalist forces at the end of the nineteenth century and the beginning of the twentieth. Because it had a mass base and a cultural dimension, that resistance was able to provide a basis for subsequent struggle for national liberation. But the bankruptcy of the various currents that led those struggles became obvious with the outbreak of the First World War. They gave way to the new nationalist formations of the twenties, formations which expressed the new social forces at work in the country and which fed upon the economic upheavals caused by colonization. The nationalist movement was not initially dominated by the communists but by the constitutionalist party of the southern rice-producing bourgeoisie and by the Viet Nam Quoc Dan Dang (VNQDD), which was strongest in the north and which recruited mainly civil servants, soldiers and teachers. But by the end of the twenties, the influence of these movements was declining rapidly. The VNQDD lost its influence because it adopted terrorist tactics and was then forced into an insurrection by the repression directed against it (the Yen Bai garrison rising of February 1930). The constitutionalist party lost its influence because in practical terms it supported the colonial regime's brutal suppression of the VNQDD (the latter survived mainly in exile and returned to Vietnam in Kuomintang army trucks in 1945).

The Yen Bai insurrection had profound repercussions throughout the country. It was the Communist Party, founded in the very month of the insurrection, that was to reap the benefit: the strike wave of 1928 had already signalled the emergence of a labour movement in both the towns and the countryside. The communists were directly involved in the setting up of trade unions and the Communist Party was thus able to make a bid for the leadership of the emerging labour movement and the nationalist movement. It did so by providing an alternative to the constitutionalist party and the VNQDD and by giving them a mass, class character. When the agrarian crisis became acute it proved capable of leading major peasant struggles.

It was during the Nghe-Tinh Soviets rising in central Vietnam between May 1930 and August 1931 that popular demands and the nationalist cause were first identified with a mass insurrectional movement under communist leadership. The Nghe-Tinh Soviets remained isolated and were subject to severe repression. The CPV was almost destroyed in 1931–2. Nevertheless, 1930 represented a major turning point for social and nationalist struggles in Vietnam.

In its early stages, Vietnamese communism owed a lot to the Comintern. But at a deeper level its emergence was an expression of processes at work in Vietnam itself: the coming together of an intelligentsia radicalized by colonial conditions, a young rural and urban proletariat involved in its first struggles and a pauperized peasantry fragmented by the impact of the agrarian crisis. The early phase of the nationalist movement was marked by a struggle between a bourgeois constitutionalist current, a radical petty bourgeois nationalist current (the VNQDD) and the communist movement. In the event the latter emerged victorious. The severity of the lasting social and national crisis, which came much earlier and was more explosive than in many colonial or semi-colonial countries, provided fertile ground for revolutionary action.

From the outset, then, the Communist Party had deep national roots. It was far from being an artificial creation of the Comintern or the Soviet bureaucracy. It was not originally Stalinist. On the contrary: in their efforts to ensure its Stalinization both Paris and Moscow came up against its national roots.

Early experiences in China

Vietnamese communist militants also learned a lot from their stay in China. It was in Canton that Nguyen Ai Quoc (Ho Chi Minh) set up the communist cell that became the core of the Thanh Nien (Vietnam Revolutionary Youth League). The communist movement also published a proto-communist newspaper in Canton. It was there that new recruits were trained to go back and establish cells in Vietnam itself.

Between 1925 and 1930 the embryonic Vietnamese communist movement was based in China. Its members were able to follow the course of the second Chinese Revolution very closely: the extraordinary rise of the mass movement, the great wave of popular mobilization, the spectacular growth of the CPC, the development of social splits within the nationalist movement, the break-up of the alliance between the Kuomintang and the CPC, Chiang Kai Shek's brutal repression of the workers' movement in Shanghai and Canton, the victory of the counter-revolution . . .

Chiang Kai Shek's victory was a severe blow for the Vietnamese revolutionaries, who saw nationalist China as their nearest and safest rear area. It was also an important lesson for them. Two members of the Thanh Ninh communist cell were officially members of the CPC. As the Vietnamese historian Nguyen Khac Vien writes, the Thanh Ninh leadership was faced with 'its first serious trial of strength . . . the failure of the Canton commune of 1927; several of its members were arrested and the Kuomintang brought pressure to bear on the organization to make it adopt a nationalist line'.[3]

The lesson of 1927 left an even deeper mark on the Vietnamese communists in that it was confirmed by developments in Vietnam itself. In 1927 the masses were betrayed by the Chinese national bourgeoisie, represented by the Kuomintang. In 1929–30, the Vietnamese national bourgeoisie, represented by the constitutionalist party, sided with the colonial repression directed against the VNQDD, the Nghe-Tinh Soviets and the CPV itself. The year 1927 also taught the Vietnamese a great deal about the policies of the Stalinist Comintern. Kremlin directives, the advice given by special advisers like Borodin and the Soviet Union's diplomatic line all contributed to the defeat: they led the CPC (and the worker-peasant mass movement along with it) into an impasse and left them defenceless against the counter-revolution. The tragic defeat of the Chinese Revolution of 1925–7 was largely the result of the policies adopted by the Stalinist leadership of the Communist International.

This dramatic experience also explains many later aspects of Maoism. The prestige and authority of Moscow – which had until then seemed quite natural – were undermined in the eyes of Chinese militants for a long time to come. The same is probably true of some Vietnamese cadres. Some of them also took part in the epic struggle of the Chinese Red Army and must have followed the long factional struggle between Mao (who became the spokesman for the CPC's 'indigenous' leadership) and Wang Ming (Stalin's envoy to the politbureau of the CPC). In the thirties and forties there were bitter factional struggles over crucial issues within the CPC. Wang Ming's faction (the 'Twenty-eight Bolsheviks' or the 'Internationalists') were trained in the USSR and were foisted upon the CPC leadership by the Kremlin to ensure that the CPC remained under the political and organizational control of the Stalinist leadership. The victory of the Maoist faction, however, gave the CPC a *de facto* independence that enabled it to bring the third Chinese Revolution to a successful conclusion.[4]

It is difficult to calculate the impact of this conflict on the Vietnamese leadership with any accuracy. But for years to come its effects were felt at every level: organizational, ideological, strategic and tactical. It is probable that it influenced the evolution of the CPV itself, especially when the leadership established the Vietminh in 1941 and began to take an increasingly 'nationalist' line and to assert its independence from Moscow.

Comintern, China and Vietnam: 1925–35

The CPV's relationship with the Comintern never resulted in anything like the traumatic experience undergone by its Chinese counterpart. On the contrary, in the twenties and thirties the communist movement in Vietnam seems to have loyally followed the Comintern's policy shifts and does not appear to have undergone any major political crises. Until 1928 it followed a 'Rightist line' and then moved to the 'Left' before adopting a popular front policy in 1935.

Links between the CPV, the PCF and Moscow (where a number of party leaders were trained) were maintained until the outbreak of the Second World War and the subsequent breakdown in international relations. During the thirties, the Communist Party defined itself in terms of the framework imposed upon Indo-China by colonialism, and not in terms of national boundaries. Even though its membership included few Khmers or Laotians, it worked in the context of a single unified state (formally divided into five regions of varying status): French Indo-China. The Communist Party was known at this time as the Communist Party of Indo-China. It called for class unity and was highly suspicious of ideological and cultural nationalism. In many respects, the line adopted by the communist movement at this time seems to contradict that adopted during the period of the wars of national liberation.

For many writers, the national character of Vietnamese communism is an acquired characteristic that appeared relatively late in the day. They argue that in the thirties the relationship between the CPV and the Comintern was one of subordination and that it was similar to the other national sections of the Communist International.[5] There is a real problem here: such analyses are based upon real sequences in the history of Vietnamese communism but they are, in my opinion, too simplistic. They tend to obscure the complexity of the relationship between the CPV and Comintern – even during the thirties – and to ignore important stages in the evolution of the nationalist movement.

The line drawn up in Moscow for the Comintern was usually forced upon the various national sections by administrative and bureaucratic means (Congress documents for the national sections were often drawn up by an ad hoc commission sitting in Moscow). For a long time the CPV probably did try to follow Comintern discipline. The pressures brought to bear by the Comintern and the PCF probably did have an effect on the practice of the Vietnamese communists. It is, for instance, possible that the 1929 crisis in the Thanh Nien (over the advisability of establishing an openly Communist Party) was in part provoked by the application of the ultra-Leftist line adopted a year earlier by the Communist International. That same ultra-Leftism probably had an effect on the Nghe-Tinh uprisings of 1930 and may well be reflected in a number of ideological themes in the first half of the thirties.[6]

But the line followed by Moscow during this crucial decade did not have the same effects in China and Vietnam. In China, Comintern policy was in open contradiction with the needs of the revolutionary struggle. This was not the case in Vietnam. Between 1925 and 1927, the Comintern forced the CPC to adopt a conciliatory attitude towards the national bourgeoisie: this at a time when the bourgeoisie was turning against its former ally and crushing the mass movement. The CPC was forced to remain within the Kuomintang at the very moment when it should have left it. In Vietnam, however, communists were told to work inside the nationalist movement and to begin to transform it from within. It should be noted that they did so by forming their own current (centred on the

Thanh Nien) and not by passively following the line of the constitutionalist party (which was in any case much weaker than the Kuomintang).

The ultra-Leftist line taken by the Communist International between 1928 and 1934 had catastrophic results in China. Most of the CPC leadership was drawn into adventurist actions at a time when the revolutionary movement was in retreat and needed defensive policies. From 1928 onwards the class content of the national movement in Vietnam became clearer as the worker-peasant mass movement grew stronger despite the treachery of the constitutionalist party. It was time for the communist movement to assert its own identity and to take control of the national movement. But it should be noted that the Vietnamese communists did not do so by following an adventurist line between 1932 and 1935. On the contrary, they moved skilfully from the defensive to the offensive, using all possible means of legal action.

Two conclusions can be drawn from a comparison of the Vietnamese and Chinese experiences. As early as 1925–7 Comintern's policies proved catastrophic in China. Until 1937 the CPV was able to follow a policy that was broadly in line with the needs of the national revolutionary movement without necessarily coming into open conflict with Moscow. As a result the CPV's policy was never divorced from developments within the nationalist movement.

The dialectical relationship between social and national demands, between communist movements and national movements, varies from one period to the next. Even in a country under direct colonial rule, like the Vietnam of the thirties, the national struggle (against French domination) does not necessarily precede the emergence of class conflict within the indigenous society itself. The Nghe-Tinh rising of 1930–31, for instance, led to conflicts between Vietnamese peasants and local Vietnamese civil servants. That revolutionary conflict was characterized by the close connection between the social and national roots of the struggle at both the local and the national level. That connection remained a basic characteristic of the struggle in Vietnam, even during the period of the liberation wars.

In general terms, the 1930s might be characterized as the decade in which a *proletarian hegemony* was established within the nationalist movement and in which the *communist leadership* established its legitimacy. In order to be able to speak for the nation – the working class, the pauperized peasantry and the rural proletariat – the communist movement had to assert their class autonomy and the need for solidarity. In the mid-thirties, the Vietnamese communist movement (which was not at that time represented by any one organization) successfully accomplished its two-fold task of asserting its class autonomy and gaining national hegemony. The fact that during the local elections the patriotic petty bourgeoisie voted against the constitutionalists and for the 'worker candidates' put forward by *La Lutte* (a united front bringing together the CPI, Vietnamese Trotskyists and Nguyen An Ninh's independent Marxists) is a striking example of its success.[7]

Far from representing an unfortunate departure from the line represented by the Thanh Nien period and the establishment of the Vietminh, the 'class struggle' line followed by the Vietnamese communist movement for almost ten years paved the way for the wars of national liberation by showing what was at stake in the fight for independence and by creating a favourable balance of power between the CPV and the bourgeois and petty-bourgeois currents. The 'class struggle' line was not artificially forced upon it by the Comintern. The CPV's experience of mass struggle throughout this period was a historical rehearsal for the national insurrection of the 1945 August Revolution.

Ambivalent Links with the Comintern

This is not to say that the first two decades of the Vietnamese communist movement were free from crises and internal tensions. The transition from one period in the development of the CPV to the next was not made without open crises (1929) and serious internal tensions (especially at the end of the thirties). The national leadership of the CPV underwent changes and it is significant that in 1934, for instance, the line taken by Nguyen Ai Quoc/Ho Chi Minh was described in very critical terms in party publications. While it recognizes Ho's positive role in the initial founding of the CPI, the review *Bolshevick* explains that 'Our comrades must not, however, forget the nationalist survivals to be found in Ho's work, his erroneous teachings as to the fundamental questions of the bourgeois democratic revolutionary movement in Indo-China or his opportunist theories.' Ho is also accused of having misunderstood or having failed to apply the Comintern's line and directives and of having recommended 'erroneous reformist and collaborationist tactics'.[8]

Between 1928 and 1935 Comintern seems to have constantly urged the CPV to combat 'nationalist survivals'. And the leadership's position on reasserting a Vietnamese national identity in the face of colonial domination was in fact ultra-Leftist.[9] It is clear that, throughout this period, there were as many conflicting tendencies and organizations within the Vietnames communist movement as there were in the CPI itself. It is also clear that representatives of the Comintern and the PCF intervened in those conflicts in the name of Comintern discipline. In theory the leadership accepted that discipline. But its relationship with the International and Moscow must already have been ambivalent.

As we have seen, the CPV definitely saw itself as part of the Stalinist Comintern. This was a matter of political conviction: the necessary link between national revolution and world-wide revolution could not be made without the Comintern. This was not an abstract profession of faith. The CPV believed that a revolution in a colonial country could not develop into a socialist revolution without the backing of the USSR. The 1930s were a very internationalist period. The hopes of Vietnamese Marxists centred upon the possible conjunction of an upsurge of workers' struggles in metropolitan France and national struggles in colonial Vietnam.

There were in fact many positive aspects to the CPV's membership of the Comintern. The consolidation of the Vietnamese communist movement owed much to the existence of its multiple international connections with Moscow, the CPC and the PCF. The defensive campaigns organized in France by the PCF and Secours Rouge (as well as by other organizations, notably those connected with the Left Opposition) were very useful in 1931–2, when the CPV was almost destroyed by repression. Similarly, pressures brought to bear in France allowed *La Lutte*, the organ of the united front, to exploit the possibilities for legal action offered by the status of Cochinchina (South Vietnam).

Although they identified closely with the Comintern, the leaders of the CPV did not apply its line mechanically. Little is known about relations between the Vietnamese communist movement and the International between 1929 (the crisis in the Thanh Nien) and April 1931 (when the CPI was recognized as a section of Comintern), but they appear to have been stormy (the name 'Communist Party of Vietnam' was rejected in favour of 'Communist Party of Indo-China', the first programme drawn up by Ho Chi Minh was rejected . . .). The concrete tactical suppleness and prudence displayed by the CPI between 1932 and 1935 is in stark contrast with the tone of the articles on Vietnam published by the Comintern. The 1932 programme ratified the ultra-Leftist line, but in practice the CPI adopted a defensive policy. Between 1932 and 1934 the Comintern press was constantly announcing 'new revolutionary upsurges' . . . but clandestine publications in Vietnam itself never mentioned them.

As early as 1932 contacts were established between the Trotskyist militants and the CPI and those contacts led to the establishment of *La Lutte* in the Saigon area. Both the Comintern and the PCF agreed to the establishment of this unique Popular Front organ, although it is clear that there were disagreements as to the importance of the initiative. Despite the bitter polemics in the clandestine press, there was a broad consensus of agreement between members of the Left Opposition and the CP during this period of exceptional activity. The leaders of the CPI resisted the pressures brought to bear by the PCF, which wanted them to leave *La Lutte*, for a long time. As late as 6 June 1937 Duong Bach Mai was still publicly defending the alliance with the Indo-Chinese Trotskyists of *La Lutte*, criticizing them for their 'sterile revolutionism' but accepting that 'they are still anti-imperialist elements who deserve all our support.'[10]

In the mid-thirties, then, the CPV's national roots enabled it to modify the Comintern line and even to resist pressures brought to bear by the PCF. After all, CPV cadres had good reason to doubt the Comintern's infallibility: the Chinese experience, the obvious failure to understand the local situation in 1932–4 (the 'new revolutionary upsurge'), the marginalization of Ho Chi Minh, the bureaucratic nature of Moscow's interventions into debates within the party . . .[11]

From the Democratic Front to the Vietminh

With the shift towards the Popular Front, Comintern's line came into open contradiction with the dynamics of the social and national struggle in Vietnam for the first time. The second half of the thirties thus represents a decisive period for relations between the CPV and the Soviet bureaucracy which dictated the Comintern's policies.

Comintern began to move to the Right in 1934. It was attempting to enter into an alliance with the imperialist bourgeois democracies, beginning with France, the colonial power in Vietnam. This radical change in policy, announced in Manuilsky's letter of 11 June 1934 to Thorez, culminated in the signing of the Stalin–Laval pact in May 1935. After the 7th Congress of the Communist International and the electoral victory of the Left in 1936 the PCF supported the government. The anti-colonialist struggle had to give way to the anti-fascist struggle. The PCF adjourned the fight for independence in the French colonies *sine die* and defended the international positions of 'democratic' imperialism against Mussolini's Italy and Hitler's Germany in Africa and against Japan in Asia.[12]

In Indo-China, the masses enjoyed few of the benefits of French democracy. It is probably significant that the CPI held its national congress and reaffirmed its previous 'class struggle' line on the eve of the Comintern's 7th Congress. It was not until later that the CPI changed its position and brought it into formal agreement with Comintern policy. The victory of the Popular Front in France had considerable repercussions in Vietnam. An unprecedented strike wave broke out, with both the clandestine organizations and the legal united front of *La Lutte* playing a very active role. An extraordinary social and national movement was getting under way in Vietnam. *Objectively*, the victory of the Popular Front in France put the resurgence of anti-colonial struggles in Vietnam on the agenda, but the PCF–Comintern line was opposed to any such development. That contradiction put the CPI in a very delicate position.

The CPV did not oppose the PCF–Comintern line openly. It compromised, modified its own line and even accepted the shameful dissolution of the Etoile Nord-Africaine. It supported the Popular Front to the bitter end, and even beyond the end. After the break-up of *La Lutte* and the end of the campaign for a Congress of Indo-China, the CPV called for the establishment of an *Indo-Chinese Popular Front* and then in 1938 for a *Democratic Front* which was in theory open to bourgeois constitutionalists and even monarchists. But a subtle distinction was made between 'ultra-colonialists' and 'anti-fascist French colonialists'. The slogans of 'Down with French imperialism' and 'Confiscate the land of the big landowners' were 'temporarily withdrawn'.[13]

Despite these compromises, the leadership of the CPV consolidated the party's clandestine structures (colonial repression was becoming severe again). In 1938 it even decided to begin underground work in the colonial army (Paris had decided to recruit 20,000 infantrymen from the colony). It was in fact trying to reconcile the irreconcilable: the PCF's support for the French government, Moscow's anti-fascist alliance and an independent policy in Vietnam to preserve its mass base and to ensure that it would be able to act in the future. It therefore became involved in a polemic against the Trotskyists on the one hand and the supporters of Franco-Annamite collaboration on the other.

Once the hopes raised by the victory of the Popular Front had been dashed, the CPV began to lose ground, although it was indisputably still the main revolutionary party in Vietnam. The break-up of *La Lutte* in 1937 worked to the advantage of the Left Opposition (which took the decision to bring about the split). The Trotskyist groups, which continued to support an active anti-imperialist policy, began to find a wider audience amongst the masses. In 1939 they won the Saigon municipal elections, standing against the CPI and the Constitutionalists.[14] Internal CP documents point to the existence of disagreements within the party at a time when its influence was declining.

It is impossible to say with any certainty just what the balance of power between the various tendencies within the CPV was at this time. It was subject to contradictory pressures which could have taken it in any one of three different directions: total support for the policies of Moscow and the PCF (which would lose it its national character), the formulation of open programmatic criticisms of the Comintern line and an official break with Moscow (possibly leading to a reconciliation with the Trotskyists) or the establishment of a new 'Ho Chi Minh line' which would in practice ensure the primacy of the nationalist line and preserve the party's international alliances (thus leading to the crystallization of a specifically national entity within the 'official' international communist movement). Given the international balance of power within the labour movement (marked by the great weakness of the Fourth International), the loyalty of CPV cadres to the Stalinist International and the national roots of the party, it was probably predictable that the third alternative would be adopted.

The setting-up of the Vietminh in May 1941 was not an extension of the Democratic Front policy of 1938: it represented a new and important policy change for the CPV. The change began in 1939 and affected the strategic line of the Vietnamese communist movement as well as the question of its basic identity:

1. The struggle for *national liberation* became the immediate and central concern of the Communist Party. As of 1939 the party took up armed struggle for the seizure of state power.

2. The renewed emphasis on the struggle for independence meant that the CPV had to distance itself from the changing policies of the Soviet bureaucracy and the PCF. The objective of the new National United Front set up by the CPV was the overthrow of *all* colonial powers, a struggle for 'the overthrow of the French imperialists and resistance against all foreign aggressors – white or yellow – for national liberation'.[15] The PCF's priorities and Moscow's temporary alliances (in August 1939 Moscow signed the German-Soviet pact; various agreements were also reached with Japan) could not be allowed to modify the dynamics of the struggle.

3. The requirements of the anti-colonial military struggle meant that the party had to give priority to the struggle for agrarian reform (distribution of the land to the tiller), as this was the only way to mobilize the peasantry on a large scale. But the importance given to broadening class alliances meant that for a long time the party had to moderate its agrarian programme. According to Vo Nguyen Giap, 'in practice we carried out our anti-feudal task' from the start 'but the influence of confused notions as to the content of the national liberation struggle was apparent both in our thinking and in the measures we took. This meant that during the early years of the resistance we tended to neglect the anti-feudal task to some extent and to give excessive attention to the peasant question. It was only in 1949–50 that the peasant question was posed with any clarity.'[16]

4. From 1936 onwards, a new emphasis was placed on the importance of anti-imperialist patriotism (as opposed to the ultra-Leftist theses of the previous period). With the setting up of the liberation fronts, the national character of the Vietnamese communist movement became obvious. Three different national fronts were in operation as early as 1941. And in

1951 the CPI was dissolved to make way for three formally independent national Communist Parties.

5. The international context was changing considerably. In the twenties, the Thanh Nien was politically and organizationally based in the East and was orientated towards China. The revolutionaries of the thirties looked westward to Europe for their inspiration. After the defeat of the Spanish revolution, the collapse of the Popular Front in France and the start of Japanese intervention in China, the East once again became the primary reference for Vietnamese communism. To a large extent that helped reinforce its Asiatic identity.

6. The new importance given to establishing a base amongst the peasantry, the new emphasis on anti-imperialist patriotism and the adoption of an overall Asian strategy meant that the CVP had to insert itself into Vietnamese cultural tradition (as it had done during the Thanh Nien period). In order to extend its popular base in a non-Western country (and especially a non-Christian country), Marxism had to find native philosophical sources. In Vietnam, those sources included Confucian sociologism, the statist tradition of the Asiatic mode of production and Chinese dialectics. Ho Chi Minh's writings provide a particularly clear example of the 'Vietnamization' of Marxism. As Nguyen Khac Vien notes,

> The Confucian moralism is instantly recognizable ... Criticism and self-criticism begin with political questions, but often lead to an extended moral analysis. It might even be said that in Vietnam (and China) Confucianism and Marxism tend to merge. Given that Marxism means both 'explanation and edification', edification can often gain the upper hand. Of all the parties in the great communist family, it is definitely the Vietnamese (and the Chinese) that uses the most moralistic tone. It is much more moralistic than parties that work in countries that were under the ideological influence of the bourgeoisie for a long time.[17]

(Nguyen Khac Vien also points out that in the West, the Communist Parties have been influenced by bourgeois cynicism and do not give sufficient importance to moral questions.)

The experience of the wars of liberation

The specific character of the Vietnamese communist movement finally took shape during the three long decades of the wars of national liberation. During these difficult years of revolutionary combat, the CPV once again realized both the importance of the aid supplied by the socialist bloc and the spinelessness of its leadership.

The victory of the Chinese Revolution in 1949 was a major turning

point for the Vietnamese revolution. It allowed Vietminh forces to take
complete control of the Vietbac (the mountainous north of the country)
and to set up secure bases to prepare for the general offensive against the
French expeditionary force. Sino-Soviet military aid (and especially
heavy material from the Soviet Union) was essential for the defence of
North Vietnam and the NFL zones against American military aggression.
The socialist countries and the 'official' Communist Parties had their
role to play on the international front. From that point of view, the
Vietnamese revolutionary movement had a more lasting and intense
experience of the effects of the international balance of power than its
Chinese counterpart. If it was to win in the face of direct intervention by
the US, the major imperialist power in the world, the Vietnamese
revolution had to work at the international level, much more so than the
Chinese. But the CPV had the bitter experience of being betrayed by the
'fraternal leaders' at that level too.

In 1945 the Vietminh proclaimed the Democratic Republic of Vietnam
and declared that the country had been liberated. In the agreements
negotiated at Yalta, Teheran and Potsdam the USSR had, however,
accepted that Indo-China belonged to the Western zone of influence.
*Moscow did not give diplomatic recognition to the Democratic Republic
until four years after its foundation – after the victory of the Chinese
Revolution!* As for the PCF, it was represented in the French government
after the Second World War. Acting 'in solidarity with the government',
the communist ministers voted in favour of the war credits required for
sending a new expeditionary force to Indo-China. The PCF's policy left
the solidarity movement in France paralysed and confused at a decisive
moment.

The line taken by Moscow and the PCF goes some way to explaining
the hesitations of the CPV leadership, which was painfully aware of its
international isolation. During this period, many nationalist elements
were killed by members of the Vietminh and the CPV (including Trotskyist leaders who had fought in the anti-French resistance like Ta Thu
Thau). But at the same time that it was negotiating with Paris, the CPV
leadership in practice refused to ratify the agreements signed by the
USSR or to conform to the demands of the PCF. Before long armed
struggle broke out in the south again.[18]

During the 1954 Geneva negotiations considerable pressure was
brought to bear on the Vietminh by the Soviet and Chinese delegations: it
was reluctantly forced into compromises which robbed it of a large part
of what it should have been able to gain, given the balance of power on
the ground and the internal weaknesses of the French government (whose
forces had been defeated at Dien Bien Phu).[19] Moscow was intent upon
reaching agreements on peaceful coexistence with the US, even if it meant

sacrificing the interests of the Vietnamese revolution. The Chinese leadership, sorely tried by the Korean War, failed to support the CPV and actively defended the policies dictated by Molotov. The fourth Indo-China war was to a large extent the result of the Geneva compromise.

When it relaunched the armed struggle in South Vietnam, the CPV found itself alone once more. The US (and France) sabotaged the political clauses in the Geneva agreements. The Diem regime's policy of repression in the southern zone was terribly effective. Despite that, Khrushchev suggested that the UN should recognize 'both' Vietnams, which was tantamount to accepting the division of the country, regardless of Hanoi's wishes. In the late fifties, the Sino-Soviet split divided the 'socialist camp' which the CPV had always seen as its major base. It was because of that split that the Maoist faction in the CPC rejected the policy of a united front with the USSR in defence of the Vietnamese revolution. The CPV had to recover the aid it needed so badly and establish a certain *de facto* unity between the leaders of the socialist world. The DRV never received heavy weapons from the Soviet Union to defend itself against US bombing (Nasser's Egypt received better quality weapons than Vietnam!). And in 1972, on the eve of the unprecedented bombing of Hanoi and the port of Haiphong, Nixon went on a triumphal visit to Peking and then to Moscow. The Vietnamese leadership saw quite clearly that a reconciliation between China and the US was on the cards. And they were very much aware that such a reconciliation was not in the interests of the revolutionary struggle in Vietnam.

Having asserted their political independence at the national level, the Vietnamese leaders tried to guarantee themselves freedom of movement at the international level. They systematically established links with all elements in the international solidarity movement – from liberals to revolutionary organizations – even if it meant displeasing 'brother-parties'. Having learned their lesson at Geneva, they took care not to invite Soviet and Chinese delegates to the Paris peace talks. They decided to launch the decisive offensives of 1972 and 1975 without consulting either Peking or Moscow.

The CPV and the 'Socialist Camp'

The CPV's long revolutionary struggle ended in victory because the party was deeply rooted in the national reality of the country. It had succeeded in asserting its political autonomy and in resisting the dictates of both the Soviet and the Chinese bureaucracies. Going against both Moscow and Peking, it used popular mobilizations in Vietnam and international support for them to establish a new balance of power within the 'socialist camp' and to assert its own line. In that sense, the CPV is very different from the majority of Communist Parties, which have always followed the changing Soviet diplomatic line (the PCF and the Soviet–German pact, the leading faction within the Greek Communist Party at the end of the Second World War, etc.).

The political independence shown by the Vietnamese leadership during the wars of liberation confirms our analysis of relations between the CPV and Comintern during the thirties. The Stalinization of the Communist International did not come about overnight. Attempts to Stalinize it met with considerable national resistance, and some Communist Parties (in China, Yugoslavia and Vietnam) succeeded in escaping the political and organizational vassalage that the Soviet bureaucracy wanted to force on them.

As we have seen, in China this resistance first became apparent during a serious factional struggle within the leadership. This does not seem to have been the case in Vietnam: even during the thirties, no truly Stalinist faction ever took control of the leadership (as did the Wang Ming faction in China). From Moscow's point of view, China was the most important strategic theatre in Asia and it was there that the Communist International concentrated its efforts. The defeat of the Wang Ming faction meant that Moscow could not use the CPC as a channel to control the CPV (the PCF's influence on the CPV was limited because of the party's predominantly Vietnamese membership).

The role of Ho Chi Minh points to a further major difference between the CPC and the CPV. Of all the Vietnamese leaders, Nguyen Ai Quoc/Ho Chi Minh was the most experienced and had the broadest knowledge of the international labour movement. He had been a party militant in France and had visited the USSR, from whence he was sent to South-East Asia by the Comintern. On several occasions he had spent long periods in China. He was both revolutionary leader and negotiator, head of state and diplomat. He could negotiate with the 'fraternal parties' on equal terms. He was a Comintern agent, but he was also the father of the 'Vietnamization' of Marxism. Even in the twenties he was a major figure in the Asian communist movement and finally became a national personality: Uncle Ho. Wang Ming was simply Stalin's agent inside the CPC. As for Mao, he spoke no foreign languages and never left China until after the revolution, when he made two brief visits to the USSR. He did not have the international experience of a Deng Xiaoping or a Chou En Lai.

The process of the Vietnamization of Marxism thus followed a very different road to the 'Sinization' of Marxism in the CPC. The breaks are less clear-cut and the long term international influences are more varied. The CPV was initially influenced by the PCF and the USSR, but the Chinese influence gradually became stronger, especially after the victory of 1949. During the fifties in particular, the CPV was politically and ideologically closer to Peking than to Moscow. The success of the 'Chinese road' to the seizure of power, their geographical and cultural proximity and a certain shared experience mean that the Chinese and the Vietnamese parties are very closely related.

But doubts as to the validity of the 'Chinese model' soon arose. The political and military experience of the Vietnamese revolution differs from the Chinese in many respects. The CPV leadership started out with a theory of 'people's war' similar to that of Mao (and directly influenced by Mao's theories), but it developed and gradually enriched it, eventually modifying it considerably. The crisis provoked in North Vietnam by agrarian reform policies in 1956 was a sharp reminder of the dangers of 'Leftism' inherent in Maoist 'mobilization campaigns'. The failure of the Great Leap Forward in the late fifties, Mao's rejection of Vietnamese proposals for a united front between China and the USSR, the chaos of the Cultural Revolution in the mid-sixties and the changes in Peking's international policies all helped to distance the Vietnamese leadership from China. Relations between the two parties almost broke down completely in 1971–2, when Nixon visited China. The CPV still has many ideological themes in common with Maoism (criticism and self-criticism for instance); but other themes with a more definitely 'Soviet' tone are also emerging (the stress on the 'scientific' nature of the political line in *every* domain, for instance).

Until the victory of 1975 the CPV did not break with either Moscow or Peking. The leadership's vision of the 'socialist camp' at this time reflects the contradictory history of its relations with its leading members. According to the CPV, the 'socialist bloc' was an essential ally in its struggle against the imperialist powers and represented an objective community of interest. It was still basically a healthy body, the representative of the historical interests of the proletariat and oppressed peoples and the privileged ally of the national liberation movement. Divisions within the socialist camp were seen as weakening revolutionary struggles throughout the world and in Vietnam in particular. This feeling of belonging to the socialist camp is very clearly expressed in Ho Chi Minh's will:

I am . . . proud to see the international communist movement and workers' movement expand, and I suffer . . . because of the dissension that at present divides the communist powers. I want our party to do its best to contribute efficaciously to the re-establishment of good relations between the communist powers on a Marxist–Leninist and international proletarian basis, always in conformity with the demands of the mind and heart.[20]

But the way in which the Soviet and Chinese leaders in turn betrayed and abandoned its struggle also convinced the CPV of their opportunism and 'national egoism'. The Vietnamese leaders usually kept their bitterness to themselves. But not always. When it was announced that Nixon was to visit Peking and Moscow, *Nhan Dan* (the CPV daily) published some very harsh articles denouncing 'manifestations of Rightism and unprincipled compromises' and stressing that 'the successes of the national liberation movement . . . are a sharp reminder to those who doubt the invincible revolutionary thought of our time and who stray into the dark muddy path of compromise.' The article denounces 'national egoism' and points out that 'the victory of the revolution in one country is not the end, but simply the beginning of a very long struggle for world communism.'[21]

The reunification of the socialist camp and the international communist movement and the rectification of its line were probably the main elements in Vietnamese thinking at the moment of victory in 1975. But it should be remembered that the Vietnamese position on the problems of the 'socialist bloc' has always reflected a 'national point of view', even though Vietnam is always ready to denounce other parties' nationalism. During the Czech crisis of 1968 the Vietnamese discreetly let it be known that they considered Soviet chauvinism to be largely responsible for the military intervention. But publicly they supported the USSR. Defence of the 'cohesion' of the socialist bloc was more important than any other consideration (notably that of defending the wishes of the Czech masses) Much the same position was expressed during the Polish crisis. Any revolutionary process in the East is seen as a divisive factor and therefore as a danger.

Although it puts forward its own positions and tries to consolidate its national autonomy from both Moscow and Peking, the Vietnamese regime has always seen itself as part of the socialist bloc and – once the break with China became inevitable – of the Soviet bloc. All the more so in that the leadership has no illusions about the difficulties of reconstruction in an isolated country that has been devastated by three decades of war and which is still threatened by imperialist revanchism. Unlike China, Vietnam is not a sub-continent. In terms of development perspectives, the current theme is not the 'construction of socialism in one country' but 'international division of labour' within the Soviet bloc.

Vietnamese communism: coherence and loss of direction

The ideological sources of Vietnamese communism were originally very varied. In many ways, the Vietnamese leadership now tends to see the country as a second Cuba: a member of the socialist block in direct confrontation with imperialism. Soviet Stalinism, Maoism and specifically national sources have probably been the most lasting influences on the ideology of the CPV. But it is the way in which it expresses a particular historical experience of a long revolutionary struggle and above all of the liberation wars that gives it its internal coherence, its strength and its unity. That experience is the source of both its strengths and its limitations. The Vietnamese leadership has never tried to make any systematic re-evaluation of the international communist movement. Whilst it is aware of the 'national egoism' of the Soviet leadership, the CPV has never looked seriously into the roots or the social nature of Stalinism and its analysis of the bureaucratic phenomenon remains superficial. This explains why it continues to identify with the 'socialist bloc' and sees the upsurge of political revolution in Eastern Europe as a threat and not as a source of inspiration for communism. In that sense, Vietnamese communism is the expression of an experience that is both geographically limited and historically dated. The very reasons that explain its coherence and richness in the sixties and early seventies explain its subsequent loss of direction. It is now confronted with a new national and international context: that of the post-victory period in Vietnam itself and of the worsening of inter-bureaucratic tensions at both the regional and the international level.

The originality of Vietnamese communism finds its expression at the theoretical and programmatic level. This is obviously true of its politico-military thinking, which is particularly dialectical. It is also true of the force of CPV's analysis of the transition from democratic revolution to socialist revolution in colonial and semi-colonial countries. In his report to the 4th Congress of the CPV in 1976 Le Duan drew the following lessons from the Vietnamese struggle:

> In our era, when national independence and socialism are indissociably linked and when the working class is playing a leading role in the revolution in our country, the victory of the popular national democratic revolution marks the beginning of the transition towards socialism, the beginning of the period in which the historic tasks of the dictatorship of the proletariat will be accomplished. It is now more than twenty years since that historic point was reached in the North [1954]. On 30 April last year [1975] the whole country reached that point.[22]

The theses of the CPV are far removed from the traditional Stalinist-Menshevik view of colonial revolution.

The CPV's conception of the dictatorship of the proletariat owes a lot to the Stalinist concept: strengthening of the state (and not the beginning of its withering away, as Lenin saw it), a one-party regime (written into the Vietnamese constitution) which places the CPV above the state itself (as opposed to the Leninist concept of the sovereignty of worker-peasant soviets), the substitution of the party for the class it 'represents' and in whose name it speaks, the absence of any real democracy within the party and the mass organizations, which have been made subordinate to a bureaucratic centralism . . .

It must, however, be stressed that Stalinism is not the only source for this conception. It also derives from statist traditions specific to Vietnam (the bureaucratic state of pre-colonial times), the experience of a long *military* struggle for liberation, the complex links between a proletarian party and a predominantly peasant social base, Maoist influences, and, after the seizure of power, the gradual emergence of a bureaucracy in Vietnam itself. The mechanisms of power are different from those prevailing in Stalin's USSR; witness the importance given to the 'mass line', 'mobilization campaigns' and 'criticism and self-criticism'. Although it has many features in common with Stalinism, the Vietnamese regime is the product of a truly revolutionary struggle. Its relationship with the masses is therefore different from that of the Stalinist regime, which was the product of a bureaucratic counter-revolution.

On two occasions, the leadership of the CPV has made a radical and public self-criticism: after the agrarian crisis of 1956 and again in 1982, during the 5th Congress. These self-criticisms reveal the differences between the Vietnamese leadership and the Stalinist regime in the USSR. But they also reveal serious problems in the present system of government. As early as 1976, Le Duan admitted that 'During the patriotic resistance we launched a powerful and enthusiastic movement against the aggressor. But we have not yet succeeded in creating a really powerful movement for the construction of socialism.'[23] Six years later, he told the 5th Congress that 'The central committee must make a sharp self-criticism' of the errors it made since the victory.[24]

The self-criticism does not deal with everything (it does not, for instance, deal with the CPV's international and Indo-Chinese policies). But it does touch upon many problems (including the economic line) and ends by concentrating upon political links between party, state and masses. Le Duan's report defends the traditional concept: the party leads, the state governs, and both are subject to popular control. But he denounces subjectivism, conservatism, bureaucratism, irresponsibility and the hypertrophy of the administrative apparatus. He criticizes party organizations which 'attach too little importance to the role and function of mass organizations' and state organs which infringe the rights of the people as collective masters of society. It follows that 'the impact of the dictatorship of the proletariat has not been directed towards the mobilization and education of the masses' and he notes that 'the fall in the revolutionary quality' of CPV cadres 'has had a negative effect on the prestige of the party amongst the masses'.[25]

The growing social and political tensions in Vietnam, the crisis in the CPV's authority *vis-à-vis* the masses and the self-criticisms of the 5th

Congress all underline the severity of the problems of the post-victory period. There are obviously objective reasons for these difficulties. Vietnam is a poor country and it has been devastated. It is subject to severe and convergent pressures from the Chinese bureaucracy and imperialism. It is therefore almost totally dependent upon aid from the socialist bloc, which means that the Soviet bureaucracy can bring even greater pressure to bear. The Cambodian crisis will also have lasting effects on Vietnam.[26] The tendency towards bureaucratization became more marked after 1975, partly because of the social exhaustion of the country after thirty years of war. In 1976 Le Duan stated that it was necessary 'to take practical measures to stop certain cadres and state employees becoming a privileged stratum'.[27] The measures he recommended were not enough.

The Vietnamese regime is the product of a revolutionary struggle. But given the difficult objective context, it is now suffering from popular disaffection and internal bureaucratization. Vietnamese communism is now subject to serious internal contradictions which threaten to destroy its former coherence, particularly as its international setting has changed considerably with the end of the liberation struggle, the final break with Peking and the crisis in Cambodia. The ideology of the CPV is changing. The changes involve many important questions, but primarily the national question.

The process whereby the Vietnamese nation was constituted has always been a subject for debate in Vietnam (mainly because of the existence of a unitary bureaucratic state prior to colonization). But at the moment the dominant theme is '4,000 years of history of the Vietnamese nation'. According to the leaders of the CPV and its most vocal historians, the history of the settlement of what is now Vietnam is *the history of the formation of the Vietnamese nation*. They claim that the history of the nation goes back 4,000 years (to the time when the Red River delta was first settled) and that it has been completed by the socialist revolution.[28]

The CPV is currently adopting themes which once belonged to the nationalists. They are beginning to turn the notion of the nation into a category which transcends the history of modes of production and social relations. The nation thus becomes a historical 'invariant' which lies outside the analytic field of historical materialism. This development in the official ideology of the Vietnamese regime is disturbing. It is quite natural that Vietnamese communism should accord prime importance to the national question. It was shaped within a national movement, made itself the spokesman of the oppressed nation and led a long struggle for national liberation. But the theme of '4,000 years of the history of the Vietnamese *nation*' makes it very difficult to take any *critical* view of nationalism, an ideology which can be either progressive or reactionary, depending upon the country and period in which it appears and upon the social groups which appropriate it. It can become a powerful weapon in the hands of an emergent bureaucracy.

In political and ideological terms, Vietnamese communism was shaped both by Stalinism and by a struggle against Stalinism and the Stalinist International. It has contradictory links with the main members of the 'socialist camp'. It remains part of the socialist bloc, but at the same time claims to be a party with a predominantly national line. During the wars of liberation it gained a definite internal coherence. It borrowed from both Stalinism and Maoism, but it is not reducible to either. Its social and national roots in the country are the source of its strength. But they are also the source of its limitations as it has been unable (or unwilling) to assimilate the lessons of the labour and communist movements of the USSR, Europe or even Latin America. It is geographically and histori- cally limited.

Since the victory of 1975, Vietnamese communism has entered a new phase in its history. Being faced with new difficulties and a new interna- tional context, it is subject to contradictory tensions. It is moving towards a crisis which reflects contradictions in Vietnam and inside the CPV itself. Its future development will to a large extent depend upon developments in the social situation in Vietnam itself and on developments in the balance of power at the regional and international level.

NOTES TO CHAPTER 14

1. The Communist Party has been known by different names at different times. Unless stated otherwise, the term 'Communist Party of Vietnam' is used throughout.
2. The adjective 'Stalinist' can be understood in several senses. Personally, I prefer to use the strict definition of Stalinism: subordination to a bureaucracy which has crystallized into a ruling caste, namely the Soviet bureaucracy. The fact that a party has links with Moscow is not sufficient to define it as Stalinist (as we shall see, there are fundamental differences between the PCF and the CPV, although both have links with Moscow). A bureaucratic style of work is by no means a prerogative of Stalinism alone. Besides, a bureaucracy does not have any coherent ideology of its own. Even the theme of socialism in one country can be found in other currents (social democratic and nationalist parties). It has in any case changed considerably since the Second World War and has in part been replaced by the theme of the 'international socialist camp'. Stalinism therefore cannot be defined in terms of a bureaucratic style of work or in terms of specific ideological themes.
3. Nguyen Khac Vien, *Histoire du Vietnam*, Paris, 1974, p. 155.
4. On this little-known but crucial aspect of the history of the CPC the reader is

referred to a book by the Chinese Trotskyist Wang Fan-hsi: *Chinese Revolutionary*, Oxford, 1980. Cf. Gregor Benton, 'The Second Wang Ming Line, 1935–1938', *China Quarterly*, no. 61, March 1975. It should also be noted that in his later writings on this period Mao often links Wang Ming with the Stalinist leadership. Cf. his talk at the Chengtu Conference in March 1958 and his speech at the 10th Plenum of the 8th Central Committee in Stuart Schram (ed.), *Mao Tse-tung Unrehearsed: Talks and Letters: 1956–71*, Harmondsworth, 1974.

5. See, for example, W. J. Duiker, *The Comintern and Vietnamese Communism*, Athens, Ohio, 1975, pp. 40–41 and J. Chesneaux, 'Les Fondements historiques du communisme vietnamien', in J. Chesneaux, G. Bondasel, D. Hemery (eds.), *Tradition et Révolution au Vietnam*, Paris, 1971, pp. 215–17.

6. On the Nghe-Tinh Soviets, see P. Brocheux, 'L'Implantation du mouvement communiste en Indochine française. Le Cas du Nghe-Tinh (1930–1931)', *Revue d'histoire moderne et contemporaine*, January–March 1977.

7. On the *La Lutte* experiment and the history of Vietnamese Marxism during this period, see D. Hemery, *Révolutionnaires vietnamiens et pouvoir colonial en Indochine*, Paris, 1975.

8. 'Quatrième anniversaire de l'unification du PCI', *Bolchevick*, no. 5, 1934, Annexe à la note périodique mensuelle No. 34 (Premier trimestre 1935), cited in P. Rousset, *Communisme et nationalisme vietnamiens: Le Vietnam entre les deux guerres mondiales*, Paris, 1978, p. 128.

9. Cf. *Bolchevick*, no. 4 on 'The Struggle on Two Fronts' which proscribes the use of clichés such as 'Weep for the loss of the fatherland and the break up of the home, for the decadence and extinction of the race' and 'Call for the restoration of the country and for the rebirth of the race of Dragons and Fairies'. Cited, P. Rousset, op. cit., p. 128.

10. Article in *La Lutte*, cited, D. Hemery, op. cit., p. 413.

11. The bureaucratic nature of these interventions can be seen in an article in *Cahiers du Bolchévisme*, 1 February 1932 (signed 'Hong The Cong'), which gives an ultra-centralist definition of Comintern discipline, arguing that Moscow can impose *tactics* on the national sections: 'All Comintern directives and decisions have the force of law for all communist comrades without exception. We simply have to *follow* them faithfully.' Cited, P. Rousset, op. cit., p. 230.

12. See for example Maurice Thorez's speech to the 9th Congress of the Parti Communiste Français (December 1937). Reprinted in J. Moneta, *Le PCF et la question coloniale*, Paris, 1971, pp. 130–31.

13. *Brève Histoire du Parti des travailleurs du Vietnam*, Commission d'histoire du PTCN, Hanoi, 1976, p. 23.

14. Cf. D. Hemery, 'Les Communistes vietnamiens et le Front Populaire (1936–1939)', *Critique communiste*, nos. 14–15, March–April 1977, p. 154.

15. Decision of the 6th Plenum of the Central Committee (November 1939), cited in *History of the August Revolution*, Hanoi, 1972, p. 14.

16. V. N. Giap, *Guerre du peuple, armée du peuple*, Paris, p. 116.

17. Nguyen Khac Vien, 'Confucianisme et marxisme au Vietnam', in *Tradition et révolution au Vietnam*, pp. 55–6.

18. Cf. the speech made by Giap in Hanoi on 7 March 1946, cited in P. Devillers, *Histoire du Vietnam de 1940 à 1952*, Paris, 1952, pp. 111–12, and P. Rousset, *Le Parti communiste vietnamien*, Paris, 1975, Chapter 4. It should be recalled that the CPV's position at this time was all the more difficult in that 20,000 Kuomintang troops were occupying the north of the country.

19. Cf. J. Lacouture and P. Devillers, *Vietnam: de la guerre française à la guerre américaine*, Paris, 1969, p. 332, and F. Joyaux, *La Chine et le règlement du premier conflit d'Indochine*, Geneva, 1954. Reprinted Presses Publications de la Sorbonne, Paris, 1979.

20. Ho Chi Minh, *Écrits (1920–1969)*, Hanoi, 1971, p. 372.

21. Reprinted in *Le Courrier du Vietnam*, no. 4 (nouvelle série), September 1972.

22. Le Duan, in Parti communiste du Vietnam, IVème Congrès national, *Documents*, Hanoi, 1977, p. 27.

23. Le Duan, op. cit., p. 137.

24. Parti communiste du Vietnam, Vème Congrès national, *Rapport politique du Comité central*, Hanoi, March 1982, p. 18 (mimeograph).

25. *Rapport politique du Comité central*, pp. 99–100, 132.

26. I cannot analyse the complexities of the Cambodian crisis here. I have published several articles on the subject elsewhere.

27. Le Duan, op. cit., p. 135.

28. On the history of Vietnam see Le Than Khoi, *Histoire du Vietnam*, Paris, 1982, and T. Hodgkin, *Vietnam: The Revolutionary Path*, New York, 1980. Hodgkin tries to situate the August Revolution of 1945 in the historical context of the constitution of the Vietnamese nation.

15. The Tragedy of Indian Communism[1]

K. Damodaran

Why do you think the CPI took such a long time to establish itself? What was its early activity and its relations with the nationalist movement: could it be that the infamous 'Third Period' of the Comintern also seriously disoriented Indian communists by isolating them at a critical phase from the mainstream of the nationalist movement?

My personal experience in this period was restricted to Kerala and I will concentrate on that, but of course the line of march throughout the country was essentially the same. I joined the CPI when it was illegal. It had been banned in 1934 after the Bombay Strike wave, which included a general strike of the textile industry. As a result even the distribution of party literature was extremely uneven and the question of organized internal discussion did not arise. But you must also understand that the CPI was an extremely small organization nationally in that period. In fact the CPI as a national political force only began to develop in 1935–6 after the worst excesses of the 'Third Period'. The politics of the Comintern certainly played a not unimportant part in disorienting the communist groups which existed regionally in the twenties and early thirties. The Comintern leaders completely underestimated the relative *autonomy* of the Indian bourgeoisie and its political instrument, the Indian Congress. They went through a stage of equating the nationalist movement and imperialism. Kuusinen, Stalin's spokesman on colonial questions, and many writers in the *Inprecor* went so far as to say that the Indian National Congress was a counter-revolutionary force in the struggle against imperialism and the Congress Socialists were branded as 'social fascists'. The attacks on nationalist leaders in the late twenties and thirties certainly were couched in an ultra-Left rhetoric and were parroted by the different communist groups which existed in India. However it is not sufficient simply to blame the Comintern: after all the Chinese party also suffered from the wrong advice of the Comintern, but they recovered and finally captured power.

So while not ignoring the importance of the subjective failures we have to look deeper and, when we do, we shall find that there was an objective basis for the existence of a strong and stable bourgeois democratic party like the Indian Congress. This was the development of an Indian bourgeoisie which was *not* a comprador bourgeoisie and which even in the heyday of the raj enjoyed a certain independence. Its interests clashed on many occasions with those of British imperialism. The Indian capitalists developed at an unusually rapid rate when Britain was tied down by inter-imperialist wars. The existence of this bourgeoisie side by side with a civil service and army that involved many Indians created the basis for the existence of a colonial state apparatus which succeeded in tying down the Congress to its structures and ensuring a smooth transition when the time for Independence came. So Indian communists confronted a unique economic and political structure which they never succeeded in analysing properly.

While the CPI was in fact properly established in 1934–5 its development was uneven. For instance the first communist group in Kerala was organized only in 1937 by five comrades including Namboodiripad, Krishna Pillai and myself. We decided that we should not openly call ourselves the Communist Party but win ourselves a base inside the Congress Socialists. I think that this was correct, but it did not happen nationally. Accordingly we disseminated communist literature inside the Congress Socialist Party, which itself worked inside the Congress, as an organized grouping. Our influence inside the Kerala Congress was not negligible: Namboodiripad, A. K. Gopalan, Krishna Pillai and, later, myself were all recognized leaders of the Kerala Congress and we held office on the leading committees. Utilizing our position in the Congress we organized trade unions, peasants' organizations, students' unions, and associations of progressive and anti-imperialist writers. We organized a regular Communist Party in Kerala only at the end of 1939. It was our mass work coupled with the fact that we were identified with the nationalist aspirations of the people which undoubtedly played a significant role in ensuring that Kerala became one of the important strongholds of post-Independence communism.

When were you first arrested as a communist?

In 1938. I was at that time a member of the party, but in the eyes of the masses was still regarded as a nationalist agitator. What brought about my arrest on this occasion was a speech I made to a conference of Youth Leaguers in Trivandrum. I had been asked to preside over the meeting and in my opening speech I mounted a diatribe against imperialism: I attacked British imperialism and the Maharajah of Travancore as embodying the oppression which was being meted out by British imperialism. The Right-wing leaders of the State Congress had been saying that the Maharajah was a great man and it was only his local satraps who were to blame and were misleading him. I attacked this absurd concept head-on and utilized the experiences of the French and Russian revolutions, observing that their method of dealing with the monarchy was rather more effective than that of the Congress leaders! I also explained to the meeting the necessity of involving the peasants and workers in the struggle and concluded with the slogan of 'Inqilab Zindabad' (Long Live Revolution) which was joyfully taken up by the whole meeting. That same day there were anti-imperialist demonstrations and clashes with the police in Trivandrum. The next morning I was naturally arrested, together with the Youth League leaders. We spent two or three months in prison and were then released. From then on prison became a regular part of my existence.

Could you briefly describe the impact of developments which were taking place in the Soviet Union on Indian communism? After all the period we are discussing was crucial: virtually the entire leadership of the Bolsheviks at the time of the Revolution were physically eliminated by Stalinist terror as the prelude to a bureaucratic dictatorship which established its total monopoly over all spheres of public life. What was the impact of all this on Indian communists?

As far as I am concerned I can speak mainly about Kerala. I was not part of the All-India party apparatus at that time and, as I have already explained, objective conditions – let alone subjective ones – did not permit horizontal contact with party members in other parts of the country. I joined the party just before the theses of the 7th Congress of the Comintern, the Dimitrov theses on the Popular Front strategy. It was after the 7th Congress that Stalin became well-known in India in the sense that he became the 'Great Leader'. In fact the theses did coincide – better late than never – with the need for us to have a united front with the Congress against the British. The sectarian ultra-Leftism of the 1929–34 period had isolated us and this was seen as an attempt to correct the mistakes. For us it was a step in the right direction. Not so much in Kerala, but in Bombay and Calcutta. After all in Kerala there was no Communist Party in the early thirties. When people ask me why the CPI became so strong in non-industrialized Kerala as compared to Bombay, I reply that the main reason is that there was no CPI in Kerala in the 1930–33 period and so it was possible to start anew. Most of the communist leaders in Kerala today were totally immersed in the Civil Disobedience movement launched by the Congress in 1930–32. It explains how they won the support of the masses and were able to shatter the Congress monopoly in a later phase.

But to answer your main question: you must understand that the communists in India were not seriously educated in Marxism. To give you one example: Lenin's theses on the colonial question were not known to Indian communists till the end of the fifties. The 7th Congress line of Anti-Imperialist United Front in India was considered not as a break from the past but a continuation of the 6th Congress line and was explained as a tactical change necessitated by the changes in the national and international situation. You may consider it strange that the disastrous colonial theses of the 6th Congress were translated into Malayalam and other Indian languages precisely in this period. But in practice the United Front was a break from the Left-sectarian line. The new line implemented by the party under the able leadership of P. C. Joshi helped us to advance rapidly. The CPI for the first time became a political force with considerable influence in the Congress, among the Congress Socialists and in the mass movements. The rival trade unions were united into a single All-India Trade Union Congress in which the CPI became the leading force. The All-India Kisan Sabha, the All-India Students' Federation and the All-India Progressive Writers' Association came into existence. The communists played an important role in uniting them and leading their struggles. National unity against imperialism, Left unity to counter the compromising and anti-struggle policies of the Right wing, socialist unity to strengthen Left unity, the CPI as the basis of socialist unity, mass organizations and mass struggles to build and strengthen the united anti-imperialist front – these were the watchwords and positive elements in the new line. This line certainly brought results and helped to build and strengthen an All-India Communist Party. The membership of the party increased from about 150 in 1934 to more than 3,000 in 1939 and its influence multiplied at an even more rapid rate. But these were also the years of Stalinism.

We were told that Stalin was the 'great teacher', the 'guiding star' who was building socialism in the USSR and the leader of world socialism. And being both new to communism and relatively unschooled in Marxism and Leninism I accepted what I was told. There is a tradition in Indian politics of political gurus enlightening the masses and this tradition suited Stalinism completely. Hence we could accept anything and everything that we were told by the party elders who themselves were dependent for their information exclusively on Moscow. This was the atmosphere in which I was brought up as a communist. However, there were some comrades who were extremely perturbed at the information on the massacres which was coming out of Moscow. Philip Spratt, one of the communists sent to help build the CPI from Britain, became so demoralized and disillusioned with Stalinism that he abandoned communism altogether and became a liberal humanist and towards the end of his life an anti-communist. He was an excellent comrade who played an invaluable role in helping us at an early stage. The Congress Left wing was also extremely critical of the purges taking place in Moscow and some of their leaders were extremely disgusted by the propaganda contained in the CPI front journal *National Front*, which depicted Trotsky as a poisonous cobra and an agent of fascism. Even Nehru, who was one of the first Congressmen who popularized the Russian Revolution and Soviet achievements, expressed his disapproval of the purges in 1938. But for us communists, in those days Trotskyism and fascism were the same. I must confess to you that I also believed that Bukharin, Zinoviev, Radek and other victims of Stalinist purges were enemies of socialism, wreckers and spies working in the interest of imperialism and fascism. In discussions with independent-minded socialists I defended Stalin vigorously. I think the main reason for this was that we identified ourselves completely with the Soviet Union, which was then under constant attack by British imperialists and by the Congress Right wing. Every strike was supposed to have been inspired by Moscow, every street demonstration was supposed to be led by agitators in the pay of Moscow. We defended the Soviet Union against these people, though, of course, completely uncritically. Hence, when the Soviet Union was attacked from the Left we used the same arguments against these critics as well. Looking back on that period I feel that all this was a big tragedy not just for us, but for the whole communist movement. Can you imagine: Trotsky had vehemently opposed fascism and had warned the German communists against the trap they were falling into and this same Trotsky was labelled by us and thousands of others as a fascist. We sincerely believed that in defending Stalinism we were defending the Russian Revolution. I remember writing articles defending Stalin in the Malayalam press in Kerala after Trotsky's assassination and utilizing that book *The Great Conspiracy* to get some factual material or what I genuinely believed to be the truth. The official history of the CPSU which was published at the end of the thirties reinforced my faith in Stalin. This book was first translated and published illegally in Malayalam in 1941 and soon became a text book of Marxism for our cadres. The study classes I conducted in jail for our comrades were very much coloured by Stalinism. In fact we identified Stalinism with Marxism-Leninism.

What was the first reaction of the CPI towards the war and in what circumstances did that change? One of your former comrades, the CPM leader A. K. Gopalan, argues in his book that the CPI became a mass party during the war. Is this correct?

The initial response of our party was to oppose the war and even before 1939 we were pressuring the Congress to step up the struggle against British imperialism. It was the Congress which hesitated immediately the war began. I remember at the Poona session of the All-India Congress Committee in 1940, I moved an amendment to the main resolution

moved by Gandhi, and was supported, incidentally, by Jawaharlal
Nehru. Opposing Gandhi's line I called for the start of a new mass
struggle against the British. This was the line of the CPI at that stage.
Soon after that I was arrested and remained in prison till the end of the
war. It is necessary to explain why I was kept in prison when most other
communists were released to implement the 'People's War' policy.
Immediately on the outbreak of war, and in the year that followed,
communists had been arrested in large numbers. In prison controversies
started on whether or not our line was correct. Then the Soviet Union was
invaded by the Nazi armies. Our controversies became ever more heated.
Professor K. B. Krishna who was with us in jail wrote a set of theses
developing the 'People's War' line and advocating that now everything
had changed and that communists should drop their anti-imperialist
activities and their opposition to war. I wrote a set of counter-theses
arguing that while the existence of the Soviet Union was vital, nonetheless
the best way to help the Russian comrades was *not* by ceasing all
anti-imperialist activity, but on the contrary by stepping it up. Our enemy
remained British imperialism. The majority of communists inside prison
supported my line and only a tiny minority was in favour of the 'People's
War' theses. Then some months later we heard that the British party had
changed its line and that Moscow was in favour of the change. Outside
the jail, the party secretary P. C. Joshi, who was initially one of the
strongest opponents of the 'People's War' line, had to change his line and
start using his oratorical skills to convince party members, and also the
masses, of the importance of helping the war effort. After the change of
line most of the pro-war communists were released, but some, including
myself, were kept in prison. British intelligence knew perfectly well who
to release and who to keep inside.

*It seems the atmosphere in jail, as far as discussion and debates within
the CP were concerned, was considerably more democratic than it was
outside. From what you have said it would appear that all CP members,
regardless of hierarchy, were involved in these discussions and that on
some subjects there were votes taken.*

Yes, that is true, but the debate inside prison did have its limits. As long
as the discussion did not directly counter the party line it took place. For
instance, even on the war issue, when a circular from the party leadership
arrived to our party Jail Committee instructing us to carry out the
pro-war line I automatically dropped my positions and was mocked by
the others who said 'You considered yourself one of the party theoreticians, but you were wrong!' This incident typifies how we were trained
as communists. I made a self-criticism and admitted I was wrong. I had to
do so because the party was always right, but doubts persisted and in later

years I was reassured that I had been correct. Today even the leaders of both the CPI and the CPM are forced to admit that 'some mistakes were made'. That phrase is meant to explain everything. However, in spite of the self-criticism the British did not release me from prison. It is possible that their intelligence services decided that my self-criticism was far too shallow. The official charge-sheet handed to me in prison gave as one reason for my continued detention the fact that I had opposed the line of the 'People's War'. This was written black on white on my charge-sheet! Of course the CP leadership made numerous representations to the British authorities demanding our release, but to no avail. I was not released until October 1945.

So when the Congress launched the 'Quit India' movement in August 1942, you were still in prison. Was there much resentment towards the CPI on the part of the hordes of Congress volunteers and leaders who filled the jails in the wake of that movement?

There is a view developed by some of the apologists for the 'People's War' line which argues that the CPI gained a lot of support as a consequence of 'swimming against the stream'. I do not subscribe to this view. Of course the party took advantage of legality granted to it by British imperialism to gain new members and increase its trade-union strength, but the point is that it was swimming against the stream of the mass movement and was to all intents and purposes considered an ally of British imperialism. It became respectable to be a communist. Many young communists joined the British army to go and 'defend the Soviet Union' in Italy and North Africa. Some of them rapidly shed their 'communism' and stayed in the army even after the war – and not to do clandestine work! It is true that the membership of the party increased from about 4,500 in July 1942 to well over 15,500 in May 1943 at the time of the 1st Party Congress. Membership of the mass organizations also increased. But most of these new members had no experience of any militant mass struggle or police repression but only the peaceful campaigns conducted by the party to 'grow more food', 'increase production', 'release national leaders', 'form a national government' and 'defend the motherland' from the Japanese invasion which never came. Strikes were denounced as sabotage. The party members also conducted social welfare operations to save the victims of the Bengal Famine of 1943. They organized medical aid for the victims of the smallpox and cholera epidemics. Of course, even this social work paid dividends in India, where there is a terrible disregard for loss of life. But we failed in our basic task, namely, to explain the roots of all the problems which confronted the masses.

On the other side, the growth of the Congress and its influence after the

'Quit India' struggle of August 1942 was phenomenal. Millions of men and women, especially the youth, were attracted and radicalized by the struggle, which was considered as a revolution against imperialism. True, we campaigned for the release of the arrested Congress leaders and the formation of a provisional national government to conduct the People's War. But at the same time we branded the Congress Socialists, Bose's followers and other radicals who braved arrests and police repression as fifth columnists and saboteurs. We appealed to Gandhi and other Congress leaders to condemn the violence indulged in by these people. After their release not only Nehru but also the apostles of non-violence, instead of condemning them, praised them as real anti-imperialist patriots – Subhas Bose, Jayaprakash Narain, Aruna Asaf Ali and even obscure figures like Colonel Lakshmi emerged as national heroes and heroines.

In reality the CPI was isolated from the mainstream of the nationalist movement for the second time within a decade. In my view the party's policy virtually delivered the entire anti-imperialist movement to the Congress and the Indian bourgeoisie on a platter. At the time, if the CPI had adopted a correct position the possibility existed of winning over a sizeable and influential section of the Congress to communism. In the 1936–42 period Jawaharlal Nehru himself went through his most radical phase and there were numerous Leftward-moving currents (such as the Congress Socialists and Subhas Bose's followers) within the Congress. On my release from prison I experienced the wrath of the Left-wing nationalists who used to chant 'Down with supporters of British imperialism' at our meetings. So swimming against the stream when the stream was flowing in the right direction resulted in drowning the possibility of genuine independence and a socialist transformation. We were outmanoeuvred and outflanked by the Indian bourgeoisie.

If the party recovered some ground it was due largely to the militant strike wave which developed immediately after the Second World War in the 1946–7 period and into which we threw ourselves, though our political line was still faulty. We supported, for example, the creation of the confessional state of Pakistan. In Bombay it was the CPI which mobilized support for the naval mutineers of 1946 only to find that our political line of supporting Congress–Muslim League unity hampered any real solidarity as the naval mutiny was broken not so much by the British as by the Congress and League leaders. They united temporarily to confront this new threat on their left flank which was uncomfortably similar to some of the events of the Russian Revolution. A number of us, including myself, were arrested once again for fomenting class struggles and we were released only on 13 August 1947, a bare twenty-four hours before Independence.

What was the logic behind the notorious Ranadive theses which drove the CPI on an ultra-Left trajectory in the period after Independence?

I think we have to carefully distinguish a number of interrelated factors. There is no doubt that the theses drafted by Ranadive and adopted by the 2nd Congress in Calcutta in 1948 were ultra-Left, but the criticism made of them in the late fifties and even today by many communists and Leftist Congressmen have a somewhat hollow ring as they are made from within a reformist problematic.

After the transfer of power there was an anticipatory outbreak of struggles in many parts of the country: these struggles had a dual nature. They both celebrated the transfer of power *to the Congress* and also expected the Congress to carry out all its radical promises. Similar struggles had greeted the election of provincial Congress governments in 1937 while the British were still in India. What these struggles tell us is that there is a link between important victories within the arena of bourgeois politics and the extra-parliamentary mass movement. There was also the struggle in Telengana (Hyderabad) which had begun before Independence and which was being waged against the Nizam of Hyderabad, his administration and their sponsored landlords in the countryside around Hyderabad. Even here the intervention of the Indian army changed the situation as it effectively removed the Nizam and at the same time blocked the development of the Left.

The post-Independence upsurge involved workers, peasants, students and teachers. Many Left-wing Congress supporters participated in these struggles for more trade-union rights, for the abolition of landlordism and for more freedoms; their character was essentially one of pressuring the Congress to move Left. If the CPI had developed a correct strategy based on an analysis of Indian conditions in the preceding years, it would have been able to play a vital role in these struggles, giving them a lead. In that eventuality the Ranadive theses would have been misplaced but would have had a greater resonance. However, given the twists and turns of the CPI, the ultra-Leftism of the 1948 Congress proved to be disastrous. The masses were not prepared to overthrow the Nehru government. On the contrary large sections of them identified with it, and the CPI slogan: 'This Independence is a Fake Independence' merely succeeded in isolating the party. The armed struggle which was launched together with this slogan led to the deaths of many cadres and imprisonment and torture of others throughout the sub-continent. The analysis of the Nehru government as a comprador stooge government of imperialism was another mistake, as it implied that there was no difference between the colonial British administration and the post-colonial Nehru government. As is now commonly accepted by Marxists, the Indian ruling class was never a comprador class in the real sense of the word. It enjoyed a relative autonomy even during the colonial occupation. To argue that it was a comprador class after Independence was not only ultra-Left in the sense that it underpinned a wrong strategic line, it also demonstrated the theoretical inadequacy of Indian communism. Many of the themes of that period were taken up again in the late sixties by the Maoist rebels in Naxalbari and other parts of India and we know with what disastrous consequences. Apart from the fact that hundreds of young people were killed, thousands tortured and the movement went from setback to setback, we still have its legacy in the shape of thousands of political prisoners imprisoned by the Indian ruling class. The tragedy here being that the prisoners are virtually bereft of any mass support.

To return to 1948: a whole number of communists, including myself, were arrested once again and it was in prison that a number of debates on the Ranadive theses were started. There was a great deal of dissatisfaction with the new line. The trade-union comrades were becoming increasingly hostile to the party leadership. The party leadership had issued a call for a national railway strike which had completely flopped. It had only succeeded in identifying the communist supporters in the railway union and many of them were arrested. Then the party leaders said that the communists who were the leaders of the union were revisionists and reformists and that is why the railway strike did not take place. But even this debate rapidly evolved in a particular fashion. There was no effort whatsoever to analyse the conditions which existed in India. It became a session of 'Stalin said . . .' to which the opponents in the discussion would respond 'But Mao said the opposite . . .' So the debate itself was largely sterile. Accordingly the result of all these disputes was not to be decided by the party Congress after a discussion throughout the party and the preparation of a balance sheet of the Ranadive line. In the best traditions of Stalinism, the party leadership decided to send a delegation to Moscow to meet Stalin. Four leaders were selected for this unique honour: Ajoy Ghosh, Rajeshwar Rao, S. A. Dange and Basava Punniah. Ranadive was eclipsed. They returned with a new tactical line and a new draft programme which were adopted by a special conference of the party held in Calcutta in October 1951. The new line formulated under the direct guidance of Stalin, Molotov and Suslov declared that the Congress government was installed by the consent of the British imperialists, that the colonial set-up still prevailed in India, the imperialists now covered their rule by the mantle of the Congress government which was completely subservient to imperialism, and that therefore the immediate task of the Communist Party was to overthrow the Indian State and to replace it by a People's Democratic State. Thus four years after the transfer of power, Stalin and other leaders of the Soviet Union considered India as a colonial country under British imperialism. Not surprisingly the party conference approved the new line, especially because it had the blessings of the 'greatest Marxist-Leninist and the leader of world revolution'. This was the thinking of the majority of our comrades at least until 1956. I, too, subscribed to this absurd view for some time, but soon doubts arose and I began to argue that India was politically free.

In practice, however, there was a new development. Along with the adoption of the new programme in 1951 the party decided to participate in the General Election which was fast approaching. While on its own this was correct, the policies adopted by the party after the elections were a more revealing indication of the turn which had been made. From ultra-Leftism the party had now embarked on a course which can only be categorized as parliamentary cretinism. The Election Manifesto as well as the new programme of 1951 stated that socialism was not the immediate aim of the party as India was still a backward colonial country. The immediate task was the replacement of the anti-democratic and anti-popular Nehru government by a government of People's Democracy, on the basis of a coalition of all anti-imperialists and anti-feudal parties and forces. The word 'class' was replaced by the word 'party' and the word 'state' was replaced by the word 'government'. They were not merely semantic changes. From 1948–51 the party had stated that its aim was the setting-up of a People's Democratic *State*, which was the starting point of the dictatorship of the proletariat. Leaving aside the ambiguities and evasions contained in the formula of 'People's Democracy', the aim was nonetheless clear. The 3rd Congress of the party at Madurai stressed that the central task of the party was the struggle to replace the Congress government with a 'People's Government of Democratic Unity'. And here quite clearly 'people's democracy' was not a synonym for dictatorship of the proletariat. It was conceived as an alliance of the CPI and the anti-Congress 'democratic' parties. The aim of the party became to acquire parliamentary majority and collect enough allies to form governments. In its different guises this remains the policy of the CPI and the CPI(M).

Could you explain why, despite all its sectarian mistakes, the CPI did so well in the 1951 general election? It had suffered repression, it was isolated from the anti-imperialist forces, it had made only a last-minute decision, obviously correct, to participate in the elections.

I think we were all surprised by the election results. We got about twenty-six or twenty-seven seats in parliament, became the largest party after the Congress and the main focus of opposition to the government. In some cases our candidates got more votes than even Nehru and overnight a whole number of comrades who had only recently been underground or in prison became members of parliament or of provincial assemblies. I think the main reason for this success was not that the people who voted for us thought that our sectarian line was correct. The major factor was that the party cadres were embedded in the mass movement. They worked in the trade unions and the peasants' organizations and many of them were respected for their honesty and courage. Thus the vote for the CPI in the 1951 election was a straightforward class vote and it revealed the potentialities which existed. The fact that these were not realized is shown on one level in the representation of the party inside parliament today, which is roughly the same as in 1951.

After the turn towards parliamentarianism was there any discussion within the party on what extra-parliamentary tactics should be adopted? Surely it would be difficult simply to switch off the involvement of party members in the mass struggles.

Yes, there were discussions on party committees. The Soviet Union had, after the Korean War, embarked once again on a policy of peace and collaboration with capitalist powers, which Khrushchev was to later theorize as 'peaceful coexistence'. Both the Soviet Union and the People's Republic of China began to praise the government of India for its 'progressive' policies, especially its foreign policy based on non-alignment. During their visits to India, Khrushchev and Chou En-lai attracted huge crowds. Nehru became one of the architects of the 'Bandung Spirit'. It was against this background that the debate in our party continued. Is India really free or still subservient to British imperialism? Who do we ally ourselves with in the political arena? I remember the debates we had in the Malabar Provincial Committee of the CPI of which I was the secretary, and in the pre-Congress discussion in the Malabar Conference of the party. Some wanted a Congress–communist coalition government, others argued for an anti-Congress front and concentrated their fire on the INTUC (Indian National Trade Union Congress) which was under the leadership of the Congress. Both conceived of the problem as essentially one of winning elections. What these comrades did not realize was that by attempting to unite the class for struggle against its oppressors we would at the same time have weakened the Congress electorally. I, therefore, disagreed with both these lines. My position at that time was for the CPI to have, first of all, a mass line for the struggles ahead. We should conceive of the struggle basically as one between classes and not parties. Accordingly we should attempt united actions between the AITUC and the INTUC and other trade unions against the capitalists with the aim of uniting the working class and other mass organizations which had been disrupted in the immediate post-war period. I argued that on the basis of class unity we should attempt to unite all progressive sections of the people, including Congress supporters, for the implementation. of land reforms, for workers' rights, for more democratic liberties, for a firm anti-imperialist foreign policy, etc. and, through these struggles, wean away the masses from bourgeois influence and build the hegemony of the working class. The political resolution moved by me on the above basis was passed by a majority in the Malabar Party Conference.

The 4th Congress of the party was held in 1956 at Palghat in Kerala. The emphasis of the majority was on an anti-Congress front. This well suited their theory that the Indian bourgeoisie was subservient to British finance capital. P. C. Joshi, Bhawani Sen, myself and a few others actually distributed an alternative resolution to the official one which Joshi moved on our behalf. Our resolution pointed out that the Congress government was not subservient to imperialism although it occasionally made compromises, that it served primarily the sectional interests of the bourgeoisie and not of the common people, that all the acute problems that plagued our people arose because of the bourgeois leadership of the country and that therefore the real remedy lay in establishing proletarian leadership in completing the bourgeois democratic revolution. It called upon the different trade unions like the AITUC, INTUC, HMS and UTOC to merge themselves into a single, united trade-union centre. It called for the united mass organizations to intervene to mould the Second Five-Year Plan in their own and the country's true interests. It stressed the need of building a United National Democratic Front as a powerful mass movement to fuse together the masses both within the Congress and outside through struggles against the remnants of imperialism and feudalism and against the reactionary policies of the Right wing. We thought that such a united democratic front was the means to build the hegemony of the proletariat. Our resolution was defeated but one-fourth of the delegates supported us. Some of the amendments moved on our behalf were incorporated into the official resolution with the result that it was later interpreted in different ways.

What was the direct impact of the 20th Party Congress of the CPSU at the CPI Congress? Was it discussed at all?

Yes, certainly. A resolution was submitted to our Congress on the changes in the Soviet Union. It approved the general drift of Khrushchev's speech, but demanded more discussion on the subjects he had raised. There was, however, not a full discussion on this either at the Party Congress or after. The reason for insisting on further discussion was because most comrades were not convinced of the correctness of the attack on Stalin. I myself began to rethink radically a whole number of questions after 1956. I wanted to defend Khrushchev for his attack on

Stalin even though I had been a staunch Stalinist up till that time. For two or three nights after the 20th Party Congress I could not sleep. A man we had been taught to worship, the idol of our world movement, had been attacked and by his own former comrades. Even after reading Khrushchev's secret report I remained in a state of shell shock; I could not believe it for some time, but after re-reading and thinking I came to the conclusion that Khrushchev was correct and I began to defend him against the supporters of Stalin. It was for Khrushchev's attack on Stalin that a number of comrades began attacking him as a revisionist, because his other theses were not too different to Stalin's own practice.

It was at the 1956 Party Congress that I was elected to the highest body of the party, its National Council. Before that I had worked exclusively at the provincial level and concentrated on building the party in Kerala.

Not long after your 4th Party Congress, the CPI won a tremendous victory in the provincial elections in Kerala, emerging as the largest party in the legislature. Its leader E. M. S. Namboodiripad formed the first ever communist government in India. The election clearly showed that the party had mass support in the province and it also struck a blow against the dominant Cold War ideology of the time. However, what in your view was the real impact of this victory both on the mass movement and on the future evolution of the CPI?

Soon after the formation of the communist government, there was a heated discussion within the leadership of the Kerala CP on the nature of the new government. The dominant view, held by the central leaders including Namboodiripad, was that the workers had captured power in Kerala by peaceful means, by winning a majority in the elections, and that Kerala would become the best example of the peaceful road to socialism. It was the first time that this had happened anywhere in the world and it showed the way to the future for comrades throughout the world. This was the initial reaction of the leadership.

I did not agree with this view. I argued that the state remained a capitalist state despite the communist victory and that it would be wrong to spread illusions to the contrary. I was supported by a small number of comrades. Ajoy Ghosh, the party secretary, was sent from Delhi to discuss with the Kerala leadership to try and solve the dispute. Both views were put to him. I spoke for the minority and argued that we were exercising governmental power in a province, but that the state both provincially and nationally remained capitalist and that the main problem which confronted us was how to use this situation in order to strengthen the party and the mass movement. In other words the working class had not come to power. E.M.S. put forward the majority view and after he had finished Ajoy Ghosh waved his finger at me and asked: 'You mean to say that E.M.S. Namboodiripad is bourgeois? Is he not a representative of the working class?' and much else along the same lines. Needless to say that was not what I had meant. The question was whether the state was bourgeois or not. Namboodiripad was only the Chief Minister of a provincial government. Ghosh backed the majority and that was that. I held my views, but all opposition ceased. It was only after the Kerala government had been dismissed that Namboodiripad wrote an article in *Communist*, which was then the theoretical organ of the Kerala unit of the CPI, in which he argued that the state had not been a workers' state. If this wisdom had dawned on him earlier it is possible that the situation would have been entirely different, as the party would have given primacy to the extra-parliamentary mass struggle which had swept it to power. But Kerala left within the CPI leaders an overwhelming desire to win power and form ministries through electoral means. We can still see it in both the segments of what used to be the CPI. Alliances are made not on the basis of principle, but to get government office.

The impact of the victory on the masses was tremendous. Immediately after the victory the workers and poor peasants, in the main, were jubilant. They felt very deeply that the new government would satisfy their demands. There was a tremendous feeling of pride and strength in the working class. I remember hearing poor, illiterate workers telling policemen on the streets: 'Now you daren't attack us because our government is in power. Namboodiripad is our leader. We are ruling.' This was not an uncommon view. The reserves of good will which existed for the government were considerable. Among the poor peasants, sections of the students and teachers there was also a feeling of joy, which increased when they saw how discomfiting the victory was for the landlords, the capitalists and for reactionaries in general. In the first weeks after the election the CP ministers made very radical speeches, constantly stressing their support for the struggle of the workers.

But these promises were in the main restricted to speeches. Namboodiripad and his ministers discovered fairly quickly that the civil service was a powerful entity and that the Chief Secretary, the top civil servant in the province, was functioning on orders from the Centre and not from the provincial Chief Minister. The same went for the police and furthermore no laws could be passed without the sanction of the Centre. So even as far as inaugurating a number of *reforms* was concerned the CP ministry found itself powerless. As it had no other real perspectives it found itself in a blind alley. Nothing radically new happened and after a while the novelty of having a communist government began to wear off. In some cases jubilation turned to passivity and in others to open and bitter disillusionment.

An important test for the new government arose a few months after it had been elected. Workers in a factory near Quilon, a town close to the capital city of Trivandrum, went on strike. The union in that factory was under the leadership of the RSP (Revolutionary Socialist Party). The strike was not against the government, but against the employer in that particular factory. It was a typical trade-union struggle. I remember vividly how the situation developed. We were sitting at a meeting of the State Council of the CPI (which consisted of about sixty comrades) when news was brought to us that three workers on strike had been shot dead by the police. We were stunned. Workers had been shot dead by the police while the communists were in office. The immediate response of *all* the comrades present was to condemn the firing, institute an immediate inquiry, give compensation to the bereaved families, publicly apologize to the workers on strike and give a public assurance that such a thing would never happen again while we were in government. This was our instinctive class response. But a discussion started which lasted for two hours and at the end of it the decisions taken were completely different to our initial response. In my view the whole business was unjustifiable, but it is necessary to understand the context of the time.

The reactionary groups and parties had started a campaign against us under the demagogic slogan of 'Join the Liberation Struggle Against Communist Rule'. They had begun to exploit our weaknesses. The movement was spearheaded by the Roman Catholic priests (as you know Kerala has a significant Catholic population) and the Nair Communalists. But all those opposed to the CPI joined them including the Right and Left social democrats (the Socialist Party and the RSP) and the movement was beginning to gather mass support. It was in this context that the police firing took place. The logic of the comrades who advocated changing the initial position on the firing went something like this: if we attack the police, there will be a serious decline in their morale; if there is a serious decline in their morale the anti-communist movement will be strengthened; if the anti-communist movement is strengthened our government will be overthrown; if our government is overthrown it will be a tremendous blow against the communist movement. The final resolution passed by the party defended the police action. It was then decided that someone must go to the spot to explain our point of view, attack the RSP and defend the police action. I was supposed to be one of the party's effective Malayalam orators and I was asked to go and speak on behalf of the Kerala CP. My response was to refuse and maintain that I had been unable to digest the decision taken by the Council and therefore I could not defend it. I was then formally instructed by the party leadership to go and defend the party. I went. I spoke for about an hour and a half and it was pure demagogy. I blamed the deaths of the three workers on the irresponsibility of the RSP and asked them to publicly explain why they had led these workers to be shot. I made vicious attacks on the strike leaders. That night when I returned home I really felt sick inside. I could not sleep. I kept thinking that I should have refused to defend the party and I felt that I was going mad. I shouted at my wife. Instead of having shouted and hurled abuse at the party leaders, who had put me in such situation, I took it out on my wife. The next day I was asked to speak at three different places and make the same speech. This time I refused pointblank and my refusal was accepted.

While the firing obviously had a traumatic effect on a number of party members such as yourself, did it also have a lasting effect on the working class?

Obviously it weakened the government and dented its mass support, but a significant section of our supporters remained solid despite the Quilon incidents. Of course the reactionaries increased their support, but, even at that stage, if the CPI leaders had understood the dialectical interrelationship between parliamentary and mass work and understood that the former must always be subordinated to the needs of the struggle we would have maintained our strength and probably increased it ten-fold. In the process we would have been dismissed from office, as we were in any case, but we would have been in an immeasurably stronger situation and we could have educated the masses in the limitations of bourgeois democracy. Real revolutionary consciousness could have been developed. None of this was done and at the same time Namboodiripad made speeches predicting a civil war, which flowed logically from his view that the working class had taken the power. These speeches were then used by the Congress leadership to further attack and weaken the government. It soon became obvious from press reports and statements by Congress leaders that the Centre was considering the imposition of President's Rule and the dissolution of the government. The growth of the reactionary-led mass movement within Kerala was also reaching its peak. It soon became difficult for CP leaders to go anywhere without being stoned and this included myself. It was at this time that Nehru decided to visit Kerala and see the situation for himself. He was besieged by petitioners demanding the immediate dismissal of the government. Of course he also met us. He had a number of separate meetings with the government ministers and a delegation of the state committee of the CP. I was one of the members of this delegation. I remember in his discussions with us the first question he asked us was: 'How did you manage to so wonderfully isolate yourself from the people in such a short space of time?' He then suggested that the communist government could continue on the condition that there would be new elections in order to let the electorate decide. The state committee convened a special session to discuss Nehru's proposal and on Namboodiripad's insistence decided to reject the proposal. We were prepared to accept new elections only in the event that they were held in all the other provinces! I felt even then that it was a wrong decision. We should have accepted Nehru's proposal, won ourselves a breathing space and then entered into battle with the opposition, which in any case was a motley collection of reactionaries, bandwagon opportunists and social democrats. Secondly the elections would have been held with the communist government in office which would have neutralized if not completely impeded the intervention against us by the state apparatus: the use of civil servants and the police. In any case we refused and in 1959 the government was dismissed. But in the next election, held a year and a half later, we increased our share of the popular vote though we got fewer seats. So while we were defeated electorally it was not a real defeat in the eyes of the masses. And this despite all our errors and mistakes.

The electoral victory in Kerala undoubtedly made the CPI into a national force; its prestige increased ten-fold and communist enthusiasts answering the stale headlines of the bourgeois commentators replied: 'After Nehru, Namboodiripad!' The importance of Kerala in that sense was the feeling that Congress could be defeated and that an alternative existed, namely, the Communist Party of India. This was not an unimportant factor given the international situation. Of course even within the CPI there were criticisms of the way in which the E.M.S ministry had condoned the killing of workers. The state committee of the West Bengal CPI wrote a letter criticizing the Kerala party. But despite all this Namboodiripad drew larger crowds than any other CPI leader and had become a national figure in his own right as the leader of the successful Kerala CPI. The CP Congress in Amritsar in 1958 also treated him as a hero and announced that power could be taken electorally, a view which was facilitated by the positions being developed by the Soviet party. There were some amendments to the main resolution and a few comrades expressed doubts, but by and large there was a consensus. The Amritsar line was to be applied nationally.

Was there never a real discussion within the leadership, even after 1959, of the problems posed on a strategic level by electoral victories won by parties pledged to some form of socialist transformation. Surely one of the key weaknesses of the CPI in Kerala, the CPM in West Bengal and, later, the Popular Unity in Chile was that there was no understanding of the necessity of helping to stimulate and create organs of popular power of a Soviet type which could organize the masses independently of the bourgeois state and could be utilized to challenge the state when the need arose. This whole dimension has been absent from the strategy of the Communist Parties for many decades.

These problems you mention are very important and vital ones, but I am sorry to say that they did not enter into the discussions which took place. One of the results of Stalinism has been precisely that the key importance of organizing the masses through their own organs of power, such as soviets, has disappeared. The party has been seen as the sole representative of the masses.

As for my own political development, I continued to develop doubts after 1956. The question of Stalin was resolved for me by Khrushchev's speech, but on international issues I was to remain totally confused. For instance on Hungary my position was completely orthodox. I even wrote a pamphlet called 'What Happened in Hungary' to answer the widespread attacks on the Soviet Union in every bourgeois newspaper. So, in spite of 1956, the change in my thinking was gradual. I felt fairly regularly the need to read more, but then the material available to one at that time in India was also very limited. I thought in 1956 that I had broken with Stalinism, but looking back it is obvious that this was not the case. The Amritsar line, the Kerala government, all strengthened my doubts, but that is the level on which matters remained: personal doubts, many of which were not expressed even internally within the party. I am convinced that this must have been the case with many a communist militant in those days. But there was no revolutionary alternative to the line of the CPI.

A further change took place in 1958 when I had the opportunity to visit the Soviet Union. I visited Tashkent in 1958 as a member of the Indian Writers' Delegation to attend an Afro-Asian writers' conference. The Chinese delegates were also present and were quite open about explaining their difference with the Soviet Union. But I also had an opportunity to see the Soviet Union and while the tremendous advances made cannot be denied, there was another side which made me uneasy. In Moscow there was a special reception for the Indian delegates which was attended by Khrushchev. During this there was a cultural show and to my surprise I discovered that the empty chair next to me had been taken by Khrushchev. So I used this opportunity to discuss with him and attempt to clear my doubts. At that time you may recall the Pasternak case had excited a great deal of attention. So I asked Khrushchev how he justified the treatment of Pasternak. How was it possible that, fifty years after the Revolution, the Soviet government still felt threatened by a novel written by Pasternak? I explained that as a writer I could not justify the treatment meted out to him even though, as a Marxist, I disagreed with his political line. I explained to him that in a country like India where many anti-imperialists had been sentenced to prison for their writings including poems and short stories, it was impossible to justify and genuinely defend the Soviet party on the Pasternak issue. Khrushchev denied all responsibility for the episode and claimed that it was done by the Writers' Union and suggested that I discuss the matter with them. It was obvious that he was not anxious to discuss the issue. We then discussed the problem of drinking in the Soviet Union and I asked if he had considered prohibition. He replied that they had, but if there was prohibition then immediately illegal distilleries would begin to spring up and it would create graver problems. I responded by suggesting that similarly if they continued to ban books illegal distilleries of books would spring up and could also create problems. Extremely irritated by now he suggested that we concentrate on the ballet! I began to understand the limits of 'destalinization'. Attempts to discuss Yugoslavia and China were also unsuccessful. Discussions with the officials of the Writers' Union were more vigorous, but equally disappointing. As a result my disillusionment began to deepen.

Did you visit any other countries apart from the Soviet Union? Did you, for instance, have an opportunity to visit the People's Republic of China, where the revolution was more recent and in one sense more relevant to the problems confronting India?

After my trip to the Soviet Union I got more opportunities to travel outside and discuss with foreign comrades. This was very vital for my political evolution. For example, in 1960 I attended the 3rd Congress of the Vietnamese Workers' Party in Hanoi. Harekrishan Konar and myself were the fraternal delegates from the Indian party. I gave the fraternal greetings from Indian communists to the Congress and afterwards discussed the situation with numerous comrades from different countries. It was a very exciting period. The NLF was about to be formed in the South and the Sino-Soviet split was beginning to dominate communist gatherings. The Soviet delegation invited us to dinner to explain their views, with which we were in any case familiar. The discussion was continued the next day as both Konar and I subjected the Russians to some extremely critical questioning. The positive feature of the early period of the Sino-Soviet dispute was that it allowed the possibility of debate and discussion on fundamentals inside the communist movement for the first time since the twenties.

The Chinese delegation invited us to go to Peking for a lengthy discussion. We were flown to Canton and from there in a special plane to Peking. We spent a total of four days in the Chinese capital including a five and a half-hour session with Chou En-lai and other party leaders. The main item of discussion was the Sino-Indian border dispute. An hour was spent with the most intricate details relating to old maps, border treaties and the like to establish China's claim to the border lands. I stated my views quite openly. I said to the Chinese comrades: 'Legally, geographically, historically you may be correct. The question which concerns me is what political purpose does this dispute over uninhabited territory serve? You have come to an agreement with Pakistan and you have given up some land. Why not do the same with India? It will prevent the reactionaries from whipping up anti-Chinese chauvinism and it will strengthen the Left movement in India. We will be able to demonstrate the superiority of the method by which socialist states settle border disputes. We could utilize this to strengthen the bond between the Chinese Revolution and the Indian masses.' I explained that this had been Lenin's attitude when dealing with bourgeois governments such as Finland or even pre-capitalist monarchies such as Afghanistan. By doing so Lenin strengthened the Russian Revolution and its appeal to the broad masses. Immediately Chou said, 'Lenin did the correct thing.' But he explained it in terms of the Soviet state's isolation and the non-existence of a 'socialist camp'. I responded by arguing that while I did not have the texts on me there was considerable evidence to show that Lenin's motives were in reality to develop friendly relations with the peoples of these countries and not to allow the ruling classes to paint the Soviet Union as a big power gobbling up their countries. Finally Chou said that he could not agree and that we should agree to disagree on this point. I had an extremely soft spot for the Chinese comrades and their revolution so I didn't want to leave matters there. I asked Chou: 'Is there any danger of the US imperialists attacking you through these disputed border territories?' He replied in the negative and said the threat was from the Nehru government and not from the Americans in this instance. The next point of discussion was on the Sino-Soviet dispute.

Here Chou stressed the betrayal they had felt when the Soviet Union, because of political disagreements, had withdrawn their technicians from China overnight. He was extremely bitter about this and complained that they had even taken the blueprints away! I felt that the Russians had been completely wrong, but I did not speak my mind as I did not want to take sides between the two giants. I returned from the discussion fairly depressed with what the Soviet Union had done, but I was not satisfied with Chou's answers on the border question. I couldn't help feeling there was a trace of chauvinism in his attitudes. Konar was much more sympathetic to the Chinese and on his return to India he organized a number of study circles to explain their views.

What was the attitude of the Vietnamese comrades in those days?

The position of the Vietnamese then was what it remains today. They saw in the dispute then the seeds of further and growing discord which they felt could only aid imperialism. On that level they were not so wrong and the attitude of both China and the Soviet Union towards the Vietnamese struggle was not as it should have been. Before I left for Peking we had a lengthy discussion with Ho Chi Minh in the course of which we discussed Vietnam, India and the Sino-Soviet dispute. On the last question he told us that he agreed neither with China nor the Soviet Union and felt that their quarrels were reaching a stage where they could harm the working-class movement internationally. He was extremely anxious and apprehensive and he suggested that nothing should be done to exacerbate the conflict. I asked why the Vietnamese did not publish their positions in their press as it could be a useful way of keeping the movement united, but he replied that they had decided not to interfere in the dispute at all. He made a few jokes about the Third World War theses and said that Vietnam was a small country and even if a few people survived in China after the war there would be no one left in Vietnam, so from pure self-interest they could not support the theses. But all this was said in a semi-ironic vein. I must confess that I found him the most cultured and charming of all the communist leaders I have met. He impressed me a great deal by speaking in six languages to welcome the delegations to Vietnam: Chinese, Russian, Vietnamese, French, English and Spanish.

He gave a characteristic reply when I asked him how in his view the Vietnamese party, which in the thirties was not much bigger than the Indian party, had succeeded whereas we had failed. He replied: 'There you had Mahatma Gandhi, here I am the Mahatma Gandhi!' He then went on to explain how they had utilized the anti-imperialist struggle to build their hegemony over the masses. They had become the leading force in the anti-imperialist struggle and moved on to socialism. The clear implication was that in India it was Gandhi and the Congress who had kept control and that the CPI was at fault. He also explained as did other Vietnamese leaders the endemic weaknesses of the Vietnamese bourgeoisie, which of course contrasted very vividly with the strength of the Indian bourgeoisie.

It was trips abroad which undoubtedly opened my mind, even though in the beginning these trips were mainly to the Soviet Union and other non-capitalist countries. I remember visiting the Soviet Union again in 1962 for health reasons. While in prison during 1940–45 I had managed to learn a bit of Russian, enough to read *Pravda*, albeit at a snail's pace. The period I was in Moscow coincided with some anniversary commemorating Napoleon's failure to take Moscow and his subsequent retreat. The very fact that a Tsarist victory was being celebrated was odd enough in itself, but what compounded the error in my view was the lengthy diatribe against Napoleon in the pages of *Pravda*. The nationalist fervour of the article was horrifying to me. Of course Napoleon was a counter-revolutionary in the context of the French Revolution, but in a war with Tsarist absolutism if one had retrospectively to take sides, it would be with Napoleon not the Tsar. After all he was carrying the bourgeois-democratic revolution, even in a distorted and impure form, to the territories being conquered. The whole of reactionary Europe was arrayed against him. If anything, there is an analogy with the Red Army's sweep into Eastern Europe at the conclusion of the Second World War and the abolition of the capitalist mode of production. I was lying in the hospital reading this article, and I did not have much else to do, so I decided to write a letter to the editor of *Pravda* expressing my shock and dismay at the reactionary nature of this article. After that I used to grab eagerly a copy of *Pravda* every day to see whether or not it had been printed and every day I was disappointed. After a week I was visited by a member of the Central Committee of CPSU who ostensibly came to inquire about my health. And then he informed me that he had read my letter to *Pravda*. I asked how he had read it, if it had been addressed to the *Pravda* editor. He preferred to ignore this question and proceeded to defend the *Pravda* assessment of Napoleon. I cut the discussion short by saying I would be happy to discuss with him or any other comrade in the columns of *Pravda*, but I would rather be spared a heavy-handed lecture in my hospital room. Of course all these things are symptomatic of a more serious disease, but this was the way in which my eyes were opened. If you want to you can learn a lot in the Soviet Union!

This evolution continued in the years which followed and I visited Western Europe twice in the period 1967–9. In Italy I discussed not only with some of the Communist Party leaders, but also with comrades of *Il Manifesto*, in France with dissident communists such as Garaudy and some comrades of the new Left. I also personally experienced the after-effects of May 1968 and then I visited Britain. It was coincidental that I happened to visit Western Europe at a time when it was experiencing new upheavals and a mass radicalization, but none the less once there my political evolution continued. I wanted to study developments taking place with an open mind and so I met all the representatives of different currents which existed and discussed with them. I witnessed for myself in France the differences on the streets between the extreme Left and the PCF and I must confess I was inclined to sympathize with the courage and conviction of the far Left demonstrators, even though I could not completely agree with them.

What was the basis for the split in Indian communism which led to the existence of two major parties – CPI and CPM? Was it a partial reflection of the Sino-Soviet split? Given the fact that the CPI lost Kerala and Bengal, its two main strongholds, to the CPM what was the impact of the split within the CPI?

Many people have written that the CPI/CPM split was a pure reflection of the Sino-Soviet dispute. This is not correct. A more substantial factor was the attitude towards the Sino-Indian conflict. As I have already told you, I was not at all convinced by Chou En-lai's explanation of the Chinese position on the border dispute. I still think that the CPI was correct in opposing the Chinese line. However, there is a big difference between not supporting the Chinese position and supporting your own bourgeoisie. I'm afraid that the statements of some of the CPI leaders were totally chauvinist and merely parroted the speeches made by the Congress leaders. There were even racist slurs of the 'yellow peril' variety directed against the Chinese leaders and some of the articles written by Dange attacking China and defending the Indian bourgeoisie were outrageous, even for a communist leader steeped in Stalinist traditions. Many of the comrades who left with the CPM were disgusted by this and correctly so, but even this was not the main reason for the split, which took place in 1964, some years after the Sino-Indian border clashes.

In my view the major reason for the split was internal differences related to the question of electoral alliances. Ever since the fall of the Kerala ministry a discussion of sorts had been taking place and it reached a head in 1964. If you study the party documents from 1960 to 1964 you can trace the real causes of the split. There is a consistent theme running through all these documents: parliamentary cretinism. On this there are no major differences between the two sides. There is agreement on the need to win more elections in the states and more seats in the Lok Sabha. That is the road to communism in India. There is a supplementary slogan embodied in the formula: 'Break the Congress monopoly'. It is around this that differences develop. Some party leaders state that the key is to break the Congress monopoly, even if this means having the Jan Sangh or the Muslim League as a partner. Others state that the best way to break the monopoly is by aligning with the progressive sections of the Congress against its Right wing. Thus the debate which led to a split in Indian communism was not on differences around how best to overthrow the existing state and its structures, but on how to win more seats. In my view it was tactical differences which led to a split.

Other differences were there: on the Sino-Indian question, on an assessment of the Soviet Union's policies, but the main reason was differences on the implementation of electoral tactics. The immediate reason for the walkout by the comrades who became the CPM leadership was the affair of the Dange letter. This was a letter supposedly written by Dange in 1924 to the British authorities offering his services to them, and a copy of this letter appeared in the national archives. The CPI National Council set up a commission to investigate the whole business. The majority of this commission absolved Dange by stating that the letter was a forgery, but a minority stated that there was no proof to indicate that Dange had not written the letter. One-third of the thirty-two members of the Council left the meeting. They were not to return. Of course it was clear that the Dange letter was merely the pretext, but it was also clear that there were no fundamental differences. I think the evolution of the two parties since that time has confirmed this fact. While on the National Council the CPI had an overwhelming majority, the situation in the state councils of the party was different. In West Bengal the CPM had the majority and in Kerala the CPI had a very narrow majority. But even this could be misleading. I'll explain why. If you went below the state council to the district committees the CPM had a majority in some, but if you went even lower down the scale of branches and cells you would see that the CPI was virtually wiped out. A large section of the base went with the CPM in Kerala. In Andhra Pradesh the situation was roughly similar. In those areas where the CP represented a mass current, the CPM gained the upper hand. The reason for this is that many of the CPM leaders after the split and the bulk of their middle cadres, including those who would in the following years break with the CPM and align themselves with Peking, explained the split in terms of the CPI being the 'Right communists' who struggled for reforms via electoral victories whereas the CPM struggled for revolution. Many of the CPM's middle cadres obviously believed this, but the CPM leadership was engaged not in revolution, but in trying to win elections. Their behaviour after the election victory of 1967 in West Bengal showed this very clearly. But the bulk of those who joined the CPM after the split did so because they genuinely believed that the latter was going to lead them towards the revolution. In addition many of those who were opposed to the line of the CPI and the CPM none the less went with the CPM because they believed that the latter had greater potential in the sense that it had taken with it the best and most revolutionary sections of the base. So in all those areas where there was a communist tradition the ranks went largely with the CPM.

Why did you personally decide to stay with the CPI?

Because I was opposed to a split. I did not see that there were any fundamental differences between the two groupings and I feared that a split would further divide the trade-union movement, which is what happened. Some time after the CPM split, the AITUC was also split, the peasant organizations were split and the student organizations were split. This weakened the Left considerably and enabled the Congress and the parties on its right to strengthen their hold on the masses. It is of course scandalous that the workers' movement has to be permanently divided in this fashion. Leaving aside the broader questions of trade-union unity, at least the two Communist Parties could have maintained a common trade-union structure in the interests of the class they claim to serve. The main reason they did not cannot simply be ascribed to sectarianism. The reason is that given the weight they attach to electoralism and the fact that they subordinate the extra-parliamentary struggles to parliament, they need their own trade unions to gain electoral support. Thus both parties utilize their respective trade-union, student and peasant organizations mainly for electoral work. The basic concept of unity against the class enemy on every front is lacking from their politics. In any case I saw no reason to split from the CPI and join the CPM and today I am still a member of the CPI. I still maintain that my decision was correct.

There were rumblings in the CPI leadership over the invasion of Czechoslovakia. I know that the CPM defended the invasion without raising any doubts, but within the CPI we heard that there was opposition and that this was not a result of the desire not to offend 'democratic allies' in India.

The National Council unanimously passed a resolution in 1968 approving the measures being carried out by Dubcek and pledging its support to 'socialism with a human face'. Then came the military intervention of the Soviet Union. Immediately a discussion began and a number of us visited the Czech embassy in New Delhi to collect all the materials of the CPCz. There was an even split on the National Council. I think that those who supported the Soviet Union had thirty-five votes and we had thirty-four (it was not a well-attended meeting of the Council in any case) with two initial abstentions. There was further discussion and both the comrades who had abstained came over to our side so that we now had a majority to oppose the Soviet intervention. Once the party leaders realized that they were going to be defeated, they became very conciliatory and suggested that we should not take an immediate vote, but should open a three-month discussion period throughout the party and circulate all the relevant documents. I agreed because I thought that it would be a good thing if all the literature on this question was discussed throughout the party. It could do us nothing but good to have a real debate. But this promise was never kept.

The next Council meeting took place four months later. In that time we had been deluged by visitors from the Soviet Union. Some of them discussed with me as well, but I was not convinced one bit. In fact I edited a book entitled 'Whither Czechoslovakia?' under a pseudonym in which all the contributors were pro-CPI, but opposed to the Soviet line. I made sure that not a single contributor could be attacked as an 'enemy of the CPI'. I do not know all the pressures that were applied. In any case at the Council meeting the party apparatus had mobilized all its forces and obtained a majority at that meeting. Immediately afterwards I was questioned about the book and I admitted that I was responsible for it. I was rebuked and an instruction was sent out that this book was neither to be distributed nor read by any CPI members. A public censure of me was proposed in the party press. A party leader suggested that before the censure was published in *New Age* I should be given fifteen days to rethink and recant. I said that it was they who should have time to rethink. They nonetheless gave me fifteen days' respite and meanwhile some people came to see me and pressure me to apologize. They said that they didn't want to censure me openly because I was a leader of the party and well-respected. I refused point blank. So the censure was published in a small corner of *New Age*. But the very next day it was reported in great detail in all the bourgeois newspapers that I had been censured for writing a book criticizing the Soviet invasion and probably more copies of the book were sold than would have been if the leaders of my party had ignored the whole business. Despite all this, however, it is worth pointing out that a discussion of sorts did take place inside the CPI in contrast to the CPM which defended the invasion wholeheartedly.

Can you tell me what are your views on Trotsky and Trotskyism?

I am not a Trotskyist. Stalin was my idol. That idol is broken to pieces. I don't want to replace a broken idol with a new idol even if it is not a broken one, because I don't now believe in idolatry. I think Trotsky, Bukharin, Rosa Luxemburg, Gramsci, Lukács and other Marxists should be seriously studied and critically evaluated by all communists. Marxism will be poorer if we eliminate them from the history of the world communist movement. I don't believe in the Stalinist falsification of history in which Trotsky was depicted as an imperialist spy and a fascist agent. It appears that even Soviet historians have now abandoned such views. In a new history of the CPSU published in the late sixties Trotsky was criticized not for being a fascist spy but for his 'incorrect views'. Even this change is not enough. As Lukács said, one will not understand the history of the Russian Revolution if one does not understand the role of Trotsky in it. I am therefore glad that John Reed's *Ten Days That Shook the World*, which gives an excellent picture of the turbulent days of the Russian Revolution and Trotsky's role in it, has recently been published in the Soviet Union itself along with Lenin's introduction to it. I think some of the important contributions by Trotsky like his essay on bureaucratization published in the *Inprecor* in 1923, *In Defence of Marxism, On Literature and Art, History of the Russian Revolution* and other works are valuable and some of his ideas are still relevant. This does not mean that I agree with everything Trotsky said or wrote. The development of Marxism needs a critical eye.

You've been involved in the communist movement for well over forty years. You've been on its leading bodies; you've represented it in parliament and at congresses of fraternal parties, you've participated in its debates, not to mention your pioneering role in helping to lay its foundations in Kerala, one of the two regions where it has been most successful. Do you think that the traditional Indian communist movement, by which I would include the CPI, CPM and the splintered M-L groups which despite differences have a common political and ideological basis, has a future in India? In other words, can these groups and parties be reformed or is there a need for a communist party of a new type?

I would reject the view that the entire past of Indian communism must be negated. Despite all the deformations and mistakes there have been hundreds and thousands of communists in India who have struggled and suffered all sorts of privations for socialism and revolution. A whole number of peasant struggles, struggles for trade-unionism and against imperialism were conducted by the finest sort of communist militants. The tragedy was that the leadership, for the reasons we have discussed, was incapable of harnessing their talents and energies in a revolutionary direction. So I would stress that the whole experience must not be written off. There are chapters of it which have to be reappropriated by any new communist movement. At the base of the CPI, the CPM and the M-L groups you have thousands of dedicated activists who want a socialist revolution. They cannot be ignored. Furthermore many of them possess experiences of mass struggles. Many young militants who did not experience Stalinism in the traditional parties are also coming forward as Marxists and communists. I firmly believe that the unification of all communist forces in the country on the basis of Marxism–Leninism is essential for the development of the communist movement. How this will be brought about, whether by a merger or unification of all these forces under a new name through a conference, or by the emergence of a new Communist Party, etc., may be left to the future. But unification cannot be brought about by breaking each other's heads but only by principled discussions and comradely debates and through united actions for a commonly agreed programme. This will succeed only if the ranks of the different Communist Parties raise their own theoretical level and enable themselves to intervene in this great debate effectively. I am an optimist and am sure that even if the leaders of the old and ageing generation fail in this task the revolutionaries of the new young generation will rise to the occasion.

NOTE TO CHAPTER 15

1. K. Damodaran was a well-known member of the Communist Party of India until his death in 1977. This interview was conducted by Tariq Ali in 1974.

16. Hungary 1956: A Participant's Account

Nicholas Krasso[1]

It must be unique for a revolution to begin with a mass demonstration in solidarity with the people of another country. Why did the demonstration in support of Poland on 23 October produce a popular uprising in Budapest?

The international context was very fundamental. In 1955 the Soviet Union had accepted Austrian neutrality, and in 1956 Khrushchev had recognized Yugoslavia as a country on the road to socialism even though it was outside the Warsaw Pact. And now suddenly Gomulka was being swept into power in Warsaw and he also seemed to be taking a neutralist position.

So it seemed that everybody around us was taking a neutralist stand and we Hungarians were again missing the bus, just as we had been the last satellite of Hitler at the end of the war.

The student demonstration in solidarity with Gomulka's Poland had been banned a day or two before, but on 23 October itself, at about midday, the radio announced that the ban had been lifted. This turned what would have been a largely intellectual affair into a mass mobilization with workers pouring out of the factories in the suburbs towards the centre of the city. Hundreds of thousands of people joined the demonstration, with the dramatic events in Poland (which filled the newspapers) fresh in their minds.

The gigantic crowd reached the Parliament building and everybody wanted to hear Imre Nagy.[2] People kept going to fetch him while actors recited Petofi poems from 1848.[3] But it was well over an hour before Nagy finally agreed to appear in front of an increasingly restive crowd, and a more incendiary speech could not have been made: he called on the people to remain calm and trust him, and return home after singing the national anthem.

This convinced large numbers of people that they would have to act themselves: Nagy was an anti-climax. A section of the demonstration went to the radio building. The AVH forces there fired on them: the uprising began.[4]

Soviet troops occupied Budapest almost straight away. What was the character of this first Soviet intervention?[5]

It was about two o'clock the following morning when I saw the first Russian tanks entering Budapest. The next morning, when I walked across the city to the Writers' Union, there were Russian tanks all along the boulevards. They were not doing anything; just standing by, making a demonstration of strength.

It is a myth to say that there was heavy fighting between the Russians and the youth during this first Soviet intervention. It is true that AVH cars were entering the small streets shooting. But apart from anything else, the tanks were too big to enter the small side streets.

Occasionally the freedom fighters would run out with Molotov cocktails and blow up a tank. Then other Russian tanks would respond by moving up and down the boulevards, firing at houses that were in no way connected with the uprising. And soon lots of tank crews raised the Hungarian flag and people were saying that they had come over to our side; but when one talked to the Russians it became clear that they had put up the flags because they didn't want to be blown up.

At the same time they did not have orders to crush the uprising during this first intervention.

What were the main forms that the uprising took?

The anti-Stalinist movement had remained a student and intellectual affair, focused on the Petofi circle debates and the various official organizations of intellectuals until the Rajk funeral on 6 October 1956, when about 200,000 people participated.[6] And it was really only during the night of 23 October that the tremendous popular uprising burst forth, spreading throughout the country.

It was the young people, including very young schoolchildren, who were doing most of the fighting in various parts of the city. The adults were organizing the general strike and the workers' councils and all kinds of revolutionary committees.

The general strike began immediately and workers' councils were set up completely spontaneously, at first on an improvised basis. They often started with the workers refusing to allow the party secretary into the factory premises and then setting up councils to run things.

The national bank had its own revolutionary council and so the workers were still paid while the general strike was on. And there was absolutely no problem with telephones, gas or electricity – these services were maintained by their respective workers' councils. Peasants were coming into the city to sell food in amazing amounts.

Of course, it was not workers' management over production because the whole task was to push forward the general strike. There were workers' councils for factories and workers' councils for districts. Their fundamental functions were to organize meetings, frame demands, keep up the general strike and organize the weekly distribution of wages.

It was extraordinary to see how identical the demands were: freedom of parties to operate, withdrawal of Russian troops, withdrawal from the Warsaw Pact, neutrality, the right to strike, and so on. There were only very occasional deviations to the right or left.

Left deviations would include demands like freedom only for those parties adhering to public ownership of the means of production – this demand came from several factories. Then there was the occasional right-wing point, like the rather silly demand for the reintroduction of religious teaching in schools.

I myself was elected to one of the district workers' councils. On Friday 26 October I spoke at a huge public meeting in Ujpest, the biggest industrial area after Csepel. Because they liked what I said, they elected me a member of the Ujpest Revolutionary Council then and there. I had never been to the district in my life before, except to watch the odd film.

The head of the council was a carpenter. I stayed in Ujpest for the next three days, and returned later after the second Soviet intervention.

The atmosphere among the intellectuals, who had played a leading role before October, was transformed after the uprising began. On the morning of 24 October I went into the Writers' Union, and the writers were just sitting there, with their heads hanging as though in mourning; and some were becoming very poetic. One told me he would just like to sit and let his tears flow and flow and flow.

I said to Dery[7] that surely the writers were at least partly responsible for what was happening, and shouldn't they consider what was to be done? And he replied: 'Why? We are writers and we just told the truth. We are not politicians, we were just telling the truth.' They really felt everything was lost.

This was in complete contrast with the total optimism of the teenagers who were making the uprising. Generally the attitude of the intellectuals was pessimistic; but the workers and the young people, feeling their power, were filled with optimism.

The period between the first and second Soviet interventions gave a breathing space for some kind of organized leadership to emerge, around Imre Nagy, or in opposition to him. Isaac Deutscher called Nagy a kind of Bukharinite, and a possible harbinger of a Hungarian Thermidor.[8] What was your attitude to Nagy, and to the problem of political leadership?

In a certain sense the analogy with Bukharin is valid. Nagy was an agrarian socialist in origin. He had participated in the civil war in Russia with the Bolsheviks, and belonged to the Landler–Lukács faction against Bela Kun's ultra-Left voluntarism in the 1920s.[9]

He spent the 1930s in an agrarian institute in Russia doing endless research to prove the feasibility of a radical agrarian reform in Hungary, against the whole record of the Kun CP, the social democrats and the reactionaries who had all in different ways opposed a land redistribution as economically disastrous.

Nagy was undoubtedly a very courageous man. In 1949 he had stood out in the Central Committee against the Stalinist plan for forced collectivization. His concern for the peasantry in the 1950s was, in itself, absolutely justified. But something of the agrarian socialist remained in him, and criticism of the one-sidedness of his preoccupation with the peasantry to the point of underestimating the problems of the workers would also be justifiable.

Moreover, in the field of political manoeuvre and organization, Nagy was very naïve, unlike Rakosi or Gero who were very acute in political intrigues.[10] Nagy's whole idea was to stand for moral purity against Rakosi's dirty ways: and this moral condemnation of Stalinist practices was, of course, absolutely justified, but it was not enough to meet the organizational and political tests of the crisis.

There was simply no leadership which represented the line that I thought should be followed, so my position was to support these 'Bukharinites', back them in forming a government, but try to build an opposition to them at the same time. But here there was this complete organizational vacuum. This was the problem, not whether Nagy might be opening the door to Thermidor – Nagy might have moved towards some kind of NEP, but this would not have been disastrous in the Hungarian context.

The unanimity of the workers' political demands was really extraordinary. But equally striking was the fact that nowhere did the workers show clear ideas as to how to achieve their demands. There is, of course, nothing remarkable about this, except to those who are submerged in a workerist mysticism.

Nowhere was the slogan 'All Power to the Workers' Councils' raised, or at least I didn't come across it. The initiative to create a central workers' council came from myself and I didn't hear about it from anyone else.

The general strike was continuing and was fully fledged. The workers felt their strength and believed that the general strike would solve everything, even after the second Russian intervention. They believed that the Russians would not be able to stabilize the situation because the workers would not start working.

This is of course true, but things become more complicated. The strike may go on, but the mass of workers are sitting at home and the force of inertia sets in. Also it will not be possible to continue to get money each week from the national bank and the children will begin to starve.

It is true that you have the active minority and they can be decisive, leaning on the support of the great mass. But then another problem came up: there was this tremendous reaction against Stalinism, against a situation where every meeting was manipulated.

Rigged meetings are obnoxious, but this does not mean that the active minority can leave things without any previous plans or arrangements, relying entirely on spontaneity. Political strategy and tactics have to be worked out and consciously put into practice in an organized way.

But here another problem arose: there was this ideology that the task of intellectuals was to get things started and then leave it to the workers to carry everything through. This is, in fact, completely alien to Marxism, to Lenin's outlook, this idea that the intrinsic virtues of the masses will sort things out. These virtues are very great but not of that kind, not of the kind to be clear about the political relationships in the situation.

What, then, is your attitude to the view that there was at least the possibility of a counter-revolution? This is the official CP position, and was also held by Deutscher at the time. Furthermore, every bourgeois commentator in the West hails the Hungarian Revolution as his own. In particular, what do you think of the view that Nagy might have given way to a Minszenty-type regime?[11]

There is a sexist German expression, '*Mädchen für Alles*', a girl for all purposes. The Hungarian Revolution was destined to be treated in this way: everyone has taken it as a justification of their outlook. This was an instant reaction to the event: for socialists of all kinds, for anarchists, liberals, fascists and conservatives it was *their* revolution.

And it could hardly have been otherwise, considering that Hungary had been dominated by a Stalinist state that was opposed by the entire population, and, having had a complete organizational monopoly, when this state crumbled it left behind a total organizational vacuum. There had been no parties, no free trade unions and even the cultural organizations could be formed only by the state.

The Hungarian masses, and in the first place the Budapest working class, rose up in a tremendous national uprising without any organized political expression on a national scale. And before the forces of the Hungarian Revolution could acquire a definite political form, the process was crushed by Russian intervention. In defeat, the uprising could serve a multitude of causes.

Kadar's own theory of the counter-revolution,[12] as outlined in the Party's December resolution, was curious. It said that the reform movement before the revolution had been correct – an anti-dogmatic, anti-sectarian thing. But when this programme was taken to the streets, it became counter-revolutionary!

The model he was following here was Stalin's line of 1927, that the Trotskyists had ceased being a working class tendency and had become an agency of imperialism by taking their programme to the streets. But Stalin's version had involved a supposedly *incorrect* line being taken to the streets. This time what was declared to be counter-revolutionary was taking a *correct* line to the masses!

As for the Kadar claim that there would have been a Minszenty-led return of the ancien regime, this was not on the cards. Minszenty had indeed protested against the land reform in 1945 and undoubtedly remained its enemy. After all the Catholic Church had been the biggest single landlord in the country. But Minszenty was not only an ultra-reactionary: he was a fool and always equivocating as cardinals do.

In his broadcast speech during the uprising, he did not actually say that the land reform should be overturned: he made allusions which could be interpreted in that way. But a return of landlordism was completely out of the question. Whoever tried to carry it through – and it is conceivable that Minszenty might have tried it later – would have committed political suicide: after all the main social base of any clerical reaction would have been the Catholic peasantry.

When I left Hungary, through the Catholic, Western part of the country, the peasants on the train were saying how much they had been attached to the Cardinal: 'After all,' they said, 'he was the only really courageous man who had stood up against the communists; and what a disappointment it was for us that his speech had called for the land to be returned to the landlords.' Actually he hadn't said this, but I was delighted to hear the peasants misinterpreting him in exactly the right way.

Of course, anti-communist moods were very obvious among the masses after the start of the uprising. But they must be put into perspective.

I remember asking a worker what he thought the chances of the Nagy-led CP were. And he said: 'Oh, nil. They might get 4 or 5 per cent. No communist has a chance, even if he is Imre Nagy.' What then was needed? 'A completely new Hungarian workers' party,' he replied.

To test the reaction, I asked: 'You wouldn't want a united workers' and peasants' party?' And his response was: 'Oh, no. It's only in full communism that the interests of the workers and the peasants will be the same, and then both classes will disappear.' This sort of thing was common: people expressing anti-communist attitudes, but at the same time showing that they had internalized many of the transformations that had taken place during the previous ten years.

Undoubtedly some kind of anti-Marxist Christian Socialist movement would have gained ground – though one cannot say to what extent. Nor can one rule out the possibility of a return of small capital, perhaps going further than NEP in Russia. All these possibilities remain in the realm of speculation, and would have been decided in the course of a political struggle which Russian intervention precluded.

Not since 1917 have we seen workers' councils of such an advanced scope and level of organization as were thrown up in the Hungarian Revolution. You played a key part in setting up the Budapest central workers' council. How was it formed?

After the second Soviet intervention I returned to Ujpest to see what was happening to the workers' council there, to which I had earlier been elected. In the town hall both the Stalinist town council and the revolutionary workers' council were operating, occupying separate rooms. And when I arrived the two councils were having a joint meeting. This was typical: they kept on arguing with the Stalinists, and I thought, what's the point?

Anyway, listening to the discussion I came to the idea of creating a central workers' council. I drafted a proclamation, and when the meeting ended I put my proposal to the revolutionary workers' council.

The proclamation simply said that at the moment there is dual power in the country: the Kadar government is just there on paper, it's non-existent. There are only two powers: one is the Russian armed forces, and the other is the Hungarian people and in the first place the Budapest working class.

One of these two powers is organized – the Russian army – but the other is still unorganized, so we must organize it. We must create a central workers' council.

They accepted it. The proclamation was handed over to the students' revolutionary council for distribution. We were calling a meeting of delegates of workers' councils to set up the central body along with a newspaper that would be its organ.

I was to present the plan to the meeting of workers' council delegates and I felt I had to have backing, otherwise people would say: who is this adventurer? What does he represent? So the carpenter chairman of the Ujpest council agreed that I should sit as part of the presidium of the Ujpest council that was convening the meeting, and speak first.

The meeting was to be at the Ujpest town hall, but when we arrived it was surrounded by Russian tanks and the members of the Ujpest council had all been arrested the previous night (as I learned later, many of them were hanged). We moved the meeting to United Electric, a big factory making sophisticated electrical appliances, with a consequently very social democratic revolutionary workers' council. So this council formed the presidium.

There were about eighty or ninety delegates from different factories: not as many as we had hoped for, but about thirty of the biggest factories were represented. Each delegation stood up in turn and read out their demands, one two three four, amazingly identical. I was alone, with no backing, and when it came to my turn the situation became almost farcical.

The elderly social democratic chairman asked: 'What factory are you from?' 'None,' I said. 'What right have you to be here?' I said that I had actually organized the meeting. The chairman replied: 'This is untrue. This meeting is an historical inevitability.' So I was demagogic in return: 'These kind of philosophical points should be discussed after the events are over. Now we have more urgent matters to confront.'

So the chairman said: 'All right, speak for ten minutes.' And he was ostentatiously looking at his watch.

There were some unpleasant noises in the hall after I had mentioned the word 'compromise'. And in fact I had started with it, saying that it was very impressive how identical all the demands were, but so far nobody had said a single word about how to win them. Ideal demands are not enough. We have to decide to get the essential thing, and be ready to compromise on other questions.

What was important was to have nothing to do with the Kadar regime and to have internal democratization. The workers' councils had to be turned into a real force for democratization. At the moment we shouldn't talk to anybody and should develop the general strike, but with a more organized leadership.

This meant organizing a really strong central workers' council in Budapest. And when the Russians realized that they couldn't stabilize without us, they would have to talk to us. Kadar was irrelevant: there is no point in talking to the servants when the masters are there. This was frankly a compromise plan – it did not take up the question of the Warsaw Pact, but concentrated on the internal question.

The speech made no impact. The meeting decided to set up the central workers' council, but the only other decision was diametrically opposite to my conception: a delegation was elected to go and negotiate with Kadar, while simultaneously insisting that it did not recognize him.

The central workers' council continued to exist and held a second full meeting, but the working class was trapped. Kadar was ready to promise just about anything *after* the general strike was called off.

The workers demand the right to strike? He fully agreed with the workers. He wholeheartedly concurred that the workers should be able to strike, but first this *particular* strike must stop.

The Russian troops must withdraw? Absolutely! And as soon as law and order was re-established, he would personally start negotiations to this effect. In short, Kadar was sufficiently trained in the art of politics to know how to concentrate on the essential and reach his objective.

The discussions went on until Kadar and the Russians felt strong enough to arrest some of the workers' leaders and then mass arrests followed. The workers' councils continued in many areas through November and into December.

In January 1957, the workers' council in Csepel, the working-class bastion, issued a declaration that they didn't want to deceive the working class any longer by a resistance that was a sham resistance. So in order to be true to their class they had decided to declare their own dissolution. The workers' council movement had ended. The repression of the leaders of the working class was terrible.

Could you sum up the meaning of the Hungarian Revolution?

I have often remembered the 19th Party Congress in the Soviet Union in 1952. Stalin kept silent throughout the Congress till the very end when he made a short speech which covers about two and a half printed pages. He said that there were two banners which the progressive bourgeoisie had thrown away and which the working class should pick up – the banners of democracy and national independence. Certainly nobody could doubt that in 1956 the Hungarian workers raised these two banners high.

NOTES TO CHAPTER 16

1. Nicholas Krasso played a central role in the formation of the Budapest Central Workers' Council in 1956. Krasso joined the Hungarian Communist Party in 1945 at the age of fourteen. He wrote the first denunciation of Cardinal Minszenty in the party daily that same year and became a frequent contributor to the party's theoretical journal from 1947–59. Banned from university in the course of the drive against the distinguished philosopher Lukács in 1950, he was drafted into the army. On his return he played a leading role in the intellectual struggle against Rakosi's Stalinist leadership prior to the 1956

uprising. Forced into exile during the aftermath of defeat, Krasso came to Britain. He has been a member of the editorial board of the *New Left Review* since the early 1960s. He was interviewed by Oliver MacDonald.

2. Purged at the end of the 1940s, Nagy returned to become Prime Minister during the thaw of 1953–5. Purged again, he came back as Prime Minister during the uprising. Kidnapped by the Russians, Nagy was imprisoned then executed in 1958.

3. Sandor Petofi (1823–49) was the great poet of the Hungarian revolution against the Hapsburgs in 1848–9. That revolution was eventually crushed by the Russian armies of the Tsar.

4. The AVH (Allamvedelmi Hatosag) was the state security authority, whose officials carried out the bloody purges of the Stalin period. Hated by the population, many suffered the same fate as this AVH officer, lynched during the uprising.

5. The tanks that entered Budapest were withdrawn after a few days, only to return on 4 November in the second Russian intervention which crushed the armed resistance movement.

6. Laszlo Rajk, the leader of the underground Communist Party during the Second World War, had been the most popular communist official in the forties before his arrest and frame-up show trial in 1949. The struggle for the rehabilitation of Rajk and other victims of the purges was one of the motor forces of the anti-Stalinist movement before October. His rehabilitation was marked by the state funeral on 6 October 1956.

7. Tibor Dery, leading communist novelist, played a prominent role in the Petofi circle. The circle was the focus of anti-Stalinist activity amongst intellectuals before October 1956.

8. Thermidor was the phase of the French Revolution which paved the way for the victory of the counter-revolution. Trotsky used the Thermidor analogy to describe the danger of capitalist counter-revolution in the Soviet Union during the 1920s. Bukharin was the leader of the Right Opposition in the Bolshevik Party in 1929.

9. Bela Kun was the leader of the Hungarian CP until his liquidation in the 1930s. A prominent Comintern functionary during the ultra-Left 'third period' at the end of the 1920s, Kun was opposed by a faction in the Hungarian CP led by the Marxist theoretician Gyorgy Lukács and the trade-union leader Landler. This faction was dissolved in 1930.

10. Matyas Rakosi was the high-priest of Stalinism in Hungary after the war, famous for his 'salami tactic' for chopping down opponents. He was suddenly removed to Moscow by the Russians in July 1956, never to return. Erno Gero, Rakosi's lieutenant and a long-time Cominterm functionary, organized the drive against anarchist and POUMists in Barcelona in May 1937 and took over from Rakosi in July 1956 until his fall during the uprising.

11. Cardinal Minszenty, Primate of Hungary from the end of the war, was jailed by Rakosi and escaped to the American Embassy in the uprising to live there until moving to the West in the 1970s.

12. Janos Kadar had supported Nagy during the early days of the revolution, but

went over to the Russians just before the second Russian intervention. He organized the Stalinist counter-revolution and remains the Hungarian Party boss today.

17. How They Crushed the Prague Spring of 1968

Josef Smrkovsky[1]

The year 1968 belongs to the past. Yet little else possesses such actuality. The Central Committee has adopted the 'Lessons'[2] *and it looks as if even among those of us who 'lost out', if one can call it that, mythology is gradually taking over. So, first, the classical question: 'Where do we start?'*

The events of January 1968 really started back in October at the Central Committee meeting where party problems were to be tackled, or were on the agenda. The tone throughout the proceedings was one of criticism of practical party policies. Internal party problems were involved, reform of the economy, relations between Czechs and Slovaks from the standpoint of power. The Slovaks expressed justifiable dissatisfaction with Prague centralism and bureaucracy. There was also the question of government practices. At that point even Antonin Novotny was sharply critical of the government when he said that the government wasn't governing.

The proceedings were so stormy that there were suggestions not to end them, but to continue at another meeting. Boruvka demanded that the proceedings shouldn't be ended, that another session be called and the discussion continued.

At the end of December 1967, these matters came before the Party Presidium and there a new point was raised, on the initiative of the secretaries, or some Presidium members, who rather simplified the whole thing, however. They put forward the demand that the posts be separated – one man as First Secretary, another as President. That was what the Presidium was concerned with, that was the argument about which we knew little enough. We heard that meeting followed meeting, but nothing was settled. Foreign radio stations reported quite a lot about these things, and towards the end of December, I asked some of the Presidium members to tell me what was actually happening. At that time I visited Jaromir Dolansky and Lubomir Strougal asking them to explain what the Presidium was arguing about, what was the point at issue.

And here the atmosphere was interesting. When I was with Dolansky in the Central Committee building, he suggested that we move over to the other end of the table – he had a conference table there – the reason being that the telephones he had round him on the table were bugged. Sitting at the other end, he whispered to me that the Presidium, its members and secretaries, couldn't really do anything, everything was strictly censored by Antonin Novotny. He stressed again the main thing – to separate the posts.

When I talked with Strougal the atmosphere was even sadder. He wanted to talk to me, but not in the Central Committee building; he asked me to come to his home, but not to drive into their street, to arrive on foot. While I was there, he was very scared, he was afraid that Antonin Novotny would take repressive measures against people who opposed him.

Before the December plenary session, the first session – the continuation was in January – it was early on Friday morning, about 7 a.m., Antonin Novotny phoned me at home asking if I would visit him that day. Naturally, I said I would.

The session began on Monday in the week before Christmas, before Christmas Eve. I saw Novotny at the Central Committee building on the Friday afternoon. I recalled that for a full two years he had found no time for me. Twice I had written to ask that he receive me, I wanted to talk with him about party problems and other things; I asked in vain. Now he had invited me. He, too, explained to me what the Presidium was concerned with in the argument which was narrowing down to the personal conflict, the separation of the posts, and he told me that he also wanted to reorganize the party leadership, the Presidium, that he wanted to make changes in the personnel. He had it in writing, jotted on a piece of paper and he said he was counting on me, too, to be in the Presidium. To convince me, he got up from that chairman's seat of his, went round the table and showed me his draft list where he had me entered for the Presidium. He didn't let me read it all, he just showed me that he had my name there.

I found the whole affair rather distasteful, because he had invited me in order to get me to support him. That I couldn't accept. When he had finished describing his personnel reorganization, as he saw it, I told him what I thought: that it was too late for that kind of thing, that in view of the situation in the party and in society, it was necessary not only to separate the two posts, but also to launch out on the whole front with the process of democratization. I referred to the October session, to the critical voices demanding that the government should be a government, not just the executive apparatus of the party, I talked about the Slovaks' problems, about economic reform, etc.

I think I shook him quite a bit with my arguments, because when he came to the separation of posts, he asked me: 'And so who would you . . .?'

I told him to remain President, let him stay on at the Castle, that was enough for one man and let someone else do the job of First Secretary. So together we thought aloud who it should be. He asked me. I had considered these things and suggested that Lenart be First Secretary. So I told him I thought this would be the best solution in view of his calm nature; from what I had known of Lenart up to then, I thought it would be a good solution.

He objected at once – Lenart was still Prime Minister then – so who would be Prime Minister in that case?

I replied that I hadn't thought it out so definitely, because I didn't know anyone would ask me about it.

We talked about this for a long time and, finally, I had the impression I had convinced him. I left with the feeling that he would do it. That was Friday. As we were driving away, I told my driver that I had had a good day and I had done a good job, Comrade Novotny was ready to listen.

Next day there was a hunt at Lany. The President always held one once a year for officers of state and party functionaries. I was there, and Chudik, Sadovsky and several Ministers were there. But Novotny wasn't present. In the afternoon, when we were sitting there after the hunt, they phoned from Prague that Comrade Novotny with Lenart were on their way to Lany and we were to wait for them. And particularly, that I was to wait, not to leave.

He arrived, we all sat round the table, then he beckoned to me to go with him.

'Now look,' – he called me Tonik, or Joska, once he said Tonda [cover name when Smrkovsky was in the resistance, 1939–45 – editor's note], as people call me; another time he used my correct name – 'yesterday we had a talk, you advised me to resign, etc. Today some old comrades came to see me, I told them what you advise, and they're against it. They're against me resigning. I think they are right.' He advised me to reconsider my attitude.

I said that of course I would think it over, but I also told him not to put much faith in his friends the so-called old comrades. I said: 'They're not your friends, Tonik, they're your gravediggers. They're not concerned about your staying in both posts. They're concerned with keeping the posts they have themselves, the jobs many of them have long, long ago not been able to cope with, or should never have had.'

For instance, Josef Němec, Klenhova-Besserova, Kozelka, he's dead now, but altogether that old gang of his Prague friends. Few of them would be in their jobs if Novotny hadn't put them there, that was common knowledge. So we parted on the note that I should think again.

On Sunday I called up Franta Kriegel, with whom up to then I had never talked personally, only on social occasions. Since he was unwilling to come to me in the office, I drove to his home, and I described the whole affair to him. He told me that he had also spoken to Novotny and had also reached no agreement with him. Kriegel and I were, on the whole, of the same opinion that things must be dealt with.

On Monday morning – by then I was to have thought things over – I went to see Lenart at the government office; I talked to him first that day because he had been informed about things by Novotny. And I told Lenart that having thought again, I was unable to change my opinion, would he explain that to Novotny.

Lenart expressed no objection to what I told him. I must stress that to that time and later, after January, my relations with Lenart were of the best. I knew him from government work and, all in all, I respected him highly – as an experienced, cool-headed, thoughtful and educated man. That is why I suggested him. And I believe he would have taken it, if Novotny had made a point of it. I wouldn't like to give an opinion today, but for a long time I felt it would have been a solution, an acceptable solution, if Novotny hadn't forced the conflict.

After seeing Lenart, I went, in the government building, to Simunek, with whom I also talked for about an hour; I gave him the whole story, too, for one thing because, as I imagined or was convinced, he was close to Novotny.

I urged him to speak to Novotny, to persuade him not to force a conflict, but to accept a solution acceptable to everyone. Simunek also expressed no objection.

The December session passed without anything being settled. It was adjourned until after Christmas. I didn't manage to speak at that December meeting. I was about thirtieth on the list, and my turn didn't come till January.

The December session, the first three days, revealed that Novotny was refusing to budge and things would not go peaceably. So the tension grew even more.

And then! During the holiday, I think it was on Boxing Day, a journalist whom I had known socially came to see me at home in the morning – he said he had an important message. Comrade Mestek was in conference at the Ministry [Mestek was a member of the Central Committee and Minister of Agriculture – editor's note] with three other comrades. He had just come from seeing Novotny and was telling these comrades about the situation and what would happen next. 'They're important matters, you must know about them', so and so (he named him to me) who was one of the three with Mestek and, so the messenger thought, one of his people, sent me this message: Comrade Novotny was going to resist, he counted on the army, he enjoyed confidence in the army, he counted on the militia, deputations from the big factories were streaming to him urging him not to retreat, to rely on them: and there was something from Vysocany, where he had his base of a kind, but there were other things, too, that he told me from this talk with Mestek: that Mestek said it was a pity they had released me, Smrkovsky, and others in the fifties from Ruzyn Prison, that we should have stayed there and orders for our arrest were prepared, only the signature was lacking. Among them, there was one for me. Further, that Comrade Mestek had made all the Ministry of Agriculture cars available for all sorts of courier services to launch this action. In short, that I should know how we stood, what to expect and what Novotny was preparing to do.

I knew then that the fight was on, there was no peaceful way out, and Novotny wouldn't give in. I had my speech ready for the December meeting, but I was not called (I have it among my papers), now for the January meeting I redrafted it, making it more militant. I refer there to the conversation I had with Novotny. Novotny confirmed that we had the talk, what I advised and what he rejected – in any case, it's printed in the report of the CC session.

There was a lot of talk at that time about Novotny's attempt to get support from the Soviet Union. What did you, members of the Central Committee, know about that?

Over Christmas 1967 I had a talk with Chervonenko at the Konopiste hunt, to which I had invited him. Svoboda, Sadovsky and others were there, too. It was between the December session and Christmas, there's always such a diplomatic hunt there at the end of the year, so Chervonenko [Soviet ambassador – editor's note] was present and we exchanged a few words in the woods about what was happening. He asked me what I thought would happen. I told him then fairly categorically that matters would be solved, because they had to be, and that included the personal matter of those two highest posts, but we also had to tackle the economy and government problems, so that the government should govern. I simply said on the general subject that things would be dealt with. He was noncommittal on all this, sceptical, because he had his own view, after all, from the outset, he hadn't much sympathy with this approach. That was Chervonenko.

At that time, of course, Brezhnev was here, too. And we begged in vain to be told what they talked about [Brezhnev and Novotny – editor's note], because it was, in fact, an intervention into party matters. We were told that having heard what was at issue, Brezhnev refused to interfere – that's the famous remark, 'it's your affair'; we all welcomed that attitude, if that's really how it was.

I remember the joy with which at least those who already knew what was happening received the news that the First Secretary was no longer

Novotny but Dubcek. Not because we knew very much about Dubcek, but because there was no longer the danger that Novotny would try to win by force. And so we were shocked when the official communiqué on the CC session appeared. We asked ourselves: How can they expect to start on a new course with such an untruth? And why?

When the meeting ended on 5 January – during the night the Presidium had agreed that, at last, Novotny would resign his post – we heard about the haggling that had gone on overnight in the Presidium. A whole lot of people were tipped for the First Secretaryship; one Novotny opposed, in another case the Slovaks were against, views clashed a lot, until finally the only candidate with a hope of being accepted was Dubcek. The Slovaks were in favour, the Czechs, too, and Novotny didn't dare to come out against Dubcek – in view of the fact that at the October meeting, and then in December and in January, over the Czech-Slovak question or, more correctly, Novotny-Slovaks, he had been on thin ice, where he had got into an unpleasant situation. So finally they all agreed on Dubcek as the sole candidate. Only, as far as I know, Dubcek was unwilling to accept. People told me afterwards how in the night from Friday to Saturday, when the meeting ended, Dubcek protested. Cernik promised him, begging him to take the job, that they would all back him up, in short, they literally shoved him into it. Dubcek wasn't prepared for a post like that, and suddenly it fell on his head.

When the Central Committee had accepted the candidate, I think with one or two votes against, the comrades from the Presidium as then constituted wanted to finish the session. After Dubcek's election there was an interval. A number of us went up to Cernik, Strougal and others to say it wasn't enough to have settled this, it was necessary to give a report to the party and the public. We wanted, too, that the main lines of future policy should be decided and declared, something said about the kind of policy the party would follow; that the gist of the discussion in the CC in January, December and October be given. I myself spoke with Cernik and Strougal. Cernik said to me, he literally begged me: 'Josef, understand, we can't carry on, we can hardly keep on our feet, we've been through endless nights, none of us have had time to think about things, we'll have to leave it for the next meeting.' The editorial commission which had been appointed had the job of proposing in general outline the main principles of party policy, which were to be put in a resolution.

In the end, we were very dissatisfied at the way things had been shelved, but we accepted it. The fact is that with that squabbling in the Party Presidium between October, Christmas and January, the Presidium of the day had really not prepared or thought about anything at all.

That is why, immediately after January, we urged Dubcek to see to it that the Presidium, or the bodies appointed or appropriate for the job should quickly work out a document about post-January policy.

I couldn't get to Dubcek at the time, he was too busy, so I saw Sadovsky, who was secretary for agriculture, and I knew, talked with Dubcek every evening or night. I reminded him that we had here in Prague a vast body of Marxist intellectuals, that here the party had people who were fully at the disposal of the Central Committee for any work it might require. Others were going to see him, too; the need was there, and those were the beginnings of the party's Action Programme.

Dubcek, of course, understood the value of working with intellectuals because he had been doing it in Bratislava – true, not brilliantly, but better than Novotny in Prague. He understood – and actually he had a similar idea – but he let himself be manoeuvred, as we all did, into a situation where instead of a simple, provisional action programme – I saw it as something on the lines of Klement Gottwald's one-time Ten Points – many comrades made an enormous work of it, where they wanted to include everything. Two or three times I went to see Dubcek, once I was alone, once with several comrades, to tell him that the party, the public, were expecting something, that the party would at last say what its policy was going to be, we urged that the Action Programme be brought forward, abbreviated and released to the public. Unfortunately, it dragged on into March.

However, several members of the CC tried to fill this information gap. You were one of them, and we know these efforts were not entirely free of obstacles.

As soon as the January 1968 session was over, party organization, public institutions, in fact everybody, were burning to know what had actually been going on in the CC. And they called meetings, they wanted speakers, members of the Central Committee, and I know that the party office had problems with that. Speakers weren't available, a whole lot of comrades were none too keen about going to the meetings. I was among those who from the start put themselves at the disposal of the central secretariat. My round of meetings started. It started in the countryside. And it was interesting that the party apparatus of the day didn't want to let me into Prague. When I had done ten to fifteen meetings outside and the Prague organizations wanted me to come to them, I called this to the attention of the comrades in the Central Committee. Dubcek noticed it, too, I'm not sure whether on his own or whether someone told him, but he insisted that they must let me speak to Prague organizations as well. So I began going to activists' meetings in the Prague districts, I was in Prague 2, then in Prague 3, then it was the CKD works, then came the whole string of Prague localities – factories, organizations, institutions. But now the interesting thing was that there were doubts about what to say and what not to say. About ten days after the CC meeting, Hendrych had invited us speakers to headquarters. We all complained that we didn't know what we could say, what we ought not to say, what was confidential and what wasn't, because it had been an unhappy decision that these matters were not to be talked about. To conceal from the party problems discussed by the Central Committee, that was a decision contrary to party principles. Hendrych informed us that the Presidium had considered the matter and decided that it was permissible to speak at members' meetings and, to a reasonable extent, at others about all questions dealt with by the CC – with one proviso, that there should be no naming of people to show what views they had expressed during the session.

Speaking from the platform of the Congress Palace[3] alongside you and other comrades was Gustav Husak. He made a good impression on the audience and evidently he had no idea of the changes life had in store for him. Indeed, no one guessed that. Did you?

Here I'd like to go back a bit. Around 16 January 1968, I asked to see Dubcek about Husak. Bilak had already taken on the post of First Secretary in Bratislava. I went to tell Dubcek that I thought it right, after all these changes, for Husak and Novomesky to be brought into activity. I recalled that in '64 and '65, when I had been rehabilitated, I tried intervening with Novotny to have Husak and Novomesky rehabilitated, too. I visited him twice, or even three times, and I got a long way with the matter, so far that Husak was to have got the job of a Deputy Minister of Justice. And the point was that he didn't want to be just one of several Deputies, he wanted to be First Deputy. That he would have accepted, and I urged him to accept even if it wasn't the post of First Deputy. In the end, he had one last condition. It was winter, sometime in February, slushy weather. He wanted Novotny to receive him, to receive him at the Castle, and that there should be an official report – about a talk at the Castle! I informed Novotny about this through Honza Svoboda (CC member and head of the organization department). And Novotny refused. He said that if Husak insisted on conditions like that, audience at the Castle, official report, then that wasn't on. And if Comrade Husak didn't want to take the job, then it was no go.

At that, Husak came to Prague with Laco Novomesky. We met in a restaurant, it was Saturday, for them to hear the answer. Husak refused to take the job on any other conditions, and Novotny didn't want to receive him there at the Castle. So it broke down over a formal matter like that. Later, at the Central Committee meeting, Novotny saw me in a corridor at the Castle and he said: 'Look here, that business of yours with

Husak, lay off it now.' Since it had been purely my initiative, the thing remained in abeyance.

And now in January '68 I went to see Dubcek and came out with it all again. He listened, said very well, he agreed. I told him that next day – 16 or 17 January, I think, a Saturday again – I was going to Bratislava anyhow, we'd arranged that; in January '68, Eugene Lobl was acting as a kind of link between Husak and myself. I went to see Bilak at the Secretariat. He had just become First Secretary for Slovakia, representatives of institutions were arriving to take the oath, and things like that. I was soon admitted, he left the others waiting, and we talked for fifteen to twenty minutes.

In the first place, it was a social occasion, where I congratulated him – I was also a minister for Slovakia. And I discussed with him those problems of Husak and Novomesky, that Dubcek agreed, and what I had done in Novotny's day, how it had turned out, etc.

And Bilak said: 'Yes, I agree.' He would look into it. And we also discussed, as I had with Dubcek already, on what lines, on what front Husak could best be brought into activity. At that time we all agreed that it would be easiest, until a load of matters had been settled, for him to work in government, to become a member of the government. Both Dubcek and Bilak agreed with that, and with that we parted. Then I dropped in on the Forestry Commission, from there I drove to Laco Novomesky's place, and we went on together to Husak's house on the outskirts of Bratislava, where he was expecting us.

We talked for about three hours. I told them about my talks with Dubcek and Bilak, and we parted in a friendly way, knowing that it had turned out well, and that Gustav Husak – Novomesky too, of course, but it was primarily a question of Husak – would be brought into activity in government, and that also happened. [In April 1968 he was appointed Deputy Premier of the Czechoslovak government – editor's note.]

It is said that Husak is well aware of all this, Laco Novomesky knows it too, as of course, does Bilak. A year later, at the Central Committee meeting, Bilak said that I had been to see him that time trying to turn him against Dubcek, and other outrageous statements. And Husak said nothing, though he knew in detail why I had visited Bilak – that I had been there on his behalf.

Following Novotny's abdication, actually before it happened, the important question arose: who would be President? There were a number of candidates, at least the public had several names in mind. General Svoboda was elected. Although many people wanted you, you supported his candidacy. Why was that?

After the January CC session Comrade Svoboda and I began to see each other very frequently. He was working at the time in the military historical institute and I was Minister of Forestry and Water Economy, our office was in Opletal Street.

Between January and the presidential election in March, around that time he approached me and then, with rare exceptions, he visited me daily in Opletal Street. Several times, twice in one day. He wanted to know what was happening in the party, what the problems were, not only about personnel, other matters too, he asked about the people in the Presidium. At that time, lots of people were unknown to him, he didn't know who was who. He kept asking me who was this Cernik, what was he like, and that Indra, and the others; up to then, in fact, he had had very little knowledge about the relations between party and government, about people, about who was in party and who in government posts. Up to then he had simply not been interested, and so I explained all this to him. And I was completely honest about it. So some time towards the end of February and in March it was generally known in party and government circles that Comrade Svoboda was going the rounds of a lot of people in the countryside, in Moravia and Slovakia, and it was then I learnt from other comrades that behind this were conjectures that Novotny would probably not last even as President, and that the choice would then fall on Svoboda. And I took, on the whole, a favourable view, I accepted the alternative and supported him in this matter.

In April, Cernik became Prime Minister and you Chairman of the National Assembly and a member of the party Presidium, despite the fact that Hager's attack[4] indicated that disagreement in some allied countries with the new Czechoslovak policy was directed particularly at yourself. What about your entry on this international arena?

On 4 May 1968, we went – Dubcek, Cernik, Bilak and I – to Moscow. On the Soviet side, Brezhnev, Podgorny, Kosygin, Suslov and some others, including Katushev, were there.

We were there for one day. On the whole, we spent the day listening to a long list of the things which the Soviet Union, or the Soviet representatives, disliked about developments in our country. In effect, it was a reading of the White Book[5] from a working draft, that is how I would describe it on the whole.

During the talk, secretaries kept coming, bringing Comrade Brezhnev more and more information about what this or that newspaper or magazine was writing about us, what this person or that had said.

It's a fact that none of us had any idea about many of the things they read out to us, especially Brezhnev. What was in some district newspaper, that there was such and such an article, a meeting some place, where somebody spoke and what he said. How could we have known it all?

They gathered the information — and here at home Ambassador Chervonenko did it — from the people who were later called the conservatives. Those people collected all kinds of gossip and handed them to the Soviet embassy — and from there the stuff went to Brezhnev.

We devoted that day to refuting and explaining. I said to Brezhnev, for instance, that in a month or two he wouldn't have such a pile of these things before him, they would have shrunk to insignificance, we could cope with matters of that kind.

We countered, especially Dubcek and others, with facts and information of much greater weight than their random assortment of so-called information. Later in 1968, Member of Parliament Dohnalova told me somewhat maliciously: 'We took care that the Soviet comrades should know everything that was happening here at that time.'

Our meeting took place a few days after May Day 1968, and we were disconcerted to find that they showed no interest whatsoever in May Day, where the participation had been so impressive, so spontaneous, altogether there were millions of people who came out so enthusiastically for the party policy. That didn't interest them. They were interested in meetings of KAN and K-23,[6] attended by fifty or a hundred people, sometimes less. We were sickened by the whole business, because we realized they weren't interested in the facts, in our overall situation, but were looking for pretexts for opposing us. Our position was made worse by the fact that Bilak took their side against us, in effect he wasn't the fourth member of our delegation, but the fifth of theirs, so instead of being four to four, we were three to five.

Didn't you have any discussion beforehand?

No.

On what basis were the talks conducted? After all, it was a delegation of one party and one state.

We were invited, we didn't know exactly why, or why they wanted to talk with us, so we went. Evidently we had been summoned to be put on the carpet. The outcome of that whole chapter was neither one thing nor the other. They demanded harsh administrative, say here police, measures against any of our people who voiced opinions not entirely in line with the documents or the policies of the party.

We, for our part, stressed that we could cope with the outburst of political activity by means of the democratic approach and discussion. Our assurance that if that failed, we would also employ administrative methods against extremes, if things went beyond the bounds of the law and attempts at agreement, that met with no success.

As for the April plenum of our Central Committee, insofar as they mentioned it, it was only touched on; they had reservations in the sense that it wasn't clear enough what we wanted. In speaking of the April plenum, I'm thinking of the Action Programme.

Did you yourselves demand anything of the Soviet representatives?

We went to the Moscow meeting on 4 May also about the matter of a loan. Cernik, as Prime Minister, explained our need to modernize our manufacturing industry, to carry out a gradual restructuring of our industry. And we also had in mind stepping up housing construction. We needed about 400–500 million roubles. We wanted to have the loan from the Soviet Union and we said that if the Soviet comrades couldn't manage to lend us that much, we would apply to the international bank or some other source. We underlined that in the event of our borrowing from the West, the deal on our side would be treated on a strictly commercial basis without political strings.

The reply to that – from Kosygin – was casual, that they would examine our request. But Kosygin didn't forget to remark – for whom did we actually want to manufacture consumer goods? For export? He said that the West didn't need our consumer goods and wouldn't want them in future. So then we'd be wanting to get our goods on the markets of the socialist countries, especially of the Soviet Union, with the help of investment capital from the Western countries. But the socialist market didn't want our consumer goods either, it needed our investment goods.

It was a very harsh and categorical attitude, favouring the old 'iron concept' of our industry which can only lead our economy by degrees not only into complete unilateral dependence, but also into a state of permanent ineffectiveness, since we lack raw materials. Their policy on trade with us was shown to be deliberately political, aimed at cutting off all our chances of sovereignty and firmly tying us to their policies. Nothing came of the loan, nothing has come of it to this day. We came back from Moscow so disillusioned that we couldn't, in all conscience, say anything to our public at home, since it was impossible to speak about the actual content of the talks.

Just one other point perhaps. It was your first visit to the Soviet Union as Chairman of Parliament. The Soviet representatives at the meeting voiced plenty of criticism. Later, however, it was said that from the outset they had warned, and indicated that they would have to intervene. Did any of them say anything at the May meeting which might have at least remotely given cause to assume that they were thinking of military intervention?

We've heard that sort of talk, too. I can say that up to 11.30 in the night of 20 August, I had heard nothing either directly from the Soviet side or from the other socialist countries, or at second-hand, that they were resolved to come in and occupy our country with their army. If I had heard anything of the kind, even at second-hand, I would certainly have dealt concretely with it, it would have to have been discussed in the Party Presidium, I simply couldn't have overlooked it. I never heard anything of the kind and insofar as I was present at several talks with the Soviet representatives, not a word was said about it.

Not even other threats, no mention of possible economic or other sanctions?

Nothing from which I could logically conclude that their words might lead to military intervention. There was just criticism, allegations, everything possible, but a threat of that kind, even indirect, veiled – I never heard it. No.

However, your Moscow talks influenced the situation. That was evident in the resolution of the May plenum. Do you still think today that the compromise was a happy one? Should it have gone further, less far, should there have been no compromise at all, or was there any other alternative?

Following our visit to Moscow there was a Central Committee meeting at the end of May where we considered the situation in the country, and where Dubcek's report and our contributions were, naturally, affected by the mood in which we had left Moscow.

I think the end of May was actually a sort of climax of the very nervous atmosphere, of the various outbursts which we said also went to extremes and where we were able to take very strong measures. It carried on into June. In those documents and speeches the Central Committee said, on the whole, openly and in warning to everyone, that things had to be calmed down and brought into legal forms.

I remember, in this connection, a discussion we had in the Party Presidium around the problem of the May Central Committee, where we thoroughly considered these excesses and none of us took the situation lightly. I myself published, I think it was on 19 May 1968, a pretty sharp article in *Rude Pravo* aimed against the extremes and the extremists. I'm not aware that any of those who were afterwards, after August, so 'courageous' and 'principled' publicly ventured anything of the kind.

In those days, in May and June – and even today I can't change anything of it – we saw things more or less like this: an outburst of popular discontent accumulated over the years had reached its height. For the time being we could not, alas, give sufficient guarantees that these negative things from the past, these distortions as they were called, would be thoroughly dealt with. That could be misused for attacking the communists altogether – which, in turn, would have incalculable consequences – including the tanks. That is why I spoke out against extremes both in public and internally. Naturally, there were sharp words; I, myself, for instance, said – and then it was used against me – that if the extremist groups refused to listen to reason, we would have to use the law against them.

When each of us had to say where we stood, we were each required to state clearly the positions we held, I also declared my attitude – that if the radical extremists wanted to push things further, maybe to conflict of some kind, I would in such a case definitely stand with the workers' militia and I would not hesitate to take harsh measures against anyone who might threaten the very existence of the Republic. May I stress again, however, that these were discussions in the most tense situation. After the May Central Committee, after those big meetings of activists, after the party documents, things definitely calmed down and the prospect of a power struggle practically vanished.

Following the resolution of the May plenum, the formulation about the main danger being from the right was in force, which was later seized upon and misused. How did it get into the resolution, what caused such a formulation to be accepted – apart from the reasons you have suggested indirectly?

In that connection I spoke, for instance, about the standpoint of our intellectuals. Many in the debate, the comrades of today who later declared themselves to be the 'healthy core', drove full tilt against the so-called Right. I took the view, and a number of other comrades did too, that we didn't have just one extreme in the so-called Right; that it was encouraged and provoked by extremes from the Left, from the so-called Left, from those conservatives. I wanted our intellectuals to come out unreservedly for the party's policy. And they said to me: where's the guarantee, what guarantee does the party give that the dogmatists won't come out on top in time? And I had to admit, more or less, that they were right, and actually I upheld this view all the time I was a member of the Presidium – that if we were to succeed at all in any measure against extremes on the Right, we had to proceed simultaneously against the extremes of the dogmatists too. They held meetings, gatherings of activists, in fact, illegal, factional activity. Unfortunately, I didn't get this view accepted, criticism of the Right was to the fore in the May resolution and the danger from the left was underestimated.

[The terms Left and Right in the Czechoslovak situation do not correspond to the classical understanding of these concepts. The dogmatists labelled as right-wing not only the negligible body of the classical Right, but also all progressive communists. For themselves, they used the term Left. The adoption of these concepts, first prefaced by 'so-called', later without it in the spoken language, was quite general and contributed to confusion of ideas and to falsifying events in retrospect. There were instances of right-wing views, but those who urged condemnation of the 'Right' were thinking of the progressive elements in the Communist Party and in other social groups – editor's note.]

The fact is that the pressure from abroad, from the Soviet Union, also helped to get that formulation in – that the main danger began to be seen coming only from right-wing excesses, without seeing the whole picture.

I recall that it was precisely this situation which had a bad effect in stirring up the feeling existing among the public at the time. The main thing was just then – to show that the party wanted to pursue a new policy. These matters threw doubt on that.

I think people's instinct was correct. And that played its part in the birth of the 2,000 *Words*, because people were afraid all the time of a return to the old times. But the measures on our part against the dogmatists were not strong enough to satisfy the other camp. I think people felt that, and anyhow it turned out that their anxiety was justified.

You've mentioned the 2,000 Words. What would you say about them today?

The 2,000 *Words!* All that business! It was Friday. I can't just recall the date. Parliament was sitting and I had popped over to the Central Committee before the opening.

There, on the steps from the street, I met Olda Svestka [member of the Party Presidium and editor of *Rude Pravo* – editor's note] with Zimyanin [member of the Soviet Party Central Committee and editor of *Pravda* – editor's note].

Zimyanin – former Soviet ambassador here – let fly at me, what did I think of it, it was outrageous . . . I stared and said: 'What?' I didn't know about the 2,000 *Words* being in the papers that day. Zimyanin was indignant, he told me it was a call for counter-revolution . . . And so I was all keyed up to learn what was in the papers. I went back to the sitting, it was at the Castle, where some Members were starting to talk about it too and during the session I, and others who hadn't read it, had a quick look at the article. There, at the instigation of several Members, we resolved that Parliament wouldn't close that day according to the programme, it was Friday, but would sit again on Saturday, that we would prolong the session and the Prime Minister would make a statement on the 2,000 *Words* on Saturday.

The same day, after Parliament rose, the Party Presidium met to consider this affair. It was agreed that Indra, on behalf of the Presidium, in the spirit of its discussion, should inform the regions by telex. That was done, but of course he wrote the message according to how he understood the Presidium's discussion.

The government met, too. I urged the Prime Minister that the government, whose job it was, should come out against the conclusions in the 2,000 Words manifesto. At one o'clock in the morning I phoned him and he told me: 'I can't convince the government, they don't want to make a statement.'

When Oldrich Cernik told me that, I asked if he and the government would object to my joining the meeting in my capacity as Chairman of the National Assembly. He said: 'Come.' So I went there, I spoke about the situation that had arisen and demanded that the government should seriously consider the matter and reject the conclusions in the manifesto. On that occasion, in view of the situation and the government's unwillingness to involve itself, I threatened them. I said: 'Comrades, tomorrow at nine or ten o'clock Parliament expects a statement from your Premier, and if you don't adopt a standpoint, then it can happen that the government will adopt one in a week. But that'll be a different government, it won't be yours any more.'

That was a strong threat. After that, just a few talks behind the scenes on the whole affair, and in the morning the Prime Minister took his seat with the government in Parliament, he spoke, his exposé was good. I think the government standpoint was good, and indeed Parliament approved it unanimously.

At the time, you wrote 1,000 Words. Did that differ from the initial reaction?

Some of us, Dubcek, Cernik, Slavik and some others, had a meeting on Wednesday of the next week with the authors, or signatories of the 2,000 Words. Vaculik was there, and others, I think it was at midday in the Hrzansky Palace. We asked, what had been their idea, what were they after?

They argued that we hadn't understood, there was a terrible misunderstanding, they wanted to help, not to cause trouble.

I think we were right in our view that the conclusions calling for certain actions were not good. In any case, it was an unfortunate business in the way it was misused, all the goings on around it, and the pretext it provided for the massive attacks on our cause.

After that discussion, I wrote the *1,000 Words* article a week later for *Prace* where I recognized that the signatories had certainly not intended any harm – definitely not any sort of counter-revolution or anything of that kind, as they were wrongfully accused later. But at the same time I was bound to say that to arouse people's passions was not the right way. I recalled what it led to in the 1950s, that in the end it meant that ten thousand resolutions came to the Party Central Committee demanding that the sentences in the trials should be even harsher, calling for more gallows, longer prison terms, and so on. I suggested that calls of any kind should be avoided; there's apt to be a big difference between a good intention and the way it may be understood. They certainly meant well, and in the end it turned against them, against us, against everyone it was horribly misused. That's about all I have to say on the 2,000 *Words*.

In those days you also encountered the students. Altogether, your relations with the students would deserve a chapter.

There was a gala performance in the National Theatre, the hundredth anniversary of the theatre, I think. The President was there, the First Secretary, I and others. As we were leaving, I met Sik in the corridor. He told me he'd heard that evening that some students were organizing a campaign for the next day. They were going to march out of the universities and colleges and they would demand that we leave the Warsaw Pact. Apparently they had talked to some writers about it, the writers had warned them, but without success, the students wouldn't be persuaded.

So I went at once to Dubcek, I managed to catch him in the street in front of the theatre. I told him I was going immediately to the City Committee of the Party, he'd better go home and go to bed, I would do what was necessary to see that nothing happened next day.

The City Committee was meeting; I spoke there and we agreed that overnight, and especially in the morning, they'd take steps in the schools and everywhere else to make sure there'd be no action. Bohous Simon [leading secretary of the City Committee of the party in Prague – editor's note] and the others arranged it. In the morning, comrades were sent to all schools and colleges, and we, with a number of comrades, were ready to go at once to the schools if these students wanted to start something. Also we took steps, in case of need, for the militia to be alerted and if the students from some schools wanted to go out on the streets, they would have to prevent them.

It wasn't a hoax. Some lads from these schools had really considered the idea, but the measures were completely effective, so that nothing happened at all, no meeting, nor any attempt to leave the schools.

I think that always when one discusses things with students one finds one can reach agreement. I've had plenty of experience of that, I've visited a great number of faculties, I went to the ones where things were hottest. And though we didn't agree one hundred per cent about everything, we always parted peacefully, having maintained a proper degree of restraint in political debate. On the whole, we always reached some agreement.

And so I had complete confidence not only in young people, but also in students. I knew that whatever happened, they wouldn't do anything rash.

While confidence was growing at home, international tension heightened. In June you led a Parliamentary delegation to Moscow. The trip caused a lot of discussion. Why was that?

The delegation to the Soviet Union had been planned long before, as a return visit to the Supreme Soviet delegation here. But the time – June – turned out to be rather inopportune for such a delegation, and for me too, because I was very busy with all the events of 1968.

We went. The reception at the airport – the Chairman of the Soviet of Nationalities was there, Chairman of the Union Soviet, Podgorny, Chairman of the Supreme Soviet were there. Then we went off on tours of the Soviet Union. On every occasion, I spoke as leader of the delegation about our country's problems, and I think I said plenty; again I stressed our unshakeable faith in brotherly relations with the Soviet Union. But I spoke about our problems, too, if only basically, not in detail, so that it didn't escape the notice of Soviet high places.

So after about three days, when we returned from Stalingrad to Moscow and were to fly to Riga, I got a new escort and he was the Zimyanin I've already referred to, the former ambassador, who told me in the plane that in my speeches I shouldn't mention the problems of the day in Czechoslovakia, those problems that we called democratization and so on. And he pointed out that the Soviet people weren't so well informed, they weren't acquainted with these matters and to explain them thoroughly at such gatherings was impossible, and just to touch on them – that would confuse people. In short, more or less a demand that I shouldn't speak on the subject.

I complied, I spoke less about it. However, on our return to Moscow we held a press conference for Soviet journalists. There were about eighty of them there, the conference lasted several hours, it was hard-hitting. The journalists put aggressive questions rather in the style of the White Book, I'd say – though not quite so sharp – and I replied, just because they were journalists, in a completely straightforward and unequivocal manner. For instance, I remember when they accused us of wanting to expand our contacts with capitalist countries, wanting a loan from them I put the question: 'Does the Soviet government take loans from the West? It does. It even has factories built – Renault, Fiat, Japanese investments.' I said: 'Is there anything strange about that? The Soviet Union does it. To my mind, it's right. But why do you criticize us for wanting to do something similar, though on an incomparably smaller scale, in line with Czechoslovakia's possibilities?'

The discussion was extremely sharp, exhaustive, but almost nothing appeared in the papers.

Brezhnev received our delegation before departure. The official part lasted about an hour. It was friendly, there was a lot of emotion, even tears, and the atmosphere was cordial. When it was over, Brezhnev asked me to stay for a private talk. Neither Koucky, our Ambassador, nor anyone else from the Soviet side was present, Brezhnev and I were alone. He reiterated his anxiety, his dissatisfaction with the way things were going with us – as in the earlier talks I've mentioned. And he spoke about leaders, too. He expressed disapproval of the elections, insofar as Comrade Dubcek's experience of life and party work was concerned. Suggesting on the whole that he wasn't the right man for the job.

On the other hand, he spoke absolutely clearly about myself. He apologized that in those first months – presumably he was thinking of Dresden and Hager's attack – the Soviet leaders hadn't known me so well, so I might have been upset by their propaganda, I should forgive them, these things happen, it's lack of information. He mentioned that I was old, I'd devoted nearly forty years of my life to the party. He put it as if I should bear the responsibility for an about-turn in our affairs, and should see to it that the turn was on the lines they had advised us and as later, in August, they took the further steps.

I was dismayed by the talk, because I knew what he was offering me. Now how to refuse so that the form was acceptable but the answer quite clear. So I defended Dubcek. Not just our policy, but Dubcek too. How he was developing quickly, of course it was a lot all at once, but he would manage and he would turn into a genuine leader of the party. I simply refused the offer which had, in effect, been made to me.

I said nothing to anyone, I returned home, and told my wife. 'What to do?' I said to myself. 'If I tell Dubcek, it'll upset him, it could cause all sorts of feelings.' So I decided to keep quiet. I wouldn't tell anyone. And I didn't. But then, when we were arrested in August and we didn't know what our end would be, then in Transcarpathian Russia where Cernik and I were interned in a forest, in a police house of some kind, I confided it to him. If he ever in his life met Dubcek again, he was to tell him that when we were in Moscow in June Brezhnev had made that offer. That I'd refused, and altogether the reasons why I hadn't told Dubcek. When we got home from Moscow, everything having turned out differently to what we had thought, it was still in the August days that I asked Cernik at the Castle whether he'd told Dubcek. He said, no, that when he saw the situation changing, that we would be going home, he had kept quiet too. Whereupon – it was after lunch in company with Dubcek,

Cernik and Svoboda – I repeated to all three the story of my talk with Brezhnev.

Perhaps we should go back a bit. What about the Warsaw letter?

The next act in the series of great events was the Warsaw letter. I don't want to tell the history of the letter myself, because Comrade Dubcek described the whole affair pretty thoroughly at the Central Committee meeting in September 1969. Because there had been so much talk about the matter, he put it on record and I shall draw on that document in my further work.

I'd like to add that it wasn't by way of being a conference for us, but a summons to give an account of ourselves. And the invitation was in a form that offended everyone. Let me mention again that I am drawing on Dubcek's account as my source, because before the CC meeting in 1969 we considered at length and thoroughly what had been the precise sequence of events, the invitation, the date and everything. And no one will be able to work out the chronology of those events, or produce better documentation than Dubcek did.

All those tales put around afterwards – if Dubcek had informed us better, etc. we would have gone to Warsaw – they're slanders. I remember, for instance, that when we received the invitation, a special letter from Chervonenko and Ceteka (Czechoslovak Press Agency) announced that the other delegations were on their way of Warsaw, the party Presidium resolved that the Presidium of our party should not leave the territory of our Republic.

I wouldn't like to attribute any deeds to anyone, to add or take away, so I ask myself: Who actually made that suggestion? Something keeps telling me that it was, in fact, Oldrich Cernik who proposed it, arguing that the Party Presidium shouldn't leave the country in the situation as it was, and on no account travel outside the territory of the Republic.

The first proposal not to go to Warsaw came from the Slovak Party Presidium and its standpoint was brought to Prague before 17 July 1968, when the Czechoslovak Presidium met, by Vasil Bilak. It was printed in *Rude Pravo*, I think, and certainly in the Slovak *Pravda* on about 16 or 17 July. Which was conveniently forgotten after April 1969.

Later there was an accusation that you had leaked the contents of the letter to the City Conference in Prague. Absurd as it is, is it worth a few words?

First, I'm hardly likely to start refuting any slanders – I don't think I shall – because there have been so many, I've lost interest.

It's nonsense. When we read the invitation to the Warsaw meeting at the Presidium meeting, twenty of us heard it, plus ten employees of the *apparat.* There were thirty of us present, and if twenty people from the Central Committee building knew it, then all five or six hundred employees knew it too. Someone leaked it. That's inevitable in a situation like that. When we'd received the official invitation in this way, learnt its content, and when I went on in the evening to the City Committee meeting and spoke about it, that can hardly be described as leaking information. Ceteka announced it that day, too. We received the information at the same time that we were to go to Warsaw, that the other delegations were arriving and there was a press report – not from us. So what price leaking – why, it's nonsense.

By then it was less than two weeks before the meeting at Cierna nad Tisou. It was the subject of much excitement and numerous misunderstandings. Until 21 August gave an apparent answer to the difficult question whether it had been successful. Nevertheless, it still isn't quite clear why, and at which moment, the policy of negotiation was dropped and replaced by military force.

The place, Cierna nad Tisou, was chosen because our Party Presidium refused to leave the territory of the Republic, as if we had sensed the Soviet representatives' intentions, which they then carried out with us on 21 August 1968. For the Soviet delegation Cierna provided the opportunity to be only a few tens of metres from the frontier, to be at home overnight, because every day their sleeping cars went back over the frontier, and they had all the services on their side, probably including regular contacts with their colleagues from the Warsaw meeting.

Our journey attracted the attention of the entire nation. A manifesto appeared at the time, I think its author was Pavel Kohout. It gave our delegation a mandate of confidence such as few Czechoslovak delegations have had for foreign negotiations, but it also set limits for our transaction. It stressed that we should hold to and defend four postulates of the Czechoslovak Socialist Republic, namely: socialism, alliance, sovereignty and freedom as the programme of our country, of our people.

In conversations on the way to Cierna, I formulated our task as containing two mandates: to defend the post-January policy as expressed in the Party's Action Programme and to prevent any break with the Soviet Union.

That's how I formulated it. Comrade Brezhnev attacked these two mandates in his speech, primarily in the sense that we were placing the negotiations of the two Presidia under the pressure of, as they said, a nationalized public.

Again Brezhnev had assistants on our Czechoslovak side – not just Bilak as on 4 May in Moscow, but also Kolder and some others.

I'd like to give one concrete example of how the whole nation was

behind us, though one could mention hundreds. A delegation came to
Cierna from a district, it was Trencin or Zilina, I must check which, with
the tension and rush of events the two names have got mixed and here in
hospital I have nothing to refer to. They wanted to see Dubcek. I received
them in his place. They had brought sheets of a petition bound into a
book, signed by all the citizens in their district. There were 20,000
signatures, in fact a few dozen over that number. They underlined that all
citizens had signed, including the sick, whom they had visited. Nobody
was missing. The petition supported the manifesto which I've mentioned.
If a national plebiscite had been possible, I think only a small percentage
would have been missing. Such a consensus and awareness by people of
what they wanted can hardly have existed before in our history. The
August days after the troops came in showed it again even more strongly.
Socialism, alliance, sovereignty, freedom, words expressing everything
for which people have fought for generations, the whole working-class
movement, what the programme of the international communist movement declares, what just wars have been and are being waged for. All this
was upheld on our side, and on the other – the whole tragic campaign on
the part of the Soviet comrades, of the whole of that 'Warsaw five'.

The talks started on Monday in the railwaymen's house. The two
delegations lived in their sleeping cars, which stood next to each other on
the track, ours on the narrow-gauge beside the Soviet one on the
wide-gauge rails. I'll never forget how our people told us to take care
about the tracks, so we didn't find ourselves suddenly on the other side of
the frontier. In my view that mistrust is a serious factor in our people's
minds and subsequent events simply intensified it very strongly.

The proceedings – it was similar to Moscow on 4 May, only much
sharper. The Soviet comrades spoke, we spoke, everyone on each side had
their say. But whereas the Soviet Presidium, with only three members
missing – Polyansky, Mazurov and Kirilenko – were united, that wasn't
the case with us.

Dubcek was our main speaker, explaining party policy, and Cernik
who explained it from the standpoint of state policy. Then each of us
spoke. Speaking from Dubcek's and Cernik's position were myself,
Kriegel and others. I have the list in my notes. But the other group of our
people – Bilak, Kolder, Svestka, again the well-known group, they spoke
from the standpoint of the Soviet arguments. So that even among us the
situation wasn't good, because they criticized everything that Dubcek
and the rest of us said.

Tuesday evening, the evening before the last day, the Ukrainian
secretary Shelest spoke, accusing us that there were even leaflets printed
in our country which were distributed in Transcarpathian Russia, they
called for the separation of Transcarpathian Russia from the Soviet

Union, and he held us responsible. And a whole lot of outrageous things, which ended in Dubcek getting up, and we with him, because we weren't willing to listen any longer to these insults.

Dubcek announced that if it was to continue like that, we would pack up and go home, we wouldn't take part any longer in proceedings of that kind. I got up, too, I went over to Chervonenko who was present, I told him to take it from me in my capacity as Chairman of the National Assembly and to convey officially to his government that I would not be party to such proceedings, if that was how representatives of the CSSR were treated, such humiliating and insulting proceedings I would not take part in. In short, the talks broke down. We rose and left the room in that railwaymen's house.

All of you?

All – it's hard to say today whether all of us, I don't know whether anyone stayed. Some went to our coach, I walked the platform and in a while one of the *apparat* people ran up to say I was to go back to Dubcek's sleeping car, that the Soviet delegation was there. Besides Brezhnev, Podgorny, Kosygin, Suslov and, I think, Shelest too were there. I'm not quite sure. They apologized, that Shelest had exaggerated. In short, we were about two hours in the waggon, trying to reconcile everything so we could carry on with the talks next day.

And there was some sort of reconciliation. Next morning, that was Wednesday, proceedings didn't start because Brezhnev was reported ill and Dubcek was to visit him in the waggon. So while they were there in the waggon, the rest of us walked around Cierna nad Tisou. I went, for instance, with Svoboda, and Podgorny and Kosygin from the Soviet side. We walked through the little town and we also carried on with the discussion.

On our return to the coach around midday, Dubcek informed us about his talk with Brezhnev, that the proceedings were to end, and they had drafted a communiqué which on the whole said nothing, and a proposal, rather a kind of resolution, that on Saturday all five partners from the Warsaw meeting, and we Czechoslovaks, so six in all, would meet in Bratislava.

So we flew back from Cierna and on Friday we left again for Bratislava, where however there were no talks, but where at the suggestion of the Soviet representatives two people were chosen from each delegation – the First Secretary and one expert colleague. Actually it was an editorial council which drafted during Saturday the famous Bratislava declaration, which had nothing to do with Czechoslovakia, but was meant to deal with the general principles for procedure by Communist Parties of the socialist countries in international matters.

But another thing about Cierna. Precautions were strict; for instance, our assistants – we could each take someone with us, a secretary, I had mine too – but they couldn't take part in the proceedings. So they weren't present. The approach to our area – to the train and the conference place – was strictly guarded, so no one could get in. Now and then somebody slipped through. People greeted us, there were crowds of people, from other places besides Cierna, as we heard.

Later it was repeatedly said that the Czechoslovak and Soviet leaders had reached agreement at Cierna, and that the Czechoslovaks then broke the agreement. What did you agree on and what was actually broken?

When I recapitulated in my own mind what the Soviet comrades had concretely wanted of us – through that flood of criticism, again this or that meeting, this or that article – it boiled down in the end to six concrete points. The actual sequence isn't important. First, the personal matters:

For instance, the categorical demand that Dr Kriegel should not be Chairman of the National Front.

Second case – Cestmir Cisar – not to be a party secretary, dismiss from the post of secretary in the Presidium.

Third case – we were not to allow the existence of the Social Democratic Party.

Fourth case – banning of KAN and K-23.

And finally, the media. We told ourselves – that'll be the hardest, because we don't want to introduce censorship again, which had been abolished shortly before, we want to do it democratically, by agreement. Discipline among journalists – on that we would take the necessary steps; and on our return from Cierna we talked a lot with them, things changed too, we even took various governmental measures to prevent various excesses in the media.

So there were those six concrete demands arising from the talks.

But – a week later Brezhnev was phoning Dubcek every day asking why they weren't being carried out. Dubcek explained again what would be happening at the CC at the end of August, what would happen at Congress, and that we couldn't use administrative means. All in vain, because they didn't want to understand us. First they took note of our arguments, then they told us we weren't fulfilling the resolution, the agreement. So those were the so-called agreements. No agreements at all – we said the points were either decided, or would be, and how the decisions would be made.

With that we left Cierna nad Tisou. In Prague I reported immediately at a meeting of functionaries in the Congress Palace, we all spoke there, objectively, concealing nothing. Only that nasty atmosphere at Cierna, of that we naturally said nothing.

Was there any mention there that the demands they made, especially with regard to personnel, and other things, showed no respect for sovereignty and meant interference in our internal affairs? At least about the principle, since the practice all over the world doesn't adhere to it?

It's all so simple today. And on the whole pointless. We knew it, but we just didn't grasp, we couldn't grasp, couldn't know that these were all merely pretexts.

There's another question here. Do you think these were definite criticisms or, at that stage, was it merely a matter of demonstrating at any price that Czechoslovakia did not fulfil agreements, thereby providing a pretext, or at least the opportunity of some false interpretation, for the entry of the troops – a step decided upon long before?

Look, I don't know if they had an absolutely clear idea about what to do – there at Cierna. Today we know they had considered the idea of occupying us. Gomulka's secretary, who emigrated, also said that in Warsaw, Zhivkov and several others demanded military intervention; I'm not really convinced that the Soviet representatives had already decided on that. I think there were still doubts, there wasn't complete unity among them, and all those things were just pretexts.

Today I see clearly that it wasn't a matter of concrete items, but of our whole political concept. That was the reason for all that went on. But it would be difficult to stand up and say: we are against democratization of the social order, we are against humanism, we are against modernizing the running of the socialist state. They couldn't do that. But that was the real issue. Those things were pretexts and that's why it was so difficult to reach agreement. They were details which couldn't be grounds for any conflict because we were tackling them and solving them. That's not why they came here. Their interpretation of 21 August has changed so often since then. Once they threatened us with the West Germans, apparently they were prepared. Their people even said: we arrived two hours before the West Germans; if we hadn't arrived, a Western army would have invaded. Then the story was that there was a threat of counter-revolution, then that God-knows-what threatened.

Was there any mention at Cierna about such things as the forged letters from Simon Wiesenthal, the weapons in the Sokolov area and so on?

There were some remarks about such things. Of course, we refuted them. You mention Sokolov. We all knew, our security was informed beforehand, that it was a provocation. And it was. Our research institutes immediately analysed the weapons, the vaseline still on them. They even left behind the rucksacks used to transport the stuff. There are photographs – a rucksack labelled *nommer* such and such. There was an immediate thorough investigation. There is no doubt – it was provocation.

Those are things culled from the White Book, there's a mass of such items, trivialities.

For instance, when we argued: in Prague 400,000 people took part in May Day. I said – I was in Brno on May Day, there were 100,000 people there, they unanimously supported my speech – and I let them have a copy of it. I said to Brezhnev: 'Come to us, Comrade Brezhnev, to Prague, to Ostrava, to Brno, to Pilsen, to Bratislava, choose where you want to go. We'll go with you. You'll see how our people support the Communist Party, socialist alliance with the Soviet Union. Come and see for yourself; why, what you have here is a collection of tittle-tattle, trivialities which in no way decide the course in our country.' They weren't concerned with the actual situation, they were concerned with something else.

When I was in Moscow with our Parliamentary delegation, I complained to Brezhnev about Chervonenko and Udaltsov. I said: 'Comrade Brezhnev, these two representatives of the Soviet Union are doing an ill service to our friendship. They're not informing you correctly.' And I indicated clearly that it would be good and our people would welcome it if these two were replaced. He looked at me without saying anything. But I said it.

Instead, came 21 August, or more precisely, the evening of 20 August.

It was Tuesday [20 August – editor], the Party Presidium had been sitting since two in the afternoon. We were discussing the preparations for the 14th Congress. Up to 11.30, I, and certainly many others, had no inkling that such dramatic events would follow.

Around 11.30 p.m. Cernik was called from the meeting to the phone in another room. He came back in about ten minutes completely crushed, he took his place, he was sitting on my left, and asked that the speaker, I don't remember who it was, should stop. Then he told us that he had just been informed that troops of the Warsaw Pact – the five, without the Romanians – that they had crossed our frontiers from all directions, from the north, the east, the south from Hungary, and that by six in the morning our country would be occupied.

The effect was absolutely crushing. Cernik himself was practically – he broke down. And Dubcek too. Neither of them was fit to talk. We started discussing, at first disjointedly, then we began to take an attitude. And during the discussion, which lasted over an hour, at first we said we must adopt an attitude and, as the Presidium, communicate it to the public. That was why instructions were given that the media be told that in a while there would be an important announcement. And the radio broadcast that.

Only time was running on and we couldn't reach any conclusions. Whereupon Zdenek Mlynar[7] was delegated, I don't know who by, it arose from the discussion, to draft a communiqué. He came out very openly with that communiqué and altogether in taking a stand similar to that then adopted by Comrade Kriegel. And, of course, I did too. Only the speakers in discussion – Kolder, Bilak, Jakes – held up the proceedings with endless debate. And Dubcek was thunderstruck. In between he announced, as has been later stated, that he really ought to resign and so on, which we refused to accept. And since he was in such a state, and Cernik too, I got up and said there'd been enough discussion, nobody would say anything new, and the public was waiting for news. And I said that since everyone had spoken three or four times, the communiqué was drafted and before us – those colleagues of ours, Bilak and Co. were against the part which spoke about the Warsaw Pact troops having infringed the Warsaw Treaty and international law, all the legal norms – so I said that we must end the debate and vote individually.

Each as we sat round the table, each individually: 'Are you for this communiqué, or are you against?' I began with the one opposite me, that was Kolder, next to him Bilak, it went all round. I noted down their votes. I came before Cernik, I said, 'I'm for – Cernik, are you for or against?' Cernik said 'for' and the last: 'Dubcek, are you for?' 'For.'

I counted it up and repeated again how many were for and against – it was seven to four.

Beside Dubcek was Comrade Svoboda, whom I had phoned earlier, immediately we got the news. His wife said that Chervonenko was with him just then: as soon as they finished, he would come to the Presidium, which happened in about an hour. But I didn't ask Comrade Svoboda if he was for or against because he wasn't a member of the Presidium at the time, and the voting was expressly by Presidium members only.

The communiqué was accepted. We'd hardly finished voting, when Sadovsky, one of the CC secretaries, asked to speak; he declared that although he wasn't a Presidium member, he asked for it to be put on record that he, too, supported this declaration by the party Presidium. I would also stress that Piller also voted in favour, because there was a sequel to that story.

The communiqué was accepted, we gave it to the media, because they were waiting for it everywhere, and now we waited for the media, mainly the radio, to send it out. We had a set, the radio started: We are announcing the resolution of the Party Presidium – and silence. It had been turned off, not on our set, but at the radio station.

In about ten to fifteen minutes, I was called to the telephone in the next room. Some radio people were calling, not from the central building, but from somewhere on the outskirts of Prague, I think it was Strahov [communications centre – editor's note]; they were waiting for the Presidium's statement. In the meantime, Comrade Hoffman [CC member and Minister of Communications, now member of the Party Presidium and Chairman of the Trade Union Council], the Minister, had declared that the report wasn't true, it was faked, so now these people were asking what was happening.

So I told them how things really were, that the Presidium report existed, that it had to do with the entry of troops, that Comrade Hoffman had disobeyed and taken the side of we knew who, he had refused to put the communications media at the disposal of the party and the state. Then I told those lads to put out the report, to broadcast it through all channels as long as possible.

That happened; they immediately put it on the air; incidentally, Vienna picked it up at once, that was by chance, and from there it went all over the world, so that within two hours the party statement had reached the whole world.

A similar episode was when, between two and three at night, it's hard to remember the time, we didn't notice it, a delegation from *Rude Pravo* came to us in the Presidium. I'm not sure now, I didn't know the comrades, but I wouldn't be surprised if Moc wasn't one [now editor of *Rude Pravo* and a member of the CC secretariat – editor's note].

I may be wrong, but it's not so important. And they told me that Comrade Svestka [then Presidium member and *Rude Pravo* editor, now a CC secretary – editor] had stopped the presses when the Presidium statement was already being printed, that this statement wouldn't be published and Svestka was sitting in his office writing a new one. Whereupon I told them how things really were and that they should arrange for *Rude Pravo* to appear and get the Presidium announcement published. They wanted me to confirm that to the chairman of their party organization; they called him, handed the phone to me, and I explained things directly to this party chairman. Then they saw to it that the paper came out.

In the meantime, a number of Presidium members and secretaries had left the meeting, including Indra, Jakes, Kolder and others. While we were overwhelmed by the event, they ran around and went to their offices, to get their hands in. Cernik also left for the government, a meeting had immediately been called, and Dubcek, myself, Kriegel, Spacek, Vaclav Slavik, we stayed, waiting for further developments.

It's also worth mentioning that some comrades came, worried about our fate. They said: 'What's this, are you waiting for them to come and arrest you, or what? Come, we'll drive you somewhere, we'll find you apartments.' I refused to go anywhere. Dubcek said he wouldn't either, without my having asked him. So we simply waited.

We heard planes roaring. They were transporting tanks and troops to Ruzyn airport. It was beginning to get light, between four and five, we waited for their troops to appear outside the Central Committee building. And we didn't wait long. Around five, cars drove up first, then the tanks, then armoured cars.

It was an 'interesting' sight when a heavy tank drove along the right bank of the Vltava, halted in front of the main entrance and turned those guns against the Central Committee building. And round it armoured troop carriers, parachutists jumped out, and covered the corners in front of the building. Others jumped out of cars, parachutists with automatics burst into the building. They already had Czech guides.

We were in Dubcek's room. They announced immediately that no one was allowed to leave, they compiled a list, they had Czechs with them, a band of volunteers, about six lads from the Ministry of the Interior. So they made a list of the people there. Some of our colleagues were there, too, for instance, my secretary, my driver, my guard, who were waiting for us, and other comrades had people there, there were quite a lot of them.

They assembled us in Dubcek's room. Then there were episodes, when someone wanted to go to the WC, for instance, a soldier with an automatic took him to the lavatory and brought him back.

In the meantime one of their men came, for instance, he was a high-ranking officer, a colonel, a small man, twice Hero of the Soviet Union. He wanted to know where 'Tovarish Svestka' was. The comrades didn't respond at all. I replied: 'Comrade Svestka is your man, he's working with you, so you find him. Probably he's at *Rude Pravo*.'

After five o'clock, big crowds of young people appeared outside the Central Committee building. They had flags, Czechoslovak, they were in ranks, about ten young people at the head. They wanted to get in front of the building, but they only got to the corner, armoured cars and tanks were there, in front of the tanks a chain of Soviet troops with automatics.

I watched from a first-floor window; they sang 'Where is my homeland?' (the Czechoslovak anthem); and I watched with a Soviet lieutenant, he was a decent boy. About ten paces in front of that line – they were giving some orders or something, with all the noise one couldn't hear – suddenly that whole line of troops fired a volley from their automatics into the air. Only one, who was on the edge, fired his volley into one of our lads, a student who was first in the row, on the right side when you faced the procession. He got it somewhere in the chest or neck, because I saw how he fell backwards. Of course, he was dead.

The lieutenant chased us away from the window, we weren't allowed to look, they shut the window. But I managed to peep for a while; through the window I saw a pool of blood around the head. Then people began to carry flowers there; they carried him away somewhere, and towards morning, before we had been taken away ourselves, a tank arrived at the spot where the blood had been. It halted, lowered one track, it moved on the spot so that everything, including the paving stones, was ground up with the blood, it made a sort of heap.

At the moment when they shot that boy, I leapt from the window to the phone next door, to Dubcek's secretary. I told her: 'Connect me immediately with Chervonenko!' She did so, Chervonenko was on the line, evidently he'd been sitting by the phone, because he took it at once. I told him – this has happened, you Comrade Ambassador, you bear the main responsibility for the blood spilt.

But – before Chervonenko could say anything to me, one of the Soviet guards seized the phone and bashed it so it flew apart. A few seconds later, Dubcek called Cernik in the government. He had that long flex on the receiver – another soldier rushed up, grabbed the phone by the flex and tore it out. I can still see Dubcek standing there holding the receiver with the flex dangling, and unable to speak. They drew their conclusion, and then they cut through all the cables. They were thick cables, even the cable for direct contact with Moscow, they gutted it all. So there was no hope of making any calls.

Couldn't you even let your family know anything?

I managed before midnight to call my wife to say what had happened. She could hardly believe it. I told her: be ready for anything, I'm staying here – I couldn't get through again. I heard later that at 7 a.m., that was Wednesday, 21 August, when we were already interned, an official car arrived at my home. Three or four men went into the building and demanded to be admitted to my flat. My wife, who had naturally hardly slept at all, refused to let them in. The door was on a chain, so she spoke through the door. Who were they and what did they want. They said explicitly that they were sent by Comrade Salgovic to ensure my protection. My wife, who had past experience, didn't above all, let them into the flat. She said: 'Why would Comrade Salgovic send you when my husband is already interned (evidently she knew or guessed it) in the Central Committee building, so what do you want here?' So they said could they at least phone, she must let them in to use the phone. And she replied there were call boxes for that, not the phone in my flat.

She just didn't let them in, but later, when she met Cisar's and Kriegel's wives, they learnt from each other that they must have gone from my place, the time fitted, to Cisar's home, they picked him up there and took him to police headquarters in Bartolomejska Street, and they went to Kriegel's too. But Kriegel was arrested as I was in the Central Committee building. So Salgovic! Those chaps mentioned specifically that they came from Salgovic – but not to protect, to arrest, because they arrested Cisar.

Afterwards Salgovic denied it all, Bilak denied it, as long as I still sat with them in the Presidium, where I said they should drop those tales, since they had definitely sent three or four fellows to my home to arrest me.

We really didn't have any illusions over the arrests. Each of us thought of our families, I said farewell by telephone. I had about a thousand crowns on me, which I gave to my secretary – that was already the situation with the soldiers there, so somehow I slipped the notes to him all crumpled, to give to my family, and asked him if he would see that if anything should happen to me, our friends didn't leave my family in the lurch. And I had some documents, congress material, a full briefcase. I shoved it at someone, saying: 'See this doesn't get into the wrong hands.' And that lad, under those conditions, actually found a place to shove the briefcase and a week later, when I was back, he unearthed it and handed it over to me in good order with all the documents.

Some reports say that you were originally meant to be put on trial. How actually?

Some time after eight, someone said it was nine, their commander came again, the two-fold hero, with some of those Czech volunteers from the Ministry of the Interior, and they called us by name. Dubcek, Smrkovsky, Spacek, Kriegel, I'm not sure who else – we were to follow them. When they called us out and we left Dubcek's room and passed through the second room where the various employees were sitting, they told us to hand over any weapons we might have on us. Well, I – they frisked us all, to see what we had in our pockets – I had a knife, I happen to have it with me now, so I put it on the table, that was my only weapon. They gave it back to me.

They led us to the other corridor, to Cestmir Cisar's office. When we got there, a Ministry of the Interior volunteer informed us, with those Soviet officers, they were all KGB officers, listening, that within two hours we would be brought before a revolutionary tribunal headed by Comrade Indra.

I exploded a bit: 'What revolutionary tribunal and what Comrade Indra is supposed to head it!' And Dubcek tugged my sleeve and said: 'Josef, it's no good. Don't say anything, keep quiet!'

So we sat in Cisar's office, we on one side of the table, opposite us KGB officers, colonels, lieutenant-colonels, those were the ranks. We each had our own by now, we sat opposite our own man. We as clients and they, who were to see to our escort to the next anabasis, which followed.

Who was there?

Dubcek, Kriegel, myself, Spacek. I'm not sure now if Simon was there. Cernik was in the government building, but I think Simon wasn't there either. There were four of us. While Mlynar, Slavik, stayed in Dubcek's office, they weren't arrested. We had been by that last act. We waited for the revolutionary tribunal. The window was open at the top, so we heard shooting from the city, we heard demonstrations, we even heard the slogans people were shouting, whereupon they went and shut the window.

We asked for newspapers, they refused, we weren't even allowed outside the door alone. When someone needed to go to the toilet, a lieutenant-colonel accompanied him. None of us had eaten since the previous day, and we had no thought of food. They brought us some salami, but nobody took any notice of it.

In the afternoon, it could have been about two, they summoned us to follow them.

As we went under those automatics past the employees, the drivers were there and our guards, they were drinking coffee – the lads hadn't slept all night – there was sugar on the table. My driver said to me then: 'Comrade Chairman, don't you want some sugar?' So I took three lumps, I thought to myself, they may come in useful. At that moment I remembered Ruzyn, when I was arrested in 1950, how hungry one was. They used to give us oats, gruel of oatmeal; you couldn't eat it unless you were absolutely starving. So I remembered Ruzyn and I took the sugar and I left it in Transcarpathian Russia, when things got better, and I'm rather sorry, because I could have given it to my grandchildren as a souvenir.

Did you know then where they were taking you?

We went down some stairs, nobody told us anything about what would happen to us. So we had all sorts of thoughts: were we going before the revolutionary tribunal, or into the cellar? They took us down dark corridors, where incidentally I had never been in my life – we've had experience of cellars, of course. Well, suddenly we found ourselves in a courtyard, a tiny courtyard in the Central Committee building. There were two armoured cars there and some of their officers. Into the first they shoved Dubcek and Kriegel from the back, and into the second armoured car they shoved me and Pepik Spacek. The door slammed, somebody was sitting beside the chauffeur and a third man was an officer who sat in front of us; and at the back Spacek and I sat.

We drove off. Where to? We didn't know. As we drove along the streets, I looked through the peephole, or whatever the military call it, and I recognized the streets – I know the Prague streets – I realized we were going in the direction of Ruzyn.

I said to myself: 'Now Ruzyn, what can that mean?' Ruzyn is the prison where I've already spent several years. Or it's the airport.

We arrived at the airport. I can't say now for certain whether it belonged to the old or the new part. I suppose I was thinking of something else at the time.

I know they took us from the cars within a few minutes. It was terribly hot in those armoured cars, the weather was hot anyhow. So we got a bit of air, and they took us to a plane, to the 'Anton', it's called the 'castle plane' because they carry the tanks in it. It was battered, there were only benches, not even fixed, it was rickety. We sat about half an hour in that plane, after which they told us to get out and they drove us in a *gazik* to another plane, and they loaded us, all four, into it. Again we wanted to know where they were taking us. And again that two-fold Hero of the Soviet Union, a short, stocky colonel, said: 'Comrades, you'll find out everything in the plane.'

It was a military plane, again battered, again the benches, the seats you have in planes had been torn out; simply a plane for field duties. So we sat in that plane, whereupon they came and told Dubcek to get out. They led him away somewhere from the airport building and I didn't see him again. He probably flew in another plane, with Cernik. When we were airborne, there were only the three of us – myself, Kriegel and Spacek – and I saw no one else.

We didn't know where we were flying. As I sat on the left side of the plane, I looked to see where the sun was, then I looked down; I saw we were over the Giant Mountains, that meant we were flying north. It was dark when we landed at the Legnica airport. I saw Legnica written on a hangar, so I knew we were in Western Poland. But Kriegel told me, somehow it had slipped my memory, that before landing in Legnica, we had landed at another airport for refuelling. I can't for the life of me remember. It's possible, it was my second night without sleep.

We stood a good half hour at that airport, perhaps three-quarters, officers were running around, evidently expecting some orders. Then they told us to get out of the plane, they put us in a car and drove us ten or fifteen kilometres to some house. It was their house, a police place, and now we each had our 'guardian angel'. I had a colonel, he introduced himself as Nikolayev.

So we sat there, each at a different table, and we talked of various things. They were interesting conversations. My man, Comrade Nikolayev, prepared me for what was to come. He said: 'Tovarish Smrkovsky, you must reconcile yourself to fate, that's how it goes in politics. And it's not our fault, we're here on duty, you know, well you must reconcile yourself to fate.' In himself, he was a cultured man.

But Kriegel sat at another table with his officer. That was, it is — terrible: they found that they had both fought in Spain. Kriegel and that Soviet officer. They spoke Spanish together – the officer could speak a bit, and Kriegel knows Spanish – and occasionally they used a few words of English. They even played chess together, because we waited there three, four hours. So both were Spain fighters!

Pepik Spacek had another colleague. They gave us a piece of salami there, or something to eat. We waited; they hadn't received orders where to fly us to. Evidently there had been some change. In the first place, after all, if they were taking us somewhere it wouldn't be Legnica. It may have been something over three hours when they drove us to the airport and put us in a new TU; it still smelt of varnish, elegant, a military plane. There were three of us; I don't know if there was anyone else in the plane, there are partitions. In short, we flew, we didn't know where, it began to get light and we landed somewhere. By the terrain, the hills, the scenery and by the sun we realized we weren't in the north, but somewhere in the south. And quite independently of each other we judged we were in Transcarpathian Russia. And we were: Kriegel knows it, I know Transcarpathian Russia, so does Cernik.

How did Cernik suddenly turn up?

Not yet, in a few minutes. At the airport they put us each separately into cars, I was in the middle at the back with a KGB officer on each side, and we drove somewhere. Each to a different place – we didn't know where. It could have been about thirty kilometres, into mountains. Suddenly we stopped at a camp of kinds, there were some buildings there, one house surrounded with barbed wire, some soldiers with automatics.

We drove into a courtyard – so that was it. Here I was in a police place, a villa of kinds. There was a garden round the house, it could have been fifteen paces in front, fifteen at the back, on average about thirty, perhaps fifty paces around was barbed wire.

I approached the door to the house, there stood Cernik. They had brought him a few seconds or minutes before me. We gazed at each other, Cernik embraced me, we greeted each other and we stayed there. Later we learnt that the other comrades were ten to fifteen kilometres away in another house of similar type.

By now the sun was rising. We washed a bit, they gave us something to eat and we went to sit in the courtyard. Of course, there was an officer right there, but they allowed us, within that space, to walk and sit together.

That was the first time they let you talk together?

Yes. The first time we could talk without being interrupted.

The sun started shining, we sat under a pine tree. It hit Oldrich Cernik, psychologically he broke down. Simply an outburst of crying, all those sort of things. I had a long talk with him afterwards on the subject and the situation; I think it helped him. He said, 'It's the end, we'll never get back, we couldn't even say goodbye to our families.' He just felt it was the end of everything. I didn't think so; and soon it turned out that it wasn't the end.

At midday they called us to lunch in the house, and in contrast to the breakfast and to the previous day, they gave us a decent meal. There were just the two of us and a girl, from the KGB, of course. We glanced at each other, I said: 'Oldrich, this means something, such a difference from the treatment yesterday and from that breakfast, this is something, this is a civilized lunch.'

After lunch we sat outside again and suddenly the officer out there called: 'Tovarish Cernik to the telephone.' So Olda Cernik went to the phone, soon he came back and he was all excited. He said – he called me Josifek at the time: 'Josifek, I've spoken to Sasha (Dubcek), he called me. Sasha has talked with Brezhnev, he's to go to Moscow and he said someone should go with him, so I'm going.' Well – we said goodbye. That was Thursday afternoon. I gave him a message for Dubcek in case I didn't see Dubcek again.

So I stayed alone for another twenty-four hours. Suddenly that young chap came, saying: 'We're off!' So I got in the car again and we drove to the airport. I was alone, we were flying somewhere again. We landed at Vnukov (Moscow airport), I've been there several times, so I know it. I wondered where we were going. Only when we left the airport for the main road, instead of turning left for Moscow we turned right away from Moscow. I think it was in the direction of Smolensk or Kalinin, anyhow not Moscow. It must have been a good forty kilometres, we drove into woods, again some kind of walled-in house in the woods. So I was given quarters there and outside – from the room allotted to me – I saw Bohous Simon, whom they had brought there before me. We spent another twenty-four hours together there, we talked about everything possible to do with the events. And he told me a little about himself, where he came from, his background, he came from a farm labourer's family in southern Bohemia.

So we were there for twenty-four hours. The table was laid, they called us – to eat – I'm not sure if it was supper or breakfast, I've forgotten. I looked at the girl who was serving us and I said: 'We know each other, don't we?' And she looked at me and said: 'No, I don't.' I said, 'Oh yes, we've seen each other, when I was in Moscow with the Parliamentary delegation in June.' In the villa for guests where we stayed, she and another woman, she was on kitchen duty, she served me, I'd seen her there. Then I realized fully that the girls who serve international guests are KGB employees. But that's just a detail.

After twenty-four hours, it was after lunch on Saturday: 'Comrades, collect your things' – we hadn't any, only what we had on – and we drove to Moscow.

So we drove to Moscow. They took us by car. We passed the Kremlin; Simon and I saw we weren't going to the Kremlin. We arrived at the Central Committee building. There they took us up to the fourth floor, we waited a moment and Pepik Spacek appeared; he had also been housed somewhere near Moscow, he was there with Kriegel, only they'd left Kriegel there and hadn't brought him to Moscow.

Well, when we were all three together, a party official told us to go in. A big hall opened up, a high conference room, and standing there were Brezhnev, Kosygin and Podgorny. So we exchanged greetings, shook hands and sat down opposite each other. Brezhnev was in the middle, to his left as I looked at him sat Podgorny, to Brezhnev's right Kosygin. I sat opposite Brezhnev, to my right was Simon, to the left Spacek.

Comrade Brezhnev let fly: A terrible thing has happened, and he started to tell us about the 14th Party Congress. And altogether we learned what we had had no idea about, because we had received no information whatever. We asked to listen to the radio. They wouldn't let us, no. Only Soviet papers and those we didn't even want to look at.

So we heard from his lips that there was the 14th Congress, there was a strike, the nation had taken its stand against this business. And we also understood that there wasn't a new government, that Comrade Svoboda was in Moscow with other comrades. We learned from them that they were taking us to the Kremlin for talks and then we would travel home.

I asked: 'Does it mean that we are not interned here any more and that we are once more representatives of the Czechoslovak Socialist Republic?'

Comrade Brezhnev – and Kosygin – told me that the 14th Congress – Brezhnev kept referring to 'Shilgan', 'What's this Shilgan?' (Venek Silhan, professor of economics, was elected at the 14th Congress to the Party Presidium and appointed to deputize for Dubcek as General Secretary in the latter's absence) – that we must go home and liquidate the 14th Party Congress, its policy, and pursue communist policies. I remarked that of course when I got back I would pursue communist policy which would be in line with my conscience and the will of our people. That angered the comrades a lot, especially Kosygin. He said: 'How can you talk like that, such an old communist?' And I replied: 'I mean precisely what I say; just because I'm an old communist, I'm more inclined now than formerly to pursue a policy which is genuinely according to my conscience.'

Again, the exchange of views was very sharp, we all spoke, Spacek and Simon, we all held the same views. Finally, Brezhnev started addressing me in the familiar form, he was so excited. Well, I also told him: 'You comrades, you've destroyed the centuries of friendship which existed between our nations; a hundred years ago our nation built up the Slavophile idea, love for Slavonic Russia, for fifty years for the Soviet Union. Our people were your most loyal friends, and in a single night you've destroyed all that.'

We talked like that, it led nowhere, and we agreed – Brezhnev said it – it would be better to stop. I said I thought so too, I remarked that history would judge who was right and who committed this tragic act. So they let us go, telling us that we'd go to the Kremlin.

Well, now, the guards at the door – there doormen are high officers or something, they had new uniforms, very fancy, greeted us most respectfully and saluted. So we realized, from that moment I realized that I was regarded again as Chairman of the National Assembly, not as some kind of prisoner.

A Chayka car was outside, I was driven to a government villa, by chance it was next to the one I stayed in in June. The Persian Shah was occupying it at the time, so now I was in the Shah's villa. There we bathed and shaved, they gave us underwear because we hadn't changed for five days, we were in a mess, it wasn't nice. So we made ourselves a bit civilized and drove to the Kremlin.

How did you meet the other Czechoslovaks?

We arrived in the Kremlin, to a wing that had been put at the disposal of Ludvik Svoboda. We went in, there were twenty, perhaps thirty people there. I saw a lot of familiar faces – Dzur (Minister of Defence), Kucera, of the Socialist Party, Jakes, Lenart and lots of others. Zdenek Mlynar was there, of course I saw Cernik. Dubcek was lying down. We quickly exchanged information, then I visited Dubcek, then Mlynar informed us about the 14th Congress and altogether about events in Czechoslovakia, we actually learned most from him. No one prevented us talking, Soviet party people were always present, but they didn't prevent us.

How did what later was called the Moscow talks start?

By now we had heard from our comrades what would be expected of us. That there would be a protocol of some kind.

When we had been acquainted with the Soviet proposal, we said it was absolutely unacceptable – what the Soviets had put before us – and we would put our own proposal. It was drafted, we gave it to the Soviet side. Now there were two proposals, the Soviet and ours.

A delegation was formed, I led it, Lenart and Svestka were in it – and I went to give the party standpoint to their Presidium, to its secretary Ponomaryov. It was late in the evening, about ten o'clock. We went to his office, where we informed him that we couldn't sign the Soviet motion, it was unacceptable for us. And he, in turn, said that the proposal we had made was unacceptable for the Soviet Union. That was on Sunday evening, another day of my stay-in Moscow. I conveyed the standpoint of our delegation, and they, Lenart and Svestka, were on the whole in agreement with it – they said nothing against it.

What were the main disagreements between the two proposals?

It's hard for me to say from memory. The Moscow Protocol is generally known, anyhow it's available. The first version was worse than this one. It began by saying they had come to prevent counter-revolution, they came to give us international aid. That we rejected, it was out of the question to include that. So it was deleted. Then we managed to get two things in, namely: about the troops – in the original draft it said they would remain. So we said, no – we got them to accept the word 'temporarily'. After some discussion, they came saying they'd accept. Then we got in as one of fourteen paragraphs that we would continue with the post-January policy, democratization, etc. Then there were some details, but they were just the result of the quarrelling. Then we told Ponomaryov that this, too, was unacceptable, that we wouldn't sign their draft.

He said: 'If you don't sign now, you'll sign in a week. If not in a week, then in a fortnight and if not in a fortnight, then in a month.'

Hard like that, saying they had time, we'd sign before we went home even if it took a month.

I reported this, Lenart and Svestka confirmed the way the talk went, and we had no alternative but to take their draft as the basis for negotiation. We worked on that then, to get those minute amendments.

Was the whole Czechoslovak delegation unanimous in rejecting the original Soviet proposal?

I've mentioned the Soviet proposal for the protocol, which the entire leadership of the delegation announced as unacceptable. Anyhow, proof of that is the delegation I led to Ponomaryov, with Lenart and Svestka on it, where we said that we couldn't and wouldn't sign. Officially, in all these negotiations, nobody from our delegation supported the original Soviet proposal. I'm not aware that anyone agreed with it, so our rejection was unanimous. Jakes and the rest rejected it too at that time.

I must say something here. It's nothing heroic. But probably each of us who took part in all this wept over it. Some people were already hit by the nervous shock in Prague, so that they broke down. I remember when we were waiting in Prague for the tanks, I saw Vaclav Slavik, Zdenek Mlynar, weeping. And then in Moscow, when we got that first Soviet proposal for each of us to read in Russian, then we collapsed one after another.

Bilak too?

Of that I'm not sure, I'm speaking of the Dubcek camp; it hit me before we got that proposal, up to then I'd held on – and there my nerve broke and simply – a kind of attack, well everyone had it. Cernik, Dubcek, the others.

Speaking about the Cierna meeting you said there were really two delegations on our side. How did it look in Moscow?

Here, when I come to work on it, I must confront my views with those of other participants, because it was so chaotic. We, that's to say the Dubcek camp, were absorbed in the negotiations themselves, with the protocol, with working out our proposals. And a number of the comrades in Moscow, who came with Svoboda, they were to-ing and fro-ing, always away somewhere. I saw little of them. Evidently they were doing – they had things to talk about among themselves, or the Soviet comrades had things to talk about with them.

Also absent from the talks was Frantisek Kriegel, then still Chairman of the National Front and a Presidium member, one of the highest office-holders in Czechoslovakia.

He was brought to the Kremlin, not to the government building, but to some police office. Pepik Spacek and I were to go with the protocol to that other building, give it to Kriegel to read so he should sign it. The Soviet people wanted that, though he wasn't admitted to the negotiations. They didn't wish him to be there.

So we gave it to him to read, time was short; he read it calmly, leafed through it again and said, 'I won't sign.' Spacek and I told him how things were going, on the whole we couldn't do more than inform him and then we had to return to the official building. He stayed where he was. There was talk about it in our delegation, but I'm not sure who proposed he should be brought to join us. So we took it up with the Soviet representatives and they gave their agreement. They brought Kriegel, he sat down, read it again and said, 'I won't sign.' And he said why.

A certain controversy broke out, quite unpleasant, between him and Svoboda. Comrade Svoboda let fly at him somewhat arrogantly, as if he were a private in the army. It was really embarrassing. Kriegel is an elderly man, he's sixty, he had to object that Comrade Svoboda shouldn't shout at him as if he were a boy. Svoboda yelled at him about not wanting to sign, about responsibility, mountains of dead in our country, that we should all realize that. Nothing came of it. Kriegel refused and that was that. He was there for a bit longer, sitting with people.

I believe that was shortly before the signing. How did you sign? Why? And what is your view today?

The final meeting began in the evening. Dubcek also came to that final meeting. Otherwise he was lying in another room, our doctors were treating him, he had some heart attacks, he was in a very bad way. And that scar on his forehead – all those rumours circulated about that – well it happened in the bathroom, he fainted and fell and as he fell he hit his forehead on the edge of the washbasin. So he had a bandage, our doctors from the military hospital whom Svoboda had brought with him looked after Dubcek. Indra didn't take part either, he was in another room, also lying down, at least he was said to be lying down, that he had some heart trouble.

We were with Dubcek constantly, we discussed everything with him, but we conducted all the business as long as he was unable to.

He took part in the last meeting. Before it started, they let in a group of film men, reporters, so they filmed it, they drove them out and the meeting started.

Brezhnev opened, Dubcek replied to him. Cernik joined in and it looked as if we would break up. In short – Moscow in May again, as I've described it, *à la* Cierna nad Tisou. Again that flood of accusations. Dubcek rejected them and it looked as if we would get up and nothing would come of the negotiations.

Svoboda spoke, he said there was no point in going over it all again, we should stop that and take the protocol, take it point by point, word by word. And he suggested that everything would turn out well and when the Soviet troops left our country they would be smothered in flowers.

The Soviet representatives said they agreed. That was Monday evening. This meeting ended around midnight, with that signing.

I wanted – before we signed, when we were negotiating in the afternoon – to have information also on the legal aspects, from the standpoint of international law. I asked Kucera, as Minister of Justice, if we were justified, in the position in which we found ourselves, in signing any protocols in the name of the Czechoslovak State, would it be legally valid. His answer was somewhat problematic. But that question of mine, which wasn't malicious and really stemmed from the question whether as Chairman of the National Assembly, I had a legal, constitutional right to sign anything of that kind – that, too, after August, in the course of my liquidation in 1969, was added for good measure, as one of my sins in the Party Presidium. Piller came out with it, that back in Moscow I had asked if our signatures had any legal value in the situation as it was.

So in the end we signed. Each of us had to state – I'll sign, or I won't sign. I think, if I'm not mistaken, that Cernik chaired it. We all hesitated. I hesitated for a long time, should I, shouldn't I, that's also why I put the question to Kucera.

I'd find it hard to say today who resisted most or who was more ready to sign, because we all resisted more or less. Nobody wanted to do it. I was aware what a serious step it was, and I said in my speech after our return that I wasn't sure whether I should have done it or not.

I did it, I stand by that of course. But I said in that speech that history will judge one day whether we were right, or whether we were guilty of treachery. I don't know. But under the circumstances then I did it by my own decisions. Though I hesitated very long.

Do you want to add any interesting incident?

When the meeting ended with the signing, as I've said, we had two or three hours before departure. As we were conferring in twos and threes with the Soviet people and so on, Lenart came up to me. He said, 'Comrade Chairman,' and then he told me that next to us, in some Kremlin Salon, 'Comrades Ulbricht, Gomulka, Kadar and Zhivkov' were waiting. They were waiting for us and wanted to have a drink with us; simply to greet us. He asked if I would organize it, our people, not all the delegates. I looked at Lenart and I said to him, 'Look here, Comrade Lenart, run and tell them that we don't want even to see them, let alone drink a glass of cognac with them. We won't go.'

He took note of that, evidently he told them, and of course I went to tell Dubcek and Cernik. They told me, 'You did the right thing.' So we refused to drink a glass of cognac with those comrades. We never saw them, so we hadn't known they were there. Only at that point we found out that they were in Moscow taking part in the whole business, that the protocol, everything, was agreed with them, with Ulbricht and Co. And we hadn't known, we were only supposed to drink cognac with them.

You flew home that night. There was an incident with Frantisek Kriegel. Can you describe it?

Now there was discussion about our journey to Prague. Svoboda wanted to call Prague and for the Castle service to arrange everything, transport from the airport. The Soviet people refused that. We weren't to do anything, they would arrange it all and in Prague Comrade Chervonenko would see to it. So we waited at least two hours for the plane before they'd made the arrangements. It was timed particularly so that in Prague no one would know; that's why Svoboda's offer, that we'd arrange things in Prague ourselves, was rejected – so we would arrive there in the dark. So we were left with two or three hours.

We sat with the Soviet people, two and two, I sat with Kosygin and Podgorny, that was in the Kremlin still. Kriegel took no part in any of this. He had refused to sign, because he hadn't been in on it and they then took him away again.

Before the meeting started, Dubcek said to Brezhnev that of course when we left, we would all go, including Comrade Kriegel. The Soviet representatives said, 'Sure.'

When we had signed, Dubcek came to me, he said, they don't want to let us have Kriegel, they're going to keep him here. I said that wasn't possible. That was breaking their word, so we'd go and demand new talks.

I called Cernik, I told him, and he said, 'We'll go to Svoboda' – who was in another room with Brezhnev. We demanded to speak to him and we told him we must talk again – that the 'fours' should meet. When there were any particular matters, then four from the Soviet side and four of ours always met: Brezhnev, Kosygin, Podgorny, Suslov; and of ours, Dubcek, Svoboda, Cernik and myself. We met. We told the Soviet representatives that we wouldn't go home without Kriegel. And they should take note of that.

They explained why they wanted to keep him, because it would cause difficulties for us, we had signed and he would act the hero, they said literally *geroy*.

We said – that's our affair, we're not going home without Kriegel, take note of that. So they went to confer, they came back and said – well, we'll give him to you.

Before we left the Kremlin for the airport, I demanded that they arrange for Kriegel to be at the airport too. And when we arrived there, in the motorcade, the Soviet people were there already and one comrade said: 'You have that Kriegel of yours in the plane.'

I called to one of our Embassy people who was with us, I told him: 'Run and have a look in that aeroplane,' it was about thirty metres from the building, so the comrade went, he came back and said: 'Yes, Comrade Kriegel is in the plane, it's all right.' That's how it ended, and we took off in the dark.

What did you feel about your first encounters after returning from Moscow?

We arrived in the dark, Soviet cars took us to the Castle, where people told us that half an hour earlier the Soviet tanks, the Soviet troops had left the Castle. Comrade Svoboda suggested that we should stay for the next few days at the Castle, possibly for security reasons. We stayed there about ten days.

The staff at the Castle, especially the women, immediately got to work on us, they brought us clean clothing. Behind a screen there I changed and as I put aside my dirty shirt and took a clean one, so the woman seized the shirt and said, 'I'm going to keep this, Comrade Smrkovsky, I shan't give it to you, I'm going to take it as a souvenir.' So she simply took it.

At dawn people started coming, journalists came to the Castle, the news that we were back spread round Prague.

Many of us were so tired, we needed to rest. I wasn't that lucky, first I gave a brief speech over the radio, then I attended a government meeting at the Castle where Cernik and others gave information about the events of our stay in Moscow, mainly about the conclusions. I wasn't there long, it wasn't necessary. Dubcek was mainly engaged with the new functionaries elected at the 14th Congress in Vysocany. Not only was Dubcek informed about the Congress, he and other comrades informed the representatives about the results of the Moscow negotiations and the undertaking contained in the protocol of the Moscow meetings that the 14th Congress wouldn't be recognized. It was a very complicated, agitated affair – actually to overturn the result of the Congress.

Finally, the Congress representatives accepted Dubcek's arguments. Dubcek asked me the same day to go to Vysocany, where the newly elected officers were meeting, certainly not all of them, and there I was, so to speak, to back up what he had agreed with the representatives in the morning. I was there in the evening, well, it wasn't a hard job, because Dubcek's arguments had been accepted.

That day, too, a delegation from the Soviet Army came to the Castle, led by General Pavlovsky with another general. I was appointed to talk with them. They brought a demand that one of us, perhaps I myself, should speak over the radio to the people of Prague calling on them to remove all the inscriptions there were in the city. I was willing to do that, to speak, and I guaranteed success, at least I thought I could, but on the condition that, at the same time, a representative of the Soviet Army would speak, assuring Prague citizens that the Soviet troops would quit the city as soon as the inscriptions disappeared.

They didn't want to accept that, to take that undertaking, so we parted on the understanding that I wouldn't speak. They then went to the Town Hall, to the Central National Committee, where they negotiated with the representatives of the city.

The same day I had a visit from a delegation from Parliament, from the National Assembly of the day, who informed me about their activity, about the continuous session from 21 August, and they asked me to go to

Parliament, where members were waiting for me. I went there. In Gorky Square an apple couldn't have fallen through the thousands crowded there. I spoke in Parliament about the outcome of our stay in Moscow, the content of the protocol we had signed, about our ideas about the future. In turn, spokesmen for Parliament recapitulated briefly the resolutions carried, in all there were about twenty resolutions of the National Assembly. They had been published as they were passed and later issued together by Parliament.

The biggest problem at that time was, perhaps, to explain to our people after the experience of that week what had been signed in Moscow and why. I remember the crowds swarming through the streets of Prague, waiting nervously for what each of you would say. How did you prepare for your speech?

It was decided that the representatives – people still spoke of the 'four' [Svoboda, Dubcek, Cernik, Smrkovsky – editor's note] – must speak to the nation. That first day Svoboda spoke as President, Dubcek spoke after him the same day. That speech had a difficult birth. Because he was completely exhausted mentally and physically, the speech is marked by that. Next day Cernik spoke, and I spoke last.

Thanks to speaking last, I was able to learn more about what had been happening, the atmosphere in our country. I had more time for the speech. Maybe I put more into it than the others. It was praised by the public in general.

On the other hand, however, my speech was not well received by the Soviet side. I was told afterwards that Ambassador Chervonenko conveyed his dissatisfaction to Moscow. And later, in 1969–70 in those familiar programmes of current propaganda, that speech of mine was criticized in our media several times as being hostile to the Soviet party, that it was emotional and the like. In that speech of mine after the return from Moscow I thought a lot about how things would develop. I based myself on that terrific unity among our people, on the authority the party enjoyed. And during those crisis days of August the party's authority was really unique, rarely to be found. I told myself that, in fact, after that whole tragedy of 21 August, all was not lost, that it would be possible, though in more difficult conditions, nevertheless to carry on to some extent with the policy we had called the post-January policy. But I was aware that it depended on whether we could maintain the unity between the top leadership of the state and the people on the one hand, and then – unity within that leadership. That was what I was really afraid of. In my speech I expressed these forebodings I felt by referring to unity, to the arch – by which I meant the leadership of the state. If we allowed one brick to fall out, another would follow and then the whole structure would collapse. And I recalled Svatopluk,[8] not as a figure of speech, but as a way of expressing my fears about what I sensed, and what later happened – that shortly after January, shortly after August and already during the August days in Moscow our unity was attacked as being a strange unity, a non-class unity, and soon after August the effects began to be seen in practice.

You are known to have taken this attitude also to people who while not taking a clear stand, did fulfil their tasks in the decisive moments. Could you give an example?

On our return to Prague, when we were living in the Castle, about the second or third day, it was about eleven in the evening, Dubcek came to me with Piller [then Presidium member and Secretary of the Central Bohemia Regional Party Committee – editor's note] to say that somewhere, I think in Kladno, the Party Regional Committee was meeting to consider the question of Piller's secretaryship. The committee hadn't any confidence in him and wanted to know how he had behaved during the voting on 20 and 21 August. So two delegates from the Regional Committee had come with Piller to get evidence from Dubcek and myself. So we saw them. Dubcek and I confirmed to the delegates that Piller had voted with us. They were glad and Piller was very moved, he thanked us warmly for bearing testimony, so we had defended his honour in the eyes of the committee. Those were the circumstances. [Piller later became active as a 'normalizer', but he was dismissed from his post, evidently because of that vote and because he had, formally, been chairman of the commission which presented to the CC the report – later not approved in 1969 – about investigation of the crimes of the 1950s, the so-called Piller Commission report – editor's note.]

When did you begin to feel that conflicts were developing, that the unity of the leadership would break up?

About the middle of September Cernik went to Moscow as Prime Minister to negotiate the military and economic matters arising from the Moscow protocol. And I was surprised when he returned on Sunday; on Monday morning he was to report, first to the inner committee, then to the Party Presidium. I assumed he would go to the Castle and we would all be called there. I waited in vain, I phoned Cernik and they told me he had left for the Castle. I got my secretary to call Dubcek, she said he had left for the Castle. I wasn't invited to that meeting. Then I realized that this was one of the things they had brought back from Moscow: the line of removing me from the 'four' and gradually from other posts as well.

It was very evident in November, when a conference was called in Kiev.

The Soviet Party leadership, and from our side the top representation – Svoboda, Dubcek, Cernik, Strougal, Husak. And I heard about it on television – that the delegation had returned. I knew nothing about their having gone. I wanted an explanation, but I didn't get it. There were excuses, that they couldn't get hold of me, for instance. That wasn't true, for I was on duty in Parliament, at home and so on. It was an embarrassing affair.

Naturally, after Kiev I wanted an answer in the party Executive, but I didn't get it. In time, I finally got it indirectly from Strougal. I'll return to that later.

A foremost point at the Kiev meeting was filling the post of chairman of the new Federal Assembly. That was an opportunity from the standpoint of the plan to change the party leadership, to get rid of me somehow. Gustav Husak played a big part in the matter. Although the question hadn't been decided in the Presidium, and still less in the Central Committee and Executive – it had even been resolved by the Executive to keep the question of Chairman of the Federal Assembly confidential until the decision was made, not to make it public – suddenly out of the blue we heard on television and the media that the Slovak Central Committee and the Presidium of the Slovak National Council had demanded that the post be filled by a Slovak. And Gustav Husak said it in a speech on television, in a statement which was not of the best.

Not only had they confronted me, and the leadership of the party and government, with an accomplished fact, but the Slovaks, that is, the leadership under Gustav Husak, had obliged the Slovak members of the Party Central Committee to support this attitude. That is, they put it as an ultimatum that I must go. At the same time, there was an embargo on news about me, nothing was allowed to be published about me, not even official news. Simply, an embargo – my name was to vanish from the Slovak media. I believe it did disappear to some extent until the decision came, until my speech on 5 May, when I spoke about these matters.

At the Executive meeting after Kiev, I questioned the comrades, would they tell me clearly and truthfully what was the Soviet attitude towards me, what did they demand or threaten. I also stressed that if I was to be a cause of complications or difficulties in normalizing the situation, in that case I would go. I said that I had thought about it a lot, because in any case I saw that I couldn't really do anything. That whatever I suggested, and what others suggested, everything was rejected and our efforts were in vain.

Although they refused to give a clear statement about the Soviet attitude to my person, to my functions, to my activity, they said it indirectly. When, for instance, Cernik said that Dubcek and Smrkovsky ought to go and have it out – he used that phrase – themselves with the

Soviets; Husak said much the same – Smrkovsky, Dubcek, they should go and have it out in Moscow, because the Soviet comrades had a critical attitude to Smrkovsky, that he wasn't adhering to the protocol, but there had been no personal and concrete demand from the Soviet side.

The Executive concentrated heavily on getting me to agree to abdicating before the event from the post in the new National Assembly – having been Chairman in the old assembly – and that the post should go to a Slovak representative.

I agreed in principle that the Slovaks had a right to the post, I wouldn't deny it to them. But in the situation and with all the implications, I argued that it was not merely a matter of right, but it also meant the gradual liquidation of the organs, the people, who had represented and personified the whole post-January effort.

The pressure in the Executive was intense. When Husak first posed the demand that they wanted the post for themselves, everyone looked as if they were surprised and that they were afraid of it. All of them. I have notes somewhere about who spoke, and how. So, at the beginning, all of them – including Svoboda, Cernik, Strougal, Erban – were afraid about the political consequences if they came out with this, how it would be received by the public. Strougal even demanded that it shouldn't be put as a Slovak demand, because they felt that it wasn't a matter of constitutional right, but an eminently political issue.

In the course of the meeting, however, after an obstruction by Husak who said that others had gone, Smrkovsky could go too, and he thumped the table and left the Executive meeting, then Dubcek objected to these practices of moral terror – the others commented variously (when I get to work on it, I shall supplement it with precise records) and during the proceedings they already changed their views, they switched. Oldrich Cernik, for instance, who had previously accepted my nomination as Chairman of the National Assembly, simply declared that he would vacate his post if I didn't want to give up this post which they counted on for them, that is, the Slovaks.

They wanted not only my agreement, but also that I should come out publicly in favour, why was I silent and things like that. And then they also criticized the campaign which had developed in the Republic after Husak's appearance on television. Up to then, things had been quiet on the whole, but after his speech, factories, public organizations, trade unions and so on raised their voices, a terrific number of resolutions came in at the time. The office of the National Assembly had an analysis made of the whole period around the election of the Chairman, some research institutes worked on it, the Institute of Computer Technology. About 4 million people gave their views.

On that occasion, in those talks, there were also attacks on me, that things would end badly if a general strike took place, there would be hundreds dead and I would bear the responsibility, and so on. I have some quotations, I'll fill it out thoroughly. Sadovsky, who often let his tongue run away with him, said: if we don't proceed in unity (he meant the eight, the Executive) if we don't support their demand, the Slovaks would leave the Executive. These threats – that they wouldn't come to meetings, that they would leave, that the Slovak delegation would come out against – these practices were very, very common in those days. They said that if the campaign for the Chairman of the Federal Assembly didn't stop in the Czech lands, that was the campaign for Smrkovsky, they would launch one against in Slovakia, etc. [Later Husak was not worried that a Czech, Alois Indra, became Chairman of the Federal Assembly, although the functions of President and Prime Minister were still in Czech hands – editor's note.]

Dubcek said that he had made no undertaking about me and had not discussed my position. But he did suggest indirectly that the situation was very dangerous and he couldn't exclude a new arrival of troops if there were to be a general strike in Czechoslovakia.

Svoboda said, among other things, that when unity had been needed in the Executive it had always been achieved. But now seven agreed, eight did not – I was the eighth. He said my name was being misused by a gang – he meant the people who voiced an opinion on who should be the next Chairman of Parliament. He, too, threw or put his authority on the scales – if we failed to agree, he would resign. And I, by keeping silent, was assisting his resignation. A personality was being put against the nation, and the like.

There were other remarks, too. Strougal: we wouldn't be able to control the situation, it was very dangerous – he spoke about the hundreds of dead.

Later, in the Presidium, some members, like Pinkava, Slavik and others wouldn't accept this argument, a polemic developed.

I tried in vain to get them to tell me what actually happened in Kiev. Finally, I learnt it in January or February 1969, from Strougal. I went to see him, we exchanged views on party policy, on various questions from the post-January past. In that connection I asked what actually happened in Kiev about the Chairman matter.

He replied: 'Well, you know how it is. Two people sit here, two talk there, we went on a hunt too, there things are said. I can tell you that when the final meeting took place between our whole delegation and the whole Soviet delegation, and Comrade Brezhnev got up to speak, he announced, "And we take note that the Chairman of the Federal Assembly will be a representative of the Slovak nation."'

So Strougal actually confirmed that the Soviet representatives had reached agreement with someone. I think it's not too difficult to guess who that was.

Following all those dramatic meetings, the campaign reached terrific heights between Christmas and New Year; I've said, about 4 million people were moving in some way. And around 3 January, I complied with the pressure in the Executive that I should come out in public – against my being a candidate, in the interests of the Slovak nation. And that I did in my speech of 5 January.

The Executive then discussed the new appointment in Parliament. Husak was obliged to present a proposal for a candidate and in first place he named Leco Novomesky, but he explained that Novomesky would not accept because of ill health. As second candidate he named Klokoc, as third Lenart, and as a last resort he suggested Golotka or Boda, but he didn't stress the fourth or fifth candidates particularly, and threw doubt on them himself.

However, the Executive decided, contrary to Husak's view, that if it couldn't be Novomesky, neither Klokoc, Lenart nor Boda should be chosen, but that Peter Golotka should be Chairman of the Federal Assembly.

Smrkovsky was to be first Vice-Chairman of the Federal Assembly and Chairman of the Chamber of the People, while Chairman of the Chamber of Nations was to be Professor Hanes – a lawyer from Bratislava University.

Do you still think today that your speech of 5 January 1969 was correct?

After that speech, Leco Novomesky sent me a telegram praising it; Eugene Erban also sent a telegram. Well, I'm not sure if I convinced the listeners. I have my doubts about that, because I had, in the end, to say in the state interest things which I was not sure were correct. To put it mildly. But – under the pressure of those circumstances – I had to do it.

NOTES TO CHAPTER 17

1. Josef Smrkovsky was one of the main initiators of the Prague Spring that excited socialists throughout the world. For once it almost appeared that socialism and democracy would coexist. Russian tanks destroyed that hope and crushed those responsible for the experiment. Josef Smrkovsky was born in 1911. He joined the Czech Communist Party in 1932 and was a leader of the underground resistance to the Nazi occupation. He was a central organizer of the Prague Uprising in 1945, which paved the way for the triumphant entry of the Red Army.

Smrkovsky was arrested by the Stalinist regime in 1951 as a 'deviationist'. He served four years of a fifteen-year sentence and worked as a forester and farmer till he was 'rehabilitated'. He was elected President of the National Assembly in 1968, from which vantage-point (as well as the Politburo) he pushed through the measures of democratization known as the 'Prague Spring'. After the Soviet invasion, he was first removed from the Central Committee and later (with Dubcek) expelled from the party along with half a million communists. This interview was conducted in Prague by a fellow dissident communist soon before his death on 15 January 1974. It was published by the Australian Communist Party as a pamphlet in April 1976. As a document it remains unique.

2. 'Lessons from the crisis development in the party and society following the 13th Congress of the Communist Party of Czechoslovakia' – a document issued in 1971.

3. One of the first mass meetings of 1968 was held in March in Prague's biggest hall.

4. Kurt Hager.

5. The propaganda booklet about events in Czechoslovakia put out by anonymous 'Soviet journalists'.

6. KAN: Club of committed non-party members; K-23: Club of former political prisoners.

7. Zdenek Mlynar – CC secretary in 1968 – resigned after the invasion, and was expelled from the party after the Husak takeover.

8. Ruler of the Great Moravian Empire, AD 870–94, who demonstrated unity of his three sons with three sticks which could be broken separately.

18. The Political Culture of Hoxha's Albania[1]

Arshi Pipa

This past Christmas Santa Claus came with an extraordinary gift, *The Titoites*,[2] the latest book in the series of Enver Hoxha's *opera omnia*. In this volume of memoirs of more than 600 pages, the author vents his spleen against his *bête noire*, Titoism. The epilogue contains a surprise.

The year is 1777, and the action takes place in the Crimea. He is the son of the Grand Vizier, she a beautiful *rayah*. The young prince falls in love with the girl and begins to court her – the citizens begin to gossip. In vain the Grand Vizier tries to dissuade his son from wooing the maiden. In the meantime the Khan of Crimea has discovered that his vizier, during a diplomatic trip to Paris, has paid a secret visit to Diderot. The Khan suspects his vizier to be contaminated by republican ideas. And when he learns that the vizier's son intends to marry the *rayah* girl, he has the vizier arrested as an agent of the *Encyclopédie*. The evidence of his high treason: the projected marriage of his son to the despicable *rayah*. The morganatic marriage would open the door to infiltration of republican and atheist ideas that will corrupt the youth, thus undermining the Khanate's social and religious order and eventually bringing the abhorrent *rayahs* to power.

This is not exactly what Hoxha relates in the epilogue of his book. There he accuses his Premier, Mehmet Shehu, of having conspired to split the Party of Labour of Albania (PLA) and to kill him. Shehu's plan for splitting the party was to have one of his sons marry a woman of a declassed family. His plan failed because the party acted promptly and the engagement was broken off. As a result, Shehu shot himself, while his son (according to rumours) electrocuted himself. Shehu's wife and another of his sons were arrested. Their imprisonment was followed by that of two other Shehu relatives: the former Minister of the Interior and the former Minister of Defence. The purge is still going on.

The story of Shehu's suicide is the subject of the volume's last chapter, 'In Open Struggle with the Titoites'. The previous chapters deal with the period 1941–8, that is, from the foundation of the Communist Party of Albania under the close supervision of the Communist Party of Yugoslavia, until the rift in which the CPA broke loose from the CPY. The last chapter begins with a review of 'the thirty-five years that have passed from the time when the Titoite betrayal was publicly denounced and unmasked' (567) and then focuses on the Shehu episode. The volume was apparently written when Shehu committed suicide (17 December 1981). A last-moment addition, in fact an appendage, the chapter functions as an epilogue.

Yugoslav leaders, Albanian nationalists and even purged Albanian communists[3] have stated that the CPA is a creation of the CPY. Hoxha begins his work by refuting that thesis. What he writes, however, only corroborates what he intends to refute. Not only was the CPA founded with the leading assistance of the CPY, but it grew and consolidated itself under the elder party's tutorship, to the point of becoming, after Albania's liberation from the Nazi troops, a mere appendage of the CPY. This Hoxha is at pains to admit. Since he was during that period the General Secretary of the party and Commander-in-Chief of the army (and already designated Premier of Albania before the country's liberation), he tries to justify his capitulation by laying the blame with influential comrades in the Political Bureau. He accuses them of plotting to dethrone him. To this effect, they became 'secret agents' of Tito and his regime, who viewed Hoxha as their main obstacle for achieving their sinister plan, the annexation of Albania as the seventh republic of the Yugoslav Federation.

The Titoites is intended to be a narrative, based on memories and occasional notes, of Hoxha's unrelenting struggle against the Yugoslav representatives in the CPA and the Albanian government, working together with their Albanian 'stooges' to enslave Albania under Tito's rule. The list of the Yugoslav representatives is a long one. It begins with Dušan Mugoša and Miladin Popović, the CPY delegates who were instrumental in founding the CPA while also acting as *de facto* members of its Central Committee for almost two years. Hoxha admits that at this time the Albanian communists 'lacked experience' (17) in organizational matters and suffered from an 'inadequate ideo-political level' (355). Yet he denies the Yugoslavs' decisive role in the CPA's leadership. Except for Popović, Hoxha's mentor, whom he praises as a real friend of Albania and a true internationalist, all the others were enemies, most of them Great-Serbian chauvinists with an endemic hatred for everything Albanian. Such were Blažo Jovanović, the official Yugoslav delegate at the CC of the PCA, and especially Svetozar Vukmanović-Tempo, Tito's 'roving ambassador' for his project of creating a Balkan Federation. Colonel Velimir Stojnić, chief of the Yugoslav Military Mission, organized the first plot against Hoxha at the Party's 2nd Plenum (the Berat Plenum, November 1944). Two Yugoslav representatives after the liberation, the 'cunning' 'diplomat of Albanian origin' Josip Djerdja and the 'ill-famed' Slavo Zlatić, were responsible for the second and major plot intended to liquidate not only Hoxha but Albania as well. Zlatić was assisted by Sergej Krajger, the person in charge of operating the 'economic union' between the two countries. General Kurešanin pressed the Albanian military chiefs hard to allow a Yugoslav division to be stationed in the Korça district, allegedly to defend the Albanian border from an impending attack by the Greek army. The move was tantamount to a Yugoslavian military occupation of Albania. At the same time Koća Popović, Chief of the Yugoslav General Staff, and Vukmanović-Tempo, its Political Director, were eagerly working for the creation of a joint Yugoslav–Albanian military command, thus eliminating Hoxha as Commander-in-Chief of the Albanian Army. Yet backed by Mehmet Shehu, then the Chief of the Albanian General Staff, Hoxha managed to foil the Yugoslav manoeuvre by writing to Stalin, who disapproved of it. As a result, Hoxha survived, whereas Shehu was dismissed for his 'anti-Yugoslavism' (439). This, of course, does not preclude Hoxha from branding Shehu, at the end of the volume, as the chief Titoist agent and even an imperialist 'superagent', the one who presided over the tripartite – cultural, military, economic – conspiracy against him during the period 1973–5. Eventually Shehu tried to liquidate his ally, with whom he had been guiding Albania on the socialist road, first as Minister of the Interior (1948–54) and then as Prime Minister (1954–81), a period of no less than thirty-three years.

This is the content of the book. Its language is not without merits. Irony and sarcasm prevail, and the narrative is spiced with anecdotes which add to the portrayal of the characters. The author's French background may be accountable to some extent for the lively sketches. And Hoxha has a knack for earthy epithets and idiomatic expressions. *The Titoites* makes good enough reading – certainly Hoxha's best literary work so far. The Yugoslavs are recipients of a great deal of muckraking, which is principally directed, however, at Albanian opponents and rivals. As rivals he deigns to consider only three: Sejfulla Malëshova, Nako Spiru and Koçi Xoxe. But while with the first two Hoxha exercises some restraint (they were, after all, intellectuals like himself), he has utter contempt for Xoxe, a 'you might say illiterate' (158) tinsmith, 'swarthy, short, podgy, with bulging eyes like those of a frog' (449) – 'his pseudonym was Trashi [the Fat], our ex-quartermaster at [the village of] Panarit' (458). Hoxha calls him, according to the circumstances, a 'gawk' (347), a 'tragicomic clown' (370), a 'plucked rooster' (556), and portrays him 'drinking with the Yugoslav comrades until four in the morning . . . but he had lasted to the end like a man and had not disgraced us' (318).

Xoxe, a longtime communist and a member of the Korçë Group, was elected member of the Political Bureau while in jail. After his release in April 1943, he was put in charge of the party cadres. He accompanied

Vukmanović-Tempo to Greece twice in 1943, and the two became friends. It was Tempo who, having clashed repeatedly with Hoxha, groomed Xoxe for the top seat. Colonel Stojnić set the stage, working behind the scenes with Xoxe, Spiru and Malëshova, unhappy with Hoxha's monopolization of power. A veteran communist who had spent his exile years in Moscow working for the Comintern, Malëshova returned to Albania in the spring of 1943, joining the partisans. He was immediately coopted as candidate member of the Politburo, due to his reputation not only as an Albanian poet but also as a Marxist theoretician, indeed the only one Albania could boast at the time. Spiru, a former student of political economy at the University of Turin, was, in his capacity as President of the Youth Organization, a member of the Political Bureau. Hoxha describes him as 'intelligent, straightforward, courageous and a good organizer' (159), but also as 'ambitious and inclined to intrigues' (160). Having been Hoxha's right-hand man during the war years, Spiru turned against him at the end of the war (hence his 'contradictory character'). The shift occurred at the Berat Plenum, where Malëshova, Spiru and Xoxe, under the baton of Colonel Stojnić, submitted the Commander-in-Chief to a volley of damning criticism. Hoxha managed to survive, but his grip on the party was gone. The victor was the proletarian Xoxe, who suddenly emerged as Albania's strong man, pushed or rather kicked ahead by the Yugoslavs (at a reception for the Albanian delegation in Belgrade in December 1946, Tito offered the seat at the head of the table to Xoxe, not to Hoxha) (399). As President of the Special Court for the Trial of War Criminals and Enemies of the People (March – April 1945), Xoxe, then Organizational Secretary of the party, set the tune for the ensuing policy of repression against opponents and critics, inside as well as outside the party. 'The first pawn to be eliminated from the game' (255) was Malëshova, who could not hide his contempt for the semi-literate Xoxe. According to Hoxha, Malëshova was purged as a right-wing opportunist: he was 'a liberal parliamentary democrat . . . a supporter of the politicians of the cafés and the secret chambers, of bourgeois elements, of the *kulak* strata and reactionary clergy . . . he was in fact opposed to the socialist revolution' (256). What he was really opposed to was a socialist revolution of the Stalinist kind, whose horrors he had experienced while in Moscow. The Yugoslavs found fault with his refusal to ban from the schools authors such as the Franciscan father Gjergj Fishta, whose epic, *The Mountain Lute*, praises the Albanians who fought against the Slavs. Malëshova's theses on the country's economy and culture (he was then Minister of Culture), at a time when writers were being jailed for expressing criticism and engineers hanged as saboteurs, made Malëshova an easy target for his rivals. The main reason, however, for his purge was his nationalism.[4]

'With the elimination of Sejfulla Malëshova, one competitor of Koçi Xoxe's ambition for absolute power was removed' (256). In fact the competition was between Malëshova and Hoxha, not between Malëshova and Xoxe, who well knew that Malëshova had no chance of gaining 'absolute power' because of his nationalism. Indeed Hoxha's report to the party's 5th Plenum (February 1946) has Malëshova as its main target. That report doomed him. Through it and with Xoxe's concurrence, Hoxha was able to get rid of a dangerous rival, his main one at the time, a person who would not bow to a – to him – upstart communist who knew little more of Marxism than the jargon of tracts and the language of Stalin's *Short Course* of the history of the Bolshevik Party. During the debates preceding the Berat Plenum, Malëshova is quoted as having defied Hoxha by saying to him, 'You are trying to stand over me . . . you want to impose your opinions on us by all means' (172).

The elimination of the second 'pawn' was a much more complicated affair. Because of the large following he had among the youth (more than once Hoxha accuses Spiru of wanting to set the Youth Organization against the party) Spiru was a serious rival to both Hoxha and Xoxe. He had, moreover, as Minister of Economy and Chairman of the State Planning Committee, the keys of Albania's economy in his hands. The Yugoslavs paid particular attention to Spiru, flattering and encouraging him in his bid for power. As a consequence, a bitter rivalry developed between the two remaining contenders for the throne, Xoxe and Spiru. No doubt their rivalry was instigated by Hoxha according to the old adage 'divide and conquer'. Their mutual recriminations gave Hoxha an opportunity to arbitrate upon their 'quarrels', thus helping him retain the reins of the government at a time when party power was rapidly slipping from his hands. And since the stronger contender was Xoxe, Hoxha made use of Spiru to check Xoxe's ascendancy. Eventually he won over Spiru to his side. This occurred when the latter began to have qualms about having signed the Economic Convention with Yugoslavia for the parification of currency, unification of prices, removal of custom barriers and creation of joint economic committees, which laid the ground for the political union. Backing away from his former pro-Yugoslav stance, Spiru oriented himself towards the Soviet Union, asking for economic and technical assistance. The arrival of Soviet advisers infuriated the Yugoslavs who felt betrayed by one whom they considered their man (Spiru had previously written a letter to Tito, asking him to use his authority for the removal of Hoxha). Xoxe availed himself of the development to settle account with his rival. Not yet strong enough to attack Hoxha frontally, he demanded Spiru's head. He had Hoxha call a meeting of the Politburo restricted to only four members: Hoxha, Xoxe, his faithful Pandi Kristo, and Spiru. In that meeting, Xoxe accused Spiru of being an 'agent of imperialism'. Spiru requested five days to prepare his reply. His request was rejected by the other three. The next day, Spiru visited Hoxha, insisting on his request and asking him for help. Hoxha's answer was negative: 'The Bureau [sic] has decided it' (385). That same day Spiru committed suicide.

Hoxha had earlier joined forces with Xoxe to liquidate Malëshova, thus reassuring the Yugoslavs who disliked both Malëshova and himself. This time, the Yugoslav pressure growing on him, he sacrificed the very person whom he had been encouraging to resist that pressure. And when the pressure reached the point of explosion with the Yugoslavs' insistent demand for the creation of a unified command of the army, Hoxha sold out Shehu, the only party leader who then stood firmly for him. In a telling passage, he admits his debt to Shehu for coming to his rescue, while minimizing it:

> Although I was Commander-in-Chief, I was virtually pushed to one side . . . Among the first measures which I decided to take was the reorganization of the General Staff. When we discussed this question, Nak Spiru proposed insistently that Mehmet Shehu should be placed at the head of the General Staff because he was 'a born soldier, well trained, who had proved himself' . . . Likewise, the fact that he was studying in the Military Academy in the Soviet Union added to my hope that Mehmet Shehu would strongly oppose the mish-mash the Yugoslavs were creating in our army' (430–31).

Which indeed he did. 'Xoxe and his clan' (495) began to attack him. 'Mehmet Shehu, who felt that his position was shaky, to save himself from this situation "opposed" the Yugoslavs openly (later I shall relate what this "opposition" was), and tried to gain my backing and support . . .' (436) (Hoxha, as usual, is inverting the roles.) Shehu is quoted as having declared to Hoxha: 'Comrade Commander . . . the Yugoslavs want to eliminate you . . . I opposed them openly' (435–6).

Spiru committed suicide on 20 November 1947. At the end of December Shehu was dismissed. In November of that year, Xoxe demanded that Hoxha 'wr[o]te a warm leading article [in a magazine founded by Xoxe] about the vital relations with the Yugoslav friends, about their aid and especially about the contribution of the Comrade Marshal Tito . . . The Yugoslavs needed my article as a "certificate of good behaviour" for Yugoslavia and Tito' (449). Hoxha complied with Xoxe's demand:

> In very general terms and with the odd 'fact' for the first years of the war, I pointed out the links of friendship between our parties and countries. However, even with this, the Yugoslavs and their agents were satisfied: the important thing for them was that the General Secretary of the CPA should write even one good phrase, even in completely general terms, about Tito's Yugoslavia, as a safe-conduct pass for the annexation (450).

In the winter of 1947, Albania's annexation by Yugoslavia in the spring of 1948 was as probable as the succession of winter by spring itself. If it did not in fact occur, this is because in the meantime Yugoslavia broke with the Soviet Union. Hoxha had been assiduously watching the darkening clouds that gradually obscured the relations between the two countries, patiently waiting for the 'thunderbolt' to strike. 'We had some signs and signals in this direction' (466). His strategy of temporization eventually bore fruit. He boasts in his book that 'at no time did it cross [his] mind to surrender' (462). Hoxha had previously approved the Economic Convention signed by Spiru, who 'did nothing in this direction without consulting me and receiving my approval' (372). Now he wrote and signed with his own hand 'a safe-conduct pass for the annexation'. Not only did he surrender, but he did so by offering up in exchange for his continued hold on power the very independence of Albania, whose champion he pretends to be. After Shehu's departure, his title as Commander-in-Chief of the Army was merely nominal. Everyone who lived through that crucial period, including this writer, was sure that Hoxha's days as a ruler were numbered. Stalin's letter to the CPY (28 March 1944) saved him. His worship of Stalin is thus understandable and, to some extent, excusable. What is inexcusable is his inflicting on the whole of Albania the Stalinist hysteria, nurturing therewith his own personality cult, a miniature of Stalin's. To that purpose, he gradually reduced the Party of Labour of Albania – the change of the name occurred at the party's 1st Congress (November 1948) – to a subservient body, ready to obey his dictates. He put his wife in control of the party's ideological apparatus[5] while entrusting Shehu, with whom he shares the responsibility for the subsequent purges, with repressing dissidents and critics of all sorts.

A review of these purges will help the reader realize the Stalinist course of Hoxha's dictatorship.

The Tirana Founding Conference (8–14 November 1941) succeeded in temporarily reconciling the conspicuous ideological differences among the three loose organizations existing at the time: the Korçë Group, the Shkodër Group and the Youth Group.[6] Hoxha, then a member of the Korçë Group operating in Tirana, was elected to direct the Provisional Central Committee composed of seven members: Enver Hoxha, Koçi Xoxe, Qemal Stafa, Tuk Jakova, Kristo Themelko, Ramadan Çitaku and Gjin Marku. Hoxha's election was a compromise solution, apparently devised by his Yugoslav advisers, based on the stipulation that 'none of the former principal leaders (chairmen and deputy chairmen) of the groups would be elected to the leadership' (H 65). The representatives of the Youth Group, Anastas Lulo and Sadik Premte, as well as older communists such as Koço Tashko and Mustafa Gjinishi, were disappointed. Premte managed to get hold of the Vlorë Regional Committee in 1943. His rebellion was quelled in May of that year – Hoxha and Shehu participated personally in the punitive expedition which ended with the death of two regional leaders (they 'accidentally fell victim of the plot they had concocted').[7] Premte escaped; later he fled abroad. Lulo was executed.[8] So was another member of the fractionist group.

The second purge struck a Politburo member, Ymer Dishnica, and Mustafa Gjinishi. They had been delegated by the party to deal with the Nationalist Front (Balli Kombëtar) at the Mukje Conference (August 1943) in view of concerted action against the fascist occupiers. Dishnica and Gjinishi signed the agreement for the formation of the Committee for the Salvation of Albania. The agreement was immediately rejected, under Yugoslav pressure, as alien to the party line. Later Dishnica was expelled from the Politburo as an opportunist (Plenum of May 1944). Opportunistic at the time was the whole party line, according to the more enlightened Politburo members such as Malëshova and Spiru as well as the Yugoslav representatives. Malëshova and Spiru tried to rehabilitate Dishnica after the liberation. He ended up in prison instead. Gjinishi, a first-rate propagandist and organizer, was the person mainly responsible for the success of the Pezë Conference (September 1942) which saw the CPA emerge as a political-military force, able to conduct guerrilla warfare. He was assassinated during the partisan conquest of Northern Albania. Hoxha accuses him of being an agent of the British Intelligence Service (135) – Gjinishi knew English, which he had learned at the American Vocational School in Tirana. Zai Fundo, though a veteran communist schooled in Moscow, was another victim. Disgusted by Stalin's atrocities, he broke with the Comintern, thus incurring the party's death verdict. Captured in Northern Albania, the 'Trotskyite' Fundo was 'shot . . . as an agent of the British and the feudals' (415).[9]

We have already commented on the purge of the 'megalomaniac' Malëshova (as a rule Hoxha exorcizes his ailments by inflicting them on adversaries). Spiru shot himself rather than suffer humiliation. Xoxe was shot when Hoxha and Shehu regained power. Xoxe's purge involved that of his clan: Pandi Kristo, Nesti Kerenxhi, Xhoxhi Blushi, and many others. They were given prison sentences. Kristo, a proletarian from Korçë like Xoxe and his closest collaborator, was apparently spared because shooting him would have been too much of an honour for that 'shitty rabbit' (482) who once, when confronted by Hoxha, 'had collapsed like a heap of cow-dung in a rain storm' (556).

The 'anti-Titoite' purge was not confined to the above-mentioned Politburo members. Pressing on Shehu to be more exacting against anti-party elements, Hoxha engineered a radical housecleaning. On the basis of official sources, it has been calculated that from 1948 to 1951, more than 25 per cent of the party membership was expelled.[10]

A second anti-Titoite purge was made public by the party's 2nd National Conference (April 1950). The scapegoats were Abedin Shehu, CC member and Minister of Industry, and Niazi Islami, Deputy Communications Minister. They were accused of having criticized the Two-Year plan as 'unrealistic' (H 263). Two army chiefs were also expelled for having undermined the role of the party in the direction of the army. They were Gjin Marku, a member of the first Politburo, and Nexhip Vinçani.

The explosion of a bomb in the Soviet Legation in Tirana (19 February 1951) prompted a wave of terrorism conducted personally by Shehu against former members of nationalist parties as well as some more outspoken critics.[11] These were the days when a party member advocating a modicum of moderation would be suspected to be an anti-party element. Such was the case of Tuk Jakova, Teodor Heba and Manol Konomi. Jakova, a leader of the Shkodër Group and a founder of the party (he was a carpenter by trade) had been, like Shehu, harassed by Xoxe and his men. After Xoxe's demise, he replaced his adversary as the party's Organizational Secretary while also holding the positions of Minister of Industry and Deputy Premier. Jakova disgraced himself by trying to win over to the party former hostile elements. He was accused of being sympathetic to reactionary individuals and groups and especially to the Catholic clergy who had born the brunt of the religious persecution (Jakova was a Catholic). His thesis that the class struggle was dying out in the country met with vigorous opposition by Hoxha and Shehu. He was dropped as the Organizational Secretary and also as a Politburo member (Plenum of February 1951). His ally Heba, the Chief of the Party's Directorate of Cadres, was expelled from the Central Committee. So was Konomi, the Minister of Justice, punished for having been lenient in administering justice to class enemies.

The improvement of Yugoslav–Soviet relations after Stalin's death set in motion a wave of opposition inside the party, led by Tuk Jakova and Bedri Spahiu. The proletarian Jakova reiterated his thesis of the extinction of the class struggle and demanded the rehabilitation of purged comrades. He was supported by Spahiu, a Politburo member and a high-ranking party leader (he had been Public Prosecutor in the Special Court presided over by Xoxe, and later was Public Prosecutor in the trial that sentenced Xoxe to death). Spahiu clashed vehemently with Hoxha at the Plenum of June 1955 (they are both from Gjirokastër). The Plenum expelled Jakova from the Central Committee but Spahiu also from the party.

Khrushchev's denunciation of Stalin at the 20th Congress of the CPSU rekindled the flames of the opposition. The dissidents came out into the open at the Party Conference for the City of Tirana (April 1956). They criticized the ruling elite for their autocratic methods, their contempt for the masses and their failure to redress the economic situation, and pressed hard for the rehabilitation of Xoxe, Jakova, Spahiu and other prominent party members. Intervening personally, Hoxha succeeded in quelling the rebellion. Reprisals ensued. In his letter to party organizations, 'The Lessons We Should Draw from the Party Conference of the City of Tirana' (21 April 1956), Hoxha mentions as 'unhealthy elements with an accentuated anti-party attitude' a group of people, laying the main responsibility on their inspirers: Pëllumb Dishnica, Hulusi Spahiu, Pajo Islami and Peço Fidhi (SW II, 456–7).

In 1956, two prominent party members, Liri Gega, a member of the first Politburo, and General Dali Ndreu, her husband, were arrested while 'attempting to cross the [Albanian-Yugoslav] border'.[12] They were both shot – the three of them, to be precise, Liri being, according to Khrushchev,[13] pregnant. In May 1957, General Panajot Plaku, former Deputy Minister of Defence, escaped to Yugoslavia.

Accused of Titoism were the alleged leaders of the 1960 'Greek–Yugoslav–US' conspiracy, Rear Admiral Teme Sejko, Commander of Albania's Naval Forces, and Tahir Demi, former Albanian representative for COMECON. They were tried and executed. Their 'revisionist-imperialist' plot occurred at a time when Soviet–Albanian relations were going from bad to worse. Only one month earlier Albania had signed an economic agreement with China according to which Peking was to give Tirana $123 million in aid and credits.[14]

The main victims of the purge following the Soviet–Albanian rift were Liri Belishova and Koço Tashko. Belishova, Spiru's widow, became a member of the Politburo after her husband's rehabilitation. She was the Number 1 woman in the party hierarchy and carried out important diplomatic missions. Tashko was discarded from the leadership when the party was originally formed. He is shown criticizing Hoxha for his handling of the Kosova question during the war (84–5). After the split with Yugoslavia, Tashko chaired the party's Central Auditing Committee. Neither he nor Belishova made a secret of their loyalty to the Soviet Union. 'Both of them were expelled from the party as enemies' (H 332).

Unlike the split with Yugoslavia, which shook the CPA to its very foundations, the rift with the Soviet Union caused no traumatic perturbations, an indication that the Albanian communists were not particularly attached to the homeland of socialism. Once Tashko and Belishova disappeared from the political scene, no spectacular purges occurred for a period of twelve years. The Sino-Albanian alliance was unlikely to cause serious ideological ruffles, given the Albanians' ignorance of the internal strife in the Communist Party of China as well as China's indifference to the PLA's ideological problems. The Hoxha–Shehu duumvirate maintained full control of the situation, despite the country's precarious economic condition following the Soviet Union's discontinuation of economic and technical aid. Beginning with the 3rd Five-Year Plan (1961–65), Albania adopted a policy of austerity, though assisted to some extent by China with credits and experts. A certain improvement occurred during the 4th Five-Year Plan (1966–70), due to stern measures taken to reduce bureaucracy, lower salaries of better paid workers, employ women in productive work, and have people do 'volunteer' work in the construction sector, farms and factories.

The stress exerted on the population by 'The Struggle of the PLA for the Further Revolutionization of the Party and the Life of the Country (1966–1971)',[15] influenced by the Cultural Revolution (1966–9), caused tension resulting in grumblings and fatigue. China's switch in the 1970s to a friendly policy towards the United States posed new dangers. Albanian intellectuals dared take liberties. A taste for new ways of expression in literature and the arts developed, backed by the mass media. Unorthodox customs spread among the youth. The censor had in the meantime grown into a writer;[16] his nostrils were particularly sensitive to literary rot. In the 4th Plenum (June 1973), Hoxha defined liberalism as 'an expression of ideological and political opportunism, renunciation of the consistent class struggle . . . acceptance of peaceful coexistence with the enemy ideology' (*SW* 4, 819). The axe fell on Fadil Paçrami and Todi Lubonja.

A crony of Spiru, Paçrami had become editor-in-chief of the party organ, *Zëri i Popullit* (The People's Voice), when only in his twenties. Hoxha had proposed him, together with Shehu and Belishova, for cooptation in the Politburo as early as 1944, to counter Xoxe's mounting influence. A Central Committee member (1952), Paçrami carried important functions in the party and the government. In his mature age he turned to writing plays. They were suddenly found polluted with liberalism. Lubonja, Director of the Albanian Radio-Television, had seconded the contagion. Their purge spread to the cadres of the Ministry of Education and Culture, including the Minister, Thoma Deljana. The leadership of the Youth Organization was particularly affected and infected – 'long hair, extravagant dress, screaming jungle music . . .' (*SW* 4, 836). It was reshuffled. So was the direction of the League of Albanian Writers and Artists.

The cultural purge raged after the 4th Plenum (June 1973). The 5th and 6th Plenums (June and December 1974) exuded the military purge. To call generals liberals wouldn't do, another name had to be found which, due to the many stripes of their insignia, had to be a string of names: 'saboteurs' – 'plotters' – 'counter-revolutionary revisionists'. Such were found to be Beqir Balluku, Minister of Defence, Petrit Dume, the Chief of the General Staff, and Hito Çako, the Chief of the Political Directorate of the army. They were charged with plotting to take power through a military putsch. As in China, the official policy on national defence was inspired by the doctrine that 'Albania could not be defended against external aggression, especially Soviet aggression, except by applying the tactics of partisan guerrilla warfare' (H 504), that 'every citizen must be a soldier and every soldier a citizen' (H 467). Accordingly, 'the key element in national defence and victory is man rather than weapons, the revolutionary consciousness of the "citizen army" rather than military technology.'[17] Apparently, Balluku and his staff wanted to build a modern army, well-trained and disciplined, and whose first loyalty was to the General Staff, not the party. The issue at stake was who would command the army: the bygone generals (Hoxha and Shehu), or those actually in charge. Lieutenant-General Balluku, a former metal-worker from Tirana, had gone through some schooling in the Voroshilov Military Academy as well as some training in the Politburo (1948–74), while also serving as Minister of Defence from 1954 on. Yet he could not match the Commander-in-Chief and the victor of the Battle of Tirana. He and his associates were found guilty of 'distributing the documents and the materials of the party and the works of Comrade Enver Hoxha, sent to the army, in very limited numbers' (H 506). The 'arch-traitor' Balluku was punished, together with his associates, 'by the laws of the dictatorship of the proletariat',[18] in other words, executed.

'Here are two, let's make them three!' rings a line in an Albanian rhyme chanted by children. The cultural and military purges – cultural and military relating pretty much like thesis and antithesis – were to lead to economic purge, their synthesis. This time the traitors were Abdyl Këllezi, Koço Theodosi and Kiço Ngjela, respectively the Chairman of the Planning Commission, the Minister of Industry and Mining and the Minister of Trade. Këllezi and Theodosi were Politburo members, Ngjela a member of the CC. Their crimes? Sundry and divers: introduction of self-management and capitalist methods, encouragement of bureaucratic and technocratic trends, waste in funds and materials, sabotage in industry and agriculture,[19] trade used as liaison with enemies. 'This group, like the others, had been engaged in clandestine activity for years,' one reads in the *History of the Party of Labour of Albania* (510), which further specifies: 'Both the group of B. Balluku and the group of A. Këllezi and Co. relied on the aid of the Chinese leadership which incited the traitorous counter-revolutionary activity of these groups' (511).

'The smashing of the enemy group' took place in the 7th Plenum (26 to

29 May 1975). Only a week later, Adil Çarçani, then First Deputy Premier and now Premier of Albania, signed a five-year pact with the Chinese for a long-term credit without interest. *HoPLA* does not mention the signing of the pact, which was, however, made public in the party's organ, *Zëri i Popullit*.[20] In other words at about the same time that an Albanian leader was conducting talks with Chinese leaders for economic aid to his country, the CC Plenum of the Albanian leadership was, according to *HoPLA*, 'smashing' the group of traitors who had tried to wreck the Albanian economy by 'rely[ing] on the aid of the Chinese leadership'. The economic aid to the Albanian government has been turned into enemy aid to Albanian 'counter-revolutionaries' plotting against their own government. 'I give you bread, and you throw stones to me,' says an Albanian proverb. Ingratitude compounded with slander.

Shams such as this adorn the Bible of Albanian Marxism–Leninism pretty much as anti-aircraft bunkers standing guard against the invisible enemy decorate the Albanian landscape. The impression one gets from reading *The Titoites* is the same: history is being continuously reinvented to please the one who detains its licence. Things that never happened are presented as facts, while facts are distorted, often to the point of being reversed. Looking for objectivity and honesty in works such as these is a desperate enterprise – scattered wreckage of truth floating in a sea of falsehood.

In 1975 Hoxha was still singing hymns to Chairman Mao, who had at that time lined up with the United States, the arch-enemy of Hoxha's pure Marxist–Leninism. His opportunism was of course dictated by economic reasons, which are likewise basic for explaining Albania's noisy love–hate affairs with her two former partners. And since the party purges in Albania have been invariably contingent on the relations between the CPA–PLA on the one hand, and the Communist Parties of first Yugoslavia, then the Soviet Union, and ultimately China on the other hand, one would be led to infer that the main cause for the purges was the country's economic dependency now on one, now on another foreign country.

Shehu's purge belies that inference. After the rift with China, Albania was, because of its total isolation, a most independent country. And here Hoxha comes to our rescue. An enlightening paragraph in *The Titoites* reads:

We know that Marxism–Leninism always regards the internal cause, the internal factor, as the main determining factor in the birth and evolution of every phenomenon. The process and birth of a communist party can never be an exception to this law, hence, the process of the founding of our Communist Party cannot be an exception to it, either. (35)

This is a time-honoured theory that goes back to Aristotle (his entelechy). The question of whether the external or the internal factor is determinant for the birth and evolution of a phenomenon boils down to the question of which comes first, the chicken or the egg. Aristotle was for the egg. But I doubt Marx shared that opinion, if for no other reason than because the poor devil could not have eaten many chickens: a rooster cost five shillings in 1867, I find in an old encyclopedia.

Hoxha's paragraph quoted above is meant to refute the thesis that the CPA was founded by the Yugoslavs. And since it was not founded by the Yugoslavs, it follows that the founders were the Albanian communists themselves. The question is, who are these founders? According to *HoPLA*, there were fifteen founders (H 64), two of them being Yugoslavs (36). Of the remaining thirteen, only four are mentioned: Enver Hoxha, Pilo Peristeri, Qemal Stafa and Vasil Shanto. The last two were killed in May 1942 and February 1944, while Peristeri, a tinsmith from Korçë, was never part of the top leadership. This leaves Hoxha a lonely star in what used to be a constellation. And if we add to the number of the purged founders – Tashko, Xoxe, Lulo, Premte, Jakova, Themelko – the number of purged builders – Dishnica, Malëshova, Spiru, Kristo, Spahiu, Gega, Belishova, Balluku, Shehu, Hazbiu, to name only the most important ones – one is left with the conclusion that Hoxha alone on the one plate of the balance weighs more than all the rest on the other. Which is not surprising, considering that the rest have been reduced to a pile of ashes.

Such being the case, if we take the lead from Hoxha's doctrine that the main determinant is the internal factor, the inference to be drawn is that the main cause for the party purges must be sought in Hoxha's innermost nature, his entelechy: his boundless and inalienable will to power, guided by his all-comprehensive and infallible mind. Is there any doubt that Hoxha considers himself a unique genius, he who acts as being the only one in the world to represent Marxism–Leninism in its immaculate purity? Read *The Titoites*. You will never catch him admitting a mistake.[21] The closest he comes to it is in a page where he defends himself from the Yugoslav charge that he once committed a 'grave' mistake. This was during the election of the Central Committee at the Labinot Conference (March 1943). 'The candidates were proposed to the delegates not by name, but, for reasons of security, by description of their characteristics' (40). This gross breach of the party rules was in fact a manipulatory device on the part of the existing leadership headed by Hoxha to elect people congenial to him: all depended on how he or a trusted comrade would describe the candidates. And here is how Hoxha justifies himself: 'The truth is that the way in which we acted over the elections at the 1st

National Conference of the CPA was not any great mistake, especially in the conditions of that time' (ibid.).

To realize who Hoxha is one needs only read *HoPLA*, the Albanian counterpart of Stalin's *Short Course* of the history of the Bolshevik Party. It begins with a description of the communist groups before the party's foundation. Hoxha is first mentioned (he joined the Korçë group shortly before the Italian occupation of the country) towards the end of the first chapter, in a section exclusively devoted to him (57–8). From that point on, however, his name structures the text. It appears rather sparingly in the second and third chapters, which deal with the party's activity during the war and after the liberation. But beginning with the fourth chapter, which focuses on the party's struggle to industrialize the country, his name and the party become increasingly interchangeable terms: *Le parti, c'est moi.* The history of the party is indeed the record of his achievements, supported by citations from his reports and speeches. In vain one looks for his closest collaborators to be given some credit. They are never mentioned, except for one or two who are dead. Those who are named are invariably dissidents, branded as plotters and traitors. One expects that at least Shehu, his ally and Premier for twenty-seven years, would crop up somewhere. Not even he. As everyone knows who is at all familiar with the Albanian war of liberation, it was Shehu who routed the nationalists, and it was he who as commander of the 1st Army Corps drove the Nazi troops from the capital. How does *HoPLA* describe that memorable battle?

> The units of the National Liberation were now engaged in the final operations against the German troops in Albania and in Kosova. Of these operations the most important was that for the liberation of Tirana. The order of the Commander-in-Chief was to wipe out the enemy, to stop the plunder and destruction of the city by the Germans and to liberate Tirana at all costs. The operation was to be led by the Command of the 1st Army Corps. (166)

The credit goes to the Commander-in-Chief who gave the 'order', not to the commander who fought and won the battle. Not only is Shehu's name omitted, but even his personality is denied, the word referring to him being 'command', an abstract collective noun. Ignoring comrades to exalt the dictator is a consistent technique in *HoPLA* (Ismail Kadare makes good use of it in his novel, *The Great Winter*). Discrediting opponents is another, parallel technique. The purges are a major theme in *HoPLA*, they constitute Hoxha's title to glory as the guardian and arbiter of orthodox Marxism–Leninism. To that effect, the victims, ghostly apparitions wrested from the limbo of shame and misery where they have been hurled, are made to parade before the throne of the victor, their judge and executioner. Once they are gone, the last of them being the economic traitors, the stage remains empty. Instead of the Leader, his picture on the wall. His communication with his worshippers will now be only through his books, approached reverently like sacred scriptures. His name will be pronounced in a formulaic clause, 'Comrade Enver Hoxha teaches ("instructs", "says", "explains"),' preceding or succeeding sentences in the form of maxims or prescriptions. The following are all found in the section 'The Revolutionary Tempering of Cadres in the School of the Working Class' (H 523–8):

'The cadre . . . first of all must be educated in the school of the working class,' teaches Comrade Enver Hoxha. (H 523)

'The cadres have their place, their role,' pointed out Comrade Enver Hoxha, 'however, they do not impose their law on the party, but the party and the class impose the law on them'. (524)

Comrade Enver Hoxha says, 'The party must immediately and unhesitatingly bring down from their high horse and break the noses and bones . . .' of cadres with the *kulak*, bureaucrat or liberal mentality . . . (525)

The struggle of the party for the revolutionary education and tempering of the cadres in the school of the working class created healthier conditions for the implementation of the teaching of Comrade Hoxha who instructed, 'The cadre should make revolution all his life, should be in revolution with himself and the others'. (527–8)

The lawmaker's injunction to his subjects blindly to obey his law could not be clearer. And if Hoxha is this kind of prophet-impostor who has reduced the party to worshipping him as the Messiah of a Marxism–Leninism which differs from that of his two masters, Stalin and Tito, in that he resolves them into a higher synthesis (synhoxhesis), then we can now explain the phenomenon of party purges in Albania in conformity with his thesis of the predominance of the internal factor: the party purges are a phenomenon of Hoxhan phagocytosis. The ogre needs fresh human flesh to thrive.

Those who were purged, in groups or individually, suffered their fate because they dared scorn or disobey his orders. Some of them, while having no qualms about expropriating the rich bourgeois and the big landowners, objected to jailing them and then harassing their families. Others who were in agreement with curbing the influence of organized religion would not condone the extermination of the clergy, scoffing at the idea that Albania be made the first atheistic state in the world. No one would hesitate to distribute the confiscated land to the poor peasants. But to persecute a peasant 'with less than 3 hectares [about seven acres] of land, 1 head of cattle and less than 10 sheep' (H 319) seemed foolish. 'In 1960 there were some 15,000 *kulak* households, or less than 1 per cent of the overall number of the peasant households. The *kulaks* had lost their former economic base,' they had 'disappeared in general as a class' (ibid.). According to Marxism, class is defined by its economic base. But if this was lost, as the text spells out, can their persecution, which raged until they were annihilated, be justified? They were annihilated as a class when they were no longer a class. This is not Marxism, but Stalinism.

When Malëshova protested against the killing without due process of former career army officers by Shehu's partisans in the first days of the liberated capital, Hoxha justified the terroristic acts by saying: 'When we appealed to them to go to the mountains and fight the occupiers together with us they didn't budge from their comfortable shelters. Now they are "repenting" too late, and we have to settle accounts with the criminals' (187). Criminals because they did not join the partisans! Malëshova is quoted to have replied: 'You have lost the heart of a communist who values another man's life and thinks deeply before he decides to wipe out someone who might be corrected and serve the country' (ibid.). A communist with a humane heart must have sounded ludicrous to Hoxha, which is his reason for quoting Malëshova's reply.

We must dwell longer on the latest purge, which hit Shehu and his family as well as his relatives.

It was suggested at the outset that Hoxha's account of the purge reads as a fanciful tale of intrigue, one, however, which is in jarring contrast with the rest of his memoirs.

Ismail Kadare has made a name for himself by writing 'historical novels' in which the blending of reality and fiction results in a third thing, the components of which can no longer be distinguished. Reality melts into fantasy while solidifying the latter. A similar – abortive – technique governs Hoxha's narrative.

He first tells us that Shehu's wife visited various capitals of Europe to consult CIA representatives about Shehu's plan to physically liquidate Hoxha. Having obtained their approval, Shehu was to have gone about implementing his plan in this way:

In this context Mehmet Shehu arranged the engagement of his son to the daughter of a family in the circle of which there were six or seven war criminals, including the notorious agent of the CIA Arshi Pipa. Such an engagement could not fail to attract the attention of the public. And it was done precisely with the aim of attracting public attention and causing a sensation. If it were accepted by the party, it would lead to splits and liberalism among others, too, in the party, the Youth Organization, etc. If it were not accepted by the party, measures would be taken against Mehmet Shehu, not imprisonment, of course, but demotion, removal from his position or even expulsion from the party. This would cause a sensation and the Yugoslavs would use it, as they needed it for propaganda purposes to discredit the leadership of the Party of Labour of Albania and especially Enver.

Hoxha, who, as they have repeated over and over again, is 'eliminating' his collaborators, as Stalin did. (p. 624)

In party terminology, the slogan of 'war criminal' applies to any person who resisted the Albanian Communist Party during the Second World War, when Albania was first a fascist- and then a Nazi-occupied territory. Some of these people, mostly bourgeois and aristocrats, had managed to flee the country during the war. Many more (mostly peasants) left after the party took over. Hoxha uses the above slogan to describe exiled persons with different ideologies but hostile to the Hoxha regime. At the same time he lumps together some of these exiles under the larger category of 'family . . . circle'. The members of this family circle in the homeland lost their privileges when the party established its dictatorship and have been ever since living in socio-economic conditions typical of declassed families.

Let us now look at the paragraph cited above. Based on an engagement that would naturally lead to marriage, the sentiments of the paragraph are structured around the concept of mixed marriage. The son of a communist leader wedded to the daughter of a declassed family is a case of miscegenation, class here substituting for race. This miscegenation will 'lead to splits and liberalism' in the party. How so? The polluted blood of the bride will first infect that of her husband and then the two together will pollute the party's collective body, which will eventually fall apart and disintegrate. And the remedy? Electrocution (fire is cathartic) of the contaminated fiancé, and quarantine of the whole family and family circle, the *pater familias*'s suicide only proving that the disease had already affected his brain.

Hoxha's concept of liberalism takes its lead from the tacit metaphor of contagious diseases:[22] plague, leprosy, syphilis. *Syphilis sive morbus gallicus* fits the picture better. A venereal disease, it is usually transmitted through sexual contact, and it decomposes the tissues of the body, eventually reaching the brain. Apparently, waves of the sexual frenzy flooding the West have been washing up on the shores of Albania. According to a colleague who recently visited the country, Albanian women are using cosmetics and youngsters are wearing jeans. A representative work of Albanian literature is much more specific.

In Kadare's novel, *The Great Winter*,[23] the main character, a journalist and a candidate for full membership in the party, is engaged to a girl who is the daughter of a vice-minister. But whereas the young man is a party hard-liner, his fiancée is more interested in buying dresses for the forthcoming wedding and furnishings for the anticipated home. The journalist, who knows Russian well, accompanies, as interpreter, the Albanian delegation, headed by Hoxha, which attends the 1960 meeting in Moscow of the representatives of the Communist and Workers' Parties. It was at that meeting that Hoxha gave the memorable speech that marks the break of Albania with the Soviet Union. The journalist was an eyewitness to what happened. But he dares not say a word before the Political Bureau decides to announce the break. His muteness has deleterious effects on his fiancée, as she suspects that he has become enamoured of a Russian girl. Worrying about her daughter's depression, the girl's mother visits the journalist's boss and tells him that her prospective son-in-law intends to break off the engagement. In the meeting of the local party organization that follows, the party secretary requests an explanation for the journalist's changed attitude towards his fiancée. He refuses angrily, on the grounds that his relation with her is his own business. But since 'a communist cannot hide anything from his organization' (358), his application for full membership in the party is shelved. Meanwhile, his fiancée has taken to drink. In a moment of laxity, she gives herself to her teacher of French, the son of a 'declassed' family. Two negative examples of party ethics on the part of the novel's main characters is much too much for Albanian socialist realism. Kadare saves the situation with a redeeming episode. The novel ends with a chapter in which the journalist's younger brother, a teenager who has been indulging in dating girls as well as attending dancing and drinking parties, is rid of these bourgeois symptoms as soon as he joins the army.

Hoxha's account of the engagement in the epilogue of his book presents affinities with the engagement episode in the novel. He must have read Kadare's modern epic, which is an apotheosis of Hoxha (the *Aeneid* comes to mind). Hoxha's towering stature makes the comrades who accompany him (Shehu, Kapo, Alia) look like shadows – Kadare achieves that effect by obliterating their names.[24] In times of dictatorship, when sources of information are rigorously controlled, literature is nearly the only way to have access to the life-style of the society it portrays. Kadare has not quite invented the unorthodox episode, which he deftly transfers to another historical period, the Khrushchev era, implicitly laying the blame there. During that era, Hoxha was still first among equals, not the Olympian figure glorified by Kadare in his novel.

A reading of Kadare's novel as a social document strongly suggests that the 'liberalism' Hoxha imputes to Shehu's intentions was rather a common phenomenon among the younger generation at the end of the 1970s and the beginning of the 1980s. And, since Hoxha associates 'liberalism' with 'splits' in the party, one can safely infer that the party was also divided at the time. The level-headed party members must have been turning a deaf ear to the virulent bombast against all sorts of revisionism from the mouth of one who believed himself to be the very incarnation of Marxism–Leninism. Party members who had read Lenin's *Left-wing Communism, an Infantile Disease,* must have realized that Hoxha's ultra-Leftism showed symptoms of the polar opposite of infantilism. In this context, it seems reasonable to think of Shehu as leading an opposition group in the party, not for a more liberal policy or a weakening of the party's role, but for a more pragmatic approach to the situation in other communist countries and parties as well as for a more moderate trend in international politics. In the past, Shehu had been, on a par with Hoxha, champion of an Albanian brand of socialism distinct from all other varieties. The downfall of Koçi Xoxe, marking the end of Yugoslav hegemony in the Albanian Party of Labour, was mostly due to Shehu. And he was, in his capacity as Premier of Albania, no less adamant than Hoxha about freeing the country from Soviet tutorship. Yet such evidence – to be found in the very books authored by Hoxha – does not prevent him from branding Shehu as agent of both the Yugoslav UDB and the Soviet KGB. He even writes that Shehu had been 'in the service of the secret American intelligence before the First World War',[25] at a time when the Central Intelligence Agency did not exist. As the 'superagent' Shehu was, he was able to fool everyone in the party, including Hoxha himself, for almost forty years, making them believe he was a party champion when he really was an 'enemy'. His secret aim was to split and liberalize the party, which is tantamount to destroying it, a split and liberalized Marxist–Leninist party necessarily stumbling to its own demise.[26] Shehu's diabolic stratagem for destroying the party was to have his son marry a woman of a formerly bourgeois origin. The marriage would inevitably have led to the *embourgeoisement* of the party and, as a consequence, to the reinstatement of the class system under the rule of capital.

What is class, according to Marxism? It is a basically economic concept, defined by the possession of the means of production and the human relations resulting therefrom. Capitalism is a social system in which the means of production are owned by a class, the bourgeoisie, which exploits the rest of society and especially those who have no other means of sustenance except their labour: the proletariat. Socialism abolishes the bourgeois system by expropriating capitalists and then by reducing to a minimum the economic differences in the rest of the population, thus paving the way for the establishment of a classless society, the goal of communism. Due especially to the party's policy of bridging the gap between city and countryside, socialism in Albania has advanced considerably. The means of production are owned and supervised by a state that is entirely controlled by the party. The aristocratic and bourgeois families of the times of King Zog and the fascist-Nazi occupation have long been liquidated and class conflict is practically non-existent. Such being the situation, does it make sense to say, as Hoxha does, that an engagement can become a propellant for reversing the historical process? An engagement is a human relation, and human relations are, according to Marxism, ultimately determined by the possession of the means of production and the mode of production, not the other way round, as Hoxha fancies. It is more than a third of a century since the party wiped out all possible opposition from the privileged classes and groups of old. Granted that these people resent the party for having expropriated and humiliated them, yet in the 99.99 per cent police state that is Albania today (as measured by poll statistics), they cannot even express their resentment, except perhaps in their dreams. Raising the ghost of their return to power will fool no one. For ever since they were liquidated, the only remaining opponents have been dissident party members, belonging to splinter groups. The splits in the party have mainly occurred because of ideological differences among party leaders, as amply documented in the official *History of the Party of Labour of Albania*. Nowhere in that text – which could not have been written without the approval of the First Secretary of the party – does one come across a single case in which family relations concerning party leaders have caused crises such as the one Hoxha portrays in his book. His argument is indeed an offence to the party. For only a straw party can be shaken by an engagement, albeit the engagement of a communist prince to a modern Cinderella.

An engagement that splits a Marxist–Leninist party? This sounds like the straw breaking the camel's back. Hoxha's saying qualifies for a collection of proverbial jokes. And what a scene for a playwright: the wranglings over an engagement in the Political Bureau of the Albanian Party of Labour!

The French edition of the *History of the Party of Labour of Albania* contains a chapter on Hoxha as a theoretician of Marxism.[27] The authors analyse various revisionistic outgrowths – Titoism, Soviet social-imperialism, Maoism, Euro-communism – as defined by Hoxha in his works. He was in the process of writing *The Titoites* when the French edition of *HoPLA* appeared. I shall supply my own brief analysis of Hoxha's latest work, limiting myself to its epilogue, where theory comes out most strongly.

The epilogue is a narrative with a theoretical core, which is to be found in the paragraph cited above. The author's thesis concerns Shehu's plan to split and liberalize the party by having his son marry a woman of a declassed family. Shehu's first move was to 'arrange' their engagement, which was bound to 'cause a sensation'. And this, in turn, 'would lead to splits and liberalism' in the party, if accepted by it. If not, Shehu's political career would be doomed. But this would still 'cause a sensation', which the Yugoslavs would then use to discredit the PLA leadership and especially Hoxha for his Stalinist methods.

The either/or argument revolves around the concept of sensation. If Shehu succeeded, this would be because of his ability to 'attract the attention of the public' by means of an engagement 'causing a sensation'. If he failed, this would be because of the party's action to forestall his planned sensation, leaving him with the surrogate satisfaction of seeing his failure made into a sensation by his patrons. The first alternative conveys Shehu's wishful thinking as attributed to him by Hoxha. The second alternative is Hoxha's reply to the first. Of the two, the first has a stronger theoretical ring, with a conceptual frame that can be described as causative attraction, that is, attraction causing sensation, which in turn causes splits and liberalism. We are faced with a chain reaction set in motion by an engagement endowed with magic. The chain is composed of several links: engagement attracting public attention causing sensation leading to party splits involving liberalism resulting in party liquidation. Is the reader getting dizzy from the chain reaction? Let me explain how the theory works in practice.

A young and beautiful couple is naturally attractive, though not necessarily sensational. 'To attract the attention of the public,' the couple needs a striking setting. A picture advertising a new brand of car with a young couple in bathing suits can serve as an illustration. Such a picture *per se* is not particularly striking and can hardly 'cause a sensation'. For the latter to occur, the persons in the picture must be unusual: he might be a well-known public figure, and she, a beauty queen. Now, have this picture published in a prestigious magazine such as *The New Yorker*. It certainly will cause a sensation and many people will rush to buy the car. This is, of course, capitalist practice. Hoxha is applying to the PLA a capitalist pattern, which he traces back to Shehu's capitalist mind. Shehu's stratagem to have his son marry a woman carrying in her blood the degenerate genes of a criminal who has become a US citizen bears, of course, a CIA stamp. The moment the picture of the newly-weds appeared in Albanian newspapers (and Shehu would see to that), Hoxha's long monopoly as a public and publicity figure would be a thing of the past.[28] Shehu would use the picture of his son and daughter-in-law so as to reflect their radiance upon himself. The newspapers and magazines of the capitalist world, including, of course, Yugoslavia, would widely publicize the picture, thus helping their agent obfuscate the figure of his rival.

The trouble with Hoxha's theoretical jewel is that it contradicts the narrative in which it is set. He does not tell when the engagement took place and when it was broken off. But even if it did not last for long, due to the prompt intervention of the party, it occurred anyway. The question arises: How is it that such a sensational event was not even mentioned in the capitalist press, which thrives, as is well known, on sensations? Hoxha himself tells us that 'Shehu arranged the engagement . . . with the aim of attracting public attention and causing a sensation.' If so, one would expect Shehu to have communicated the sensational news to his patrons, the CIA and the UDB, who would have been only too glad to spread it. The news could have been easily transmitted by Shehu's wife, Fiqret Shehu, who, Hoxha writes, consulted various CIA representatives during her European trip. He also writes that Feçor Shehu, Minister of the Interior, was in close touch with the Yugoslav Embassy in Tirana. Was it not in the interest of the Yugoslavs to let the world know that Hoxha and Shehu had clashed on a question directly regarding Shehu's family? Hoxha himself states that the Yugoslavs 'would use' the sensational news of Shehu's political disgrace, 'as they needed it for their propaganda purposes to discredit the leadership of the Party of Labour of Albania and especially Enver Hoxha'. If anything stands out clearly in what Hoxha himself tells us in his narrative, it is the exact opposite of what he writes, that is to say, that Shehu wanted to attract public attention and cause a sensation. It is Hoxha himself who, with a 'spectacular' piece of news about a plot against him, has managed to attract public attention and cause a sensation through reports in the international press.

What the author narrates as his memoirs would certainly be more credible as fiction. Perhaps he should write fiction to be credible at all. From memoirs to historical novels, the distance is short. And he could easily take the step, having shown himself to be also a literary critic.[29] He could write political novels, as Disraeli did, or perhaps political thrillers. Witness the following excerpts (pp. 625–7):

> Meanwhile, the question of Kosova was becoming dangerous. The Yugoslavs were being unmasked before international public opinion, while the authority of our country was rising . . .
>
> On the eve of the meeting of the Political Bureau, at which the grave political mistake [the engagement] was to be discussed, the Yugoslav Embassy in Tirana, acting on orders which it had received from Belgrade, sent its agent and contact man Feçor Shehu to Mehmet Shehu to transmit the 'ultimatum' of the UDB that 'Enver Hoxha must be killed at all costs, even in the meeting, even if Mehmet Shehu himself is killed.' So hard-pressed were the UDB, the Great-Serb and Titoite clique with the situation in Kosova, so gloomy seemed the future, that they decided to 'destroy' their trump card, their superagent, provided only that something spectacular would occur which would shake socialist Albania and the Party of Labour of Albania to their foundations!
>
> At ten o'clock at night, on 16 December 1981, Feçor Shehu went to Mehmet Shehu's home and transmitted the order of their secret centre.
>
> On 17 December the discussion commenced in the meeting of the Political

Bureau. All comrades, old and new, took part in the discussion, and resolutely condemned Mehmut Shehu's act of engaging his son to a girl in whose family there were six or seven war criminals . . .

At the end of the discussion on the first day, I said to Mehmet Shehu:

'Reflect deeply all night and tomorrow tell us in the Political Bureau from what motives you have proceeded. Your alibi for the engagement does not hold water, something else has impelled you in this reprehensible act.'

What I said alarmed Mehmet Shehu, he suspected that the crime he was preparing might have been discovered . . .

Apparently he judged matters in this way: 'I am as good as dead, the best thing is to save what I can,' and he decided to act like his friend Nako Spiru, to kill himself, thinking the party would bury this 'statesman', this 'legendary leader', this 'partisan and fighter in Spain' with honours . . .

Together with his wife he flushed the poison down the WC . . .

Fiqret Shehu, as the agent she was (she who trembled and wept over nothing), agreed to the suicide of her husband coolly and cynically, provided only that their 'historic' past and she and her sons were saved.

However, they had reckoned their account without the innkeeper. As soon as they informed me about Mehmet Shehu's final act, within moments I proposed that his suicide be condemned, that he had acted as an enemy, and the Political Bureau expressed its unanimous condemnation of the act of this enemy.

. . . He was buried like a dog.[30]

I shall spare the reader comments on this diatribe, the language of a mind run amok with insatiable revenge – calling a rival an 'enemy' *because* he killed himself! The 'alibi for the engagement' Hoxha attributes to Shehu was his own 'trump card' to bring down a rival in a power struggle that had been brewing for some time in the party and that came to a head with the Kosova demonstrations in spring 1981.

The trial following the unprecedented purge will reveal more details such as those just recited but not the truth of what happened. The Bolshevik leaders who were publicly tried by Stalin in the 1930s confessed of having been traitors to the party and even agents of imperialist countries. They did so to spare themselves further torture and to save their families. Saving her sons is a phrase Hoxha attributes to Fiqret Shehu in the cited excerpts. Family ties continue to be strong in socialist Albania, despite the party's efforts to have family loyalty superseded by party loyalty. Because of family ties, when a person commits a party crime, his or her family shares the consequences. The sins of the fathers are visited on their children, as in Biblical times. It is well known that families of political prisoners and even fugitives have been persecuted. Persecution that reaches this point takes on a tribal character, similar to the vendetta once practised by North-Albanian tribes. First exercised against reactionary and declassed families, revenge, grown into a habit, shifted over to comrades and their families. A case in point is Hoxha's revenge against Shehu. Hoxha's rage does not stop at his target, but extends from an individual to his family and from his family to his kin, constrictor-like, embracing even prospective relatives. Such emphasis laid on kinship in matters regarding the party degrades the latter – one is reminded of Engels words about 'the decisive role that kinship plays in the social order of all peoples in the stage of savagery and barbarism'.[31]

One must add, to be fair to savages and barbarians, that their tribal vendetta is less cruel by far than a Stalinist vendetta. They kill, but they do not torture. In a Stalinist regime, invidious revenge tends to nestle in that section of the party which performs police functions, the state security apparatus. When Albania recovered its independence, the dreadful Albanian Security became the fief of Koçi Xoxe, Organizational Secretary of the Party and Minister of the Interior. After Xoxe's demise, Mehmet Shehut became the Minister of the Interior. Under his leadership, the Security apparatus was instrumental in ruthlessly enforcing the party's policy. When Shehu moved to the premiership, the previous position was assumed by Kadri Hazbiu, his brother-in-law. And when Hazbiu became Minister of Defence, the key position was occupied by Feçor Shehu, Mehmet's nephew. Now, in record time, the clan has been liquidated, by methods similar to those used by Stalin and, to some extent, by King Zog. Ahmet Zogu became King of Albania after eliminating his actual and potential rivals, thanks to his tribal craftiness and the fanaticism of his mountaineer retainers, the core of his personal guard. Enver Hoxha eliminated his collaborators thanks first to Shehu and later to Hazbiu. Hoxha allied himself to Shehu when his position as Secretary General of the party was threatened by Koçi Xoxe. From that time until the recent clash, Hoxha and Shehu together ruled socialist Albania. But, whereas Shehu concentrated his efforts on consolidating his grip on the state machine through the State Security network, the more clever Hoxha devoted his energies to building a cult around his person. He achieved that aim through his charisma, his oratorical skill, his French manners and, last but not least, his good looks. Opportunistic and servile writers and artists hailing him as the father of socialist Albania helped create a halo around his figure. In his old age, he had produced a corpus of literary works in which he appears as historian of the PLA, a memorialist, and chief ideologist of Albanian Marxism–Leninism. His ambition is to secure a seat in the pantheon of Marxism–Leninism, alongside Lenin, Stalin and Mao. He certainly will be remembered, and not only for his theory of causative attraction.

NOTES TO CHAPTER 18

1. The Communist Party of Albania (CPA) was formed only in November 1941, two and a half years after the country was invaded by Mussolini's troops. It

united several groups, based on the main urban centres, which had hitherto
been in mutual competiton for the loyalty of the numerically small working
class and even smaller intelligentsia. The role of catalyst in the process was
played by the Communist Party of Yugoslavia (CPY), on behalf of the
Comintern. A national liberation struggle closely coordinated with that led by
Tito in the north was conducted, as in Yugoslavia, simultaneously with a bitter
civil war which brought the CPA to power within three years of its foundation: Tirana was liberated from the Nazis by Albanian partisans on 27
November 1944. Although Yugoslav partisans never fought on Albanian
territory, CPY influence was dominant until 1948, when Yugoslavia was
expelled from the Soviet bloc as a punishment for its independent line. The
Albanian party now turned against its erstwhile ally, to become one of the
staunchest and by far the most lasting of Stalin's followers. Apart from
Georgia and Manchuria, Albania is today the only country where Stalin's
portraits and statues adorn public places.

The speed of the historic change that engulfed the country in 1944–5 was all
the more remarkable given that the civil war had started in earnest only in
August 1943, after the breakdown of talks between the communist-led
National Liberation Front and the bourgeois Balli Kombetër, supported for a
time by the British. The imposition of communist rule was as swift as it was
violent, the urgency of power underscored by the uncertain future which the
country faced in the European settlement following the war's end. By mutual
agreement, the Western Allies' policy in the Balkans had been in British hands.
Albania was not apparently a subject of discussion between Churchill and
Stalin, either at Teheran (November 1943), or in Moscow (October 1944,
when Churchill omitted Albania from the notorious piece of paper he shoved
across the table to Stalin, indicating a possible division of spheres of influence
in the Balkans), or at Yalta (February 1945). The strong Yugoslav influence in
Albania, however, ensured that the country would remain part of the system
then in formation in Eastern Europe.

In 1946, after an incident in Albanian waters off the island of Corfu, first
Great Britain and then the United States withdrew their diplomatic missions
from Tirana, never to return. In 1948, forces within the CPA hostile to the
projected federation with Yugoslavia, used the occasion of the Yugoslav–
Soviet split to sever links with the hegemonic northern neighbour. This in turn
provoked a serious crisis inside the Albanian party, followed by a large-scale
purge of pro-Yugoslav elements. Close links with the Soviet Union were
maintained until the 20th Congress of the CPSU, after which Soviet–Albanian
relations cooled rapidly: the dominant wing of the Albanian party felt
mortally threatened by the Tito–Khrushchev rapprochement. By 1962 Albania was in open alignment with China, which filled the economic and military
gap created by the withdrawal of Soviet and Eastern European aid and
personnel. The change of orientation necessitated another party purge. Ten
years later, however, Albania broke with China as well, ostensibly in protest
against the latter's decision to re-establish diplomatic links with the United
States. At each turn, the core of the old central leadership shrank further, and
the missing coherence was supplemented by reliance on family ties: a tendency

encouraged further by continuing influence of the clan tradition in the organization of Albanian social life, as well as by the country's growing isolation. The negative effect of this on the Albanian ruling polity is clearly brought out in this essay.

Arshi Pipa, one of the foremost contemporary Albanian poets (who ironically was taught French by Enver Hoxha in secondary school before the war), wrote for cultural and literary journals produced in Shkodër after Liberation. In 1946, when a comprehensive drive against all independent intelligentsia was initiated by the party, he was imprisoned and confined in various labour camps for the following decade. Barely surviving the harsh prison life (his brother, a Communist Party sympathizer, was killed and he himself contracted tuberculosis during his confinement), Pipa was released in 1956 to ,the humiliating and insecure existence of a former political detainee, at a time of great political upheaval in Eastern Europe. He left Albania in 1957 and finally settled in the United States, where he teaches Italian literature at the University of Minnesota. He has published several collections of poems and a number of scholarly works on Albanian culture and society, most notably *Trilogia Albanica* (Munich, 1978).

2. *The Titoites.* The Institute of Marxist–Leninist Studies at the Central Committee of the Party of Labour of Albania: Tirana, 1982. Citations are from this edition, the figure in parenthesis indicating the page.

3. Tuk Jakova, a Politburo member and the party's Organizational Secretary (1948–51), fell into disgrace for maintaining, among other things, that 'it was they [the Yugoslavs] who had created the Communist Party of Albania' (*History of the Party of Labour of Albania*, the Institute of Marxist–Leninist Studies at the CC of the PLA, 2nd edn, Tirana, 1982, p. 287). The citations are from this edition, identified by *H* preceding the page number in parentheses. *HoPLA* is an abbreviation referring to this work when in context.

4. In one of his poems, Malëshova clearly expressed his nationalism: 'I love Albania/from Skoplje to Yannina' (I quote from memory, his works having been long suppressed).

5. Nexhmije Hoxha headed the Agitation and Propaganda Directorate of the Party's Central Committee beginning 1952. Later she directed the Institute of Marxist–Leninist Studies and is still director of that institute.

6. A fourth, Trotskyite organization, *Zjarri* (The Fire), was not invited.

7. Enver Hoxha, *Selected Works*, vol. 1. The Institute of Marxist–Leninist Studies at the CC of the PLA, Tirana, 1974, p. 140. Four volumes have already appeared: vol. 1, 1974; vol. 2, 1975; vol. 3, 1980; and vol. 4, 1982. Citations from these volumes are identified in parentheses by the initials *SW*, followed by the volume number and the page number.

8. This is how Ismail Kadare portrays his execution in his novel, *The Great Winter*:

> 'Anastas Lulo, you have betrayed the International.' He stood before them, pale, looking with empty eyes on now one now another. Partisan court martial. 'Don't hurry, my boys, wait a moment, you don't know what the International is. You are young. Don't rush, summon here a competent comrade. I want to discuss with him questions of principle. A comrade from

the centre, one who is conversant with theory.' They listened to him for a while. His imploring voice kept increasingly repeating resonant foreign words, which sounded more and more absurd in that scorched plain. 'This comrade here is conversant with theory,' the company commander finally interrupted him, pointing to a young man with blondish hair and a snubbed nose, a partisan 'from the village of Brataj. The partisan lowered his eyes. 'Çoçol, explain to him the question from a theoretical viewpoint,' the company commander said. 'And you, Muqerem, assist him.' The man charged with treason opened wide his eyes, twisting his mouth. And instead of uttering resonant foreign words, he only said, 'no, no.' They took him to a place some fifty steps away. And there they gunned him down. (*Dimri i madh* (*The Great Winter*), Tirana, 1981, pp. 105–6.)

9. Fundo was then an adviser to Seit Kryeziu, a landowner from Gjakovë (Djakovica), who had close contacts with the British Military Mission at the time when they were trying to set up Abbas Kupi and an alternative to the CPA.

10. Stavro Skendi (ed.), *Albania*, New York, 1956, p. 86.

11. Among the twenty-eight victims executed without due process were a writer, Manush Peshkëpia, and a woman professor, Sabiha Kasimati.

12. *Documenta kryesore të PPSH*, III (Main Documents of the PLA, vol. 3). Mihal Duri: Tirana, 1970, p. 449 (quoted by Prifti – see no. 16 – p. 276).

13. Khrushchev mentioned her case in his speech at the 22nd CPSU Congress (October 1961). See William E. Griffith, *Albania and the Sino-Soviet Rift*, Cambridge, Mass., 1963, p. 235.

14. Nicholas C. Pano, *The People's Republic of Albania* (The Johns Hopkins Press: Baltimore, 1968), p. 148.

15. Title of Chapter 7 of *HoPLA*. The chapter is divided into five subchapters (a total of seventy-three pages). Subchapter 4, 'Revolutionizing in the Field of Economy', occupies less than seven pages. The titles of all five subchapters include a derivative of 'revolution' (-ary, -izing, -ization) as their leitmotif: 'revolutionization' of the party and the state power, education and literature and the arts; 'revolutionizing' foreign policy and economy, social and ethical life (emancipation of women and abolition of religion).

16. The first two volumes of Hoxha's Works were published in 1968. By 1971, eight volumes had appeared.

17. Peter Prifti, *Socialist Albania since 1944: Domestic and Foreign Developments*, Cambridge, Mass., 1978, p. 215.

18. Hoxha's *Raport në Kongresin VII të PPSH* (Report to the 7th Congress of the PLA), 8 Nëntori, Tirana, 1976, p. 95.

19. Pirro Dodbiba, Minister of Agriculture and Politburo Candidate member, was dismissed in April 1976.

20. See also *Peking Review*, no. 28 (11 July 1975), p. 7.

21. *Il Duce ha sempre ragione.* In the past, for tactical reasons, he would admit having made mistakes. In his 'Theses on Re-Examining the Work of the 2nd Plenum of the CC of the CPA' (June 1946), he confessed to having acted improperly in not reacting to the criticism of Malëshova, Spiru and Xoxe, implicitly accusing himself of sharing 'qualities and shortcomings inherited

from our old work', in other words, opportunism (*SW* 1, 564). He was even more explicit in his 'Report to the Party Activists in Tirana on the Analysis and Conclusions of the 11th Plenum of the CC of the CPA' (October 1948) (*SW* 1, 752, 762). The admitted mistakes, however, refer to the Yugoslav-dominated period of the CPA, during which not he, but Xoxe, held real power.

22. Disease as an attribute of revisionism (the *genus* of liberalism) is spelled out in the following sentence: 'What is the explanation for this custom of revisionists? Do they all copy each other, or does their disease drive them to find the same cause?' (498).

23. See note 8 above.

24. Mehmet Shehu, Hysni Kapo and Ramiz Alia are never mentioned by name, only as 'member(s) of the Albanian delegation' (Shehu is also referred to as 'Premier of Albania', and 'the man . . . who fought in Spain' (176). On the other hand, the members of the Soviet delegation, Mikoyan, Andropov and Kozlov, are singled out by name.

25. Enver Hoxha's Electoral Speech to Voters of Zone Nr. 120 in Tirana, *Rruga e Partisë* (The Party Road) 11 (1982), p. 6. In the following sentences, Hoxha accuses Shehu of being a (Yugoslav) OZNA (later UDB) agent from the time he was Commander of the First Brigade (in 1943–4). Later, Hoxha maintains, he became a (Soviet) KGB agent. In the following excerpt from *The Titoites*, Shehu appears also as an agent of the British Intelligence, while at the same time being a *persona grata* of the German Gestapo and the Italian secret police (SIM): 'From the investigations following the suicide of Mehmet Shehu and from the documents in the possession of the party, it appears that Mehmet Shehu was an agent recruited by the Americans from the time he attended Fultz's school [the American Vocational School] in Tirana [from which Shehu graduated in 1932]. On Fultz's orders, Mehmet Shehu went to study in a military school in Italy; on the orders of the American secret service he was sent to Spain to penetrate into the ranks of the International Brigades. The aim of the American secret service was to provide its agent with the 'aura' of an 'internationalist fighter' so he could be used for long-term aims in Albania later. After the defeat of the anti-fascist war in Spain, Mehmet Shehu went to a refugee camp in France where he stayed for three years, at a time when many of his comrades escaped from it. In the camp he was recruited as an agent of the British Intelligence Service also. He was taken out of the camp by an officer of the German Gestapo and one of the Italian SIM, passed through Italy, where he was held two months, and was then handed over in Durrës to the notorious Albanian spy in the pay of the Italian secret service Man Kukaleshi, who released him after twenty days, and Mehmet Shehu went to Mallakastra and linked up with the organization of our party there. During the National Liberation War, Mehmet Shehu and his wife Fiqret Sanxhaktari were recruited as agents of the Yugoslavs, too, by Dušan Mugoša' (pp. 596–7).

26. That a split and liberal Marxist–Leninist party ceases to exist as such is made clear by Hoxha himself: 'The Marxist–Leninist party . . . is not a party of words, but a party of revolutionary action. If its members are not engaged in concrete actions and struggle it will not be a genuine Marxist–Leninist party, but a Marxist–Leninist party only in name. At given moments such a party will

certainly be split into different factions, will have many lines which will coexist, and it will be turned into a liberal opportunist and revisionist party' (E. Hoxha, *Eurocommunism is Anticommunism*, Institute of Marxist–Leninist Studies at the CC of the PLA, Tirana, 1980, p. 258).

27. *Histoire du Parti du Travail d'Albanie*, Institut des Études Marxistes-Léninistes, Tirana, 1982 (2nd edn).

28. Chapter 2 of Kadare's novel contains an episode that illustrates Hoxha's role as a publicity figure. The editor-in-chief of the journal for which the journalist works, dissatisfied with a series of pictures figuring Hoxha among women workers, has the head of the photography laboratory look for another picture that is to be printed in the journal. The head wonders why, the development of the film having been faultless. The journalist provides the answer: 'Perhaps we should look for a shot where Comrade Hoxha is seen smiling a little' (32).

29. One of the volumes in Hoxha's *Works* is entirely filled with ideological speeches and addresses to writers and artists as well as with conversational remarks about literature and the arts.

30. This sentence, expunged from the English edition, is found in the Albanian edition of the volume, written by Hoxha himself: '*u fut në dhe si qen . . .*' (*Titistët*, Tirana, 1982, p. 578). The sentence is a repetition of the sentence Hoxha attributes to Xoxe when the latter announced to him that Spiru had committed suicide: 'He killed himself and *died like a dog*' [emphasis added] (387).

31. *Origin of Family, Private Property and State*, chapter on 'The Family' (2nd paragraph).

19. The Polish Vortex: Solidarity and Socialism

Oliver MacDonald

The greatest and most sustained popular upsurge in Europe for decades has left both bourgeois and working-class opinion in the West profoundly bewildered as to its basic historical meaning. A standard formula – used by both *The Times* and miners' leader Arthur Scargill – has been that Solidarity was an excellent thing but that it was going too far, or travelling too fast. Yet the deeper implicit worry on all sides was not so much the speed or extent of Solidarity's journey, but its point of departure and the nature of its ultimate destination. The main purpose of this essay is to try to discover the answer to this question. A second aim will be to try to explore the issue of Solidarity's defeat in December 1981: why it was possible for this huge mass movement to be driven underground by the imposition of martial law.

What follows is not an attempt to encompass the history of Poland between 1980 and the beginning of 1982. Our analysis will omit serious considerations of important regions and dimensions of the story: notably the peasantry and rural Solidarity, internal Church politics, events in the Sejm, international reverberations and so on.[1] Throughout, the focus of our attention will be on Solidarity, its antagonist and the main intermediary political forces within Poland.

Introduction: class and state in Eastern Europe

The fundamental feature of the Polish upheaval that has been so difficult for socialists (and anti-socialists) in the West to grasp has been the fact that the Polish workers combine a tenacious political opposition to continued monopolistic rule by the Polish Communist Party (PZPR) with a no less tenacious defence of a group of rights never guaranteed by any capitalist state. Opposition to a pre-democratic political order is less difficult for people in the parliamentary states of the West to grasp than the fact that the workers in Eastern Europe possess certain post-capitalist social rights (whose preservation is, in the end, of critical importance in the stable maintenance of these states). We must therefore begin by looking at these social rights to which Eastern European workers are strongly attached, and which, for obvious reasons, bourgeois writers working within the Cold War consensus tend to gloss over.

The starting point of any serious analysis of Eastern European societies is that the decisive means of production within them are nationalized, and with the suppression of the class of private capitalists has gone the suppression of the capitalist market as the regulator of economic activity. Instead, the forms of economic activity become matters of political struggle and political decision. The distribution of factors of production and the ways they are related to each other are decided, and can only be decided, by the predominant powers in the political field. Indeed an enormously wide range of socio-economic issues excluded from the political system's jurisdiction by capitalist class relations are brought within the field of politics by the nationalization of the means of production. The distribution of wealth and income and the entire price structure become matters for political manipulation, together with the length of the working day, the intensity of work, the extent of unemployment, and the allocation of investment resources.

In the classical Marxist conception of socialist transition, the nationalization of the economy would be accompanied by its socialization through the political control of the working class in a new type of democratic regime. This has, of course, not happened in Eastern Europe. Instead, the political field has been occupied by the monopolistic Communist Party while all other political trends have been excluded from the political system. Within the Communist Party power is concentrated in the hands of an elite of party and state officials, essentially appointed from above to these positions through the so-called *nomenklatura* system. All instruments of state power are tightly controlled by the party elite and members of the party are not allowed to engage in any organized struggle for alternative policies to those of the party leadership.

All this is widely recognized by socialists and non-socialists alike in the West. But the conclusion that has traditionally been drawn from this, particularly by devotees of American totalitarian theories of Eastern European states, is that the regimes are virtually omnipotent, that they have near total freedom to mould an atomized mass in any way they please. Yet for Marxists such notions are absurd. The party-state leaders of Eastern Europe do indeed wield enormous power, but within a framework of socio-economic relationships established when the new states were constructed in the late 1940s, a framework which places strict limits on the exercise of this power.

It would be possible to conceive of nationalized property relations coexisting with massive unemployment and the progressive immiseration of the working class. This is a theoretical possibility, but it does not describe the actual history of these states. In practice, nationalized property has entailed a number of social and economic corollaries: full employment and economic security; very low and largely stable prices for essential items such as food, housing, transport, etc.; rising living standards; a large and generally growing degree of social egalitarianism (in comparison with capitalist states), a lower level of work intensity; and, for a minority of the manual working class, prospects of social privileges and upward mobility considerably greater than under capitalism. Moreover, the rule of the party requires a degree of active involvement by its members, and corresponding recruitment from the working class, at every level in the workplace and the locality in order to invigilate and propel the plan.

Almost all these phenomena are indeed registered in Western bourgeois literature on the states of Eastern Europe, but they are mentioned overwhelmingly in the context of the supposed economic evils of these state systems. Thus we hear an unending stream of scorn for the arbitrary prices, the slack work rhythm, the supposed absurdities of full employment in terms of rational use of labour resources, and so on. The micro-economic rationality of the capitalist enterprise is held up for comparison with what goes on in a Soviet factory: ignoring, of course, the gigantic macro-economic waste generated by the irrationalities of the capitalist system as a whole.

What is less often registered is that these supposedly irrational social features of the Eastern European states are perceived by their own working populations as important social gains and rights. All the evidence indicates that workers in Eastern Europe place a high value on economic and social security, price stability, social egalitarianism and rising living standards. And these phenomena, presented in the capitalist world as economic gains contingent upon capitalist economic conditions, are perceived by workers in Eastern Europe as socialist *rights*, guaranteed by the very foundations of the state.

All the historical experience of these states demonstrates that any attempt to tamper with these rights is liable to produce a political crisis, and consequently the regimes must operate within the framework of these given social conditions. In order to do so, they seek to mobilize the working class for production by other methods than those of the capitalist economic whip of insecurity and the threat of unemployment. Instead they have had to rely upon explicitly political instruments, above all the Communist Party and its satellite organizations. Workers wishing to improve their economic position substantially have been able to do so by subscribing to the norms laid down by the Communist Party, meeting individual work norms, and carrying out all the various economic and social directives of the party. Those who do so and join the party or become activists in one of the satellite organizations can gain very substantial privileges – promotion eventually out of manual labour, better housing, holidays abroad and a range of queue-jumping possibilities. Only a minority of the working class, though often a large one, does in fact join the party or play a role in satellite institutions, but the requirement that the regime binds such a minority to itself is not an arbitrary element in the system, but is indeed at least as important as the regime's complementary capacity to use repression against those sections of the working class which refuse to subordinate themselves to the system.

An important consequence of these arrangements should be stressed: when they work effectively, there is little rational, economic basis for Western, capitalist-style trade unionism in the Eastern European states. In the West, workers confront a vast array of commodities and services available on the market in condition of general inflation. They have a permanent pressure upon them, therefore, to increase their money wages in order to maintain and strengthen their purchasing power. But typically in Eastern Europe essential items are governed by frozen prices, and while workers have rising money wages, they must confront shortages and various forms of official and unofficial rationing. Furthermore, access to goods is a problem of tackling queues, most of which are controlled by political authorities. It therefore makes little sense for workers to engage in collective action to demand higher money wages. Their attention must rather be turned towards the political authorities as targets of individual or collective pressure.[2]

Yet while the economic and social systems bring the party–government right into the factories and into the centre of everyday life, and push the workers towards involvement within the political structures of the state, the internal mechanisms of Communist Party rule do not give the working population an effective voice in the affairs of the state. Political participation is encouraged but only in the field of *implementing* policies agreed at the top. No effective channels exist for the workers to play an active and conscious part in formulating policy and taking the strategic decisions about how resources should be allocated. This political passivity and subordination weighs increasingly heavily upon the working class, the more that living standards and cultural levels rise, but the enormous concentration of institutional power in the hands of the central authorities makes it possible for them to prevent the frustrations and humiliations of the non-party workers from finding any open means of expression.

An open challenge from below can occur under three conditions: first, when what are conceived by large numbers of workers to be basic social rights underpinning 'real, existing socialism' are undermined by government policy; secondly, where workers acquire a sense of their capacity to engage in collective action with some chance of success; and thirdly, where they acquire a sense of their own independent identity as a class, on a national scale. For various reasons these conditions all came to be present in Poland at the end of the 1970s.

I. The Prelude to August

Two alternative frameworks jostle for our attention in trying to make sense of the forces that produced August 1980 and Solidarity. One urges us to view the upheaval in terms of East–West relations, incorporating both the phase of détente of the early and mid-1970s and the intensifying 'war of manoeuvre' between Washington and Moscow towards the end of the decade. The second urges us to see the crisis primarily as a domestic confrontation between those at the base and those at the summit of the Polish state.

The international conjuncture

An adequate account of the origins of Solidarity would have to intertwine both perspectives. The Polish crisis of 1980 was the first challenge to Stalinism in an Eastern European society in which both direct and indirect Western influence was strongly present in its origins. In the economic field, Poland became heavily indebted to Western banks and governments to the point where it could no longer meet its obligations by 1980; central control over foreign trade was loosened; important sectors of industry became dependent on Western companies for components, materials and spare parts; sectors of the economic administration became deeply involved in networks of corruption involving capitalist companies (and no doubt intelligence services); and a parallel dollar economy flourished; moreover, in the late 1970s the government managed to make itself directly dependent upon the US government for tackling the most sensitive issue of domestic politics – the market supply of meat. American credits for grain shipments, supplied by the Carter administration for political rather than economic reasons, rose massively in the last three years of the 1970s. And it was as a direct consequence of the changed line from Western financial centres made clear to the Polish government in May 1980, that Gierek was forced to raise meat prices on 1 July and thus triggered the working-class movement.[3] Increasing economic integration with the West was abetted by the Carter administration's strategy of using economic incentives ('most favoured nation' trading status, commodity credits, and so on) to promote a more general political and cultural 'open door' to the West.

A further crucial influence from the West was the election of Cardinal Wojtyla as Pope in October 1978 and his visit to Poland the following June. As he had shown in his encouragement for the growing political opposition currents around the KOR when he was still Archbishop of

Cracow, Wojtyla was an entirely new force in the Catholic hierarchy. The aging Primate, Wyszynski, had ruled the Church autocratically since the late 1940s, reviving it as a great national symbol but also keeping it in the mould of pre-industrial, peasant religion. Wyszynski had been failing to make an effective religious appeal to the growing urban population, and his relations even with the Catholic liberal intelligentsia were stormy. With little interest in 'Western' social or political values, he paid scant attention to directives from Rome, and combined thunderous affirmations of traditional peasant cultural values with great flexibility in compromising with the state, being ready to help calm political tensions during the periodic political crises, in return for practical, institutional benefits for the Church. Wojtyla, much more attuned to the West and loyal to Vatican requirements, was also, almost uniquely in the episcopate, an intellectual at home in urban intellectual circles. In contrast to the majority of the Polish hierarchy who feared (and fear) urban, secular, mass movements, and have been much happier trying to seal off their flock from outside influences while sorting out problems with the state through closed bargaining at the top, Wojtyla aimed to win the ideological battle for the urban population by harnessing their desires to his own brand of populist religion.

Wojtyla's June 1979 visit to Poland was designed to exert a profound impact on the entire political climate of the country. He sought to strengthen popular yearnings for an improvement in their lives and give them a sense of the great power of the Church. He emphasized the theme of human rights and presented the Church as their guardian. And, while formally referring to the need for realism, he gave the overwhelming impression that miracles were possible so long as the people followed him, a theme that culminated in his astonishing vision of being able to unite Europe, enunciated at Gniezno: 'Is not the Holy Spirit disposed to see that his Polish Pope, this Slav Pope, should at this very moment reveal the spiritual unity of Europe?'[4]

These ideological, political and economic influences from the West have been widely reported in the media here, and form the 'common-sense' background for most people trying to understand why Solidarity emerged. But they are very far from being an adequate explanation. They do not tell us why the Polish government deliberately opened up the country to such influences – in other words, the domestic social and political reasons for this turn. Nor do they explain why these influences contributed towards the creation of a very specific and unprecedented social phenomenon – an organized, independent working-class movement struggling for very distinctive social goals. To explain such phenomena we must turn to the domestic situation in Poland in the 1970s.

The domestic configuration of forces

The starting point for any analysis of the evolving relationship of forces in Poland in the 1970s was the outcome of the Baltic crisis of 1970 and Gierek's decisions at that time. The political changes of that time gave the Polish working class, at least along the Baltic, a sense of their independent identity as a class with considerable potential power. For the government to give way by removing Gomulka in the face of the Baltic workers' protests was a momentous event. And to surmount the crisis's consequences in a state with a nationalized and planned economy, the PZPR leadership gave a commitment massively to re-enforce the workers' economic and social rights. To try to meet these promises, Gierek utilized détente to make a bold opening to the world capitalist economy, massively borrowing credit and buying technology. During his first five years, economic growth did increase dramatically (in 1975 GNP 50 per cent up on 1970) along with living standards (real wages up 40 per cent), and there were signs of upward social mobility. But in face of rising expectations, he couldn't hold the line on the single most important front of all in 1970 – food prices. Wages soared from 473.4 billion zloty in 1971 to 883.0 billion in 1975 – 300 billion more than planned – with enhanced consumer demand concentrated especially on meat, whose per capita consumption rose from 53 kilos in 1970 to a staggering 70.3 kilos in 1975 (equivalent British figures for the two years showed a drop from 50.4 kilos to 46.2 kilos!). But with meat prices frozen, the government was forced to pay a fortune in subsidies while simultaneously being unable to guarantee increased supply.[5]

The government tried to break out of this social relationship of forces with the working class, which amounted to a virtual economic state of siege, by attempting a 60 per cent rise in food prices in June 1976. But the working class would have none of it and got its way, after strikes and demonstrations. The government suffered a massive loss of authority which added a renewed political crisis to the economic one. The Gierek leadership's response to this double crisis from the summer of 1976 set in motion the dynamics that led to August 1980. It had offered the working-class socialist social rights and had gone deep into debt to the West in order to provide them. Gierek's gamble on export-led growth – without serious reformation of internal corruption or significant democratization of planning – miscalculated both the structural contradictions of Polish society and the prospects of the world market. After 1976 the situation deteriorated spectacularly: the government became even more dependent economically on the West; Western involvement disrupted the functioning of centralized planning; living standards stopped rising and then fell slightly; spending on social services was cut back; the black market and social differentiation grew; and the working class became increasingly angry, not only at the frustration of its quantitative demands, but especially at what it saw as the violation of its socialist social rights.

The PZPR leadership's initial political response to this social crisis was a considerable departure from classical Stalinism. It allowed an intellectual opposition to grow to levels of sustained and protracted activity never before seen in post-war Eastern Europe. It sought a new level of cooperation and understanding with the Church hierarchy. And it generated what the Polish sociologist Jadwiga Staniszkis has called a politics of 'lame, bureaucratic pluralism', with separate social groups able to engage in limited collective protests without being crushed, provided they sought a solution to them through the mediation of the central bureaucracy. During the last three years of the 1970s about a thousand strikes took place, the great majority settled in the strikers' favour.

But perhaps most important was Gierek's policy towards the country's 3.5 million industrial workers concentrated heavily in very large factories (over half of them in factories with more than 1,500 employees). Without actually listening much to what they were saying Gierek went out of his way to pay court to these workers. Their wages were kept high, their canteens cheap and well stocked, their plants hailed as the 'citadels of Polish socialism'. After 1976 an intense and successful effort was made to recruit industrial workers into the party: between 1975 and 1979 the proportion of workers increased from 42 to 46 per cent, the highest percentage in the Soviet bloc. And these members were heavily concentrated in the big plants – 27 per cent of all manual worker PZPR members were in the 164 biggest plants. Furthermore it was by no means necessarily the case that PZPR activists in the factories were looked upon with suspicion by the non-party workers. A sizeable proportion of them enjoyed workers' confidence and were ranked on the side of labour rather than management. In 1979, the founder of the unofficial workers' paper *Robotnik*, Jan Litynski, a leading KOR activist, described the working-class party members' attitudes:

They are convinced that it is the workers who rule Poland – the term 'rule' expressing both their need for prestige (workers sit on the executive committee) and a genuine feeling of responsibility for the fate of the country. However they really feel tied to the cause of the working class, not hesitating to show their solidarity with strike movements, and even take the head of such movements by turning to account the organizational experience they acquired in the party.[6]

Litynski also confirmed that the PZPR was far less compromised in the eyes of workers than the official trade unions. (At the same time as seeking to integrate the working class in industry into the PZPR, the party leadership also used repression to try to stamp out unofficial, external political or trade-union activities within the working class, such as the movement around *Robotnik*.)

If the PZPR managed to integrate such a large proportion of workers into the party – one in every nine workers was a PZPR member – and if these members retained a great measure of trust among the non-party workers, why did August 1980 need to happen at all? The answer to this lies partly in the general bureaucratic-centralist functioning of Stalinized Communist Parties and partly in three specific features of the party–state regime in Poland in the late 1970s. These can be briefly listed:

1. The generalized growth of corruption within the ranks of party and state officialdom produced by the opportunities offered by the economic crisis and by cynicism and political demoralization amongst such officials.

2. An administrative reorganization carried out by Gierek which simultaneously broke down the state administrative structure from seventeen major provinces to forty-nine, while massively recentralizing the structure of enterprises into large national conglomerates, whose managements were given powers to deal directly with Western companies and with the central ministries. The effect of these parallel changes was to make the factory and provincial party executives incapable of effectively controlling economic management. Plant management could trump local party directives with decisions from higher conglomerate management, while the latter, with plants in many provinces, were beyond the jurisdiction of any mere regional party secretary.

3. Into this picture we should insert Gierek's cadre policy within the party apparatus. During the 1970s Gierek massively purged the apparatus of its staff from the Gomulka period, replacing the old guard with young university graduates in such subjects as public administration, fitted only for a career as a professional party official. Such a policy had the 'merit' from Gierek's perspective of making such functionaries utterly dependent on the will of the central secretariat with its monopoly on promotions – after all, their training left them no other alternative career.

Together these three ingredients comprised a formidable formula for undermining the 'leading role of the party apparatus'. Instead of the party organizations controlling their professional apparatus, which in turn controlled the economic administration and trade unions, a pattern developed along the following lines: the local party apparatus ignored pressure from the membership; plant management ignored the local party apparatus and turned the official union apparatus into its passive tool; the national conglomerate management manipulated the central ministries, and the central ministries presented the party centre with *faits accomplis* rubber-stamped by Gierek. The wheels of the whole system were kept turning by powerful and often corrupt lobbies operating beyond any form of public control. Thus Gierek's so-called 'economic manoeuvre' after 1976 was simply sabotaged by such forces.

Thus the principal result of recruiting young, skilled industrial workers into the party was to enable them to see a good deal of what was going on and to prove to them how impotent the local PZPR apparatus was in the face of this informal power structure. Opposition to this situation did develop within the party hierarchy, led by figures like Olszowski and Grabski who appealed for support to frustrated provincial party secretaries[7] in the run-up to the Party Congress of February 1980. But the Congress was Gierek's last chance as far as the PZPR's working-class base was concerned. He failed to grasp it. So the politically aware sections of the working class gave up thinking about action above and started pondering action from below. August was on the agenda.[8]

II. Solidarity: a workers' movement *sui generis*

The events in Gdansk during August 1980 are sufficiently widely known to require no narrative here.[9] However, before turning to the rise of Solidarity itself, we should stress certain crucial (and indeed obvious) features of the August strike movement too often overlooked in journalistic accounts.

The first key point is that the strike movement immediately spread from Gdansk to other centres until it became a *national* movement encompassing all the main industrial centres of the country and no less than 4,000 enterprises, including the great majority of large enterprises. If it had not spread, the strike could not conceivably have been victorious. The workers in the Lenin Shipyard played a critically important role as a trigger and a focus for the whole movement, but to say this does not explain why workers throughout the country were ready to respond to the lead from Gdansk. Nor do theories of a 'dissident' conspiracy tell us anything. Gdansk was *unique* as the only industrial centre where previously active opposition groups played a significant role in organizing the August strikes. They played no role in Szczecin nor Silesia. And the two cities where oppositional groups were by far the strongest – Warsaw and Cracow – were among the least affected by the August movement. So what was the social agency that spread the strikes? Certainly not the Church. In Gdansk itself, Bishop Kaczmarek's first response to the strike committee's appeal for a mass to be said in the Lenin Shipyard was to refuse until they gained permission from the provincial party secretary. The Bishop of Szczecin was equally conservative (and in any case the whole issue of holding a mass in the Warski yard was initially contentious among the strike leadership). Wyszynski himself in his only public speech during the crisis broadcast on TV caused bitter resentment among the strikers by urging a return to work.

The truth is that there was no organized agency at all spreading the strike movement. But a cursory glance at the forces initiating the big leaps in the strike movement beyond Gdansk shows a very strong presence of PZPR members – workers, technicians and foremen – among the leaders of the strike movement and, in many cases, among its initiators. This was the case in Sczcecin, Wroclaw, Poznan, Walbrzych, Jastrzebie, Torun and many other centres.[10]

At the PZPR Central Committee meeting at the height of the strike on 24 August, Edward Pustelniak, a CC member from the Szczecin Repair Shipyard participating in the strike, told the plenum something about the attitudes of many working-class party members:

> As a worker and as a member of the party, I have to say that there are certain things that I do not understand. Because when all is said and done, the majority of the problems at present being raised by the strikers have already been raised several times within party meetings, in particular in the meetings preparatory to the 8th Congress of the PZPR. The non-party members knew this and they supported us; furthermore, they believed that our voices would finally be listened to. Unfortunately this proved not to be the case . . . But to carry on like this gives the lie to what we have been saying and repeating in public, namely that the party listens to the opinions of its members, as well as those of non-party members, and that it draws from these opinions the necessary conclusions.[11]

The August strike movement was thus very far from being either the product of some 'anti-socialist' group or a spontaneous outburst of despair or primitive plebeian revenge. It could much better be described as the collective effort by the elite industrial and transport workers of the country – party and non-party workers – to lead the society out of its crisis. The Gierek leadership was seen as utterly incapable of solving a crisis it was seen to have created. It was the Gomulka story all over again. What way out? The collective thinking of the politically aware Polish workers was transparently clear in its practical logic based on experience. There was no point in leaving matters to a new leadership of the party. The workers needed a new instrument under their control for ensuring change. Thoughts went back to Gdansk and Szczecin in 1970–71 and the demands then for independent trade unions, the right to strike, and free information. How could this be achieved? The strikes of 24 June 1976 had shown a way provided workers occupied their plants and didn't flood uncontrollably on to the streets. And the Gdansk workers were using the organization of an inter-factory strike committee: again a weapon that had proved successful on the Baltic in 1971.

One final element in the August strikes is too often glossed over: the social demands of the movement. Formulated democratically with great care, they bound together the more politically conscious section of workers with the broad majority and they indicated principles which were by no means the common sense of some undifferentiated 'society': workers should be compensated for striking; there should be a flat-rate increase for all employees (helping the lower paid); the 'commercial' shops and hard-currency shops should be closed; the privileges of the police and party apparatus should be abolished, as should special stores; family subsidies should be equalized; there should be rationing rather than free-floating prices, and a massive shift in spending towards social welfare. This social programme was classic in the socialist egalitarian assumptions underlying it. So too were the radical democratic freedoms called for in the twenty-one demands: freedom of speech, the press and publication; 'availability of the mass media to representatives of all faiths' (the sole demand relating to the Church), the release of all political prisoners; and measures to enable 'all sectors and social classes to take part in discussion of the reform programme'.

The social and political radicalism of the workers on strike was not matched by the majority of the politically aware Polish intelligentsia, among whom a broad consensus had developed in the late 1970s that accepted the necessity of market reforms and attendant inequalities (including unemployment, price rises and special hard-currency shops). The bulk of the intelligentsia initially considered the prospect of independent trade unions as wildly unrealistic and viewed the potential of working-class actions as a destructive and chaotic force. When the power and discipline of the strike movement revealed itself, however, the intelligentsia moved towards it with the aim of assuming influence over its direction. Similarly, the Church hierarchy followed behind the example of the local priests who were already involved in supporting the movement. For their part, the workers welcomed such support unreservedly, gained enormous confidence from it, and hoped that their own lack of political experience outside the PZPR and their exclusion from theoretical culture could be compensated for by assistance from the intelligentsia and the Church. With such help they hoped to be able to steer the country out of its crisis, using independent trade unions to force the PZPR to transform its egalitarian and democratic rhetoric into practical reforms.

The organization of the working class
Solidarity was in large measure created pragmatically out of the very difficult conditions of September 1980 when, despite the Gdansk Agreements, many sectors of the state and party administration were trying to resist the formation of new unions. This official harassment accounted in

large measure for the fact that one single national union was formed – against the initial resistance of the Gdansk strike leadership – and it also helped ensure that the regional structures of the movement remained based upon the model of the Inter-Factory Strike Committees of August. The structure combined the external pattern of organization used by the PZPR (factory, regional and national instances) with an internal pattern that was the PZPR's polar opposite: initiative from below, great autonomous power in the regions and a purely coordinating role for the national leadership, as opposed to 'democratic centralism' and the *nomenklatura* system of appointment from above. Solidarity's structure was thus highly political, emphasizing the unity of the workers as a class, rather than their sectional diversity (which was expressed only in industrial commissions without decision-making powers). This proletarian unity and distinctiveness was further enhanced by the exclusion of other social groups apart from wage earners from Solidarity's ranks – party and state officials, private peasants, students, small craftspeople and traders.

Solidarity grew with extraordinary rapidity, reaching 3 million by the end of September, some 6 million by the end of October and 8 million by the end of November. According to the union's own figures published at its first Congress in October 1981, membership stood at 9,410,005 out of a total work-force of 12.5 million in the nationalized sector of the economy. There is no precise figure of the number of party members in the movement, but the Soviet leadership put it at about 1 million out of just under 3 million.[12] Starting out with more than eighty regional centres, Solidarity eventually consolidated these into thirty-nine regions, with two-thirds of its membership in ten key regional organizations reflecting the main industrial centres of the country:

Katowice	1,400,000
Warsaw	911,000
Wroclaw	910,000
Cracow	645,000
Gdansk	532,000
Lodz	463,000
Poznan	429,000
Szczecin	353,000
Lublin	332,000
Bydgoszcz	275,000
TOTAL	6,250,000

During the August strikes, it was the industrial and transport workers who played the leading role and it was they also who took the lead in building Solidarity. Other sections of the workers flooded to join after seeing the movement's strength in the August conflict, in the 3 October national strike, in the episcopate's support and in the union's registration on 10 November. But throughout Solidarity's legal existence, the 3.5 million industrial workers continued to be the dominant social group in the movement, determining basic programmatic aims and methods of struggle. Their influence was expressed throughout the key large plants in each region such as Huta Katowice and the July Manifesto mine in Upper Silesia, the Lenin and Paris Commune yards in the Gdansk-Ddynia area, the Warski yard and Police chemical plant in Szczecin, Huta Lenina in Cracow, FSO Zeran, Ursus and Huta Warszawa in Warsaw, the Pafaweg railway wagon plant and the Thorez mine in Lower Silesia, the ZISPO works in Poznan, the Marchlewski works in Lodz, and so on. The regional leaders tended to come from these plants, and the workers in each region tended to take their cue from the decisions of the workers in these plants. Previously hailed by the party leadership as Poland's 'citadels of socialism', they contained the most highly paid sections of manual workers, the largest factory party organizations, and generally the most able and flexible plant managements. In classic proletarian fashion, the workers in these plants tended to be much more stable, self-confident and disciplined, and much less given to volatile swings of mood from extreme radicalism to passive resignation than the weaker sections of the working class (or the intelligentsia).

Given its roots in the industrial working class, Solidarity from the beginning contained a very high proportion of employees from the large factories who had a background in the PZPR, the SZMP (the Polish Komsomol), and as departmental officials or workplace delegates in the official trade unions. An estimate by a Gdansk Solidarity leader in December 1980 put the proportion of regional activists of Solidarity who were in the PZPR at about 50 per cent. Among manual workers in the PZPR, the bulk of them seem to have devoted their energies to Solidarity activity rather than the internal struggle within the PZPR, without initially resigning from the party in large numbers. A majority of regional activists on regional executives tended to be technicians and white-collar personnel who were often much more active in the internal debates and internal activities of the movement above shopfloor level. On the other hand the manual workers in industry tended to see themselves as more steadfast than the white-collar sections in conflicts with the authorities.[13]

Patterns of working-class opinion

As in any mass proletarian movement, Solidarity embraced an extremely complex pattern of opinion reflecting all the myriad strata of wage earners in different trades, social and geographical settings, generational cohorts and so on. Local histories played a very important role in working-class thinking in relation to the PZPR, the Church, the intelligentsia, and the state administration. Yet the preponderance of the big industrial plants in each region and the preponderance of the ten main industrial regions in the national thinking of the movement makes it possible to make some general statements about the dominant trend of working-class opinion within the movement, for it was this trend that tended to assert itself in the demands around which Solidarity as a whole struggled during its sixteen months of existence.

Although for large numbers of wage earners economic issues and grievances remained a central concern, the weight of the skilled industrial workers ensured that after August, particularly as the scale of the economic crisis was revealed, Solidarity limited its purely economic demands drastically and was ready to compromise on economic points already won in the Gdansk Agreements. Furthermore, there was a strong sense of the importance of using the strike weapon sparingly because of its economic consequences. The number of working hours lost through strikes had no significant impact on the economy. There was, indeed, a growing awareness of the need for the workers to accept some cuts in living standards in order to try to surmount the crisis.

But such economic restraint only sharpened the industrial workers' fiercely egalitarian thrust against social differences, privilege, waste and corruption. They opposed the dollar shops and black markets, and they favoured rationing rather than free-floating prices. There was strong opposition to unemployment and a merciless assault on managerial perks and privileges which are on the whole taken for granted by workers under capitalism. Clubs for management personnel, leisure centres for party officials, private clinics for the police or party functionaries, new conference centres for exclusive party use, company cars, the use of company materials for building private villas, the acceptance of 'commissions' by managers buying equipment from the West, the payment of everybody from football teams to party officials out of company funds, the unequal distribution of housing and of coupons for buying cars, the distribution of prizes for meritorious work according to political or clique loyalties – all these became the object of merciless attack and of strikes involving demands for the sacking of officials. It was part of a wider thrust for public property to be firmly under public control and for resources to be allocated according to efficient work and according to need.[14]

The political thinking of the industrial workers underwent profound changes during the course of Solidarity's legal existence, but it is important to define the membership's standpoint in Solidarity's first months of existence. The most fundamental political idea was that Solidarity must remain absolutely free from the administrative control of the party–state apparatus. Without such independence workers felt – whether their concerns were economic defence or social and political reform –

that all would be lost. This was why the membership was ready to risk everything in an unlimited general strike in October 1980 rather than have the PZPR's 'leading role' written into their statutes.

Another principle was that the party–state authorities had to be brought under some form of public, social control from below if there was to be any chance of overcoming the country's crisis. This did not at all necessarily imply removing the PZPR from power or changing the central political institutions in any structural way, but it did imply radically altering the way these institutions related to the mass of the population. In the first phase of Solidarity's existence this control from below involved largely a negative power of veto over decisions that the government took which the workers considered to be against their interests. There was a strong reluctance on the part of the membership to allow Solidarity to get drawn into participatory or co-responsibility schemes, either at the level of enterprise or government decisions. They viewed Solidarity's influence as being exerted through possessing its own press, having direct access to the mass media and being able, in the last resort, to strike in order to press home its views. The membership was also acutely sensitive to the movement being accorded full national status and dignity on a par with all other institutions in the country. All attempts to deny Solidarity this recognition brought massive opposition from its working-class base, which also strongly supported the right of other social groups to win similar organizations and powers.

The most important and problematic area of working-class political thought concerned its conception of Solidarity itself. The August strikes and Gdansk Agreements had formally given birth to a purely trade-union body. This formal definition governed membership requirements: any employee in the nationalized sector of the economy, regardless of ideology, could join. Yet the actual role widely ascribed to the union by workers even while Solidarity was merely defending the Gdansk Agreements went far beyond merely looking after the socio-economic interests of employees. They saw it, rightly, as the main driving force behind general political reform. Furthermore, the union's organizational structure, which placed a premium on working-class unity, underlined this class-political role. Yet in the consciousness of workers, politics was almost totally identified with the activities of the PZPR and, thus, there was a tendency to reject any idea of Solidarity being transformed into a political movement or party based on a political programme. Yet, to add a further dimension, Solidarity grew to such scope that for many workers it was not simply a party or a union, but the corporate expression of the entire urban population of the country – an institution expressing, so to speak, the popular will, or what Western Marxists would call a Soviet-type body. In face of the evidently non-representative character of the political system, the all-embracing structure of Solidarity around elected regional assemblies reinforced a vision of the movement as something little short of being an alternative system of national state authority.

Solidarity's ideological horizons

This leads us to some consideration of the more general ideological currents within the working class: its attitudes towards socialism, capitalism and the international order. Such a survey is especially difficult in a situation where there were no substantial organized political currents, where there was a powerful impulse to suppress ideological differences for the sake of political unity, and where political and international conditions led to a good deal of care being taken over the repercussions of general ideological statements. Nevertheless, certain points can be established. For example, although at no time during its existence did Solidarity declare itself formally to be a socialist union or movement, evidence from both opinion polls and from talking to Solidarity activists indicates a general readiness among workers to support not only socialist values but also the idea of a socialist state. Yet there was no sign of workers vigorously claiming socialism as their own against the PZPR leadership. Nor were the classic socialist symbols – the red flag, socialist songs, and so on – embraced by the movement. Instead, the movement's symbols and rituals were drawn from three sources: previous post-war upsurges of the Polish working class (Poznan, the Baltic, 1976, August 1980 itself); pre-1944 Polish national traditions; and the Catholic Church.[15]

The central reason why Solidarity did not embrace a socialist ideological commitment lay in its evolving relationship with the PZPR and in the way in which that party had successfully appropriated the terminology of socialism. The birth of Solidarity *ipso facto* signified that the Polish workers were no longer putting their faith in one wing of the PZPR leadership to carry the country out of a crisis created by another wing of the party. This meant that there was no strand within the PZPR's own tradition which the workers could make their own, as there previously had been, for example, with the Gomulkist tradition as it was perceived by the working class in 1956. At the same time, the regime's propaganda hammered home the iron link between the economic and social basis of socialism and the PZPR's monopolistic supremacy over society. From the cradle to the grave Polish workers were taught – by Western radio stations as well as by the official media – that socialism and the party monopoly were inextricable: you could not have one without the other. Given that the PZPR leaders were unable from mid-August 1980 onwards to justify their monopoly by reference to working-class consent – as Solidarity effortlessly established its hegemony – the integral link supposedly existing between the party monopoly and the very existence of socialism became a vital ideological bastion for the authorities to defend. (An attempt by one of the expert advisers to the Gdansk strike committee, Jadwiga Staniszkis, to substitute a non-institutional, socio-economic definition of socialism for the formula about the party's 'leading role', was repudiated by the other experts who carried the day with the strike committee.)

Neither did the workers possess any living alternative socialist political tradition to that of the PZPR. A good deal of work was done by intellectuals to disinter the traditions of the Polish Socialist Party, but this made little impact on a working class with no living PPS tradition. Nor, finally, was there any strong socialist political tradition outside the PZPR within the Polish intelligentsia. 1968 had put paid to 'revisionism' as a vital theoretical force within the intelligentsia, giving way either to Catholic Nationalist trends expressed in such groups as ROPCIO, the KPN, Young Poland or the Macierewicz wing of KOR, or to Catholic liberal or social-democratic liberal trends such as the current represented by Mazowiecki in the KIKS or the Kuron—Michnik wing of the KOR.[16] Radical socialist trends were very weak and, apart from in Warsaw, Szczecin and Lodz, had almost no contact with Solidarity's membership.

This near-void in the field of socialist ideological alternatives to Stalinism presented the workers with a choice between generating a new ideological tradition and turning towards pre-war nationalist traditions, still present within the Catholic Church and the population at large, and indeed within the state bureaucracy in the form of Polish equivalents of Ceausescism. As the political crisis deepened, a large section of Solidarity's working-class membership turned from militant trade unionism towards a form of what might be called anarcho-syndicalism, essentially derived from the structure of Solidarity itself as an organization embracing the overwhelming majority of wage-earners, stressing their unity as a class and counterposing themselves to a single huge political party. This produced a vision of a self-managed republic in the hands of the producers, organized through their union without the need for parties, running an egalitarian society and a nationalized urban economy. This indeed was the vision expressed within the programme adopted at the Solidarity Congress in October 1981.[17]

To this vision was married one strand of Polish nationalism, the romantic, revolutionary-insurrectionary nationalism of the nineteenth-century aristocracy, the Szlachta. The workers took over, in many ways, the aristocracy's self-image as the heroic leading class of the nation and applied this to themselves, the industrial workers. In this way they interpreted their struggle to bring about basic change in the teeth of evident opposition from the Soviet leadership. This strand of nationalism had indeed been present within the early Polish socialist movement, bringing out the wrath of Rosa Luxemburg who was in turn repudiated by Lenin for her failure to grasp the difference between progressive and reactionary nationalism.

Against this strand of nationalist ideology was set the nationalism of the inter-war Polish bourgeoisie and Catholic Church: the integral nationalism of Dmowski and National Democracy with its central emphasis on ethnic purity and anti-semitism; its corporatist rejection of classes and class conflict; its reactionary social philosophy; its hatred of political radicalism of any sort; and its emphasis on organic change combined with authoritarian order and unity. This strand of nationalism continued to be strongly present in some sections of the Church and also within the state bureaucracy. It was to be used to some considerable effect as a weapon against the social and political aspirations of the working class during the crisis. And in the context of Solidarity's defeats in the late autumn of 1981 a small minority within the industrial working class turned in despair towards such ideas, assisted in this direction by the black anti-semitic propaganda spread by agencies controlled by the political police. But such ideas were born of defeat and a search for alternatives to Solidarity and mass working-class struggle. They were the product of the movement's incipient disintegration, not of its development. The industrial workers in Solidarity identified themselves certainly with the Polish eagle, but it was in the service of popular, working-class sovereignty, with the crown removed. And as for a return to capitalism, so the joke went, nobody was in favour of returning the Lenin Shipyard to the Lenin family.

III. Forces and strategies

The Gdansk Agreements and rise of Solidarity as a multi-million strong social movement placed one fundamental issue before all social and political forces involved in the Polish crisis: how, if at all, was this movement to be integrated into a political and social structure shaped up until then by the management of all public life by the PZPR? We will try very briefly to summarize the stance on this issue of some of the other key actors in the drama: the Soviet leadership, the PZPR and state leaderships, the Church hierarchy, and the main reformist currents within the politically active sections of the intelligentsia, especially the Catholic intelligentsia.

The CPSU leadership
The Soviet leadership had two central concerns following the August events: a military-security requirement dictated by Poland's absolutely pivotal position in the USSR's European defences; and a political-

security requirement dictated by the need to ensure that the Polish 'disease' didn't spread to other Warsaw Pact countries, including the USSR itself. The solution to both these problems lay, for the Soviet leadership, in the full restoration of party–state control over the Polish population and this in turn required ending trade-union independence. *Pravda* spelt this out in unequivocal terms on 25 September, the day after Solidarity had applied for legal registration. The article stated that 'independent unions' were a violation of 'Leninist principles' and a 'bourgeois provocation' and insisted that 'trade unions can only fulfil their tasks in close collaboration with and under the direct leadership of the party'. Secondly, the Soviet leadership strongly opposed any changes in the ideological and organizational principles of the PZPR itself – thus the party should not achieve its ascendancy by a Czechoslovak-style move towards inner-party pluralism that would enable the impulses from Solidarity's base to flow freely into party organizations. Thirdly, the binding together of the PZPR and the working class could not, in Soviet opinion, be achieved by giving a new political role to the Church hierarchy, making the PZPR dependent on the Church to integrate the workers.

To achieve its strategic task of resubordinating the Polish working class, the PZPR leadership was to be allowed, in Soviet eyes, some tactical flexibility over methods and timing (more, at least, than either the CPCZ or the SED leaders felt happy with). But the *direction* of these tactics was what mattered: was the PZPR elite fighting to *subordinate* Solidarity, or was it seeking to *reconcile itself* to Solidarity, succumbing to the enormous pressure from the party rank and file to cooperate with Solidarity? This was the cardinal question for the CPSU leadership throughout the crisis. And when it became convinced that the PZPR as a political apparatus was incapable of pursuing this struggle to victory, it was prepared, however reluctantly, to seek other solutions.

The PZPR and state leaderships

Bourgeois literature tends, for obvious reasons, to equate the ruling Communist Party – a mass political apparatus – with the professional bureaucracy of the state and party. But by conflating the two it is impossible to make sense of the real political dynamics of the Polish crisis. In terms of membership the PZPR embraced some 3 million people at the start of the crisis, located in every sphere of social life, including over 1.25 million workers. The PZPR's own professional bureaucracy numbered only about 10,000 officials, the bulk of whom were involved in seeking to manage the activity of the mass membership in all spheres of life. There were then about a million state officials, mostly within the PZPR but largely involved in very different activity from politics proper: they were rather involved in public administration through the ministries, and provincial state bodies, in the internal security apparatus, in the army, and judiciary, and so on. The task of the central party bodies was to reconcile all these functions and personnel through furnishing them with an overall policy line. In seeking to do so, the Politburo and CC members tended to reflect very different social and political trends and pressures from the different quarters.

Two types of fissure revealed themselves sharply in what might be called the sociology of the PZPR during the crisis. First, there was that between the mass membership of the party and the state bureaucracy and much of the party bureaucracy. Secondly, there was a deep-going struggle between the different functional elements of the state apparatus and a tendency for each of them to try to free themselves from the central political control of the PZPR apparatus leaderships.

The split between the state bureaucracy and the party membership can be briefly summarized. The former social stratum was vividly described in a report by critical Polish sociologists before the August events as

what might be called the socialist middle classes or a socialist petit bourgeoisie. They have unquestionable influence on the party and government apparatuses, the greater part of which are staffed by these middle classes. Do they have an interest in common with the working classes? Absolutely not. They grow richer and richer but still they are not as rich as they would like. They are hampered by the remnants of socialist phraseology at the top . . . and socialist ideology at the bottom . . .[18]

Their general reaction to Solidarity was one of fear and horror. As for the party membership, its main thrust was to cooperate with Solidarity (indeed, join it), and to struggle to bring this state bureaucracy under effective democratic *party* control. For this purpose it sought to bring massive pressure to bear on the PZPR leadership to gain a Politburo majority that reflected its will. Insofar as the political elite wished to govern the country principally through the PZPR as a mass force, it had to bend to this rank-and-file pressure or risk a split, if not a collapse of the mass party.

Intertwined with this conflict was the institutional struggle within the different functional components of the state and the efforts by powerful institutional groups to break free from control by the given PZPR leadership. Each institution, so to speak, generated its own institutional interests and programme and they were not bound together by any class principle of social organization such as private capitalist property and its defence, which binds together state bureaucracies in the West. Thus while the party apparatus had an interest in preserving the planned economy, this was far less clear for, say, the judiciary; and while the central party apparatus was preoccupied with responding to political pressures from the rank and file of the party, this was by no means the main preoccupation of the officer corps of the military. Eventually, as both Moscow and a large part of the state bureaucracy lost confidence in the efficacy of the mass party as the key apparatus of rule, a coalition of forces within the state machine (all of whom, of course, were party *members*) pushed the civilian party apparatus to one side and opted for other means of government, at least temporarily.

But for the moment we will concentrate upon summarizing the main political currents within the PZPR Central Committee as they began to crystallize in the late autumn of 1980 in the party leadership's efforts to reunite and assert its authority over the PZPR membership and the state machine.

1. *The Kania-Barcikowski Grouping:* Kania, the new First Secretary, who immediately raised the slogan of 'Socialist Renewal', on 8 September offered the membership the promise of a new PZPR Congress and sanctioned secret ballot elections for executive positions in the party. He supported a purge of corrupt officials, and backed the removal of unpopular officials. His political line began with the affirmation that the August strikes 'were not directed against socialism but against its distortions', went on to sanction party members joining Solidarity but called for the condemnation of 'anti-socialist forces' within and around the union. He repudiated the use of force to resolve conflicts, but did not advance any programme of political reform. Instead he offered a style of political management through which the party's 'leading role' would be assured, a style which was, in truth, a continuation of Gierek's own style of conflict resolution in the late 1970s: a pluralistic corporatism with the party apparatus as the sole body for harmonizing all the various particular interests in society. Those who sought to replace this corporatist consensus with adversary politics were branded as anti-national extremists. In this framework, the Church was placed firmly within the range of healthy forces, while Solidarity was partly in, partly out. The unacceptable forces were depicted as the anti-socialist intellectuals while the workers were presented as the healthy force. (In reality, of course, it was the industrial workers' militant syndicalism that was the real source of adversary politics, but the Kania group sought to displace the origin of conflict to KOR and other non-working-class political groups.) Beyond this, in the field of actual policy, Kania's politics was 'centrist', moving between the pressures from the Soviet leadership and those from social forces below.

2. *Olszowski, Grabski, Zabinski:* this was less a stable group than a trend, differing from Kania in two respects. First it wanted a more militant, adversarial style of politics to be pursued by the PZPR, as

against Kania's corporatism. It wanted a greater distance from the Church, a greater emphasis on Marxist–Leninist ideological struggle against counter-revolution, a sharper polarization to subordinate Solidarity, and an effort to instil in the ranks a 'will to win'. Secondly, and in this context, it was far less attached to the central plan than Kania and favoured decentralization and marketization of the economy along with plant-level 'workers' self-management. For this current, the PZPR could afford to lose a big part of its working-class base and become a slimmed-down, militant, anti-clerical but also technocratic and managerial force.

3. *Fiszbach and Popular Consent:* this trend, smaller and less influential on the CC than the others, found its clearest expression in the Gdansk provincial secretary, Fiszbach. It favoured the party seeking to establish a real mechanism of popular consent and legitimation within the political system and it favoured strategic cooperation with Solidarity and its working-class base. In this way the PZPR would establish its 'leading role' rather as the Czechoslovak party had done but with greater emphasis on the link with the independent union. This was the one trend within the leadership that was unacceptable on principle to the CPSU leadership.

4. *The Bonapartist Role and Moczar:* this trend wanted to reconstruct the political system around a 'strong' nationalist leader cast in a Bonapartist role. Combining populism with authoritarianism this current wished to play down official Marxism–Leninism and to stress a nationalist drive for discipline, unity, the workers' welfare and puritan morality. Partisan General Moczar, aided by his newly promoted (or repromoted, after being in the doldrums during the Gierek years) supporters, offered himself to the nation in this role up until the spring of 1981. But in the eyes of the intelligentsia, with vivid memories of his activities in 1967–8,[19] he was disqualified from playing this part. The role was thus eventually assumed by another figure with better military credentials, and a less tainted political record: Defence Minister and Army Commander-in-Chief General Jaruzelski. Like Moczar, Jaruzelski was to ally himself initially with the Kania group, but his institutional base lay right outside the PZPR civilian political apparatus.

The Church and the Catholic intelligentsia
The Church was a huge institutional structure which for twenty-five years had been leading a highly routinized existence within the Republic under the autocratic leadership of Cardinal Wyszynski. With 19,913 priests in 1978, 447 monasteries, 2,349 convents, forty-eight seminaries, a fully fledged Catholic University and a university-level theological academy in Warsaw, about 20,000 centres of religious instruction and

fifty-seven Catholic periodicals – with all this, the Polish episcopate, far from being a militant centre of 'anti-socialist counter-revolutionary mobilization', was a settled, conservative and prosperous establishment without any active project for upsetting the *status quo*.

In Poland's successive political crises, the episcopate had always proved its loyalty by appealing for calm and order in the cities; its message on social questions was a mixture of calls for sober hard work and respect for the family coupled with denunciations of worldly, secular (and pro-Western) life-styles, as well as a strong appeal for Poles to love their country and build up its resources. There was no trace of radical democratic ideology within the episcopate. Wyszynski was fiercely independent of Rome and he comforted his priests with the thought that the Church had survived for one thousand years and would continue to flourish for another millennium provided they kept out of politics and left everything of that sort to the Primate and central Church bureaucracy. Not for nothing did Gierek strongly support Wyszynski when the Vatican had to decide whether the Primate could stay on after his seventy-fifth birthday. In return for this posture, the episcopate was guaranteed that there would be no forced collectivization of agriculture and it was given substantial institutional freedom in the religious sphere. The overwhelming bulk of Church funds came from congregations' contributions and payments for births, marriages and funerals, though it also gained some income from agriculture and some funds from the Vatican.

All of this produced a strong tendency within the episcopate towards what the KOR activist Adam Michnik has called 'Paxization' – in other words towards full integration into the existing political structure of the state. This current strongly influenced, and influences, the central Church bureaucracy including such figures as Glemp (to succeed Wyszynski in the summer of 1981), Bishop Dabrowski (the secretary to the episcopate), Abbot Orszulik (the episcopal spokesperson), Bishop Modzelewski of Warsaw, Kaczmarek of Gdansk, and so on. Picked by Wyszynski these men have throughout the crisis exercised decisive sway within the domestic Polish Church.

For this current, Solidarity's rise presented both a powerful potential threat and a possible, though dangerous, opportunity. Solidarity could have become a rival centre of gravity and of authority for the urban masses outside the orbit of the PZPR. It was also potentially ideologically subversive within the Church, with its radical democratic and egalitarian thrust. And the Church leadership feared Solidarity might provoke a counter-revolution or Soviet invasion that could sweep away the Church's own institutional rights. Wyszynski evolved a series of objectives for the hierarchy to meet this situation. First, the Church would present itself as mediator between the party leadership and Solidarity, thus occupying a nationally unifying supra-political position. Secondly, Solidarity should confine itself to strictly economic issues, should not meddle in politics and should remove such secular political groups as KOR from positions of influence. If Solidarity had some political grievances it could approach the Primate to intercede with the authorities. Thirdly, the Church's key base the peasantry was pressing for its own rural Solidarity and Wyszynski felt constrained to champion this cause and thus assure the Church firm control over that movement. Fourthly, the Church should try to spread its ideological influence within the urban popular movement through taking great pains to give the movement religious symbols. And finally, Wyszynski entertained the idea that the Church might, in addition to Rural Solidarity, acquire a new political instrument through which to entrench further into influence. This would have involved merging the existing pro-regime Catholic groups – Pax, OdiSS, the Christian Social Association, Neo-Znak, and so on – with other independent Catholic forces into a new Christian party within the National Front and the Sejm. The Cardinal unsuccessfully pursued this idea unofficially both with the government and with such groups as Pax.

Two other currents were visible within the Church. The most important of these was represented by the Pope himself. Far less nervous of the popular movement than Wyszynski, the Pope was interested in cooperating with and hegemonizing its secular forces. Compared to Wyszynski he downplayed traditional Polish nationalism and instead encouraged the movement to look to the Western bourgeois states as its home. While strongly opposing impulses within the working-class movement towards political confrontation, the Pope and his allies in the hierarchy were interested in an ideological confrontation between urban populist Catholicism and the PZPR. This involved encouraging a much more dynamic and combative thrust within the working class than Wyszynski's mixture of economism and traditionalist piety. The Pope's close co-thinkers within the hierarchy itself were remarkably small in number – among them Archbishop Macharski of Cracow and the extremely energetic philosopher, Abbot Tischner. His support came more from the Catholic liberal intelligentsia in the KIKs, the Znak group and the Catholic weekly, *Tygodnik Powszechny*.

But if such forces played a subordinate political role, their intellectual influence was substantial. Despite political rivalry and differences of tactical nuance, their objectives were similar to those of the Kuron–Michnik wing of the KOR: *de facto* political pluralism and a greatly reduced role and power for the PZPR. The party would retain control of the army, police, foreign policy, etc., but through plant self-management plus the marketization of the economy, economic regulation would be removed from the control of the PZPR apparatus. The judiciary also would become independent and while censorship would remain it would be limited and there would be genuine pluralism in the media. Through marketization and self-management, the workers would face austerity, Solidarity would be not simply a trade union but a broader 'social movement'. It would not challenge for power but would be *de facto* an indispensable political factor of the first order which any PZPR government would have to cooperate with. This was the programme of the so-called 'self-limiting revolution' or 'New Evolutionism' which united a wide spectrum of opinion stretching from the agnostic Kuron through to close collaborators of the Pope.

The third trend of opinion within the Church was what might be described as the *endecja* current – reactionary Catholic anti-communist nationalism of an anti-semitic and strongly authoritarian character. This had been the strongest trend within the Church in the pre-war period. As a political trend within the episcopate it was largely extinguished in the 1950s – a good example of the political transformation of that time was Bishop Kaczmarek of Gdansk – but some elements among both priests and laity still subscribed to such thinking in the late 1970s, together with some elements of the state bureaucracy itself. Figures like Andrzej Czuma from ROPCIO, Leszek Moczulski, the leader of KPN and other similar groups entertained hopes of liquidating the communists and establishing a new authoritarian regime embodying the 'true Polish' 'ethnic spirit'. They wished to restore the past and strongly identified with a thousand years of Catholicism. Throughout the crisis they maintained a shadowy, semi-clandestine existence, operating largely on the fringes of Solidarity, and their political orientation involved extreme tactical moderation, and hostility to the social militancy of Solidarity, with a perspective of infiltration of influential institutions and the organization of networks of cadres. They lacked unity and leadership, but in the context of defeats and demoralization within the working class in the late autumn of 1981, one of these groups, the KPN, started to pick up some following among a significant minority of workers in some cities.

IV. Solidarity's struggle for survival

Phase one: A failed party offensive and its consequences
The critical political events of the autumn of 1980 were the emergence of Solidarity as a class-wide organization with a structure that emphasized class unity and the failure of the party–state authorities' attempt to polarize society around the issue of Solidarity's political subordination to the PZPR. This confrontation took the form of a battle over whether the

movement's statutes should affirm the party's leading role. The authorities tried to make this a condition for Solidarity's legal registration. In doing so they were evidently reflecting an understanding between the PZPR and CPSU leaderships. Solidarity's regional organizations overwhelmingly rejected this proposition and rallied to the call for an unlimited general strike rather than submit to a demand that seemed to destroy the union's autonomy. The Solidarity leadership suggested a compromise putting the section of the Gdansk agreements that recognized the party's leading role in society as an appendix to the statutes, but this was initially rejected by the authorities. Only after Kania flew to Moscow on 30 October, when it was clear that Solidarity could carry out its threatened strike, and gained the Soviet Politburo's approval for Solidarity's suggested compromise, was the domestic crisis defused. Solidarity was legally registered on 10 November, almost two months after it was founded.

The internal compromise was swiftly to produce an external crisis as the Czechoslovak and DDR governments, along with a powerful segment of the Soviet elite, interpreted the compromise as a capitulation on the part of the PZPR, necessitating military intervention. This campaign for an invasion was fuelled by sections of the Polish state apparatus in some regions who were banking on the swift, surgical removal of Solidarity from the scene. Within the Soviet leadership, the military commanders and political directorates of Soviet ground forces in Europe seem to have been strongly supporting the campaign, presumably because of worries about Soviet communications with the front line in the DDR. Warsaw Pact forces were mobilized along Poland's frontiers in late November, but the majority within the Soviet Politburo allegedly repudiated invasion and called a Warsaw Pact summit meeting at the start of December to lay down alternative guidelines for restoring control over the domestic Polish situation. (Subsequently, between 2 December and 16 January there was a sweeping reorganization of Soviet military commanders, involving the transfer of the C-in-C Soviet Ground forces, the Chief of the Political Directorate of Soviet Ground forces, the C-in-Cs of Soviet forces in the DDR, Czechoslovakia, Belorussia and the Baltic states as well as the chiefs of the political directorates in the DDR and the Baltic.)[20]

Throughout these autumn events, the Solidarity leadership was struggling to maintain the movement within strictly trade-unionist limits. Walesa repeatedly declared that Solidarity was not concerned with political questions and that even on trade-union questions the movement could not operate like a militant Western European movement. Walesa's most influential adviser at this time, the Catholic liberal Mazowiecki, was striving, as he put it, to 'create a trade-unionist ideology' for the movement. During the Narozniak affair in Warsaw in late November, when

workers in the big factories were threatening a general strike against the
activities of the political police, Kuron and Walesa intervened heavily and
in the end successfully, to block such action.

This orientation was strongly reinforced by the episcopate, which
echoed the PZPR's appeals for national unity and in December called
upon the population in unprecedented terms to repudiate 'irresponsible
extremists' such as the KOR and KPN and to support Poland's existing
state structure. What might be called a corporatist national consensus
emerged strongly over Christmas. The Solidarity leadership called for
and achieved a moratorium on all strikes until 15 January, when the
commemoration ceremonies for the dead of 1970 were turned into
extraordinary spectacles of national unity and reconciliation between
Solidarity and the government, presided over by the episcopate.

Phase two: A second party offensive
The Christmas consensus rapidly disintegrated at the start of January.
After the Moscow summit, there was a notable hardening of the government's positions in the various negotiations over implementing the
specific clauses of the Gdansk Agreements, many of whose provisions
should have come into force on 1 January. This hardening was noticeable
on two issues especially which were, for different reasons, crucial: the
granting of free Saturdays, and the legalization of Rural Solidarity. On
the legalization of Rural Solidarity, a new union law already agreed
between the government and Solidarity provided for the right of such a
peasant union. But it was not issued by the government, apparently
because of Soviet objections. On the free Saturday issue, the Solidarity
leadership was ready, because of the economic crisis, to retreat from the
Gdansk Agreements, and agree to three Saturdays off in the month. But
the PZPR leadership insisted upon only two free Saturdays. This was a
long-standing grievance among Polish workers who remembered
Gierek's long past promises of a five-day week and could see both Czech
and DDR workers already enjoying such rights. The issue raised even
more feeling given the binding promise of a five-day week in the August
Agreements. A test of strength was inevitable, and was turned by
Olszowski into a drive to assert, for the second time, the PZPR's
ascendancy over Solidarity. The episcopate and Walesa sought to accept
the government's terms on free Saturdays, and throughout the first four
months of 1981 Cardinal Wyszynski sought to pressurize the Solidarity
leadership to concentrate its efforts on one question: the legalization of
Rural Solidarity. But such pressure was not successful. Solidarity struck
twice, and when, on 24 January, it pulled out between 75 and 95 per cent
of workers in the large plants (according to the official news agency PAP),
the government moved towards a compromise more or less along the

lines of Solidarity's original proposals. Once again, in the eyes of Poland's neighbouring governments, the PZPR leadership had failed to assert its authority.

Meanwhile, serious tensions were appearing within Solidarity itself. The Gdansk adviser Bogdan Borusewicz pointed to one of their sources in an interview with the official press in December:

At this moment people expect more from us than we can possibly do. Normally, society focuses on the party. In Poland nowadays, however, society gathers around the free trade unions. That's a bad thing. Thus there is an increasing necessity to formulate a political programme. It would be good if the party took the lead and removed people's social expectations from our shoulders. But will it do so now? In the eyes of the people, the new trade unions should do everything: they should fulfil the role of trade unions, participate in the administration of the country, be a political party and act as a militia, that is, detain drunkards and thieves, they should teach morals – and that's a great problem for us . . .[21]

Solidarity's rise had brought millions of people into open political life for the first time and the consciousness of these newly awakened masses was extremely difficult for the Solidarity leadership, committed at this time to a purely trade-unionist posture, to handle. On one side this consciousness was expressed in vast numbers of specific grievances: in individual regions it was possible for literally thousands of isolated demands to be assembled. On the other side, it was expressed in terms of what might be called a fundamentalist attachment to various absolute values: freedom, the nation, democracy, equality, unity, and so on. Kuron described the consequences of this type of consciousness in pointing out that 'when any conflict arises between Solidarity and the government, no matter on what question, we always get tremendous support. On the other hand, any agreement, however favourable to the union it may be, arouses dissatisfaction, or – to use a perhaps better word – disappointment among the people.'[22]

This popular consciousness has been mistaken by some on the Left as a revolutionary consciousness.[23] This has a superficial appearance of truth in the sense that these masses yearned for a swift, total solution to all their problems. But in a deeper sense it was very far from being a revolutionary political consciousness. It did not at all express confidence in their own strength in collective action, far less a will to power or any programmatic unity over popular objectives. Indeed this popular mood was highly volatile, liable to swing between fervent confidence in supporting the almost miraculous powers of Lech Walesa to a loss of hope for any change and a drift into a rejection of collective action in the political field.

In the large industrial plants and among the skilled workers, on the other hand, there was both a more pragmatic conception of politics, as being a struggle to defend definite social interests and achieve particular goals, together with a strong sense of their collective strength. By the early months of 1981, these workers had developed what might be called an attitude of political syndicalism to achieve the necessary reforms. They did not believe that the reforms would be achieved by waiting and trusting the good will of the government, but they did believe the government would grant them under pressure from below. As to the reforms that were necessary, these were at this time overwhelmingly limited to implementation of the Gdansk Agreements as the industrial workers understood them, above all freedom of action for Solidarity, an effective voice of the movement in the mass media, and a clear readiness on the part of the government to cooperate with Solidarity and respect the opinion of the workers. Finally and crucially, there was a growing awareness of the scale of the economic crisis and in the need for austerity, but an equally strong insistence that any austerity programme had to be policed by the workers' trusted leaders to safeguard their social and political interests. As to how this was to be done was not yet clear.

Against this background, during January and February, a mass of local struggles on a variety of issues broke out while the movement's main centres concentrated on the issue of free Saturdays. The national leadership of Solidarity was overwhelmingly involved in rushing from one dispute to another, seeking to rein in the movement towards purely trade-unionist objectives, while leaving it up to the government to unveil a programme of political reform and hoping by its moderation to strengthen the hand of the reform-minded elements in the government. Their model was not that of political syndicalism but rather what might be described as corporatist trade unionism, with Solidarity retaining complete independence from the PZPR but operating a social contract with the government in the 'national interest'.

These different layers of thinking were beginning to produce strains and tensions within Solidarity. In the less industrial regions, the local leaderships, under intense pressure from their mass base on a wide range of issues, were being pushed into local struggles. In Solidarity's main centres, tensions were being channelled outwards towards frustration with what was seen as the national leadership's lack of vigour and militancy, while on the national leadership itself an incipient split was developing between those favouring militant syndicalism and Walesa and his advisers' more corporatist approach, itself in line with the perspective held by the Church hierarchy. Meanwhile, there was a tendency for Walesa himself to rise above the constituted committees, resting on the growing popular confidence in his supposed powers, amounting almost to a cult, particularly outside the movement's main industrial bastions.

Phase three: The Bydgoszcz crisis

The turmoil of January and the first half of February was followed by the sudden and unexpected appointment of military Commander-in-Chief General Jaruzelski as Prime Minister on 10 February. While Walesa swiftly welcomed the appointment, Jaruzelski moved to settle outstanding conflicts and calm prevailed in Poland as the 26th Congress of the CPSU took place in Moscow at the end of the month.

Jaruzelski's appointment must be seen against the background both of the Soviet leadership's rejection of invasion as a method of resolving the crisis, and of the demonstrative failure of the PZPR leadership's two efforts to establish its ascendancy over Solidarity through political polarization (the statutes and the free Saturdays campaigns). After the Moscow summit, Warsaw Pact attention shifted to Poland's internal security forces and the Pact's Commander-in-Chief Marshal Kulikov arrived in Warsaw on 14 January 'on a fact-finding mission to establish the loyalty of Poland's armed forces'.[24] From this time, serious preparations were under way to establish the option of an internal crackdown against Solidarity. General Jaruzelski's elevation made it possible for such plans to go ahead outside the framework of the PZPR's civilian apparatus and utilizing the lines of communication of the Warsaw Pact military structure rather than Central Committee links.

Secondly, Jaruzelski's appointment and the subsequent infusion of other military personnel into government positions was designed to help break the real circuit of the political process that had led to the failure of the PZPR's leadership's political offensives. This circuit had not at all involved government retreat under the pressure of economic losses from strikes or under the pressure of the threat of the strikes becoming insurrectionary. It had involved the swing of the PZPR's base organizations on to Solidarity's side on both the statutes and the free Saturdays and the consequent build-up of intolerable political pressures on the Central Committee of the PZPR. The officer corps of the army was under no such civilian political pressures, was the most socially conservative wing of the apparatus and could be counted on to stand firm in a confrontation.

The great irony of Jaruzelski's appointment was that in popular consciousness he was seen as being more amenable to the aspirations of the masses than the PZPR's civilian apparatus. Jaruzelski was presented as a 'non-political', patriotic and strong military leader, above what was seen as the sordid infighting of PZPR factions. He took over the role to which Moczar had aspired, and the official media were not squeamish in surrounding him with the aura of traditional Polish military nationalism and evoking the mantle of Pilsudski (even to the point of naming workplaces after the pre-war dictator). Jaruzelski avoided the phraseology of Marxism and presented himself as the standard-bearer of national welfare, national unity and national independence. His programme was presented as a combination of order and reform. He thus appealed precisely to the fundamentalist and only semi-political values of broad masses of the population that we spoke of earlier. And as his lieutenant he brought in as Deputy Prime Minister, Mieczyslaw Rakowski, a reformist journalist with no background in the PZPR apparatus (and no base there either), who exhibited a political style that was Jaruzelski's polar opposite: politics as complete relativism, as pure tactics, as infinitely flexible manoeuvre at the top in the cause of compromise and reform – *realpolitik* in a good cause.

But the real accompaniment of these governmental changes was the Bydgoszcz crisis, a dramatic provocation marking the replacement of the party apparatus by the political police as the initiator of political events. This crisis had been preceded by an important meeting between the Soviet and Polish party leaderships in Moscow on 4 March, at the end of the CPSU Congress. Up to this time, the Soviet line had been that despite problems and anti-socialist forces, Poland was moving towards national renewal and the PZPR had the resources to carry it out. But now the communiqué said the Soviet leaders were convinced that the PZPR had 'both the opportunity and the strength *to reverse the course of events* and to eliminate the peril looming over the socialist achievements of the Polish nation'. This was a new tune.

Then on 19 March while Kania was on a visit to Budapest and large Warsaw Pact manoeuvres were starting, came the incident that plunged the country into its gravest political crisis until martial law: the beating up of Solidarity leaders in Bydgoszcz. The details of the affair are sufficiently well known to need no further recounting here. It is important to recognize that the crisis was caused as much by the government's refusal to condemn the attack and expose its causes as by the incident itself. Solidarity's membership treated the affair as a challenge to the movement's existence. For the broad masses, it was a test of Solidarity's credibility as a force for change. At the same time the affair sharply revealed the insufficiency of the Solidarity leadership's established political conceptions.

The leadership quickly agreed five limited, piecemeal demands: the punishment of those responsible for the attack, the legalization of Rural Solidarity, security for union members and the union's right of reply to media attacks on it, full pay for strikers, and the dropping of all charges against those arrested for political offences between 1976 and 1980. At the same time, the KKP (National Coordinating Commission) was thrown into turmoil over *the form of action* on those demands. At first the majority wanted an immediate, unlimited general strike, but by threatening to split the movement, Walesa and his Catholic advisers won the day for immediate negotiations, then a four-hour warning strike on Friday 27 March, then an unlimited general strike from Tuesday 30 March.

In terms of the extremely limited demands involved, an unlimited general strike – that objectively posed the question of power – made little sense. This was the underlying logic of Walesa's position. On the other hand, Solidarity's regional activists and Walesa's opponents on the KKP had logic on their side in feeling that only a basic structural change in the situation like that which had occurred in August 1980 was appropriate. But they could express this will only in terms of the forms and timing of struggle, without articulating an appropriate structural political objective. They had no equivalent of the August demand for independent trade unions, a demand that bridged the gulf between immediate, partial issues and some all-out struggle for power. And the reason why they lacked such an objective was because of their own self-definition as a trade union which did not and should not possess any overall programmatic objective.[25]

In the absence of such a positive programmatic perspective appropriate to the interests of the working class, the Solidarity leadership was under strong pressure to adopt the priorities of the Catholic hierarchy. The Church was strongly opposed to a head-on confrontation for further structural political reform. On 28 March, the Pope sent a message saying that 'voices reaching him from Poland were stressing that working men wanted to work and not to strike.' Wyszynski moved into the centre of the stage as a mediator, moving between meetings with Walesa and Jaruzelski and agreeing with the latter on a peaceful settlement. Walesa himself later explained the Solidarity leadership crisis in the following way: 'What really happened was that we were in danger of splitting up; splitting away from the Church especially. At times like that you've got to turn back ... But these are all behind-the-scenes machinations which will be brought to light by future generations.'[26] The key objective of the Primate was to use the crisis to gain the legalization of Rural Solidarity, and this indeed was the single substantive outcome of the crisis.

Meanwhile, at the base the crisis brought a thunderous display of popular unity and discipline behind Solidarity. And the salient political feature of this was the great shift of the PZPR's basic organizations. The Politburo banned PZPR involvement in the Friday warning strike and the ban was overwhelmingly flouted, with factory PZPR organizations often explicitly placing themselves under the discipline of the strike committees (future Politburo member Zofia Grzyb was one of the factory party leaders involved in this). The central committee meeting that weekend was besieged by pressure from the base as regional conferences of PZPR delegates monitored proceedings around the clock and bombarded the CC with telegrams and resolutions. Only hours before the Tuesday general strike was due to start, Gwiazda appeared on TV to read out an agreement, consisting of general promises from the government and admitting that in Bydgoszcz the 'principles for solving social conflicts by political means' had been violated.

Among the working population in general there was at first relief that the tension was over; among Solidarity's activists in the large plants, however, there was outrage at the perceived insufficiency of the agreement. In the longer term, the movement was never again able to rally the overwhelming majority of the population behind its defence. The masses tended to drift in other directions as the economic crisis weighed ever more heavily and as Solidarity did not seem strong enough to resolve their problems. Some began to yearn for a strong government of any sort, others launched into wild-cat action on their own, out of the Solidarity leadership's control. As for the movement's activists, they began to search for more radical political answers to the crisis, moving beyond purely trade-unionist objectives. In the meantime, between April and June, the Solidarity leadership sought to contain pressures from below while the PZPR Congress approached and concentrated upon internal Solidarity affairs – regional elections, preparations for its own Congress and programmatic debate. The locus of political contestation shifted to the internal struggle within the PZPR itself.

Phase four: The rise and fall of the party reform movement
One of the most important features of the whole Solidarity experience was the union leadership's eschewing of any effort to stimulate a mass tendency within the PZPR with a shared reform programme. In 1979, Kuron had forcefully made the case for such an orientation, arguing for a movement of social pressure from below that would then become 'the social base of the grouping within the party whose programme most fully recognized the demands of society'. He went on: 'The problem of whether this type of activity constitutes participation in the game of party factions is not new. But it is naïve . . . there isn't any public activity in our country which would not become the object of clique activity within the ruling circles of the party. The object of these struggles is precisely public life . . .'[27] And he went on to explain that in a society such as Poland, the fundamental arena in which political decisions are made is the party. If there had been the danger of small opposition groups becoming the playthings of party factions before August 1980, this was far less possible a fate for a huge social movement such as Solidarity.

But this orientation was rejected (including by Kuron himself) in favour of what was called, in Michnik's phrase, the 'New Evolutionism', dealing with the government rather than the PZPR or in dealings with the latter, confining them to external relations between Solidarity and PZPR leading organs. Solidarity members in the PZPR were not discouraged from leaving the party. There were a number of distinct contributory arguments to this approach: the fear among workers of the PZPR apparatus returning to dominate them; the desire of the Church hierarchy to minimize the influence of party ideology within Solidarity; the belief that Solidarity was strong enough, and the governing authorities were reform-minded enough gradually to gain the necessary reforms from above; and a socio-economic reform programme shared by wide layers of Solidarity intellectuals and advisers that involved marketization of the economy (along with plant self-management), taking it out of the control of the party *apparat* in alliance with those sections of the state bureaucracy not institutionally tied to plan management. Finally, there was the argument that Czechoslovakia showed that structural change in the PZPR would lead to invasion.

Yet throughout its first nine months of existence, Solidarity and the PZPR rank and file could not be disentangled. The number of workers who actually resigned from the party between May 1980 and May 1981 was remarkably small: out of 1,400,000 workers in the PZPR only 180,000 resigned (resignations from other social groups in the same period were 126,000). The really mass exodus from the PZPR did not occur until after the June Party Congress (official figures give the losses from then up to December as being 500,000). After Bydgoszcz, these continuing links between the PZPR base and the Solidarity rank and file suddenly revealed themselves in a dramatic way, as the CC finally announced that the 9th Emergency Party Congress would take place in June. Writing in the party's theoretical organ in April, Rakowski explained, 'For the first time since September, a mass bloc has been created of the main party organizations together with Solidarity.' The Solidarity leadership itself was largely taken by surprise. At the beginning of May, Kuron stated: 'This entire programme (of self-limitation) has fallen to pieces, because a revolution has started in the party . . . This revolution has reached the party and now it is proceeding inside the party. And I don't know yet what should be done in this situation.'[28]

The reform movement within the PZPR should not, in fact, be seen *purely* in horizontal terms, as a revolt of base against summit. There were individual leaders at all levels of the party interested in structural political reform and strategic cooperation with Solidarity, while there were substantial elements at the base, particularly in rural and small-town communities, and also in institutions such as the army and security police, not touched by reformism. But the main *form* of the reform movement was the so-called 'Horizontal Structures' movement, started in Torun in the autumn of 1980. It involved party units breaking democratic centralism by establishing horizontal links with each other, outside the mediation of higher party bodies. The movement was not programmatically based: the sole criterion for a party unit joining was that it had elected its First Secretary in a democratic secret ballot. (The idea was launched by the leader of the August strike in Torun, Zbigniew Iwanow, who drew it directly from the model of the MKS and applied it to PZPR internal politics.)[29] The overwhelming thrust of the horizontal movement was towards internal democratization within the PZPR – 11,000 proposals for changes in the statutes were sent in from the base! – plus cooperation with Solidarity. A second source of the movement for reform was the party intelligentsia and notably leading figures in the Higher Party College of Social Sciences, like Lamentowicz, who were seeking to establish new ideological principles for the PZPR, moving it from Stalinist conceptions towards new theoretical foundations presented as more in keeping with its name and formal origin: a Polish United Workers' Party stemming from a fusion of the Polish Socialist and Communist Parties in the late 1940s. Such ideas gained wide currency in some regional party organizations, notably Cracow. Yet a third trend was represented by Tadeusz Fiszbach and the Gdansk regional organization. This presented a new draft programmatic document whose central idea was the need of a democratized PZPR to establish a mechanism for gaining popular consent to its main policy proposals, suggesting for this purpose the use of referenda. Finally we should mention as a fourth current the more amorphous trend of 'Party liberals' who sought to retain the formal accoutrements of a Moscow-style Leninist vanguard party, while transforming its style of work. This, broadly speaking, was the stance of the Kania–Barcikowski grouping within the leadership.

In April delegates representing about half a million PZPR members held a national conference of the 'horizontal movement' in Torun and championed internal democratization and a call for the Congress to be held in two parts: the first should elect a new leadership and agree new statutes; the second should agree a new party programme. The Politburo majority sought to respond to this movement by seeking to incorporate it on the Politburo's terms. These involved strictly defined democratic changes – above all the election of party executives by secret ballot – but a repudiation of new ideological principles or of new programmatic conceptions concerning the structural relations between the working class and the party–state authorities. At the same time the Kania group gave *de facto* recognition of the horizontal movement and sought to develop a centrist political course balancing between its activity and the thoroughgoing anti-reform elements within the bureaucracy.

The Moscow letter

A week after Torun the first high level CPSU delegation to visit Poland since August arrived in Warsaw led by Mikhail Suslov. Discussion focused on internal party affairs. On Suslov's return to Moscow, TASS reported a revisionist threat within the PZPR 'seeking to paralyse the party of Polish communists as the leading force in society'. During May factory and regional elections of party executives and Congress delegates returned strong reformist majorities. To counter this a serious attempt was prepared to topple Kania. On 26 May a so-called Katowice Forum published a document saying the Politburo majority was under the influence of 'bourgeois liberalism'. This was denounced on all sides within the PZPR but was followed up by a political bombshell that transformed the mood inside the party. On 5 June a letter to the PZPR arrived from the Soviet Central Committee. It made a frontal attack on the party leadership saying, 'One position after another is being surrendered . . .' to the counter-revolution, and 'so far no measures have been taken to counter it . . .' It called the horizontal movement a 'tool for dismantling the party . . .' It accused Kania and Jaruzelski of saying one thing and doing another and ended by saying that the situation 'demands first and foremost a revolutionary will from the party, its members and its leadership – yes, its leadership. The party can and should find within itself the forces to reverse the course of events and restore them to the right path before the Congress.'

The effect of the letter was both to raise Kania's standing in the country and to drive the party's reform movement into wholesale retreat. A dividing line was drawn through it between those ready to dissolve into the Kania current and those not, and the latter were effectively marginalized at the Congress. Fiszbach, for example, was not even elected to the Central Committee at the Congress, while more radical reformers such as Stefan Bratkowski were not even elected as delegates (unless they had received their mandates before 5 June). Fiszbach told the Congress that the PZPR had achieved 'negligible results' since August and blamed this on the fact that 'we have wasted too much time defending positions we simply could not defend and did not need to . . .' He went on: 'I think the trade unions must be guaranteed the right to co-participation in taking strategic decisions . . . Our Congress must map out a political programme for overcoming the crisis . . . But it will not be possible to regain public trust by means of a programme . . . The programme has to be implemented and proved right.'

But the Congress produced no such programme and was entirely devoted to the struggle over CC and Politburo elections. The turnover of personnel was sweeping, but no new political course emerged and the crucial party secretariat was recomposed as even more anti-reformist than before. Bratkowski summed up the political colour of the delegates with the word 'magma' — vaguely reform-minded but ideologically and politically inchoate. As soon as the Congress was over, the state authorities unleashed an unparalleled offensive against Solidarity, using the judicial apparatus, the central economic ministries and the newly remuzzled media. The military had strengthened their control over key posts, the party apparatus was increasingly bypassed and Kania himself reportedly became ill and torpid, sinking into depression.

As for Solidarity, it had stood aside from the dramatic battle in the party, throwing its enormous moral support behind none of the contending forces. It is impossible to say what would have happened if it had entered the fray. The obstacle to doing so was no longer the Solidarity leadership's rejection of an explicitly political involvement. But intervention would have involved giving at least implicit ideological support to forces within the orbit of Marxism.

Phase five: Solidarity seeks a political solution

By the summer of 1981, the Solidarity leadership had decided that a purely trade-unionist posture was no longer tenable for the movement. The general population ever more urgently needed positive solutions to the economic and social crisis, while the Solidarity activists were no longer prepared to wait for a government reform programme. They were moving from the politics of militant trade-union reformism towards what can best be described as an anarcho-syndicalist outlook, whereby Solidarity itself could directly establish a new political order without the need for the PZPR or parties of any kind.

The solution that emerged from the Solidarity leadership was the slogan of 'self-management' elaborated into the Programme for a 'Self-Managed Republic' endorsed at Solidarity's Congress in September —October. The programme was designed to fulfil a number of quite separate, and in certain respects profoundly conflicting, requirements. In the first place it appealed to the ideological trend growing within the industrial working class towards an anarcho-syndicalist vision of a self-managed and at the same time self-governing republic (the words management and government being interchangeable in Polish in this context) without subordination to a monopolistic party. It also contained a strong theme of social egalitarianism. But at the same time the self-management idea incorporated a socio-economic programme which involved the more or less sweeping replacement of the planned economy by marketization in which completely autonomous, self-managed enterprises would struggle for their existence on a more or less free market, supervised by the banks. And the third component of the programme was that progress towards a self-managed republic would proceed *gradually* through the ever-widening existence of self-management in the work-places (along with marketization).

The critical elements in this programme were plant self-management and gradual evolutionism since they were the points of entry of the whole programme into the field of practical politics. Yet the social logic of plant self-management plus marketization ran directly counter to the social aspirations of the working class since August, especially in the context of a catastrophic economic crisis. Free-floating prices would have rocketed, large numbers of enterprises would have gone bankrupt, unemployment would have reached millions, rapid social differentiation would have divided the working class, and Solidarity itself would have almost certainly fragmented. It is one thing for the Western Left to champion self-management at plant level in a capitalist context, on the road towards a planned economy and national self-management. It is quite another to champion self-management plus marketization in the context of a centrally planned economy which still protects the workers from unemployment and the effects of free-floating prices.

This indeed was the advantage of plant self-management from the standpoint of the Polish government itself (which even now has not dismantled all the self-management structures set up in 1981).[30] It saw this as a way of carrying through austerity and no doubt dividing the working class. What the authorities feared was that self-management would destroy the *nomenklatura* system and indeed the party apparatus itself at the local level. It therefore pushed, successfully, between the first and the second part of the Solidarity Congress for the Solidarity leadership to accept the *nomenklatura* within the government's new self-management law. (At the second part of the Congress, Walesa and Kuron were pilloried for accepting this point.)

The alternative thrust towards self-management in the economic field involved an attempt to bring the planned economy itself under effective *national* working-class control. This was argued theoretically only by a very few – inevitably Marxist – Solidarity advisers, such as Michal Kawecki in Szczecin, and was largely opposed by the professional economists among the Solidarity intellectuals. But in a practical way this thrust was strongly expressed at the Congress in the notion that Solidarity should take over control of food distribution, in the notion that a 'Social Council' should invigilate economic activity nationally. But the critical problem about such a practical course from the standpoint of the Solidarity leadership was that democratic working-class control over the plan, either in the form of a Social Council or through a second chamber being created in the Polish parliament with this task, was that it could involve a central political challenge to the country's political structure. And despite the very radical rhetoric at the Congress itself, the move-

ment's national leadership around Lech Walesa were very far from
believing they could or should mount such a challenge. Thus the slogan of
self-management did not in fact resolve the contradictions within Solidarity, it simply obscured them linguistically. When the Congress ended,
Solidarity had a formally more centralized structure and a presidium
much more solidly under Walesa's control. But the movement's reality
was very different. It lacked a clear practical perspective and was deeply
and increasingly divided.

From October until 13 December, the working-class movement was
entering a deep crisis. The strike wave from below that had begun in July
and reached its peak in October declined rapidly thereafter. On 8
November an opinion poll reported that only 30 per cent of people were
prepared to contemplate a general strike for any purpose. Another poll in
Warsaw at this time showed that 26 per cent of the population supported
abolishing the right to strike, according to *Tygodnik Solidarnosc*.[31] A
delegate at a national leadership meeting in early December reported that
one-third of the workers counted Solidarity as well as the government as
being to blame for the crisis. Modzelewski added at the same meeting:
'The Union is not as strong as it was. It is weaker, and every activist
knows it.' Ten days before the coup, *Tygodnik Solidarnosc* published a
balance-sheet of the self-management movement. After many months of
vigorous propaganda it affected only 15 to 20 per cent of enterprises. In
Oldz, an advanced region in this field, self-management committees
existed in only 150 out of 1,500 enterprises. Henryk Wujec reported
from the Warsaw area, 'As long as it was a matter of drawing up our
statutes, the movement was extremely active. But now that it has become
a matter of putting them into practice, the movement has gone a bit
slack.' In Bydgoszcz it was reported, 'We have observed among the
workers a weakening of the self-management dynamic; hesitations are
setting in. It is as if people had lost faith in continuing the movement.'[32]
Against this background, the state authorities were planning something
very different from either self-management or anarcho-syndicalism.

Phase six: Preparations for the state of war
The government offensive against Solidarity from August, consisting of
hundreds of small challenges to its rights, opened up a growing gap
between the increasingly radical and political rhetoric of Solidarity's
activists and the mass of the population, increasingly weary of politics,
increasingly preoccupied with the daily struggle for existence, and looking for strong leadership to overcome the crisis. General Jaruzelski
moved ever more prominently into the centre of the political stage to
assume this role. While still proclaiming the need for reform, Jaruzelski
brought increased vigour to the theme of order and iron – national unity

to ensure Poland's independent salvation – and branded Solidarity as a force for chaos and national disintegration. The Solidarity Congress was characterized in this light.

Within the regime itself, the party apparatus was increasingly paralysed and bypassed, as the military and the security apparatuses assumed an ever greater role in policy-making. At the October Plenum of the CC, Kania as the representative of the party apparatus made a last bid to re-assert his authority by demanding a vote of confidence. He was defeated by 104 votes to seventy-nine in a secret ballot and Jaruzelski was appointed to replace him by 180 votes out of 184. This was a decisive turning point on the road to 13 December, greatly weakening those for whom it was a point of principle that the PZPR should manage the state as a mass political organization engaging in an interplay of political forces between itself and the population.

Yet the switch from Kania to Jaruzelski was welcomed by Walesa on behalf of Solidarity. Preparations for a possible military coup were known to the Solidarity leadership at least since July. On the other hand, Jaruzelski was genuinely in favour of economic decentralization and marketization. He was also ready to respect the power and the role of the Church and was little given to serving up large doses of Moscow-style Marxism–Leninism.. Jaruzelski was himself fairly explicit about the alternative he was presenting. He offered the possibility of a national accord between himself, the Church and Solidarity, on his own terms, and he warned that the alternative would be martial law. Walesa entered discussions for such an accord but it was evident to Solidarity activists that this could only result in an authoritarian regime massively restricting Solidarity – the very opposite of a self-managed republic. Solidarity's main industrial regions strongly opposed Walesa's participation in such an accord and the stage was set for 13 December. In the last days, some of Solidarity's strongest regions, such as Szczecin, Wroclaw and Lodz, saw attempts by the movement's activists to prepare for pre-emptive local efforts to take power. On a national level, Solidarity made a last minute call for free elections to the Sejm, but such an appeal had a purely propagandistic significance.

When the blow fell on the night of 12–13 December, Poland's industrial workers found themselves alone. The Catholic hierarchy immediately issued a statement appealing to the population not to resist. In all the industrial bastions of Solidarity, the workers nevertheless threw themselves into occupation strikes. But their spirit was closer to that of a willingness to sacrifice themselves than a will to win. The proof of this is that in no single case was the loyalty of the troops put to the test by active working-class resistance in December. The occupation strikes were broken through the action of ZOMO's 25,000 troops with the army playing only a back-up role. The explanation for this is not hard to find. The industrial workers saw the division in their own leadership, the way Solidarity had been weakened over many months, the lack of any clear vision of its practical way forward. They saw also the demobilization of the population around them and the regime's determination to crush them.

Jaruzelski's success on 13 December did not signify the Polish workers' abandonment of the traditions of Solidarity. They saw the movement as part of their own identity and no one with any experience of a working class's attachment to its own independent traditions can doubt that Solidarity has sunk deep roots in the historical experience of Polish workers. But 13 December has ensured that the course of Polish history has entered new, obscure and undoubtedly tortuous paths.

V. Conclusions

Any attempt to draw conclusions about the extraordinary and tragic Polish drama must await the passage of time, and indeed the drama itself is still being played out. All we will attempt here are some points for further discussion, in the form of theses.

1. August 1980 and Solidarity represented, in social terms, a great constructive effort by Poland's industrial working class to overcome the crisis generated by the Gierek regime in a progressive and objectively socialist direction. The origins, self-definition, structure, composition and methods of struggle of Solidarity, as well as its internal democracy, all ensured that the movement could retain its integrity and cohesion only by respecting the interests of the industrial workers; and the social weight of the working class in Polish society ensured that Solidarity was the fundamental political factor in the popular upsurge. Throughout the crisis it was pitted objectively against the resistance of the state bureaucracy and the state leaderships of the surrounding countries. These were the two fundamental forces in the conflict, with all other socio-political groups occupying intermediate positions – the mass membership of the PZPR, the Church, the reformist intelligentsia, the peasantry. This configuration of forces was starkly revealed in December 1981, as the state bureaucracy cast aside the PZPR and turned its repressive apparatus against a largely isolated industrial working class. The Church hierarchy far from being the driving force behind the working class in a putative holy war against communism, was in many ways the main beneficiary of 13 December, gaining sweeping new financial privileges from the regime and the right to greatly extend its apparatus, while

managing to preserve and, in the medium term even strengthen, its hold over the population as it looks in despair for solace.

2. But if the state bureaucracy and the Church hierarchy are the main beneficiaries of 13 December, and both Solidarity and the PZPR rank and file the main losers, this in turn highlights a serious ideological weakness and political deficiency within the working-class movement. For by-and-large, the workers saw the episcopate as a close and powerful defender of its rights and they viewed the military leadership with far greater sympathy in the last months than they viewed the PZPR organizations. Our analysis of the events leading up to 13 December has shown that the driving of Solidarity underground at that time was simply the violent culmination of a political and social struggle in which Solidarity had already been thrown into retreat and some political disarray. Without this preparatory series of political defeats, General Jaruzelski's military triumph in December would have been inconceivable. Indeed, if it had not been for the very severe disintegration within the PZPR and the established political order, Solidarity might have been split and defeated without the necessity for the blitzkrieg. We must therefore look for the causes of Solidarity's earlier political defeats.

3. Our attempt to analyse the course of events during Solidarity's sixteen months of legal existence points inescapably to the conclusion that these defeats were not the result of the superior social weight of Solidarity's enemy within Polish society. On the contrary, the social balance of forces was overwhelmingly in Solidarity's favour. And in the global crisis, or if you like the revolutionary crisis, of any state, it is social forces, not technical apparatus whether of a military, administrative, financial or communications variety, that counts. The problem must therefore have been whether Solidarity had the political capacity to unite these social forces along a common path of action to surmount the crisis and overcome those seeking to destroy it.

4. The most pressing programmatic problem that Solidarity faced was how to maintain the social cohesion of the wage-earning population through the economic crisis and the inevitable severe and protracted period of austerity that would have to accompany any solution to the crisis. It is hard to escape the conclusion that a programme of marketization would have both destroyed the social cohesion of the working class and violated its strongly articulated egalitarian and socialist social values and interests. Ideas which meet the aspirations of active working-class movements catch on and spread with extraordinary rapidity, but plant self-management plus the market did not at all seize the imagin-

ation of Poland's manual workers. Indeed their preference for rationing rather than floating prices, full employment, and the equalization of rewards all pointed towards the preservation of the planned economy as well as its subordination to effective working-class political control. On such terms, the workers would in their majority have been prepared to make substantial quantitative sacrifices in income without losing their cohesion and active unity.

5. But if marketization and plant autonomy was not a viable socio-economic programme for a movement dominated by the industrial workers, then the socio-political premises of the entire strategy of 'New Evolutionism' were called in question. These premises entailed the idea that the working class could disengage itself from the PZPR in the same way as the Church had and could then coexist with an evidently weakened but fundamentally unreformed and authoritarian bureaucratic state structure. Such an orientation assumed that the economy would be taken out of the PZPR's control and also implied that those sections of the state bureaucracy not involved in operating the plan were in essence more progressive than those who were, despite the fact that they included precisely the most authoritarian and repressive sections of the state apparatus – the security forces. In this scheme of things a Jaruzelski appeared in some ways closer to Solidarity than a Fiszbach. There were impulses from within Solidarity counterposing to this disengagement of the 'New Evolutionists' a drive towards a democratic-central mechanism of economic management – a vision of this sort could be perceived within such ideas as national working-class control over the distribution system and in the idea of a workers' chamber of the Sejm. The conception had been raised, somewhat half-heartedly, before in Yugoslavia, and in its abstract form it could be presented as a national council made up of democratically elected delegates from workplaces. But whatever its form it would have involved a political thrust in the opposite direction from disengagement.

6. This in turn raises the question of whether Solidarity's leaders and advisers were right to largely ignore, or even turn their backs on, the forces struggling for ideological, political and organizational change within the PZPR. In the context of any strategy for democratizing the central mechanisms of economic management, such an orientation would have been indispensable. But more generally, Kuron's arguments of 1979 in favour of such an orientation then contained even greater force in 1980–81. The social premise for such an orientation was present from the start in the huge numbers of PZPR members within Solidarity, and within the party reform movement there were large forces ready to respond to pressure and support from Solidarity. But the inescapable

consequences of such an orientation should also be registered. These were not so much that Solidarity, or a section of it, might have become the plaything of this or that faction of the PZPR leadership, however understandable such fears were among workers who had lived through 1956 and the early 1970s. Such problems could have been handled tactically. The real consequence was rather an ideological one: insofar as Solidarity, or a wing of it, linked up and tried to publicly encourage any tendency within the PZPR, it would have had to explicitly embrace and indeed champion, socialist ideological principles, and identify with global socialist programmatic conceptions. This did not mean it would have had to adopt Stalinist views of any variety, but it would have had to champion the cause of the anti-Stalinist socialist and Marxist currents growing at the base of the PZPR. This would in turn have brought about an open, ideological and political pluralism within Solidarity, as those forces most closely linked to the Catholic hierarchy's project would have resisted such socialist democratic trends.

7. This raises, of course, the question of the nature of the relationship between Solidarity and the Church hierarchy. In the 1960s and 1970s, the independent existence of the Church unquestionably opened up space for debate and the circulation of information in Polish society not available in other Eastern European states. And the episcopate's readiness, for its own reasons, to oppose the suppression of intellectual opposition groups in the late 1970s, played an objectively progressive role. At the same time, it would be a crime for socialists to fail to respect the religious rights of believers or to treat Christians as in any sense *ipso facto* opponents of socialism and democratic rights. But this does not at all exhaust the subject of Solidarity's relationship with the episcopate. If the latter played a partially progressive role in defending civil liberties before August, it was dwarfed by Solidarity's own role in this field after it emerged. Throughout the crisis the hierarchy repeatedly intervened to weaken working-class resolve – in August, in the Bydgoszcz crisis and again in December 1981. It was ready to attack non-Catholic political currents within the movement – as with the KOR in December 1980 – and was resolute in its refusal to subordinate its own narrow institutional interests to those of the popular social movement, avoiding doing so by equating the interests of its own authoritarian bureaucracy with the interests of the Church as a Christian community and even with the interests of 'the nation'. The workers gained great confidence from the hierarchy's verbal gestures of support early in the crisis but the episcopate had little choice in the matter if it wished to maintain its popular, and indeed financial, base. It is, in truth, impossible for an institution which crushes dissent within its own ranks and seeks to impose monolithic unity

on its followers in their beliefs as well as their actions to be a trustworthy ally of any democratic popular movement for social progress.

8. Solidarity did not at any time become a passive tool of the Church hierarchy, however much the latter's real social role may have remained a powerful impediment to the movement. Instead the industrial workers at the movement's core generated an independent ideological conception of their historical trajectory that we have called anarcho-syndicalism, linked to a strain of revolutionary, romantic nationalism in which the workers conceived of themselves as the leading force in Polish society. But however mistaken it would be to equate such ideological conceptions with reactionary anti-socialist ideas, this vision contained within it contradictions which played a part in weakening the movement's unity. In the first place, though generated by Solidarity's own structure, anarcho-syndicalism simply obliterated the real tensions over whether Solidarity was to play the role of a trade union, of a political party or of a quasi-state institution – it did not resolve these tensions. Large sections of the working class were not prepared to abandon a purely trade-unionist conception of Solidarity and were not politically won over to a perspective of anarcho-syndicalist revolution. Secondly, the nationalist vision of the workers tended to presuppose a unity of social interests and of programmatic objectives which had not been present in the crisis, and whose absence was brutally revealed on 13 December.

9. Finally, we must consider the basic issue of reform and revolution in the states of Eastern Europe. The capacity of the domestic Polish state bureaucracy to challenge the working-class movement militarily might suggest that this bureaucracy possesses the independence and homogeneity of a ruling class akin to the Western bourgeoisie and that the working class must enter the road of social revolution and insurrection in order to achieve socialist democracy. Yet in our view, the superficial similarities between 13 December and military coups in the Third World obscure more than they reveal. In the first place, the crackdown bears no comparison with the scale of carnage in Chile or Argentina or Turkey. This is not to suggest that there are not elements within the Polish regime capable, subjectively, of killing large numbers of workers. It is simply that experience teaches these bureaucratic regimes that even a few hundred deaths – as opposed to tens of thousands or hundreds of thousands in individual bourgeois states since the war – can spell catastrophe for their perpetrators within a few short years, because of the socio-economic structure of these states and the place of the working class within them. The Polish regime has thus had to put up with continuing political resistance on a wide scale. The extraordinarily rapid growth and consolidation of the working-class movement in 1980

and its capacity to pull all other sections of the masses behind it, while thoroughly disorganizing the internal mechanisms of the political system, is a further testimony to this social balance of forces in Eastern Europe. And while the state bureaucracy is a real social antagonist of the workers that will not reform itself, its subordination to popular sovereignty involves essentially a political revolution drawing strength from the socio-economic foundations of the state. If such a political revolution need not necessarily entail insurrection, what it does require, however, is a break with the ideological, political and organizational principles of Stalinism and of the Stalinized party. This cannot be achieved by the manoeuvres of factions at the top. But the Polish events do not exclude the possibility of such a transformation being carried out through the combination of a mass movement outside and an allied mass current inside the CP. It leaves the question open. Open too is the most fundamental issue of all: whether under some circumstances the hostility of the CPSU leadership to movements towards socialist democracy could still remain below the threshold of military invasion.

These attempts to explore some of the factors involved in Solidarity's defeat should not be taken to imply that socialists and Marxists here should take their distance from the Polish working class, blame it for its own defeat and wag a disapproving finger at its leaders. Exactly the opposite conclusion must be drawn by socialists here in the West. The working-class movement and the struggle for socialism must be international in character for its historic project to be realized. A crucial part of that project entails the search for a path beyond Stalinism towards socialist democracy in Eastern Europe. When Poland's workers rose in August 1980 in a genuinely heroic collective effort constructively to create such a path beyond the authoritarian–bureaucratic political order that Stalinism had bequeathed, what did they find on the Western Left in the way of coherent programmatic conceptions to help them in this task? Where were such conceptions for democratic workers' states on the road towards socialism being elaborated and translated into the languages of Eastern European people by the Socialist and Communist Parties of Western Europe? The truth is that beyond general doctrinal points, the Western socialist Left was and remains almost totally unprepared to provide aid for the enormous theoretical and practical tasks the Polish workers face. It has been the Kilakowskis, Brzezinskis and the ideologues of NATO who devote massive efforts towards working out the intellectual and practical problems of breaking up the regimes of Eastern Europe, and their schemes are always directed above all at destroying the planned economies–and the concomitant social gains and rights of working people in these states.

The Polish workers were thus forced back on their own resources and on the ideas current in other social groups within Poland. The really outstanding feature of the Polish crisis is the extraordinary resourcefulness of their movement. Any Marxist theory of the transition from Stalinism to socialist democracy must depend on our ability to learn from their experience. And the defeat of 13 December and its international consequences shows that if we do not make this task of learning from Solidarity's experience an urgent one, the future of socialism will involve further tragic defeats.

NOTES TO CHAPTER 19

1. The best overall account of the crisis available in English is Neil Ascherson, *The Polish August,* Harmondsworth, 1981. Also see the often brilliantly illuminating writings of the Polish sociologist Jadwiga Stanisykis, some of which are collected in *Pologne: La Révolution Autolimité,* Paris, 1982.

2. There is, of course, another channel of access to desirable goods and services other than those mediated through the political institutions – the black market. And in almost all East European societies all sections of the population do participate in the black market. But for many sections of the working class access to really important goods and services through this channel is not open because transactions require Western currencies. Thus the industrial workers are continually brought back to their relationship with the party as the really crucial relationship in their efforts to improve their own and their family's standing.

3. See Juan Cameron, 'What the Bankers Did to Poland', *Fortune,* 22 September 1980. On the more general economic crisis in the 1970s, see my article, written under the name 'Peter Green', 'The Third Round in Poland', *NLR 101/102* (February–April 1977).

4. From Peter Hebblethwaite's excellent critical analysis, *Introducing Pope John Paul II,* London, 1982, p. 48. The considerable influence of the Polish Pope over the subsequent course of events is difficult to gauge in its concrete effects. There is, however, evidence to show that it seriously worried the hierarchy of the domestic Polish Church, which in subsequent months from the Pope's visit sharply distanced itself from oppositional activities it had previously endorsed and embarked upon negotiations to establish – for the first time ever – formal relationships with the *pro*-government Catholic lay organizations.

5. The meat price subsidy alone rose from 12.3 billion zloty in 1971 to 91.4 billion in 1979, despite special shops selling 18 per cent of all meat at higher prices by that time.

6. Interview in *Labour Focus on Eastern Europe,* III, 5 (November 1979–January 1980), p. 12. Also see Alex Pravda's important article, 'Poland 1980' (*Soviet Studies* [April 1982]) for a mass of valuable information on working-class attitudes at this time.

7. One such figure, Zabinski in Opole, took his local struggle to the point of banning all plant managements within his province from carrying out any central ministerial directive without first gaining his personal clearance: a

clearly illegal ban which gave him the credentials to sweep into the Politburo along with Olszowski as soon as Gierek fell.

8. It was not difficult for outside observers to see it coming. In November 1979 we reported: 'Out of the corners of their eyes, all political forces noted an incident in Gdansk: workers in department K2 in the Lenin Shipyard struck for two days in October. A central committee representative rushed north to negotiate a settlement. Unnecessary jitters? Perhaps. But with workers' living standards falling many nerves are strained in Warsaw at the thought that the subterranean giant of Poland's politics may again move out and stamp its will on the country's history.' (*Labour Focus*, III, 5. See also my 'The Struggle for Independent Workers' Organization in Gdansk' in the subsequent issue of *Labour Focus*.) And those ready to pore over the debates in the election campaign in the official unions during these pre-August months would have been able to read advance notices of most of the demands raised by the Inter-Factory Strike Committee later in the year. (See George Kolankiewicz's important article, 'The Working Class under Anomic Socialism', in *Blue-Collar Workers in Eastern Europe*, Jan F. Triska and Charles Gati (ed.), London, 1981, p. 136.)

9. The most evocative account in English can be found in Jean-Yves Potel, *The Summer Before the Frost*, London, 1982. The complete set of Gdansk strike bulletins is translated in *Labour Focus*, IV, 1–3.

10. About one-third of the Inter-Factory Strike Committee (MKS) delegates in Gdansk itself were estimated to be PZPR members, and the two vice-chairpersons of the Szczecin MKS were PZPR members as were five of the fifteen members of the MKS presidium. The Walbrzych mines, the first Silesian pits to go on strike, were led by PZPR members (one-third of the miners, in fact, were party members) and the same was true in the key strike centre in Upper Silesia, the Jastrzebie mines. In Szczecin the Parnicza shipyard was brought into the strike within hours of the Warski yard on the initiative of its party secretary.

11. Potel, pp. 144–5.

12. Leonid Zamyatin, 20 June 1981, quoted in Kevin Ruane, *The Polish Challenge*, London, 1982, p. 199.

13. With the exception of Karol Modzelewski in Wroclaw and Zbigniew Kowalewski in Lodz, the number of former political oppositionists who became prominent in the leadership of Solidarity's regional organizations was very small, except in Warsaw and Gdansk. Although former oppositionists did come to exert influence as advisers (especially in Solidarity's press organs), the working-class membership was generally extremely wary of involvement with any of the various organized groups such as KOR on the grounds that they did not wish to have any political line 'imposed on them from the outside' – whether by the PZPR or anyone else.

14. Another very strong belief amongst workers was that the health, safety and social welfare of the working class had been widely ignored by the authorities under Gierek. These issues were a source of bitter resentment, not least because official propaganda and legal requirements told an opposite story (Poland, for example, had on paper some of the toughest and most compre-

hensive anti-pollution laws). In the late 1970s Poland had the second highest incidence of TB in Europe and in 1976, according to government figures one in four workers worked in unhealthy conditions.

15. There was also to a considerable degree an identification with the trade-union movements of Western Europe, one which expressed itself in the many local links established between Solidarity branches and trade-union branches from the West. But a purely trade-unionist ideology was not enough to sustain a movement continually involved in general confrontations with the government and threatened with invasion from neighbouring countries.

16. The Kuron–Michnik trend tended to present itself as a purely democratic ideological current with a strong sympathy for Western parliamentary democracy, rather than as a socialist current linked up to any international socialist or working-class tradition.

17. *Labour Focus*, V, 1–2, contains the full English translation of Solidarity's Programme.

18. The report by DIP (the 'Experience and the Future' Group) is published in English in *Poland: The State of the Republic*, Michael Vale (ed.), London, 1982. The quotation is from p. 65.

19. Moczar at that time used anti-semitism and chauvinism in a drive against the cultural intelligentsia as part of this factional campaign within the PZPR.

20. R. D. Anderson, 'Soviet Decision-Making in Poland', *Problems of Communication* (March–April 1982).

21. *Labour Focus*, IV, 4–6, p. 15.

22. *Spiegel* interview (15 December 1980).

23. See Colin Barker and Kara Weber, *Solidarnosc from Gdansk to Military Repression*, London, 1982.

24. See Leslie Collitt in *Financial Times* (15 January 1983). *The Economic Bulletin East–West*, edited for Western bankers by Jan Syoublek, reported in the Spring that sources in Moscow spoke of preparations for a military coup in Poland.

25. The contrast with August is crucial. On that earlier occasion, the workers had not fought either for piecemeal minimal objectives nor for the general overthrow of the bureaucracy, but rather for the essential *intermediate political objective* of an independent trade union. This was a demand that was grasped by the mass of working people as both reasonable and necessary, while ensuring, if won, a formidable practical advance for the consciousness and organization of the class. Such an intermediate or transitional political objective was lacking during the Bydgoszcz crisis. Despite a far more massive national mobilization than in August, as well as the dramatic shift of the PZPR's urban base into the mass movement, Solidarity's leadership was led into a strategic impasse, unable to channel the popular will to *defend* Solidarity at all costs (something different from a will to conquer state power) into an advance of the scope and organization of popular power.

26. See *The Book of Lech Walesa*, Harmondsworth, 1982, pp. 192–3.

27. See Kuron's 'The Situation in the Country and the Programme of the Opposition', *Labour Focus*, III, 3 (July–August 1979). His argument brought a polemical response from Michnik and Lipski.

28. Interview with *Intercontinental Press*, given on 2 May and published on 1 June 1981.

29. On the origins of the movement see the interview with Iwanow in *Labour Focus*, IV, 4–6, p. 51.

30. One of the earliest and most succinct proposals for self-management came from none other than Tadeusz Grabski. In January 1981 at a meeting of party leaders from the largest enterprises, he argued, 'Under the new economic system, the enterprise becomes the basic, independent economic unit . . . It must operate on the basis of cost accounting and face the consequences of its activities, while observing workers' self-management. It means the right of the workforce to decide independently on all essential matters as regards the functioning of the enterprise, starting with the organization of production and ending with staff policy, pay policy and the distribution of earnings.' (Ruane p. 113.) Exactly the same formula could have been heard from some of Solidarity's economic advisers months later, although by no means all of them.

31. 13 November 1981.

32. *Tygodnik Solidarnosc* (4 December 1981). Much of the material here is drawn from the afterword of Jean-Yves Potel's *The Summer Before the Frost*. See also Jadwiga Stanisykis, 'Poland on the Road to the Coup', *Labour Focus*, V, 1–2. For a contrary view of Solidarity's last weeks, see Zbigniew Kowalewski, 'Solidarnosc on the Eve' in the same issue of *Labour Focus*.

20. Solzhenitsyn: The Witness and the Prophet

Daniel Singer

'No, don't! Don't dig up the past! Dwell on the past and you'll lose an eye.'
   But the proverb goes on to say: 'Forget the past and you'll lose both eyes.'

Solzhenitsyn, Introduction to *The Gulag Archipelago*

'How could anyone possibly say that the October Revolution was in vain?'

Tvardovsky, in *The Oak and the Calf*

In literary history there can be few cases of such a sudden rise of a writer to national and then international fame. In November 1962 the 92,000 copies of the Soviet magazine *Novy Mir* were snapped up as soon as they reached the stands. The public knew, by one of those mysterious channels, that the eleventh issue of that year contained something exceptional, a short novel or long story called *One Day in the Life of Ivan Denisovich*. The author, the unknown zek Alexander Solzhenitsyn, became famous in the Soviet Union almost overnight and in the world at large within months.

For millions of Russians, unfortunately, the subject matter of the book – the universe of the concentration camp – was neither strange nor abstract; it was a fact of life. Yet for the first time these Russians could recapture in a novel the mood and the quintessence of their season in hell. Foreigners, naturally, had no such intimate knowledge. On the other hand, they had every facility to read about repression in Russia, though most of them, it must be admitted, did not bother. Now *Ivan Denisovich*, through its artistic concision and power, was compelling everybody to look at the cruel past and its current implications. For both Russians and foreigners the publication of the book was also an event in yet another sense. The decision to publish such a sober indictment, a decision taken by none other than Nikita Khrushchev himself, was hailed as a significant extension of the Soviet frontier of freedom, a step on the road towards the dismantlement of the Stalinist heritage.

The hopes of such a smooth transition from Stalinism, carried out largely from above, have been dashed. Eighteen years later, the author of *Ivan Denisovich*, though a Nobel Prize-winner, lives in exile in Vermont. In the intervening years he has produced a tremendous amount to justify his sudden reputation. From his prolific pen as well as from his drawer (or more accurately from his secret hiding places) manuscripts have been flowing unceasingly: poems in prose, plays, short stories, three full-length novels, the monumental *Gulag* trilogy, a volume of literary memoirs, and a host of more directly political and polemical writings. Admittedly, out of this impressive output only three short stories were officially published in the Soviet Union. Solzhenitsyn's Russian readership has been limited to the restricted circles of the deliberately circulated illegal manuscripts, the *samizdat*. Outside the Soviet bloc, by contrast, his books are sold by the million. Alexander Solzhenitsyn is now arguably the most famous living writer in the Western world, subject of endless controversy, in the form of theses, studies, essays, and innumerable articles. And yet, in a curious way, he remains an ambiguous, contradictory, and controversial figure.

Paris was a good vantage point to watch this confused controversy. The French communists took out of context some passages in *The Gulag Archipelago* about General Vlasov and his soldiers to dismiss Solzhenitsyn as a traitor, although they could perfectly well have argued, within context, about Solzhenitsyn's reactionary outlook. However, any serious treatment would have compelled the Communist Party to deal in earnest with Solzhenitsyn's charges about the horror of concentration camps, their impact on political life in the Soviet Union, and the survival of Stalin's system well beyond Stalin. For the party, therefore, the cruder – and the shorter – the better. The Right, for its part, welcomed Solzhenitsyn with open arms and hailed his every work as gospel truth. After a time, some of his more awkward pronouncements – say, about the virtue of authoritarian rule when tempered by Christian beliefs – had to be played down. But his main message, namely that the revolution is the root of all evil, has been a godsend for the conservatives of the Western world. Coming from a man with his talent and his experience, it is a perfect weapon for the establishment.

The two contrasting reactions were thus true to form. More puzzling was the attitude of that part of the Left unburdened with a Communist Party card. In dealing awkwardly with the subject it has given the impression of being paralysed by a Manichean pattern. The non-communist Left acted on the absurd assumption that to dissociate itself from Solzhenitsyn's philosophy would prevent it from attacking his torturers. It has behaved in this strange fashion as if calling a spade a spade and Solzhenitsyn a reactionary meant giving one's blessing to Brezhnev or whitewashing Stalin. This tortured mental paralysis was well illustrated when Alexander Solzhenitsyn came to Paris in the spring of 1975 for his first appearance on French television.

On the eve of his performance, Solzhenitsyn gave a press conference at his publisher's. As this was at the time of the impending collapse of the puppet regime in Saigon, he lectured his bewildered audience about the victory of brute force over the values of culture and civilization. The very idea of Thieu as the defender of any values – other than those of the dollar or the piastre – was so grotesque that the journalists present at the conference, presumably out of sympathy for Solzhenitsyn, chose not to mention it in their reports. Only Jean Daniel, editor of the Leftist *Nouvel Observateur*, in front of the cameras the following evening, dared to raise the issue and to deplore Solzhenitsyn's stand. As a result he was clubbed from Right, Left, and centre, despite the fact that he had wrapped up his criticism in all sorts of regrets and had added his hope to resume a 'common struggle' with Solzhenitsyn. To fight *for* Solzhenitsyn is one thing. But can a progressive, even a liberal, let alone a radical or a revolutionary, envisage a common struggle *with* the Russian preacher, now that his views, his outlook, his *Weltanschauung* have been spelt out fully? The confusion springs from the duality of Solzhenitsyn's works and struggle.

Is there anything more moving and inspiring than this victim defying the mighty and ruthless establishment, this zek emerging from eight years in the concentrationary universe and, in the dangerous circumstances of exile, getting down at once to his work and his mission? The sudden fame after *Ivan Denisovich*, even the Nobel Prize, are merely means for accomplishing his task, allowing him to speak for the silent, to be the voice of the downtrodden. He does not rest on his laurels. In secrecy, permanently threatened by police spies, with only the help of a handful of fellow victims, he painstakingly gathers the corpses, the bones carried by the rivers of the Archipelago, to erect a monument that will bear witness and that nobody will be able to dismantle. Is there anything more moving than the sight of this undaunted individual refusing to yield to the threats and the corrupting power of the ruling Leviathan?

But the moving witness is also a strange preacher and a false prophet. The defender of the oppressed in the Soviet Union is the champion of the torturers in Vietnam and of the executioners in Indonesia. The most famous Russian rebel despises the Western establishment because it is not, in his view, sufficiently repressive and authoritarian. In his frequent declarations on world problems he stands 'to the right of Goldwater', to borrow a quip attributed to his fellow Nobel Prize-winner, Henry Kissinger. Nor is Solzhenitsyn's attitude due to his sheer ignorance of the West. On his home ground, too, picking up the struggle of the Slavophiles against the Westerners, he is a reactionary in the etymological sense of the term. He is hankering after an idealized, imaginary past, after a land ruled by a benevolent Tsar and inhabited by happy Russian peasants – *muzhiks* – a Mother Russia without the stench, the knout, and the pogroms. And the two visions fit into a coherent, if irrational, whole. If Russia's troubles seem in his writings to go back to the evil of the October Revolution, Solzhenitsyn makes it quite clear that the original sin must be sought further back in time and space, that one must go back to the French Revolution – which he equates with Nazism – and beyond. We are doomed because we are godless.

Solzhenitsyn's credo as summed up here is not the fruit of my imagination; it will be backed up with chapter and verse. Enough has been said, however, to suggest that both his critics and his admirers within the Western Left have landed themselves with a dilemma of their own invention. It is patently absurd to endorse Solzhenitsyn's philosophy because his description of the horrors of the gulag is accurate. It is equally irrational to reject his testimony because of his outlook. Dostoyevsky in *Crime and Punishment* attacks the corrupting power of money in the budding capitalist economy from the point of view of a reactionary romantic. His indictment is none the less devastating. So is Solzhenitsyn's. He is at his best describing the scene, conveying through one day the full horror of life in the camp. In his novels, and not just in *The Gulag Archipelago*, he shows how the concentration cancer grew, how it spread, attacking the whole social fabric, and how the entire body politic is still infected, even if the camp population is now incomparably smaller than in the past. To ignore Solzhenitsyn's heart-breaking contribution because one disagrees with his diagnosis would be sheer folly. On the contrary, those who reject his vision must follow him to the bitter end, and only then move beyond to find out what went wrong and when and why. This is the price that must be paid by those who see in October 1917, whatever happened afterwards, the birth of a new era and not a calamity. Communists, trying to conceal the whole matter under the threadbare cloak of the 'personality cult', are merely helping our rulers who are only too glad to confuse Marxism with the barbed wire.

But Solzhenitsyn is significant for us in more ways than one. Alexander Isayevich, born in the second year of the Soviet regime, is almost literally a child of the revolution. His ideological journeys cannot be put down to the heritage of the past. True, this exceptional man had a rather exceptional life, and I shall try to retrace briefly his itinerary, if only to explain some of the apparent contradictions in his work and his outlook. Nevertheless, when a young man starts by criticizing Stalin in the name of Leninism and ends by seeking a solution in heaven, his journey tells us a great deal about the 'socialist' environment in the Soviet Union. Solzhenitsyn, for all his peculiarities, is also a symptom, the sign of decay of

Russian society, of its inability to move beyond a certain point in its abortive attempt to get rid of the Stalinist pattern. And this, in turn, explains why the Soviet rulers could answer Solzhenitsyn only through censorship and banishment. The central thesis of this essay is that Solzhenitsyn, physically and mentally a victim of Stalinism, does not point to the future, that his voice — tragic and moving as it is — is a voice of the past. Why then is it still relevant in Russia today? Why does it frighten the rulers in the Kremlin and their henchmen at all levels in the party hierarchy?

Finally, there remains the problem of treating Solzhenitsyn in political terms. No attempt will be made here to assess whether Solzhenitsyn is 'worthy' of the Nobel Prize (after all, many writers of smaller stature obtained this award) or to argue whether as a novelist he can be called the equal of Dostoyevsky (though such a claim, in my opinion, can only be backed by political passion). This is not my purpose. But to look at Solzhenitsyn and his work as a political phenomenon seems perfectly natural. It is by now a cliché to recall that in Russia, in the absence of a political opposition, prominent writers have often taken it upon themselves to act as national spokespeople. Today in the Soviet Union no political opposition is tolerated and Solzhenitsyn chose to challenge the authorities on his own. Though a master craftsman of the Russian language, he is no innovator, no explorer of uncharted literary roads. He is neither Joyce nor Kafka. His greatness lies in his concentration on major themes, or rather on one of the great issues of our time. Solzhenitsyn is essentially a moralist, and politics lies at the heart of most of his writing. Critics who choose to treat him in purely literary terms — and they alone — must justify their approach.

Let us start with the easiest, though not least indispensable, aspect: Solzhenitsyn the prophet and his message for the Western world. Easiest because some of Solzhenitsyn's statements are so preposterous as to speak for themselves. Indispensable because, if his message carried in millions of copies goes unchallenged, our establishments will have achieved their purpose — turning Solzhenitsyn into a public warning against any radical action. Strange though it may seem, Solzhenitsyn is not particularly valid as a weapon of anti-Soviet propaganda. Few people in the West, even among members of European Communist Parties, still view the Soviet Union as a workers' paradise or even simply as a model of socialism. Since the end of the old Cold War the points that can be scored against Soviet rulers are of lesser importance, and it requires Solzhenitsyn's passion still to see Moscow as the headquarters of world revolution. But greater changes loom ahead for Western capitalism. If the French rising of May 1968 and the 'hot autumn' that year in Italy herald the revival of revolutionary hopes in Western Europe, if the economic crisis marks the end of a quarter of a century of exceptional prosperity and false euphoria, if a whole rising generation questions the rules of the game, then it is indispensable for the establishment, as part of a counter-offensive on the ideological front, to persuade the new rebels that any attempt to change society radically is doomed in advance. And who is better placed to proclaim that you start with Marxism and inevitably end up with barbed wire than the articulate and passionate survivor of the gulag?

Solzhenitsyn in his writings often addresses the West, sometimes directly, sometimes in polemical asides. The zek, faithful to his past, has a contemptuous hatred for all those distinguished visitors, the notorious 'friends of the Soviet Union' who at the end of their superficial journey were only too eager to praise Stalinist freedom and democracy. That the Western Left must take the blame for its shameful silence – and more – at the time of wholesale purges and mass deportations is undeniable. But Solzhenitsyn tends more and more to reserve his bitterest comments for those European Leftists who dare to protest crimes committed not just in the Soviet Union but also outside the Soviet bloc, for 'the zealous champions of Greek democracy and North Vietnam', for the 'anti-fascists and the existentialists, the pacifists, the hearts that bleed for Africa'. His favourite targets are Bertrand Russell and Jean-Paul Sartre (not the fellow traveller of the post-war period but the Sartre who in the last twenty years of his life could not be described as tender towards the Soviet leaders). In rather irritating remarks, Solzhenitsyn accuses them and their like of hypocrisy, of perceiving imaginary crimes in the West and turning a blind eye on Soviet atrocities. In his passion – understandable considering his background – he does not seem to perceive to what extent he himself is guilty of such double standards.

Take, for instance, the forced feeding of prisoners. Solzhenitsyn treats this as a horrible crime and compares it in a vivid metaphor to rape. Yet when the same thing is perpetrated in Germany against members of the Baader-Meinhof group, Solzhenitsyn keeps silent. Indeed, he tacitly approves, choosing as the publisher for the journal with which he was connected Axel Springer, the most outspoken supporter of such a system of repression. Or take Indo-China: human beings literally caged like animals in Poulo Condor, one would imagine to be something comparable to Kolyma, something to excite the sympathy, the fellow feeling, of a zek. Yet Solzhenitsyn ignores their very existence, preoccupied as he presumably is with Thieu's culture and civilization. Back in 1965, feeling down and disheartened, he was cheered by the news of the communist defeat in Indonesia. What was the human cost of that defeat? According to Western estimates, about half a million people perished. Considering the population of the country and the speed of the massacre, the mincing machine must have been working as fast in Indonesia as in the Soviet Union at the height of Stalin's purges. Not all the victims being equal for the ex-zek Solzhenitsyn, this massacre is for him a source of rejoicing.

This is still humanly understandable. Victim of 'communism', Solzhenitsyn cannot extend his Christian charity to communist victims. Let us therefore pick a different case. The latest appeal of Solzhenitsyn to his fellow citizens is not a call for rebellion. Instead, he makes a case for passive resistance. He pleads with his brethren, whatever their position, to speak the truth and damn the consequences. Daniel Ellsberg, product and servant of the American establishment, reaching breaking point and then putting his love of truth above the interests of his masters, would seem just the man for Solzhenitsyn's heart. Quite the contrary, however. Far from feeling sympathy for this American 'seeker after truth', he is angry with Ellsberg's judges because of their leniency. He blames America, 'in which a judge, flouting his obligatory independence to pander to the passions of society, acquits a man who, during an exhaustive war, steals and publishes War Ministry documents'. Here the victim borrows not only the language but the mentality of his torturers.

His Christian charity may be selective but our crusader is at least consistent in one respect. Unlike most Soviet dissidents, he is no admirer of the West. He pleads with Western rulers to break economic relations with the Soviet Union, to stand up to that country in order not to lose the 'fourth world war'. But he thinks Russia's salvation must come from its own moral regeneration. He is not envious of Western riches, which he finds merely corrupting ('excessive ease and prosperity have weakened their will and their reason'). He has no special love for democracy, bourgeois or otherwise ('when unlimited freedom of discussion can wreck a country's resistance to some looming danger and lead to capitulation in wars not yet lost; when the historical democracies prove impotent, faced with a handful of snivelling terrorists'). He has no objection to authoritarian rule as such, as he repeats time and again: 'The autocrats of earlier and religious ages, though their power was ostensibly unlimited, felt themselves responsible before God and their own conscience.' In any case, if the twentieth century has a lesson for humankind it will not come from the morally debased West, but from the East regenerated through suffering. If there is to be salvation, Russia will be the redeemer.

Alexander Solzhenitsyn, in rejecting Western influences, explicitly links up with an old tradition, that of the Russian Slavophiles. This, on its own, does not make him a reactionary: in Russia's famous ideological struggle of the nineteenth century one cannot neatly divide the protagonists into Left and Right, into progressives and reactionaries. Among the

Westerners some were dreaming of a socialist world of 'free and equal' people while others were simply striving for capitalist exploitation on the Western model. Among the Slavophiles a good number were undoubtedly seeking an ideological cloak for the preservation of existing privileges. Yet others were genuinely hoping that Russia would be able to jump from the *mir*, the commune, into a socialist commonwealth, bypassing capitalism, 'history, like a grandmother, showing a partiality for the youngest grandchildren'. Solzhenitsyn, however, opts proudly for the most backward wing of the movement. He glances nostalgically back beyond Peter the Great and Ivan the Terrible. He dreams of a pastoral past, of a peasant Russia with its happy serfs. Solzhenitsyn is not just appalled by the barbarian means used to modernize Russia; he is opposed to modernization whatever the methods. He goes on fighting the old battle and produces a modern toy – ecology – to clinch the argument. Teilhard de Chardin, the Club of Rome report, zero growth – he chuckles slyly. Weren't we reactionaries wise before the event?

The West can bring no salvation; it is the source of poisonous modern germs which infected and contaminated Russia's happy pastures. Russia's undoing began when 'the intelligentsia repudiated religious morality and chose for itself an atheistic humanism'. Solzhenitsyn is ready to admit that through the October Revolution Russia brought 'its share of evil'. 'But did the so-called Great French Revolution, did France, that is, bring less? Is there any way of calculating? What of the Third Reich? Of Marxism as such? Not to go any further.'

A strange equation. Nevertheless, among humankind's many sins Solzhenitsyn has, naturally enough, picked Marxism as his target. He preaches on the subject, if not with authority, at least with assurance. Thus he asserts categorically that 'in contemporary economic works – Lubell and others – it is proved that since the end of the manufacturing period, capitalism – belying Marx – has ceased to exploit workers . . .' In any case, Marxism is anachronistic, a vestige of the nineteenth century! Whereas the ideology of the Orthodox Church is, by contrast, the latest product of the modern mind, even if according to Solzhenitsyn one should stick to the version preached in the fifteenth century, before the Church got involved with modernizing tsars. It is unfair always to expect consistency and coherence from a reactionary romantic.

But from where does Solzhenitsyn draw his knowledge of Marxist theory? Certainly not from the principal work of the revolutionary thinker. Alexander Isayevich Solzhenitsyn, usually so contemptuous of people talking out of their hat, so full of scorn for instance for the editors of *Novy Mir* who dared to criticize an old émigré publication, *The Landmarks*, without having read it, admits with full candour that he has never read *Das Kapital*. The passage in 'An Incident at Krechetovka

Station' is autobiographical. Like Vasya Zotov, Solzhenitsyn made many attempts to read the 'book of wisdom' but found it too hard going. His knowledge of the 'progressive doctrine', about which he lectures so often, is thus based on Soviet practice rather than on Marx's theory. In other words, to recognize his competence we must accept the one point on which Solzhenitsyn agrees, for once, both with the professionals of anti-socialist propaganda and the masters of the Kremlin, namely that what is happening in the Soviet Union is socialism on earth and Marxism incarnate.

If Solzhenitsyn's value as prosecutor of socialism rested on his grasp of Marxism or on his increasingly unreal versions of world history, this whole section would have been superfluous. Our establishments have shrewder spokespeople. Faced with a rising generation questioning the established values of the ruling ideology, they have been forced to elaborate more sophisticated weapons of propaganda. They know that to appear plausible it is wiser to cover the anti-socialist message with a liberal coating, that it is cleverer to say a word against apartheid and not to show undue enthusiasm for the most notorious torturers of the Western world. By comparison, Solzhenitsyn's message is crude, full of visible special pleading and obvious half-truths. It is the sort of stuff that one only hears in the West on the lunatic fringe of the Right. But this is merely half the story. We should not confuse Solzhenitsyn with our home-bred reactionaries. Whereas they have class interests to defend, profits to collect, advancement to think of, Solzhenitsyn – a victim and spokesperson for the victims – has nothing to gain. His courage cannot be compared with their hypocrisy. Solzhenitsyn's distorted world outlook is the product of his bitter experience. The universe of the Soviet concentration camp is not for him an abstract proposition.

'Don't break the mirror because the mug is ugly.'

Gogol, *The Government Inspector*

No literate and politically minded adult in the West had to wait for Solzhenitsyn to discover the Soviet concentration camps. A detailed bibliography of books published on the subject would fill more space than this essay: memoirs, eye-witness reports, analytical studies have been pouring out at least since the 1920s. Only for a short period, during the last war, were Western publishers reluctant to print material 'libelling' Uncle Joe, the indispensable ally. The refusal of a large part of the European Left to read or to believe that literature is another matter. It raises the whole question of the success of Stalinism outside Soviet frontiers, a problem much more complex than the now fashionable books by former practitioners suggest and one which can be explained only in the context of the social conflicts, the political struggles, and the ideological climate of the period. Here all that can be ventured is that the greater readiness of the European Left to listen today has probably less to do with Stalin's crimes than with the double failure of his successors: their inability to liberalize the Stalinist heritage beyond a certain point and their failure to preserve the illusion that what they are building is a different world, a socialist alternative.

All this in no way diminishes the importance of a great writer, his ability to render vivid what was abstract, significant what was vague; his capacity to force the reader to penetrate a strange world and there to look at its workings through the eyes of the victim. Solzhenitsyn is the first great novelist of the universe of the concentration camp and it is as such that he will go down to posterity. He had written constantly about the gulag and its shadow over the country at large, well before the *Archipelago*. (His only novel based not on his experience but on history, *August 1914*, I personally found uninteresting, as I did *Lenin in Zurich*, but judgement must be suspended since the whole work is unfinished.)

In *Ivan Denisovich*, his early masterpiece, Solzhenitsyn gives us a glimpse of everyday life in hell, plain, ordinary, and horribly true. Though *The First Circle* is set in a relatively privileged detention centre for scientists, a *sharashka*, drawing on a bigger and looser canvas the author can show us different kinds of inmates, trace their background, suggest their fears and hopes, the mainsprings of their struggle for survival. It is there, too, that we best perceive the thin frontier separating the outsider from the inmate in Stalin's time, the ease with which the mighty dignitary could be turned overnight into a helpless prisoner. In *Cancer Ward*, the gulag is apparently distant in the background. Only Oleg Kostoglotov, one of Solzhenitsyn's several semi-autobiographical heroes, is a former political prisoner, a 'fifty-eighter'. Nevertheless, the gulag looms large over the whole story, particularly as it is set in 1954, when the entire system seemed for an instant threatened from within. Thus, Rusanov, the successful climber from working-class origin, suddenly remembers with fear how years earlier he had denounced a neighbour simply to get his apartment, while Shulubin, faced with death, accuses himself unjustly of cowardice because he merely had the courage to refuse a career, not the guts openly to defy the authorities. It is in this book, with its eloquent title, that we are best shown how the diseased cells invade the whole organism, and why Soviet history cannot be comprehended without the gulag.

Translating his own experience into a literary indictment was not in Solzhenitsyn's view enough to repay his debt to his fellow victims, especially when it became clear that the post-Stalinist process of change had come to a stop (the refusal to publish his own works was one of the signs of that reversal). He then decided to prepare for a more direct attack against Stalin's heirs. The Gulag Archipelago is, in one sense, a collective work of a unique kind: 220 testimonies were gathered secretly in a police state. But it is also very much a personal work, bearing the mark of its author, reflecting his outlook, his talent, his style. Solzhenitsyn is at his greatest telling a story, describing things seen, choosing the significant detail, investing a small fragment with significance for life at large. In Gulag he lends his pen to other sufferers and makes their experience come to life. Each reader will be haunted by a different scene: the young, blonde girl standing in the night, swallowing her tears and waiting helplessly for her fate to be decided by a bully in uniform, whose whim will mean life or death to her; or the agony of the train journeys to the camp of the suckers, the frayers, in Russian camp slang, robbed of all their possessions by the pitiless old-timers, thieves and crooks, the subservient masters of this kingdom; or kids turned into literally murderous little devils by their early struggle for survival. Yet it is the cumulative effect of such scenes which turns the reading of The Gulag Archipelago into such a harrowing and indispensable experience, as if the description of hell lay in the accumulation of detail. No, nobody has the right to write the history of the Soviet Union treating the Archipelago as a side issue or even merely as a seamy side. It is an integral part of the whole.

Although naturally more gifted in describing the concrete than in conveying the abstract, Solzhenitsyn is forced in Gulag to venture into generalization. He is the historian of the gulag, its geographer, its sociologist. He analyses its legal providers, its police supervisors ('the bluecaps understood the makings of the meat-grinder and loved it'), its slave-drivers. He has a chapter on the 'magical work' of women and he does not forget the children. At the end of the second volume he even turns anthropologist to discover, bitter tongue in cheek, the strange habits of the tribe of zeks.

To sum up the work of a brilliant writer is a waste of time; he had better be read. Yet to recommend the reading of a best-seller is even more ridiculous. The recommendation should be taken metaphorically, as an appeal to the Left to take Solzhenitsyn seriously – despite the hysterical absurdity of some of his latest pronouncements on world affairs. The Right is a different matter. Its passion for freedom is always curiously awakened when bourgeois interests are threatened. It was greatly bothered by democratic niceties in Portugal after the overthrow of Salazar's dictatorship or in Chile during the presidency of Allende. But it was blind to the performance of the Pide, Salazar's political police, as it now prefers to hear as little as possible about the atrocities perpetrated in Chile by the Pinochet regime. For the Right such an attitude is normal, since it can only rule by fooling the people. The Left can indulge in such hypocrisy only at its own peril, however. Not that a revolution in any of the advanced capitalist countries would face handicaps comparable to those experienced by the Soviet pioneers. But their precedent must stand as a permanent warning of what can happen when a movement departs – allegedly for a while, because of exceptional circumstances – from the principles of socialist democracy. And Solzhenitsyn's testimony, whatever his own views on the subject of revolution, is a reminder of the tragic catastrophe that may follow.

The mirror, therefore, should not be broken. Indeed, it should be kept as precious, showing that the mug was more terrible than even we imagined. But it still remains to be seen whether Solzhenitsyn's picture is complete and whether it does not contain its own distortions: is the prophet guiding the pen of the witness? We must now look at the limitations of Solzhenitsyn the historian.

The Gulag Archipelago, in the words of its author, is a literary investigation and as such cannot be judged by normal historical standards. After all, a Soviet historian who asked the authorities for access to the secret archives would either have his head examined or, more likely, would be deported to a camp to study his subject from inside. Inaccuracies and approximations are thus inevitable. Solzhenitsyn's figure for the number of the victims of terror, for instance, seems very far-fetched. In *Gulag* he put it at between 40 and 60 million. Recently, in *From Under the Rubble*, he has raised the figure to over 70 million. To this one must add Soviet losses in the Second World War, usually estimated at about 20 million people. The total should be compared with the Soviet population which, during the period under consideration, averaged less than 200 million. Since the dead were predominantly male and essentially adult, we must conclude that within less than half a century Russia lost well over half its labour force. If this account were true, Stalin's economic achievement – very questionable by socialist standards – would be fantastic, extraordinary, unbelievable; indeed, as unbelievable as Solzhenitsyn's figure. But the doubtful nature of this figure does not invalidate the indictment: if the number of victims were a tenth of that figure, the tragedy would still be there. Its causes still would have to be searched and studied with passion by all those who, like myself, believe that what the Bolsheviks intended to carry out was a socialist revolution.

More worrying are Solzhenitsyn's biases, often setting at odds the analyst and the chronicler. Some of his prejudices are perfectly understandable. For example, the ex-zek has a contemptuous hatred for the orthodox, the *bien-pensants*, the Stalinists. He therefore tends to minimize their massive presence among the victims of their own system, playing down for instance the importance of the purges of the mid-1930s.

He also tries to describe them all as time-servers, bullying their subordinates and bootlicking their superiors, as privileged guests of the Archipelago. This just does not square with his own description. The deported Stalinists were fifty-eighters and as such shared the hardships with which 'politicals' had to put up in the camps. Besides, if they were as 'pampered' as he suggests, it is difficult to see why the waves of suicide he writes about should have been particularly frequent among them.

Whatever one thinks of Stalinism – and however passionately one was against it in its heyday – the phenomenon is not so simple, so uni-dimensional, as it is now being painted, often by its former admirers. If Stalin had relied only and exclusively on the fear of the masses and the avidity of the climbers, undoubtedly two important ingredients of his system, he would not have ruled for so long. The drama of the men who faced the Soviet execution squads with the name of their beloved tyrant on their lips, of thousands who perished in the name of the principle 'right or wrong, my party', or of those who assumed that there was no way to fight the established system without endangering the revolution – this drama adds a vital dimension to the Russian tragedy, even if the illusions and scruples of the victims look strange in retrospect. It is a dimension missing from Solzhenitsyn's vision.

It is asking much even from a Christian preacher to feel sympathy for his persecutors the day when they in turn are swallowed by the meat-grinder. But strangely, or rather not so strangely, Solzhenitsyn hates with ever greater passion all members of the Bolshevik opposition, of whatever faction. He goes out of his way to taunt them, to insult them, inventing imaginary charges to strengthen his argument. His attitude is best summed up in his own words:

If you study in detail the whole history of the arrests and trials of 1936 to 1938, the principal revulsion you feel is not against Stalin and his accomplices, but against the humiliatingly repulsive defendants – nausea at their spiritual baseness after their former pride and implacability.

Is this not just the reaction of a man of courage disgusted by the apparently grotesque behaviour of the defendants in these ghastly trials? It is nothing of the sort. Solzhenitsyn has no more love for oppositionists whose courage was, to put it mildly, no less than his own, for men who were not deported by accident but because they refused to abjure their principles and who in the camp did not just try to survive but went to their death sticking to their convictions. Whatever his prejudices, the author was bound to mention the resistance of the anti-Stalinist opposition, the strikes in Kolyma, the hunger strike which began in the autumn of 1936 in Vorkuta and lasted 132 days. The authorities gave the impression of merely yielding in order to gain time to prepare for savage reprisals.

Solzhenitsyn describes this 'final solution'. Early in 1938 over a thousand remnants of the Trotskyist and 'decemist' (that is, democratic centralist), oppositions were gathered at the Old Brickyard in the Vorkuta. Gangsters were introduced into their tents with specific orders to humiliate and provoke the protesters; whenever they fought back they were shot by the guards. The survivors were marched off to a new destination: they were mowed down by machine guns in the tundra. Elsewhere opponents were literally buried alive. Solzhenitsyn the narrator tells their story briefly but movingly. The prophet cannot help interrupting with undisguised gloating: 'At the old brickyard, in cold and tattered shelters, in the wretched unwarming stove, the revolutionary gusts of two decades of cruelty and change burned themselves out.'

Clearly, Solzhenitsyn's dislike for the opposition has nothing to do with their cowardice or courage. It has less to do with the past of the concentration camp than with the author's present convictions and with the political prospect for Russia. If all Bolsheviks were not bloodthirsty thugs, if all revolutionaries are not scoundrels, if all was not doomed from the start by definition, then the opposition to the present regime could be carried in the name of a socialist alternative. This, as we shall see, is a perspective Solzhenitsyn now refuses to envisage. The only possible opposition must be moral and religious.

Once the spell is broken and Solzhenitsyn's political bias perceived, everything falls neatly into a pattern. The priests, the nuns, the believers in general, are upright, brave, and decent. This can be taken for granted. Should a free thinker possess any virtue the case must be stressed almost like a miracle. ('He had never been a believer, but he had always been fundamentally decent.') Our populist also discovers the moral superiority of the aristocracy: 'And here is the kind of self-control this meant, the sort of thing we have forgotten because of the anathema we have heaped upon the aristocracy, we who wince at every petty misfortune and every petty pain.' No wonder that for him the White Guard officers who shoot workers and whip peasants are 'the exceptional few' as opposed to the 'soldierly majority', whereas for the Bolsheviks the opposite is true. This stands to reason, since the Bolsheviks are the godless.

The contrasted description of Red and White guards gives the game away. For ideological reasons Solzhenitsyn must prove that Lenin equals Stalin, that the early 1920s were no different from the late 1930s. If the White Guards were on the side of the angels, if foreign intervention is not even mentioned in the story, then the action of the Bolsheviks, the writings of Lenin, the first detention camps, and so on, are taken completely out of their context. If the Bolsheviks were not besieged, if they were not struggling desperately for survival and then coping – however inadequately – with major social upheavals, then their actions can be portrayed as the ravings of madmen driven by some metaphysical hatred of humanity, and hence Solzhenitsyn can argue that everything was bleak, bloody, and hopelessly cruel from the very start. Yet however hard the prophet tries to prove his equation the task is beyond him. The witness contradicts him time and again.

The relationship between Leninism and Stalinism is a crucial element in any writing on the Soviet Union and I want to make my point perfectly clear. Only writers with an axe to grind – opponents of any radical, revolutionary change or Stalinists disguised – can blur the line between the two. Only they can confuse the political and moral climate of the early revolutionary period, when the pioneering Bolsheviks, besieged in their backward fortress, betrayed by the international labour movement, faced with a situation for which classical Marxism had no real counsel, had to improvise just to hold on, with the Stalinist period, when the allegedly necessary vices had been turned into virtue, into the model for the world at large, and a massive police state had been built to quash the faintest sign of dissent. No true historian of the Soviet Union will ignore this division. Yet just drawing the great divide will not do either. The seeds of the Stalinist nightmare must have been sown earlier. Where did things start going wrong? With the disbanding of the soviets? With undemocratic social relations in the factory? In the light of what was to happen, no concept, no instrument, no individual should be sacrosanct. The party as a vanguard, the 'dictatorship of the proletariat', the action of Lenin, or even the teachings of Marx must be looked at again critically from our position of hindsight. Russia's backwardness alone cannot explain it all, though any judgement, however stern, will have to be set against the background of the country's primitive conditions. To pronounce a verdict in a social void is to condemn oneself to empty moralizing.

The fundamental weakness of Solzhenitsyn's approach is the divorce between the history of the gulag and the changing social and economic shape of the Soviet Union. Not that he does not bother about life outside the Archipelago. He mentions, for instance, the post-war famine, 'to the point of cannibalism, to the point at which parents ate their own children – such a famine as Russia had never known, even in the Time of Troubles in the early seventeenth century'. But the gulag remains a product of its own, or Bolshevik, wickedness somehow unrelated to the upheavals and calamities affecting the outside world.

What would we say of a historian of Nazism who would explain its rise without taking into account the galloping inflation and the economic crises, driving the middle classes into their hysterical frenzy? Yet the social conflicts tearing the Soviet Union apart were even more tremendous: the bloody collectivization, equivalent to a second Civil

War, the breakneck industrialization, the turning of millions of *muzhiks*, accustomed to the pace of rural life, into workers responding to the rhythm of the industrial machine. This whole process of 'primitive accumulation', as Marx called it, had taken cruel centuries in England, the birthplace of the Industrial Revolution. In Russia it was to be packed into barely a few decades. The misfortunes that were to follow were summed up in advance by Preobrazhensky in a formula that speaks for itself in its tragic contradiction: 'primitive socialist accumulation'. Was the speed indispensable? Was post-revolutionary society bound to perform the capitalist task and, in doing so, was it not condemned to pervert the ends for which the revolution had been carried out? Today, when the USSR generates over 1,000 billion kwh of electricity and cannot show the shadow of a soviet, our answers to these questions are more disillusioned and probably wiser than they would have been in the past. But it is only in tackling such questions in their proper context that one can hope to understand the gulag and not view it as a freak, as a cruel and mysterious monstrosity.

A season in hell – the metaphor was used on purpose at the beginning of this essay. Hell, too, needs no beginning, no end, and is merely related to its imaginary counterparts: heaven and purgatory. We emerge from Solzhenitsyn's *Gulag* volumes like from a nightmare – shaken, guilty, terribly aware of what life in this hell is and at the same time ignoring its origins, utterly unarmed to fight against this phenomenon or its repetition. Naturally, Solzhenitsyn tells us incomparably more about the horrors of the concentration camp universe than Nikita Khrushchev did in his 'secret' speech, but he adds little to our understanding of its causes. This is not surprising. God's wrath, the original sin, or Bolshevik wickedness are no more explanations than the euphemistic 'cult of personality'.

True, no history of Soviet Russia will be genuine unless it includes the gulag at the heart of the narrative, not as an epiphenomenon but as an intrinsic part of the system. The reverse is even more true. No history of the Archipelago will make sense unless it is conceived as part of a broader whole, as one of the elements in Russia's transformation, with its political conflicts, the social forces unleashed on a stupendous scale, its terror and its achievements, its broken hopes and twisted aspirations – in short, the more than half a century of Soviet history. This monumental modern tragedy is still to be written and, to avoid any fatalistic whitewashing, it should have as its motto: *tout comprendre n'est pas tout pardonner*. In any case, Alexander Solzhenitsyn, for all his experience, talent, and passion for his fellow victims, was ill-equipped to face this wider task. Indeed, by the time he was writing *The Gulag Archipelago*, his vision of the world meant that he did not even feel the need for such a rational explanation of the seemingly irrational.

*

One and the same human being is, at various stages, under various circumstances, a totally different human being. At times he is close to being a devil, at
times to sainthood. But his name does not change, and to that name we ascribe the
whole lot, good and evil.

The Gulag Archipelago (vol. I, p. 168)

A full-length portrait of Solzhenitsyn would present problems. He has
violently dismissed his only biography published in the West, and has
often protested against the forgeries, half-truths, and plain lies about his
past spread by the Soviet police and its stooges. In fairness to a man for so
long slandered by the professional machinery of a powerful state such
materials must be dismissed. But for our purpose the obstacle is
irrelevant. For a sketchy outline of his life, helping to understand his
ideological journey, it is enough to draw on Solzhenitsyn's own writings,
including some of his fiction, handled with due care.

Child of the new regime, Alexander Isayevich was born on 11 December 1918, in Kislovodsk, a Caucasian spa. He never saw his father, a
former student of philology at Moscow University who had survived the
First World War, during which he had served as an artillery officer, but
died from the sequels of a hunting accident before the birth of his son. His
widow took young Alexander to Rostov-on-the-Don when he was six
years old. There, in the capital of the Cossack country, he was brought up
in very modest surroundings, his mother eking out a meagre wage doing
all sorts of minor office work.

There must have been a religious background in the family, since years
later, ashamed retrospectively of his own role as a bully, Solzhenitsyn
exclaims: 'And where have all the exhortations of grandmother, standing
before an ikon, gone!' This, however, significantly is balanced at once:
'And where the young pioneer's daydreams of future sacred equality.'
Everything seems to indicate that his early days as a pioneer left an
imprint on Solzhenitsyn who, apparently, was a very politically-minded
adolescent. Did he, like Zotov, consider that 'his insignificant life only
meant something if he could help the revolution'? And did he, too,
volunteer to fight in Spain? This may be going too far. But it is very
probable that, like his other alter ego, Gleb Nerzhin, 'he did not run out
to play after he had done his homework but sat down to read the
newspapers. He knew the names and positions of all the party leaders, all
the commanders of the Red Army . . .' The analogy with Nerzhin springs
to mind because, like Solzhenitsyn, by the end of his secondary school 'he
could clearly detect the falsity in all the inordinate, gushing praise of one
man, always that one man.' And it was this refusal to take part in the
Byzantine cult which was to lead Solzhenitsyn to his destiny.

But let us not anticipate. It was not all politics for Solzhenitsyn. The
youngster was so gifted that he faced an *embarras de choix*. By 1941 he

had taken his degree in mathematics, a diploma he rightly claims really saved his life. He had also studied, by correspondence, at the Moscow Institute of History, Philosophy and Literature. He might even have become an actor had it not been for some disease of the throat. War did not leave him much time for choosing. Newly married, Solzhenitsyn spent the first winter of war as an ordinary soldier in charge of horse-driven vehicles, but shortly after he was sent to an officers' school. The days of an army without epaulettes were gone and Solzhenitsyn emerged from the school proud of his rank and in no way perturbed by the hierarchical power it gave him over subordinates – a weakness he was later to describe in touching terms and to deplore. This is the sin admitted. The insinuations about Solzhenitsyn's 'doubtful' war record are a pure fabrication of the official scoundrels ready to stoop to any level to discredit their accuser. In fact, Solzhenitsyn was in the front line as commander of a company searching for the artillery positions of the enemy. He fought the Germans almost to the end, until that fateful day in February 1945, the turning point in his life.

However learned and politically minded, young Solzhenitsyn must have been extraordinarily naïve, a real innocent. Otherwise he would not have included in his letters to a friend thinly veiled criticisms of the Father of the People and Fountain of All Wisdom. Whatever his other qualities, Stalin remained the all-seeing, even in wartime, thanks to the secret police. The inevitable happened. The Smersh counter-intelligence officers were waiting for him that February. Proud Captain Solzhenitsyn, cashiered on the spot, began at once the journey that was to take him to Moscow, the infamous Lubyanka prison, and beyond.

The rest is public knowledge. Five months later, he was sentenced for anti-Soviet activity (under the notorious Article 58) to eight years in corrective labour camps. He had just time to get acquainted with the gulag and its convoys when mathematics came miraculously to his rescue. To his great surprise, his background was taken into account and Solzhenitsyn was admitted to a special prison for scientists, the *sharashka* described in *The First Circle*. He was to stay there, near Moscow, between 1946 and 1950. We do not know whether he was to be sent away from these relatively privileged surroundings anyhow or whether, like Nerzhin, he really helped his fate in order to take his place among the 'dead on probation'. ('As the proverb says, "You won't drown at sea, but you may drown in a puddle." I want to try swimming in the sea for a bit,' Nerzhin replies to a suggestion that he might stay in Mavrino.) Be that as it may, Solzhenitsyn was to spend the next three years in the labour camp for political offenders at Ekibastus in Kazakhstan, working with trowel and mortar, a brother of Ivan Denisovich; and he survived this ordeal. He was freed, the date is symbolical, in March 1953, just after Stalin's death, the beginning of the thaw. Freed, however, is too strong a word, since he was sent into exile to Kok Terek in South Kazakhstan.

What did this descent into the 'sewers' of Soviet society do to Solzhenitsyn's outlook? He claims that in the first year he still assumed his opposition to Stalin was in the name of some form of 'purified Leninism'. He considered himself a Marxist. But his intellectual defences were very weak indeed. More than a child of the October Revolution, Solzhenitsyn was a product of the Stalinist thirties, when the study of Marxism had been reduced to the veneration of the Holy Gospel and the learning by heart of its reduced authorized versions – *The Short Course, The Problems of Leninism,* and particularly the chapter on Diamat (dialectical materialism). Faced in prison with men talking a different language, Solzhenitsyn felt like a ventriloquist's dummy having to find his own voice. He was particularly shaken by his contact – in the Butyrki prison – with two men younger than himself, former Komsomols, or young communists, rebels, and believers in God:

> I don't recall that Ingal and Gammerov attacked Marx in my presence, but I do remember how they attacked Tolstoy and from what direction the attack was launched. Tolstoy rejected the Church? But he failed to take into account its mystical and its organizing role. He rejected the teachings of the Bible? But for the most part science was not in conflict with the Bible, not even with its opening words about the creation of the world. He rejected the State? But without the State there would be chaos. He preached the combining of mental and physical work in one's individual life? But that was a senseless levelling of capabilities and talents.

The Marxism taught at Rostov University must indeed have been sterile if Solzhenitsyn was taken aback and unable to answer arguments so old and unoriginal. From one gospel and catechism to another the distance is surprisingly short. Solzhenitsyn was already ripe, but the actual conversion came much later, in the seventh year of confinement, during a scene worthy of Dostoyevsky.

Solzhenitsyn lies in the camp hospital after an operation. Everybody is asleep. At the bedside of the feverish patient is a doctor, Boris Nikolayevich Kornfeld, a Jew converted to Christianity, who explains to Solzhenitsyn the reasons for his conversion and passes on to him his credo: 'There is no punishment that comes to us in this life on earth that is undeserved. Superficially it can have nothing to do with what we are guilty of in actual fact, but if you go over your life with a fine-tooth comb and ponder it deeply, you will always be able to hunt down that transgression of yours for which you have now received this blow.'

Dr Kornfeld preached so passionately because he was frightened. That very night he was to be murdered, hammered to death by unknown prisoners. Does it mean that the saintly man was a stool pigeon? Solzhenitsyn leaves the question ambiguously unanswered, but he is struck by the last words of the dead man, especially that he himself was maturing towards a similar conclusion. In the very same hospital bed he writes a poem celebrating his religious resurrection which ends:

> God of the Universe! I believe again!
> Though I renounced you, you were with me!

There too, he discovers his new fundamental belief: Good and Evil are to be found in every person. Hence the 'truth of all the religions' which fight the evil in individuals (every individual). Hence the 'lie of all the revolutions', which merely suppress contemporary carriers of evil (and carriers of good, too, in their undiscerning hurry); but they inherit 'the actual evil itself, magnified still more'.

God had given Solzhenitsyn his message; the sense of mission was to follow soon after. Life in camp had left its mark on Solzhenitsyn's body. In the autumn of 1953, plagued by a malignant tumour, he had to leave his distant place of exile to travel, like Kostoglotov, to Tashkent, expecting to die there in a cancer clinic.

In December the doctors – comrades in exile – confirmed that I had at most three weeks left . . . I did not die, however (with a hopelessly neglected and acutely malignant tumour, this was a divine miracle; I could see no other explanation. Since then all the life that has been given back to me has not been mine in the full sense: it is built around a purpose).

He has been fulfilling this mission ever since, with the pen as his weapon. We now know that Solzhenitsyn had actually started writing in the second year of his confinement in appalling conditions. For him the 'pains of creation' had a more literal sense than for Flaubert. There was no question of re-reading, pruning, polishing. One portion of the text memorized, the bit of paper on which it was written had to be destroyed; the penalty for absent-mindedness would have been death. Once out of camp Solzhenitsyn got down to writing with the passion of a man possessed and the caution of a crafty zek. 'Rehabilitated' in 1957, he moved from Kazakhstan to Ryazan, south of Moscow. In both places he worked as a teacher during school hours and devoted the rest of his time to writing, or rather to writing and concealing his work. All drafts burned, the final version had to be microfilmed in primitive fashion in order to be hidden from the secret police. Solzhenitsyn seemed to write for eternity, or rather for the record.

Then, in the autumn of 1961, after the 22nd Congress of the Communist Party, he suddenly changed his mind and decided to stick his neck out. He sent the manuscript of *Ivan Denisovich* to the relatively liberal review, *Novy Mir*, edited by the poet Alexander Trifonovich Tvardovsky (or, to be more accurate, he had it submitted by Kopelev, the model for Rubin in *The First Circle*). It took a year between the first contact and the final publication. The complicated tug-of-war is vividly described in *The Oak and the Calf.* Here it is enough to recall that the timing was opportune, that *Ivan Denisovich*, as Solzhenitsyn put it, conquered the 'superior *muzhik*' Tvardovsky, and appealed to the 'supreme *muzhik*' Khrushchev. Indeed, in the hands of the latter the booklet became a weapon in the struggle against Stalinism.

Overnight the unknown Solzhenitsyn became a famous author (and, incidentally, the money advances enabled him to drop teaching in favour of full-time writing). But the honeymoon between Solzhenitsyn and the regime, or rather the period of diplomatic relations between the two, did not last long. By the end of 1964, and certainly in the following year, it became obvious that what Solzhenitsyn intended to publish – particularly his two novels – would not get past official censorship. Indeed, the mid-sixties mark an ideological divide in his writing. Naturally, the break is not neat and the dividing line is blurred. Thus, *Cancer Ward*, begun three years earlier, was only completed in 1965, whereas in the previous winter Solzhenitsyn was already hard at work on the *Gulag*. Yet it can be argued that in his earlier works, including *The First Circle* and *Cancer Ward*, he still seems to be driven by his original beliefs, attacking Stalin in the name of Lenin, contrasting the reality of the Soviet Union with the promises and hopes of the revolution. Later, and particularly today, he sends a plague on both their houses and curses all revolutions.

It may be objected that there is a difference between books written in the hope of official publication and those conceived when all such hopes are given up. Granted. But however much I may disagree with Solzhenitsyn's views, I would never accuse him of lack of courage. To have concealed his thoughts and withdrawn some passages from publication is one thing. It was not cowardice but wisdom. Once bitten, twice shy, Solzhenitsyn knew that for an unknown, a former zek, to reveal some of his views would have been useless suicide. Yet actually to write what he did not believe would have been quite a different matter and Solzhenitsyn would be the last person I would dare to suspect of performing such action just for profit or glory. To avoid any ambiguity, I will not quote from 'For the Good of the Cause', the only short story Solzhenitsyn claims to have written to measure, for immediate tactical reasons. In fact, the two main novels provide more than enough material to prove my point.

Equality – to be more precise, its promise contained in the revolution and its absence in Soviet society – is an important theme running through both books. Thus, in *The First Circle*, Yakonov, the future MVD (Ministry of Internal Affairs) officer, explaining to Agniya why one should be on the side of the Bolsheviks: 'But the main thing is they stand for equality! . . . Nobody will have any privileges based on income and position.' And much later, Ruska, the young rebellious zek, talking to

Clara, the daughter of public prosecutor Makarygin: 'Why did we have a revolution? To do away with inequality! What were the Russian people sick and tired of? Privilege! Some were dressed in rags and others in sable coats; some went on foot and others rode in carriages; some slaved away in factories while others ate themselves sick in restaurants . . .' And he goes on to explain how privilege persists and 'spreads like the plague'.

And here is the portrait of an old Bolshevik, hardly consistent with the views of the author of the *Gulag*: 'Thus it seemed to Adamson that none of these people in the room was remotely comparable to those giants like himself who at the end of the twenties had chosen deportation to Siberia rather than to retract what they had said at party meetings . . . They had all refused to accept anything that distorted or dishonoured the revolution and were ready to sacrifice their lives to make it pure again.' Or this comment about Makarygin's first wife, a Bolshevik revolutionary: 'If she hadn't died when Clara was born it is difficult to imagine how she would have coped with today's world at all.' Or the comment of Radovic about a young officer who did not want to have special privileges: 'This boy had been brought up a Leninist like us.'

The same theme runs through the passionate discussion in *Cancer Ward*:

'I haven't got a bean and I am proud of it,' says Kostoglotov. 'I don't want a huge salary, I despise such things.'

'Sh-sh,' hissed the philosopher, trying to stop him. 'Socialism provides for the differentiation in the wage structure.'

'To hell with your differentiation!' Kostoglotov raged as pigheaded as ever. 'You think that while we're working towards communism the privileges some have over others ought to be increased, do you? You mean that to become equal we must first become unequal, is that right? You call that dialectics, do you?'

Shulubin joins the discussion, quoting the April theses of the Bolsheviks: ' "No official should receive a salary higher than the average pay of a good worker." That's what they began the revolution with.' And Kostoglotov brings the discussion back to his time: 'It was called the Workers' and Peasants' Army then. The section commander got twenty roubles a month, but the platoon commander got six hundred.'

I could go on quoting, but I do not want to overstate my case. An author is not responsible for the views of all his personages. In the same *Cancer Ward*, when Shulubin, after the moving confession of a man who just weathered the storm, preaches his wishy-washy version of 'ethical socialism', it has more to do with the religious teachings of Soloviev than with the thinking of Marx. Throughout this novel and its predecessor one can already perceive the germs of Solzhenitsyn the Christian crusader. Nevertheless, the emphasis is entirely different. Then the author seemed to suggest that Russia could begin its resurrection by reverting to the early ideals of the revolution. Since then he has been preaching with increasing passion that all the misfortunes can be traced back to that revolution and to its ideas.

This is why Lukács, in an essay published in 1969, was entitled to maintain: 'Nowhere [in the two novels] is there a figure whose thoughts and feelings are even remotely connected with a restoration, with the overthrow of the socialist regime, to say nothing of the reintroduction of capitalism.' He was wrong, and Solzhenitsyn told him so (to be more accurate, Solzhenitsyn was talking to himself while facing Tvardovsky): 'If the novel [The First Circle] contained "nothing against the communist idea" . . . you've missed the point! It's much more dangerous than you think.' Still, Lukács' error was at least understandable. The critics who today try to paint the portrait of a 'progressive' Solzhenitsyn have only their imagination and their own prejudices to build their case upon.

Why Solzhenitsyn changed so profoundly and roughly at that time can only be guessed, though the history of post-Stalinist Russia helps us to grasp his evolution. In the first ten years or so after Stalin's death hopes ran high and illusions prospered. It was then possible to imagine that the barbarian and anachronistic system built in primitive conditions had been artificially preserved by the aging tyrant and would somehow be dismantled after his departure. Various hypotheses were advanced in the West about the possible historical reversal towards democracy. The process of 'substitution', analysed by Trotsky and Deutscher – the proletariat standing for the nation, the party for the proletariat, the central committee for the party, and, finally, the general secretary for the society at large – was now expected to unfold in the opposite direction. As the frozen Stalinist society began to be affected by the thaw; as Khrushchev to defeat his rivals in the Politburo had to appeal to the central committee in 1955; as Stalin's statue was toppled from its pedestal; as hundreds of thousands of political prisoners emerged from the camps and timid moves were made to loosen the ideological strait-jacket – it was not entirely absurd to assume that the road, however tortuous, full of zigzags and ambushes, might lead to a reforming of Soviet society. Then the advance got bogged down. Any further steps threatened not just the top leadership but all its accomplices and fellow profiteers, the whole mighty apparatus of the party. It became apparent, or at least it should have become obvious, that the system would not reform itself from within and from above, that Russia would have to go through a social upheaval from below.

That Alexander Solzhenitsyn, cautious, sceptical, mistrustful though he was, was himself influenced by this mood of hope is undeniable. About the year 1956 he wrote: 'these were the freest months our country had known in half a century.' He hailed 'the splendid promise' of the 20th

Congress and the 'sudden fury, the reckless eloquence of the attack' against Stalin launched by Khrushchev after the 22nd Congress. Later, through *Ivan Denisovich*, his fate was in a way linked with that of Khrushchev, and after the latter's fall, Solzhenitsyn watched the tug-of-war attentively, fearing the victory of 'Iron Shurik' otherwise known as Alexander Shelepin. In fairness, it must be added that Solzhenitsyn was among the first – long before the Soviet intervention in Czechoslovakia – to perceive the intrinsic inability of the regime to move beyond certain boundaries. This awareness may partly explain the shift in his own position.

The shift itself is shown vividly in *The Oak and the Calf*. This is a strange book. It offers us a portrait of Solzhenitsyn himself, a complicated man, an *illuminé* mixed with a clever zek, a visionary with an eye on the main chance, an author claiming to have reached detachment, distance, charity, yet really feeling in his element with a club, a *dubinushka*, angrily raised above his head. The book also provides an insight into the Soviet literary establishment, its liberals and its diehards, its servitudes, its degrading subservience to the cultural section of the party. But above all *The Oak and the Calf*, half duel and half love story, is a record of Solzhenitsyn's relations with Tvardovsky and the latter's beloved journal, *Novy Mir*. Naturally, it is a one-sided record, since we hear only Solzhenitsyn's version. He is too clever a craftsman not to steal the limelight and too convinced of his mission not to see himself as the centre of the world. But any genuine stage manager would have had to put Solzhenitsyn in a favourable light. After all, while Tvardovsky and others more or less dirtied their hands during the Stalin era, the only mud Solzhenitsyn gathered was the mud of the camp. And even in the years described in the book, they are the *insiders* straining for compromise within the system, whereas Solzhenitsyn is the *outsider* seeking justice, and revenge, for the victims of oppression.

For all the author's efforts, the contrast to the reader is not so plain. This is probably due to the fact that Solzhenitsyn attacks his opponents not only for what they were and are, but also for what they pretend to be, for their aspirations. When Tvardovsky, during a discussion over *The First Circle* at the *Novy Mir* office, argues that the book raises the question, 'What does socialism cost and is the price within our means?' nobody objects that the Russian regime has little to do with socialism, least of all the author. When Tvardovsky claims, 'But we are defending Leninism. In our situation it takes a lot of doing. Pure Marxism-Leninism is a very dangerous doctrine (?!) and is not tolerated,' Solzhenitsyn does not question the value or coherence of their alleged Marxist critique, he merely sneers with the question and exclamation marks shown above. And when Tvardovsky and his team are finally kicked out of *Novy Mir* and some of them send a text to the *samizdat* assessing the historical role of the review, Solzhenitsyn is a ruthless critic. He rightly contrasts their boasts about the achievements of the review with concrete examples of its timidity (for example, its silence over Czechoslovakia). Yet what drives him really mad is the epigraph taken from Marx and the suggestion that socialism alone can offer 'the progressive historical alternative to the world of capital', while the perversions of socialism may have something to do with the Russian heritage. 'Are we, by chance, going to admit, comrades,' he thunders, 'that socialism *itself* is inherently flawed?' The anger is not surprising, since by that time, Solzhenitsyn is searching his own 'progressive alternative' and quoting as an example the Raskolniki, the Old Believers.

This was the period of unrest among intellectuals, of the *samizdat*, of Solzhenitsyn's growing fame in the outside world, culminating in the Nobel Prize for literature bestowed upon him in 1970. But these were also the years of Solzhenitsyn's exclusion from the Writers' Union, years of harassment and slander. Unable to answer argument with argument, unwilling to embark on a debate bound to go beyond the meaningless condemnation of the 'personality cult', the Soviet leaders resorted to the well-tried methods of the witchhunt. Solzhenitsyn's books remained unpublished in Russia, yet in public or confidential meetings they were being presented by the stooges of the regime as the work of an informer, a German agent, or even – who knows the prejudices of the public? – the Jew Solzhenitzer. Alexander Isayevich stood up magnificently to the mounting pressure. After a moment of panic in 1965, when part of his archives were seized by the police, he recovered with a renewed confidence in the power of the written word and a challenging contempt for the allegedly almighty rulers. From then onward he was ready to behave in keeping with the dictum of Innokenty that 'for a country to have a great writer . . . is like having another government.' Here for example is his reply to rumours about the Soviet leaders' readiness to allow him to emigrate: 'I have the permission of my benefactors to abandon my home. And they have mine to go to China.' He did not yield to corrupting offers nor to bullying. He answered threat with threat, coolly calculating the weight of his response.

Unfortunately, while the stature of Solzhenitsyn as a resister was thus growing, his contact with Soviet reality was getting looser. He was no longer studying the present and the recent past in order to grapple with the future. He was looking further and further back into the past of Mother Russia for current solutions, dreaming nostalgically of a 'future' in which the *muzhik* once again would be the backbone of society and not an 'operetta *muzhik*'. While gaining respect as a resister, he was also losing touch with a good number of the small though brave band of

Soviet dissidents. Bitterly conscious of this divorce, he pins his hopes on the future – as if unaware of the fact that his new posture really cuts him off from the incomparably stronger potential movement of Russian resistance:

> It is not from this letter, but earlier, from the appearance of *August 1914*, that we must date the schism among my readers, the steady loss of supporters, with more leaving me than remained behind. I was received with 'hurrahs' as long as I appeared to be against Stalinist abuses only; thus far the entire Soviet public was with me. In my first works I was concealing my features from the police censorship – but, by the same token, from the public at large. With each subsequent step I inevitably revealed more and more of myself: the time had come to speak more precisely, to go even deeper. And in doing so I should inevitably lose the reading public, lose my contemporaries in the hope of winning posterity. It was painful, though, to lose support even among those closest to me.

However strong or weak Solzhenitsyn's influence on the young generations is likely to be, his collision with the heirs of Stalin was inevitable. The question was only when and how. Stalin had carried Shaw's dictum that extermination is the extreme form of censorship to its practical conclusion. In his time there was no space for Solzhenitsyn, or for any form of open dissent. His successors, in spite of their camps and their psychiatric wards, did not quite know how to cope with an opponent too famous to be silenced without a major international outcry, a fuss particularly inconvenient for leaders whose whole policy rested on the premise of a détente with the United States. On the other hand, they could not leave Solzhenitsyn quiet either. When in August 1973 the secret police forced a poor old woman to reveal where one manuscript of *The Gulag Archipelago* was buried (and drove her for this reason to suicide), Solzhenitsyn replied by lighting the fuse of his time bomb: he asked his Western publishers to release this very book. The conflict was reaching its climax (or anticlimax). On 12 February 1974, Solzhenitsyn was once again taken to a Moscow prison. Nineteen years earlier, for the young army officer coming from Germany, it was merely the beginning, the first of nearly 3,000 nights behind bars. The celebrated writer was to spend only one night in jail and then, ironically, was to be sent back to Germany, as an exile. Deportation, it will be objected, is better than death. Undoubtedly. But for a man like Solzhenitsyn exile, a break with his native soil, was a particularly bitter and dangerous blow.

As a novelist Solzhenitsyn is, in a way, the social historian of the end of the Stalin era and of the beginning of its aftermath. He shows the stirrings below the surface, the contrast between the official image and the Russian reality, the hypocrisies which pretend to reconcile the two. But he is also the product of the period which he describes, of a Russia apparently unable to reform itself. When society is thus in stalemate, when its institutions no longer correspond to its stage of development but no social force is yet capable of breaking the deadlock, when the road forward looks as if it is blocked for ever, many people feeling trapped invent their own ways of escape. They seek God, find a nostalgic shelter in distant history, confuse past and future – just like Solzhenitsyn, though not, as a rule, with his talent and passion.

Some writers, even novelists, more intellectual, more abstract, can prosper in exile. Not so Solzhenitsyn. Naturally, with his sense of God-given mission and his prodigious gifts, he would have gone on writing even if exiled to the moon. But what hitherto kept this visionary from a total flight into fancy was the shrewd and brilliant observer within him, in permanent contact with his Russian environment. Cut off from his roots he is bound, if I may say so, to take off, to proceed inexorably on his already well-advanced journey into the past and the irrational.

> The *mushik* can only be resurrected in opera houses?
>
> Solzhenitsyn, *From Under the Rubble*

It remains to explain why a writer whose political message is so obviously anachronistic remains so subversive in the Soviet Union, so unbearable to the men in the Kremlin fifty-eight years after the Revolution and already twenty-two years after the death of Stalin. The answer, we have seen, lies in the witness, the shrewd observer, hidden but hitherto not yet stifled, by the prophet. Even his maddest proclamations usually contain passages of plain, and for the Soviet leaders unpalatable, truth. *Letter to the Soviet Leaders*, to which we shall return, is a good example. The migration to Siberia, proposed by Solzhenitsyn, may be irrelevant, his appeal to the peasant soul and to the nationalism of the Russian leaders may be naïve or unpleasant, according to taste. But in the same text Solzhenitsyn says that members of the Communist Party in the Soviet Union are not a heroic vanguard, merely a host of time-servers, because the party card is a passport to promotion. He adds that in the Soviet Union the ruling ideology is 'a sham, a cardboard theatrical prop', that 'everything is steeped in lies and everybody knows it – and says so openly in private conversation and jokes and moans about it but in their official speeches they go on hypocritically parroting what they are supposed to say.' Turning to the Soviet leaders, he asks: 'Do you yourselves really believe for one instant that these speeches are sincere?'

What can they answer? jiaa country where for decades heretics were exterminated and dissent was a form of suicide, where even today an open debate with both sides stating their cases is unthinkable, and at the end of each conflict within the leadership we merely hear the version of the victors, in such a country Solzhenitsyn's plain speaking was dynamite. In a literary world in which for years, as a critic put it, it was enough to drive on a tractor into an editorial office to get published and in which the other function of the writer was to act as a social make-up specialist and remover of warts, the charge of realism – call it socialist or otherwise – contained in Solzhenitsyn's works was explosive. *Ivan Denisovich* got through. If other critical books were allowed into print, where would it all end? There can be no genuine freedom in literature alone.

Solzhenitsyn is particularly dangerous for the establishment in two respects. The first is his determination to explore the recent past. He has staked his claim to be the 'historian of the revolution', in other words, to tell the true story of the last sixty years. The ambition is perfectly legitimate. A nation is politically paralysed by collective amnesia just as an individual is and in the Soviet Union the basic facts about the development of the Soviet regime have been buried under layer after layer of successive distorted versions. The ordinary Russian does not really know what his revolution stood for, who made it, and how. Nobody has told him how the soviets were deprived of all meaning in the Soviet Union and how the workers were stripped of all power in the allegedly workers' state. He or she has only the faintest idea of how collectivization was precipitated and carried out, how the industrialization was conceived, how the party was purged and purged again, what the views of the 'enemies of the people' were who stood in the dock. No wonder that one of the first temptations of many dissidents, such as Roy Medvedev or Solzhenitsyn himself, is to break through the wall of official lies in order to reconquer the collective memory. How badly this exercise was and is needed may be gathered from the gaps, loopholes, and errors in their works. But here again the reconstruction of history is impossible without a free debate, while relevant questions about the recent past have a dangerous bearing on the present.

The scrutiny is the more subversive since Solzhenitsyn puts the emphasis on the bleakest and the bloodiest in the recent past. The ex-zek has heroically taken it upon himself to speak for those who have not lived to tell their woes, to seek redress for all the victims, and his accusing finger points in the direction of the guilty men in the Kremlin. So many years after Stalin's death are his accomplices still there? The revolution opened the gates to the young. The hierarchical system that evolved subsequently means that the prospective leader must climb all the rungs of the ladder to the top: the average age of the members of the Politburo is seventy. These men were in their prime in Stalin's day and were in some way cogs in the mincing machine. Nor were they just a handful. The Rusanovs, the Makarygins, the profiteers of the regime described by Solzhenitsyn are legion, and ready to defend their interests. The revelation of the whole

truth about the camps, the terror, and their function in society threatens
the entire edifice and is resisted accordingly.

The second and even more dangerous weapon Solzhenitsyn wields is
his egalitarianism. We saw how, as a novelist, he contrasts the revolutionary promise of equality with the glaring inequalities of Soviet fulfilment
and how he fully illustrates this contrast. Ruska, for instance, in the
above-quoted conversation from *The First Circle*, goes on to tell Clara
about the wives of bigwigs who never go to ordinary shops, about the full
crate of macaroni he delivered to a party secretary in half-starved
Kazakhstan, about special shops, special clinics, clubs for members only,
and so on. A heresy for half a century, egalitarianism still haunts the
Russian rulers who do not dare to throw the limelight on their privileged
positions.

'He who drives in a car is incapable, absolutely incapable of understanding a pedestrian, even in a symposium,' Solzhenitsyn comments
wittily. It is metaphorically from the point of view of a pedestrian that he
attacks his fellow dissidents for their haughty contempt for the ordinary
people. The intelligentsia, the 'smatterers' as he calls them, pour scorn on
the workers and peasants, guilty of political apathy, ready to sell their
political birthright for a glass of vodka. This group forgets to look at itself
in the mirror to see the one social group which does not bend its back to
survive, but simply to preserve its privileges.

In the most penetrating parts of *From Under the Rubble*, Solzhenitsyn
makes an important point, though he does not carry the argument to its
logical conclusion. The professional intelligentsia, in the wide sense of the
term, is now incomparably more numerous than in tsarist times. The
democratic slogans of its dissident spokespeople are not at all irrelevant.
The snag is that these slogans are devoid of social content, that they
sound like the abstract preoccupations of an elite. In a profoundly
divided, hierarchical country, in which the gap between the mighty and
the mass of the people is still very deep, they look to the ordinary Russians
as part of the struggle among the privileged. The intelligentsia will have a
following if it dares to look beyond its own narrow interests and attack its
own privileges in the process.

It is necessary to look at Solzhenitsyn's egalitarianism again to see
whether it can provide such a lead. His feeling of equality goes back to his
childhood and youth, to the enthusiasms of the young pioneer recalled by
Solzhenitsyn (and Nerzhin). It grew, deepened, and consolidated itself in
the camp, where the zek Solzhenitsyn shared the work, the dangers, the
humiliations and hopes of people thrown on to the very bottom of
society. The resulting profound sympathy for the poor and the downtrodden, the genuine warmth towards the weak and the victims of
injustice, are one of the most attractive features of Solzhenitsyn's writing,

and this Christian 'populism' finds a response among many young readers in the West. But this sentimental egalitarianism is not integrated into Solzhenitsyn's political outlook, nor is it universal. Having blamed the present rulers for thus betraying the ideals of the revolution, he now proceeds to attack the Bolsheviks because they had tried to apply their principles. In the first volume of *The Gulag Archipelago* he takes the defence of the engineers downgraded by the new regime. He not only approves their resentment as they, the possessors of knowledge (science) were stripped of their hierarchical superiority ('How could the *engineers* accept the dictatorship of the workers, the dictatorship of their subordinates in industry, so little skilled or trained and comprehending neither the physical nor the economic laws of production, but now occupying the top positions, from which they supervised the engineers?'), he is really incensed because 'engineers were paid immeasurably low salaries in proportion to their contribution to production' (presumably, salaries not much higher than the wages of the workers). Privileges of the 'upstarts' under the present regime apparently disturb our author, while social differences under tsardom or in the West leave him unperturbed. In any case, he has now come to the conclusion that the 'suppression of privileges is a moral not a political problem' and where this doctrine leads we may gather from his fellow crusader Igor Shafarevich, who in the same collection of essays sings the virtues of 'spiritual equality' preached by the Church and points out the vices of 'material equality' sought by socialism. Justice in heaven is a message our own priests find today too crude to serve unvarnished and we shall not swallow it because it is served by eastern redeemers.

The absence of a plan of action, of a plausible political solution, is also striking in Solzhenitsyn's *Letter to the Soviet Leaders*. What does he tell them in substance? Remember that you are Russians. Forget that silly Marxist nonsense. Leave it to the Chinese, God help them. Stalin was almost fine when he was just a patriot during the war. I, Solzhenitsyn, I am against revolutions, upheavals, and I have little faith in democracy for Russia. I believe in social order and discipline. I don't want you to be swept away by a movement from below. It could be dangerous. Just stay Russian and drop your 'progressive ideology'. Solzhenitsyn gives here a good example of his split mind. Having told us that the ruling ideology in Russia is a pretence, a sham, he then picks one item of that ideology – internationalism – and wants to convince us that this is the driving force of Soviet policy, domestic as well as foreign. He must be one of the last people genuinely to believe that Moscow is the headquarters of world revolution and that Leonid Brezhnev spends sleepless nights dreaming of true soviets from the Atlantic to the Pacific. He is actually asking the leaders in the Kremlin to drop one of the weapons in their arsenal of power politics and not any 'proletarian internationalism' to which, at best, they never did more than pay lip service. While finding Solzhenitsyn's nationalist language quite congenial, they have no reason to yield to his entreaties. Dangerous as a critic, he looks less threatening as the inspirer of a political movement since historically, his political constituency – the peasantry – is dwindling.

For many years before and after the last war the Soviet leaders saw the main threat to their regime in backward, rural Russia, in the mass of forcibly collectivized peasants hankering after private property. No wonder. When Captain Solzhenitsyn was thrown into jail, collective farmers and their families accounted for roughly half the Soviet population. Now they account for less than one-fifth. Here we may warn against expectations of instant results. The political future is not a crude and immediate reflection of statistical change. Indeed, judging by the performance of an admittedly young, small, and slowly growing dissident movement, the trend is in the opposite direction. Amid Russian dissidents, both within Soviet frontiers and in exile, the Westerners associated with the academician Sakharov have gained less ground than the Slavophiles following in the footsteps of Solzhenitsyn. In his footsteps and, unfortunately, beyond. Some of the apostles of Orthodox Russia as the only Messiah capable of bringing redemption to this rotten world have carried Solzhenitsyn's premises to their logical conclusions. They are admirers of an authoritarian state, contemptuous of the rights of non-Russian minorities, and openly anti-semitic. Together with its voice, the old Russian Right has recovered the language of the tsarist pogrommongers, the Black Hundred.

Less surprisingly, it is this jingoist opposition which managed to gain a sympathetic echo in sections of the ruling establishment. The Medvedev twins once assumed that 'party democrats', as they called themselves, might be able to rely on the support of liberal and modernizing elements within the party hierarchy. The hoped-for alliance between a democratic opposition and a technocratic wing in the leadership never really materialized. On the other hand, the reactionary opposition dreaming aloud of rural Russia, of the ikon and of traditions going back to tsarist times, obtained space for its views in *Molodaya Gvardya* (Young Guard) and *Krasnaya Zvezda* (Red Star). Thus, the journal of the Communist Youth Movement and the newspaper of the armed forces offered their columns to the preachers of Great Russian nationalism and when, the propaganda having gone too far, this whole campaign came under official attack, there were still men in the top leadership to protect the culprits.

Solzhenitsyn, therefore, is not preaching entirely in the wilderness. The religious revival in Russia is a yardstick, the measure of the ideological desert created by the regime. The nationalism has stronger Soviet roots.

Stalin resurrected Great Russian chauvinism and the cult of national heroes – Ivan and Peter, Kutuzov and Suvorov – as part of preparations for the last war. The conflict over, he discarded the crude nationalism and replaced it, once again, with 'Marxism–Leninism' taught as a gospel. Stalin's successors are in a worse predicament. They have to serve the same primitive creed to a more sophisticated audience. Khrushchev's indictment of Stalin shook the believers, who were then not allowed to examine critically the new system and their own position. Threatened by the alternative of cynicism or religion, the authorities hoped to fill the ideological void by their own version of the doctrine of growth and prosperity. Hence, they are particularly alarmed by the slowdown of the economy. The combination of ideological emptiness with economic stagnation leads inexorably to a deadlock, and one can no longer exclude the emergence of a Bonaparte, not as a peasant emperor, but as a marshal produced by the social stalemate and designed to solve the deadlock. Adding the ideology of the Dark Ages to modern means of repression, his regime could inherit the worst features of both its predecessors.

The worst is never sure, and in this case the napoleonic solution is actually rather unlikely. The Communist Party has every reason to fight against a regime which would deprive it of its absolute power. The military dictatorship, with no obvious answers to major questions facing Soviet society, would at most be a stopgap. It is not illogical to expect that far from the spotlight turned on the star dissidents, far from the centres attracting foreign correspondents, in factories, laboratories, offices, and colleges as well as in the camps, a new generation is rising which may cast aside the bastards of October in the name of some new councils of urban and rural, manual and intellectual workers – a modern version of the soviets which back in 1917 not only shook the world but seemed to offer it new hope.

In order to move forward, this new generation will have to reassume its past, if only to grasp how the dream was twisted into nightmare, and in doing so it will pay tribute to the countless victims of this tragic period. Alexander Isayevich Solzhenitsyn will figure prominently in this metaphorical monument. He will figure there as an ex-zek who has somehow survived the horrors, as the heroic writer fighting passionately so that these crimes should be neither forgotten nor forgiven. But he will be there, too, as the mental victim of both Stalin and his successors, who, unable to reform Soviet society, have driven this man, for all his courage and talents, into an irrational deadend. In other words, they will show gratitude to the unflinching witness and compassion for the twisted prophet. Only when such reinvented soviets take over will the voice of Solzhenitsyn become what it should have been for a very long time – a tragic voice from the past. Until then, for all his aberrations, it will unfortunately remain relevant.

Epilogue
The Heirs of Stalin

Yevgeni Yevtushenko

Silent the marble. Silent the glass scintillates.
Silent stand the sentries in the breeze like bronzes poured.
And the coffin smoulders slightly.
                              Through its chinks breath percolates,
as they carry him through the mausoleum doors.
Slowly floats the coffin, grazing bayonets with its edges.
He was silent too – menacingly silent indeed.
Then grimly his embalmed fist clenches,
through the chinks peers a man pretending to be dead.
He wanted to remember by whom he was carried out:
those juvenile recruits from Kursk and Ryazan,
so that, somehow later, gathering strength to sally out,
he'd rise up from the earth and get that brainless band.
He had conceived a plan. But to rest was having a nap.
And I turn to our government with a request:
to double, treble the guards over that gravestone slab,
so that Stalin should not rise, and with Stalin – the past.
I don't mean that past, noble and treasured,
of TurkSib, and Magnitogorsk, and the flag over Berlin invested.
Now I have in mind the past that is measured
by the people's good neglected the innocent slandered and arrested.
In honesty we sowed,
in honesty metal smelted,
and honestly marched in soldierly formation.
But he feared us. Believing the mighty
that the means
                    should be worthy of that mighty consummation.
He was farsighted. In the laws of struggle well-instructed,
and many heirs he left in this world's precincts.
It seems to me to that coffin a telephone's connected:
To Enver Hoxha Stalin transmits his latest edicts.
To where else is that direct line linked up?
No – Stalin didn't surrender. Death's to him a rectifiable mistake.
Out of the mausoleum we resolutely took him.
But Stalin out of Stalin's heirs how do we take?
In their retirement some heirs prune roses,
but in secret think retirement's a temporary phase,
From platforms at Stalin, others even hurl curses,

Epilogue: The Heirs of Stalin

But at night-time pine for the good old days.
The heirs of Stalin, not for nothing, apparently
have heart attacks now. Being one-time pillars of society,
they don't like the times when prison camps are empty
and halls are overfull of people

       listening to poetry.
My people

   have commanded me –

       no complacency.
I can't be calm –

    though some repeat 'Calm down'

        ad nauseum
As long as Stalin's heirs on this earth exist,
it will seem to me

    that Stalin is still in the mausoleum.

Select Bibliography

There are many books on Stalinism. The following are only a very few intended to lead to more specialist reading.

Perry Anderson, *Arguments Within English Marxism*, London, 1980.
Rudolf Bahro, *The Alternative in Eastern Europe*, London, 1978.
Robin Blackburn (ed.), *Revolution and Class Struggle*, London, 1975.
E. H. Carr, *Socialism in One Country* (3 vols.), London, 1958–64.
    Twilight of the Comintern, London, 1982.
Fernando Claudin, *The Communist Movement*, London, 1975.
Richard B. Day, *Leon Trotsky and the Politics of Economic Isolation*, Cambridge, 1973.
    The 'Crisis' and the 'Crash', London, 1981.
Isaac Deutscher, *Stalin*, Oxford, 1949.
    The Prophet Armed, Oxford, 1959.
    The Prophet Unarmed, Oxford, 1959.
    The Prophet Outcast, Oxford, 1963.
Chen Er-Jin, *Crossroads Socialism*, London, 1984.
Moshe Lewin, *Lenin's Last Struggle*, London, 1969.
Marcel Liebman, *Leninism Under Lenin*, London, 1975.
Michael Löwy, *The Politics of Combined and Uneven Development*, London, 1981.
Livio Maitan, *Party, Army and Masses in China*, London, 1975.
Ernest Mandel, *Marxist Economic Theory* (2 vols.), London, 1968.
    Inconsistencies of State-Capitalism, London, 1969.
    Revolutionary Marxism Today, London, 1979.
Roy Medvedev, *Let History Judge*, London, 1972.
Zhores Medvedev, *The Rise and Fall of T. D. Lysenko*, New York, 1969.
Christian Rakovsky, *Selected Writings on Opposition in the USSR*, London, 1980.
Pierre Rousset, *Le Parti Communiste Vietnamien*, Paris, 1972.
Su Shaozhi, *Marxism in China*, Nottingham, 1983.
Victor Serge, *Year One of the Russian Revolution*, London, 1972.
Leon Trotsky, *The Revolution Betrayed*, New York, 1972.
    My Life, London, 1975.
    In Defense of Marxism, New York, 1976.
    History of the Russian Revolution, London, 1976.

For a view that is radically different to the one reflected in this volume and which either regards Western capitalism as a superior form of society or sees no qualitative difference between the USA and the USSR, the following books are recommended.

Otto Bauer, *Bolshevism and Social-Democracy*, Vienna, 1925
Charles Bettelheim, *Class Struggles in the USSR*, New York, 1978.
Franz Borkenau, *World Revolution*, London, 1948.
Tony Cliff, *Russia: A Marxist Analysis*, London, 1955.
Milovan Djilas, *The New Class*, London, 1957.
Chris Harman, *Class Struggles in Eastern Europe*, London, 1983.
Nigel Harris, *The Mandate of Heaven*, London, 1979.
Karl Kautsky, *Bolshevism at a Deadlock*, London, 1931.
Alex Nove, *Stalinism and After*, London, 1975.
Max Shachtman, *The Bureaucratic Revolution*, New York, 1952.
Paul M. Sweezy, *Post-Revolutionary Society*, New York and London, 1980.

Also available from Haymarket Books

The Bolsheviks Come to Power
The Revolution of 1917 in Petrograd
  Alexander Rabinowitch

The Comintern
  Duncan Hallas

The German Revolution, 1917-1923
  Pierre Broué, Eric D. Weitz (Introduction)

How Revolutionary Were the Bourgeois Revolutions?
  Neil Davidson

Imperialism and War
Classic Writings by V.I. Lenin and Nikolai Bukharin
  Phil Gasper (Editor), V. I. Lenin, Nikolai Bukharin

Lenin's Political Thought
Theory and Practice in the Democratic and Socialist Revolutions
  Neil Harding

The Lost Revolution
Germany 1918-1923
  Chris Harman

The Nazis, Capitalism and the Working Class
  Donny Gluckstein

On Changing the World
*Essays in Marxist Political Philosophy, from Karl Marx
to Walter Benjamin*
  Michael Löwy

History of the Russian Revolution
  Leon Trotsky

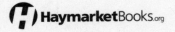